# computers
# and
# data
# processing

## second
## edition

## THE CAPRON/WILLIAMS INSTRUCTIONAL SUPPLEMENT PACKAGE

*Guide for Instructors*, H. L. Capron

*Interacting with Computers and Data Processing*, Zoe Groulx
and H. L. Capron

*Guide to Testing*, Carole Colaneri
 Computerized Testing Service (mainframe and mini)
 TestGen (microcomputer)

*Guide to Subscriptions, Films, and Videos*

*Transparency Masters*

*Transparencies*

*Instructor's Resource Manual* (containing all of the above)

For more information on the above titles please call 800-227-1936 or (in
California) 800-982-6140.

*second edition*

# computers and data processing

## H. L. Capron
## Brian K. Williams

**The Benjamin/Cummings Publishing Company, Inc.**

Menlo Park, California • Reading, Massachusetts • London • Amsterdam • Don Mills, Ontario • Sydney

Sponsoring Editor   **Susan Nelle**

Production Manager   **Margaret Moore**

Production Coordinator   **Pat Franklin Waldo**

Interior Design   **Dare Porter,** with second edition modifications
   by **Paul Quin**

Color Galleries   **Dare Porter**

Cover Design   **Alan Springer**

Photo Research   **Roberta Spieckerman Associates**

Illustrations   **J & R Art Services,** new art by **John Foster**
   and **Kirk Caldwell**

**Library of Congress Cataloging in Publication Data**

Capron, H. L.
   Computers and data processing.

   Includes bibliographical references and index.
   1. Computers.   2. Electronic data processing.
I. Williams, Brian K., 1938–     . II. Title.
QA76.C357   1984     001.64     83-15756
   ISBN 0-8053-2214-0
   ISBN 0-201-32238-8 (SD)

DEFGHIJ-DO-8987654

The Benjamin/Cummings Publishing Company, Inc.
2727 Sand Hill Road
Menlo Park, California 94025

*To our fathers*
*Robert Capron*
*and*
*Harry A. Williams*

# brief
# table
# of
# contents

# *detailed table of contents*

## Reviewers and Consultants for First and Second Editions

Ronald Anderson
Carlotta Appleman
James Arnold
Jeanne Barry
Robert Behling
Nona Berghaus
Jacqueline Bishop
Marilyn Bohl
Eugene Bumgarner
Jack Castek
Augusta Chadwick
Carole Colaneri
William Cornette
Rosemary Damon
Robert Dashner
Barbara Denison
Robert Dickey

Mary Dirkin
Kevin Duggan
Ronald Eaves
Gary Eerkes
Ray Fanselau
Alice Fischer
Richard Fleming
David Godderz
Michael Goldberg
Howard Granger
Zoe Groulx
Kerry Hayes
Donald Henderson
Ruby Holliday
Randy Johnston
James Kasum
Richard Kerns

John Lloyd
Richard Matson
Allan Maynard
Richard McCalla
Michael McCandless
Linda J. Metcalf
Susan Nycum
William O'Hare
Tony O'Truk
Sherril Overfield
Alex Prengel
Buck Rader
Edward Rattigan
George Rice
JoAnn Robison
Gary Schmidt
Harold C. Sellers

William Shockley
John Schrage
Dennis Severance
Lee Smith
Ronald Suprenant
Nabil Takla
Steve Teglovic
Julie Tinsley
George Vlahakis
Gerald Wagner
Barry Weinmann
Caroline Welter
David Wen
James Wilson
Richard Yankofsky
Phyllis Yasuda

# *the galleries*

Just as a museum has galleries devoted to different themes or subjects, so in this book we have presented nine "galleries" of *full-color* photographs for the reader to tour. These photographs are organized around themes relevant to the book and, usually, to the chapters in which they appear.

Computers now permeate our lives, extending from NASA space shots of the further reaches of space, down through links with the country and the city, to involvement in all aspects of people's pastimes and productivity.

An overview look at four types of computers—super, mainframe, minicomputer, and microcomputer—and examples of hardware demonstrating the four parts common to all computer systems: input, processing, output, and storage.

An integrated circuit begins with a large drawing of electrical circuitry, which is then photographically reduced so it is more than 500 times smaller. It is then reproduced many times on a 3-inch-diameter piece of silicon, which is finally cut into individual pieces or "chips."

Data, the often unorganized stuff of life, can be symbols, shapes, colors, or other raw material. Various input devices have been developed to put data into machine-processable form.

Printers and CRT terminals are perhaps the most pervasive output devices associated with computers, but there are other intriguing devices and forms of output, from computer graphics to robots.

GALLERY **6**

*The "All-Purpose Machine":* The Many, Often Hidden, Uses of Computing
follows p. 198

John von Neumann said that the device should not be called the computer but the "all-purpose machine." This gallery—twice as long as others—offers proof that the computer can be put to any number of applications besides calculations. Examples show uses in government, education, the military, transportation, science and medicine, the automated office, manufacturing, energy, and food and agriculture.

GALLERY **7**

*Global Search:* Computer Use Around the World follows p. 230

Computers are being used in Europe, Asia, and the Third World. North Americans have no cause to feel smug about innovation, for many exciting developments are happening elsewhere, particularly in Europe and Japan.

BUYER'S GUIDE

*How to Buy Your Own Microcomputer* follows p. 278

Choosing among 150 to 200 microcomputers is not easy. This Buyer's Guide helps readers determine why they need a computer, what to look for in hardware and software, where to buy, and other matters.

GALLERY **8**

*Personal Computers:* The Personal Convenience Machine follows p. 294

The Computer Revolution comes home in a small but spectacular way. The uses to which microcomputers may be put seem boundless—from number crunching to music making, from running a house to running a boat. Several models of personal computers are shown.

GALLERY **9**

*The Last Picture Show:* Computers and Imagination follows p. 390

New machines. New ideas. New ways of seeing. The future may be evident in today's recent developments: wider communications, increased robotics, more computer-assisted labor-saving and entertainment devices. And new ways of perceiving the world as the computer assists the artist's and scientist's imagination.

# *preface*

*Computers and Data Processing*, wrote our publisher in the 1983 catalog, "sold over 100,000 copies in its first year of publication, making it one of the most successful new college textbooks of all time in any discipline." We are, to say the least, overwhelmed by this enthusiastic reception—and, of course, immensely gratified.

What were we trying to do that apparently elicited this response? Let us describe our objectives and accomplishments here, for they apply to the second edition as well—and constitute the reasons we urge you to adopt this book.

1. **This book offers a substantive but not overly technical treatment of computers and data processing.** The book was designed as a textbook for an introductory course in computers and data processing, but it will also be of interest to anyone who wants to learn about computers. Our purpose is not to saturate the reader with numbers and small details, most of which are made obsolete anyway by fast-moving technological changes. Our purpose, rather, is to show the breadth, depth, and fascination—in a word, the excitement—of computers. Accordingly, whether your students are in the course as majors in business or a computer-related field or are there as general education students, we believe you will find this book suitable.

2. **Many instructors provided input to the book's content.** Before we wrote the first edition, our publisher sent out more than 3000 detailed questionnaires to data processing instructors throughout North America. Several of these instructors participated in discussion panels and some reviewed the manuscript—both for the

first and for the second edition. The result, we believe, reflects the current needs and preferences of instructors and students nationwide, such as up-to-date coverage of programming methods, data base systems, distributed data processing, microcomputers, and computer careers.

3. **We offer distinctive coverage.** This text covers many subjects not frequently covered in one book—for example, structured programming, data communications, personal computers, the automated office, operating systems, robotics, data bases, management information systems, security and privacy, and computer and data processing careers. We also present, in Appendix A, enough material for a complete mini-course in BASIC.

4. **We have tried to make the subject matter interesting and meaningful to students.** There is no reason why a textbook cannot have an impact on people's lives for reasons other than being "required reading." Thus, we have tried to communicate our ideas with liveliness and style, using extensive and vivid examples, illustrations, and color photographs. We have also incorporated a number of learning aids, such as particularly complete summaries. Our publisher has happily retained the successful typographical design of the previous edition, which makes the book easy to read and pleasing to look at.

5. **We have expanded coverage since the first edition.** Those who used the earlier version of this book will find that a number of changes have taken place. We have extended the historical discussion to coverage of not only the Fourth Generation but also Japan's Fifth Generation. Dvorak keyboards are compared with QWERTY keyboards. Ergonomics, that new buzzword, is given more play. A section has been added on microcomputer storage in our chapter on storage devices. At the request of many users, we have reversed the sequence of Chapters 10 and 11, so that the discussion of structured program design now precedes the discussion of languages. Ada is now described fully, and other languages, such as LOGO and Smalltalk, are also included. The chapter on operating systems describes Unix, Pick, and CP/M.

Office automation is given greater prominence, as evidenced by the title of Chapter 13. Word processing, in particular, is covered more fully. The chapter on personal computers, as one might expect, is greatly revised to reflect the latest in that field's tumultuous developments, such as types of chips, electronic spread sheets, and 16-bit microprocessors. Networking is updated to reflect voice mail, personal networks, Local Area Networks, and other innovations. The chapter on MIS and data base systems has been significantly enhanced with the addition of discussion about decision support systems, information centers, and microcomputers for executives.

The careers chapter cautions students on expectations for entry-level positions while at the same time pointing out the opportunities for freelancers and entrepreneurs with some experience. Software piracy, copyright infringement, and other security matters are enlarged upon in Chapter 18. The last chapter is considerably revised to cover automation and robotics, artificial intelligence, and new technological developments.

We are also proud to point out two important features for this edition. The first is the addition of the **Buyer's Guide: How to Buy Your Own Microcomputer,** which appears following page 278. As we point out in our notes to the student, this unique section may be read by itself; no prior knowledge of microcomputers is required. It is protected from datedness because it describes how to evaluate parts of a microcomputer system rather than particular models.

The second feature is the addition of **new color photo galleries.** Eight of the nine original galleries (the popular Gallery 3, "Making of a Chip," has been left as is) have been completely revised from the first edition. Moreover, we have introduced new themes we think will stir student interest: Gallery 1, "From Cosmos to Consciousness: The Sweep of the Computer Revolution"; Gallery 7, "Global Search: Computer Use Around the World"; Gallery 9, "The Last Picture Show: Computers and Imagination." In addition to these color pictures, the reader will find that the black and white pictures have been extensively revised throughout.

6. We have been able to make last-minute changes so that we could include the latest information. By putting the publication of this book on a special production timetable using word processing and state-of-the-art computerized production techniques, our publisher has enabled us to include many late-breaking developments. Book production is normally a 12- or 18-month process, but a glance through this book will assure the reader that a great many of the boxes, margin notes, and photographs are of very recent date. Indeed, writing and production *together* took only 10 months!

### Organization: Options for Using This Book

*Computers and Data Processing* is divided into five parts. **Part 1, You and Computer Literacy,** describes the tremendous presence and influence of computers in our lives and gives a brief overview of a computer system. **Part 2, Hardware,** presents a one-chapter history of computers and data processing, then goes on to cover the four principal facets of a computer system: the central processor, input, output, and storage and file processing. **Part 3, Software,** covers some of the nonhardware side of computing, including programming, systems analysis, operating systems, and the various programming languages. **Part 4, The New Story of Computing,** branches out to explore the computer industry, personal computers, data communication systems, management information systems, and data bases. **Part 5, Computers and Us,** concludes with an examination of the computer in relation to society: careers in the field, security and privacy issues, and the future of computing. **Appendixes A and B,** respectively, present a course in BASIC and a brief coverage of number systems.

The chapters may be covered in other than in chronological order, if that suits your particular course organization. Chapters are often *modular,* which is to say that to some degree they may be taken out of sequence and read independently of other chapters. The history chapter (Chapter 3), for example, may be taught at any time. For instructors who wish to teach programming early in their course, we have written Chapter 8 so that it may be taught immediately after Chapter 2. We recommend that Appendix A on BASIC be taught only after Chapter 8 is covered. Chapters 9 through 19 may all be taught out of order; also, any of these chapters may be omitted without loss of continuity.

Detailed course outlines and further discussion of chapter interdependence may be found in the Instructor's Guide supplement, which is available from our publisher.

### Supplements Available

Our supplements package offers a complete system of instruction that is sensitive to the needs of part-time instructors and teaching assistants as well as full-time instructors. The supplements include the following:

**Guide for Instructors**  To help instructors, particularly the part-time instructor and teaching assistant, the *Guide for Instructors* by H. L. Capron offers many practical suggestions for using this textbook in the classroom. Alternative schedules are given for quarter and semester courses. For each chapter in the text, the instructor's guide offers:

- Learning objectives
- Chapter overview
- Lecture outline, with suggestions for time priorities for each topic
- Marginal examples, anecdotes, and other topics to add extra flavor to the lecture
- Glossary terms
- Information on how to use photo galleries from text

**Guide for Students**  Written by Zoe Groulx and H. L. Capron, the *Guide for Students* is available for students interested in more directed and intensive study of the textbook's contents. More than the usual student guide, it includes what we believe to be *useful* aids for study. For each chapter, it includes:

- Learning objectives
- Why this chapter is important
- Key words

- Chapter outline
- Study hints
- Multiple choice chapter test
- True/false chapter test
- Matching chapter test
- Fill-in chapter test
- Answers to chapter tests
- "Close to home"—a paragraph or two relating material to the student's career or personal environment
- Special notes

**Guide to Testing**  This includes more than 3500 items in the following test formats:

- True/false
- Multiple choice
- Matching
- Sentence completion

A *computerized testing service* is available from our publisher for qualified adopters. Two types are available: one a computerized testing service designed for mainframes and most minicomputers, or, TestGen, designed for IBM PC or Apple II microcomputers. Further information is available from our publisher.

**Transparency Masters and Transparencies**  Transparency masters and transparencies included are of three types: key graphics that appear in the text, adaptations of graphics from the text, and totally new art that does not appear in the text. All the transparency masters and transparencies have been drawn with thick lines and large type for highly readable projection.

**Guide to Subscriptions, Films, and Videos**  Compiled from more than 200 suppliers of videotapes, films, and film strips and many periodical publishers, this guide offers audiovisuals conveniently keyed to the appropriate part number of the text.

## To the Student: The Promise of This Book

For the rest of your life, you will live in the Computer Age. Whatever your career, therefore, your future depends on knowing something—perhaps knowing a great deal—about computers and data processing. To learn what computers do and how they affect society and your life, to be able to find your way between the sunny and the dismal forecasts about what computers will bring, you need to achieve some semblance of *computer literacy*. That is the major promise of this book: with your participation, we will help you become computer literate.

To help you succeed in this, we have employed a number of devices:

1. **We have tried to write with liveliness and style.** We want this book to speak directly to you, and we want you to *enjoy* reading it. Thus, we have tried to write in a conversational style and to offer information in a way you can understand. We have also used many devices to make this book interesting for you to read.

2. **We have included an extensive and varied assortment of examples and applications that stress human interaction with computers.** Computers and data processing permeate practically all aspects of life in the twentieth century. Therefore, we show applications and examples not only in business, science, and engineering but also in the arts, farming, and law. We also show computers being used not only as research and organizational tools but for fanciful and entertaining purposes as well. Throughout the book, we show how computers work and the impact they have on our lives.

We have tried to present these applications in the most effective, dramatic ways:

● **Through the use of "galleries."** Color photographs grouped in themes vividly illustrate such subjects as the uses of computers or how a microprocessor chip is made. See page xviii for a description of the galleries.

● **Through margin notes.** The immediacy and pervasiveness of computers is often best conveyed in press accounts and reports. Thus, we included many excerpts in the margins of our book from a wide range of periodicals and books. These are listed in the Detailed Table of Contents.

● **Through in-depth boxes.** Throughout, we have presented material boxed off from the text, such as case studies, how-to tips, and analyses, to personalize the material for you. These, too, are listed in the Detailed Table of Contents.

● **Through vivid in-text examples and illustrations.** Wherever we have introduced a concept, we have tried to incorporate examples that show the extensive involvement of the computer in modern life— and in your life.

3. **We have provided a great many learning aids throughout the text.** The following are designed to help you grasp the material. **In This Chapter** is a "preview" that appears at the beginning of each chapter, to help orient you to the main topics to be covered. **Summary and Key Terms** appears at the end of each chapter. This section will be particularly valuable for reviewing material before examinations. All material covered in the chapter is summarized in very specific terms. In addition, this section lists **key terms** in boldface type; these are the same key terms that appear in boldface throughout the text. **Review** consists of questions found at the end

of each chapter designed for self-testing before examinations. **Suggested Readings** appear at the end of most chapters, listing appropriate books for further study. The **Glossary/Index** at the back of the book provides a concise definition of each key term and refers you to the appropriate discussion of these terms and other key concepts in the text.

4. **Special bonus: We have provided a buyer's guide to microcomputers.** One of the most exciting developments in computers is the appearance of the personal computer or microcomputer—the kind you see advertised so widely on television and in magazines. As declining prices make these machines more accessible to everyone, the choices become more bewildering. To help you make these choices, we have provided a special section that appears following page 278, the **Buyer's Guide: How to Buy Your Own Microcomputer.** Note: We have deliberately designed the Buyer's Guide to resist datedness (if that's possible at all with computers) by avoiding specific brands of equipment or software, which are fast-changing, and describing instead categories of equipment to evaluate. The Buyer's Guide requires no prior knowledge of computers, and it may be read by itself; it is not necessary to read the text first.

Your reactions to this book are important to us. In developing this second edition, we have taken to heart the comments and suggestions of students and instructors who have used the first edition. Thus, any comments, favorable or unfavorable, will be welcomed and will be read with care. Write to us in care of the publisher, whose address is listed on the copyright page.

## *Acknowledgments*

As before, we are grateful to the many hardware and software companies and computer and data processing users without whose generosity we could not have provided the pictorial treatment we have attempted. Their names are listed on pages 449–453. Our thanks are also due to those who were kind enough to grant permission to reprint excerpts from previously published material; they are listed on pages 447–448.

Many instructors responded to our questionnaire, participated in discussion groups, or reviewed the material in manuscript form, and we are grateful for their suggestions. The reviewers and consultants are listed on page xvii.

Many publishing professionals assisted in the design, graphics, editorial, and production phases of the second edition, and we are deeply appreciative of their efforts: Louise Billotte, Debbie Bowman, Ken Butler, Jenny DeGroot, the Derman brothers, Deborah Gale, Louise

Sessions, Steve Sorensen, and Alice Spears. As on the first edition, we are greatly indebted to Roberta Spieckerman for her many original ideas, without which this book would be the less. We would also like to thank her staff, especially Marsha Shenk, who performed extraordinary photo research efforts in a very short period of time. Dare Porter once again provided exciting design and layouts of the photo color sections, and we are extremely appreciative of his talent. Alan Springer has given us another dynamic, eye-catching cover, for which we are grateful. Kirk Caldwell, John Foster, and Paul Quin did highly professional work in art and production matters.

At Benjamin/Cummings, we are grateful to Margaret Moore for her production management and to Wayne Oler, Allan Wylde, and Jim Behnke for the kind of strong publishing support that makes a project of this magnitude possible. Pat Waldo as production coordinator was fantastic to work with, and we can only marvel at the way she kept so many balls in the air so successfully. Pat, thank you for everything. We felt a special bond with Susan Newman, our sponsoring editor on the first edition of the book. However, we have been fortunate in her successor, Susan Nelle, who came to the project with new vigor, enthusiasm, and dedication. Susan, we are very appreciative of your ideas and support.

Finally, we are very grateful to all the men and women at Benjamin/ Cummings in promotion, marketing, and sales who did such a superb job of making the book known in its first edition. We hope we have done well enough on the second edition to deserve their renewed efforts.

H. L. Capron
Brian K. Williams

ch 1 the
unfinished
revolution:
the future
now

ch 2 overview
of a computer
system:
hardware,
software,
and people

# part 1

# you and computer literacy

"We should all be concerned about the future," wrote scientist Charles F. Kettering, "because we will have to spend the rest of our lives there." This book is about your future, a future rapidly becoming present.

It is about a technological revolution that will make— in fact, is making now—profound changes in your life. It is a revolution that will affect all parts of society. Indeed, it will probably make the Industrial Revolution, which has given us so many of the joys and ills of our time, pale by comparison. The instrument of this new revolution is, of course, the computer. For many, the computer promises greater ease and an end to drudgery. For others, it is a source of dread and represents the ultimate takeover of a machine society. The key to survival in the Computer Age, however, is not to ignore the computer's existence or to cheer its failures. Rather, survival lies in attaining *computer literacy*—in learning enough about computers so that control remains in our hands, not in the hands of others or with the machines themselves.

**IN THIS CHAPTER**

The Computer Revolution may well be far more sweeping than the Industrial Revolution—and certainly far more sudden. The effects of the computer are now seen in spectacular ways: in the graphics it produces; in its use as an industrial robot; and in its effect on such areas as transportation, money, paperwork, commerce, the professions, and our personal lives. Despite computer anxiety, we cannot turn back the clock, nor would we want to. Liberation lies in computer literacy.

# ch1

# the unfinished revolution

## the future now

How sweeping is the Computer Revolution? A few examples show the high drama of the times we live in:

- If cars had developed as computers have, today you would be able to buy a Cadillac for under $3, get three million miles to a gallon, and park up to a half dozen cars on the head of a pin.

- In the early 1950s, a computer containing the same number of functional elements as the human brain would have had to be the size of New York City and draw more power than the city subway system. Today, such computers exist—and they are the size of a TV set.

- Already we can see the antiques of the future: Slide rules, used for three centuries, have been supplanted by powerful pocket calculators. Typewriters are giving way to so-called word processors—electronic typewriters married to computer video screens. Rotary-dial telephones, which cannot transmit computer-to-computer signals, will someday be as quaint as vacuum-tube radios.

The Industrial Revolution, building on the development of the steam engine, the dynamo, and the factory system, took place relatively rapidly. In less than 100 years, human society was changed on a massive scale. To live between 1890 and 1920, for instance, was to live with the dizzying introduction of electricity, telephones, radio, automobiles, and airplanes—perhaps a far more tumultuous period than the times we live in today. But the Computer Revolution is also irreversible and massive and will probably bring about dramatic shifts in the way we live, perhaps even in the way we think. This revolution, however, is happening a great deal more quickly than the Industrial Revolution, and its effects will be felt well before the end of the century. Though the Computer Revolution is far from finished, it is well along. Let us try to glimpse the future.

## The Computer as Artist

There is no better place to get a sense of the computer's impact than in the area of design and graphics, some examples of which are shown in Gallery 1, the first section of color photographs in this book. Breathtaking photographs of the rings of Saturn are beamed back over nearly a billion miles of space. Color-coded portraits of solar flares and different gases reveal violent fireworks on the sun. Meteorological satellites photograph the births and deaths of hurricanes and other forms of weather. Technically, however, none of these transmissions from space is a photograph at all. Rather, they are all electronic impulses assembled by computers.

Closer to home, the computer as artist is evidenced in medicine, where brain scanners produce color-enhanced "maps" to help diagnose mental illness. Biochemists use computers to examine, in three

# *F*rom *C*osmos to *C*onsciousness
## *The Sweep of the Computer Revolution*

**①** "Stargate": Artist David Em's computer graphic artwork not only expresses the feeling of space, but grew out of work in computer programs developed at the Jet Propulsion Laboratory, in Pasadena, Calif., which pioneered many space explorations.

The universe may be immeasurable in its age, whereas computers are less than four decades old. Yet computers allow us to view the long ago and far away: pictures from space vehicles are converted into dots representing various colors; the dots are then given numbers, which are radioed to earth and reassembled by computer. Although not always evident, computers now permeate our lives. As this gallery shows, they extend from the cosmos to the commonplace—and even to human thought itself.

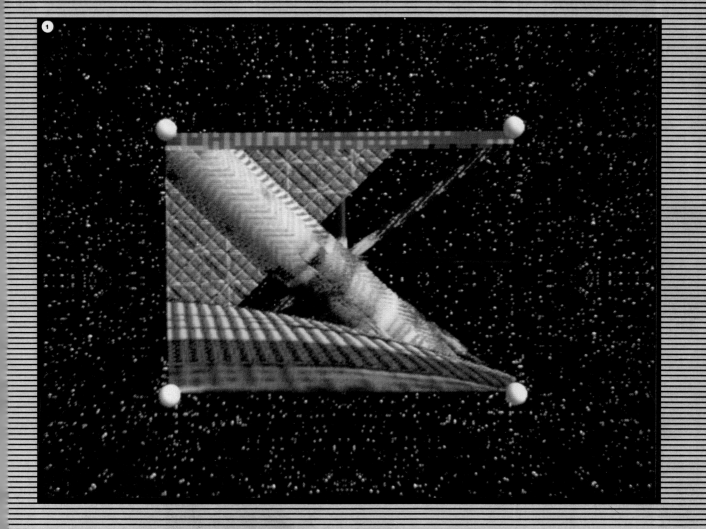

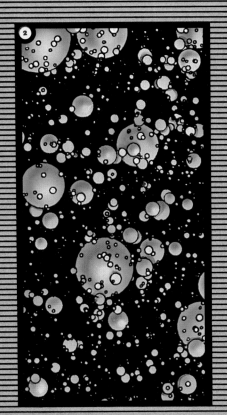

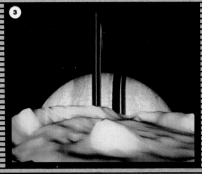

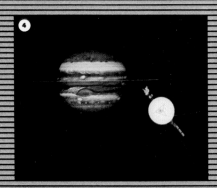

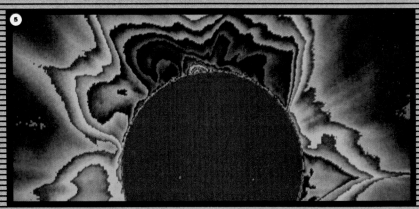

Space graphics: **2** Imaginary closeup views of Saturn's rings, developed by the National Aeronautics and Space Administration. **3** Saturn viewed from its innermost moon. **4** Jupiter taken from Voyager 2. **5** Eclipse of the sun, taken from Solar Maximum Mission spacecraft. **6** View of Mars with Viking 2 Lander. **7** Souvenir from a space mission that never was: this "fractal planetrise" is not a photograph but a geometric shape, generated on the computer, at IBM, by Dr. Richard F. Voss. It illustrates the theories of the mathematician and IBM Fellow Dr. Benoit B. Mandelbrot, and is excerpted from his book *The Fractal Geometry of Nature*, publisher W.H. Freeman, Copyright 1982 by Benoit B. Mandelbrot. **8** Astronaut Sally Ride on Space Shuttle Challenger. **9** China taken by photo from **LANDSAT** satellite; red represents wooded areas and other vegetation.

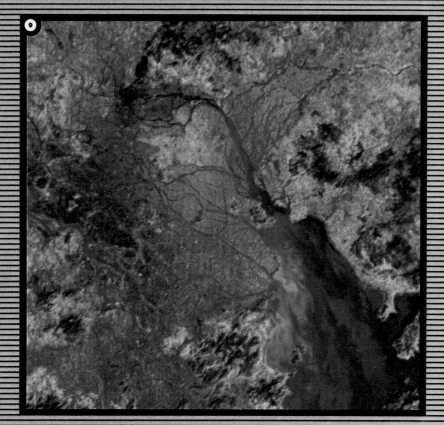

**The country: ⑩ to ⑱** *(counter-clockwise)* **There are no computers in nature, of course, and none are shown here, although the center-piece seascape illustration was executed as computer graphic art. Nevertheless, computers are instrumental in connecting the land with the city—to sort oranges, improve crop yields, aid in breeding livestock, distribute electric power, shear sheep, and many other uses.**

**The city: 19 to 27** *(clockwise)* Take away computers and you take away the modern city—offices, communications, manufacturing, and transportation systems.

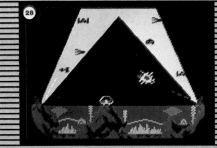

People, pastimes, and productivity: **28** to **39** Computers have changed the nature of play, introducing video games, computerized amusement-park rides, and sophisticated manipulation of sports statistics. They have also come into use to enhance education, increase production, and improve public services such as mail, fire protection, water quality, and health care.

**Mindgames:** 40 41 Ultimately, the computer affects human consciousness and our view of ourselves. Chess, once exclusively the domain of human intelligence, can now be played with a computer. Likewise, art—as in this painting-like graphic by David Weimer of Bell Laboratories—can now be rendered on a computer. For all that, however, it is the human being who is still in charge.

dimensions, the structure of genetic molecules. Architects use computer-animated graphics to give clients a visual walk-through of proposed buildings, to show possible exteriors, and to subject buildings to hypothetical earthquakes. Aircraft designers use such graphics to create experimental aircraft and put them through practice flights without having to resort to model building and wind tunnels. Business executives play artist, making bar graphs and pie charts out of tedious figures and using color to convey trends with far more impact than numbers alone can do. Finally, a whole new kind of artist has emerged, the so-called graphicist, who uses computers to create cartoon animation, landscapes, and still lifes.

## Rolling Out the Robots —and Other Uses

With the age of the computer has arrived the age of the robot. These are not vaguely human-shaped robots like *Star Wars's* C3PO or even R2D2, but rather information machines with the manual dexterity to perform tasks too unpleasant, too dangerous, or too critical to assign to human beings. Examples are pattern-cutting robots in garment businesses, which are able to get the most apparel out of several bolts of cloth; robots used in defense to handle underwater military missions; remote-control arms for removing radioactive nuclear fuel rods; and medical robots to aid physicians and surgeons and to furnish patients with orthopedic devices.

Especially controversial are the robots that do tedious jobs better than human beings do, such as welding or paint spraying in new-car plants. Clearly, these signal the end of jobs for many factory workers— a troublesome social problem and one we will return to in the final chapter of this book.

Whether encased in a robot or in some other form of "smart" machine, the computer is a workhorse. It is generally capable of laboring 24 hours a day, does not ask for raises or coffee breaks, and will do the ten-thousandth task exactly the same way it did the first one—and without complaining of boredom. In the world of work, the uses for computers are as varied as we can imagine (see the box, "Tales from the Computer Age"), but the following are some of the principal ones.

**Paperwork** There is no doubt that our society runs on paper. While in some ways the computer contributes to this problem—as in adding to the amount of junk mail you find in your mailbox—in many other ways it cuts down paper handling. The techniques of word processing, for example, allow letters and reports to be done in draft form and placed in storage accessible by computer. Corrections can be made to the draft and entered into the computer. The letter or report does not need to be completely retyped. Instead, the whole text regenerates automatically, with all errors eliminated. Computerized bookkeeping, record keeping, and document sending have also made paperwork more efficient.

**8**

## Tales from the Computer Age

The uses of computers range from the grand to the trivial. Examples:

### Burger Science

Ray Kroc purchased the McDonald's hamburger business in 1960 from the McDonald brothers of San Bernardino, California. One of his first acts as the new owner is described as follows:

Instead of hiring chefs for his restaurants, Kroc hired engineers. He told them to create a space-age food-preparation system that would depend on machines, not people. He wanted a hamburger served in Portland, Maine, to taste exactly like one served in San Diego, California.

The engineers came through. They designed computer-controlled machines that would stamp out identical patties, each one weighing exactly 1.6 ounces, each one measuring 3.875 inches in diameter. They invented transistorized grills that told the burger-turner exactly when to flip the burgers.

—Murray Suid and Ron Harris,
*Made in America*

### Digital Diagnosis

A physician sits before a video screen on which appears a detailed picture of a human hand. He types some numbers into a keyboard, and the hand begins to change. The joints swell, the fingers curl inward, the bones twist. The hand withers into the gnarled claw of an arthritic. The doctor types once more, and the video hand's condition improves remarkably. The doctor smiles with satisfaction; through the computer he has practiced surgery on his crippled patient's hand and knows that the operation will help before he ever touches a scalpel.

Such scenes will be common among orthopedic surgeons within a few years as a result of studies that use electronic sensors and computers to create accurate working models of the human machine. Called computer biomechanics, this new branch of medical research prom-

ises to revolutionize the diagnosis and treatment of muscle and bone diseases.     —Michael Edelhart,
*Omni*
October 1982

### Tubaduba

At a castle-like mansion in north Berkeley [California] a crowd is gathered around a long table, on which a row of television sets perches over several rectangular wood-framed devices, to hear the first cries of a new breed of musical instrument.

Among them is Don Buchla, 45, a tall, neatly bearded man with pale blue eyes and an intense manner. It is Buchla who invented the electronic instrument that is generating the sound emerging from speakers at each corner of the room, a tone at once alien and pure. Inside the instrument's computer "library" are 24 voices, with names like pipeorgy, bong, tubaduba, glider, swisher, jungle, moonhowl, birds and squeaky. The music they make chatters, meows, rumbles, then passes through an ornate jazz segment, the voices crossing and breaking into each other. You might hear sounds like this in dreams, the way you glimpse images from the corner of your eye. Buchla has devised a means to capture these wisps of imagination and turn them into music.

—Mark Hunter,
*California Living Magazine,*
October 24, 1982

### Need a Model?

NEW YORK—Wanted: A good-looking young man who can read four lines promoting furniture polish while walking on his hands.

That's the kind of specific request model agencies increasingly are getting from clients. Long gone are the days when an advertiser stipulated little more than hair and eye color, so Ford Models Inc. has switched from portfolios and resumes to a computer. . . .

The computer system first divides

the models into five categories based on their general "look," which ranges from "pre-teen" to "very sophisticated." Next, it separates them according to nine shades of eye color, 10 shades of hair color, and various vital statistics.

After that, the computer gets brutal. It rates on a 0-to-9 scale each of 32 characteristics, from how attractive the legs are to how nice the smile is. And then there's a listing of 40 activities and who does which, including shooting, scuba-diving, sidesaddle riding, mountain-climbing, and singing.

—Dennis Kneale,
*Wall Street Journal,*
February 15, 1983

### Duplicating Scientists' Thinking

PITTSBURGH, Pa.—Learning by tracing the steps of the masters is a time-honored practice and researchers at Carnegie-Mellon University (CMU) here are using the same techniques to teach a computer to repostulate theorems set down by early scientists.

The program, called Bacon, . . . has been able to rediscover a series of principles set down by such noted scientists as Johannes Kepler and George Simon Ohm.

The program is fed the same raw data that early scientists had at their disposal. From that information, the program has been able to draw fundamental conclusions that accurately resemble the original theories.     —*Computerworld,*
February 1, 1982

### Monopoly

Computer analysis by Irvin Hetzel of Iowa State University has revealed the 10 squares most likely to be hit during a game of Monopoly. In order they are: Illinois Avenue, Go, B&O Railroad, Free Parking, Tennessee Avenue, New York Avenue, Reading Railroad, St. James Place, Water Works, and Pennsylvania Railroad.

—Murray Suid and Ron Harris,
*Made in America*

✶**Money** Computers have revolutionized the way money is handled. Once upon a time it was possible to write a check for the rent on Tuesday and cover it with a deposit on Thursday, knowing it would take a few days for the bank to process the rent check and debit it against your account. With computers, however, the recording of deposits and withdrawals can be done more quickly. Computers have also helped fuel the cashless economy, enabling the widespread use of credit cards and instant credit checks by banks, and by department stores and other retailers. Interestingly, at the same time that some oil companies have done away with credit cards for car gasoline sales (on the grounds that processing the paperwork adds to the cost of gasoline), others are going in for credit-card activated, self-service gasoline pumps.

✶**Commerce** Products from meats to magazines are now packaged with zebra-striped symbols that can be read by scanners at supermarket checkout stands to determine the price of the products. This Universal Product Code is one of the highly visible uses of computers in commerce; however, there are numerous others.

Electric companies use computers to monitor their vast power networks. Energy companies use them to locate oil, coal, natural gas, and uranium. Modern-day warehousing and inventory management could not exist without computers. Take your copy of this book, for instance. From printer to warehouse to bookstore, its movement was tracked with the help of computers.

**Transportation** Computers are used to help run rapid transit systems, load container ships, fly and land airplanes and keep them from colliding, and schedule airline reservations. They are also used in cars and motorcycles to monitor fluid levels, temperatures, and electrical systems and to improve fuel mileage.

**Agriculture** The computer a farm implement? Absolutely. Farming is a business, after all, and a small computer—which can be a lot cheaper than a combine—can help with billing, crop information, correct fertilizer combinations, cost per acre, and so on. Cattle breeders also may use computers for breeding and performance information about livestock. In addition, it is predicted that computers may end the isolation of country living and the movement of younger farm generations to the cities by giving people the option of working at home instead of in city offices.

**Education and Training** Computers have been used behind the scenes for years in colleges and school districts for record-keeping and accounting purposes. Now, of course, they are rapidly coming into the classroom— elementary, secondary, and college. Many parents and teachers feel that computer education is a necessity, not a novelty. The pressure is on school districts to acquire computers and train teachers and students in their use. In addition, computers are also being used as training devices in industry and government. It is

## THE COMPUTER AND THIS BOOK

This book *could* have been produced and distributed without the help of the computer, but the process would have been much less efficient. Some contributions:

- The manuscript was typed on word processing equipment.

- Type was set using computerized typesetting equipment.

- Warehousing, shipping, and inventory were handled by computer.

- Complimentary copies of the book were distributed to professors whose names appeared on computerized lists.

- Orders were placed with computer-generated customer-service labels.

- Finally, the text of the book was placed in computer-accessible storage so that it can be updated quickly for future editions.

much cheaper, for instance, to teach aspiring pilots to fly in computerized "training cockpits" or simulators than in real airplanes. Novice engineers can also be given the experience of running a train with the help of a computerized device.

**Health and Medicine** Computers have been used on the business side of medicine for some time; but in addition, they are being used in the healing process itself. For instance, computers are used in an electronic imaging capacity to provide ultrasound pictures and types of X-rays, to help pharmacists test patients' medications for drug compatibility, and even to help internists make diagnoses. We have also begun to see the use of computers in health maintenance, in everything from weight-loss programs to recording heart rates.

**The Sciences** As you might imagine, computers are used extensively in the sciences, but consider this pair of examples involving the scientific investigation of two different kinds of "communication": The Human/Dolphin Foundation in Redwood City, California, has used a computer system to translate human words typed on a keyboard into high-frequency sound patterns that dolphins seem to understand and in turn to analyze dolphin sounds. The National Aeronautics and Space Administration has developed a computerized system for use in Arecibo, Puerto Rico, to scan the heavens and listen in on eight million narrow-band radio frequencies in an attempt to find signs of communication from alien beings in outer space.

**Government and Politics** The federal government is the largest single user of computers. The Social Security Administration, for example, gets out 36 million benefit checks a month with the help of computers. Computers are also used for air traffic control, for fighting wars, and for collecting taxes. The machines are also used (fortunately or unfortunately, depending on your point of view) to help political candidates direct their fund-raising and vote-getting appeals to various groups.

**The Human Connection** Although computers are bloodless, of course, they can be used to assist humans in areas in which we are most human. Can the disabled walk again? Perhaps, with the help of computers. Can dancers and athletes improve their performance? Maybe they can by using computers to monitor their movements. Can we be helped in learning more about our ethnic backgrounds, our cultural history, even spiritual matters, with the aid of computers? Indeed we can.

## The Personal Computer

Perhaps the opening wedge was the pocket calculator, introduced on a wide scale in the mid-1970s. Or maybe it was digital watches or microwave ovens, or video or electronic games. Whatever it was, the computer has now entered our individual lives in many ways. Consider toys and games. The widespread use of new technological devices is often heralded by their use as toys or playthings, as was the case with the automobile, for instance. Cars were quite expensive toys at first, affordable only by the wealthy. But as many people became interested in them and more cars were manufactured, the costs went down, making them available to even more people.

From the wide range of electronic games that beep, buzz, chirp, test strategy and memory, and launch missiles at enemy space ships have come a host of other computerized gadgets and uses for the computer. Now personal computers of desktop size or smaller are available not only to be playthings but also to help you keep track of your bank account, write papers and letters, teach yourself foreign languages, design artwork, turn on lawn sprinklers or morning coffee, monitor temperature and humidity, and organize your Christmas card list.

Clearly, the computer user no longer has to be a Ph.D. in a laboratory somewhere. We are _all_ computer users.

But just how happy are we with this new-found sophistication?

## Computer Anxiety

The plane from Chicago to Seattle is late boarding and passengers are grumpy. Finally, all are on the plane and settled in their seats. A flight attendant switches on the public-address system.

"Sorry for the delay, everybody," she says. "We had a computer breakdown."

A chorus of groans rises throughout the plane.

"But," she goes on triumphantly, "we managed to get you on board anyway. Guess that shows we can still get along without computers, right?"

Loud cheers.

This story is true, but the conclusion that we can get along without computers is not.

"We are reaching the stage where the problems that we must solve are going to become unsolvable without computers," says prolific science and science fiction writer Isaac Asimov. "I do not fear computers. I fear the lack of them."

But clearly not everyone feels the same way. When computers fail or goof, we often take secret pleasure in the mistakes. We snicker when a computerized subscription-solicitation letter arrives for an eight-year-old child that begins, "Because your name is on a special list of inventive, creative thinkers. . . . " Or when we read in the newspapers about a computerized bank teller machine that spilled $20 bills into the street for more than 15 minutes.

We can sympathize with the California sheriff who shot his computer when it started spewing out arrest records, apparently uncontrollably, or with the person who attacked a New York life insurance company computer and murdered it with a screwdriver. Indeed, as

---

### PERSONAL COMPUTERS AND PERSONAL CARS

Seventy years ago the automobile had just begun to have a major impact on how people lived, worked, played, interacted. There are now more owners of personal cars than there were owners of personal horses. . . .

Has anything influenced the texture of our lives more than automobiles? The personal computer is going to be a rival to the automobile. . . .

Car ownership in 1911, for instance, was about the same density as personal computer ownership in 1981. There was about one car per thousand persons in the U.S. in 1911 and the same personal computer ownership density in 1981. However, by 1921, there were one hundred people per car in the U.S. It only took a year or two for personal computers to go from one computer per thousand people to one hundred.

—H.E. James Finke,
ISO World,
January 10, 1983

these last two incidents show, some people are inclined to attribute human qualities to computers, to personify them, like HAL (note the letters alphabetically precede the letters IBM), the computer gone mad in the movie *2001: A Space Odyssey*. Computers are not just fancy adding machines, we think; sometimes they actually seem to have a will of their own.

Terms such as *computer anxiety* and *computer phobia* have now entered the language. One study found that at least 30 percent of the business community that deals with computers on a daily basis experiences some form of "cyberphobia"—fear of computers—which is characterized by such symptoms as nausea, sweaty palms, and high blood pressure. Another survey found that 34 percent of all Americans expressed lack of confidence in doing business with computers and that an amazing 89 percent disliked doing business with automatic teller machines at banks, preferring instead to deal with real, live tellers.

What are people afraid of? Some people are nervous about the mathematical sound of the word *computer*. It seems to suggest that only a person with high analytical and quantitative skills can use the machine. In fact, however, as we see all around us, computers are becoming more and more accessible to more and more people.

Many people are fearful of the whole environment of computing. The machinery looks intimidating to them. The programming languages appear incomprehensible. There is a notion that computers are temperamental gadgets, and that once a glitch gets into a computer system it may wreak all kinds of havoc, from fouling up bank statements to launching nuclear missiles by mistake. People are nervous that computers might be used to "get" them in some way—by the Internal Revenue Service, by credit bureaus, by privacy invaders of one sort or another.

Many people are worried about computers in relation to their jobs. A nationwide survey by ITT Educational Services, Inc. found that four out of five Americans doubt they have the skills to find jobs and keep them in the technological labor market of the future. A good many present-day executives whose companies are installing computer terminals in their offices worry about typing, either because they do not know how or because they are afraid they will lose status if they use a keyboard. Some people are edgy about missing face-to-face contact if separated from other people by video terminals.

Finally, people are fearful of depersonalization, of being turned into numbers. Sometimes these are the very people who are installing computer systems. ("Incidentally, I hate numbers," a former Postmaster General was quoted as having said. The occasion was an interview in which he was enthusiastially describing the benefits of expanding zip codes from five to nine digits.) Could we, in fact, get along without number identifications for people? Perhaps. But consider that in any given year the admissions office of a major West Coast university has to deal with the following: 20 to 30 pairs of applicants will have the same first and last names; about six pairs will have the same first, middle, and last names; one or two pairs will have the same first,

## COMPUTER ANXIETY HITS MIDDLE MANAGEMENT

. . . Executives feel that sitting at a computer terminal ill-suits the executive image. Secretaries type; managers feel foolish and unprofessional when they do. . . .

Still another unexpressed fear stems from the widespread notion that computer systems are temperamental gadgets. Managers are afraid that a missed keystroke will result in a nasty headquarters memo that reads in effect: "Who was the jerk who blew up the system?"

Booz Allen senior vice president Harvey Poppel points out that a computer's ability to give instantaneous notice of mistakes further intimidates many managers. "In a corporate environment, people sugarcoat the ways they tell you you're wrong," Mr. Poppel says. "The computer just comes out and says you're wrong with blinding speed. It is an immediate rebuke."

—Mary Bralove,
*Wall Street Journal*,
March 7, 1983

middle, and last names and the same birthdate. A number, by contrast, can be a unique identifier. This kind of depersonalization is part of the price we pay for the convenience of the computer.

Eventually, the number of people suffering from computer anxiety will probably decline. The availability of cheaper, easier-to-use personal computers will reduce the intimidation factor. But probably more important, a new generation of children is growing up who are perfectly comfortable with the computer. This has lessons for the rest of us who are not so young. As one writer put it, "Perhaps our most significant problem is that adults take a natural negative view of mistakes. This is why children take to computers with few of the frustrations shown by adults; children are not as concerned with . . . the possibility of appearing foolish in front of a computer."

## Human Nature and Computer Nature

It is human nature to be worried about the encroachments of the computer, and indeed there *are* some things to worry about. One pervasive problem is the computer billing error. Despite efforts to alleviate this irritation, which usually results from mistakes made by the people putting data into the computer system, setting the record straight is often frustratingly slow. An even more serious problem is invasion of privacy. Think of all the forms you have filled out for schools, jobs, medical matters, credit, taxes, and so on. There is scarcely any data related to your daily life that is not on a computer file somewhere. Might this information be obtained by unauthorized persons? The computer industry has been trying to deal with the privacy matter, but it is an expensive and difficult issue. We shall touch on problems such as these throughout the book and discuss them in more detail in Chapter 18.

Some people have worried there might be some computer-smashing revolts, much like the Luddite uprisings in England in the early 1800s. The Luddites were workers in industrial centers who went on a rampage and destroyed textile machines, to which they attributed unemployment and low wages. Today there are people who think wistfully that, if we wished to, we could still reorganize society and return to the precomputer days. The truth is, however, that the computer is not a luxury any more, and unplugging it would have enormous consequences—most of which we are not prepared to live with.

There are at least five reasons why we cannot—indeed, should not—turn the clock back:

• First, by now it is human nature to be resentful if service is not fast. But it is "computer nature" that provides that fast service. Thus, unless we are prepared to do a lot more waiting—for paychecks, grades, telephone calls, travel reservations, and many other things—we need the split-second processing of the computer.

• Second, computers are extremely reliable. Of course, you might not think this from the way stories about "computer mistakes" are handled in the press. Unfortunately, what is almost never brought out in these stories is that *the mistakes are not the fault of the computers themselves.* True, there are sometimes equipment failures, but most errors supposedly made by computers are really human errors. Although one hears the phrase "computer error" quite frequently, the blame usually lies elsewhere.

• Third, computers are able to perform boring, dangerous, or highly sensitive jobs that people should not perform or, in some cases, cannot perform, as in working with nuclear fuel rods. Granted, computers will eliminate some jobs; automation is a tough societal nut to deal with and always has been. But computers free human beings for other kinds of productivity. We can also turn this idea around: If we were to abolish computers, we would have to hire millions of people to do what computers are now doing and ask them to perform some very tedious tasks.

• Fourth, because of expanding technology, communications, and the interdependency of people, we suffer from an information deluge. Although this is in part brought on by the computer, it is also the computer that will help solve it. To make essential business and governmental decisions, managers need to take into account a variety of financial, geographical, logistical, and other factors. The computer helps them sort wheat from chaff and make better choices.

• Finally, for all of these reasons, the computer helps hold costs down—for labor, energy, paperwork, and waste—thereby increasing productivity and reducing the costs of goods and services.

## The Future Now: Toward Computer Literacy

The Computer Revolution is an unfinished revolution, one that will continue to roll throughout our lifetimes. But its seeds are already apparent, which is why we subtitled this chapter "The Future Now." Throughout the rest of this book, we will describe the implications of the near future for the tasks we must learn today. In the final chapter, "Computers and Society: The Future Then," we will look to the far horizons to see what forms the Computer Revolution may take and how they may affect your life.

We have written the book with two kinds of readers in mind. If you are contemplating a computer-related career, you will find a great deal of discussion about the technology, the applications, and various associated jobs. If you are not interested in a career in computers, this book will, we hope, provide you with some computer literacy. For if the computer is to liberate us rather than confound us or threaten us, we have to assume some responsibility for understanding it.

## Summary

- Like the Industrial Revolution, the Computer Revolution is irreversible. It is making massive changes in society. Though unfinished, the revolution is well under way and its effects are seen in graphics, robotics, transportation, paperwork, money, commerce, the professions, and the surge in use of the personal computer.

- The computer as artist is seen in space photography, photographs by meteorological satellites, brain scanners in medicine, biochemists' study of genetic molecules, architectural graphics, and graphics of aircraft designs. Business executives use computer graphics to illustrate sales figures and the like.

- Robots are used in auto plants to do welding and painting, and in many other jobs people cannot or should not do.

- In paperwork tasks, computers are used in word processing to handle repetitive drafts and for bookkeeping, record keeping, and document sending.

- In the world of money, computers are used to speed bank withdrawals and deposits and have ensured the widespread use of credit cards.

- In commerce, computers are used to read the Universal Product Code symbols on groceries, help locate energy sources, monitor electric power networks, and maintain day-to-day warehousing and inventory management.

- In transportation, computers are used to run rapid-transit systems; load container ships; fly, land, and guide airplanes; and monitor auto fluid levels and mileage.

- For agriculture, computers can be used not only for business uses but also to provide crop information, help cattle breeders, and for other farm-related tasks.

- Computer education is becoming more and more a necessity, in the view of many parents and teachers. The machines are also used as training devices, in teaching pilots to fly and engineers to drive trains, for example.

- In medicine, computers are used to provide ultrasound pictures and types of X-rays, to help pharmacists test patients' medications for drug compatibility, and even to help internists make diagnoses.

- Scientists use computers in many ways, but two dramatic examples are for attempts to communicate with dolphins and with possible alien beings in outer space.

- The federal government is the largest single user of computers—for example, for issuing Social Security checks, for air traffic control, for fighting wars, and for collecting taxes. Computers are also used by politicians to target voting and fund-raising appeals to certain groups.

- Despite their bloodlessness, computers are used for very human purposes—to help dancers and athletes, for example, or to help us learn about our cultural backgrounds.

- The computer has entered our lives in the form of electronic games, microwave ovens, and digital watches, and as personal-convenience home computers that can help with personal finances, learning, and hobbies.

- Some people suffer from "computer anxiety" or "computerphobia," fearing that computers will invade their privacy, start nuclear war, eliminate or change jobs, turn people into numbers, or be too complicated to cope with.

- Some serious computer-related problems, such as billing errors, are being addressed. Since most of us have extensive personal data on computer files, the privacy issue is particularly important.

- There are five reasons we cannot and should not try to do without computers: (1) They provide fast service. (2) They are extremely reliable. (3) They can perform boring, dangerous, or highly sensitive jobs. (4) They can help us sort through the deluge of information and make better decisions. (5) They can help increase productivity and reduce waste and labor and paperwork costs.

## Review

1. How are computers used to do things that people cannot and should not do?

2. What are some of the ways computers have already revolutionized our lives?

3. What are the fears people have about computers? (What discomfort or anxiety, if any, do you feel about computers?)

4. Give five reasons why we cannot do without computers.

**IN THIS CHAPTER**

A computer system consists of three main areas of data handling—input, processing, and output—and is backed by a fourth, storage. Whether the system is centralized or decentralized, machines (hardware) and programs (software) turn unprocessed data into usable information. A computer system also requires people. Data may be collected and processed in groups (batch processing) or it may be processed as it occurs to provide immediate results (direct access real-time processing).

*ch2*

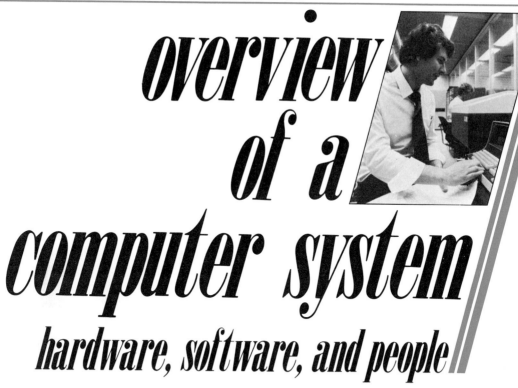

# *overview of a computer system*
## *hardware, software, and people*

You sit down at what looks like a television set connected to a typewriter keyboard. You type:

```
100 REM ***CAR RACING GAME***
110 REM
120 REM DESCRIBE GAME TO PLAYER
130 PRINT "THIS GAME PITS YOUR CHOSEN CAR"
140 PRINT "AGAINST A CAR CHOSEN BY THE COMPUTER."
150 PRINT "YOU WILL CHOOSE TYPE OF CAR AND SPEED."
160 PRINT "YOU WILL BE ADVISED OF ROAD CONDITIONS,"
170 PRINT "GAS CONSUMPTION, AND OTHER FACTORS."
180 REM TELL PLAYER WHICH CARS AVAILABLE
190 PRINT "HERE ARE THE CARS AVAILABLE:"
200 PRINT "1. PORSCHE"
210 PRINT "2. CORVETTE"
220 PRINT "3. DATSUN 280 ZX"
230 PRINT "CHOOSE YOUR CAR BY TYPING ITS NUMBER."
240 REM GET THE CAR NUMBER
250 INPUT N
     •
     •
     •
```

What you are doing is "talking" to a computer through the keyboard, using a programming language known as BASIC. In this case, you are using the computer for one of its more entertaining purposes—playing a game. But the process you are using is essentially no different from that used for any other, more serious purpose, as we shall see.

The set of instructions you have just typed is part of a program. A **program** is a series of step-by-step instructions that directs the computer to do the tasks you want it to do and produce the result you want. (The numbers on the left are called line numbers, and the text on the lines forms program statements.) The purpose of a program is to take data, or raw facts, and turn them into useful information.

Programs available to run a computer system are called **software.** The machines in the system are called **hardware.** When outsiders think of computer personnel, they tend to think of them as people who operate machines. Actually, many people who work in the computer field are involved in some aspect of software. However, before you begin to work with software, it is helpful to understand the machines on which it runs.

As the title of this chapter indicates, what follows is an *overview,* a look at "the big picture" of a computer system. Therefore, you will be exposed to what may seem to be a blizzard of new terms. Indeed, there are more new terms introduced here than in any other chapter in the book, and they are defined in only a minimal way. Do not despair. In subsequent chapters we will discuss the parts of a computer system more leisurely and in greater detail.

## A Tour of the Hardware

The computer system consists of three main areas of data handling—input, processing, and output—and is backed by a fourth, storage. The hardware responsible for these four aspects, diagrammed in Figure 2-1, operates as follows:

- **Input units** take data in machine-readable form and send it to the processing unit.

- The **processor** is the central processing unit, which has the electronic circuitry that manipulates input data into the information wanted. The processor actually executes computer instructions. Main storage contains the instructions and data needed by the processor.

- **Output units** make the processed data available for use.

- **Storage units** are secondary devices outside the processor itself that can store additional data and programs. That is, they *supplement* the main storage in the processor.

Now let us consider the equipment making up these four parts.

### Input: What Goes In

**Input** is the data that is input—put in—to the computer system for processing. Some of the most common ways of feeding input data into the system are by:

- Floppy disk, through a floppy disk reader

- Magnetic tape, through a key-to-tape device

- Your fingers, typing on a terminal

- Documents, through optical character recognition devices such as "wands"

- Bar codes, through a bar code reader

- Punched cards, through a card reader

There are some other interesting ways of entering data into the system (such as by voice), but for the moment let us consider those just listed.

A **floppy disk** looks something like a 45 rpm record, an oxide-coated plastic disk. However, it is called "floppy" because it is somewhat flexible. The **floppy disk reader** (Figure 2-2) translates data on the disk into electronic impulses. These data-containing impulses are sent to main storage.

**Magnetic tape,** which comes on a reel, looks like cassette tape or reel-to-reel tape that one plays on a tape recorder. The data may have been keyed on the tape using a **key-to-tape device** (Figure 2-3). The data can be sent to main computer storage.

**20**

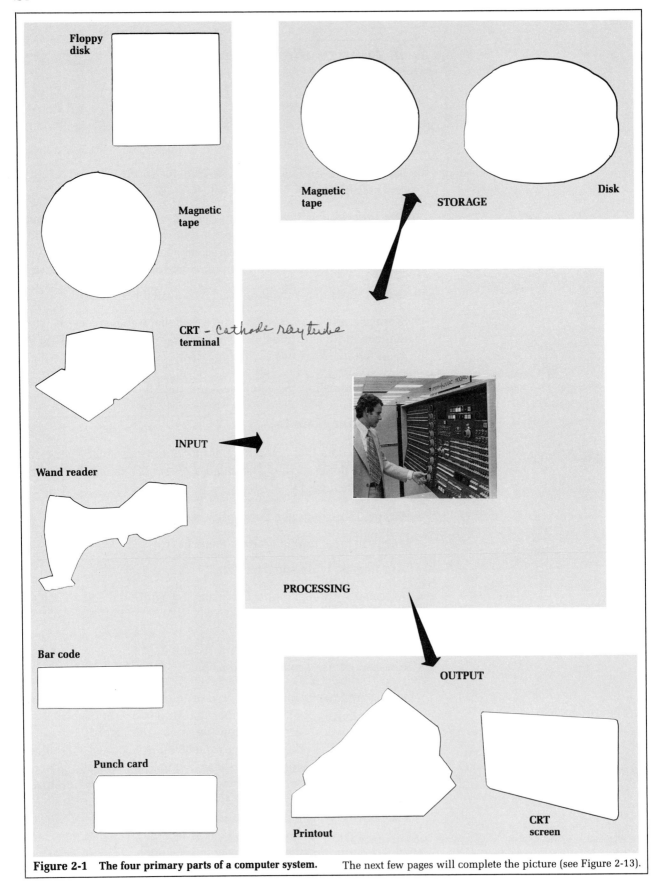

Floppy
disk

Magnetic
tape

CRT - *Cathode ray tube*
terminal

Wand reader

Bar code

Punch card

Magnetic
tape                    STORAGE                    Disk

PROCESSING

INPUT

OUTPUT

Printout

CRT
screen

**Figure 2-1   The four primary parts of a computer system.**     The next few pages will complete the picture (see Figure 2-13).

**Figure 2-2 Floppy disk reader and floppy disks.** *Left,* cutaway version of floppy disk shows part of protective jacket removed.

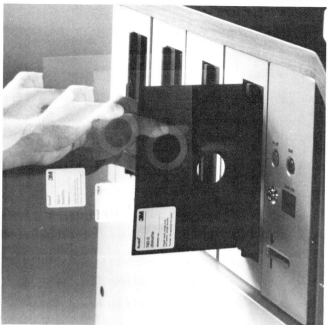

**Figure 2-3 Magnetic tape and key-to-tape device.** Tape is shown on the reel left of the keyboard.

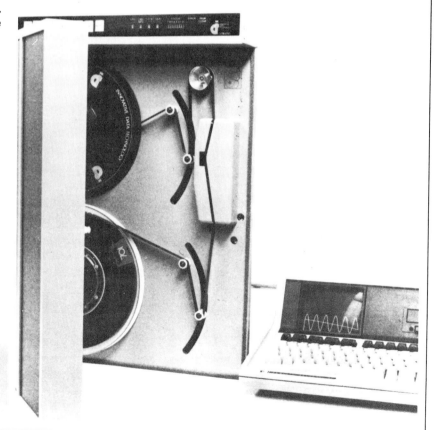

**Figure 2-4    A CRT terminal.**   The CRT (cathode ray tube) device consists of a televisionlike screen coupled to a typewriterlike keyboard.

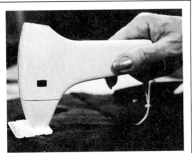

**Figure 2-5    An OCR wand reader.** This device "reads" data on price tags. It is often found in department stores.

**Terminals** are of many kinds, but the most common is the television-screen kind (Figure 2-4). Terminals usually have keyboards like an electric typewriter and operate much the same way, except that the computer terminal responds to what you enter on the keyboard; that is, it "talks back" to you.

Television-screen terminals are usually called **CRTs,** for **cathode ray tubes.** These terminals are also called **video display terminals (VDTs).** With the CRT, you can enter data into the computer from the keyboard. You read and respond to information displayed on the CRT screen by the computer.

**Optical character recognition (OCR)** devices are able to read data directly from an original document, thus eliminating the costly data preparation step. Data that can be input directly comes in many forms. One of the most common forms is the price tag that can be scanned by a **wand** to input data about goods being sold (Figure 2-5). Another is the **bar code,** the zebra-striped symbols now carried on nearly all products from meats to magazines, which can be read by a **bar code reader** (Figure 2-6). The advantage of OCR and bar codes over other ways of inputting data is that they eliminate (or at least significantly reduce) the chance for human error in transcribing the data.

**Punched cards,** which contain small holes representing data, are read by a **card reader,** as shown in Figure 2-7. The cards contain data that will be manipulated by the computer.

Sometimes, before data can be input to the system, it must be manually prepared in some way. **Data entry operators** (Figure 2-8), using machines, prepare the data by recording it on punched cards, magnetic tape, or magnetic disks. The data is then sent to the computer room, which houses the processor, for processing.

Figure 2-6   Bar code and bar code reader.

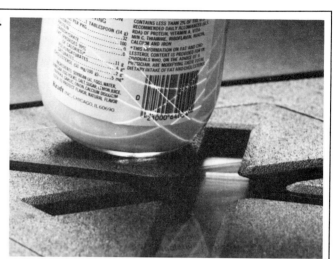

*1234567890*

Figure 2-7 Punched card, card keypunch machine, and card reader.

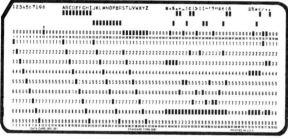

**Figure 2-8 Data entry operators.** Some large organizations have data entry departments in which data is prepared for processing on the computer system.

## The Processor: Data Manipulation

The **processor** is the computer's center of activity. The processor is also called the **central processing unit,** or **CPU.** The central processing unit consists of electronic circuits that interpret and execute program instructions, as well as communicate with the input, output, and storage devices. The computer's **main storage** holds the data after it is input to the system and before it is to be processed. It holds the data also after it has been processed but before it has been released to the output device. Also consisting of electronic circuits, main storage electronically stores letters, numbers, and special characters such as dollar signs and decimal points.

The processor is usually contained in a cabinet or housing that also contains the computer **console.** This is the panel of switches and dials and colored buttons and winking red and green lights that has inspired the control rooms of so many Hollywood-built space ships. The console (Figure 2-9) allows the computer system to signal the operator when something needs to be done—for example, resupplying the printer with paper. The console also permits the operator, through a **console terminal** such as a CRT, to have two-way communication with the computer system, for example, to check on which programs the system is executing.

**Figure 2-9 The computer console.** The array of switches and lights, which indicates the status of processing occurring in the computer, is less dramatic on the most recent models of computers.

## Output: What Comes Out

The results produced by the processor are, of course, a computer's whole reason for being; **output** is raw data processed into usable information. Some ingenious forms of output have been devised, such as music and synthetic speech, but the most common forms are words and numbers. Two common output devices are terminals and printers.

Terminals are the same as those described under input—they are usually CRTs. However, they can vary in their forms of display: Some may produce lines of written or numerical display; others may produce color graphical display.

**Printers** (Figure 2-10), machines that produce printed reports under the control of a computer program, vary in several ways. Some printers form images on paper as typewriters do, striking a character against a ribbon, which makes an image on the paper. Other types of printers form images by using specially coated papers that respond to electrostatic impulses. Printers also vary based on how much is printed at one time—a character at a time or an entire line of characters at a time. Other variable factors are speed, cost, and noise.

### Storage

By **storage** we mean **auxiliary** or **secondary storage,** not main storage. For instance, it would be unwise for a college registrar to try to house the grades of all the students in the college in main storage; if this were done the computer probably would not have room to store anything else. Hence the need for auxiliary storage.

The two most common auxiliary storage media are magnetic disk and magnetic tape. **Magnetic disk** is an oxide-coated disk like a phonograph record on which data is recorded as magnetic spots. The disk can be floppy disk (which can be used not only for storage but also, as we mentioned, as an input device) or **hard disk,** which is not

**Figure 2-10   Two types of printers.** The high-speed printer on the left typically is used in businesses with high volume output. The printer on the right is much slower and would often be used with a word processor.

**Figure 2-11 Disk pack and disk drives.** Disks are contained within the round disk packs shown on top of the cabinets containing the disk drives. The disks are lowered into the opened drawer when they are to be used.

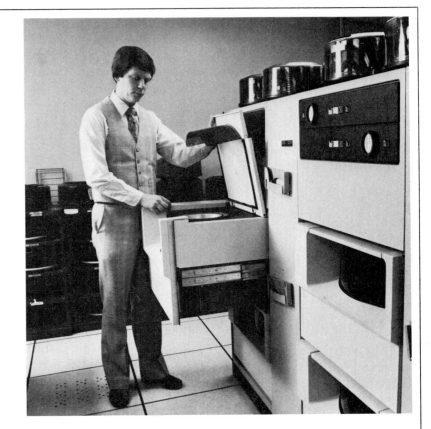

**Figure 2-12 Magnetic tape reels and tape drive.** Magnetic tape is traveling off one reel onto another.

flexible but holds more data and has faster access than a floppy disk. Hard disks are usually contained in **disk packs** (Figure 2-11), and the data on them is read by **disk drives** (Figure 2-11). On some disk units, the disk packs can be removed from the drives. This permits unlimited storage capacity by use of interchangeable disk packs.

**Magnetic tape** can also be used for auxiliary storage. Magnetic tape reels are mounted on **tape drives** (Figure 2-12) when the data on them is to be read by the computer system.

When not in use, tape reels or disk packs—at least in large installations with lots of reels or disk packs—are stored in a room called a **tape** or **disk library.** It is the job of people in the library to catalog the tapes or disks and to store them so that they are safe and away from dust, heat, or static electricity that might disturb the magnetization on their surfaces—and hence the data.

## *The Complete Hardware System*

Figure 2-13 shows the system we sketched at the beginning of this chapter (in Figure 2-1) with the pieces filled in with the equipment we have been discussing. Although the equipment may vary widely, from the simplest desktop computer to the most powerful supercomputer, by and large the nature of the hardware remains the same. Gallery 2, "A Little Gallery of Hardware," shows various forms of computer hardware in use.

Nearly all large systems run 24 hours a day to meet the users' data processing needs. However, the size of the computer an organization needs depends on the organization's requirements. Clearly, the U.S. Weather Bureau, keeping watch on the weather fronts of many continents, has different requirements from those of a car dealer's service department, for instance, that is trying to keep track of its parts inventory.

In the jargon of the computer trade, large computers are called **mainframes.** Mainframes are capable of processing data at very fast speeds and have access to billions of characters of data. The most powerful mainframes are often known as **supercomputers.** There are only a few supercomputers in existence, and they are used principally for such mammoth data manipulation as worldwide weather forecasting.

Smaller computers, smaller than mainframes in storage capacity, are called **minicomputers.** Minicomputers are slower and less costly than mainframes, but they fall within the price range of many small businesses. The advent of the minicomputer greatly expanded the potential computer market.

The smallest computers, such as desktop and personal or home computers, are called **microcomputers.** This is the class of computers represented by the Apple, the TRS-80, and the IBM Personal Computer, which have taken the country by storm during the last few years.

**SUPERCOMPUTERS: AS FAST AS THE ENTIRE HUMAN RACE**

To qualify as a supercomputer, a machine must be able to perform more than 20 "megaflops," meaning 20 million floating-point, or arithmetical, operations per second. (The fastest IBM computer, by contrast, can do only about a single megaflop.) Lowell Wood, who heads an advanced supercomputer project at Lawrence Livermore National Laboratory in California, offers a vivid illustration of the machines' number-crunching power: Already, he says, a supercomputer does high-precision arithmetic as fast as "the entire human race could, with each person using one of the best available hand calculators."

—Bruce Schechter
*Discover,*
January 1983

**28**

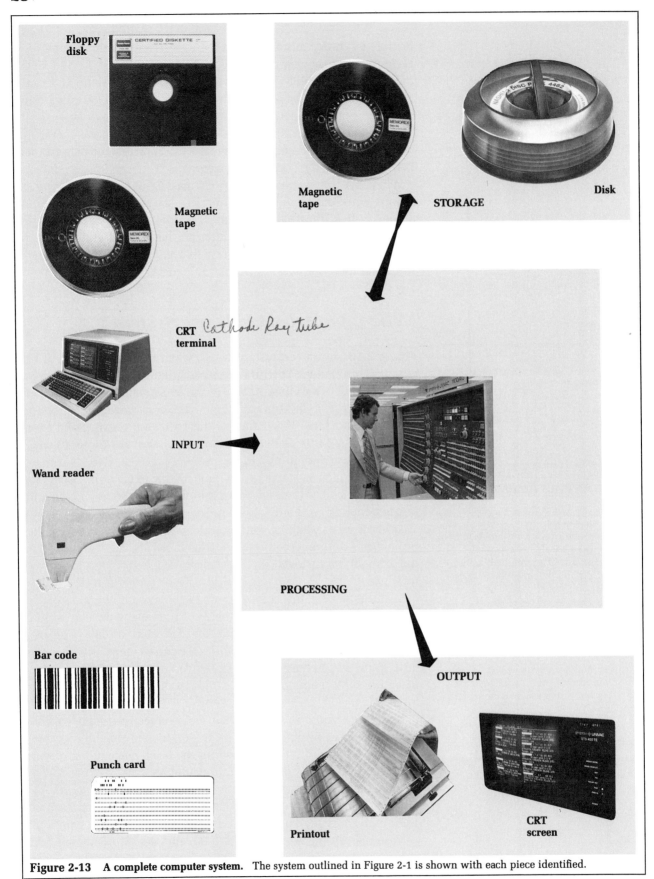

Floppy disk

Magnetic tape

CRT terminal *Cathode Ray tube*

INPUT

Wand reader

Bar code

Punch card

Magnetic tape

STORAGE

Disk

PROCESSING

OUTPUT

Printout

CRT screen

**Figure 2-13   A complete computer system.**   The system outlined in Figure 2-1 is shown with each piece identified.

**Figure 2-14   A microcomputer, with CPU, screen, keyboard, and disk drives contained in the same unit.** Only the printer (right) is separate. This is a TRS-80 ™ Model II microcomputer with a typewriter-quality printer.

## PERSONAL COMPUTERS REDUCE TV VIEWING

Home computers reduce television viewing by more than a half hour daily, a study of 77 computer families at Stanford [University] shows.

"This change represents a rather major shift in the use of time. It suggests that home computers may be more addictive than television," Prof. Everett M. Rogers, Hugh M. Daley and Thomas D. Wu declare. . . .

More than half the families studied (56 percent) reported no change, but four out of ten (40 percent) said they decreased their viewing by an average of 1.5 hours daily.

The average U.S. household has TV turned on about six hours per day. A separate study of Stanford faculty and staff this fall indicated their sets were on only 2.7 hours per day.

When asked what changes their home computer had caused, the most common response was "facilitates my work" (29 percent), followed by "increased my awareness of the computer world" (17 percent), "changes my recreational activities" (14 percent), "saves time" and "allows me to spend time at home" (12 percent each).

—*Stanford Observer*,
April 1983

Unfortunately, none of the definitions of mainframe, minicomputer, and microcomputer can be said to be fixed because computer technology is changing so rapidly.

The hardware devices attached to the computer are called **peripheral equipment.** Peripheral equipment includes all input, output, and secondary storage devices. In the case of microcomputers, most or all of the input, output, and storage devices are often built into the same physical unit. In the popular Radio Shack TRS-80, for instance (Figure 2-14), the CPU, keyboard, CRT screen, and disk drives are all contained in the same housing; only the printer is separate.

## Centralization versus Decentralization: The Rise of the Computer Commuter?

Originally, computer hardware was all kept in one place; that is, it was centralized in one room. While this is still often the case, more and more computer systems are, in a broad sense, decentralized. That is, the computer itself, the CPU, may be in one place, but the devices to access the computer, usually terminals, may be somewhere else in order to serve users better. The terminals are usually connected to the computer by telephone lines. For instance, the computer and storage that has the information on your bank checking account may be located in one place, but the terminals are located in branch banks all over town so a teller can find out what your balance is. It is precisely this kind of decentralized access to information that has permitted the growth of another banking service, the automated self-service teller machine.

In its strictest sense, "decentralized" refers to a system whereby computers and data storage are placed in dispersed locations, a system known as **distributed data processing.** In this arrangement, a local office usually uses its own small computer for processing local data but is connected to the larger organization's central computer for other purposes. For example, an insurance company headquartered in Denver, with branches throughout the Midwest, might process payments, claims, and the like through minicomputers in local offices. However, summary data could be sent regularly by each office for processing by the mainframe computer in Denver.

The ultimate form of decentralization is the home computer terminal that is connected by telephone lines to the mainframe computers of companies selling all kinds of services—instantaneous news, stock market reports, encyclopedic facts. The growth of home computers has already led to some "computer commuters"—people who work at home on home computers or terminals connected via phone lines to computers at their office. Indeed, it has been suggested we may begin to see a new bumpersticker—I'D RATHER BE TELECOMMUTING—on the cars of people who are still required to drive to work instead of being allowed to work at home.

## Software

As we mentioned, when most people think about computers, they think about machines. The blinking lights on the console, the clacking of the printers, the whirling tape reels, the changing lines on a CRT screen—these are the attention getters. However, it is really the area of **software**—the planned, step-by-step instructions required to turn data into information—that we wish to emphasize in this book.

Programs—software—can be written in a variety of programming languages. Most programming languages in common use today are English-like in appearance, although there are very definite rules for using them. Some languages are used specifically for business or for scientific applications; we will present some such languages in Chapter 11. BASIC, used at the start of this chapter, was designed for beginners but has become popular for use on mini- and microcomputers. (BASIC is described in some detail in Appendix A.)

Programmers must understand how to use a programming language so that they can convey the logic of a program to the computer. The program must be made available to the computer in a form it understands. Sometimes it is punched on cards, but more often it is keyed (typed) in line by line on a CRT terminal. The program is then stored in some form of auxiliary storage, such as disk, from which it can be called into main storage for testing and execution. Besides being able to use a programming language, programmers must also understand what the program is supposed to do and design it accordingly, test it to remove errors, and document—write about—what they did.

### TELECOMMUTING AND PERSONAL POWER

The personal computer offers access to information, which in the modern world is an emerging form of power. So, in effect, the personal computer is also a means of gaining power. The kind of power which once belonged only to large institutions can now belong to the individual.

In many ways telecommuting is an extension of the virtues found in personal computing. There is also increased freedom and control—in this case, over time and space. You can now work at your own pace in the environment of your choice. . . .
—Evan Peelle,
*Personal Computing,*
May 1982

Because of miniaturization, standardization, and the growing popularity of computers, the cost of hardware is going down. The cost of software, however, is going up, for a variety of reasons. Unlike hardware, the making of software depends chiefly on labor, and labor costs keep rising. In addition, the story of the Computer Revolution is that computers are becoming easier, not harder, for people to use. That is, computers are becoming accessible to more people, and less training is required to use them. But it takes complicated software to give uncomplicated access to the computer—another reason why software costs are going up. For most readers of this book, then, particularly those interested in careers in the computer field, we suggest that the future lies in understanding software.

## _Organizing Data for Processing_

Up to this point, we have been using the word _data_ in a loose sense, as unorganized information. Now let us give a specific definition.

**Data** is the raw material to be processed by a computer. Such material can be letters, numbers, or facts—such as grades in a class, baseball batting averages, or light and dark areas in a photograph. Processed data becomes **information**—data that is organized, meaningful, and useful. Data that is very uninteresting to one person may become very interesting information to another. The raw facts of births, eating habits, and growth rates of calves, for instance, may mean nothing to most people. But the computer-produced relationships among feed, growth, and beef quality are critical information to a cattle breeder.

To be processed by the computer, raw data must be organized into characters, fields, records, files, and data bases (Figure 2-15).

A **character** is a letter, number, or special character (such as $, ?, or *). One or more characters comprise a field.

A **field** contains an item of data. For example, suppose a health club was making address labels for direct mailing. For each person, it might have a date-joined field, a name field, a street address field, a city field, a state field, and a zip code field.

A **record** is a collection of related fields. Thus, on the health club list, one person's date-joined, name, address, city, state, and zip code would comprise a record.

A **file** is a collection of related records. The entire list of address labels for the health club would be a file.

A **data base** is a collection of interrelated data stored together with minimum redundancy. Specific data items can be retrieved for various applications. For instance, the health club data could be obtained according to state or zip code or alphabetically by last name. The concept of a data base is complicated; we return to it in more detail in Chapter 16.

Whenever a change is to be made to stored data, a record is generated containing the new data. The record is called a **transaction.**

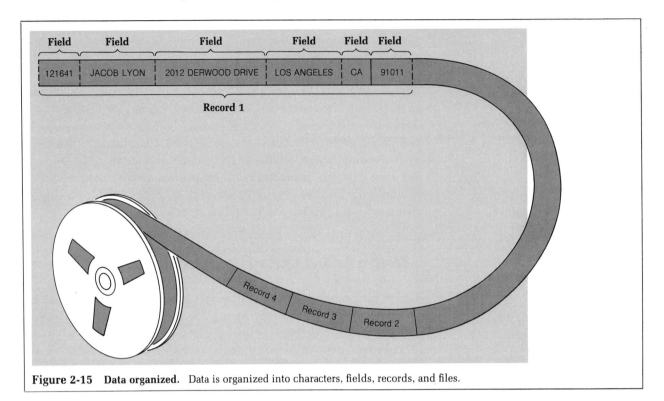

| Field | Field | Field | Field | Field | Field |
|---|---|---|---|---|---|
| 121641 | JACOB LYON | 2012 DERWOOD DRIVE | LOS ANGELES | CA | 91011 |

**Record 1**

Record 4

Record 3

Record 2

**Figure 2-15   Data organized.** Data is organized into characters, fields, records, and files.

Whenever files are changed to reflect new information, the process is called **updating.** Files of records are stored on some form of medium, usually magnetic disk or magnetic tape, so they can be read into main computer storage for processing.

A file can be a **transaction file,** one that contains modifications to existing records. For example, in our address label list, a transaction would be a change in a label (a new address), an added label (a new member), or a deleted label (a member resigns). Or a file can be a **master file,** which contains relatively permanent data—the master address label list, in this case—that is updated by a transaction file.

## Types of Processing

There are several methods of processing data in a computer system. We shall briefly describe some of the common methods and the related concepts. In general, we are distinguishing between processing data transactions in groups and processing the transactions one at a time.

### Batch Processing

**Batch processing** is a technique in which transactions are collected into groups, or batches, to be processed. Let us suppose that we are going to update the aforementioned address label file—that is, process changes to the file. The master file is the list of all members of the health club and their addresses. It is updated (batch-processed) monthly with these transactions: additions (transactions to create new master records for new names added), deletions (transactions with instructions to delete master records of people who have resigned from the health club), and changes or revisions (transactions to change fields such as street address or phone numbers on the master records).

In batch processing, when a transaction file is matched against a master file, it is processed in some sequential order by a field called a key. The **key** is a unique identifier for a record. It is used to locate a specific record within a file and to sort the transaction records before processing. In updating the address label file, the key might be member number.

One advantage of batch processing is that it is usually less expensive than other types of processing because it is more efficient: A group of records is processed at the same time. One disadvantage of batch processing is that you have to wait. It does not matter that you want to know what the gasoline bill for your car is *now*; you have to wait until the end of the month when all your credit card gas purchases are added up. Batch processing cannot give you a quick response to your question.

Another disadvantage is that batch processing requires an extensive manual support system. Let us say your department store credit card does not allow you to charge a purchase over $50 without further verification, and the new coat you want costs more than that. The sales clerk must call the store's business office, where someone will have to leaf through the printout of the results from the most recent batch processing, which was perhaps done the night before, to see if you are creditworthy.

Figure 2-16 shows an example of batch processing, using a common example of a payroll system.

### Direct Access Processing

**Direct access processing** is a technique of processing transactions in random order—that is, in any order they occur. No presorting of the transactions is required.

A common form of direct access processing is real-time processing. **Real-time processing** can obtain data from the computer system in time to affect the activity at hand. In other words, a transaction is processed fast enough that the results can come back and be acted upon quickly. (Usually "quickly" means "immediately.") Processing transactions one at a time, as they occur, is also called **transaction processing.** An example is a teller at a bank (or you at an automatic teller machine) finding out immediately what your bank balance is. For processing to be real-time, it must also be **on-line;** that is, the user's terminal must be directly connected to the computer.

The great leap forward in the technology of real-time processing was made possible by the development of magnetic disk as a means of storing data. With magnetic tape, it was not possible to go directly to the particular record one was looking for—the tape might have to

**34**

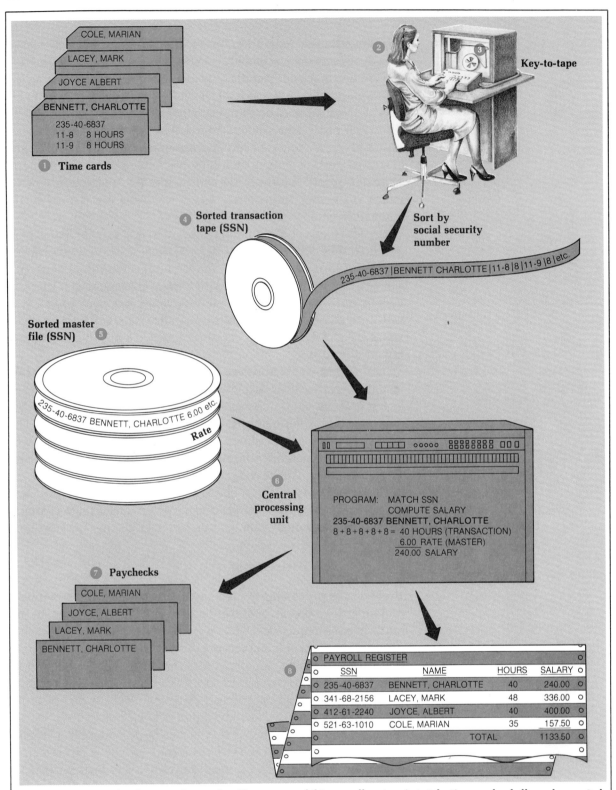

**Figure 2-16  How batch processing works.** The purpose of this payroll system is to take time cards of all employees and sort them, then print out paychecks and a payroll register. ❶ Time cards showing hours worked are in input on ❷ key-to-tape equipment, which produces ❸ a tape. That tape is sorted by a computer onto ❹ another tape, which is a transaction tape sorted according to social security number. The key on this transaction tape is a social security number, and the transaction file contains these numbers in sequential order, from lowest to highest. ❺ The master file, which is also organized by social security number, supplies the pay rate of each employee. ❻ The computer matches transaction-file information and master-file information by social security number, producing ❼ paychecks and ❽ a payroll register, a listing of employees and their related payroll data.

be advanced several feet first. However, just as you can move the record arm on your stereo directly to the particular song you want on an LP record, so with disk you can go directly to one particular piece of data. The invention of the disk means that data processing is more likely to be **interactive,** a word meaning that the user communicates with the computer through a terminal, maintaining a dialogue or conversation back and forth. The direct access to data on disk dramatically increases the uses for interactive computing.

There are several advantages to real-time processing. The first is that you do not need to wait. A department store sales clerk, for instance, can ask, "What is the balance in customer number so-and-so's account?" and get an immediate reply—a distinct plus, since everyone expects fast service these days. Second, the process permits continual updating of a customer's record. Thus, the sales clerk can not only verify your credit but also record the sale on your computer record, and you will eventually be billed through the billing process.

Real-time systems are one form of time-sharing. **Time-sharing** is a system in which two or more users can, through individual terminals, share the use ("time") of a central computer and, because of the computer's speed, receive practically simultaneous responses. Thus, an airline can have reservation clerks in far-flung cities interact with the same computer at the same time to keep informed on what flights are scheduled and how many seats are available on each.

Real-time processing does have some drawbacks. One is expense. Unlike batch processing, which uses the computer only for the amount of time needed to get the job done, real-time gives you access to the computer at all times. The result is that real-time processing uses more resources and so it costs more. However, when weighed against the alternative, such as lack of quick service, the added expense may be a minor matter.

A more serious drawback is the potential for security exposure. If many users have access to the same data, it is more difficult to protect that data from theft, tampering, destruction by disgruntled employees, or unauthorized use. It has become necessary, therefore, for the computer industry to take greater precautions to protect the security of computer files.

An example of real-time processing is given in Figure 2-17, where a patient has submitted a prescription for processing.

### Batch and Real-Time: The Best of Both

Numerous computer systems combine the best features of both these methods of processing. A bank, for instance, may record your withdrawals during the day at the teller window in real-time. However, the deposit that you leave in an envelope in an "instant deposit" drop may be recorded during the night by means of batch processing. Many oil company credit card systems also combine both: A garage manager can instantaneously check the status of your credit by calling your card number into a computer facility; but for billing purposes all your gasoline purchases may be totaled at one time.

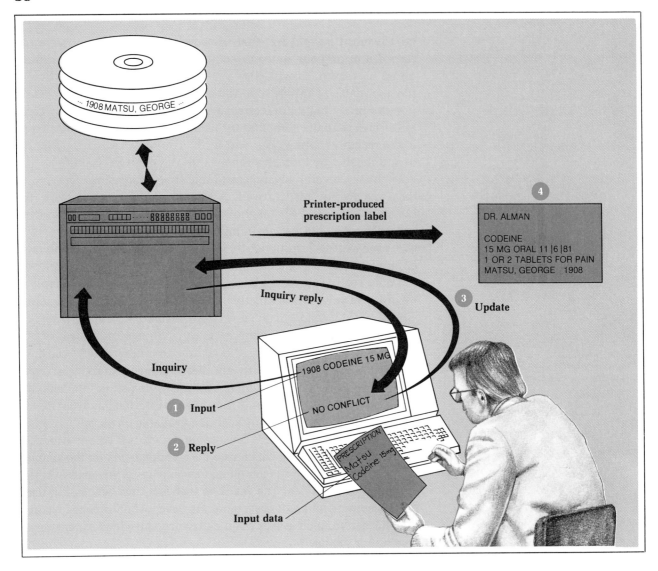

Police license-plate checks for stolen cars work the same way. As cars are sold throughout the state, the license numbers, owners' names, and so on, are updated on the motor vehicle department's master file, usually via batch processing on a nightly basis. But when police officers see a car they suspect may be stolen, they can radio headquarters, where an operator with a terminal can do a real-time check with the master file to see if the car was reported missing.

## Processing Operations: Campbell Goes to College

There are several operations common to the processing of data. With a computer, you can:

- Input
- Store
- Update
- Output
- Summarize
- Inquire
- Sort
- Compute
- Classify
- Retrieve

The best way to explain these is to use an example. Figure 2-18 shows what happens when Joan Campbell fills out two forms for college—the application form, which gets her name and personal data on file, and the registration form for a particular quarter. The following steps take place, corresponding to the processing operations we just listed. Notice the system is a combination of batch and real-time.

**Input** Data is entered into the computer system for processing. Joan's college application and registration forms are **input** by a data entry clerk into the file, which we will call the student master file.

**Inquire** A computer user **inquires** about data in the computer through the computer terminal. Here the data entry clerk makes an inquiry to find out if there is room in the classes Joan has said she wants to take, and the computer replies there is.

**Store** To **store** means data that has been processed is to be retained for future reference. Here Joan's application and registration data are stored in records on secondary storage in the student master file and class master file, respectively.

**Sort** Student records are sorted by the computer into alphabetical order within a class. For DAT 102, "Introduction to Computer Programming," Campbell, Joan, is second on the class roster. To **sort** means to arrange data into a particular sequence.

**Update** The preceding steps took place at the start of the school quarter. At the end of the quarter, when Joan's instructor turns in the grade sheet, Joan's master-file record is **updated** with new data: She received an "A" in DAT 102.

**Compute** Add, subtract, multiply, and divide are arithmetic operations— computations that the computer can perform. Here the computer equates Joan's letter grades to numerical values, adds them, divides them by the number of credit hours, and **computes** a total grade-point average of 3.6.

**Output** The computer produces the processing result in usable form. Joan's list of grades is printed out and mailed to her home.

**Classify** **Classify** means data is categorized according to characteristics that make it useful. The computer program classifies all students enrolled in the college according to age, to help college administrators in their planning.

**Summarize** The computer summarizes the total number of students in the various schools and also gives an overall enrollment total— again, to help administrators in their planning. To **summarize** means to reduce data to a more concise, usable form.

**Figure 2-17   How real-time processing works.** The purposes of this hospital-clinic pharmacy system are to verify that a patient's prescription is safe, produce a prescription label for the medication bottle, and update the patient's medical records so the physicians in the hospital-clinic can see what kind of medication the patient is taking. Because of the possibility of patients having the same name, the file is organized by patient number rather than by name. Here George Matsu, patient no. 1908, brings his prescription to the pharmacist. The pharmacist ❶ queries the computer system through the terminal as to whether the codeine prescribed is apt to conflict with other medication he might be taking. The terminal ❷ responds, "No conflict," meaning there are apt to be no adverse side effects. The computer then ❸ updates Matsu's file so other physicians will see later that codeine was prescribed for him. The machine also ❹ prints out a prescription label that the pharmacist can place on the codeine bottle. All this is done while the patient is waiting.

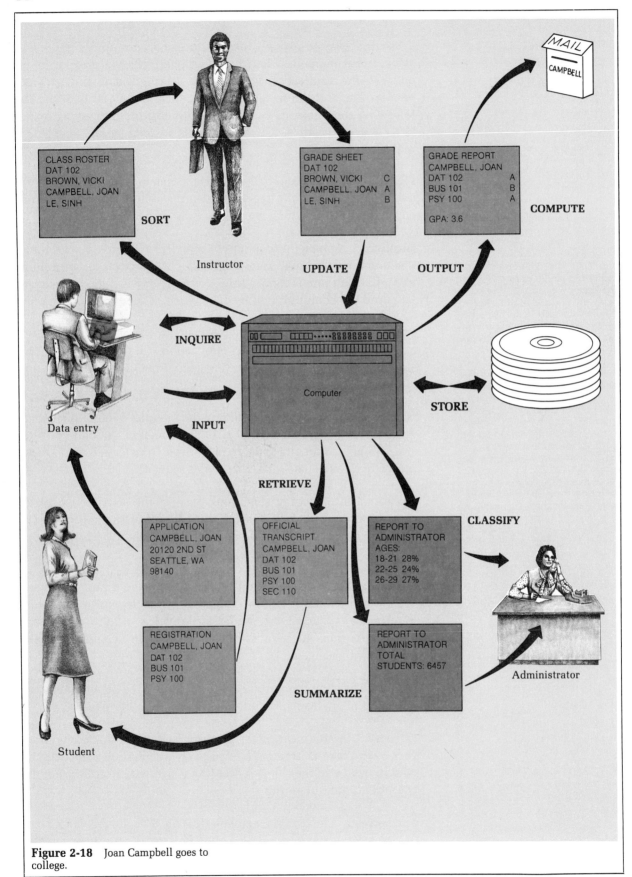

**Figure 2-18**  Joan Campbell goes to college.

# A Little Gallery of Hardware
## The Main Parts of a Computer System

**①** Computer color: Although not all can provide both text and graphics or even color, terminals are one of the most common ways of communicating with the computer.

Whether it is a huge supercomputer or a small hand-held computer, the essential activities are the same. This gallery takes a look at four types of computers—supercomputer, mainframe, minicomputer, and microcomputer—then presents examples of hardware demonstrating the four parts common to all computer systems: input, processing, output, and storage. One other essential component of a computer system is also shown: people.

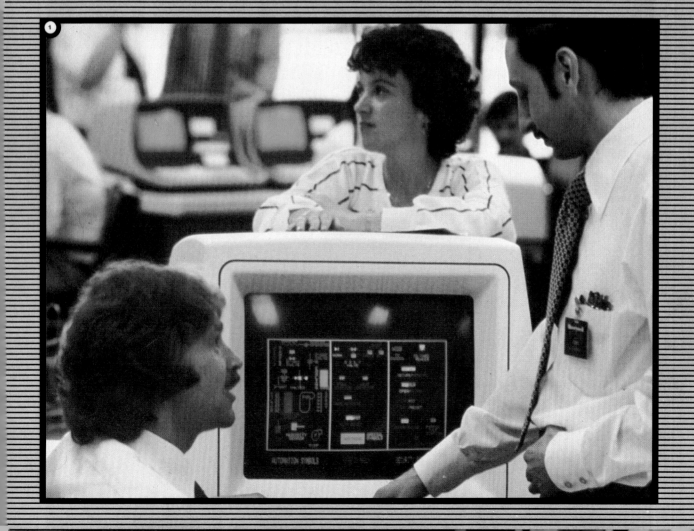

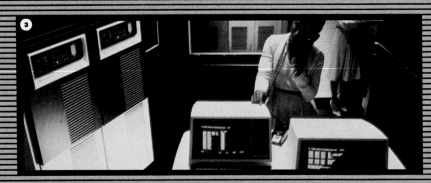

Computers come in four basic sizes: ❷ Microcomputer: The smallest category often has central processing unit and terminal in the same unit. This one is built by Zenith. ❸ Minicomputer: The intermediate computer, such as this Honeywell DPS 88, is popular with small- and medium-sized businesses. ❹ Mainframe system: This IBM 370, in use at Bell Helicopter/Textron, is representative of the class of large computers. ❺ Supercomputer: Slightly resembling a form of public seating, this Cray-1 computer system is one of the world's most powerful computers, useful in weather forecasting and weapons research because of its enormous computational power.

Input: Data can be input to the computer in many ways; two are shown here. **6** Somewhat resembling a 45 rpm phonograph record, the floppy disk enters data through a floppy disk reader. **7** With a CRT (cathode ray tube) terminal, data is input through the keyboard.

**8** Data entry operators: Operators can input data simultaneously, each using a separate terminal.
**9** Processing: Computer consoles, located in the main computer room, allow operators to monitor the system during processing.

**10** Output: Processed information from the computer can be output in many forms, but this picture shows two of the most common: as so-called "soft copy" or images on a CRT screen, and as "hard copy" or printed images on paper.

Storage: Secondary storage of data—that is, outside the computer itself—is frequently on magnetic tape or disk. ⑪ ⑫ Disk storage: Looking somewhat like long-playing phonograph records, disks are transported as disk packs in containers and are lowered into disk drives for recording or retrieval of data. ⑬ Magnetic tape storage: Magnetic tape is placed on a tape drive for recording and retrieval of data.

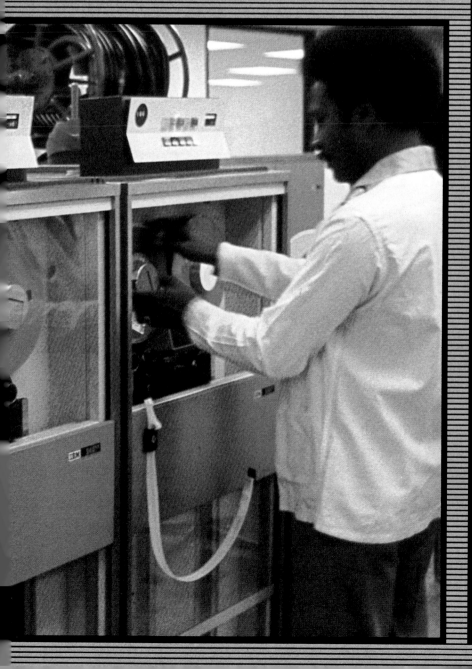

**14 15** Most data processing organizations maintain a tape (or disk) library. The woman here works in a U.S. Postal Service computer center.

**Retrieve** Data stored in the system can be **retrieved** later for use. Here, when Joan decides she wants to transfer from this college to another, the computer is able to retrieve an official transcript showing all her grades and courses.

Incidentally, it might seem that there is not much difference between inquiring and retrieving. Normally, however, making an inquiry involves asking (and the computer answering) a brief question at the terminal in real-time, whereas retrieving usually produces a paper printout and is usually done in batch processing.

## People and Computers

We have talked about hardware, software, and data as though these three elements were all that were necessary to make a computer system work. Anyone nervous about a takeover by computers will be relieved to know, however, that none of these three elements can amount to much without people—both the people who help make the system work and the people for whom the work is done.

Beyond the level of home computers or personal computers, the best way to think about computers and people is within the context of a data processing organization. The data processing organization is an information resource. Whether it exists within a university, government bureau, or corporation, this organization may well be the institution's most important asset. Most of the knowledge of what that institution does is contained in its computer files: research data, engineering drawings, marketing strategy, accounts receivable, accounts payable, sales information, manufacturing specifications, transportation plans, warehousing data—the list goes on and on. Small wonder, then, that corporations, universities, and government bureaus are so sensitive about the security of their computer files.

### Computer People

Because of the data processing organization's importance, there are several levels of management associated with it. We will discuss these in detail in Chapter 17, the computer careers chapter. Here, however, let us touch on the essential personnel required to run the system.

We have briefly mentioned the data entry people, who prepare data on cards, disk, or tape for processing; the computer operator, who monitors the console, reviews procedures, and keeps peripheral equipment running; and the librarians, who are in charge of cataloguing and keeping secure the processed disks and tapes.

Two other types of trained personnel are programmers and systems analysts. **Computer programmers** design, write, test, and implement the programs that process the data on the computer system. **Systems analysts** are knowledgeable in the programming area but have broader responsibilities. They plan and design not just individual programs, but entire systems of programs. Systems analysts maintain a working relationship with the user organization. This relationship contributes to the systems analyst's knowledge of the user requirements. The systems analyst must have a good understanding of user requirements to plan new systems.

To make their work as useful as possible to other computer personnel and the users, programmers and systems analysts spend a fair amount of time writing reports and procedures.

### Users

**Users** are we, the people the computer systems are supposed to serve. Whereas once computer users were an elite breed—high-powered Ph.D.s, research-and-development engineers, government planners—today the advent of small, less costly computers has widened the population of users considerably.

The most elementary user is the novice, the person with no training on computers. He or she may be just learning, such as a child playing computer games. A more sophisticated user is one who uses a personal computer for home finances or as a hobby.

Above this level, users are those who, to varying degrees, use the computer for business or professional reasons, although they are not computer professionals themselves. For instance, a person may be trained well enough to make the inquiries required in, say, customer service, banking, or airline reservations. At a slightly higher level, a person may know what data is available for the computer and what information is expected from it. He or she may have direct contact with the data processing organization's systems analyst and assist the analyst with developing and monitoring the system.

The most sophisticated user is a person who has written some computer programs, understands computer jargon, and is well equipped to deal with most insiders in a data processing organization.

---

### Summary and Key Terms

* The machines in a computer system are called **hardware.** The **programs** or step-by-step instructions that run the machines are called **software.** Most people in the computer field are involved with some aspect of software.

* Hardware in a computer system consists of devices to handle input, processing, output, and storage. **Input units** take data and send it to the processor. The **processor** is the central processing unit, which manipulates the input data into the information wanted. Main storage holds instructions and data needed by the processor. **Output units** make processed data ready for use. **Storage units** store additional data outside main storage.

* Data may be **input** in various ways: **floppy disk** through a **floppy disk reader, magnetic tape** through a **magnetic**

**tape drive,** original documents through **optical character recognition** devices such as a **wand** that scans price tags or **bar code reader** that reads **bar code** symbols on packages, or input may be typed in through a **cathode ray tube (CRT) terminal** (also called **video display terminal**). Data may also be input on **punched cards** through a **card reader.** Data is prepared for processing by **data entry operators.**

* The **processor,** also called the **central processing unit (CPU),** interprets and executes program instructions and communicates with the input, output, and storage devices. **Main storage** holds data after it is input and before and after it is processed but not yet released to output. The processor is usually contained in a cabinet that also contains the **console,** the controls that allow the computer system to signal the operator when something needs to be done. Through the **console terminal,** such as a CRT, the computer operator can have two-way communication with the system.

- **Output** can take a number of forms, most commonly printers or terminals. **Printers** have various characteristics: the method of forming images on the page, the amount of data printed at one time (character or line), speed, cost, and noise.

- **Storage,** by which we mean **auxiliary** or **secondary storage,** may be on **magnetic disks,** which are combined as **disk packs** and read by **disk drives,** or on **magnetic tape reels,** which are read by **tape drives.** Both disk packs and tape reels may be stored in a **library** for safekeeping.

- Large computers are called **mainframes,** and the most powerful of the mainframes are called **supercomputers.** Smaller computers are called **minicomputers,** and desktop and personal computers are called **microcomputers,** although the distinctions among the classes of computers are somewhat blurred. Hardware devices attached to computers are called **peripheral equipment.**

- Computer systems may be centralized in one place or they may include terminals located in different places. **Distributed data processing** decentralizes the processing itself by using computers in remote locations.

- **Software,** or programs, is the growth area in the computer field. Because of miniaturization, standardization, and the growing popularity of computers, the cost of hardware is going down, but the cost of software is going up.

- **Data** is the raw material to be processed by a computer. It consists of **characters** (letters, numbers, special characters), which in turn are organized into **fields,** which in turn are organized into **records** (collections of fields), which in turn are organized into **files** (collections of records). A **data base** is a collection of data that can be used for different applications. **Information** is data processed into organized, meaningful, useful form.

- A **transaction** is a record containing fields that represent changes to a master file. **Updating** is the process by which files are changed to reflect new information. Files can be **transaction files,** which are those that contain modifications to existing master records, or they can be **master files,** which contain relatively permanent data.

- The two major ways to process data are **batch processing,** in which transactions are saved and processed at one time, and **direct access processing,** in which transactions are processed randomly.

- In batch processing, transaction files are processed against a master file in some sequential order by a field called a **key,** a unique identifier for a record. The advantage of batch processing is that it is less expensive than other processing methods; the disadvantages are that one must wait for the processing results and that it requires an extensive manual support system.

- **Real-time processing,** also called **transaction processing,** is a form of direct access processing that produces output fast enough to affect the activity at hand. For processing to be real-time, it must be **on-line,** with the user terminal directly connected to the computer.

- Real-time processing was technologically advanced by the development of disk as a means of storing data, since disk permitted quicker access to a particular record than did magnetic tape. Computing became more **interactive;** that is, users were able to maintain a dialogue back and forth with the computer. The advantage of real-time processing is that it allows for faster results and continual updating of records. The drawbacks are that it is more expensive and more vulnerable to breaches of security.

- **Time-sharing** is a system in which several users can share use of a central computer practically simultaneously.

- Several operations common to processing are: **input, inquire, store, sort** (arrange in particular sequence), **update, compute** (perform arithmetic calculations), **output, classify** (categorize data), **summarize** (reduce data to concise form), and **retrieve** (request and receive paper printout).

- Computer people include **data entry people, computer operators, librarians, programmers** (who design, write, test, and implement programs), and **systems analysts** (who plan and design entire systems of programs). Computer users range from novices, with no training, to experts, who are able to communicate with computerm professionals.

## Review

1. Name some common ways of inputting data to a computer system.

2. What are the functions of the processing unit?

3. What are the most common ways of outputting from the computer?

4. What are two forms of auxiliary or secondary storage?

5. How is data organized for batch processing? Give an example, such as payroll by social security number.

6. Distinguish between batch processing and direct access processing. What are the advantages and disadvantages of each?

7. Name ten common processing operations and define them.

# part 2
# hardware

"The future ain't what it used to be," remarks science writer Arthur C. Clarke wryly. Of course, the future never has turned out to be quite what people anticipated. Perhaps nowhere is this more evident than in predictions about the computer. One computer pioneer said in the early 1950s that he felt "only four or five giant firms will be able to employ these machines usefully." But by 1955 there were 1000 computers in use in the United States. In 1960 government engineers predicted that 15,000 computers might be in use within five years. Instead, there were 25,000—and two years later, 15,000 more. We cannot pretend to be more foresighted than they. Unquestionably, the numbers and uses of computers will continue to change dramatically. However, the four basic components of a computer system—input, processing, output, and storage—will probably remain the same. In this part, we take a closer look at the hardware that goes into such a system today and try to suggest the directions hardware will take.

The principles are old, but the
first computer generation actually was born only
about three decades ago. It was not long before this
generation of vacuum tube computers was replaced
by second-generation computers using transistors
and then by third-generation machines using
integrated circuits. The fourth generation of
general-purpose microprocessors may yield to a
fifth by 1990. The dynamism of the field continues.

*ch3*

*evolution*

*from finite to infinite*

To those who like stories of risk and of ideas that create a breakthrough in some field, the story of how computers evolved is just as exciting as the new computer uses emanating from the current onrush of technological developments. And it is appropriate to discuss the history of the computer in this part on hardware because the touchstone of the computer revolution has been its rapidly changing technology—its hardware. However, it is by no means just a history of machines; it is also a history of people.

We could start with the history of methods of representing numbers or quantities—methods such as making marks on wood or piles of stones or perhaps employing instruments like the abacus, which was used for 5000 years in the Orient (Figure 3-1). Or we could start with the idea of numbers being represented by a mechanical gear wheel, as they are on car odometers and old-fashioned adding machines; this idea was first developed in 1642 by Blaise Pascal (Figure 3-2), who built an adding machine based on it. However, it was not until 180 years after Pascal's invention that someone was able to advance significantly the cause of mechanical computation. That someone was Charles Babbage, called the "father of the computer." We therefore start with him.

**Figure 3-1   The abacus.** Consisting of beads strung on wires, the abacus is still used in places such as Shanghai. People have been as nimble at manipulating abacuses as their Western counterparts have been in operating mechanical calculating machines.

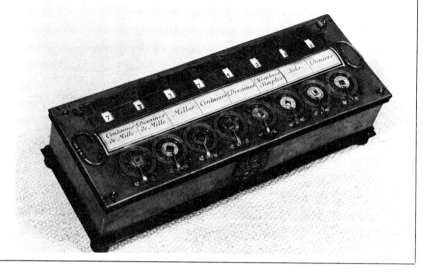

**Figure 3-2 Blaise Pascal and his adding machine.** This cigar-box-sized mechanical adding machine, called the "Pascaline," involved a set of interlocking cogs and wheels. People dialed the numbers they wanted, and the wheels and cogs inside turned to the appropriate amount; the result was displayed in the little windows above. Fifty Pascalines were built, but they found few buyers, because—an interesting reason, in light of today's anxieties about computers—clerks and accountants refused to use them, fearing the machines might do away with their jobs.

## ✴*Babbage and the Countess*

Born in England in 1791, Charles Babbage was an inventor and mathematician. When solving polynomial equations, he found the hand-compiled mathematical tables he used filled with errors. He decided a machine could be built that would solve polynomial equations more easily and accurately by calculating the successive differences between them. He therefore set about making a demonstration model of what he called a **difference engine** (Figure 3-3). The model was so well received that he enthusiastically began to build a full-scale working version, using a grant from the British government.

However, Babbage found that despite tight design specifications and exhortations to workers, the smallest imperfections were enough to throw the tons of brass and pewter rods and gears of the ambitious larger machine out of whack. Finally, after spending £17,000 to no avail, the government withdrew its financial support. (A British prime minister later stated that the only use he could see in the difference engine was for calculating the large amount of money spent on it.)

Despite this setback, Babbage was not discouraged. He conceived of another machine of cogs and wheels, christened the **analytical engine,** which he hoped would perform many kinds of calculations. This, too, was never built, at least by Babbage (a model was later put together by his son—see Figure 3-4), but it embodied five key concepts of modern computers:

- Input device
- Processor or number calculator
- Control unit to direct the task to be performed and the sequence of calculations
- Storage place to hold number waiting to be processed
- Output device

**Figure 3-3  Charles Babbage and his difference engine.** This shows a prototype model. Babbage attempted to build a working model, which was to have been several times larger and steam-driven, but he was unsuccessful.

**Figure 3-4  The analytical engine.** This model was built by Babbage's son.

Part of Babbage's device was similar to an invention built in 1801 by Frenchman Joseph Jacquard. Jacquard, noting the repetitious nature of the task required of weavers working on looms, devised a stiff card with a series of holes punched in it; the card blocked certain threads from entering the loom and let other threads go on to complete the weave. Babbage realized that the punched card system could also be used to control the order of calculations in his analytical engine, and he incorporated it in the machine.

If Babbage was the father of the computer, then Ada, the Countess of Lovelace, was the first computer programmer (Figure 3-5). The daughter of English poet Lord Byron and of a mother who was a gifted mathematician, Ada went to work with Babbage when she was 27 and helped develop the instructions for doing computations on the analytical engine.

Lady Lovelace's contributions cannot be overvalued. Not only did her interest give Babbage encouragement—since she was able to see that his theoretical approach was workable—but also she published a series of notes that eventually led others to accomplish what Babbage himself had been unable to do.

# Hollerith Helps the Census

**Figure 3-5  The Countess of Lovelace.** Augusta Ada Byron, as she was known before she became countess, was Charles Babbage's colleague in his work on the analytical engine and has been called the world's first computer programmer. A programming language sponsored by the Pentagon has been dubbed Ada in her honor.

Since 1790 the U.S. Congress has required that a census of the country's population be taken every ten years. For the census for 1880, tabulation took seven and a half years because all the counting had to be done by hand. Accordingly, there was considerable anxiety in official circles as to whether the counting of the next census, to be taken in 1890, could be completed before the turn of the century.

A competition was held to find some way to speed the counting process. In the final test, involving a count of the population of St. Louis, Missouri, Herman Hollerith's tabulating machine completed the count in only five and a half hours. As a result of his system's adoption, an unofficial count of the 1890 population (62,622,250) was announced only six weeks after the census was taken.

Like the Jacquard cards, which Babbage had adopted, Hollerith's punched cards involved stiff paper with holes punched at certain points. In his tabulating machine (Figure 3-6), rods passing through the holes completed an electrical circuit, which caused a counter to advance one unit. This capability pointed up the principal difference between Hollerith's and Babbage's machines: Hollerith was able to use *electrical* rather than mechanical power to drive his device.

Hollerith, who had been a statistician with the Census Bureau, realized that punched card processing had considerable commercial potential. In 1896 he founded the Tabulating Machine Company, which

**Figure 3-6  Herman Hollerith and his tabulating machine.** This electrical tabulator and sorter was used to process punched cards.

became successful in selling services to railroads and other clients. In 1924 the successor to this company merged with two others to form the International Business Machines Corporation—IBM.

## *"The Old Man" of IBM*

For over 30 years, from 1924 to 1956, Thomas J. Watson, Sr. (Figure 3-7), ruled IBM with an iron grip. Before becoming its cantankerous, autocratic head, he had worked for the Tabulating Machine Company. There he had carried on a running battle with Hollerith, whose business aptitude, he felt, did not match his technical ability. Under supersalesman Watson, IBM became a dominant force in the business machines market, first as a supplier of calculators, then as a developer of computers.

IBM's entry into computers was sparked by a young Harvard professor of mathematics, Howard Aiken. In 1936, after reading Babbage's and Lady Lovelace's notes, Aiken began to think that a modern equivalent of the analytical engine could be constructed. The important difference now would be that it would not be mechanical but *electromechanical*. Because IBM was already such a power in the business machines market, with ample money and resources, Aiken

### NO PRETENSIONS

In her series of notes entitled "Observations on Mr. Babbage's Analytical Engine," Lady Lovelace wrote: "The Analytical Engine has no pretensions whatever to originate anything. It can do whatever we know how to order it to perform. It can follow analysis; but it has no power of anticipating any analytical relations or truths." In other words, a computer by itself cannot be considered creative. As Christopher Evans writes in *The Micro Millennium:* "It was a very perceptive comment and seems to be the first ever statement of the argument which today crops up unfailingly whenever the intellectual potential of computers is discussed—*a computer can only do what you program it to do.*"

**Figure 3-7** **"The Old Man."** Thomas J. Watson, Sr., of IBM. The original IBM building is shown at right.

worked out a careful proposal and approached Thomas Watson. In one of those autocratic make-or-break decisions for which he was famous, Watson gave him $1 million. As a result, the Harvard Mark I was born.

## *The Start of the Modern Era*

Nothing like the **Mark I** had ever been built before. It was 8 feet high and 55 feet long, made of streamlined steel and glass (Figure 3-8), and it emitted a sound during processing that one person said was

**Figure 3-8** **The Mark I.** *Top left:* Howard Aiken in white shirt. *Top right:* IBM's Watson, pointing out the Mark I.

"like listening to a roomful of old ladies knitting away with steel needles." Unveiled in 1944, the awesome sight of Mark I was accentuated by the presence of uniformed Navy personnel. It was now World War II and Aiken had become a naval lieutenant, released to Harvard to help build the computer that was supposed to solve many of the Navy's problems.

Actually, the Mark I was never very efficient. But it had such enormous publicity value that, when the security wraps came off after the war, it received a great deal of public attention and so strengthened IBM's commitment to computer development. The company released sums with which to build a Mark II model.

Meanwhile, technology had been proceeding elsewhere on separate tracks.

## *Of Code-Breakers and Computers*

During the war, German scientists made impressive advances in computer design. In 1940 they even made a formal development proposal to Hitler, who rejected further work on the scheme, thinking the war already won. In Britain, meanwhile, scientists succeeded in devising a special-purpose computer called Colossus, which helped crack supposedly uncrackable German radio-communications codes. The Nazis unsuspectingly continued to use these codes throughout the war. It is sobering to think what the outcome of the war might have been if the British and German experiences in computer development had been reversed.

In the same period, American military officials approached Dr. John Mauchly at the University of Pennsylvania and asked him to build a machine that would rapidly calculate trajectories for artillery and missiles. Mauchly and his student J. Presper Eckert relied on the work of Dr. John V. Atanasoff (Figure 3-9), a professor of physics at Iowa State University.

During the late 1930s, Atanasoff had spent time trying to build an electronic calculating device to help his students solve complicated mathematical problems. One night, the idea came to him for linking the computer memory and the associated logic. Later, he and an assistant, Clifford Berry, succeeded in building the first digital computer that worked electronically; they called it the "ABC," for **Atanasoff-Berry Computer** (Figure 3-10). After Mauchly met with Atanasoff and Berry in 1941, he used the ABC as the basis for the next step in computer development. From this association ultimately came a lawsuit, based on attempts to get patents for a commercial version of the machine Mauchly built. The suit was finally decided in 1974, when a federal court determined that Atanasoff had been the true originator of the ideas required to make an electronic digital computer actually work. (Some computer historians dispute this court decision.) But during the war years, Mauchly and Eckert were able to use the ABC principles to dramatic effect in creating the ENIAC.

**Figure 3-9   Dr. John V. Atanasoff in 1960.** As a young man, Atanasoff and his assistant, Clifford Berry, developed the first digital electronic computer.

**Figure 3-10**  **The "ABC."**  The Atanasoff-Berry Computer.

### The ENIAC

Although Mauchly and Eckert owed much to Atanasoff, they still faced an awesome task. The machine they proposed, which would cut the time needed to produce artillery and bombing trajectories from 15 minutes to 30 seconds, would employ 18,000 vacuum tubes— and all of them would have to operate simultaneously.

No one had ever had any experience with a project of such magnitude. One critic noted that because "the average life of a vacuum tube is 3000 hours, a tube failure would occur every 15 minutes. Since it would average more than 15 minutes to find the bad tube, no useful work could ever be done." Even so, at a cost of $400,000, funding was approved to develop the project.

The ENIAC was not built in time to contribute to the war effort (even though it was worked on 24 hours a day for 30 months). Nevertheless, work continued, and when the world's first general-purpose electronic digital computer was turned on in February 1946, it *was* impressive. Filling a huge room (Figure 3-11) and drawing 140,000 watts, enough electricity for a small power station, the **ENIAC**—short for Electronic Numerical Integrator And Computer—was able to multiply a pair of numbers in about three milliseconds (three-thousandths of a second).

However, the heat generated by this enormous system posed serious cooling problems, and the storage capacity was ridiculously small. Worst of all, the system was quite inflexible: Each time a program was

**Figure 3-11   The ENIAC.** Occupying 1500 square feet and weighing 30 tons, the ENIAC could handle 300 numbers per second. Co-inventors J. Presper Eckert, Jr., and John W. Mauchly are shown foreground left and center, respectively.

**Figure 3-12   Dr. John Von Neu-mann,** Hungarian-born mathematician, made many contributions to the development of flowcharting, and also proposed that computer memories be used to store programs. In addition to being a great mathematician, he held degrees in chemistry and physics, was a great storyteller, and had total recall. A computer called JOHNNIAC was named for him.

changed, the machine had to be rewired. This last obstacle was overcome by the work of world-famous mathematician Dr. John Von Neumann.

### Von Neumann and EDVAC

One day in 1945, while waiting for a train in Aberdeen, Maryland, a member of the ENIAC development team ran into Von Neumann (Figure 3-12), who was then involved in the top-secret work of designing nuclear weapons. Since both persons had security clearances, they were able to discuss each other's work, and Von Neumann began to realize that the difficulties he was having in the laborious and time-consuming checking of his advanced equations could be solved by the high speeds of ENIAC. As a result of that chance meeting, Von Neumann joined the University of Pennsylvania as a special consultant to the ENIAC team.

When the Army requested the university to build a more powerful computer than the ENIAC, Von Neumann responded by proposing the **EDVAC** (for *E*lectronic *D*iscrete *V*ariable *A*utomatic *C*omputer), which would utilize what he called the **stored program** concept. The idea, Von Neumann said, was to make the new machine more flexible than ENIAC by allowing it to store all program instructions inside the computer. That is, instead of having people laboriously rewire the machine to go to a different program, the machine would, in less than a second, "read" instructions from computer storage for switching to a new program. The significance of this is noted in *The Micro Millennium* by Christopher Evans:

# *The Making of a Chip*
## *Miniaturization Miracles*

**❶** Looking like caterpillars with nine pairs of legs, these two carriers each hold a tiny Intel "computer on a chip."

Take a large drawing of electrical circuitry that looks something like the map of a train yard. Photographically reduce it so it is more than 500 times smaller. Reproduce it many times on a 3-inch diameter piece, or "wafer," of material called silicon. Cut the wafer into individual pieces, or "chips." Mount each chip in a protective package. That, in brief, is how a chip is made. It will be a thousand times faster than the old room-sized ENIAC computer.

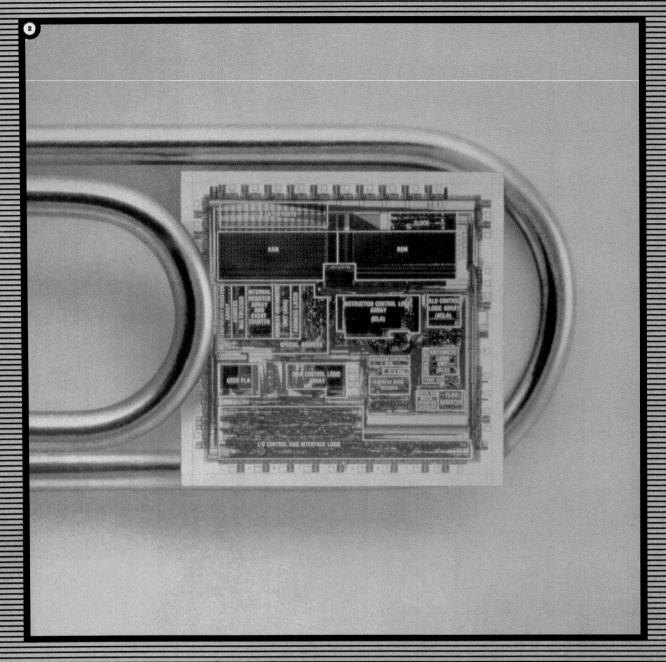

How small is "tha-a-at small"? ❷ This one-chip computer contains everything needed for processing and storing data, yet it is smaller than a standard paper clip. Here the chip's numerous functional areas are labeled. ❸ An integrated circuit that is slightly smaller than the push button on a telephone, this Bell Labs microelectronic chip can make over a million calculations per second.

**4** One thin dime: The size of an Intel chip's carrier is dramatically illustrated in this picture. **5** A striking mass of color, this high-performance microprocessor is made by National Semiconductor.

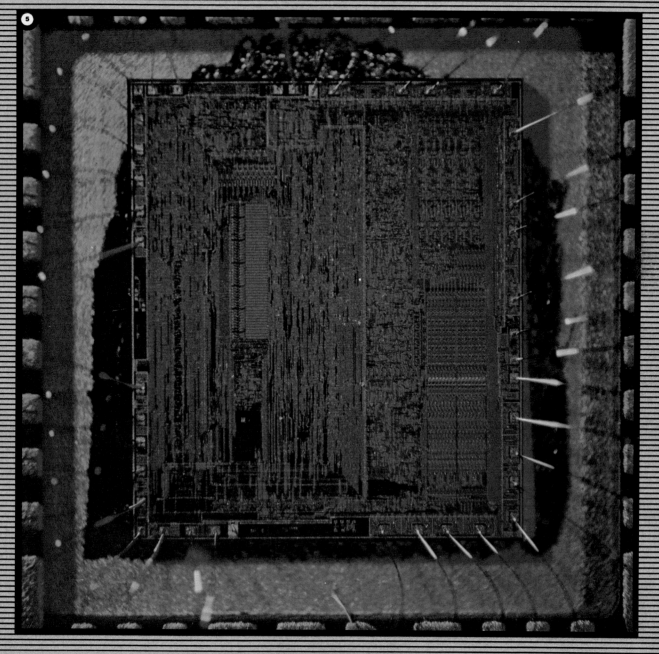

How a chip is made: These and the following two pages show the steps in the design and manufacture of a chip. **6** A circuit designer translates rough layouts into drawings that may be as large as 8 feet square. **7** These intricate lines form the basis for the complex circuitry—the pathways for electrical impulses—contained in a single chip. **8** The wall-size drawing is then "digitized" (through the vertical movable device shown toward the middle of the upright mounted drawing here), a process that translates each portion of the image into coordinates within a computer. The complete result is stored on magnetic tape, which will then be used to reproduce a photomask. **9** The large mask will ultimately be scaled down photographically to the size of a chip and then reproduced, like a sheet of postage stamps, on a 3-inch-diameter silicon "wafer," producing several hundred chips. For comparison, the wafer here is shown next to a chip on its carrier, the end stage of the manufacturing process. **10** A technician checks a photomask before it is reduced. Any flaw could significantly affect the storage and information-processing capabilities of the final chip.

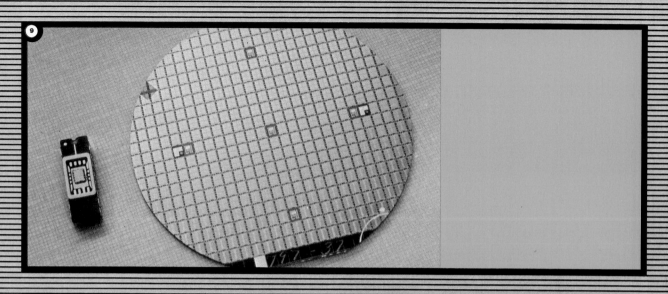

**11** "Dip and wash": Silicon wafers are bathed in photoresist, a photographic-type emulsion, and a scaled-down photomask is then placed over each wafer. After exposure to ultraviolet light, parts of the photoresist are washed away in an acid bath; other (unshielded) areas harden and form an outline of the circuit. **12 13** Wafers are baked in an oxygen furnace. Oxygen reacts with the silicon to form an insulating layer of glass on the circuits etched on the wafer surfaces.

**14 15** Silicon wafers: A wafer actually consists of two types of silicon—an N-type (for electrically negative) to which is added a P-type (for positive), in order to make the chip electrically conducting and nonconducting at the proper junctures. Since dust can ruin a chip, work is done in "clean rooms," special air-filtered laboratories where workers dress like members of a surgical team. **16** At this point, only one layer of circuit design is complete. Sometimes as many as 10 layers of etched photographed circuits are placed on top of one another. With each layer the process begins again with photoresist (as shown here), another photomask, and so on. **17** The wafer is inspected through a microscope for flaws and scratches. Circuits are also tested electrically. **18** An automated die-cutting machine cuts the wafer into separate chips. At this point the chip is ready for metal or plastic protective packaging.

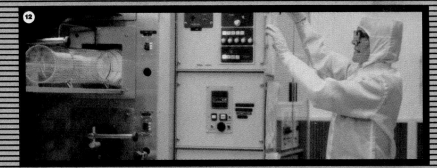

**Table 3-1   Generations of the computer.**   The chronology of the Computer Age is the chronology of America's recent past.

| Period and primary electronic hardware | Principal features |
|---|---|
| *1951—First generation: the vacuum tube* | |
| 1951  President Truman fires MacArthur<br>1952  The hydrogen bomb; Eisenhower president<br>1953  Korean War ends; Stalin dies<br>1954  Supreme Court outlaws school segregation<br>1955  The Beat Generation; Davy Crockett craze<br>1956  Ike reelected; Grace Kelly princess of Monaco<br>1957  Sputnik launched; Ike sends troops to Little Rock<br>1958  John Birch Society founded; hula hoop craze | • Punched card input<br>• Punched card files<br>• Magnetic tape introduced<br>• Programming language—machine language<br>• Scientific applications |
| *1959—Second generation: the transistor* | |
| 1959  Nixon-Khruschev "kitchen debate" in Moscow<br>1960  U-2 downed over Russia; Kennedy president<br>1961  Bay of Pigs invasion; Freedom Rides in South<br>1962  Marilyn Monroe dies; John Glenn orbits the earth<br>1963  JFK assassinated; Martin Luther King march<br>1964  Johnson elected president; Civil Rights Act | • Card and tape input<br>• Tape files<br>• New programming langues—COBOL, FORTRAN<br>• Batch processing of business applications |
| *1965—Third generation: the integrated circuit* | |
| 1965  Watts riot; troops committed to Vietnam<br>1966  Supreme Court *Miranda* ruling on suspects' rights<br>1967  Haight-Ashbury "Summer of Love"; Arab-Israel Six-Day War<br>1968  Tet offensive; Martin Luther King and Robert Kennedy assassinated; Nixon beats Humphrey<br>1969  Apollo II on moon; Woodstock rock festival<br>1970  Kent State shootings; women's liberation | • Tape and disk input<br>• Tape and disk files<br>• Advanced software systems<br>• Microcomputers<br>• New programming language—BASIC<br>• On-line processing<br>• Data communications |
| *1971—Fourth generation: the microprocessor* | |
| 1971  Cigarette ads taken off TV; Pentagon Papers<br>1972  Watergate burglary; Nixon beats McGovern<br>1973  *The Sting* wins Oscar; Vietnam War peace accord<br>1974  Patty Hearst kidnapped; Ford president; gas pump lines<br>1975  *Jaws* popular movie; New York financial crisis<br>1976  Carter elected; U.S. bicentennial<br>1977  *Star Wars* hit movie<br>1978  Sadat and Begin at Camp David; Jonestown deaths<br>1979  Iran takes 52 hostages<br>1980  Reagan elected; Mount St. Helens erupts<br>1981  Reagan and Pope John II shot<br>1982  High unemployment; artificial heart<br>1983  Sally Ride—First American woman in space; Korean 747 shot down | • Source data entry—OCR, bar codes<br>• Disk files, mass storage<br>• Microprocessors, microcomputers<br>• VLSI<br>• New programming languages—Pascal, Ada<br>• Distributed data processing |

In the first generation, **vacuum tubes**—electronic tubes about the size of light bulbs—were used as the internal computer components (Figure 3-14). However, because thousands of such tubes were required, they generated a great deal of heat, causing many problems in temperature regulation and climate control. In addition, although all the tubes had to be working simultaneously, they were subject to frequent burnout—and the people operating the computer often did not know

From this moment on, computers were no longer fast but blinkered work-horses, woodenly proceeding down one track, but had become dynamic, flexible information-processing systems capable of performing multitudes of different tasks. In one conceptual jump, the true power of computers moved from the finite to the potentially infinite. . . .

# ＊ _The Computer Age Begins_

The remarkable thing about the Computer Age is that so much has happened in so short a time. As Table 3-1 shows, we have leap-frogged through four generations of technology in just over 30 years—a span of time whose events are within the memories of many people today. The first three "generations" are pinned to three technological developments—the vacuum tube, the transistor, and the integrated circuit—each of which has drastically changed the nature of computers. Defining subsequent generations has become more complicated because the entire industry has become more complicated.

### The First Generation, 1951–1958:
### The Vacuum Tube

The beginning of the Computer Age may be dated June 14, 1951. This was the date the first **UNIVAC**—short for _Universal Automatic Computer_—was delivered to a client, the U.S. Bureau of the Census, for use in tabulating the previous year's census. It also marked the first time that a computer had been built for data processing applications rather than for military, scientific, or engineering use. The UNIVAC (Figure 3-13) was really the ENIAC in disguise and was, in fact, built by Mauchly and Eckert, who in 1947 had formed their own corporation (later sold to Remington-Rand).

**Figure 3-13 The UNIVAC.** The familiar but younger figure of Walter Cronkite (right) is shown here with J. Presper Eckert and an unidentified operator of UNIVAC during vote counting for the 1952 presidential election. UNIVAC surprised CBS executives by predicting—after analyzing only 5 percent of the vote counted—that Eisenhower would defeat Stevenson. CBS withheld announcement until it could be confirmed by the complete vote. Thus began the use of computers in predicting election outcomes—a practice that evoked criticism in the 1980 Reagan-Carter election, when NBC forecast the winner with only 1 percent of the vote counted and long before polls had even closed in many western states.

**19** An automated wire-bonding machine attaches gold wires to circuit chips; the wires connect the chips to their individual holders. **20** This National Semiconductor integrated circuit and package, with attached bonding wires, are ready to be plugged into a printed circuit board, along with resistors, capacitors, and switches, to perform useful work.

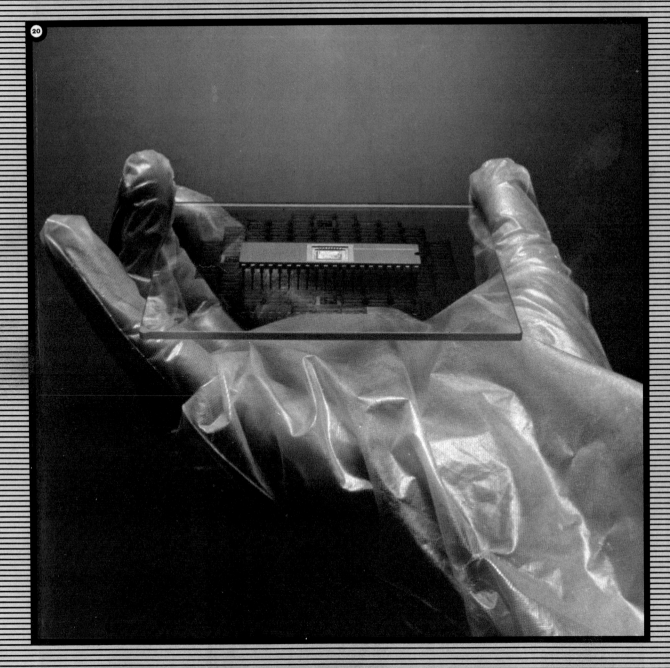

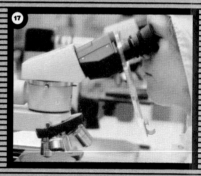

**Figure 3-14 Three generations of technology.** *Left,* an array of vacuum tubes. *Right,* the first-generation vacuum tube is shown next to the smaller, second-generation transistor, which was replaced in the third generation by the tiny integrated circuit.

*Vacuum tube*
*1. Created too much heat*
*2. Many tubes - burn out - difficult*
   *to find*
*3. Programming difficult - mach.*
   *lang was numbers.*

whether the problem was in the programming or in the machine. In addition, input and output tended to be slow, since both operations were generally performed on punched cards.

Another drawback was that the language used in programming was machine language, which uses numbers, rather than the present-day higher-level languages, which are more like English. Programming with numbers alone made using the computer difficult and time-consuming.

For primary storage, **magnetic core** was the principal form of technology used. This consisted of small, doughnut-shaped rings about the size of a pinhead, which were strung like beads on intersecting thin wires (Figure 3-15). Magnetic core was the dominant form of primary storage technology for two decades. To supplement primary

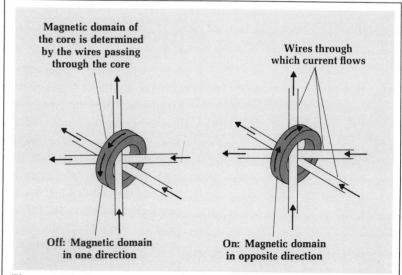

Magnetic domain of the core is determined by the wires passing through the core

Wires through which current flows

Off: Magnetic domain in one direction

On: Magnetic domain in opposite direction

**Figure 3-15 Magnetic cores.** Each a few hundredths of an inch in diameter, magnetic cores were mounted on wires. When electricity was passed through the wire on which a core was strung, the core could be magnetized as either "off" (above) or "on," which could be used to represent a zero (off) or a one (on). Combinations of zeros and ones could be used to represent data.

storage, first-generation computers stored data on punched cards. In 1957 magnetic tape was introduced as a faster, more compact method of storing data.

As Table 3-1 shows, the early generation of computers was used primarily for scientific and engineering calculations rather than for business data processing applications. Because of the enormous size, unreliability, and high cost of these computers, many people assumed they would remain very expensive, specialized tools, not destined for general use.

But at Bell Laboratories there had already been a new technological development—the transistor.

## The Second Generation, 1959–1964: The Transistor

TRANSISTOR:
1. Much smaller than vac. tube
2. no warm up time
3. used less energy
4. faster / more reliable

Three Bell Lab scientists—J. Bardeen, H. W. Brattain, and W. Shockley—were later to receive the Nobel prize for developing the **transistor,** a small type of electrical circuitry. The transistor revolutionized electronics in general and computers in particular. Not only did transistors shrink the size of computers—the first transistors were about one-hundredth the size of the vacuum tube—but they also had numerous other advantages: They needed no warm-up time, consumed less energy, and were faster and more reliable.

During this generation, another important development was the move from machine language to **assembly languages**—also called **symbolic languages.** Assembly languages use abbreviations for instructions (for example, "L" for "LOAD") rather than numbers. This made programming less cumbersome.

After the development of the symbolic languages came **higher-level languages.** The first language to receive widespread acceptance was **FORTRAN** (for *FOR*mula *TRAN*slator), developed in the mid-1950s as a scientific, mathematical, and engineering language. Then in 1959 **COBOL** (for *CO*mmon *B*usiness-*O*riented *L*anguage) was introduced for business-programming use. Both languages, still widely used today, are more English-like than assembly language. Higher-level languages allowed programmers to give more attention to solving problems. They no longer had to cope with all the details of the machines themselves. Also, in 1962 the first removable disk pack was marketed. Disk storage supplemented magnetic tape systems and enabled users to have fast access to desired data.

All these new developments made the second generation of computers less costly to operate—and thus began a surge of growth in computer systems. In 1960 Bethlehem Steel became the first corporation to use a computer on a real-time basis to handle orders, inventories, and production control. In 1963 the *Daily Oklahoman—Oklahoma City Times* became the first newspaper to use the computer to set type for all its editorial and news matter, as well as for classified advertising. In 1964 American Airlines instituted a real-time reservation system. Throughout this period, however, computers were being used principally by business, university, and government organizations. They had not filtered down to the general public. The real part of the revolution was about to begin.

### ✳ The Third Generation, 1965–1970: The Integrated Circuit

One of the most abundant elements in the earth's crust is silicon, a nonmetallic substance found in common beach sand as well as in practically all rocks and clay. The element has given rise to the name "Silicon Valley" for Santa Clara County, which is about 30 miles south of San Francisco. In 1965 Silicon Valley became the principal site of the electronics industry making the so-called **silicon chip.**

An **integrated circuit** (abbreviated IC) is a complete electronic circuit on a small chip of silicon. The chip may be less than 1/8 inch square and contains hundreds of electronic components (Figure 3-16). Beginning in 1965 the integrated circuit began to replace the transistor in machines now called third-generation computers. An integrated circuit was able to replace an entire circuit board of transistors with one chip of silicon much smaller than one transistor. Gallery 3 shows how silicon chips are made.

Silicon is used because it is a **semiconductor.** That is, it is a crystalline substance that will conduct electric current when it has been "doped" with chemical impurities shot into the latticelike structure of the crystal. A cylinder of silicon is sliced into wafers, each about 3 inches in diameter, and the wafer is "etched" repeatedly with a

**Figure 3-16  The integrated circuit.** The picture at left shows the chip magnified several times. At right a quarter-inch-square chip is compared with a 6-by-11-inch magnetic core memory.

IC (Silicon chip)
1. Reliable - used over (over
    no moving parts
2. Compact - circuitry in tiny
    space · reduces size of
    equipment
    · Mach. speed increased /circuits
      closer together - travel time to
      electricity reduced.
3. Low cost · small size · mfg.
    cheaper · More prod. improved.
4. Low power use - less power
    needed to operate

pattern of electrical circuitry. Up to ten layers may be etched on a single wafer. The wafer is then divided into several hundred small chips, each with a complete circuit so tiny it is half the size of a human fingernail—yet under a microscope looks as complex as a railroad yard. A chip 1 centimeter square is so powerful it can hold 10,000 words—the length of a daily newspaper.

Integrated circuits entered the market with the simultaneous announcement in 1959 by Texas Instruments and Fairchild Semiconductor that they had each independently produced chips containing several complete electronic circuits. The chips were hailed as a generational breakthrough because they had four desirable characteristics:

- **Reliability.** They could be used over and over again without failure. Whereas vacuum tubes failed every 15 minutes, chips rarely failed— perhaps once in 33 million hours of operation. This reliability is due not only to the fact that they have no moving parts but also to the fact that semiconductor firms give them a rigid work/not-work test.

- **Compactness.** Circuitry packed into a small space reduces the equipment size. The machine speed is increased because circuits are closer together, thereby reducing the travel time for the electricity.

- **Low cost.** Mass-production techniques have made possible the manufacture of inexpensive integrated circuits. That is, miniaturization has allowed manufacturers to produce many chips inexpensively.

- **Low power use.** Miniaturization of integrated circuits has meant that less power is required for computer use than was required in previous generations. In an energy-conscious time, this is important.

---

### ANY MACHINE IN THE WORLD

Computers can be hooked up to any electrical device in the world; and any machine can be run by electricity. Thus the computer can be made to run any machine in the world.... Computers can activate printers, picture screens, lawn sprinklers, musical instruments, juke boxes, music synthesizers, rocket launchers, atomic weapons, electric trains, cameras, water pistols, puppets, exhibits, theater lights, fish feeders, cattle gates, movie projectors, bells, whistles, klaxons, foghorns, and chimes.

—Ted Nelson,
*The Home Computer Revolution*

---

The small-is-beautiful revolution moved from the integrated circuits of 1965 to **large-scale integration (LSI)** in 1970. Thousands of integrated circuits were crammed onto a single quarter-inch square of silicon.

The beginning of the third generation was trumpeted by the IBM 360 series, first announced April 7, 1964 (Figure 3-17). The System/ 360 family of computers, designed for both business and scientific use, came in several models and sizes. Also offered were about 40 different kinds of input and output and secondary storage devices, all compatible so customers could put together systems tailor-made for their needs and data processing budgets.

The 360 series was launched with an all-out, massive marketing effort to make computers a business tool, to get them into medium-sized and smaller business and government operations where they had not been used before. The result went beyond IBM's wildest dreams. The reported $5 billion the company invested in the development of the System/360 repaid itself, and the system rendered many existing computer systems— including some former IBM systems—obsolete.

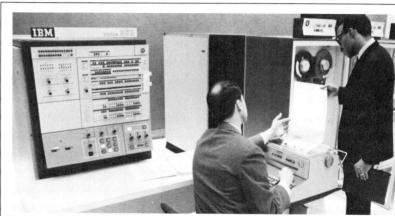

**Figure 3-17    The IBM System/360.** This $5 billion system marked the beginning of third-generation computer systems.

Software became more sophisticated during this third generation, permitting several programs to run in the same time frame, sharing the computer resources. Under this type of system, one program could be processing, another reading from a tape, and a third printing a record. This approach improved the efficiency of the computer system by decreasing CPU idle time. Software systems were developed to support interactive processing, in which the user is in direct contact with the computer through a terminal. This kind of access caused the customer service industry to flourish, especially in areas such as reservations and credit checks.

Large third-generation computers began to be supplemented by **minicomputers,** which are functionally equivalent to a full-sized system but are somewhat slower, smaller, and less expensive. These computers have become a huge success with medium-sized and smaller businesses.

Although the beginning of the third generation can be pinpointed by the introduction of the integrated circuit, actually there was extensive overlapping of the second and third generations. Yet the distinctions between the two seem crystal clear compared with the distinctions between the third and the fourth generations.

## The Fourth Generation, 1971–Present: The Microprocessor

Through the 1970s, computers gained dramatically in speed, reliability, and storage capacity, but entry into the fourth generation was evolutionary rather than revolutionary. The fourth generation was, in fact, an extension of third-generation technology. That is, in the early part of the third generation, specialized chips were developed for computer memory and logic. Thus, all the ingredients were in place for the next technological development, the *general-purpose* processor-on-a-chip, otherwise known as the **microprocessor.** First developed by an Intel Corporation design team headed by Ted Hoff in 1969, the microprocessor became commercially available in 1971.

*c p u - Central Processing unit*

Nowhere is the pervasiveness of computer power more apparent than in the explosive use of the microprocessor. In addition to the common applications of digital watches, pocket calculators, and **microcomputers**—small home and business computers—microprocessors can be anticipated in virtually every machine in the home or business. (To get a sense of how far we have come, try counting up the number of machines, microprocessor controlled or not, that are around your house. Would more than one or two have been in existence 50 years ago?) In 1975, **very large scale integration (VLSI)** was achieved. As a result, computers today are 100 times smaller than those of the first generation, and a single chip is far more powerful than ENIAC.

Computer environments have changed, with climate-controlled rooms becoming less necessary to ensure reliability; some recent models (especially minicomputers and microcomputers) can be placed almost anywhere. Table 3-1 lists other principal features of the fourth generation.

Large computers, of course, did not disappear just because small computers entered the market. Mainframe manufacturers have continued to develop powerful machines, such as the UNIVAC 1100, the IBM 3080 series, and the supercomputers from Cray.

Countries around the world have been active in the computer industry; few are as renowned for their technology as Japan. The Japanese have long been associated with chip technology, but recently they announced an entirely new direction.

### The Fifth Generation: Japan's Challenge

In 1980, signaling a bold move to take the lead in computer technology, the Japanese announced a ten-year project to develop a so-called fifth generation. Although the plan is as yet rather vague, its ambitious hardware and software goals have captivated the computer industry.

So far the Japanese government and Japanese private industry have each contributed $300 million toward the project, in an attempt to develop radically new forms of computer systems. The real significance is not the money itself, however, but the cooperation among government and Japanese industries and the writing of a blank check for computer development.

There has been much speculation about whether "Japan, Inc."—the name given the project—can really succeed. Even if the total aims are never achieved, however, there are apt to be at least two results: First, there will certainly be some significant side effects. Second, the American computer industry will respond to the challenge.

### The Computer Industry Diversifies

As we said, the development of the System/360 cost IBM $5 billion. Clearly, with that kind of astronomical investment, it is extraordinarily difficult for many firms to compete effectively in the main-

---

## THE OLD COMPUTERS' HOME

In this age of superspecialization, even the museum, that much-loved haunt of the dilettante, has been forced to narrow its scope . . . . The Computer Museum in Marlborough, Massachusetts, about forty miles west of Boston, . . . is a stupendous collection of old and not-so-old calculators, famous old computers and part of computers, from ENIAC to ILLIAC, photographs and assorted memorabilia, computer-generated murals, and even a computer made of Tinkertoys that plays ticktacktoe. . . .

Unlike science museums that have a couple of microcomputers programmed to play games, the Computer Museum takes a strictly historical approach. "One thing we *don't do*," explains Gwen Bell, the director, "is to say 'Line up here, folks, for your hands-on experience.'" The museum is more for looking than touching; it is a scholarly place, a thorough catalogue of man's struggle to hand his dreariest figure work over to amenable machines.

But scholarly does not mean stuffy. On the contrary, Bell jokingly refers to the museum as a sort of Salvation Army for obsolete computers, and she feels about each machine she saves from the scrap heap the way someone does who takes in a stray pet. "If it weren't for us," she declares, "all this stuff would be gone, thrown away, and industrial archaeologists fifty years from now would be the poorer for it."

—Natalie Angier,
*Discover,*
February 1983

frame market. Indeed, some big names in American industry have gone into mainframe manufacturing, then changed their minds and pulled out—among them General Electric and RCA. The survivors of the early manufacturers are Burroughs, NCR, Sperry-Univac, Honeywell, and IBM—and IBM today has about 70 percent of the mainframe market.

In the 1960s and 1970s, however, other companies emerged to give IBM a run for its money. One was Control Data Corporation (CDC). Another was Cray, formed by Seymour Cray (Figure 3-18), formerly with CDC, who developed the "supercomputer" called the Cray-1. A third, Amdahl Corporation, was formed by former IBM employee Gene Amdahl. His Amdahl 470V/6 was one and a half times as fast as a comparable IBM 370 computer and occupied one-third the space, yet cost less and was still compatible with IBM equipment and software.

Hundreds of other manufacturers have entered the computer industry in ventures requiring less capital outlay than the mainframe business. Today a wide range of diverse products and services are offered. The field includes mini- and microcomputers, peripheral equipment, software, and various service industries. Many companies provide specific support for particular aspects of the industry such as data communications or word processing. Digital Equipment Corporation and Hewlett-Packard began the trend to minicomputers in the early 1970s. Microcomputers joined the scene in the mid-1970s, led by products from Radio Shack, Apple, and Commodore. Others have joined the fray, with the IBM Personal Computer in the forefront.

## Problems of a Flourishing Industry

The growth of the computer industry has been unprecedented. Yet, for all the spectacular gains, it has not been without growing pains.

### The Software Crisis

While the miracles of miniaturization and technology were proceeding with hardware, users were encountering ongoing crises with software. As hardware capabilities and large memories were extended, computer industry researchers assumed they could easily develop massive, complex programming systems to match.

They were wrong. The complexities were greater than anyone had imagined. As a result, during the 1960s there were terrible traumas throughout the industry, as schedules and budgets slipped. Programming was found to be unreliable, often not meeting the specifications called for by clients. Complex software projects were poorly planned. Definitions of problems to be solved often were incomplete, leading to time-consuming and costly changes later on. It became apparent that the difficulties stemmed largely from inadequate management techniques, that managers lacked tools to monitor projects properly.

**Figure 3-18** Seymour Cray, developer of the supercomputer, Cray-1.

In addition, users began to discover that paying for an expensive programmer did not necessarily guarantee good programs. Sometimes a person who supposedly had ten years' experience might turn out to be, as someone said, a programmer "with one year of experience ten times." It became clear that new software techniques were needed. Eventually some new approaches were developed. One approach is structured programming, which, it has now been shown, produces fewer errors and reduces the cost of developing and maintaining programs.

### A Shortage of Qualified People

As we discuss in Chapter 17, on careers in computing and data processing, the whole field has grown so explosively that there has been a never-ending shortage of trained personnel. Indeed, the National Science Foundation expects the shortage to persist beyond 1990. As an indication of the problem, the NSF projected approximately 550,000 openings in the United States between 1978 and 1990 for programmers, systems analysts, and other computer professionals. Yet only about 157,000 persons will receive bachelor's and master's degrees in computer-related fields.

## From the Whole to the Parts

History is still being made in the computer industry, of course, and it is being made incredibly rapidly. A book cannot possibly pretend to describe all the very latest developments. Nevertheless, as we indicated earlier, the four areas of input, processing, output, and storage describe the basic components of a computer system—whatever its date.

In the next four chapters we consider each of these parts, beginning with the most fundamental, the processor.

## Summary and Key Terms

- The principles of a computer system—including input, processor, control unit, storage, and output—were embodied in the early nineteenth century by Charles Babbage in his **analytical engine.** This idea for a machine for performing calculations was an outgrowth of an earlier machine devised by Babbage called a **difference engine.**

- To control the order of calculations on his analytical engine, Babbage utilized an invention by Frenchman Joseph Jacquard, who devised a punched card for weavers working on looms. Countess Ada Lovelace helped develop instructions for carrying out computations on Babbage's device.

- The first computer to use electrical power instead of mechanical power was Herman Hollerith's tabulating machine, which was used in the 1890 census in the United States. Hollerith founded a company that became the forerunner of International Business Machines Corporation (IBM).

- Thomas J. Watson, Sr., built IBM into a dominant force in the business machines market. He also gave Harvard professor Howard Aiken research funds with which to build an electromechanical computer. The result was the Harvard **Mark I,** unveiled in 1944. The public reception to this machine strengthened IBM's commitment to computer development.

- John V. Atanasoff, with assistant Clifford Berry, devised the first digital computer to work by electronic means, the **Atanasoff-Berry Computer** ("ABC").

- During World War II, American military officials approached Dr. John Mauchly at the University of Pennsylvania about building a machine to compute missile trajectories more rapidly. Mauchly and his assistant, J. Presper Eckert, used ABC principles to build the **ENIAC.** The ENIAC (*E*lectronic *N*umerical *I*ntegrator *A*nd *C*omputer), made operational in 1946, was the world's first general-purpose electronic digital computer.

- John Von Neumann devised what he called the **stored program** concept, by which a computer read instructions from computer storage for switching to a new program. This principle was successfully utilized on the **EDVAC** (*E*lectronic *D*iscrete *V*ariable *A*utomatic *C*omputer).

- The Computer Age consists of four generations, primarily attached to four technological developments: the vacuum tube (1951–1958), the transistor (1959–1964), the integrated circuit (1965–1970), and the microprocessor (1971–present).

- The first generation began June 14, 1951, with the delivery of the **UNIVAC** (*U*niversal *A*utomatic *C*omputer) to the U.S. Bureau of the Census. To operate first-generation computers, thousands of **vacuum tubes** were required. Their drawbacks were that they caused temperature-control problems and frequently burned out. First-generation computers had slow input/output, were programmed only in machine language (rather than English-like higher-level languages), and were unreliable and expensive. Primary storage was via **magnetic cores.** Data was also stored on punched cards. Magnetic tape was introduced in 1957 as a faster, more compact storage method.

- The **transistor,** developed at Bell Laboratories, was only one-hundredth the size of a vacuum tube, needed no warm-up, consumed less energy, and was faster and more reliable. During the second generation, **assembly languages** or **symbolic languages** were developed, which used abbreviations for instructions rather than numbers and so made programming easier. **Higher-level languages,** such as **FORTRAN** (*FOR*mula *TRAN*slator) and **COBOL** (*CO*mmon *B*usiness-*O*riented *L*anguage), which are more English-like than machine language, were also developed. In 1962 the first removable disk pack was marketed. All these developments made the second generation of computers less costly to operate.

- The third generation emerged with the introduction of silicon, which could be sliced into wafers and etched with electrical circuitry, as a **semiconductor** of electric-

ity. These small **silicon chips** of **integrated circuits (ICs)** were hailed as a generational breakthrough because they met these four desirable characteristics: they were reliable, compact, and inexpensive, and they used less power. Large mainframe computers have been supplemented by **minicomputers,** conceptually equivalent to full-sized computers but slower and less expensive.

- The integrated circuits of 1965 moved on in 1970 to **large-scale integration (LSI),** with thousands of ICs on a single chip, and then in 1975 to **very large scale integration (VLSI)**—with a single chip being far more powerful than ENIAC.

- With the third generation, IBM announced the System/360 family of computers, comprising several models and sizes. After an all-out marketing effort, the system was accepted overwhelmingly in large- and medium-sized business and government operations. During this period, more sophisticated software was introduced that allowed several programs to run in the same time frame and enabled users to interact with the system.

- The fourth-generation **microprocessor**—general-purpose processor-on-a-chip—grew out of the specialized memory and logic chips of the third generation. Microprocessors have led to the development of **microcomputers**, expanding computer markets to smaller businesses and to personal use. Computer environments have become less rigid.

- In 1980 Japanese government and industry began collaborating on a ten-year project to develop a "fifth generation," radically new forms of computer systems.

- Some of the mainframe manufacturers—General Electric and RCA—have pulled out of the business because of the astronomical investments required, leaving IBM (with a 70 percent share of the mainframe market), Burroughs, NCR, Sperry-Univac, and Honeywell. These firms were joined in the 1960s and 1970s by Control Data Corporation, Cray, and Amdahl Corporation.

- Other companies began to offer products and services requiring less capital outlay than the mainframe business; these included minicomputers (pioneered in the early 1970s by Digital Equipment Corp. and Hewlett-Packard) and microcomputers from the Radio Shack, Apple, Commodore, and IBM companies.

- Software problems were a major concern in the computer industry in the 1960s owing to poor management and inadequate programming techniques.

- A shortage of trained personnel has haunted the computer industry and will probably continue through the 1980s.

1. Explain the contributions of the following people to the development of computers in the pre-electronic era: Charles Babbage, Joseph Jacquard, Ada Lovelace, Herman Hollerith, Thomas J. Watson, Sr.

2. Explain the contributions of: Howard Aiken, John V. Atanasoff and Clifford Berry, John Mauchly and J. Presper Eckert, John Von Neumann.

3. What was the significance of the following computers: Mark I, ENIAC, EDVAC, UNIVAC?

4. Give the principal technological development associated with each of the generations of computer development.

5. What are the four desirable characteristics of integrated circuits?

6. Explain the meaning of IC, LSI, and VLSI.

7. Name the principal mainframe manufacturers now in business.

**Selected References for Further Reading**

Austrian, Geoffrey. *Herman Hollerith: Forgotten Giant of Information Processing.* New York: Columbia University Press, 1982.

Feigenbaum, Edward, and Pamela McCorduck. *The Fifth Generation.* Reading, Mass.: Addison-Wesley, 1983.

Fishman, Katherine Davis. *The Computer Establishment.* New York: Harper & Row, 1981.

Goldstine, Herman H. *The Computer from Pascal to Von Neuman.* Princeton, N.J.: Princeton University Press, 1972.

Hanson, Dirk. *The New Alchemists: Silicon Valley and the Microelectronics Revolution.* Boston: Little, Brown, 1982.

Sobel, Robert. *I.B.M.: Colossus in Transition.* New York: Times Books, 1981.

Stern, Nancy. *Eniac to Univac.* Bedford, Mass.: Digital Press, 1981.

## IN THIS CHAPTER

The problem-solving part of the computer is the central processing unit, made up of the control unit, which directs the computer system, and the arithmetic/logic unit, which controls arithmetic and logical operations. Primary storage holds data and instructions for processing. Registers, addresses, storage capacity, coding schemes, and types of memory are also explained.

# ch4

# the central processor

## the intelligent machine

Can computers think?

This fascinating question has stirred a great deal of interest, not only among fiction writers (remember HAL in *2001*?) but also among scientists. Indeed, there is now a field of study known as **artificial intelligence,** which explores tasks computers do that previously were reserved for human intelligence, imagination, and intuition (see the box "Artificial Intelligence: Can Computers Think Like People?").

Leaving aside for the moment the problem of what we mean by "thinking," let us see how the processor works to do a kind of thinking—namely, problem solving—as it processes raw data into information. Incidentally, you will find this one of the more technical chapters, with a great many new terms. Once you get beyond this point, however, the going should be easier.

## The Central Processing Unit

The central processing unit is the part of the computer whose operations we cannot see. The human connection is the data input and the information output, but the controlling center of the computer is in between. The **central processing unit (CPU)** is a highly complex, extensive set of electrical circuitry that executes stored program instructions. As Figure 4-1 shows, it consists of two parts:

- The control unit

- The arithmetic/logic unit

Computers actually use *two* types of storage components, primary storage and secondary storage. **Primary storage** holds data only temporarily, at the time the computer is executing your program. It is not feasible to keep your data in primary storage when your program is not running because other people will be using the computer and will need the primary storage space. **Secondary storage** holds data that is permanent or semipermanent, stored on tape, disk, or (as explained in Chapter 7) mass storage. The CPU interacts closely with primary storage, referring to it for both instructions and data. Primary storage will be discussed with the CPU in this chapter. Since the physical attributes of secondary storage devices are related to the way data is organized on them, we wiil discuss these two topics together in Chapter 7.

Let us consider these components.

### The Control Unit

The **control unit** contains circuitry that, with electrical signals, directs and coordinates the entire computer system in carrying out, or executing, stored program instructions. Like an orchestra leader, the control unit does not execute the instructions itself; rather it directs other parts of the system to do so.

## Artificial Intelligence: Can Computers Think Like People?

"The spirit is willing, but the flesh is weak," goes the Biblical verse. When the verse was translated from English to Russian and back again, the computer interpreted it as: "The wine is agreeable, but the meat has spoiled."

This anecdote illustrates the difficulty of teaching a computer the subtleties of human language, for so much about understanding in language depends on context and experience. Even so, some programs have been devised that allow computers to carry on a conversation on a limited subject. For instance, a UCLA psychologist invented PARRY, which was supposed to act like a 28-year-old horse player with paranoid ideas about being pursued by a vengeful bookie. When interviewed via a terminal by six psychiatrists, PARRY was so successful in its role that the psychiatrists as often as not guessed it was human.

In a demonstration of another form of "thinking," in a chess match played between David Levy, the International Chess Master, and Northwestern University's computer chess champion, CHESS 4.7, the computer made some moves that Levy later said were such that he found it hard to believe he was not playing with an outstanding human opponent.

Several years ago, British mathematician Alan Turing proposed a test of thinking machines, which (in a narrow sense) both PARRY and CHESS 4.7 might be said to have passed. In the *Turing Test,* a human being is seated before two hidden terminals, one operated by another person and one by a computer, and asked to guess, by carrying out conversations through the terminals, which is the person and which is the computer. If the human judge cannot tell the difference, the computer is said to have passed and to be considered *for all practical purposes* a thinking machine.

It may be argued that some computers have passed the Turing Test in one or two areas of knowledge, such as chess, but that no computer has been programmed in the enormous range of topics that would enable it ultimately to fool the human tester. Yet it has been shown that computers can be programmed to learn new concepts, to understand simple drawings, to understand simple English, to work as robots, and to do some expert problem solving. At M.I.T., MACSYMA does high-level algebra. At Stanford, DENDRAL analyzes mass spectrograms and finds molecular structure, and MYCIN is helping physicians diagnose and treat certain blood infections. At SRI International, PROSPECTOR is aiding in mineral exploration. These programs clearly demonstrate the problem-solving power of computers.

To develop a clear understanding as to whether or not computers are really capable of thinking, it might be well to review the following seven myths offered by M.I.T. professor Patrick Henry Winston.

*Myth: Computers Can Never . . .* This sentence, Winston says, can be restated and completed as, "Computers cannot . . . , because no one has thought of a way to make them. . . ." This argument maintains a belief in human superiority. "Beware of those who think it can never happen," Winston writes. "Their ancestors hassled Galileo and ridiculed Darwin."

*Myth: Computers Are Not Intelligent Because They Do Not Write like Shakespeare, Compose like Beethoven, or Explore Science like Newton.* The rejoinder is neither do we ordinary writers, musicians, and scientists. Computers need not be superhuman to meet the test of intelligence.

*Myth: Computers Can Do Only What They Are Programmed To Do.* Computers are indebted to human programmers, but humans are indebted to the genetic code. Winston believes that once people bring computer intelligence up to the level beyond which learning from the environment takes place, computers will "augment their directly programmed gifts by the same means humans do: by being told, by reading, by asking questions, by doing experiments, and by being curious."

*Myth: Software Can Never Equal Brainware Because Transistors Are Different from Neurons.* Studying neurons, says Winston, can no more produce understanding of intelligence than studying transistors can produce understanding of how a computer, say, responds to English. Besides, an intelligent computer program is built on a hierarchical structure, of which transistors are only a part.

*Myth: Probabilistic Machinery Causes Inspiration and Explains Free Will.* In other words, some persons like to believe that deep, inexplicable thoughts come from random neural behavior and that computer intelligence cannot draw on similar randomness or disorder. However, says Winston, "It is more likely that increased randomness of neural behavior is the problem of the epileptic and the drunk, not the advantage of the brilliant."

*Myth: Computers Can Never Appreciate Aesthetics.* " . . . Smart computers will undoubtedly find art a challenge," writes Winston, "since descriptions and interactions of descriptions must surely be central to understanding why any art form is interesting, moving, pleasing, disquieting, or new."

*Myth: Intelligence Can Never Be Understood.* "To be intelligent is to be mysterious. . . . As long as the origin of an idea is obscure, its invention seems profound. . . ." However, says Winston, once a process "is dissected, studied, and grasped, the intelligence invariably seems to vanish."

We shall come back to a consideration of artificial intelligence in Chapter 19.

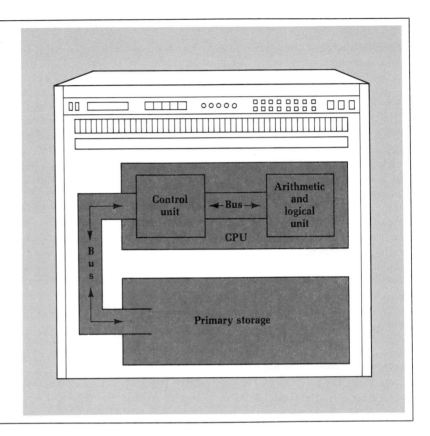

**Figure 4-1   The central processor in the computer system.** The two parts of the processor are the control unit and the arithmetic/logic unit. Primary storage holds data and instructions temporarily, at the time the program is being executed. The CPU interacts closely with primary storage, referring to it for both instructions and data.

Notice in Figure 4-1 that the control unit must communicate both with the arithmetic/logic unit and with primary storage. These communications are usually made through physical connections called a **bus line** or **data bus.** A data bus consists of parallel data lines with, usually, as many lines as bits in the computer's word size; bear with us for the moment, we will describe these terms in a subsequent section.

### The Arithmetic/Logic Unit

The **arithmetic/logic unit** (abbreviated **ALU**) contains the electronic circuitry that controls all (1) arithmetic and (2) logical operations.

Four kinds of **arithmetic operations,** or mathematical calculations, can be performed on data by this unit:

- Addition
- Multiplication
- Subtraction
- Division

**Logical operations** are usually comparing operations. The arithmetic/logic unit is able to compare numbers, letters, or special characters and take alternative courses of action. This is a very important capability. It is by comparing that a computer is able to tell, for instance, whether there are unfilled seats on airplanes, whether charge-card

< *less than*
> *greater than*
= *equal to*
<= *less than or equal to*
=> *greater than or equal to*
<> *not equal to*

customers have exceeded their credit limits, and whether one candidate for Congress has more votes than another.

There are three basic comparing operations: *logic*

- **Equal to (=) Condition:** Comparing to determine if the values in two fields are equal—for example, "If the number of tickets sold equals the number of seats in the auditorium, then the concert is declared sold out."

- **Less Than (<) Condition:** Comparing to determine if the value of one field is less than the value of another—for example, "If the number of speeding tickets on this driver's record is less than three, then insurance rates are thus-and-so; otherwise the rates are higher."

- **Greater Than (>) Condition:** Comparing to determine if the value of one field is greater than the value of another—for instance, "If the hours this person worked this week are greater than 40, then multiply every extra hour by 1-1/2 times his or her usual hourly wage to compute overtime pay."

These three comparing operations may be combined to form a total of six commonly used operations: equal to, less than, greater than, less than or equal to, greater than or equal to, and less than or greater than. Note that "less than or greater than" is the same as "not equal to." (These comparing operations are used frequently in the decision boxes in flowcharts, as we will show in Chapter 8.)

### Primary Storage Unit

The **primary storage unit** is also known as **main storage, internal storage,** and **memory**—all terms used interchangeably by people in computer circles. The primary storage unit is the part of the computer that holds data and instructions for processing. Primary storage is used only temporarily—it holds your program only as long as your program is in operation. It must then be yielded so that other people can use it for their programs.

Data and instructions are put into primary storage by the control unit. After being processed, the data is held in primary storage until it is ready to be released to the output unit.

The chief characteristic of primary storage is that it allows very fast access to data and instructions in any locations in it.

### Registers: Temporary Hardware Storage Areas

**Registers** are temporary storage areas for instructions or data. Registers are part of the CPU, but they are *not* in primary storage. Rather, they are special, additional storage locations whose advantage is speed. They can operate very rapidly in accepting, holding, and transferring instructions or data, or in performing arithmetic or comparisons, all under the direction of the control unit of the CPU. In other words, they are temporary storage areas that assist transfers and arithmetic/logical operations within the CPU.

There are different kinds of registers, including:

- An **accumulator,** which collects the results of computations

- A **storage register,** which holds information taken from or sent to primary storage

- An **address register,** which holds the address of a location containing an item of data called for by an instruction

- A **general-purpose register,** which is used for several functions— for example, arithmetic and addressing purposes.

## How Computer Program Instructions Are Executed

Let us examine the way the central processor executes a computer program. First, the control unit gets an instruction, examines it to figure out what is to be done, and then turns control over to the arithmetic/logic unit. This process is called instruction time, or **I–time.** Then the ALU executes the instruction. This process is called execution time, or **E–time.** The combination of I-time and E-time is called the **machine cycle.**

The following description of the machine cycle is for just one instruction in a program. In fact, most computers can execute *only* one instruction at a time (see Figure 4-2).

After data and instructions are read by the input device and placed into the primary storage unit, the control unit then does the following, one instruction at a time, in four steps:

❶ The control unit "fetches" (gets) the instruction from primary storage. (It should be noted that storing results in main memory is not universal; leaving the result in a high-speed register is also common.)

❷ The control unit decodes the instruction (decides what it means), and makes available to the arithmetic/logic unit any data needed for the operation to be performed.

❸ The control unit directs the arithmetic/logic unit to execute the instruction. That is, the ALU is given control and performs the actual operation on the data.

❹ The control unit then places the result of this operation into the primary storage unit.

After the appropriate instructions are executed, the control unit directs the primary storage unit to release the results to the output device.

Each CPU has an internal **clock,** which produces pulses at a fixed rate to synchronize all computer operations. A single machine code instruction may be made up of a substantial number of subinstruc-

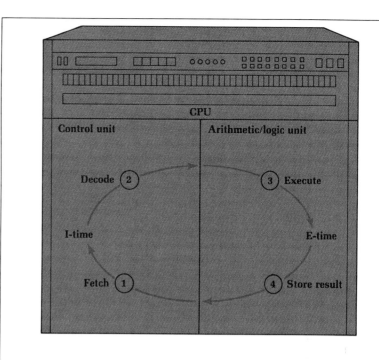

**Figure 4-2** **The machine cycle.** How an instruction is executed (*see text*).

tions, each of which must take at least one clock cycle period. These instructions are controlled by the lowest level of the program, called **microcode.** Microcode instructions are executed directly by the computer's electronic circuits. The microcode instructions are permanently set inside the control unit; these detailed operations are invisible to the user and cannot be altered.

## Computer Processing Speeds

The attribute speed is universally associated with computers. Certainly all computers are fast, but there is a wide diversity among computer speeds.

The execution of an instruction on a small computer may be measured in less than a **millisecond,** which is one-thousandth of a second (see Table 4-1). Many computers can execute an instruction measured in **microseconds,** one-millionth of a second. Modern super-

**HOW FAST IS A NANOSECOND?**

| If one nanosecond is . . . | Then one second is . . . equivalent to . . . |
|---|---|
| one mile | 2000 trips to the moon and back |
| one person | population of China and the United States |
| one minute | 1900 years |
| one square mile | 17 times the land area of the entire world |

**Table 4-1** **Units of time:** How fast is *fast*?

| Unit of time | Fraction of second | Mathematical notation |
|---|---|---|
| Millisecond | Thousandth: 1/1000 | $10^{-3}$ |
| Microsecond | Millionth: 1/1,000,000 | $10^{-6}$ |
| Nanosecond | Billionth: 1/1,000,000,000 | $10^{-9}$ |
| Picosecond | Trillionth: 1/1,000,000,000,000 | $10^{-12}$ |

computers are approaching the **nanosecond** range—one-billionth of a second. Still to be broken is the **picosecond** barrier—one-trillionth of a second.

## Storage Locations and Addresses: How to Find Instructions and Data

It is one thing to have instructions and data somewhere in primary storage and quite another for the computer—that is to say, the control unit—to be able to find them. How does it do this?

The location in primary storage for each instruction and each piece of data is identified by an **address.** That is, each location has an address number, like the mailboxes in front of an apartment house or numbers on bank safe deposit boxes. And, like the mailbox numbers, the address numbers of the locations remain the same, but the contents (data and instructions) of the locations may change. That is, new data or new instructions may be placed in them.

Figure 4-3 shows how a program manipulates data in primary storage. As a programmer, it is up to you to keep track of which data are in which locations.

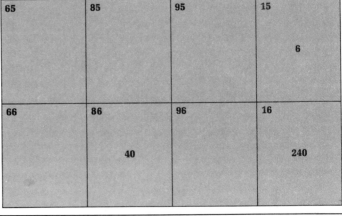

**Figure 4-3 Addresses like mailboxes.** The addresses of primary storage locations are like the identifying numbers on apartment house mailboxes (photo). Suppose we want to compute someone's salary as hours times rate. Rate ($6) goes in primary storage location 15, hours (40) in location 86, and the computed salary ($6 x 40 hours, or $240) in location 16. Thus, *addresses* are 15, 86, and 16, but *contents* are $6, 40 hours, and $240, respectively. Note that the program *instructions* would say to multiply the contents of location 15 by the contents of location 86 and move the result to location 16. (A computer language used by a programmer would use some kind of symbolic name for each location, such as R or RATE or PAY-RATE instead of the number 15.) The *data* is the actual contents—what is stored in each location.

**BINARY EQUIVALENT OF
DECIMAL NUMBERS 0–15**

| Decimal | Binary |
|---------|--------|
| 0 | 0000 |
| 1 | 0001 |
| 2 | 0010 |
| 3 | 0011 |
| 4 | 0100 |
| 5 | 0101 |
| 6 | 0110 |
| 7 | 0111 |
| 8 | 1000 |
| 9 | 1001 |
| 10 | 1010 |
| 11 | 1011 |
| 12 | 1100 |
| 13 | 1101 |
| 14 | 1110 |
| 15 | 1111 |

**Figure 4-4   Bit as light bulb.** A light bulb operates as a binary digit, with "off" representing 0 and "on" representing 1. Light bulbs, of course, are not used in computers, but vacuum tubes, transistors, silicon chips, magnetic bubbles, or anything else that can stop or start an electronic signal can be used. The eight on and off bulbs above represent the letter *A* in the EBCDIC code.

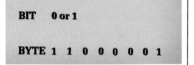

**Figure 4-5   Bit and byte.** The byte shows the letter *A* in EBCDIC.

# Data Representation: "On/Off"

People are accustomed to thinking of computers as complex mechanisms, but the fact is that these machines basically know only two things: "on" and "off." This "on/off," "yes/no," two-state system is called the **binary system.** Using the two states—which can be represented by electricity turned on or off, or a magnetic field that is positive or negative—sophisticated ways of representing data are constructed.

Let us look at one way the two states can be used to represent data. Whereas the decimal number system has a base of 10 (0, 1, 2, 3, and so on, to 9), the binary system has a base of 2. This means it has only two digits, 0 and 1, which can correspond to the two states "off" and "on." Combinations of these zeros and ones can then be used to represent larger numbers. The binary system is discussed in more detail in Appendix B.

## Bits, Bytes, and Words

Each 0 or 1 in the binary system is called a **bit** (for binary digit). The bit is the basic unit for storing data in primary storage—0 for "off," 1 for "on" (see Figure 4-4).

Since single bits by themselves cannot store all the numbers, letters, and special characters (such as "$" and "?") that must be processed by a computer, the bits are put together in groups, usually of six or eight, and called **bytes** (see Figure 4-5). Each byte (pronounced "bite") usually represents one character of data—a letter, digit, or special character.

Computer manufacturers express the capacity of primary storage in terms of the letter **K.** The letter was originally intended to represent the number 2 to the tenth power, which is 1024, but the meaning has evolved so that now K stands either for 1024 or is rounded off to 1000. A **kilobyte** is K bytes—that is, 1024 bytes. Kilobyte is abbreviated **KB.** Thus, 2KB means 2K bytes. Main storage may also be expressed in **megabytes,** or millions of bytes ("mega" means million). Recently some large computers have expressed main storage in terms of **gigabytes**—that is, *billions* of bytes.

A small, pocket computer may have less than 2K bytes of primary storage, but most microcomputers have between 4K and 64K bytes. Minicomputers usually range from 64K bytes to 1 megabyte. Mainframes range from 512K bytes (more than half a megabyte) up to 16 megabytes and more.

In advertising computers, the use of the letter K can be confusing. A microcomputer billed as having a "4K memory" may have 4096 *bytes* or 4096 *words.* A computer **word** is defined as the number of bits that constitute a common unit of information, as defined by the computer system. The length of a word varies by computers. Common word lengths in bits are 8 (microcomputers), 16 (traditional minicomputers and some microcomputers), 32 (full-size mainframe computers and some minicomputers), and 64 (supercomputers).

A computer's word size is very important. In general, the larger the word size, the more powerful the computer. A larger word size means:

- The computer can transfer more information at a time, making the computer faster.

- The computer word has room to reference larger addresses, thus allowing more main memory.

- The computer can support a greater number and variety of instructions.

The internal circuitry of a computer must reflect its word size. Usually, a bus line has the same number of data paths as bits in its word size. Thus, a 16-bit processor will have a 16-bit bus, meaning that data can be sent over the bus lines a word at a time.

**COMPUTER WORD SIZES**

| Bits per Word | Representative Computers |
|---|---|
| 8 | Atari, PET |
| 16 | IBM PC, HP-3000, Lisa |
| 18 | PDP-15 |
| 24 | Harris H100 |
| 32 | IBM 370, VAX 11/780 |
| 36 | Honeywell DPS8, Univac 1100/80 |
| 48 | Burroughs 6700 |
| 60 | CDC 7600 |
| 64 | Cyber 205, Cray-1 |

### Fixed-Length and Variable-Length Computers

Some computers are designed to be character-oriented; that is, data is addressed as a series of single characters. When an instruction calls for data to be accessed from a memory location, the data is moved a character at a time, until the required number of characters has been read. In other words, the length of the data being processed may vary. Computers that process data this way are said to use **variable-length words.**

Other computers move data a word at a time. These computers are said to use **fixed-length words.** As we mentioned, the size of the word depends on the computer.

### Coding Schemes: EBCDIC and ASCII

There are two commonly used coding schemes for representing numbers, letters, and special characters—EBCDIC and ASCII.

**EBCDIC** (usually pronounced "EB-see-dick") stands for Extended Binary Coded Decimal Interchange Code. Established by IBM and used extensively in the IBM 360/370 models, as well as in the 4300 model series, it uses eight bits to represent a single character. The letter *A*, for instance, is represented by 11000001.

Another code, **ASCII** (pronounced "AS-key"), which stands for American Standard Code for Information Interchange, uses seven bits for each character. The ASCII representation has been adopted as a standard by the U.S. government and is found in a variety of computers, particularly minicomputers and microcomputers. Two examples are the minicomputers marketed by manufacturers Hewlett-Packard and Prime. Figure 4-6 shows the EBCDIC and ASCII codes.

| Character | EBCDIC | ASCII |
|:---:|:---:|:---:|
| A | 1100 0001 | 100 0001 |
| B | 1100 0010 | 100 0010 |
| C | 1100 0011 | 100 0011 |
| D | 1100 0100 | 100 0100 |
| E | 1100 0101 | 100 0101 |
| F | 1100 0110 | 100 0110 |
| G | 1100 0111 | 100 0111 |
| H | 1100 1000 | 100 1000 |
| I | 1100 1001 | 100 1001 |
| J | 1101 0001 | 100 1010 |
| K | 1101 0010 | 100 1011 |
| L | 1101 0011 | 100 1100 |
| M | 1101 0100 | 100 1101 |
| N | 1101 0101 | 100 1110 |
| O | 1101 0110 | 100 1111 |
| P | 1101 0111 | 101 0000 |
| Q | 1101 1000 | 101 0001 |
| R | 1101 1001 | 101 0010 |
| S | 1101 0010 | 101 0011 |
| T | 1110 0011 | 101 0100 |
| U | 1110 0100 | 101 0101 |
| V | 1110 0101 | 101 0110 |
| W | 1110 0110 | 101 0111 |
| X | 1110 0111 | 101 1000 |
| Y | 1110 1000 | 101 1001 |
| Z | 1110 1001 | 101 1010 |
| 0 | 1111 0000 | 011 0000 |
| 1 | 1111 0001 | 011 0001 |
| 2 | 1111 0010 | 011 0010 |
| 3 | 1111 0011 | 011 0011 |
| 4 | 1111 0100 | 011 0100 |
| 5 | 1111 0101 | 011 0101 |
| 6 | 1111 0110 | 011 0110 |
| 7 | 1111 0111 | 011 0111 |
| 8 | 1111 1000 | 011 1000 |
| 9 | 1111 1001 | 011 1001 |

**Figure 4-6    The EBCDIC and ASCII codes.** Shown are binary representations for numbers, letters, and special characters. These may be thought of as a series of light bulbs. In the first generation of computers, when vacuum tubes were used, they could be seen to light up.

## The Parity Bit: Checking for Errors

Suppose you are transmitting data over a telephone line, say, or even within the computer system itself. How do you know it arrived safely—that is, that nothing was lost or garbled? Sometimes data *is* lost in transit, owing to bit synchronization, hardware failure, and the like.

To signal the computer that the bits in a byte have stayed the way they are supposed to, another bit is added to the byte as a check. This bit is called a **parity bit** or **check bit.** Thus, in an eight-bit EBCDIC byte, the parity bit is a ninth bit.

As Figure 4-7 shows, the parity bit stored with each byte alerts the computer system if any EBCDIC bits are flawed or missing because—since we are using an odd parity system—the number of 1 bits must add up to an odd number. (If even parity were used, the number of 1 bits would have to add up to an even number. Computers vary: some use odd parity, some use even.)

As you might suspect, a parity check is not infallible. For instance, for any of the letters in Figure 4-7, if *two* 1s were dropped, the number of 1 bits would still add up to an odd number—and the computer would not notice that the byte was erroneous. But two bit failures within one byte in one move are not likely to occur.

# Primary Storage Components: Memories Are Made of This

As we saw in Chapter 3, primary storage components evolved from vacuum tubes to magnetic cores to semiconductors.

## Semiconductor Storage

Most modern computers use semiconductor storage because it has several advantages: reliability, compactness (hence increased speed), low cost, and lower power usage. But it has one major disadvantage: It is volatile. That is, semiconductor storage requires continuous electric current to represent data. If the current is interrupted, the data is lost.

As Gallery 3 shows, **semiconductor storage** is made up of thousands of very small circuits on a silicon chip. The circuits etched on these chips can be in one of two states—either conducting a current or not, "on" or "off." The two states can be used to represent binary digits 1 and 0. *Large scale integration (LSI)* means a chip has a large number of circuits and they are integrated. More recently, chips are described as *VLSI,* for *very large scale integration.* A chip is also described as *monolithic* because the circuits on a single chip comprise an inseparable unit of storage.

Since semiconductor memory can be mass-produced economically, the cost of primary storage has been considerably reduced. Chips that

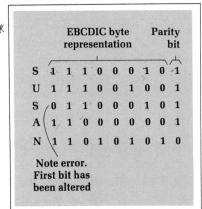

| | EBCDIC byte representation | | | | | | | | Parity bit |
|---|---|---|---|---|---|---|---|---|---|
| S | 1 | 1 | 1 | 0 | 0 | 0 | 1 | 0 | 1 |
| U | 1 | 1 | 1 | 0 | 0 | 1 | 0 | 0 | 1 |
| S | 0 | 1 | 1 | 0 | 0 | 0 | 1 | 0 | 1 |
| A | 1 | 1 | 0 | 0 | 0 | 0 | 0 | 0 | 1 |
| N | 1 | 1 | 0 | 1 | 0 | 1 | 0 | 1 | 0 |

Note error.
First bit has
been altered

**Figure 4-7 Example of odd parity.** A 0 or a 1 is added as a parity bit to the EBCDIC byte so that each byte always comes out with an odd number of 1 bits. Thus, with the second S here, the absence of the first 1 will produce an even number of bits—signaling the computer that there is an error.

once cost $80 to $90 each to build can now be made in volume for less than $1 each. In addition, miniaturization has reduced the memory required to store a million characters of information from 400 cubic feet in 1953 to 0.03 cubic feet in 1981. The continued trend toward miniaturization means that future semiconductor storage will become even smaller, faster, and less expensive. By 1990, engineers expect to squeeze 10 million transistors on a chip, making it as complex as a city of 1000 square miles.

The current generation memory chip is the 64K chip. Japan has been dominant in chip production. The U.S. Department of Defense worries that computers, weapons, and telecommunications may grow dangerously dependent on foreign memory chips. In recent years, Japan and the United States have been running neck and neck in the chip race.

### Bubble Storage

A **magnetic bubble memory** (see Figure 4-8) consists of a chip coated with a thin layer of magnetic film. On this film, a microscopic "bubble" is formed when a uniform magnetic field is applied. The presence of a bubble represents a 1, its absence a 0, the basis for a binary system of representing data.

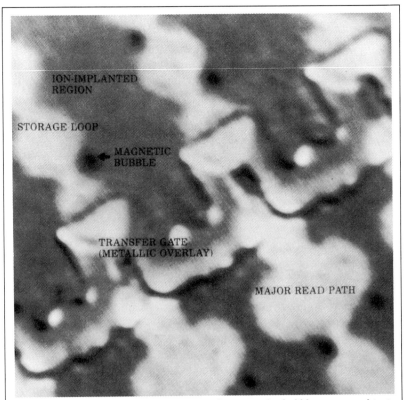

**Figure 4-8 Magnetic bubble memory.** This part of a bubble memory chip is magnified 3000 times. Individual bubbles are visible as dark dots.

The advantages of the bubble memory are twofold: It has a great deal more capacity than even the most powerful integrated circuit chip now on the market. And it is *nonvolatile,* meaning that it can retain data even when the current is turned off—something present-day chips cannot do.

Bubble memory was introduced by Bell Laboratories in 1966, but the technology never seemed to live up to the expectations. Many companies that followed Bell tried to develop its potential but abandoned the effort. However, not long ago, Intel announced the development of a magnetic bubble memory chip that could store the equivalent of 240 typewritten pages—four million bits of information.

# RAM, ROM, PROM, and EPROM

The above do not represent some mystical chant. Rather they are acronyms describing four different types of storage.

**RAM** stands for **random-access memory** and refers to storage in which data and programs can be written in and read from main storage locations readily and speedily. **ROM** stands for **read-only memory.** This type of storage contains programs and data that are permanently recorded into the memory at the factory and cannot be changed by the user. The contents of ROM can be read and used, but they cannot be changed.

RAM is the type of memory that we have been describing in this chapter. Unlike the magnetic bubble memory, RAM is usually *volatile*—that is, data is lost once the power is shut off. ROMs, often called **firmware,** are used to store programs that will not be altered. For example, a pocket calculator might have a program for calculating square roots in ROM; a microcomputer might have a BASIC interpreting program in ROM. ROM is nonvolatile.

Some further variations in types of memory are seen in PROM and EPROM. The term **PROM** is an abbreviation for **programmable read-only memory.** It is like ROM in that its contents cannot be altered while a program is being processed. PROM has been programmed by the manufacturer to satisfy specific customer software needs; in hardware form these programs can execute much more quickly.

EPROM chips are like PROM, only erasable; **EPROM** stands for **erasable, programmable read-only memory.** Information stored on EPROM chips can be erased by ultraviolet light beamed into a window of the chip package. This means that EPROMs can be reprogrammed repeatedly.

If you have seen some advertisements for microcomputers, you may have noticed that a computer can have both RAM and ROM. For instance, an ad may offer a personal computer with "16K RAM and 4K ROM with a BASIC language interpreter" or some similar enticement. We come back to this in a bit more detail in our discussion of personal computers, Chapter 14.

## *Next: Putting in Input*

The future holds some exciting possibilities. Would you believe computers that are actually *grown* as biological cultures? So-called "bio-chips" can replace the present billions of molecules that make up today's silicon chip with a single atom brewed in a test tube. As far-fetched as this sounds, that is precisely the direction of some present ongoing research. Tomorrow's processing unit may well be an organic computer.

A central processing unit is nothing, of course, without data to process. In the next chapter we will describe how input data is put into the computer.

## *Summary and Key Terms*

- **Artificial intelligence** is a field of study that explores how computers can be used for tasks of intelligence, imagination, and intuition.

- The **central processing unit (CPU)** is a complex set of electrical circuitry that executes program instructions. It consists of the control unit and the arithmetic/logic unit.

- The **control unit** directs and coordinates the entire computer system in executing stored program instructions.

- A **bus line** or **data bus**—parallel data lines—helps the control unit communicate with the arithmetic/logic unit, and the primary storage unit, described below.

- The **arithmetic/logic unit (ALU)** controls all arithmetic and logical operations. There are four kinds of **arithmetic operations:** addition, subtraction, multiplication, and division. **Logical operations** are usually comparing operations, and there are three basic kinds: equal to, less than, and greater than.

- The **primary storage unit,** also called **main storage, internal storage,** and **memory,** holds data and instructions for processing. Unlike **secondary storage** (tape, disk, or mass storage), which holds data that is permanent or semipermanent, primary storage holds data only temporarily—that is, it holds data for a particular program and that program is being run.

- **Registers** are temporary hardware storage areas for instructions or data. They are part of the CPU. Their advantage is their speed in manipulating data under the direction of the control unit.

- **Accumulators** are registers that collect the results of computations; **storage registers** hold information taken from or sent to primary storage; **address registers** hold the address of a location containing an item of data; **general-purpose registers** are used for arithmetic and addressing purposes.

- A program instruction is executed with a combination of **I-time** (instruction time), in which the control unit gets an instruction, examines it to see what is needed, and turns control over to the ALU; and **E-time** (execution time), in which the ALU executes the instruction. A **machine cycle** is a combination of I-time and E-time.

- The CPU executes an instruction as follows: the control unit (1) fetches the instruction from primary storage, (2) decides what the instruction means and makes the data available to the arithmetic/logic unit, (3) directs the ALU as to what to do with the data, and (4) places the result of the computation back into the primary storage unit.

- The CPU **clock** produces pulses at a fixed rate to synchronize computer operations. Machine code instructions and subinstructions are controlled by **microcode** instructions permanently set inside the control unit and executed directly by the computer's electronic circuits.

- Computer processing speeds are expressed in terms of **milliseconds** (one-thousandth of a second), **microseconds** (one-millionth of a second), **nanoseconds** (one-billionth of a second), and—still to come—**picoseconds** (one-trillionth of a second).

- The location in primary storage for each instruction and each piece of data is identified by an **address.** Address numbers remain the same, but the contents of locations change.

- Data is represented on a computer by means of a two-state on/off system called the **binary system,** which has a base of 2 (the decimal system we generally use has a base of 10). Each 0 or 1 in binary is called a **bit** (for binary digit) and is the basic unit for storing data in primary storage, with 0 for "off" and 1 for "on".

- A group of bits (such as six or eight) is called a *byte.* Each byte represents a letter, number, or special character.

- Storage capacity is expressed in **kilobytes (KB),** which are equal to 1024 bytes, and **megabytes** (millions of bytes). Computer storage can range from 2K to 16 megabytes and more. The letter **K** stands for 1024, but is often rounded to 1000. Some large computers have expressed main storage in **gigabytes,** or billions of bytes.

- Some computers divide primary storage into sections called **words,** each holding a certain number of binary digits, such as 8, 16, 32, or 64. The larger the word, the more powerful the computer, for a large word size means the computer can transfer more information at a time, can have more main memory, and can support a greater number and variety of instructions.

- **Fixed-length computers** move data a word at a time, whereas **variable-length computers** move data a character at a time.

- Commonly used coding schemes for representing characters are **EBCDIC** (Extended *Binary Coded Decimal Interchange Code*), which consists of eight-bit characters, and **ASCII** (*American Standard Code for Information Interchange*), which uses seven-bit characters.

- A **parity,** or **check, bit** is an extra bit added to a byte to signal the computer if a bit is flawed or missing. A computer may use either odd parity or even parity.

- Most modern computers use **semiconductor storage,** which is mass-produced as integrated circuits etched on silicon chips. Large-scale integration (LSI) means that a chip has a large number of circuits and that they are integrated. Very large scale integration (VLSI) means the circuits on a single chip comprise an inseparable unit of storage. The current generation memory chip is the 64K chip.

- **Bubble memory storage** is a chip of garnet coated with thin magnetic film that forms a "bubble" when a mag-

netic field is applied, and has more than ten times the capacity of today's most powerful integrated circuit chip. Bubble memories retain data even when the current is turned off.

- **Random-access memory (RAM)** means that data and programs can be both written in and read from any storage location. **Read-only memory (ROM)** means some programs are permanently recorded in the hardware by the manufacturer and cannot be changed by the user. ROMs are often called **firmware. Programmable read-only memory (PROM)** means that the user can program the data into the memory before it is assembled with the computer system. **EPROM** stands for **erasable, programmable read-only memory;** information on such chips can be erased by ultraviolet light, so that the chips can be reprogrammed repeatedly.

*Review*

1. Describe the two parts of the CPU and their functions.

2. Distinguish between primary storage and secondary storage.

3. Describe four kinds of registers.

4. Describe the steps to execute a program instruction.

5. Differentiate among millisecond, microsecond, nanosecond, and picosecond.

6. Why is the binary system used in data representation?

7. Define bit, byte, kilobyte, megabyte, gigabyte, word.

8. What are the two principal coding schemes for representing bits and characters?

9. Write this sentence first in ASCII and then in EBCDIC: "If the only tool you have is a hammer, you tend to see every problem as a nail." (Abraham Maslow)

10. Describe how a parity check works.

## IN THIS CHAPTER

Input is the bridge between "data" and "processing." It includes the long-used punched cards on the one hand and the newly developing technology of voice recognition on the other. In between are such methods as key input to magnetic tape and disk, magnetic-ink character recognition, optical recognition of various kinds (marks, characters, handwriting, and bar codes), touch-tone telephones, data collection devices, and light pens.

# ch.5

## input
### what goes in

How would you like to open a bill from the electric company, to which you usually pay about $45 a month, and find you were asked to pay $613,051? That is what happened to a Belleplain, New Jersey, woman as a result of an input error. (A secretary at the company added insult to injury by telling the woman not to worry, she could pay it off a little each month.)

This true anecdote illustrates the importance of input—and demonstrates the truth of **GIGO,** the programmer's acronym for *garbage in, garbage out.* That is, the quality of the information the computer produces can be no better than the quality and accuracy of the data given to it in the first place.

*ch5*

## The Forms of Input

Have you talked to your computer recently? Has it talked to you?

One of the fascinating methods of input is computer voice recognition, which, as we shall see, represents a modern refinement in data entry. Research scientists at IBM have used a computer to transcribe speech consisting of sentences from a vocabulary of about a thousand words, read at a normal speaking rate. The computer transcribed these spoken sentences into printed form with a 91 percent accuracy rate.

Voice recognition is a newly emerging method of input, but there are many others:

- Punched cards

- Magnetic-ink character recognition, which is used with the account numbers on checks

- Optical-mark recognition, which is used with machine-scored tests

- Optical-character recognition, which is used in department stores on sales tags read by "wands"

- Optical recognition of handwritten characters and bar codes

- Touch-tone telephones

- Light pens for altering data directly on a CRT screen

Some of the data can go directly to the computer for processing, as in voice input. Some data goes through a good deal of intermediate handling, as when it is copied from a *source document* (jargon for the original source of data) and keypunched on cards, which may then be verified for accuracy.

In this chapter, we consider the various methods of gathering data to be processed by the computer—sometimes called *raw data*—and converting it into some form the computer can understand. We begin by studying punched cards, then consider the improved input techniques of key-to-tape and key-to-disk. Finally, we look at the most direct form of input, source data automation. Several kinds of input are shown in Gallery 4 following page 86.

# *Punched Cards*

The Jacquard loom, invented about 1800, used a deck of punched cards to control the patterns of the weave automatically. Even earlier, rolls of punched paper had been programmed to control some musical instruments, such as player pianos (see Figure 5-1). However, it was Herman Hollerith, as we have seen, who applied Jacquard's punched card principle to information processing.

When, in the 1950s, computers began to be widely used, the punched card was the main form of input. It served well through the first, second, and third generations of the Computer Revolution and even into the fourth. Because the punched card is significant from a historical perspective and because it is still often used as a learning tool, we will describe it here. However, it should be noted that cards have been largely phased out, and many organizations do not use them at all.

### *The 80-Column Card*

The standard **punched card** is shown in Figure 5-2. Note that whatever is being described on a card, whether name and address or a variety of cornflakes, can be only 80 characters long, because that is the number of character positions available on a card. Thus, if your name is Alfred North Whitehead and you live at 12345 West Susquehanna Boulevard, Apartment 10, East Rockingham, Richmond County, North Carolina—109 characters and spaces, without zip code— some abbreviations will be required. Or the excess data could be continued on a second card (which means that matching identification must be used on both cards so that the data can be combined later by the processing program).

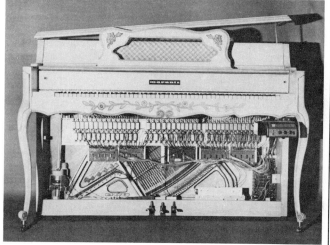

**Figure 5-1   The player piano, old and new.** *Left,* an old-fashioned player piano, with punched roll. *Right,* a 1980s version of a computer player piano, which uses a cassette recorder.

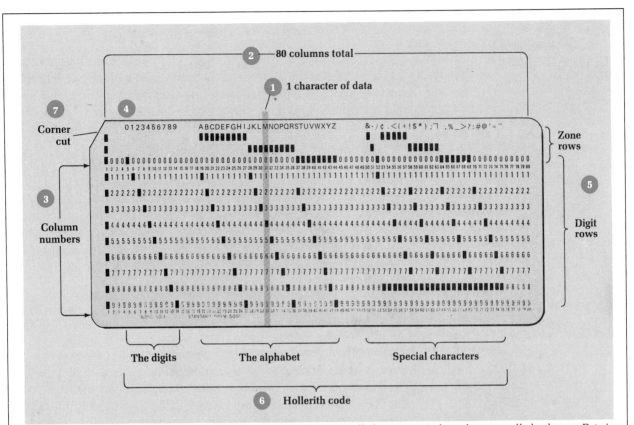

**Figure 5-2    The 80-column punched card.** Horizontal numbers are called rows; vertical numbers are called columns. Data is incorporated on the card as follows: ❶ One character of data—we have highlighted the letter M here—is represented by the punches in one column. ❷ There are 80 columns on the card. ❸ The column numbers are indicated in two places on the card—at the very bottom and near the top, as shown. ❹ As holes are punched in the card, the symbol reproduced is typed across the top of the form as standard numbers, letters, or special characters so that you can tell what was punched. ❺ There are 12 rows, the top three called *zone rows* (12, 11, and 0) and the bottom ten called *digit rows* (0 through 9). Note that 0 is considered both a zone and a digit row. Each letter has a zone punch and a digit punch (for instance, the letter M has an 11 punch for zone and a 4 punch for digit). ❻ Data is represented on the 80-column card using **Hollerith code.** Each digit, letter, or special character is represented by a unique combination of punched holes. The digits 0 through 9 are punched in the corresponding digit rows. Letters A through I use zone punch 12, but digit punches vary from 1 to 9. Letters J through R use zone punch 11 and digit punches 1 through 9; letters S through Z use zone punch 0 and digit punches 2 through 9. Special characters use 1, 2, or 3 punches. ❼ The *corner cut* is to help the person working with the cards make sure they are always facing in the proper direction.

Frequently, organizations use cards that have preprinted areas, indicating what fields are to appear where on the cards.

### Keypunching and Card Reading

Data is recorded on cards by means of a **keypunch,** or **card punch,** by which a keypunch operator punches holes by pressing typewriterlike keys on a keyboard. The mechanics of the keypunch are explained in Figure 5-3 on p. 87.

After a deck of cards is punched, it is taken to a **card reader** (see Figure 5-4 on p. 87). This machine translates the holes in the punched cards into electrical impulses, which in turn are input to the computer for processing.

Card readers are classified according to their different characteristics. A card reader can be a brush type or a photoelectric type. A

# *I*nput

## *Capturing the Stuff of Life*

"Data" can be nearly any-thing—letters, numbers, symbols, shapes, colors, temperatures, sounds, or whatever raw material needs processing. A great deal of ingenuity has gone into developing ways of representing and capturing data—the often unorgan-ized stuff of life—and putting it into machine-processable form. Most input devices, of course, are designed to read num-bers, letters, and special characters. However, there are also some fascinating machines that input data that is drawn or spoken.

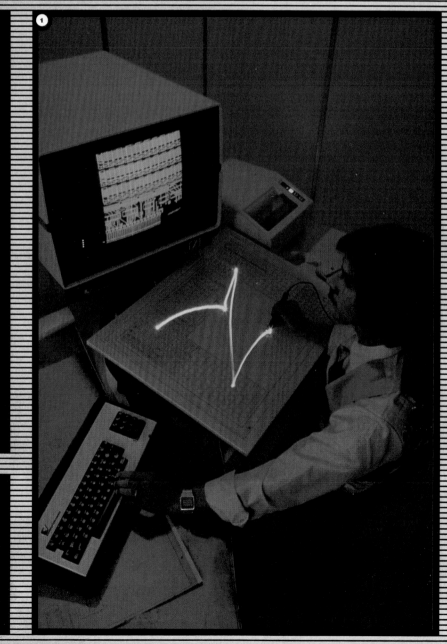

❶ Input magic: A keyboard and graphics tablet with an electronic pen helps this man design a computer chip. This graphics generation system by Paradyne permits several automated design, drafting, and manufacturing activities.

The inner game of input:
**2** Flying fingers: The best known way of inputting data is through a keyboard, as on this Wang word processor. **3** "Help me up": Automatic banking is made possible with automated teller machines. **4** A visually handicapped student operates a computer terminal. **5** Data entry operators: Some offices have departments with a number of operators sitting at workstations and entering data onto disks or tape. **6** Small business: Executives can perform computations with hand-held computers such as this Hewlett-Packard model. **7** Inputting data in factories and warehouses: Data entry devices are now found on shop floors and loading docks. This Prime terminal is being used in a General Electric aircraft engine shop.

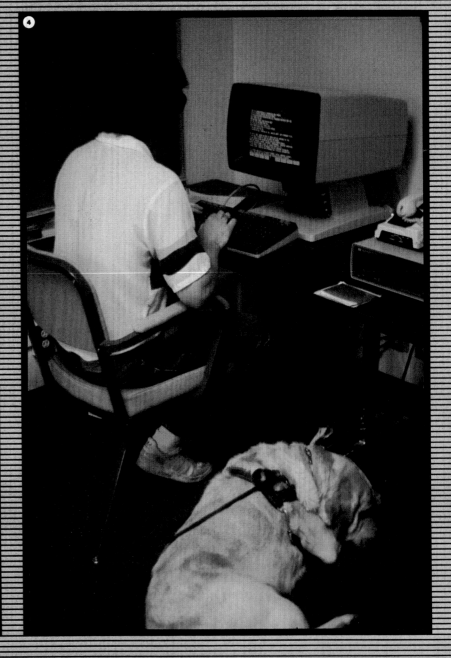

Retail input: **8** Point-of-sale (POS) terminals are used as cash registers—this one is in New York's Metropolitan Museum of Art—but may also input sales data to a central computer. **9 10** A wand reader reads optical characters on a product's retail tag; data is used for billing and reordering. **11** The supermarket bar code scanner reads the Universal Product Code on each product.

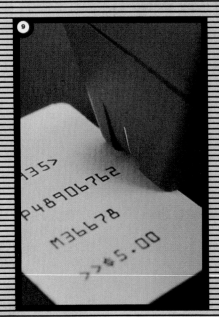

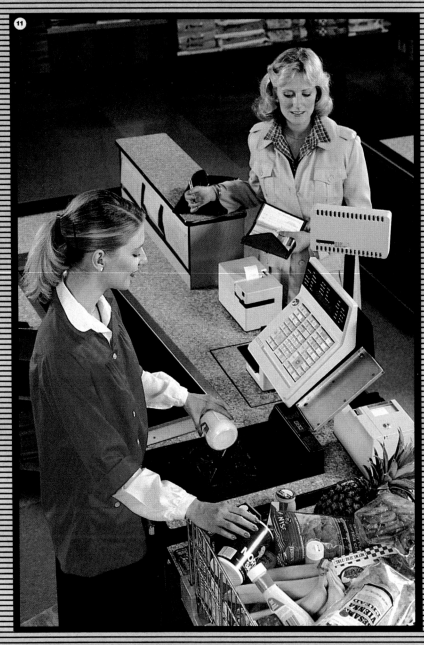

Bar code benefits: **12** At Miami Valley Hospital in Dayton, Ohio, a bar code system keeps track of medical equipment used during the day. **13** **14** At Todd Shipyards, bar codes and scanners monitor whereabouts of tools during shift changes.

Specialized kinds of input devices:
**15** Drawing tablets and electronic
pens are used here for circuit
design, but they can also be
applied to a range of other artistic uses. **16** Light pen: Data is
entered with a light pen, whose
light-sensitive cell closes a photoelectric circuit when placed
against the screen. **17** Pushbutton screen: This Xerox 5700
allows users to give instructions
simply by touching a finger to
areas of the screen. **18** Optical-
mark recognition: Machine-
readable order forms may be
marked with a pencil for recording
cosmetics purchases. **19** Voice
data entry: Users must "train"
the system to recognize their
individual voice. The principal
advantage of voice-input devices
is that they permit users to keep
their hands free for other tasks.
**20 21** Digitizer: This device converts graphic images into digital
data, which can be represented
on the terminal screen or printed
out on a printer.

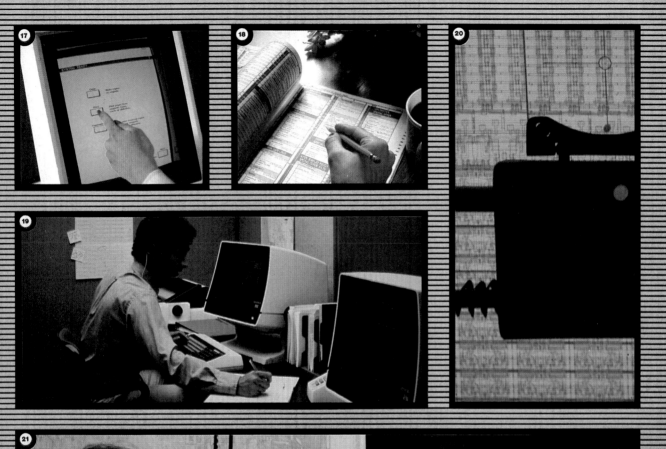

**22 23** Direct input: Exercises performed on this Nautilus physical fitness equipment are input to a computer, which gives a digital readout indicating the number of repetitions and the force required.

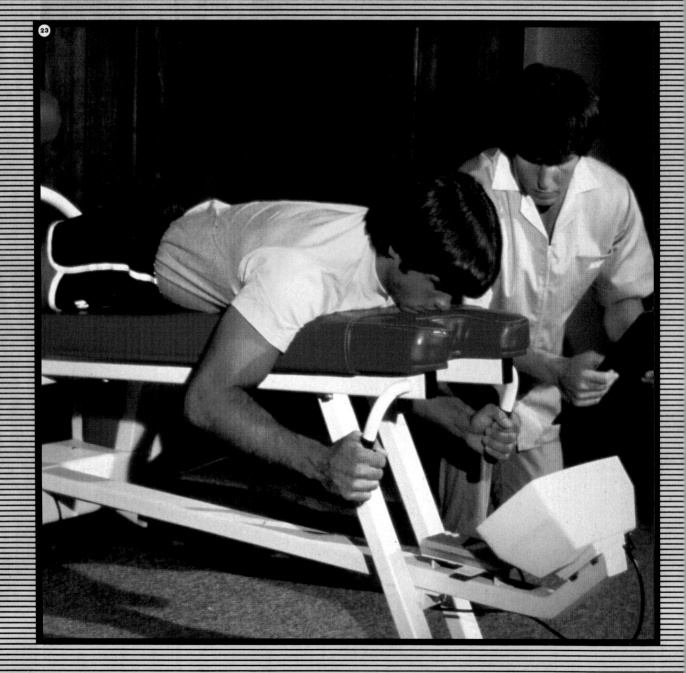

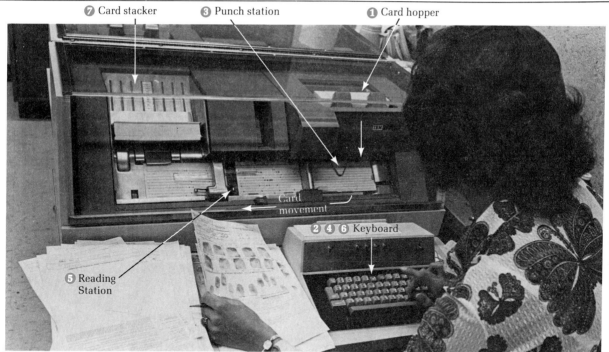

⑦ Card stacker ❸ Punch station ❶ Card hopper

Card movement

❷❹❻ Keyboard

❺ Reading Station

**Figure 5-3   Using the 80-column-card keypunch machine.** After turning on the power switch, ❶ Load card hopper with blank cards. ❷ Press feed key on keyboard, which feeds cards from hopper to punch station ❸. ❹ Punch card, then press REL KEYP key, which moves punched card to read station. ❺ Another card will descend to card punch station. ❻ Typing and releasing cards will cause them to accumulate in card stacker ❼. This photo by the Royal Canadian Mounted Police shows a keypunch operator punching cards from source documents containing fingerprint data.

**Figure 5-4   Card reader.** Keypunched cards are being placed in card reader and printer at Fisher-Price Toys.

## THE BEAUTY OF QWERTY (BUT DVORAK IS BETTER)

The beauty of QWERTY is that it is pretty much universal. QWERTY is the name given to the arrangement of the typical typewriter and computer keyboard, and describes the beginning keys in the top row of letters. Patented in 1867, it became the standard of the typewriter industry even though there are many failings: more keystrokes above the home row than on it, lots of jumping around from row to row, commonly used letters away from the home row—all of which add up to relatively slow speed and more errors.

Designed in the 1930s, the Dvorak keyboard (see drawing) is supposed to be 5 to 25 percent faster than QWERTY and produce only half the number of errors. The world speed record for typing, 186 words per minute, was set on a Dvorak-style computer keyboard. The design is also better for right-handed typists: right-hand keys are struck 57 percent of the time with Dvorak, only 43 percent of the time with QWERTY.

Dvorak keyboards are available from the principal typewriter companies, but only a minuscule number are sold. Indeed, it is estimated that there are only about 5000 Dvorak keyboards in the entire world. However, recently Dvorak was accepted as an ANSI (American National Standards Institute) standard, which could change everything and make Dvorak a far more popular design than it is now.

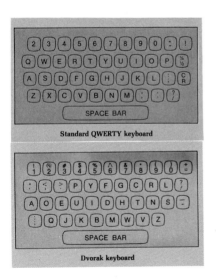

**Standard QWERTY keyboard**

**Dvorak keyboard**

brush reader has metal brushes that pass over the cards; whenever they find a hole, an electrical connection is made. The electronic signal is then sent to the CPU. More common now is the second kind, the **photoelectric reader.** Because the cards are made of heavy paper, light cannot pass through them except through the punched holes. The light sent through these holes causes electronic signals representing data to be transmitted to the CPU.

Card readers are also classified as *serial* or *parallel*. A serial card reader reads cards from one side to the other, a column or character at a time. A parallel card reader starts at the top or bottom of the card and reads all columns in parallel. A parallel card reader is usually faster than a serial card reader.

### *Advantages and Disadvantages of Cards*

Because they are made of sturdy, heavy paper, cards are fairly economical to store and use. However, cards are also heavy and bulky. They take up a good deal of space. It is hard to carry more than a couple of boxes with a couple of thousand cards per box. Cards are also easy to drop or to misplace on a messy desk. Compared to other forms of input, they are also slow to process; typical reading times range from 600 to 900 cards per minute.

Perhaps the biggest disadvantage of cards, however, is that so many intermediate steps are required to use them. The source document must be written carefully, the keypunching done carefully and then verified, the cards gathered and put in a card reader—all these represent a series of bottlenecks between source document and processing. Therefore, as we mentioned, though cards are still used, they are being phased out in favor of more efficient input methods.

## *Key-to-Tape and Key-to-Disk*

A significant improvement over cards, in terms of reducing intermediate steps, has been the development of key-to-tape and key-to-disk input methods.

### *Key-to-Tape*

A **key-to-tape** device (see Figure 5-5) operates much like a keypunch, except that, instead of data being represented by punched holes in cards, it is represented by magnetized spots on magnetic tape. Usually, several people prepare small reels of tape, which are then pooled together on a magnetic tape that can be processed by the computer at a later date.

A variation on the key-to-tape device is the **key-to-cassette** device (Figure 5-6). Data is input directly on a small magnetic cassette tape or cartridge, which, along with other cassettes, is later converted to

**Figure 5-5** Key-to-tape device.

**Figure 5-6  Key-to-cassette device.** Operator is about to insert a data cassette into a portable terminal.

a full-sized magnetic tape for processing by the computer. With cassettes and cartridges, data can be recorded at regional offices, for example, then mailed to a central office for processing.

### Key-to-Disk

A **key-to-disk** device (see Figure 5-7) is similar to a key-to-tape device but has several advantages. Actually, we should think of it as a key-to-disk *system* because, as the figure shows, it consists of a key-to-disk shared processor system. Shared processing means that users have access to the same processor or computer. In this system, several keyboard consoles, or keystations (as many as 64 in some large computer shops), are connected to a common computer. The computer edits—checks the reasonableness of—the data prior to storing it temporarily on a magnetic disk. After the data is keyed in, the data on the disk may be transferred to magnetic tape for processing by the computer system.

Some key-to-disk keyboard consoles are equipped with screens that allow operators to do a sight verification of data before it is entered into the computer. An operator can then correct any errors that were made during the keying process.

A variation on key-to-disk is **key-to-diskette** (Figure 5-8). The diskette, also called **floppy disk,** looks like a 45-rpm record and comes encased in a heavy-paper jacket. Floppy disks are, because of their size, easy to handle, store, and mail. For home computers, they usually come in 5¼-inch-wide size, for word processors, in 8-inch-wide size. A typical 5¼-inch floppy disk holds the equivalent of about 123,000 bytes or characters. To give you an idea of what that means,

**Figure 5-7** **Key-to-disk device.** Several operators at workstations typing on key-to-disk devices.

**Figure 5-8** **Key-to-diskette device.** Operator is inserting floppy disk into key-to-diskette system.

consider that a normal double-spaced typewritten page contains about 2000 bytes. Thus, a floppy disk will hold the equivalent of about 62 manuscript pages. Recently, "microfloppy" disks of approximately 3 inches have been developed for microcomputers. These will be discussed in Chapter 7.

### *Advantages of Key-to-Tape and Key-to-Disk*

Key-to-tape and key-to-disk have many advantages over cards. From the data entry operator's point of view, tape or disk input methods are much quieter. The machines in a keypunch room make an incredible racket, so much so that many keypunch operators feel obliged to wear earplugs. Although sitting in front of a CRT all day may lead to other problems, notably eyestrain, at least there are not the nerve-jangling problems associated with constant noise. Data entry people also like the improved control over the data resulting from the editing capability.

Some of the advantages of tape or disk are as follows:

- Tapes and disks can be reused for different data.

- Initial record lengths need not be limited to a specific number.

- Errors on data intended for tapes and disks can be corrected during the keying process by simply backspacing and rekeying. Moreover, detection of errors is easier because of sight verification.

- Keying is fast because key-to-tape and key-to-disk are electronic, not mechanical, processes.

- Productivity is increased. The keystrokes per hour can range from 5000 up to 18,000, with disk at the higher end.

## *Source Data Automation: Collecting Data at the Source*

By now the challenge to productive data entry must be clear: cut down the number of intermediate steps required between the two words *data* and *processing* so that "data processing" becomes more efficient. This is best accomplished by **source data automation**—the use of special equipment to collect data at the source and send it directly to the computer. Since data about a transaction is collected when and where the transaction takes place, source data automation improves both the speed and accuracy of the input operation.

One characteristic of source data automation is that the data entry equipment needs to be fairly easy to use, reliable, and maintenance-free. The kind of people who will use it are often data entry personnel who are less skilled and require less training time—meter readers, shop clerks, grocery clerks, and the like. A phrase that encompasses these dispersed data entry techniques is **distributed data entry**. Distributed data entry simply means that data entry points are physically removed—distributed—from the central computer operation. It makes more sense to enter data to the system at the point where the data is prepared, rather than to transfer data manually to the computer and enter it there.

For convenience, we shall divide this discussion into three areas related to source data automation: magnetic-ink character recognition, optical recognition, and remote terminals. A magnetic-ink character recognition process can read data that has been coded in magnetic ink. An optical recognition system can read characters or bar codes by exposing the data to a light source. Remote terminals are hardware devices used to collect data at the source.

Let us consider each of these in turn.

### *Magnetic-Ink Character Recognition*

Abbreviated **MICR** (pronounced "miker"), **magnetic-ink character recognition** is a method of machine-reading characters made of magnetized particles. The most common example of magnetic characters is the array of somewhat futuristic-looking numbers on the bottom of your personal check. Figure 5-9 shows what these numbers and attached symbols represent.

The MICR process is, in fact, used mainly by banks for processing checks. Checks are read by a machine called a **MICR reader/sorter** (see Figure 5-10), which sorts the checks into different compartments and sends electronic signals, read from the magnetic ink on the check, to the computer.

Most magnetic-ink characters are preprinted on your check (account numbers and so on). If you compare a check you wrote that has been

*MICR - used primarily by banks for processing checks*

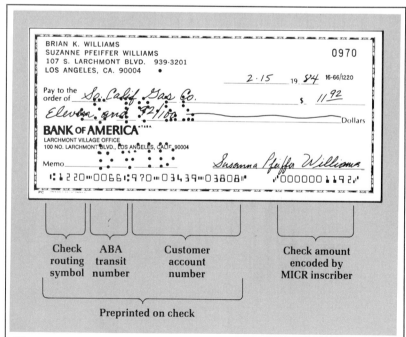

Check routing symbol

ABA transit number

Customer account number

Check amount encoded by MICR inscriber

Preprinted on check

**Figure 5-9  The symbols on your check.** Magnetic-ink numbers and symbols on a check are not always self-evident. Note that the MICR characters in the lower right-hand corner of your cashed check *should* correspond to the amount for which you wrote the check.

**Figure 5-10   MICR reader/sorter.**  This machine processes checks and other documents with MICR-encoded information at speeds up to 1200 documents per minute. The documents are sorted into the different compartments.

**Figure 5-11   Magnetic-character inscriber.**  Checks with numbers newly inscribed on them are being removed on the right.

cashed and cleared by the bank with those that are still unused in your checkbook, you will note that the amount of the cashed check has been reproduced in magnetic characters in the lower right-hand corner. These characters were added by a person at the bank using a **MICR inscriber** (see Figure 5-11). (If you find a discrepancy between the amount you wrote on your check and the amount given on your bank statement, you might wish to look at this lower right-hand number on the check. Maybe someone had trouble reading your handwriting.)

When your check is run through the reader/sorter, it is sorted by account number and put in order so that it can be stored along with all other checks and returned to you with your statement at the end of the month. Checks that are torn or otherwise mutilated and cannot be read by the machine are sent to a separate compartment of the machine. The banking transaction is later recorded by a person who reads the check directly.

### Optical Recognition

**Optical recognition** systems read numbers, letters, special characters, and marks. An electronic scanning device converts the data into electrical signals and sends the signals into the computer for processing. Optical recognition may be categorized according to:

- Optical marks  _O M R_
- Optical characters  _O C R_
- Handwritten characters
- Bar codes  _UPC ( Universal Product Code )_

**Optical-Mark Recognition** Abbreviated **OMR**, optical-mark recognition is sometimes called "mark sensing," because a machine senses marks on a piece of paper (see Figure 5-12). As a student, you may immediately recognize this approach as a technique used to score certain tests. Using a pencil, you make a mark in a specified box or space that corresponds to what you think is the answer as in multiple-choice questions. The test answer sheet is then machine gradable by a device that uses a light beam to recognize the marks and convert them to electrical signals, which are sent to the computer for processing.

**Optical-Character Recognition** Abbreviated **OCR**, optical-character recognition also uses a light source to read special characters and convert them into electrical signals to be sent to the CPU. The characters—letters, numbers, and special symbols—can be read by both humans and machines. They are often found on sales tags in department stores or imprinted on credit card slips in gas stations after the sale has been written up.

_OMR - Pencil marks made in a specified box ; read by a light beam ; signal sent to computer for processing_

_OCR - The light source, usually a "wand" reads the special characters ; sends signals directly to computer for processing_ OCR-h

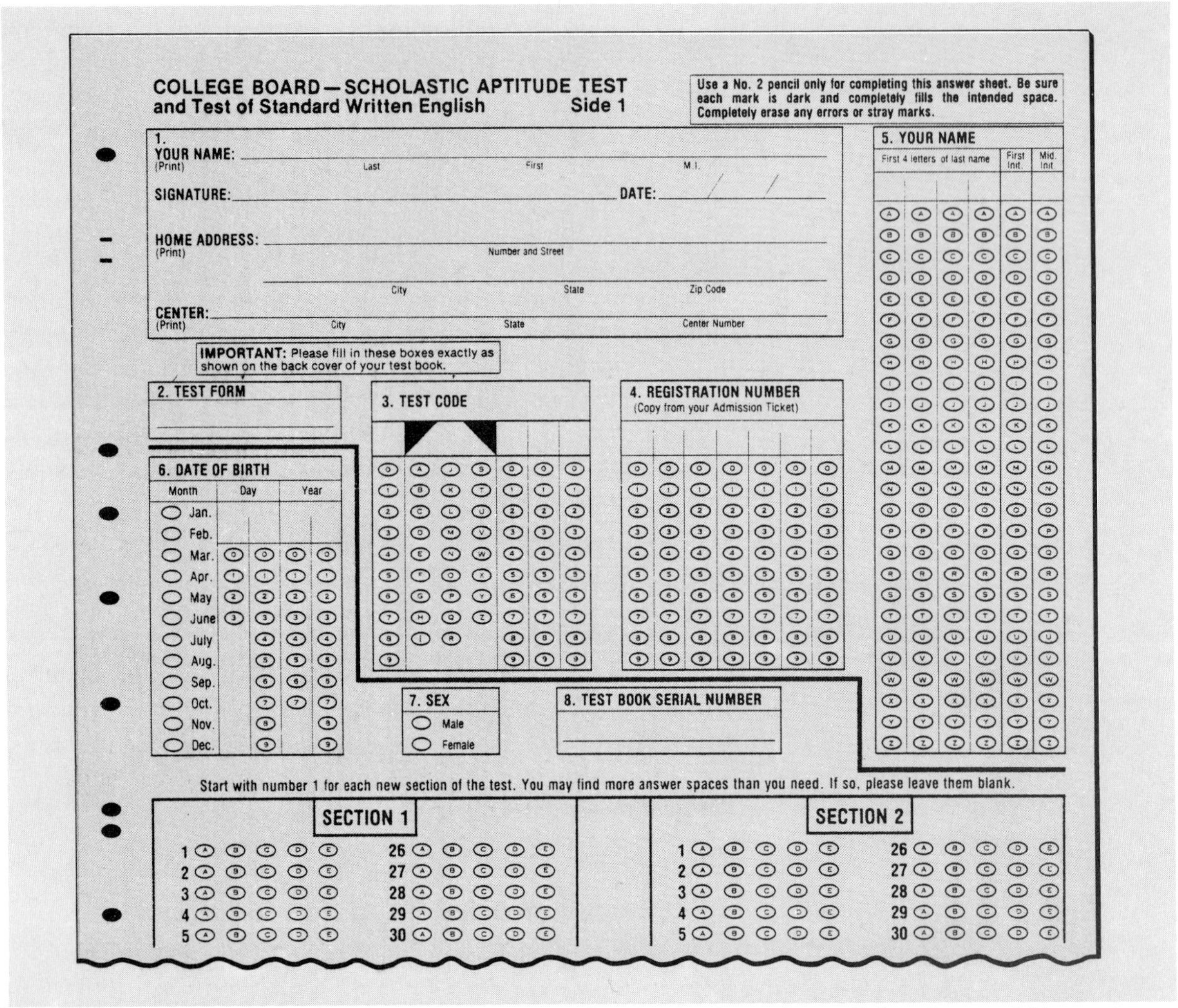
COLLEGE BOARD—SCHOLASTIC APTITUDE TEST
and Test of Standard Written English Side 1

Use a No. 2 pencil only for completing this answer sheet. Be sure each mark is dark and completely fills the intended space. Completely erase any errors or stray marks.

1.
YOUR NAME: (Print) Last First M.I.
SIGNATURE: DATE: / /
HOME ADDRESS: (Print) Number and Street
City State Zip Code
CENTER: (Print) City State Center Number

IMPORTANT: Please fill in these boxes exactly as shown on the back cover of your test book.

2. TEST FORM

3. TEST CODE

4. REGISTRATION NUMBER (Copy from your Admission Ticket)

5. YOUR NAME
First 4 letters of last name | First Init. | Mid. Init.

6. DATE OF BIRTH
Month | Day | Year
Jan. Feb. Mar. Apr. May June July Aug. Sep. Oct. Nov. Dec.

7. SEX
Male
Female

8. TEST BOOK SERIAL NUMBER

Start with number 1 for each new section of the test. You may find more answer spaces than you need. If so, please leave them blank.

SECTION 1

SECTION 2

**Figure 5-12 Example of optical-mark recognition.** Most students are familiar with so-called machine-readable test sheets, such as this one used by the College Board, considered as part of the admissions criteria for many colleges. Pencil marks must be dark and completely fill the intended spaces, and all mistakes must be completely erased to prevent errors in machine scoring.

A standard typeface for optical characters, called **OCR-A,** has been agreed upon by the American National Standards Institute (see Figure 5-13).

An input device that is gaining in popularity is the hand-held **wand reader** (Figure 5-14), seen in large department stores. The wand reader is capable of reading OCR-A optical characters. After data from a retail tag has been read, the computer system can automatically and quickly pull together the information needed for billing purposes. This data can also be used to alert the store regarding merchandise sales so that intelligent decisions can be made about reordering.

Wands are an extremely promising alternative to key input because they eliminate one more intermediate step between "data" and "processing"—that of key entry. We are seeing an increasingly frequent use of wands in libraries, hospitals, and factories, as well as in retail stores.

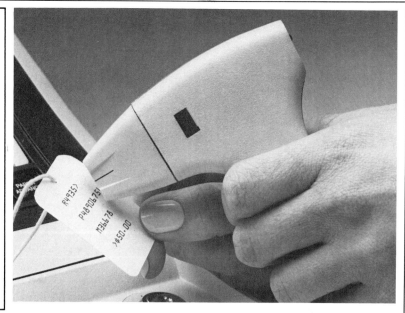

**Figure 5-13    OCR-A typeface.** This is a commonly accepted standard font for optical-character recognition.

**Figure 5-14    Wand reader.** An example of optical-character recognition often used in department stores, the "wand" is a hand-held photoelectric scanning device that can read special OCR characters.

Modern OCR data entry systems often operate as stand-alone units. With their microcomputers, these systems not only read but also edit and format data at its source.

**Handwritten Characters**   Yet another means of reducing the number of intermediate steps between capturing data and processing it is the use of handwritten characters for data entry. There are many instances where it is preferable to write the data and immediately have it usable for processing rather than key it or otherwise treat it for data entry. However, as Figure 5-15 makes clear, not just any kind of handwritten scrawl will do; the rules as to the size, completeness, and legibility of the handwriting are fairly rigid.

*Handwritten characters — used by Postal Service: manually punch zip code of each letter to direct the sorting operation*

| | Good | Bad |
|---|---|---|
| 1.  Make your letters big | TAPLEY | TAPLEY |
| 2.  Use simple shapes | 25370 | 25370 |
| 3.  Use block printing | STAN | STAN |
| 4.  Connect lines | B5T | 13ET |
| 5.  Close loops | 9068 | 9068 |
| 6.  Do not link characters | LOOP | LOOP |

**Figure 5-15    Handwritten characters.**   Legibility is important in making handwritten characters readable by optical recognition.

Handwritten optical-character reading has many uses, but one area in which it could be particularly productive is the postal service. At present, postal workers manually punch the zip code of each letter to direct the sorting operation. The optical character readers being acquired will eliminate this step.

**Bar Codes** Most of us are familiar with the "zebra-striped" Universal Product Code, which appears on most supermarket products. **Bar codes** are vertical marks, or bars, printed on prerecorded tags, that represent data and that can be sensed and read by a wand or by a **bar-code reader,** a fixed photoelectric scanner that reads the code by means of reflected light (see Figure 5-16). When you buy a jar of, say, mayonnaise in a supermarket and take it to the cash register, the checker moves it past the photoelectric scanner, which reads the bar code. The bar code merely identifies the product to the store's computer; it does not list the price, which may vary from month to month and so is stored in a file that can be accessed by the computer. (Obviously it is easier to change the price once in the computer than to have to repeatedly restamp the price on the mayonnaise jars themselves.) The computer automatically tells the cash register what the price is and prints the product and price on a tape for the customer.

When the Universal Product Code was first introduced, there was a great deal of unhappiness among both store employees and consumers. The employees realized that the new system would substantially reduce the effort to price-mark grocery items, thereby threatening their jobs. Consumers were afraid supermarket managers would

*BAR CODES - UPC - (Universal Product Code) used in grocery stores. Photoelectric scanner or wand reads the bar code which identifies the product to the computer; computer sends the price to cash register; prints the name of product, price on tape for customer.*

*other uses:*

*By railroads - keep track of box cars*

*By libraries - charging out/in of books/materials.*

*By Boston Marathon*

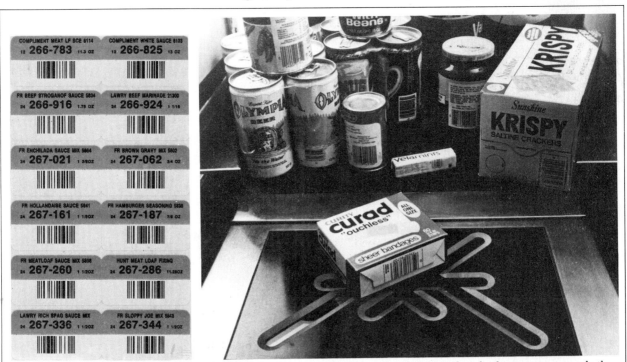

**Figure 5-16  Bar-code scanner.** This photoelectric scanner (*right*), often seen at supermarket checkout counters, reads the "zebra-striped" bar code (*left*), which identifies the product to the store's computer for price information. The price is then automatically rung up on the cash register.

sneak price changes (different from prices displayed on the shelves) into the computer. Indeed, there have been reported instances of grocery chains advertising items on sale but forgetting to reflect these sale prices in the computer; however, these are the exceptions. There are a great many benefits in the UPC system that can help slow the rise of grocery prices:

- Prices determined at the cash register by scanning are more accurate than those rung up by human checkers, who allegedly err in favor of the buyer on 7 percent of all bills over $9, according to research by one cash register company. Of course, such inadvertent generosity by the store is bound to be reflected in higher overall food prices.

- Checkout is faster.

- Checkout training is easier, since the machine does most of the work previously done by people punching keys.

- Cash register tapes are more complete, since they identify not only prices but also their corresponding purchases.

- Labor costs are reduced.

- Inventory control is easier: As goods are moved through the checkout stands, the computer can keep a tally of what is left on the shelves, and signal the store manager when restocking and reordering are necessary.

Although the principal use of bar codes has been in retail business, there are other interesting applications. One of the original uses of bar codes was as identifiers on railroad cars; the scanned data helped the computer system keep track of lost cars. More recently, the codes have been useful in libraries, keeping track of books checked in and out. Bar codes also have been officially embraced by the promoters of the Boston Marathon: as each runner completes the 26-mile course, he or she turns over a bar code tag that helps officials tabulate the final results swiftly. It seems likely that new applications for bar codes will continue to be developed.

### _Remote Terminals_

The hardware devices used to collect data at the source are called **remote terminals,** terminals at a different location from the computer itself. Data collected at these terminals is transmitted to the computer for processing.

There are two kinds of terminals—intelligent and dumb. A **dumb terminal** does not process data; it is merely a means of entering data into a computer and receiving output from it. Some remote terminals, however, are **intelligent terminals;** that is, they perform some processing. Many supermarket point-of-sale terminals are of this nature. They have CPUs in them that can execute programs right at the checkout stand.

We can group remote terminals according to type—for example:

- Point-of-sale terminals  *POS*
- Touch-tone devices
- Data collection devices
- Graphic display devices
- Automated teller machines  *ATM*
- Voice input devices

*[handwritten margin note: POS Terminals  1. Retail stores  2. Grocery chains]*

**Point-of-Sale Terminals** Abbreviated **POS, point-of-sale terminals** (see Figure 5-17) are like cash registers in many ways; in addition, they can be used to relay sales and inventory data to a central computer. Some POS terminals read the supermarket bar codes described previously. Now seen frequently in grocery and department stores, a POS terminal consists of a keyboard and a screen for displaying dollar amounts and a printer that prints out a list of items and prices for the consumer. No doubt we will be seeing many more such terminals in retail stores by the end of the decade.

*[handwritten margin note: Touch-Tone - use telephone lines  1. Small business - check on supplies  2. Verify customers credit cards - card dialer]*

**Touch-Tone Devices** It is possible to walk into a pay phone booth, open your briefcase, attach the telephone receiver to what is known as a **touch–tone device** in the briefcase, and send data directly over the phone wires to a central computer (see Figure 5-18).

*[handwritten margin note: Data collection devices:  1. Warehousing inventory  2. Reading shipping labels  3. Recording job costs]*

**Figure 5-17  Point-of-sale terminal.** The sales clerk is using a wand reader, but data may also be keyed indirectly on the POS terminal. The terminal is used to prepare sales slips and approve check purchases.

**Figure 5-18   Portable touch-tone device.** General Automotive Parts store owner matches parts requests to warehouse supplies and monitors inventory levels using this portable remote terminal, which communicates with a computer over standard telephone lines.

There are several kinds of touch-tone devices, but all of them can use ordinary telephone lines to send data from remote locations to a central computer. One touch-tone device, called a **card dialer** (see Figure 5-19), reads holes punched in plastic cards. It is useful to merchants who want to verify customers' credit cards with a central source.

**Data Collection Devices** Data entry once was done exclusively in a centralized keypunch department by operators copying source documents. Today the source documents themselves can become forms of data entry through the help of remote **data collection devices,** which may be located in the warehouse or factory or wherever the activity that is generating the data is located. This process eliminates intermediate steps and ensures that the data will be more accurate.

Such devices must be sturdy, trouble-free, and easy to use since they are often located in dusty, humid, and hot or cold locations. They are used by people such as warehouse workers, packers, forklift operators, and others whose primary work is not clerical. Examples of remote data collection devices are machines for taking inventory, reading shipping labels, and recording job costs (see Figure 5-20).

**Figure 5-19   Card dialer.** A credit card check is being performed over telephone lines.

**Figure 5-20  Data collection device.** Such devices are designed for use in demanding factory environments for collection of source data such as this card.

Graphic display devices

1 digitizer - converts picture
into digital data according
X-Y coordinates that can be
presented on screen.

2. light pen - has light sensitive
cell at the end. when placed
on screen - closes a photoelectric circuit and terminal
identifies X-Y coordinates.

3 joy stick - knob - allows
fingertip control of figures on
the screen

4. Mouse - directs movements
on screen

**Graphic Display Devices** With this form of remote terminal, we begin to consider some of the exciting and sophisticated new forms of data entry. **Graphic display devices** are often CRTs that display not only letters and numbers but drawings and graphs as well. Many graphic display devices are output only, but some allow people to interact with drawings directly on the CRT screen.

People trained as graphic display designers work by breaking the screen into pairs of X-Y coordinates that represent points, so that any given point on the screen can be identified. There may be as many as 1000 points per square inch. A graphic image—whether a color drawing of a bar chart or an X-ray photo of the human brain—can then be scanned by a device called a **digitizer** (see Figure 5-21), which converts the picture into digital data, according to X-Y coordinate numbers, that can be represented on the screen. This digital data can also be processed on a computer system.

Pictures or data on the screen can be entered or modified using a **light pen** (see Figure 5-22), which has a light-sensitive cell at the end. When the light pen is placed against the screen, it closes a photoelectric circuit and the terminal can identify the X-Y coordinates there.

Another well-known graphic display device, the **joy stick** is that gadget dear to the hearts of—indeed, we might say the *joy* of—video game addicts. It is, of course, a knob that allows fingertip control of figures on a CRT screen (see Figure 5-23).

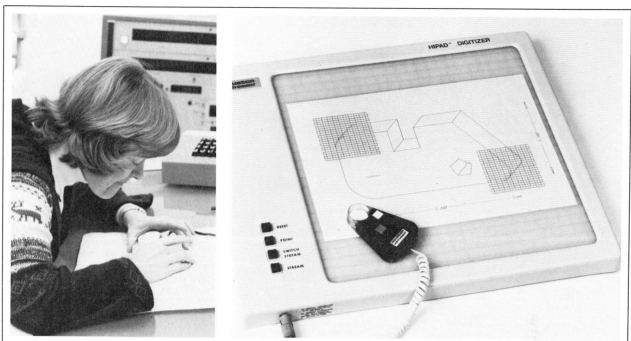

**Figure 5-21  Digitizer.** This device scans pictorial material such as maps and converts it to digital data that can be represented on a CRT screen.

**Figure 5-22  Light pen.** When a pen with a light-sensitive cell at the end is placed against the screen of this graphic display terminal, it closes a photoelectric circuit, enabling the terminal to identify the point on the screen.

**Figure 5-23    A joy stick.**

A **mouse** is a computer input device that indeed actually *looks* a little bit like a mouse (see Figure 5-24). The mouse wheels are rolled on a flat surface, usually a table near your computer terminal, and this rolling movement causes a corresponding movement on the terminal screen. The screen location so moved is called the **cursor.**

If you wanted to draw a circle on the screen, for example, you would roll the mouse on the table, keeping your eye on the screen until the cursor was in the desired place on the screen. You would then signal

**Figure 5-24    Lisa's mouse.** Lisa's integrated operation uses a rolling "mouse" (*lower right*) to move a cursor on the screen. The user can move the cursor to a selected function and usually open a list of options by pressing the button on the mouse.

the computer that this cursor point is to be the center of the circle. You would next roll the mouse away from the center, to a point that you want to be on the circumference of the circle, then send another signal to the computer, which would cause the circle to be drawn.

Mice have become a hot item for personal computers, beginning with that made for Lisa, announced in 1983 by Apple.

**Automated Teller Machines**  With these devices, the term "banker's hours" is bound to disappear, for customers no longer have to worry about appearing between 10:00 and 3:00 to transact banking business. **Automated teller machines (ATMs)** are complicated systems of electronics, pulleys, and wires (see Figure 5-25) that dispense money, usually $20 bills, to customers meeting three criteria: possession of a credit-cardlike ATM card, which is inserted into a slot on the outside of the machine; a secret code number, which is punched in on the machine's key pad; and, of course, enough money in their checking accounts. ATMs also accept deposits and make transfers of funds between accounts. The machines may be located anywhere, but are usually found on the outside walls of banks or in shopping malls, and are tied electronically to the bank's mainframe computer.

**Voice Input Devices**  What could be more direct than speaking to a computer? Speech input is about twice as fast as keyboard input by a skilled typist. **Voice input devices,** also known as speech recognition devices, convert voice input into digital code that can be accepted by the computer (see Figure 5-26). Obviously, there are a great many uses for this process, quite apart from being an aid to status-conscious executives who hate to type. Among current uses are:

- Use in airplane cockpits for such non–flight control jobs as changing radio frequencies

**Figure 5-25   An automated teller machine.**

**Figure 5-26   Voice recognition.** The speaker has "trained" the system to recognize her enunciation of the words in the vocabulary. Voice recognition has been accomplished (in a limited way) of words spoken not only in English but also in Tagalog, Armenian, Czechoslovakian, Japanese, and Swahili, among other languages.

## COMPUTERS THAT LISTEN TO YOU—AND TALK BACK

Listen to Hugh Tucker of Interstate Electronics Corp., talking through a microphone to his computer screen that's empty save for the words, "System relaxed."

Tucker speaks: Ready! Attention!

The computer comes alive as letters zip into place on its screen.

Computer: What is your first and last name?

Tucker: Hugh Tucker.

Computer: Where were you born?

Tucker: In a hospital.

Computer: How old are you?

Tucker: Old enough.

Computer: I don't like the sound of you. Who do you think you're kidding? You're not Hugh Tucker. I quit! (The screen goes blank.)

Tucker had "trained" his computer to distinguish his own natural voice from all others, and in this dialogue he was speaking with only the slightest distortion. If his nuances had been natural, the computer would have been ready to obey his slightest command. He alters his voice to repeat the sequence.

Now, without touching a finger to the keyboard, Tucker can talk pleasantly to the computer, asking it to display graphically his company's sales figures for widgets, to list the defects his inspectors may have detected along the assembly line and announced to the computer through their own microphones or to tabulate the day's inventory of gizmos in the company warehouse.

Tucker was using what the gurus of computerland call a Voice Data Entry System. . . .

—David Perlman,
San Francisco Chronicle,
September 27, 1982

- Phone-in orders from field sales representatives
- Sorting of packages
- Factory inspections of items coming along an assembly line
- Action commands from physically disabled users

In each of these cases, the voice recognition system "learns" the voice of the user, who speaks isolated words repeatedly. The voiced words the system "knows" are then recognizable in the future. The package sorter, for instance, could speak digits representing zip codes. The factory inspector could voice the simple words "Good" or "Bad," or "Yes" or "No." In a recent experiment, a physically disabled man instructed a computer-controlled robot to move a cup toward him by issuing voice commands: "Up," "Down," "Right," and "Left." Today voice input is even available on some personal computers. Video games that anyone can talk to will be here soon, accepting verbal commands like "Bombs away!", "Dive! Dive! Dive!", and other important instructions.

As we will see in the next chapter, however, computers are frequently like people in the sense that they find it easier to talk than to listen. Voice recognition is a lot more difficult than voice synthesis—the process of enabling machines to talk to people.

What are the problems in voice recognition? First of all, speech communication is a very subtle process. Its fundamental bases are not all that well understood. (The workings of the inner ear and the auditory nerve, for example, are somewhat of a mystery.) Thus, there is the problem of what elements in speech to pick out for the computer to recognize. Second, there is the problem of distinguishing voice from background noise and other interfering sounds. Third, most speech recognition systems must be separately trained for each individual talker; they can recognize only isolated words, and they have a relatively small vocabulary.

Even so, research continues on this sophisticated form of data entry. Scientists and engineers, for instance, are working toward the goal of automatic transcription of spoken English into typed text. On the far horizon are some even more fascinating data entry technologies. The ultimate, for instance, may be use of laser beams to scan a person's eyeball so that the computer can tell what the person is looking at and translate that into a form of data entry.

## Onward

It may begin to be clear by now that many means of input are also means of output. Indeed, some of these forms—such as voice and graphics—are more impressive in their output than in their input, as we shall see in the next chapter.

## Summary and Key Terms

- **GIGO** stands for garbage in, garbage out. It means the quality of information a computer produces is no better than the quality of the data given it in the first place.

- Common forms of input include punched cards, magnetic tape, magnetic disk, magnetic-ink character recognition, optical-mark recognition, optical-character recognition, optical recognition of handwritten characters and bar codes, touch-tone telephones, data collection devices, light pens, and voice input.

- The 80-column **punched card** is organized into three zone rows and ten digit rows. Data is recorded on a card by means of a **keypunch.** A deck of cards is read by a **card reader,** which translates the data holes into electrical impulses, which are input to the computer for processing.

- Card readers may be classified as **brush readers** or **photoelectric readers.** They may also be classed as serial (reading a column at a time) or parallel (reading all columns in parallel).

- The advantage of cards is that they are sturdy and easy to handle. The disadvantages are that they are heavy, bulky, slow to process, and require many intermediate steps to use.

- **Key-to-tape** devices record data as magnetized spots on magnetic tape. **Key-to-cassette** devices record data on a cassette tape or cartridge. **Key-to-disk** devices are usually combined into a system, with several keystations connected to a common minicomputer. This permits data to be edited prior to its being stored on a magnetic disk. A variation is **key-to-diskette,** in which data is recorded on a **floppy disk.** Key-to-tape and key-to-disk have several advantages: they are quiet, they can be reused for different data, record lengths need not be limited, keying errors can be corrected during the keying process, keying is fast, and productivity is increased.

- **Source data automation** uses special equipment that collects data at the source and sends the input directly to the computer. Data entry equipment must be easy to use, reliable, and maintenance-free. **Distributed data entry** means the data entry points are physically removed from the central computer operation.

- **Magnetic-ink character recognition (MICR)** readers read characters made of magnetized particles, such as the preprinted characters on a bank check. Checks are read by **MICR reader/sorters.** Characters are put on documents with **MICR inscribers.**

- **Optical recognition** systems' electronic scanners read data and convert it to electrical signals, which are sent to the computer. Optical recognition may be categorized according to: optical marks, optical characters, handwritten characters, and bar codes.

- **Optical-mark recognition (OMR)** senses marks on paper, such as machine-readable test forms. **Optical-character recognition (OCR)** uses a light source—sometimes a **wand reader**—to read special characters, such as the standard typeface called **OCR-A.** Handwritten characters may be read, using optical recognition, provided the writer follows certain careful rules. **Bar codes,** such as those found on products adhering to the Universal Product Code, are read by **bar-code readers,** and allow stores to reduce errors, speed checkout, reduce labor costs, and control inventory more easily.

- **Remote terminals,** devices removed from the computer itself and used to collect data at the source, are of two types—dumb and intelligent. **Dumb terminals** do not process data; **intelligent terminals** can do some processing.

- Remote terminals can be grouped according to several types, including point-of-sale terminals, touch-tone devices, data collection devices, graphic display devices, automated teller machines, and voice input devices.

- **Point-of-sale (POS) terminals** are like cash registers; in addition, they can relay data to a central computer. Portable **touch-tone devices,** which can be carried in briefcases, can be used to send data directly over telephone wires from remote locations to a central computer. Remote **data collection devices,** such as those located in warehouses and factories, use source documents as forms of data entry. **Graphic display devices** can display graphs and drawings as well as letters and numbers; pictures or data can be entered on the screen using a **light pen.** A picture or photograph can be scanned by a **digitizer,** which converts it into digital data. **Joy sticks** are knobs that allow fingertip control of figures on CRT screens. A **mouse** is a device that is rolled on a flat surface; its movement causes a screen location called the **cursor** to move on a CRT screen. **Automated teller machines (ATMs)** are remote terminals, usually on bank outside walls, that permit withdrawals, deposits, and transfers of funds. **Voice input devices** convert voice input to digital code that can be accepted by the computer.

## Review

1. List several forms of input.
2. Explain the principle behind punched cards and their advantages and disadvantages.
3. Explain how key-to-tape and key-to-disk devices work.
4. What is source data automation?
5. Describe how magnetic-ink character recognition works.
6. Name the types of optical-recognition systems and describe how they work.
7. List different types of remote terminals and describe how each one works.

## IN THIS CHAPTER

Output is the human connection with computing. One popular form is paper, or hard copy, such as printed reports produced by printers, both impact and nonimpact. CRT terminals are also popular. They are used to provide displays of both alphanumeric and graphic material. Special output devices include computer output microfilm, plotters, robots, and voice output.

# ch6

# output

## the human uses of computing

Suppose you were writing this book. Not only writing it, but simultaneously setting the type for it, using a computer terminal. You might design your own typeface, varying the length, shape, and weight of loops, crossbars, and so on, so that no two letters in this chapter were identical. It would be an individualized typeface to suit your whim and mood.

Although it is doubtful that publishers and their art directors would permit such typographic anarchy to reign, computer programs have been devised that demonstrate it is technically possible for writers to design their own typefaces. And although type design is a field requiring years of study, this new technique is a tool that allows type designers many more opportunities to experiment than they have had before and allows them to shape results much more quickly.

*ch6*

## Output: The People Connection

The preceding example shows what computing is supposed to be all about: output that improves productivity. Output is what all data processing efforts so far have been directed toward and what makes

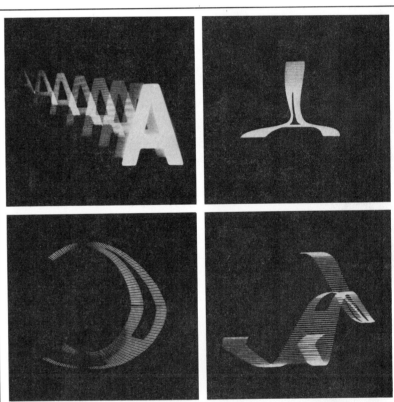

**Give me an A!**   This series of type imaging experiments by Samuel N. Antupit shows how the letter *A* can be modified typographically using computer and electronic design. As one writer stated, such equipment is "literally an electronic idea machine. It multiplies options for the designer's taste and judgment, and its output is useful in all graphic media."

computing useful to human beings. With output, data becomes information.

Output can take many forms, such as printing on paper, color graphics, microfilm, electronic signals, and sounds. Even within the same organization there can be different kinds of output. You can see this next time you go to a travel agency that uses a computer system. If you ask for airline flights to Toronto, Calgary, and Vancouver, say, the travel agent will probably make a few queries to the system and receive output on a CRT screen indicating space availability on the various flights. After the reservations have been confirmed, the agent can ask for printed output of three kinds: the tickets, the traveler's itinerary, and the invoice. The agency may also keep historical records, which may be output on microfilm, of your and other customers' travel plans. In addition, the agency may periodically receive printed reports, such as monthly summaries of sales figures, for management purposes.

As you might already suspect, perhaps the principal medium used for computer output is _paper._ While the intent of data processing is to increase productivity, its misuse has contributed to a scourge of the modern world—paper pollution. The computer may enhance the productivity of direct-mail advertisers, but it may inhibit your own productivity, if, as an executive, you find your in-basket clogged with computer junk–mailings. (Of course, not all of it is the computer's fault; the rise in popularity of the photocopying machine may be even more to blame.)

Still, our complex society depends on paper, or at least on the information that usually comes to us on paper, and one of the most important forms of computer-produced paper consists of reports.

### Printed Reports

Reports can be classified several ways. **Periodic reports** are planned reports, usually related to scheduled or recurring events. Typical periodic reports are payroll register, monthly sales report, and accounts receivable. **Demand reports,** as the name indicates, are prepared on a nonscheduled, as-needed basis. Demand reports are a powerful management tool. For example, the manager of a steamship company interested in ships available to transport an upcoming large cargo might have a file of up-to-date information on a fleet of ships. The manager then could "demand" a report on their current locations and arrival dates.

Business and nonbusiness organizations produce two kinds of printed reports: external and internal.

**External reports** are reports produced by an organization for people outside it, such as customers and shareholders. Just as a company's waiting room tends to be nicer than its offices, so external reports tend to be more attractive in appearance than those intended for internal use.

**Internal reports** are usually not as attractive in appearance and are concerned with inventory, quality control, payroll, personnel, and

**TAKE ME OFF YOUR MAILING LIST!**

Tired of getting junk mail? Of course, you can always write directly to all those institutions you do business with and ask not to be included on any mailing lists they lease or lend.

Or you can write to the Direct Mail-Marketing Association (6 East 43rd Street, New York, NY 10017) and request that a so-called "mail preference form" be sent to you free of charge. When you return the form, it will be circulated to 180 mail-order houses and other institutions. After a few months your unsolicited mail should diminish. The same form can be used to get more mail-order advertising, if you check off any of the 24 categories of merchandise of interest to you.

other matters related to the organization. Even a bank notice to a customer regarding insufficient funds may be nicer looking than an advisory to bank officers about the same thing.

Traditional printed reports are of three kinds (see Figure 6-1):

- **Detail report.** In this report, every record is printed—for instance, every item in an inventory. Generally, detail reports are used by people in an organization who need them to do day-to-day operations. The shipping clerks in the book publisher's warehouse, for

Detail Report

```
      DAILY SALES REGISTER BY TYPE OF SALE              11/30/83   PAGE 1

SHIP-TO ADDRESS            CODE AUTHOR-TITLE          LIST QUANTITY TOTAL
                                                     PRICE         AMOUNT
THE SOUTH MAIN             36990 WILSON ANATOMY       22.95    10   229.50
BOOKSTORE                        & PHYSIOLOGY
209 SOUTH MAIN
CHICAGO ILL 60625

UNIVERSITY BOOKSTORE       50239 LYON TRIGONOMETRY     17.95    30   538.50
OLD STATE COLLEGE
800 W VICTORIA ST
STAMFORD CT 06903

EASTERN ARCATA UNIV        34102 SPENCE GENETICS       17.95    40   718.00
BOOKSTORE
P O BOX 8769
ARCATA CA 95521
```

Exception Report

```
AVAILABILITY DATE LISTING-
TITLES TEMP OUT OF STOCK AND NOT YET PUBLISHED 11/30/83
CODE AUTHOR-DESCRIPTION                               AVAIL

00089 BYRNE ELEM STATISTICS                          MAY 10, 84
00093 BLUESTONE ANTHROPOLOGY                         JAN  5, 84
00156 ALBRIGHT INFECTIOUS DISEASES                   APR 17, 84
```

Summary Report

```
THREE-YEAR SALES TITLE REPORT AS OF 11/30/83
MATHEMATICS-AUTHOR & TITLE

50239 LYON TRIGONOMETRY
1982 QTY 1981 QTY 1980 QTY 1979 QTY
    1581     1623     8587     1891

50240 SMITH LINEAR MATH
1982 QTY 1981 QTY 1980 QTY 1979 QTY
    2503     5250     7919     2210

50241 ANDREWS COLLEGE MATH
1982 QTY 1981 QTY 1980 QTY 1979 QTY
    2001     4892     5993     2320
```

**Figure 6-1  Three kinds of printed reports.** The detail, exception, and summary reports shown here are examples of the kinds of reports a book publisher might use to keep track of books shipped to bookstores, number of copies sold, and titles not yet published or temporarily out of stock.

example, need to know how many books of a particular title are supposed to be shipped to a particular bookstore.

- **Exception report.** This report calls attention to unusual situations and is usually intended for management. For example, an exception report might alert the publisher as to what books are out of stock.

- **Summary report.** This report, as its name suggests, summarizes numerous records. Generally, the higher up the manager is in the organization, the less detailed the reports need to be. The report the publisher gets about a book, for instance, will be more general than the report the marketing manager or the warehouse manager will get.

### Paper

The output you produce may be listed on a variety of different kinds of paper—cheap newsprint, simple lined stock tabulating (called **stock tab**) paper, shaded-band paper (called **green-bar paper**), or even fancy preprinted forms with institutional logo and address.

Paper may come in letter-sized shape, as in xerographic printing. More likely it will come from a roll or be one continuous folded form (see Figure 6-2). Continuous folded paper comes with sprocket holes along the sides, which help feed the paper rapidly through the printer without slippage.

**Figure 6-2    Continuous forms printer.** Printout paper is on continuous form Z-fold.

A computer operator will put a box of continuous paper on the floor, feed the paper through the printer, and allow the printer output to accumulate, folded, in another box. The separation of continuous paper is called **bursting.**

An advantage of impact printing is that if multiple copies are required, carbon copies may be made. The process of removing the carbon paper from between the layered copies is called **decollating.** A special paper called **NCR paper** (NCR stands for "no-carbon-required"—not, as many people think, National Cash Register) allows several copies to be made without the need for carbon paper. NCR paper is more convenient and more expensive than carbon-lined paper.

As we shall discuss, output can come from different kinds of equipment—terminals, printers, and plotters, for instance. Not all output devices can be categorized so neatly, however. There is considerable overlap. Certain types of terminals, for instance, provide printed output. Many graphics terminals are connected to small printers; you can press a button on the terminal keyboard to get a printed copy of the image on the screen. Some terminals even have voice output. For convenience, however, we shall discuss output devices in three groups: printers, terminals, and special output devices.

## Printers: The Image-Makers

A printer, as we have seen, is a device that produces printed paper output—known in the trade as **hard copy,** because it is tangible and permanent (unlike "soft copy," which is displayed on a screen).

There are two principal ways of classifying printers:

- According to the means of making an image on the paper.

- According to the amount of information they print at a time.

There are two ways of making an image on paper—impact and nonimpact. An **impact printer** is much like a typewriter. It forms characters by physically striking paper, ribbon, and characters together. A **nonimpact printer** forms characters by using heat, lasers, photography, or ink spray. It may use a special kind of electrostatic or sensitized paper. In a nonimpact printer, physical contact is never actually made between the printer and the paper.

Let us take a closer look at these differences.

### Impact Printers

Impact printers are of two kinds: character and line.

**Character printers** (also called "character-at-a-time" or "serial" printers) are like typewriters. They print character by character across the page from one margin to the other. A typical character printer is the **daisy wheel** (see Figure 6-3). Noted for high-quality printing,

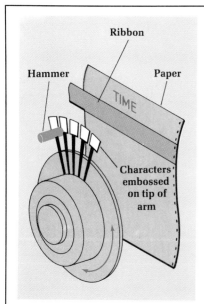 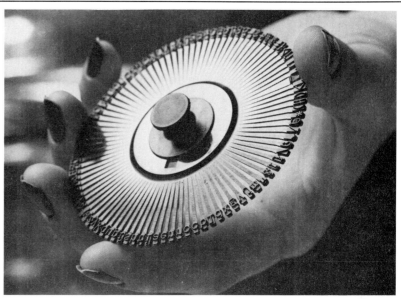

**Figure 6-3    Daisy wheel printer.** The daisy wheel consists of a rotating wheel with a set of spokes, each spoke containing a raised character.

this kind of printer is useful for word processing and professional correspondence. The daisy wheel consists of a removable wheel with a set of spokes, each containing a raised character. The entire wheel rotates to align the appropriate character, which is then struck by a hammer. A different type of font (printing type) may be used by changing the wheel. Recent daisy wheel printers print up to 70 characters per second.

**Line printers** (or "line-at-a-time" printers) assemble all characters on a line at one time and print them out practically simultaneously.

In both cases, there is some sort of physical contact with the paper, which is why the process is called impact printing. The impact may be by a print hammer and character striking a ribbon against the paper or by a print hammer hitting paper and ribbon against a character.

Printing can form either a solid character or a dot-matrix character. **Dot-matrix printers** construct a character by activating a matrix of pins that, following the principle of lights on a basketball scoreboard, produce the shape of the character. Figure 6-4 shows how this works. The matrix principle also works in nonimpact printing, as we shall see. It should be noted that the daisy wheel printers are being challenged by new dot-matrix printers in which the dots are placed more closely together than previously, which eliminates the "polkadotted" look of older dot-matrix printers. At 150 characters per second, the new printers are more than twice as fast as the daisy wheel printers, but they are about the same price.

There are several types of impact line printers:

**Band** The **band printer** (also called a "belt printer") uses a horizontally rotating band that contains characters, as shown in Figure 6-5.

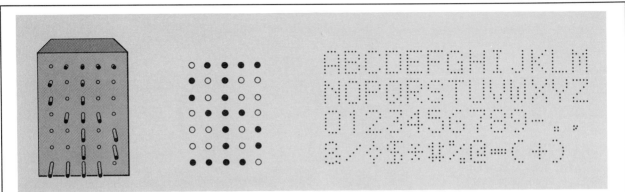

**Figure 6-4    The shape of dot-matrix characters.** The standard dot-matrix character print head (*left*, example of dollar sign) is composed of a rectangle of pins, usually seven high and five wide. Like a bank temperature sign or basketball scoreboard, different combinations of pins are activated, by electronic signals sent by the computer, for each character.

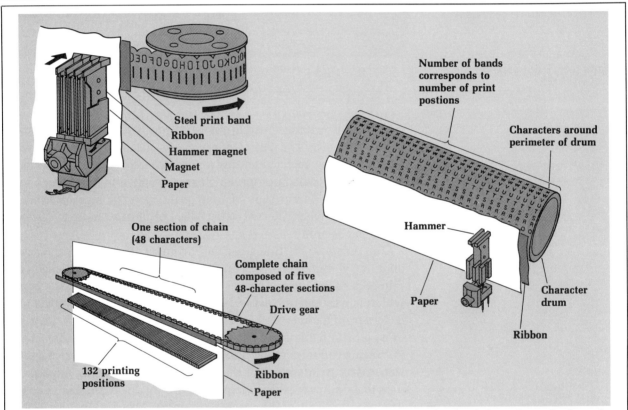

**Figure 6-5    Three kinds of printer mechanisms.** *Top*, band printer mechanism. The band or belt can be easily changed to make different styles of type available. Some band printers can print up to 600 lines per minute. *Right*, drum printer mechanism. Some print up to 3000 lines per minute. *Bottom*, chain printer mechanism. Some of these also print up to 3000 lines per minute.

The characters on the band are struck by hammers through paper and ribbon. An advantage of band printers is that the bands can be changed for different type fonts.

**Drum**   A common kind of line printer, the **drum printer** consists of a cylinder with embossed rows of characters on its surface (see Figure 6-5). Each print position has a complete set of characters (64) around the circumference of the drum. As the drum turns, a hammer strikes paper and ribbon against the drum. Drums do not have interchangeable fonts.

**Chain**  The **chain printer** consists of characters on a chain that rotate past all print positions (see Figure 6-5). Hammers are aligned with each position, and when the appropriate character goes by, each hammer strikes paper and ribbon against it. Chain printers have a variety of type fonts available.

### *Nonimpact Printers*

The wave of the future is the nonimpact printer, although we will no doubt see a lot of impact printers around throughout this decade. The reasons for the growing popularity of the nonimpact printer are simple: It is faster and quieter.

Speed derives from the fact that nonimpact printers have fewer moving parts. They have no type elements or hammers physically moving around. As you might guess, the lowering of the noise level results from the absence of the impact—the striking of print hammers against ribbon and paper.

Nonimpact printing has grown enormously in popularity in recent years—up from a $1 billion market in 1980 to an expected $3 billion in 1986. Because such printers they have so many mechanical parts and are so complex, they are very expensive (some high-speed printers cost over $100,000). Although the price is not apt to come down significantly, the printers are still expected to stay in demand—mainly because large organizations need printers that can produce a lot of printed-out material quickly. IBM and Siemens are the major vendors of nonimpact printers.

Nonimpact printers are of several kinds: electrostatic, electrothermal, laser, xerographic, and ink-jet. Let us briefly consider each of these.

**Electrostatic**  Like some impact printers, this printer uses a dot-matrix device. However, instead of using dot-matrix pins to strike the paper, the **electrostatic printer** supplies an electrical charge through the pins, in the desired shape of the character, onto special paper. The paper is then passed through a solution, or toner, containing ink particles with the opposite charge. The ink particles stick to the charged areas on the paper, producing the visible image.

**Electrothermal**  Like electrostatic, **electrothermal printers** use dot-matrix print devices. They produce characters using heat in the pins in the print head and heat-sensitive paper. The process is essentially one of burning characters into the paper.

**Laser**  In **laser printers,** laser beams are reflected off a rotating disk, which contains the range of characters, onto the paper (see Figure

**Figure 6-6** **Laser-electrophotographic printer.** Laser beam image is transmitted to moving belt, to which dry ink is applied. The dry-ink image is then transferred from the belt to the paper and is then fused to the paper. Laser printers can print up to 21,000 lines per minute.

6-6). The laser beam forms an electrostatic image on the paper, which is then processed through a toner. The result is extremely high-quality images.

**Xerographic** The method used by **xerographic printers** resembles those used in photocopying machines such as the Xerox copier. The complicated process involves the electrical transfer of the printed image onto a photoconductive surface, to which ink is then applied. Electrically charged paper passed over the surface will attract the dry ink, forming the printed image. One advantage of this type of printer is that it can print on ordinary letter-sized paper.

**Ink-jet** Also using the dot-matrix principle, the **ink-jet printer** sprays ink from a jet up to ten times the speed of impact printers. The ink, which is charged, passes through an electronic field, which deflects it and produces a dot-matrix character. Ink-jet printers, by using multiple nozzles, can print in several different colors of ink.

### Printers and Their Uses

Printers range from reasonably inexpensive (only a few hundred dollars) to incredibly expensive ($300,000), from slow (10 characters per second for some impact printers) to fast (21,000 lines per minute for a laser printer), from just barely readable characters to sharply delineated characters.

Printers may have maximum line lengths as short as 20 characters or as long as 160. The type fonts and styles available may range from only all capital letters in one kind of typeface to both upper- and

**PRINTER SPEEDS:
LINES PER MINUTE**

Impact printers:

- Band—up to 600

- Drum—up to 3000

- Chain—up to 3000

Nonimpact printers:

- Electrostatic—up to 5000

- Electrothermal—up to 5000

- Laser—up to 21,000

- Xerographic—up to 4000

# *Output*
## *The Products of Computing*

**①** Free-form brilliance: This example of computer-generated graphic art was produced at the Los Alamos Scientific Laboratories in New Mexico.

Computers can be hooked up to operate nearly anything, from vending machines to power plants. This gallery demonstrates some of the output devices most commonly associated with computers. Although, as we have seen, printers and CRT terminals are the most widespread, there are many other intriguing forms of output, from spoken words to robots.

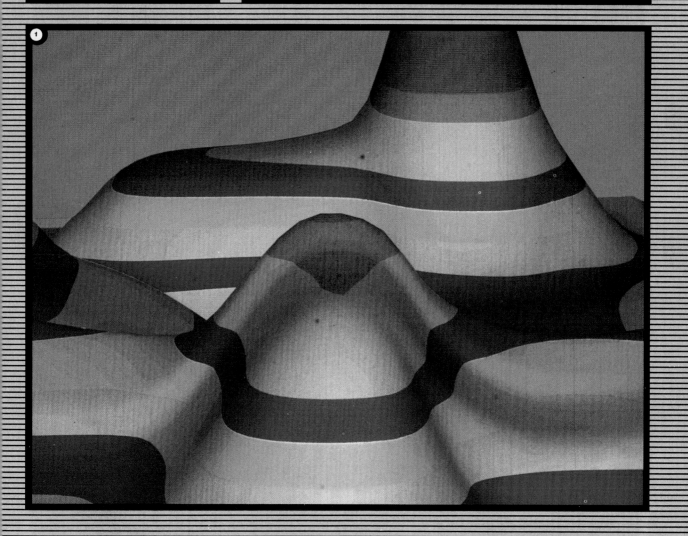

**2 to 6 Printer products:** Printers can be small, hand-held ones or large, free-standing ones. The printouts can be words or numbers printed in a single color or graphic output of several colors.

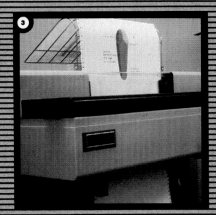

**7** Drum plotter: This Calcomp four-pen plotter operates at a speed of 30 inches per second.
**8** Flatbed plotter: This has a four-pen liquid inking system.
**9** Example of plotter graphics.

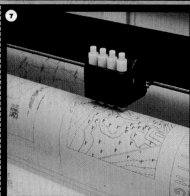

**10** Computer output microfilm: A real space saver, COM allows college transcripts to be stored and later read on a microfiche viewer, as here. **11 12** Robots: Dramatic output devices, robots allow such tasks as sorting and welding.

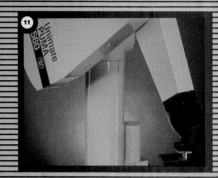

Output images: **13** A U.S. Senator's computerized reply to a constituent's letter. **14** Computer graphics county breakdown of Republican party registration in New Mexico. **15** Graphic image of Washington volcano, Mount St. Helens.

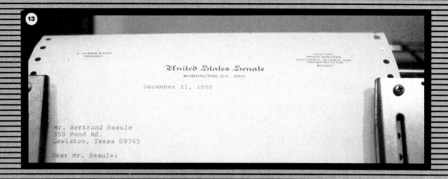

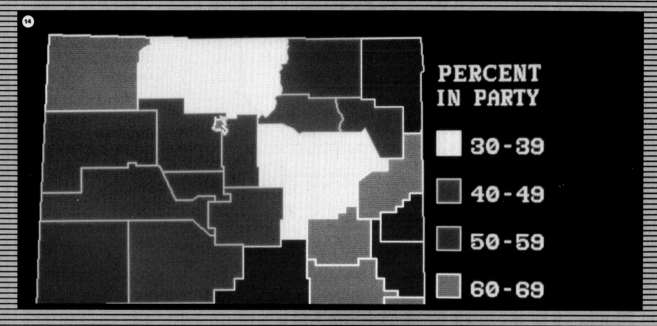

PERCENT IN PARTY

30-39

40-49

50-59

60-69

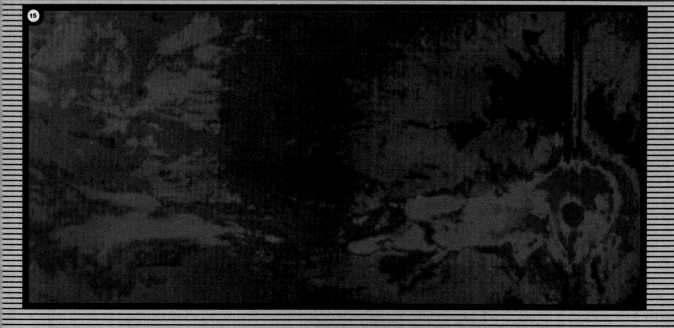

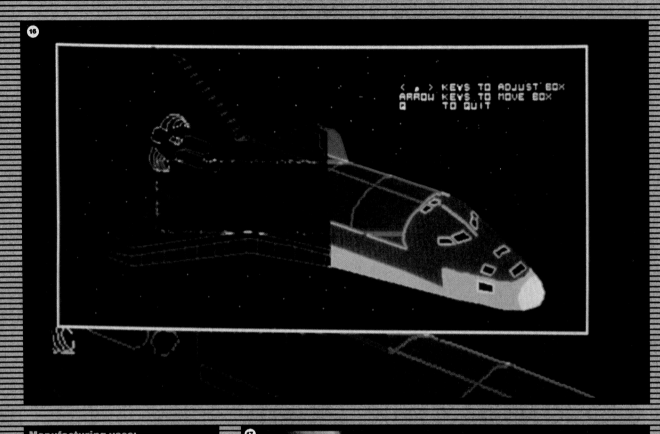

**Manufacturing uses:**
**16 17 18** Computer-aided design and computer-aided manufacture (CAD/CAM) has become important in industry, such as aircraft design.

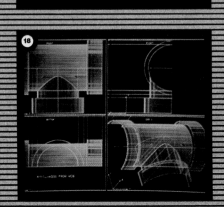

More graphics: ⓳ Military command and control of troop movements. ⓴ Cubic color. ㉑ A chemical molecule in three dimensions.

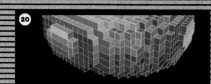

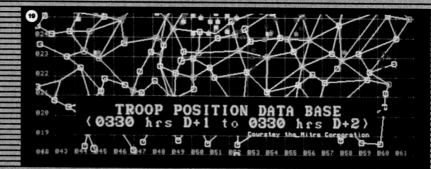

TROOP POSITION DATA BASE
(0330 hrs D+1 to 0330 hrs D+2)
Courtesy the Mitre Corporation

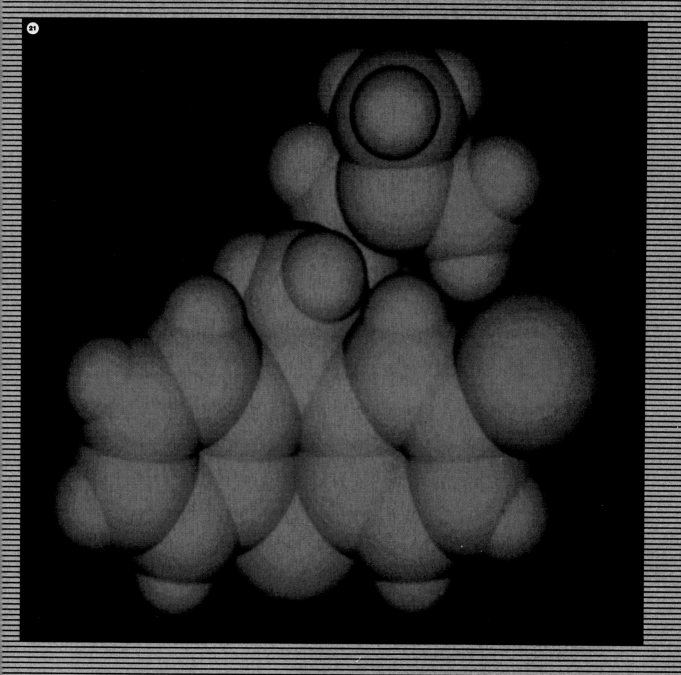

The imagination of computer graphics: 22 23 24 The range of styles of output graphics is shown in these pictures.

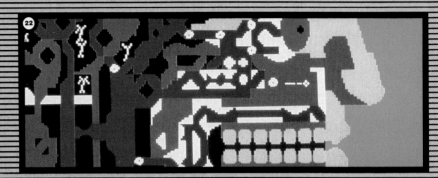

lowercase letters in a variety of type fonts. While some printers use ordinary paper, others (particularly nonimpact printers) require expensive special paper. Impact printers can produce carbon copies. Nonimpact printers cannot, yet nonimpact printers may print so fast that they can make multiple printings of the same page faster than an impact printer can make multiple copies of one page—and do it a lot more quietly.

If you are considering buying a microcomputer, incidentally, you may be surprised to discover that it is as difficult to choose a printer as it is to choose the computer itself. Some people are also startled to find that the printer they want may cost twice as much as the computer. However, Coleco and Atari have made complete home computer systems, including a printer, available for under $600.

Clearly, then, there is a range of printers for a range of uses. Printers are being developed and marketed to suit many different users. For the typical microcomputer, with low-volume output, a relatively slow, inexpensive printer is satisfactory. For a high-volume batch operation, a high-speed, expensive printer is needed.

Until recently, technological developments for printers have been somewhat behind the times. Whereas Silicon Valley engineering genius had succeeded in making central processing units cheaper and cheaper, printers have been comparatively expensive. The pressure has been on printer manufacturers, therefore, to find ways to reduce costs. In the future we may see more nonimpact than impact printers, since nonimpact printers are capable of producing higher quality output at a wider range of speeds—some of them as high as 120 pages a minute.

**I believe in music** ... Stanford University music professor Leland Smith examines music printer.

## Terminals

Printers are more useful in showing the results of batch processing than in providing real-time output. After all, who wants to make an inquiry and then wait the length of time it takes a printer to play back the answer? For real-time transactions, it is best to have a cathode ray tube (CRT) terminal, which can be used as both an input and an output device.

CRT terminals are used for two principal forms of output—alphanumeric and graphic. Let us discuss these.

### Terminals for Alphanumeric Output

**Alphanumeric terminals** display alphanumeric output—letters, numbers, and special characters (such as ?, $, *)—and resemble 9- or 12-inch television screens. Some allow 80 characters per line, with 24 lines visible on the screen at one time. Some can display letters in both upper- and lowercase; as we shall see, this feature is particularly desirable for word processing uses.

**Features** Several features affect the display of the output on the screen—scrolling, paging, and highlighting are among them. In some cases, color is also offered as a feature.

- **Scrolling.** This is the ability to move lines displayed on the screen, up or down, as though you were reading a scroll.

- **Paging.** With this feature, you can display an entire new screen ("page") full of data—a helpful feature when you are searching for a particular piece of information.

- **Highlighting.** This feature calls a portion of the text to the reader's attention. It can consist of underscoring (on the electronic display, but not on any output later printed out), increased intensity in a particular area, blinking letters, or **reverse video,** in which brightness and darkness are reversed. In reverse video, sometimes an entire screen is reversed, sometimes single areas such as words or characters (see Figure 6-7).

**Inquiries and Prompts** How do you communicate with the computer in a real-time system? You make what is called an inquiry. An **inquiry** is a request by a terminal operator for information. The result is usually displayed on the CRT screen very quickly.

Sometimes the computer will request information of *you,* as the user at the terminal. This is known as a **prompt.** Suppose you work in police communications and receive a report that a police officer has sighted a suspicious car with a license plate beginning AXR. You might make an inquiry of the computer and ask it to display a list of

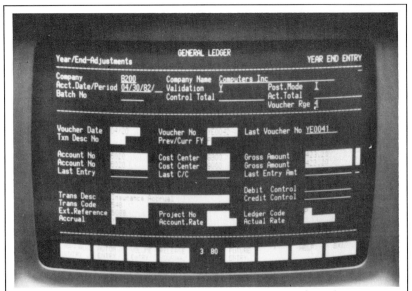

**Figure 6-7   Reverse video.** On this CRT screen, reverse video—the reversal of brightness and darkness—highlights certain information or provides a guide for operators.

all stolen cars in your state with licenses beginning AXR. The computer might do this and then provide a prompt, such as:

```
DO YOU WISH DETAILS FOR A SPECIFIC NUMBER?
YES (Y) OR NO (N)
```

If you typed Y, it might say:

```
TYPE SPECIFIC LICENSE NUMBER.
```

If you did so, you might receive details about the make and the year of the car, its owner, address, and so on.

### Terminals for Graphic Display

As Gallery 5 shows, computer output in the form of graphics has come into its own in a major—and spectacular—way. What reader of this book could possibly be unaware of clocks or watches with **LED (light-emitting diode)** numbers? Or of the form of graphics known as video games? Who has not seen TV commercials or even movies (such as Walt Disney's *Tron*) that use computer-produced animated graphics? Even cars now sport this special form of output; Ford's Concept 100 electronic car offers a 5-inch CRT screen that can produce a road atlas and visually chart a driver's progress. And computer graphics have been used for **computer-aided instruction (CAI)** of various kinds in industry and education for some time. (Every computer graphics area has its unique set of problems; in one CAI program for young children, a fire-breathing dragon acted so much more interestingly when students gave *wrong* answers to exercises that educators had to redesign the software to avoid reinforcing incorrect behavior.)

For more than a decade, computer graphics have also been part and parcel of a field known by the abbreviation **CAD/CAM**—short for **computer-aided design/computer-aided manufacture.** In this area, computers are used to create two- and three-dimensional pictures of everything from hand tools to tractors. Today, however, sales of **graphics terminals** are booming, and the entire graphics marketplace is expected to increase 35 percent a year to $4.6 billion by 1985. The reason: quite simply, graphics make it easier to do business.

It might seem wasteful to buy terminals merely to display in color graphics what could more cheaply be shown to managers as numbers in standard computer printouts. However, colorful graphics, maps, and charts can help managers compare data more easily, spot trends, and make decisions more quickly. Business graphics, in fact, is a merger of financial reports with graphic art. The use of color also has an emotional impact that helps people "get the picture"—literally. Finally, although colored graphs and charts have been used in business for years—usually to make presentations to higher management or outside clients—the computer allows them to be rendered quickly, before information becomes outdated.

*LED - Light emitting diode*

*CAI - computer aided instruction*

*CAD/CAM - computer aided design computer aided manufacture*

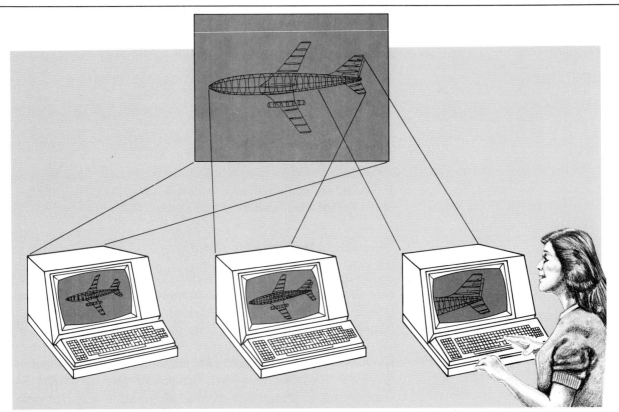

**Figure 6-8 Windowing.** An airplane designer or artist could use this technique to get various "windows" of the same picture: full view, enlarged view, tail section only.

**Figure 6-9 Viewporting.** The CRT screen shows three pictures displayed simultaneously: (1) user action, (2) user instructions, and (3) drawing to be revised.

**Windowing** is a feature that permits the user to view, on the screen, different portions of a picture. You can choose the dimensions and contents of the "window" somewhat like a photographer might choose to view a scene with a zoom or telephoto lens, zeroing in on the object of interest (see Figure 6-8). The **viewporting** feature allows the user to place any selected picture in a chosen location on the screen. This is particularly useful when several pictures or selection lists are needed together; the user can decide which items shall be where on the screen (see Figure 6-9).

Most graphic display terminals can also display alphanumeric data, but the reverse is not true. Few alphanumeric terminals offer color capabilities or are able to display data in graphic form.

### Ergonomics: The Human Factor

**Ergonomics** is defined as the human factors related to computing. That could cover a great many subjects related to both hardware and software, but we have chosen to introduce it here in this chapter because one of the places it is particularly important is in relation to terminals. From an ergonomic standpoint, a terminal should have a high-resolution screen that is easy to read, should have minimal glare, and be built in such a way that it can be tilted, swiveled, and adjusted for height. If such ergonomic concerns are addressed, it should increase job satisfaction and productivity and decrease fatigue and errors. Obviously, managers are very interested in ergonomically designed terminals, and many manufacturers of terminals are careful to use the word "ergonomic" in their ads because it has become such a vogue word in the 1980s.

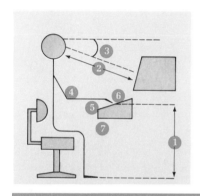

**WORKSTATION DESIGN**

❶ The European recommendation for the height of the home row keys is 28-1/4 to 29-1/2 inches. The U.S. military standard is 29-1/4 to 31 inches. ❷ The viewing distance should be between 17-1/4 and 19-3/4 inches, with a maximum of 27-1/2 inches. ❸ Generally, the center of the screen should be at a position between 10 and 20 degrees below the horizontal plane at the operator's eye height. One researcher recommends that the top of the screen be below eye height, another that the top line of the display be 10-15 degrees below the horizontal, with no portion of the screen at an angle greater than 40 degrees below the horizontal. ❹ One researcher recommends that the angle between the upper and lower arms be between 80 and 120 degrees. ❺ The angle of the wrist should be no greater than 10 degrees. ❻ The keyboard should be at or below elbow height. ❼ Don't forget enough room for your legs.

—Taken from *Potential Health Hazards of Video Display Terminals*

# Special Output Devices: Machines That Draw, Speak, Etc.

As time goes on, the forms of output have become more and more sophisticated, and there is every likelihood of more to come. Among those being widely used are:

- Computer output microfilm, which allows a great deal of printed material to be reduced into an extremely small volume.

- Graphics drawn on paper by devices called plotters.

- Other forms of graphic display, such as photographic.

- Robots of one sort or another, used in industry, medicine, the military, and elsewhere.

- Voice output devices.

Let us describe some of these fascinating devices and their output.

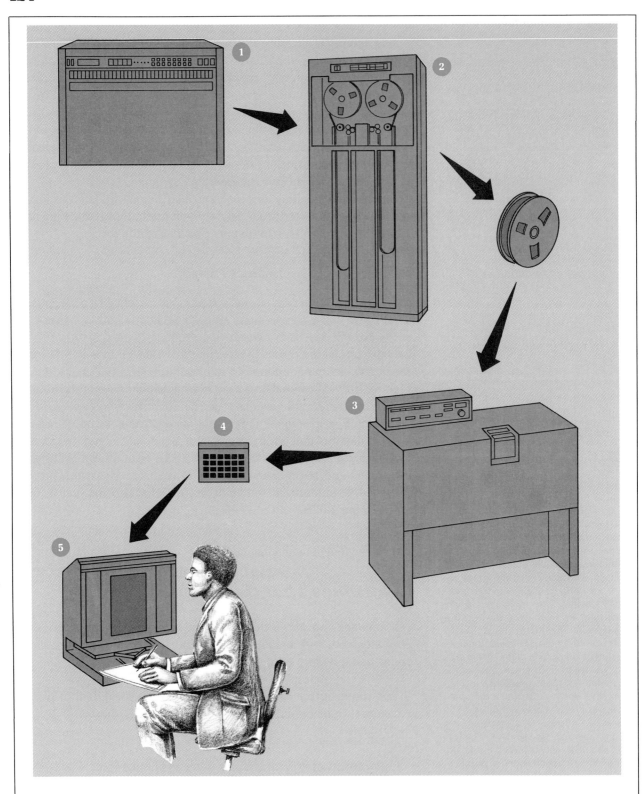

**Figure 6-10  Computer output microfilm off-line and on-line.** In the **off-line** version, data comes directly off ❶ the computer and onto ❷ magnetic tape on a tape drive. The data on the tape is then run through ❸ a microfilm recorder, which converts the data to images stored on the film. Some recorders also develop the film ❹, making it available for immediate viewing. After the film is developed, it can then be displayed ❺ on a viewer or CRT. The **on-line** version works much the same way except that the data goes directly from the computer to the microfilm recorder, rather than via magnetic tape. Some COM recorders offer many fonts, sizes of print, underlining, and retrieval codes for each page.

_COM_

## MICROFICHE DISCS: MANHATTAN PHONE BOOKS ON AN LP RECORD

Electron beams, laser beams, electronics, and optics have been combined in a unique micrographic mass storage and retrieval system. E-beam lithography and laser technology are used to shrink over 6000 documents—the equivalent of three Manhattan telephone directories—onto a paper-thin, clear-plastic, $12 disc that's the size of an LP record. The discs are inserted into a microprocessor-controlled workstation that uses keywords to locate desired images and magnify them back into a readable format.

Intended for parts catalogs, service and technical manuals, abstracts, and reference manuals, the system is expected to fill a niche between conventional micrographic media like fiche and film and other forms of bulk storage such as magnetic disks and tapes, optical discs, and video discs.... The system should be cost-effective enough to archive information for customers such as stock analysts, pharmacists, and patent attorneys—an emerging market termed "database publishing."

—John G. Posa,
*High Technology,*
February 1983

*COM - disadvantages:*
*1. Unable to write on*
*2. Need reader to read*
*3. Incompatible with fast chang-*
*ing data*
*4. Poor file integrity - can be removed*
*+ not detected.*

## Computer Output Microfilm: Small "Fish"

How many warehouses would it take to store all the tax-return forms of everyone in this country? Or all census data? Or all FBI criminal records? In industry, how many rooms in an insurance company or major bank would be required to hold all the customer records?

Computers can produce reams, even miles, of printed output, and although this is the easiest form for people to use, the space required is enormous. To save space, **computer output microfilm** (generally referred to by its abbreviation, **COM**) was developed. Printed output is photographed as very small images on sheets or rolls of film. A microfilm record can be preserved on a roll of film (usually 16, 35, or 105 millimeter) or on 4-by-6-inch sheets of film called **microfiche;** users often call them "fish." Microfilm is produced from magnetic tape (off-line) or directly from the computer (on-line). Both of these ways are shown in Figure 6-10.

COM has many advantages, not the least of which is space savings. At 200 pages per microfiche, this book, for instance, could be stored on three 4-by-6-inch microfiche. A 1-ounce piece of microfiche is equivalent to 10 pounds of computer printout, and the contents of a file drawer full of paper could be contained in only 2 percent of that space if transferred to microfiche (see Figure 6-11).

Space savings also translate into savings in handling, distribution, and, of course, dollars: whereas it costs $6 to print a thousand pages on paper, it costs only 75¢ to print the same amount on microfilm.

COM does have limitations, however. For one thing, you cannot write on it as you can paper. For another, it cannot be read without the assistance of a microfilm reader (like those used in libraries for back issues of newspapers). It is incompatible with fast-changing data systems such as airline reservations. Finally, COM has what is known

**Figure 6-11** **Microfiche.** *Left,* a sheet of microfiche is compared with a catalogue of inventory records. A single sheet of microfiche might well store the equivalent of 200 pages. *Right,* information is displayed on a microfiche viewer.

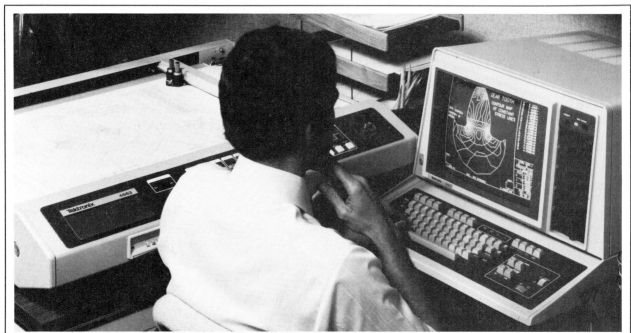

**Figure 6-12    Flatbed plotter.** This digital plotter allows designers of electronic circuit boards, street maps, schematic diagrams, and similar applications to work with fine detail at the scene and then print the results on a flatbed printer as shown here on the left.

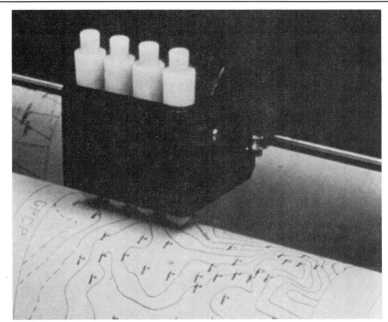

**Figure 6-13    Drum plotter.** Four pens in four different colors—usually black, blue, red, and green—enable the plotter operator to draw multicolor drawings, such as maps.

as poor "file integrity"; that is, it is easy to have one microfiche removed without its loss being detected. Even so, from the standpoint of paper, it is clear that COM helps to save a lot of trees.

### Plotters

**Plotters** draw hard-copy output in the form of maps, bar charts, engineering drawings, and even two- or three-dimensional illustrations. Plotters are of two types: flatbed and drum.

A **flatbed plotter** looks like a drafting table with a mechanical pen suspended over it (see Figure 6-12). The pen is at an angle to the table and can move around, operating under the control of a computer program. The flatbed is commonly used for engineering drawings.

A **drum plotter** is like the flatbed in that it uses the same size paper, except that the paper is rolled on a drum (see Figure 6-13). A pen is poised over the drum. If the pen is placed on the paper while the drum unrolls the paper (to be taken up temporarily on another drum), a straight line will be drawn along its length. On the other hand, if the pen is moved *across* the paper while the paper remains in place, a line will be drawn across the paper. You can visualize the various diagonal lines and curves that may be drawn with combinations of drum and pen movement.

Plotters often come with a set of four pens in four different colors. Most plotters also offer shading features. An example of a plotter output is shown in Figure 6-14. Flatbed plotters can cost up to $150,000, drum plotters up to $250,000.

**Figure 6-14   Mount St. Helens—before and after.** These examples of plotter graphics show the famed Washington volcano before it erupted May 18, 1980 (left) and afterward (right), when the top 400 meters of the mountain had been removed, leaving a crater 750 meters deep.

**Figure 6-15 "Soaring Gulls."** One of the first instances of computer art, this was produced in 1966 by Bell Labs engineers Leon D. Harmon and Kenneth C. Knowlton. They used a TV camera to scan the original image and break each row into points, each of which was assigned a number for brightness—from 0 for white to 15 for black, with 14 intermediate shades of gray. Each number was assigned a symbol; the higher the number the more it filled its allotted space when printed.

**Figure 6-16 The Mona Lisa as "seen" by a computer.** This image, prepared by Ed Manning, shows how microelectronic television-camera eyes spatially quantize a picture and break it up into different shades of brightness.

## Photographic Images and Other Computer Art

As was shown in Gallery 1, the method whereby satellites send pictures back from space to reproduce photographic images has been extended to other forms of graphic art (see Figure 6-15 and Figure 6-16). A great deal of work is now being done with the computer as a tool of art. Even as far back as *Star Wars* (remember the famous "Death Star" trench?), movie settings were being produced using a light pen, a so-called electronic tablet, and a computer.

We have mentioned the use of business graphics. However, computer art can also be used in business and government in many other ways. For example, the ability of electronic circuits to "see" an image has been put to use in Israeli police work. A program called PATREC (for "pattern recognition") mathematically analyzes a police artist's sketch of a criminal suspect and then picks out a group of similar photographs from a large police file.

As Gallery 5 shows, the uses for this kind of output are many.

### Robots

Robots conjure up a picture of intelligent, humanlike figures. Although it is possible to design a machine that walks and talks, most industrial robots are built to be positioned in one place and programmed to do a fairly limited task. **Robotics**—the study of the design, construction, and use of robots—is a serious technological field. Research on robotics has intensified in large universities, and there is even a Robotics Institute. Robots used as mechanical welders and paint sprayers (see Figure 6-17) promise to be an important part of the economy in the years to come; indeed, some observers feel that by 1990 *half* of manufacturing work will be done by robots. Robots have also been developed for consumer and hobbyist markets.

The two key aspects of robots are that they are *reprogrammable* and *multifunctional*. Multifunctional means the machines are built to be able to do more than one task, unlike standard assembly-line components, which are engineered for one function. Reprogrammable means just that: robots can be reprogrammed to carry out new kinds of tasks. Both of these qualities can mean substantial savings for users since robots are not in as much danger of becoming obsolete as are traditional kinds of machinery.

Most robots operate by electronic impulses through a claw, but others use hydraulic pressure for heavy work. Some robots "see," using TV camera vision systems; others operate by touch, measuring size, shape, temperature, hardness, and so on.

The uses for robots become more imaginative all the time. Robots are used not only in car assembly plants, but also to wash windows, mine coal, and transport highly radioactive substances. Future uses include underwater exploration and mining, space exploration and repair of satellites, replacements for human limbs and organs, and assistance to surgeons as aids to dexterity. Robots have even been

### HERO THE ROBOT WON'T WASH WINDOWS BUT IT WILL HAPPILY STROLL AROUND AND CHAT

NEW YORK— . . . Hero I, which looks like a cross between a gray plastic vacuum cleaner and a garbage can is one of the first personal robots to hit the market. It is made by the Heath Co. unit of Zenith Radio Corp., which has just started selling it in kit form. . . .

In a little more than a week of trying, I got Hero to talk, to move more or less where I wanted it to (it ran into the wall a few times on the way down the hall); to detect sound and respond accordingly ("You're a bucket of bolts," I would say; "I heard that!" Hero would retort); to detect motion; and to measure levels of light. Better programmers will be able to combine a lot of these things so that Hero could, for instance, turn on the lights in the morning, turn them off at night or stand guard at the front door and yell if an intruder gets in.

But even ace programmers won't be able to get this robot to do a lot of things that people think robots ought to do. "You'd have a tough time making Hero serve drinks, feed the dog or wash the windows," concedes Douglas M. Bonham, Heath's director of educational products, who is in charge of selling Hero and other devices. "That's not the intent of it. There are a lot of easier ways to wash the dishes than with this robot."

Hero was designed to be a teaching aid for Heath's 1,200-page course on industrial robotics, as its name, an acronym for Heath Educational Robot, suggests. Mr. Bonham says, however, that Hero has captured the imaginations of a lot of people who have seen it or heard about it, and Heath will be happy to sell it to anybody.

"It now appears that there is a personal robotics market just starting up," Mr. Bonham says. "We think it's similar to where home computers were eight years ago. The tinkerers, experimenters and backyard inventors seem interested, and they'll modify and enhance it."

—Philip Revzin,
*The Wall Street Journal*,
January 5, 1983

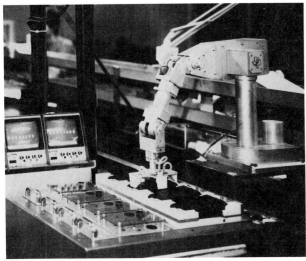

**Figure 6-17   Factory robots.** *Left:* Visually aided robot arms are used on a production line for calculators at Texas Instruments to perform pick-and-place operations. *Right:* Welding robot on Chrysler K-Cars automatically welds together the two sides and underbody panel of each car body.

### NORMI, CALL HOME

MIAMI BEACH, FLA.—Dade County school officials said yesterday they are applying a space age solution to one of the oldest problems in education—truant students.

When a student is absent from school, a [voice output] robot calls home to see if the reason is legitimate. The robot can contact up to 400 parents a day, in Spanish or English.

The robot, called NORMI, called the homes of 200 Miami High School students Monday night as part of a month-long test the Dade County school board is running to see if the device can effectively combat truancy.

Parents at first weren't sure what to make of the robot's calls.

"I called back Tuesday and said, 'Did you call or was somebody pulling a prank?' " said Connie Bird, whose 18-year-old son Kenneth was absent for a legitimate reason—a cold. . . .

On its first day in use, the robot drew more than 40 return calls from parents, about double the response the school gets with more conventional communications, such as writing letters to parents.

—Reported by United Press,
*San Francisco Chronicle,*
March 24, 1983

designed to pluck chickens and shear sheep. Perhaps most fascinating, the day is coming soon when robots will design and build other robots.

### *Voice Output: "Speak . . . to . . . Me"*

"The door is ajar," your car says to you in a male voice. Why male necessarily? Because male voices have a narrower range than do female voices and thus—an interesting, nonsexist reason—require less capacity in the memory of the microprocessor from which the voices originate!

These are not, after all, real, human voices. Rather, they are the product of **voice-output devices** (also called **audio-response units**), which convert data in main storage to prerecorded vocalized sounds understandable to humans. Voice output—which is nowhere near as difficult to produce as voice input, discussed in the last chapter—has become common in such places as airline and bus terminals, banks, and brokerage houses. It is typically used when an inquiry is followed by a short reply (such as a bank balance or flight time). However, it has also found some other creative uses, as in an automatic telephone voice ("Hello, this is a computer speaking . . . ") to remind consumers that they have not paid their bill—an activity that has allowed one utility company to save on hiring people to call the thousands of subscribers who do not pay their bills on time.

The Texas Instruments Speak & Spell educational toy, which helps children learn to spell, has been available for several years, and the company also has a Touch & Tell learning aid to help preschoolers in language development. Electronic translators are also available that can accept plug-in modules for Spanish, French, and German so that one can press buttons and produce spoken words in a foreign

**Figure 6-18** **Talking Language Translator.** Designed for world travelers as an aid to communicating in foreign countries and for language students learning to pronounce a foreign language, this device by Texas Instruments contains about 1000 words, half of which are spoken and displayed (the other half are displayed only). The Language Translator can form 25 common phrases (such as "I need a doctor"), as well as assorted partial phrases. Modules are available in English, French, German, and Spanish.

language (Figure 6-18). Other new devices promise not just a pre-programmed vocabulary of a few hundred words and phrases, but a way of collecting the 45 sound segments called phonemes (pronounced FO-neems) that English-speaking people use. The phonemes could be combined into spoken words as fast as a person could punch the sounds into the keyboard.

In addition, a reading machine has been devised that is of considerable help to the blind. Scanning a page, it recognizes letters and words, applies phonetic rules, and produces spoken sentences, even putting in stress and accents. A CRT terminal has been developed that delivers spelled speech output in audible form as an aid to blind keyboard operators.

## Yet to Come

Almost monthly, new forms of computer output are announced, with an array of benefits for human use. As we shall see in the chapters on personal computers and data communications, they promise to have an enormous impact on our lives. Their effectiveness, however, depends on two components that we have not yet discussed: storage and software. We shall study the first of these in the next chapter.

## Summary and Key Terms

*Review Summary*

- Output can be from CRT terminals, printers, and plotters, to name a few devices, and can take the form of printed paper, color graphics, electronic signals, and sounds.

- The principal form of output is paper, such as printed reports. **Periodic reports** are planned reports, usually related to scheduled or recurring events. **Demand reports** are nonscheduled, as-needed reports. **External reports** are produced by an organization for people outside the organization. **Internal reports** are produced for people within the organization. These reports are of three kinds: (1) **detail reports,** listing all items; (2) **exception reports,** calling attention to unusual situations; and (3) **summary reports,** summarizing numerous records.

- Paper that comes off a printer may be cheap newsprint, stock tabulating (**stock tab**) paper, shaded band (**green-bar**) paper, or preprinted forms. It may be letter-sized, come off a roll, or be one continuous folded form (which is separated by **bursting**). Impact printers may produce multiple copies. **NCR** ("no-carbon-required") **paper** may be used to print the copies. The removal of carbon paper from standard multiple forms after printing is called **decollating.**

- Printers, which produce **hard copy**—printed paper output—can be classified according to the means of making an image on the paper and the amount of information they print at one time.

- There are two ways of making an image on paper—impact and nonimpact. An **impact printer,** like a typewriter, forms characters by physically striking paper, ribbon, and characters together. A **nonimpact printer** forms characters using heat, lasers, photography, or ink spray.

- Impact printers can be either **character printers,** which print character by character across the page, or **line printers,** which assemble all characters on a line together, then print them simultaneously. One type of character printer is the **daisy wheel printer,** which has a removable wheel with a set of spokes, each containing a raised character that is struck by a hammer when in the print position. With both types of printers, printing can be of a solid character, like the type produced by a typewriter, or of a **dot-matrix character,** constructed by activating a matrix of pins.

- Common types of impact line printers are: band, drum, and chain. The **band** (or belt) **printer** uses a horizontally rotating band of characters; bands may be changed for different type fonts. The **drum printer** consists of a cylinder with embossed rows of characters; as the cylinder turns, a hammer strikes paper and ribbon against it. A **chain printer** rotates characters on a chain past all print positions; hammers strike the appropriate character as it goes by.

- Nonimpact printers promise to gain in popularity because they are faster and quieter than impact printers. Nonimpact printers can be electrostatic, electrothermal, laser, xerographic, and ink-jet. **Electrostatic printers** use a dot-matrix device that supplies an electrical charge to the paper, which is then passed through toner to produce the image. **Electrothermal printers** also use dot-matrix devices, but they use heat instead of electrical charges. **Laser printers** reflect laser beams off rotating mirrors containing characters onto the paper, which is given an electrostatic image that is then processed through a toner. **Xerographic printers** use a process resembling that used in Xerox photocopying machines. **Ink-jet printers,** using the dot-matrix principle, spray ink that is charged through an electronic field.

- Printers can range in price from under $400 to over $300,000, in speed from 10 characters per second to 21,000 lines per minute, and from hard copy limited in type styles and characters per line to those with an array of upper- and lowercase characters, type fonts, and lines as long as 160 characters.

- Printers are useful for batch output, but CRT terminals are more useful for real-time output. CRT terminals are used for two principal forms of output—alphanumeric, which displays letters, numbers, and special characters; and graphic, which displays drawings and charts.

- **Alphanumeric terminals** have several features: **scrolling,** which moves lines up and down on the screen; **paging,** which displays an entire screen of data; and **highlighting,** which consists of underscoring, blinking letters, or **reverse video** (brightness and darkness reversed). Alphanumeric terminals allow the operator to make an **inquiry** of the computer, the answer to which is displayed on the screen, or the reverse, for the computer to make a **prompt**—that is, request information from the operator.

- **Graphic terminals** can display both alphanumeric data and graphic data, such as colorful maps, charts, and graphs. **Light-emitting diode (LED)** numbers are an example of graphic display. Computer graphics have been used in **computer-aided instruction (CAI)** and in **computer-aided design/computer-aided manufacture (CAD/CAM)** to create two- and three-dimensional engineering drawings. Some graphic features are **windowing,** which allows the user to view different portions of the picture; and **viewporting,** which allows the user to place any selected picture in a chosen location on the screen.

- **Ergonomics,** defined as the human factors related to computing, is concerned with increasing job satisfaction and productivity by making hardware and software easier to use.

- Special output devices include computer output microfilm, plotters, photographic display, robots, and voice-output devices.

- **Computer output microfilm (COM)** allows printed output to be photographed as very small images on rolls (16, 35, or 105 millimeter) or sheets (called **microfiche**) of film. Microfilm is produced by magnetic tape (off-line) or directly from the computer (on-line). The advantages of COM are space and dollar savings, but it cannot be read without a microfilm reader, cannot be used with fast-changing data systems, and has poor file integrity.

- **Plotters** draw hard-copy output in the form of maps, bar charts, and engineering drawings in two or three dimensions. There are two kinds: **flatbed,** which are like drafting tables, and **drum,** which have rollers.

- Computer art may appear as photographs or as business graphics, among other uses.

- Robots are mechanical devices that can be used in factory, medical, and hazardous environments. The study of the design, construction, and use of robots is called **robotics.**

- **Voice-output devices (audio-response units)** usually take keyboarded input or programmed input and produce spoken output.

_Review_

1. Describe the uses of different kinds of printed reports.

2. Describe the differences between impact and nonimpact printers.

3. What is a character printer? What is a line printer?

4. Describe the types of nonimpact printers.

5. What kinds of paper may be used with printers?

6. What are the principal forms of output from CRT terminals?

7. What are some features of alphanumeric terminals?

**IN
THIS CHAPTER**
Secondary storage allows data
to be stored economically, reliably, and
conveniently outside the computer itself, using
magnetic disk, or mass storage. Ways of
representing data, organizing it, filing it, retrieving
it, and protecting it are described.

# ch7

# storage devices and file processing

## facts on file

Picture, if you can, how many office filing-cabinet drawers would be required to hold the millions of files of, say, criminal records held by the U.S. Justice Department or employee records kept by General Motors. The rooms would have to be enormous (see Figure 7-1). Computer storage—the ability to store many records in extremely compressed form and to have quick access to them—is unquestionably one of the computer's most valuable assets.

## Why Secondary Storage?

Secondary storage, you will recall, is necessary because primary, or main, storage can only be used temporarily: Once your program has been run, you must yield main storage to someone else. However, you may wish to store the data you have used or the information you have derived from processing, and that is why secondary storage is needed. (As we stated, secondary storage is also called auxiliary storage.)

The benefits of secondary storage are:

- **Economy.** It is less expensive to store data on magnetic tape or disk, the principal means, or media, of secondary storage, than in filing

**Figure 7-1    Millions of file drawers. . . .**

cabinets. This is primarily because of the cost savings in storage space and the increased accuracy in filing and retrieving data.

- **Reliability.** Data in secondary storage is basically safe, since (1) the medium is physically reliable and (2) the data is stored in such a way that it is difficult for unauthorized people to tamper with it.

- **Convenience.** Authorized people can locate and access the data quickly with computer help.

The two primary media for storing data are, as mentioned, magnetic tape and magnetic disk. Let us consider each of these and then consider how data is organized and accessed.

## Magnetic Tape Storage

**Magnetic tape** looks like the tape used in home tape recorders—plastic Mylar tape, usually one-half inch wide and usually wound on a 10½-inch-diameter reel. The tape has an iron oxide coating that can be magnetized. Data is stored as extremely small magnetized spots, which can then be read by a tape unit into the computer's main storage. Some tapes ("minitapes") are only 600 feet in length, but the most common length is 2400 feet.

The amount of data on the tape is expressed in terms of **density,** which is the number of **characters per inch (cpi)** or **bytes per inch (bpi)** that can be stored on a tape. (A byte is essentially the same as a character.) Although some tapes can store as many as 6250 bpi, a common density is 1600 bpi.

### Data Representation

How is data represented on a tape? As Figure 7-2 shows, one character is represented by a cross section of a tape. As the figure also shows, the tape contains **tracks** or **channels.** On most modern computer tapes, one cross section of the tape, representing one character, has nine bits, one on each of the channels. There are nine locations. Each location has either a magnetized spot, which represents the 1 bit, or no magnetization, which represents the 0 bit. The most common data-representation code is the **Extended Binary Coded Decimal Interchange Code (EBCDIC,** which we discussed in Chapter 4). Eight of the nine bit locations are used to represent a character in EBCDIC; the ninth bit is a parity bit, which we explained in Chapter 4.

Figure 7-2 describes how the tracks are used, but you should note that the tracks that are used most frequently are clustered toward the middle of the tape. This is to protect the data from dirt or damage, which are more apt to affect the outer edges of the tape.

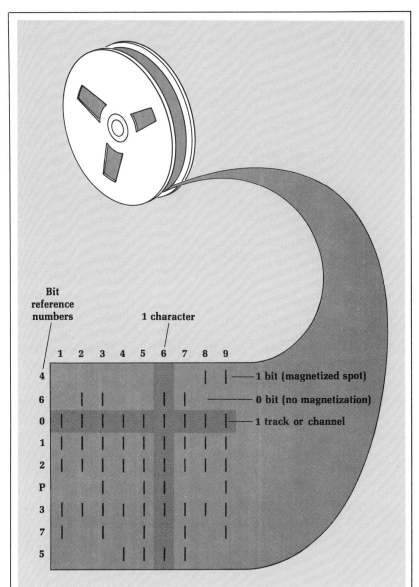

**Figure 7-2  How data is represented on magnetic tape.** This shows how the numbers 1 through 9 are represented, using combinations of 1 bits and 0 bits. For each character, there are eight bits. The ninth bit—represented here under the bit reference numbers by the letter P—is a parity bit. In the odd parity system illustrated here, each byte is always made up of an odd number of 1 bits. In an odd parity system, an even number of 1 bits would suggest that something is wrong with the data. Note that the parity-bit track appears in the middle of the tape.

### The Magnetic Tape Unit

As Figure 7-3 shows, a **magnetic tape unit** is about the size and shape of a refrigerator and indeed may even have a door that opens in the front. The purpose of the unit is to read and to write—that is, to record data on and retrieve data from—magnetic tape. This is done by a **read/write head** (see illustration), an electromagnet that *reads* the magnetized areas on the tape and converts them into electrical impulses, which are sent to the processor. The reverse is called *writing*. When the machine is writing on the tape, the **erase head** erases any data previously recorded on the tape.

Two reels are used, a **supply reel** and a **take-up reel.** The supply reel, which has the tape with data on it or on which data will be recorded, is the reel that is changed. The take-up reel always stays with the magnetic tape unit. As Figure 7-3 illustrates, the tape is allowed to drop down into vacuum chambers, airless chambers that lessen drag on the tape and prevent it from breaking if there is a sudden burst of speed. When operations are complete, the tape is rewound onto the supply reel.

Several precautions are used in the design of the tape reel and the tape to prevent mixups and loss of data:

- **File protection ring.** This plastic ring, also called a **write-enable ring,** is shown in Figure 7-4. The name "file protection ring" seems to imply that the ring is supposed to protect the file. Actually, it is the reverse: The *absence* of the ring protects the file. That is, if you try to record data on a tape, you will not be able to unless you have a ring, so you cannot erase and write new data over data already stored.

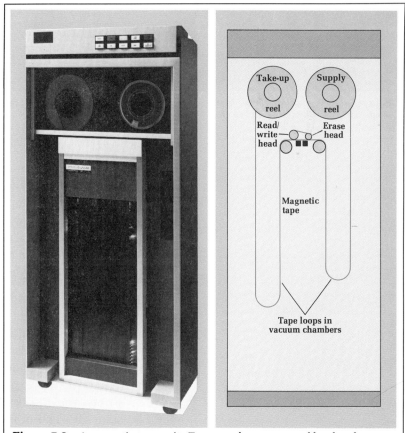

**Figure 7-3    A magnetic tape unit.** Tapes are always protected by glass from outside dust and dirt.

**Figure 7-4  Tape precautions.** Tapes are shown with external labels to help prevent mixups. *Inset:* File protection ring. This plastic ring must be placed in the groove in the tape reel before the tape can be recorded on—hence the expression, "No ring, no write."

- **Leader and load point.** The first 10- to 15-foot portion of a tape has no data and is called the **leader.** The reason no data is recorded here is that the tape may touch the floor or people's fingers, or otherwise be treated in ways that disturb the data. After the leader comes the **load point,** the place where the data starts. At the end of the file is an *end-of-file record.* There can be more than one file on a reel; if so, there will be one end-of-file record for each file.

- **Labels.** There are two kinds of tape labels, external and internal. The **external label** consists of a sticky piece of paper placed on the side of the tape reel, which identifies the tape (see Figure 7-4). **Internal labels** are records on the tape itself and are of two types. The **header label** appears on the tape right after the load point and before the first data record; it contains such identifying information as the file name and date written. The **trailer label** is at the end of the file, before the end-of-file marker, and includes a count of the number of records in the file to be checked against current processing information.

### Fixed-Length Records Versus Variable-Length Records

It might be obvious to you that data on tape is stored *sequentially;* that is, records are written onto the tape one after the other—as the tape travels past the read/write head—in a particular order by **key.** The key is a field or fields (such as social security number) selected by you. Its value may be unique within each record; the key serves as an identifier.

Records may be either fixed length or variable length. The term **fixed-length** means that all records on a file are of the same length—that is, have the same number of characters. We have already seen an example of this in the fixed length of punched cards. Each record is usually 80 characters in length. It is also common to have fixed-length records on tape and disk because the program logic to handle fixed-length records is simple and straightforward.

Sometimes the records on a file have different numbers of characters—they are **variable-length** records. While this complicates the programming, variable length is appropriate in some cases. For example, for its airplane parts file, an aircraft manufacturer might plan a fixed number of characters on each record for the part's inventory number, part name, assembly number, and so forth (see Figure 7-5). Each record will have at least these fields. However, not every part is used by every customer buying airplanes. The name of each customer using the part—for example, Pan American, United, and Northwest—is added to the fixed number of characters. The variations in the number of customer names added to each part record make the records variable in length. As shown, there are differences between the number of customers who order standard parts and those who order an isolated luxury item.

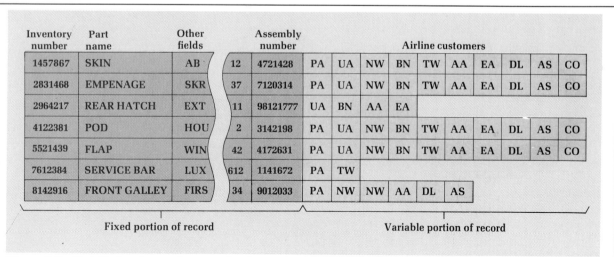

| Inventory number | Part name | Other fields | | Assembly number | Airline customers | | | | | | | | | |
|---|---|---|---|---|---|---|---|---|---|---|---|---|---|---|
| 1457867 | SKIN | AB | 12 | 4721428 | PA | UA | NW | BN | TW | AA | EA | DL | AS | CO |
| 2831468 | EMPENAGE | SKR | 37 | 7120314 | PA | UA | NW | BN | TW | AA | EA | DL | AS | CO |
| 2964217 | REAR HATCH | EXT | 11 | 98121777 | UA | BN | AA | EA | | | | | | |
| 4122381 | POD | HOU | 2 | 3142198 | PA | UA | NW | BN | TW | AA | EA | DL | AS | CO |
| 5521439 | FLAP | WIN | 42 | 4172631 | PA | UA | NW | BN | TW | AA | EA | DL | AS | CO |
| 7612384 | SERVICE BAR | LUX | 612 | 1141672 | PA | TW | | | | | | | | |
| 8142916 | FRONT GALLEY | FIRS | 34 | 9012033 | PA | NW | NW | AA | DL | AS | | | | |

Fixed portion of record          Variable portion of record

**Figure 7-5  Variable-length records.** Most of each aircraft part record is of fixed length, but the portion for airline customers varies, depending on the number of customers.

Any given file will have records that are either fixed-length or variable-length. The two types of records cannot be recorded on the same file.

### Blocking

Speed of access to a record is important; therefore, magnetic tape units are designed to provide fast access to records processed one after another on tape. However, just as you cannot stop a car on a dime, so you cannot stop a tape instantly. Thus, it is necessary to have some room between records for stopping space. This space is called an **interrecord gap (IRG)** or **interblock gap (IBG).** Typically, it is a blank space on the tape three-fifths (0.6) of an inch long.

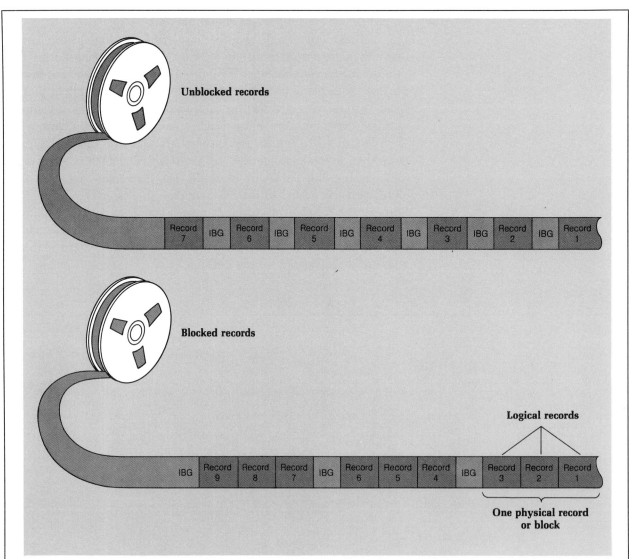

**Figure 7-6** **Blocking.** In the *unblocked* records, each record is a physical record and also a logical record. Each physical record (block) is separated from the next by an IBG. In the *blocked* records, three logical records are grouped into one physical record. This saves space, because of fewer IBGs, and increases processing speed.

However, many such IRGs on a tape waste space and add to processing time. To avoid this, records are grouped together, using a process called blocking. Figure 7-6 shows how this works. **Blocking** consists of putting together logical records into one physical record, or block, followed by an interblock gap. By **logical record** here we mean the record written by the application program; it is called "logical" because it is related to the logic of the program. The **physical record,** otherwise known as a **block,** is the collection of logical records grouped together on the tape. Programmers use the term **blocking factor** to refer to the number of logical records in one physical record. That is, for the tape shown in Figure 7-6 they would say "The blocking factor is three"—there are three logical records in a physical record. The number of records blocked together—that is, the blocking factor—depends on the amount of main memory available to the program, the size of each logical record, and also (if disk is being used) the size of a track on the disk containing the file. With some experience, programmers become adept at selecting the blocking factor for a particular file.

Although blocking saves time and space, there are costs involved: the time spent to block and deblock, and the extra memory needed to hold the larger records.

## ✳ *Why Magnetic Tape? Why Not?*

Tape has many advantages as a method of storing data:

- It is compact. One 2400-foot reel of tape (at 1600 bpi) can hold as much data as 240 *boxes* of punched cards (at 2000 cards per box), which would fill a closet.

- It is portable—a reel of tape can be carried or mailed.

- It is reusable. Data on tape can be erased.

- It is relatively inexpensive. A reel of 2400-foot tape costs less than $15.

- It can hold records of different lengths.

Still, tape does have at least two drawbacks:

- It is vulnerable to physical damage from heat, dust, stretching, and tearing.

- It is limited to sequential organization. This disadvantage is particularly important. It means that you cannot always go quickly to a particular record (you might have to read the contents of an entire reel, for instance). It also means that you cannot simply add, delete, or revise a particular record on the same tape. You have to rewrite the entire file to make even one of these changes to a single record.

## STORAGE STORIES: THE USES OF COMPUTERIZED INFORMATION

The computer's storage capabilities promise to revolutionize our way of life, as we will see in the chapter on data bases. Even now computer data banks are having an impact in ways we might not imagine.

### Gigs by Computer

John Ullman [a musicians' agent] runs the nationwide Traditional Arts Services from Portland, Oregon. He finds audiences for such artists as bluegrass pioneer Bill Monroe, folk musicians Mike Seeger and Elizabeth "Libba" Cotten, and a variety of black, Irish, Cajun, and Celtic performers. He knows that an agent's biggest problem is knowing who to call or write to line up gigs. By teaming with a computer programmer, Ullman has been able to automate his agency.

Here's a typical problem, as Ullman explains it: "Let's say someone calls me and wants Libba Cotten in Carlsbad, New Mexico, in July. It's just one gig, and it pays well, but it's months in advance. We don't want to pass it up, but we couldn't send her there from her home in Syracuse, New York, without some connecting dates along the way. My problem is to put together a tour—to find every potential sponsor who could put her onstage in the Southwest in July.

"Now, before we got the computer, I would have to scratch my head and say, 'Where are some other sponsors around Carlsbad?' I'd have to go through my Rolodex file, start looking up names and making phone calls. . . . "

For help, Ullman turned to an old friend, Robert Harper of Seattle, Washington. . . . Together they worked out a system for booking artists with an IBM computer that is now installed in Ullman's office.

In the case of booking Libba Cotten, the computer helps Ullman find those potential sponsors around Carlsbad. By typing out what category of venues [locations] he wants, Ullman instructs the computer to identify those sponsors whose zip code or area code is in the southwestern states. It will then look for those among them who have expressed interest in folk artists like Ms. Cotten, and it may also include any venue whose "season" covers the month of July, and who can be expected to meet her fee. What Ullman eventually gets is a printout of mailing labels which he can stick on promotional flyers for Ms. Cotten. When he sends those flyers out, he knows that the sponsors will be predisposed to considering her.

—Hal Glatzer,
*Frets Magazine,*
March 1983

### Customized Vegetable Gardens

A Minneapolis seed producer, Northrup King Seeds, has a new service . . . which provides customized information on how to plan and plant a vegetable garden to any plot, no matter how small, in any of the 50 states.

Mike Dowell, product manager for Northrup King, said the Smarter Garden Plan (delivered as a computer printout) takes into account most of the major variables associated with home gardens: plot size and shape, orientation to the sun, weeding method, and soil type.

It also determines the amount of each requested vegetable to be grown, based on family size, even taking into account whether the harvest is to be frozen or canned.

"Our computer form provides a listing of 41 vegetables (not all grown from seed). The gardener makes his choice, stating how many people he wants to feed, preferences, etc. . . . What he gets back is a list of vegetables he has selected . . . a timetable that takes into consideration the altitude and climatic conditions within his zip code and the amount in pounds or numbers of vegetables he can expect to harvest."

"In addition, he receives a picture of his garden with everything laid out in place with exact measurements for spacing between plantings."

—Evelyn Dewolfe,
*Los Angeles Times,*
reprinted in
*San Francisco Chronicle,*
January 2, 1982

### A Computerized Catalog of Catalogs

In today's increasingly hectic society, shopping by catalog has become almost a necessity: a hurried customer can look at hundreds of pieces of merchandise merely by flipping pages. Now retired inventor-entrepreneur Hazard Reeves has taken the concept into the electronic age. Last month he fed the contents of 100 different catalogs into a computer [file] and opened the first computer catalog store in the country. At Reeves's Catalogia store in Montvale, N.J., a walk-in customer looking for a pink negligee—or even a decorative suit of armor—need only tell a clerk and in seconds he receives a computer print-out showing which of the catalogs carries the goods he wants. If the shopper decides to buy, the clerk places an order, gives him a receipt and confirms a delivery date. The store takes 20 percent of each sale as a commision. Since Catalogia creates "extra" sales for the catalog outfits, Reeves claims the charge is really quite reasonable.

—*Newsweek,*
March 8, 1982

As we shall soon see, magnetic disk has many advantages over tape. Even so, because of its compactness and economy, tape is still a viable storage medium. The chief uses of magnetic tape are in standard sequential processing (for example, payroll) and as a convenient backup medium for disk files. "Backup" copies of disk files are taken regularly on tape as insurance against disk failure.

## Magnetic Disk Storage

Magnetic disk storage is another common form of secondary storage. A **magnetic disk** is a metal platter coated with ferrous oxide that looks something like a long-playing stereo record but is typically 14 inches in diameter. Generally, several disks are assembled together in a **disk pack** (see Figure 7-7), which looks like a stack of phonograph records, except that daylight can be seen between the disks. There are different types of disk packs, with number of platters varying by model. Each disk has a top and bottom surface on which to record

**Figure 7-7   Disk pack.** The 11 disks or metal platters in this disk pack provide 20, not 22, surfaces on which to record. The top and bottom surfaces of the stack are not used for recording.

data. Many disk devices, however, do not record data on the top of the top platter or on the bottom of the bottom platter.

As Figure 7-8 shows, the surface of each disk has tracks on it. Data is recorded as magnetic spots on the tracks. The number of tracks per surface varies with the particular disk pack model.

But note how a disk differs from a phonograph record: Whereas the track on a long-playing record allows the stereo arm to move gradually from the outside toward the center, a track on a disk is a closed circle, so the arm on a particular track always stays the same distance from the center. All tracks on one disk are *concentric*; that is, they are circles with the same center.

The same amount of data is stored on every track, from outermost (track 000) to innermost (track 399 of a 400-track disk), and it takes the same amount of time to read the data on the outer track as on the inner, even though the outer track moves faster. (The disk can be compared to a chain of ice skaters playing "crack the whip": the outside skater will be racing, whereas the inside skater will only be inching around—but both take the same amount of time to go around.) Disk drives rotate at a constant speed.

Disk storage belongs to a class of devices called direct-access storage devices. With such a device, you can go *directly* to the record you want at any point on the disk. With tape storage, on the other hand, you must read all preceding records on the file until you come to the record you want. A **direct-access storage device** (abbreviated **DASD**) is a secondary storage device on which data can be stored either sequentially or randomly.

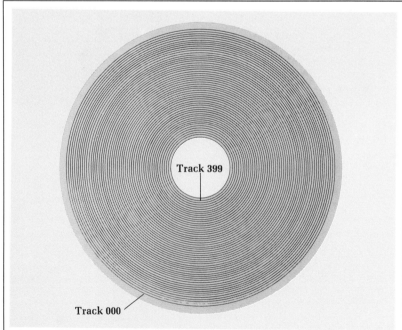

Track 399

Track 000

**Figure 7-8   Surface of a disk.** Note that each track is a closed circle, unlike the tracks on a phonograph record. This drawing is only to illustrate the location of the tracks; you cannot actually see the tracks on the disk surface.

**Figure 7-9   Disk drive units.** Looking like cake covers, these disk pack containers sit atop Control Data Corporation disk drive units in Ford Motor Company's Engineering Design Center in Dearborn, Michigan. The disk packs themselves are seated beneath the top-loading glass doors when being run. The information stored here is used to help Ford meet government-mandated emissions, fuel-economy, and safety standards.

## HEAD CRASH: THE SOUND AND THE FURY

As the poet said, the best laid plans of mice and men often go awry, and disk storage is no exception. One sometimes has the impression in reading about computers that all is quiet efficiency, but that is not always the case. A disk drive in operation, for instance, is like a washing machine during the spin cycle, which means the unit may shake.

In addition, accidents sometimes happen. A machine malfunction such as a drop in pressure or a warped disk can create a form of havoc known as a "head crash," which is fatal to a disk pack.

This happens when a read/write head actually touches a disk, which it is not supposed to do, of course. The result is a metal-on-metal kind of sound (as when a driver hits the brakes in a car at 60 mph), a strange odor and smoke, an eighth-of-an-inch gouge in the disk—and the loss of data and disk pack.

This is one of the reasons why important data on disks is also stored on tape, for backup purposes.

## The Disk Drive

A **disk drive** (see Figure 7-9) is a mechanical machine with a spindle in it on which a disk pack can be mounted. All the disks in the pack rotate at the same time and at very fast speeds (up to 3600 revolutions per minute).

The mechanism for reading or writing data on a disk is called an **access arm** (Figure 7-10); it moves a read/write head over a particular track. The access arm acts like the needle arm on a stereo, except that it never is supposed to touch the disk. It comes just close enough to detect the magnetized data. Actually, as the illustration shows, there are a *series* of access arms, which slip in between the disks in the pack. Two read/write heads are on each arm, one facing up for the surface above it, one facing down for the surface below it. Only one of the read/write heads can operate at one time.

Some disk packs are removable. That is, the access arms on the disk drive can be retracted, so that the pack can be lifted out of the machine. However, there are also nonremovable disk packs, which remain attached to disk drives. Generally, such packs are used in cases where several users are sharing data. A typical example would be a disk used for files containing flight information, to be used by several airline reservations agents. In addition, there is a type of disk drive that has a **sealed data module** (see Figure 7-11), which has disk, access arms, and read/write heads sealed within it. In some drives,

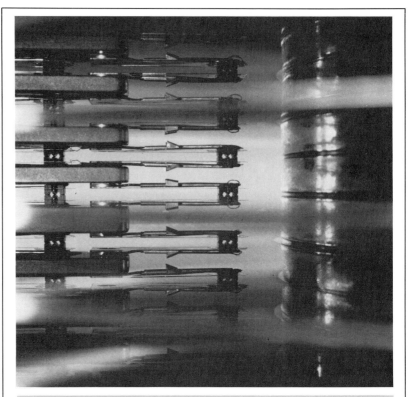

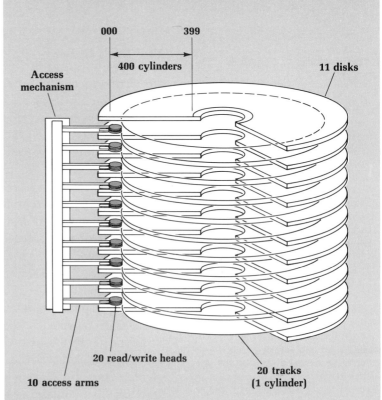

**Figure 7-10   Access arms and disk pack.** Note there are two read/write heads on each arm, which slips between the disks in the pack. The ten access arms move simultaneously, but only one read/write head operates at any one time.

**Figure 7-11    Sealed data module.** This Nashua removable data module is a sealed cartridge containing disks, access arms, and read/write heads.

### IMPROVEMENTS IN DISK CAPACITY AND SPEED

|  | IBM 2314 | IBM 3350 |
|---|---|---|
| *Capacity:* | | |
| Bytes/pack (millions) | 100 | 317.5 |
| Cylinders | 200–400 | 555 |
| Tracks/cylinder | 20 | 30 |
| *Speed:* | | |
| Average seek time (milliseconds) | 135 | 25 |
| Average rotational delay (milliseconds) | 12.5 | 8.4 |
| Data transfer rate (bytes/ second) | 624,000 | 1,198,000 |

these are removable. The technology for the data module is commonly referred to as **Winchester technology.** A Winchester disk is often called a **Winnie.**

Until 1980, the most common type of high-speed storage consisted of removable disk packs. Since then, that technology has been supplanted by Winchester disks, and it is expected that by 1985 around 85 percent of all disk storage units sold will be of the fixed, Winchester variety. The principal reasons are that Winchester disks cost only about half as much and can go twice or more as long between failures compared to removable disk packs. This increased reliability stems from the fact that operators do not handle the Winchester disk at all and that the disk's being sealed prevents the read/write heads from contamination.

Tremendous progress has been made in both speed and capacity of disk devices. We can see this evolution easily by comparing two representative devices, known by their IBM origins: the IBM 2314, which became the standard industry technology in the mid-1960s, and the IBM 3350 (see Figure 7-12), which was introduced in 1977 and has become popular in many medium to large installations. No doubt disk technology will continue to improve in both speed and capacity. For instance, the recently introduced IBM 3380 has a storage capacity nearly four times that of the 3350.

### Disk Access to Data

Four primary factors determine the time needed to access data:

- **Seek time.** This is the time it takes the access arm to get into position over a particular track. (On an IBM 3350, for instance, it averages about 25 milliseconds.) Keep in mind that *all* the access arms

**Figure 7-12  The IBM 3350 disk pack.** Introduced in 1977, this nonremovable disk pack consists of 555 cylinders, with 30 tracks per cylinder. It has a capacity of 317.5 million bytes.

move as a unit, so that actually they are simultaneously in position over a *series* of tracks.

- **Head switching.** The access arms on the access mechanism do not move separately; they move together, all at the same time. However, only *one* read/write head can operate at any one time. Head switching is the activation of a particular read/write head over a particular track on a particular surface. Since head switching takes place at the speed of electricity, the time it takes is negligible.

- **Rotational delay.** With the access arm and read/write head in position, ready to read or write data, the read/write head waits in position for a short period of time until the record on the track moves under it. (On the IBM 3350, average rotational delay is about 8.4 milliseconds.)

- **Data transfer.** This activity is the transfer of data between primary storage and the place on the disk track—to the track, if you are writing; from the track to primary storage, if you are reading. The data transfer rate for the IBM 3350 is 1,198,000 bytes per second.

With these four motions, users can quickly get at any particular record any place on a disk, provided they have a method of finding where it is. (That method is called direct access file processing, as discussed later in the chapter.)

### How Data Is Written on a Disk

There is more than one way of physically writing data on a disk, but the method we will consider here is the **cylinder method,** shown in Figure 7-13. The organization here is vertical. The purpose is to minimize seek time, the movement of the access arms. It is clear that once the access arm is in position, it is in the same vertical position on all disk surfaces.

To appreciate this, suppose you had an empty disk pack on which you wished to record data. You might be tempted to record the data horizontally: start with the first surface, fill track 0, then track 1, track 2, and so on, then move to the second surface and again fill tracks 0, 1, 2, and so forth. Each new track and new surface, however, would require movement of the access arms, a relatively slow mechanical process. Recording the data vertically, on the other hand, substantially reduces access arm movement: The data will be recorded on the tracks that can be accessed by one positioning of the access arm, that is, on one **cylinder.** By using cylinder organization, it is as though you dropped a cylinder (like a tin can) straight down through all disks in the disk pack: The access arms mechanism would have equal access to track 0 of all surfaces, then with a single movement would have access to track 1 of all surfaces, and so on. The cylinder method, then, means all tracks of a certain cylinder on a disk pack are lined

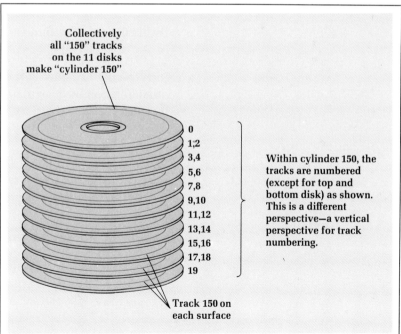

**Figure 7-13  Cylinder data organization.** To visualize the cylinder form of organization, imagine that a cylinder such as a tin can were dropped straight down through all the disks in the disk pack.

up one beneath the other—30 tracks on 30 surfaces—and all 30 vertical tracks are accessible by the read/write heads with one positioning of the access arms mechanism. Using this vertical perspective, we can now number the tracks vertically within one cylinder: A 30-surface pack would number the tracks of a cylinder 0 through 29, top to bottom.

### Disk Addresses

Now that we have seen how data can be written vertically on disk, we can also see how we would establish a disk address for a particular record. The disk address would be cylinder number, surface number, and record number, in that order. For example, the disk address of a record might be cylinder 40, surface 16, record 4. If we wanted to consider this address as a single number, it would be 0401604. This concept of disk address becomes important as we consider file organization and processing.

## File Organization: Three Methods

There are three major methods of storing files of data in secondary storage:

- **Sequential file organization** simply means records are organized in sequential order by key.

- **Direct file organization** means records are organized randomly, not in any special order.

- **Indexed file organization** is a combination of the above two: Records are organized sequentially, but, in addition, indexes are built into the file so that a record can be accessed either sequentially or directly.

These are three forms of *file organization*—that is, how the files can be set up. Let us now see how these translate into *file processing*—that is, how the files are used.

### Sequential File Processing

In **sequential file processing,** records are usually in order according to a key field. If it is an inventory file, the key might be part number. A people file might use social security number or credit card number as the key.

To understand how sequential organization works, let us see how a master file of personnel records might be updated by a transaction file, as shown in Figure 7-14. A master file, you may recall from Chapter 2, is a set of records that represents the current status of data

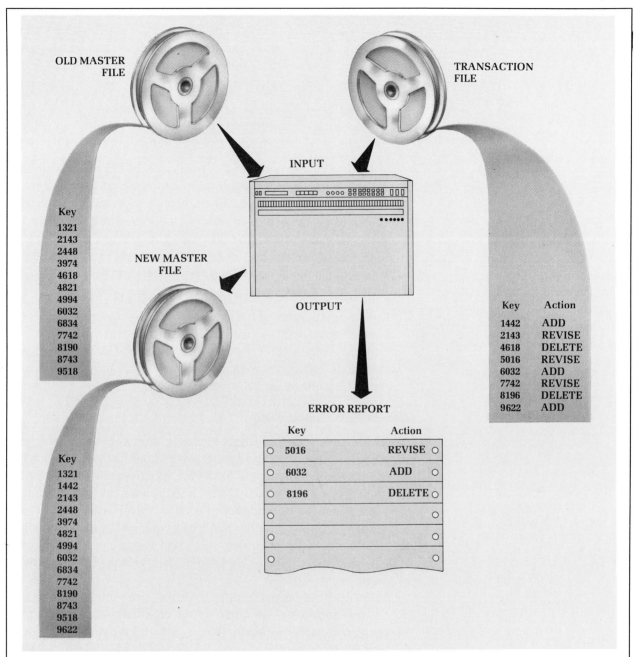

**Figure 7-14  Sequential updating of auto maker's personnel files.** Each key here represents an entire employee record: employee name, address, salary rate, job title, and so on. The master file consists of semipermanent data. The transaction file (which has been presorted so that keys are in numerical order from lowest to highest number) consists of new actions to be taken with the master file.

for a business or organization. Master files may be changed by additions, deletions, and revisions. A transaction file is the most recent gathering of such additions, deletions, and revisions. The points to observe about this updating process are as follows:

- Records—in this case, employee records—for both master file and transaction file, must be in order by key, perhaps arranged from low numbers to high, before the updating can be done. (This means the numbers on the transaction tape had to have been presorted, since it is doubtful that matters requiring attention would have occurred quite so conveniently as to be in numerical order.)

- The changes to the master file required by the transaction file consist of additions, deletions, or revisions. (An addition would result from someone's being hired, a deletion from someone's job termination, and a revision from a promotion, new address, or the like.)

- During processing, the computer reads records from the master and transaction files and takes action on whichever of the two keys is lower in number. If the keys are the same, the record in the master file should be revised or deleted. If the master file record key is higher, the transaction should be added to the master file (if it is not an add, it is some sort of error); if the master file record key is lower, there is no change of any sort to that master file record.

- As the processing takes place, a new master file is produced; this new file incorporates all the changes from the transaction file. Also, an error report will be printed. The error report calls the user's attention to requests for deletions and revisions for personnel records that do not exist and requests for additions for personnel records that have been added previously.

### Direct File Processing

**Direct file processing,** or **direct access,** allows you to go directly to the record you want, using a record key, without the computer having to read all preceding records in the file, as in sequential file organization. (Direct access is sometimes called **random access,** indicating the records can be in random order.) It is this ability to access any given record instantly that has made computer systems so convenient for people in service industries—for travel agents checking for available flights, for example, or bank tellers determining individual bank balances.

Obviously, if we have a completely blank area on the disk and can put records anywhere—in other words, randomly—then there must be some predictable system for placing a record at a disk address and for retrieving the record at some subsequent time. In other words, once the record has been placed on a disk, it must be possible to find it again. This is done by choosing a certain formula to use on the record key, thereby deriving a number to use as the disk address. **Hashing,** or **randomizing,** is the name given to the process of applying a formula to a key, yielding a number that represents the address.

There are various formulas, but a simple one is to divide the key by a prime number and use the remainder from the division operation as an address. A prime number is any number that can be divided evenly only by itself or 1; it cannot be divided by any other number. Examples of prime numbers are 7, 11, 13, and 17. Figure 7-15 shows how dividing a key by a prime number produces a remainder that, in

```
                          74
Prime number   17/ 1269  Key
                   119
                    79
                    68
     Remainder      11
```

**Figure 7-15 A simple hashing scheme.** Dividing the key number 1269 by the prime number 17 yields a remainder of 11, which can be used to indicate track location on a disk.

this case, indicates the track location. Now the record can be written on the first available location on that track, or, if reading, that track can be read until the desired record is found.

The reason for using remainders is that they produce disk addresses of manageable size. Some keys, such as social security numbers, are quite long; indeed keys may run 20 digits or more. The main reason for using a key is that it is predictable: by applying the same hashing formula to the same key you can obtain the exact same address and therefore always find that record again. For instance, if our hashing formula is to divide the key by prime number 13 and use the remainder as the address, then key 54 would yield address 2 (54 divided by 13 gives remainder 2). The record for key 54 would then be placed on the disk in "location 2." (This example is intentionally simple to illustrate this point.) At some later time, this record can be found by

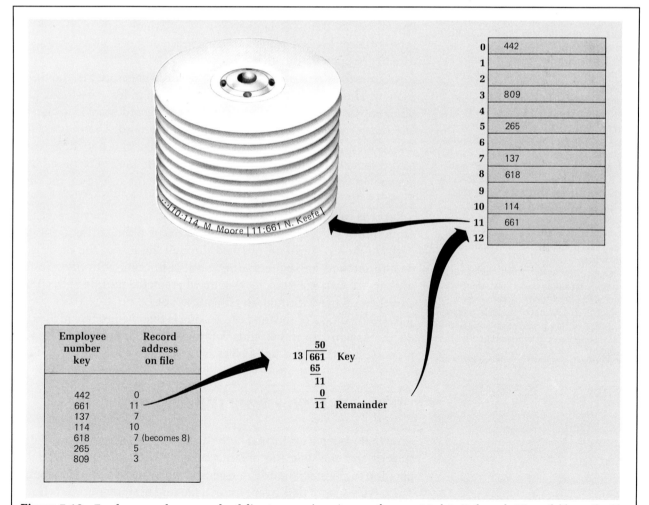

**Figure 7-16  Employee number; example of direct processing.** Assume there are 13 slots (0 through 12) available on the file. Dividing the key number 661, N. Keefe's employee number, by the prime number 13 yields a remainder of 11. Thus, 11 is the address for key 661. However, for the key 618, dividing by the prime 13 would yield the remainder 7—and this address has already been used (by the key 137); hence, the address becomes the next number, that is, 8. Note, incidentally, that keys (and therefore records) need not appear in any particular order. (The 13 record locations available are, of course, too few to hold a normal file; a small number was used to keep the example simple.)

applying the same formula to key 54 and again coming up with 2 as its address.

What happens, you might ask, if two keys divided by the same prime develop the same remainder so that you have duplicate addresses? (For instance, 7 divided by 3 has a remainder of 1, but so does 10 divided by 3.) Records with duplicate addresses are called **synonyms.** One approach is to put each synonym in the closest available location—the next address, or, if that one is full, the address after that, and so on.

Figure 7-16 gives a very simplified example of how direct processing works.

### Indexed File Processing

**Indexed file processing** or **indexed processing** is a third method of file organization and represents a compromise between sequential and direct methods. It is useful in cases where files need to be in sequential order but where, in addition, you need to be able to go directly to specific records.

An indexed file works as follows: Records are stored in the file in sequential order, but the file also contains an index. The index contains entries consisting of the key to each record stored on the file and the corresponding disk address for that record. The index is like a directory, with the keys to all records listed in order. To access a record directly, the record key must be located in the index; the address associated with the key is then used to locate the record on the disk. Figure 7-17 illustrates how this works.

Records can also be accessed sequentially. The file may be accessed sequentially in two different ways. To retrieve the entire file, begin with the first record and proceed through the rest of the records. A second method for sequential retrieval is to begin with the retrieval of a record with a certain key—somewhere in the middle of the file—and then proceed through the file as before.

A disadvantage of indexed processing is that the process of looking up the key in the index adds one more operation to the retrieval process. It is therefore not as fast as direct file processing.

## Why Disk Storage? Why Not?

Now that we have examined both the physical characteristics of disk storage and possible file organization methods, we are in a better position to evaluate the advantages and disadvantages of disk storage. The advantages of disk over tape as a method of storage are as follows:

- Disk files may be organized directly, which allows immediate access to any given record. This is the biggest advantage and is basic to real-time systems such as instant credit checks and airline reservations.

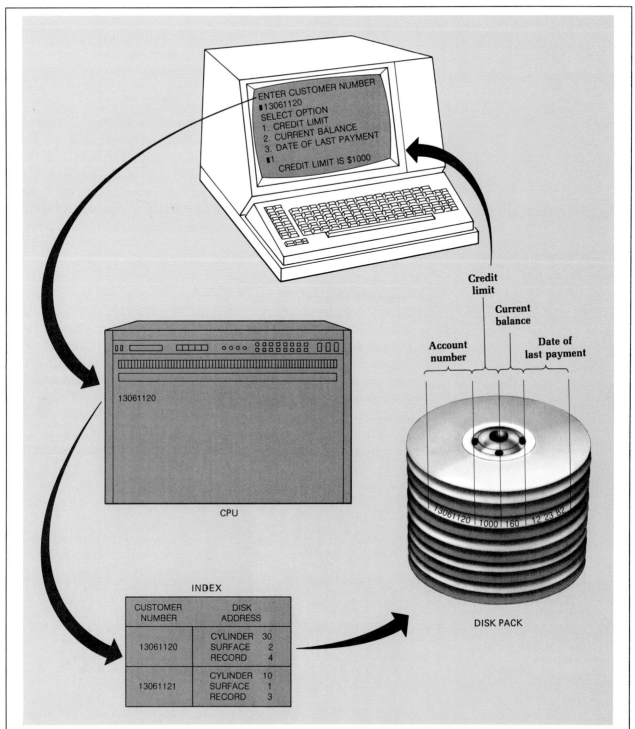

**Figure 7-17** **Customer balance example of indexed processing.** At a retail store, a terminal operator can make an inquiry about a customer by typing in the customer number on the terminal. The index then directs the computer to the particular disk address, which indicates the customer information.

Using direct access, information may be updated easily. A single record may be read, updated, and returned to the disk—what is called "updated in place"—without the necessity of rewriting the entire file, as is the case in sequential processing.

- No presorting of records is necessary for direct updating because, unlike sequential processing, transactions need not be processed as a group with one reading of the master file. Instead, the master file can be updated one record at a time as the transactions occur.

There are also disadvantages to disk storage. Perhaps the most obvious one is the cost of the medium: One disk pack typically costs $300 and up. The disk storage unit can cost many thousands of dollars. Disk packs are cumbersome to transport or to mail. Another consideration is security: If it is so easy for authorized people to access a record, then unauthorized people may very well access it. As we will see in Chapter 18, computer security and computer crime are important concerns.

## *Mass Storage*

Mass storage is a third form of secondary, or auxiliary, storage. **Mass storage devices** are able to store enormous volumes of data, such as census records or Internal Revenue Service records, but their drawback is that they are relatively slow—their speed of information retrieval is measured in seconds rather than milliseconds.

As Figure 7-18 shows, the IBM 3850 Mass Storage System consists of a honeycomblike apparatus. Each cell of the honeycomb contains a cartridge that is 2 inches in diameter and 4 inches long—and with

**Figure 7-18  A mass storage device.** The IBM 3850 Mass Storage System. The cartridges shown inside each honeycomblike cell are about the size of an individualized fruit juice can.

a magnetic tape inside it that is 770 inches long and holds 50 million bytes of data.

Neither the honeycomb nor the cartridges themselves are connected directly to the CPU. When data is needed, a mechanical arm must retrieve the cartridge from the cell and the data on the cartridge is transferred to a magnetic disk, a process that takes 3 to 8 seconds. The data on the disk is then available to the CPU. Mechanical action of any sort is always slower than electronic action, and in this case it can take up to 15 seconds to retrieve the data. This makes the process 600 times slower than the average seek time on IBM 3350 disk storage. Clearly, then, mass storage devices are most useful in situations where fast access time is not required.

We have mentioned the large data volumes of government files, but many private industries also maintain large files. A large, national insurance company, for example, needs considerable file storage for applications, policies, claims, and related data. It is feasible to use mass storage devices for these files, moving appropriate files to disk when needed for processing.

## Storage for Microcomputers

The market for data storage is being profoundly affected by the surge in popularity of personal computers or microcomputers. Storage media are available in three basic forms: cassette tapes, diskettes, and hard disk. Let us look at each of these.

**Cassette tapes** are the same as the audio tapes you use on a home portable tape recorder. Their advantage is that there are many cheap tape recorders around, so if you are putting together a home computer system for the first time, this is a way to save money. Their disadvantage is the same as all tape storage: you cannot access the tape file directly—that is, request any one record. Moreover, tape is slow.

**Diskettes**—commonly known as **floppy disks**—are more popular than cassettes with most microcomputer users. Diskettes started out as 8 inches in diameter, but were supplanted by 5¼-inch diskettes called **minifloppies**, which generally hold about 250K bytes of data and sell for under $4. More recently, some shirt-pocket-sized diskettes known as **microfloppies** have appeared on the market (see Figure 7-19). Because of the lack of standardization (microfloppies are being marketed in four different sizes—3, 3¼, 3½, and 3.9 inches) it remains to be seen how popular they will be. Most users of diskettes are in small businesses; the rest of the market is divided between word processing and personal computer users.

**Hard disks,** which is to say 5-inch Winchester disks in sealed modules, are expensive—between $2000 and $3000 per unit—but, with a capacity of 5 to 15 megabytes of storage, may be worth the price. At 56 miles per hour, hard disks are also ten times faster than floppy disks. As mentioned, hard disks are more reliable, since they are sealed against contamination by outside air or human hands.

**Figure 7-19 Microfloppy disk.** Diskettes in the 3-inch range are intended to fit in a shirt pocket.

## *Onward*

What is the future of storage? The technical literature mentions terms such as *optical memory* and *laser memory*. Perhaps the closest to actualization are magnetic bubble memories, as we mentioned in Chapter 4.

The biggest advantage of bubble memories is that when power to the memory is turned off, the data does not disappear. Moreover, they are also resistant to harsh environments such as radiation, contamination, and extreme temperatures, which can be fatal to tape or disk. Whatever the technology, it seems likely that we will be seeing greater storage capabilities in the future. Such capabilities have awesome implications, with their huge data files—for law, medicine, teaching, for large government files, and ultimately for you.

None of this is possible, however, without software. To which we now turn.

## *Summary and Key Terms*

- Secondary storage (also called auxiliary storage) is necessary because primary (main) storage must be yielded to other users once one's program is executed.

- The benefits of secondary storage are economy, reliability, and convenience.

- Two common secondary storage media are magnetic tape and magnetic disk.

- **Magnetic tape** is usually one-half inch wide plastic Mylar tape usually wound on a 10½-inch-diameter reel. The tape has an iron oxide coating that can be magnetized. Data is stored as small magnetized spots. The most common length tape is 2400 feet.

- The amount of data on tape is expressed in terms of **density,** the number of **characters per inch (cpi)** or **bytes per inch (bpi)** that can be stored on tape.

- A character of data may be represented on tape as a cross section of nine bits, one bit for each of the nine **tracks** or **channels** on the tape. A magnetized spot represents a 1 bit; no magnetization represents a 0 bit. The most common data-representation code is the Extended Binary Coded Decimal Interchange Code (EBCDIC).

- A **magnetic tape unit** records data on tape and retrieves data from it. It utilizes a **read/write head,** an electromagnet that reads the magnetized areas on the tape and converts them into electrical impulses; the reverse is called writing. When a machine is writing on the tape, the **erase head** erases any data previously recorded on the tape.

- Two reels are used. The **supply reel,** which has data on it or on which data will be recorded, is changed. The **take-up reel** always stays with the magnetic tape unit.

- Several precautions are taken to prevent mixups and loss of data. One is the use of the **file protection ring.** Also called a **write-enable ring,** this plastic ring must be on the tape reel to record data. The first 10- to 15-foot portion of the tape, the **leader,** has no data on it. The **load point** is the place on the tape following the leader, where the data starts. At the end of the file is an end-of-file record. A sticky piece of paper, an **external label,** is placed on the outside of the tape reel to identify it. **Internal labels** are on the tape itself and are of two types. The **header label** follows the load point and contains such information as the file name and date written. The **trailer label** is at the end of the file, before the end-of-file marker, and includes a count of the number of records in the file.

- Records may be either fixed length or variable length. **Fixed length** means that all records on a file have the same number of characters. **Variable length** means that they may have different numbers of characters.

- Magnetic tape units are designed to provide fast access; however, a tape cannot be stopped instantly at an exact point. Some stopping space between records is needed. This space, typically three-fifths (0.6) of an inch long, is called an **interrecord gap (IRG)** or **interblock gap (IBG).**

- To avoid wasting space on a tape, **blocking** is used. That is, **logical records,** the records written by the application program, are blocked, or put together, into **physical records,** or **blocks.** The term **blocking factor** refers to the number of logical records in one physical record.

- The advantages of magnetic tape as a medium for storing data are that it is compact, portable, reusable, relatively inexpensive, and can hold records of different lengths. Disadvantages are that it is vulnerable to physical damage from heat, dust, stretching, and tearing and that it is limited to sequential organization.

- Magnetic disk storage is another common form of secondary storage. A **magnetic disk** is a metal platter, typically 14 inches in diameter. Generally, several disks are assembled in a **disk pack.** Each disk has concentric tracks on it, so that each track is a closed circle, but the same amount of data can be stored on each track.

- Disk storage belongs to a class of devices called **direct-access storage devices (DASDs).** With such a device, one can go directly to the record one wants, without having to read all preceding records on the file.

- A **disk drive** is a mechanical machine with a spindle in it on which a disk pack can be mounted; all disks in the pack rotate at the same time and at up to 3600 revolutions per second.

- The mechanism for reading or writing data on disk is called an **access arm;** it moves a read/write head over a particular track. There are a series of access arms, which are between the disks in the disk pack. Only one read/write head on the access arms operates at a time.

- Some disk packs are removable. Some are nonremovable and remain attached to the disk drive; generally, these are used in cases where several users are sharing the data. There is also a **sealed data module,** with disk, access arms, and read/write heads sealed within it; the unit may be removable. The technology for the data module is commonly referred to as **Winchester technology.**

- Records may be ordered by **key,** a chosen field (such as social security number), which serves as an identifier.

- Four primary factors determine the time to access data: seek time, head switching, rotational delay, and data transfer. **Seek time** is the time required for the access arm to get into position over a particular track. **Head switching** is the activation of a particular read/write head over a particular track on a particular surface. **Rotational delay** is the time for the record on the disk to rotate under the read/write head. **Data transfer** is the transfer of data between primary storage and the place on the disk track.

- The **cylinder method** is a way of physically organizing data on a disk pack that minimizes seek time. Access arms are in the same vertical position on all disk surfaces. The disk address for a particular record would be cylinder number, surface number, and record number, in that order.

- The three major methods of storing files of data in secondary storage are sequential file organization (in sequential order by key), direct file organization (randomly organized), and indexed file organization (records are organized sequentially, but indexes also permit access directly).

- In **sequential file processing,** records may be in order by key field.

- In **direct file processing,** or **direct access** (sometimes called **random access**), one can go directly to the record one wants, using a record key, without the computer having to read all preceding records in the file. **Hashing,** or **randomizing,** is the process of applying a formula to a key, yielding the number that represents the address of a record. Records with duplicate addresses are called **synonyms.**

- In **indexed file processing,** or **indexed processing,** records are stored in sequential order, but the file also contains an index, which acts as a directory, with the keys to all records listed in order.

- The advantages of disk over tape as a method of storage are that disk files may be organized for immediate access to any given record (which is basic to real-time systems), information may be updated easily, and no presorting of records is necessary for updating. The disadvantages of disk storage are the costs, the cumbersome nature of disk packs for shipping purposes, and the possibilities for breach of security because of their being more accessible.

- **Mass storage devices,** a third kind of secondary storage, store enormous volumes of data, such as census records. An example is the IBM 3850 Mass Storage System. A disadvantage is that retrieval of information is measured in seconds rather than milliseconds.

- Media for microcomputer storage take three basic forms: **cassette tapes,** like audio tapes for portable tape recorders; **diskettes,** known as **floppy disks,** which may be 8 inches in diameter, 5¼-inch (**minifloppies**), or between 3 and 3.9 inches (**microfloppies**); or **hard disks,** which are 5-inch Winchester disks.

## Review

1. What are the physical characteristics and most common length of magnetic tape?

2. Explain how a tape unit works.

3. List and describe the types of tape labels.

4. Explain fixed-length and variable-length records.

5. What is an interrecord gap?

6. What differentiates logical records and physical records?

7. List the advantages and disadvantages of magnetic tape.

8. Describe the physical characteristics of magnetic disk.

9. What is DASD?

10. What are four primary factors that determine the time needed to access disk data?

11. Describe a cylinder.

12. What are three methods of file organization in secondary storage?

13. What happens to synonyms in direct file processing?

14. In indexed processing, how are records accessed directly?

15. What are the advantages and disadvantages of disk storage?

16. Explain how mass storage devices work.

17. What advantages does floppy disk have over cassette tapes for microcomputer storage?

ch 8 beginning
programming:
getting your
fingers wet

ch 9 systems
analysis and
design: the
thrust of
change

ch 10
structured
program
design:
up from
"spaghetti"
code

ch 11
languages:
communicating
with the
computer

ch 12
operating
systems: the
traffic cop

# part 3
# software

The Software Decade—that is what the 1980s will turn out to be, suggests *Computerworld*, a computer industry trade magazine. Hardware has grown in spectacular technological leaps, as we have seen. Twenty years ago, who would have predicted the growth of microchips, robots, and other electronic wizardry? But, as many people found to their sorrow during the sixties and seventies, gigantic storage capacity and speedy input and output notwithstanding, hardware is no better than the software used with it. In the following five chapters, we will discuss software-related topics, including flowcharting, systems analysis and design, structured programming, languages, and operating systems. Here you can begin to understand the excitement and challenges of telling the computer what you want it to do.

## IN THIS CHAPTER

We describe how programmers work: define the problem; plan the solution; and code, test, and document the program. Some basic flowcharting techniques—ways of representing a program as a picture—are also shown. The control structures of structured design and programming are introduced. Pseudocode is presented with some of the control structure examples. A problem solution expressed in flowchart form is developed into a program.

*ch8*

# *beginning*
# *programming*

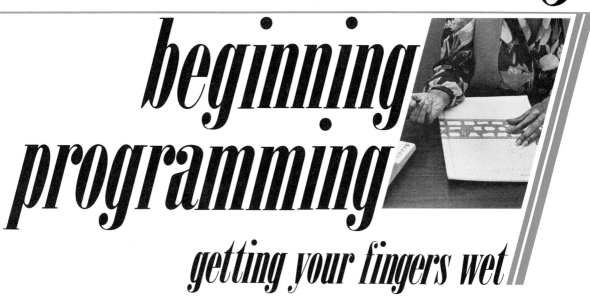

## *getting your fingers wet*

By now you may be starting to feel the excitement associated with computers and are ready to begin using them to solve problems. This chapter will introduce you to the programming process. When used in conjunction with a guide to a specific language (such as BASIC, which is described in Appendix A), this chapter should help you use the computer for a variety of activities.

## Why Programming?

There are at least two good reasons for learning programming at this point:

- Programming helps dispel the mysteriousness of the computer. The computer is simply a tool. Although some training is required, learning to use it is like learning to drive a car: You can learn how to use it without knowing every detail of how it works.

- Learning programming will enable you to find out quickly whether you like it, and whether you have the analytical turn of mind needed. Even if you decide that programming is not for you, trying your hand at it will certainly increase your computer literacy and give you an appreciation for what programmers do.

An important point before we proceed, however: You will not be a programmer when you finish reading this chapter or even when you finish reading the final chapter. Programming proficiency takes practice and training beyond the scope of this book. But you will have written programs, if you put into practice what we are about to describe, and you will have a good idea of what programmers do.

## "Programmers Keep Out!": What Programmers Do and Do Not Do

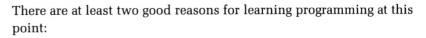

People visualize programmers as working with computers, throwing switches and reading printouts in a computer room. Actually, the computer room is one of the last places a programmer should be. Among the people who *do not* belong in a computer room are programmers. One reason for this is security: The fewer people allowed in the computer room, the lower the risk of having anyone tamper with data or programs. Another reason is that individual programmers, in their zeal to make sure *their* programs are running right, are apt to get in the way of computer room operations and the running of other programs.

In general, programmers work less with hardware than they do with people. Indeed, often they are stationed away from computers and in the offices of users. Thus, having people skills is as important as having programming skills. The programmer most likely to be hired for a given job is one who can communicate as effectively with people as with computers.

But what *does* a programmer do? In general, the programmer's job is to convert user problem solutions into instructions for the computer. That is, the programmer prepares the instructions of a computer program and runs, tests, and corrects the program. The programmer also writes a report on the program. These activities are all done for the purpose of helping a user fill a need—pay employees, bill customers, admit students to college, and so forth. Programmers help the user develop new programs to solve problems, weed out errors in existing programs, or perform changes on programs as a result of new requirements (such as the five-digit postal zip code being replaced by a nine-digit code).

At present, a great many people are working as programmers and a great many programming jobs are going unfilled. However, over the years there have been periodic prophecies that the need for programmers will disappear. The most recent version of this prophecy is that there will be less need for programmers in the future because the distinction between users and programmers is fading. This version argues that improved software makes it possible for more and more users to use a computer without having to engage the services of a programmer. In effect, "user" can be "programmer," perhaps without even realizing it. Hence, the need for professional programmers will decline.

Actually, the converse may be true, for two reasons. First, the more user-oriented the field of computers and data processing becomes, the simpler things have to be—but to produce powerful software that anyone can use requires skilled programmers. Second, the computer market is expanding. As hardware becomes cheaper, more computers will be purchased for businesses and organizations. And more programmers will be needed to serve these additional users.

In Chapter 17, we will discuss computer careers in more detail. Let us turn now from programmers to programming.

 ## *The Programming Process*

Developing a program requires five steps:

1. Define the problem.
2. Plan the solution.
3. Code the program.
4. Test the program.
5. Document the program.

Let us discuss each of these in turn.

## 1. Defining the Problem

As a programmer, you may be contacted because your services are needed. You, as a programmer (or through the systems analyst), meet with users from the client organization and analyze the problem. Eventually you come to an agreement that, among other things, specifies the kind of input, processing, and output required. This is not a simple process. It is closely related to the systems analysis function, discussed in Chapter 9.

## 2. Planning the Solution

Two common ways of planning the solution to a problem are to draw a flowchart and/or write pseudocode. A flowchart is an important tool of programming. Essentially, a **flowchart** is a pictorial representation of an ordered, step-by-step solution to a problem. It is a map of what your program is going to do and how it is going to do it. **Pseudocode** is an English-like language that you can use to state your solution with more precision than you can in plain English but with less precision than is required when using a formal programming language. Pseudocode is an alternative to flowcharting as a design tool.

In the latter part of this chapter, we shall consider the construction of flowcharts in detail. Some flowchart examples are accompanied by the corresponding pseudocode.

### SOME PSEUDOCODE RULES

1. Break the program into small procedures. Name each procedure. Start each procedure with BEGIN. Indent the statements within the procedure. Terminate each procedure with an END statement.

2. Use IF-THEN-ELSE for decisions. Indent THEN and ELSE statements. End each IF with ENDIF, in the same margin as the IF.

3. Use DOWHILE or DOUNTIL for iteration. Indent the statements after the DO statement. End each DO with ENDDO, in the same margin as the DO.

## 3. Coding the Program

Your next step is to **code** the program; that is, to express your solution in a programming language. There are a great many programming languages. BASIC, COBOL, Pascal, PL/I, and FORTRAN are common examples. You may find yourself working with one or more of these. These languages operate grammatically, somewhat like the English language, but they are much more precise. To get your programs to work, you have to follow *exactly* the rules of the language you are using. Your coded program must be keyed, often at a terminal, into a form the computer can understand.

## 4. Testing the Program

After coding, you test the program. This step involves these phases:

- **Desk-checking.** This phase, similar to proofreading, is often avoided or short-cut by the programmer. He or she is dying to run the program on the computer, now that it is written. However, with careful desk-checking, you may discover several errors, possibly saving yourself several computer runs. In **desk-checking**, you simply sit down and mentally trace, or check, the logic of the program to ensure that it is error-free and workable. In the process, you may also discover keying errors and errors in the use of the language.

- **Translating.** A translator is a program that translates your program into language the computer can understand. A by-product of the process is that the translator will tell you if you have improperly used the programming language in some way. If you have, the translator will produce descriptive error messages. For instance, if in FORTRAN you mistakenly write, $N = 2*(I+J))$—which has two closing parentheses instead of one—you will get a message that says, "UNMATCHED PARENTHESES." Programs are most commonly translated by a **compiler** or an **interpreter.** A compiler translates your entire program at one time, giving you all the error messages—called **diagnostics**—at once. An interpreter, often used for the BASIC language, translates your program one line at a time. A BASIC interpreter will signal errors as each line is keyed in. This translation process is described in more detail in Chapter 12.

- **Debugging.** A term used extensively in programming, **debugging** is detecting, locating, and correcting "bugs" (mistakes) by running the program. These bugs are logic errors such as telling a computer to repeat an operation but not telling it how to stop repeating. In this phase, you run the program against test data. Since the test data is planned by you, you should try to test every part of the program.

### 5. Documenting the Program

Documenting is an ongoing, necessary process—although like many programmers you may be eager to pursue more exciting computer-related activities. **Documentation** is a written detailed description of the programming cycle and specific facts about this program. Typical program documentation materials include the origin and nature of the problem, a brief narrative description of the program, logic tools such as flowcharts and pseudocode (to be discussed), data record descriptions, program listings, and testing results. Comments in the program itself are also considered an important part of documentation. In a broader sense, program documentation could be part of the documentation for an entire system, as described in Chapter 9.

The wise programmer will continue to document the program throughout its design, development, and testing. Documentation is needed to supplement human memory, to help organize program planning, and to communicate with others who have an interest in the program. Documentation also is needed so that those who come after you can make any necessary modifications in the program or track down any errors that you missed.

### Programming Teams

Many computer installations organize individual programmers into programming teams. Within this framework the programmers conduct formal reviews of each team member's program design and coding. The reviewers look for flaws and make suggestions for improvement. The atmosphere of these reviews is one of mutual assistance.

The primary goals of the programmer team technique are to minimize development costs and to ensure quality programs. The team concept will be discussed more fully in Chapter 10.

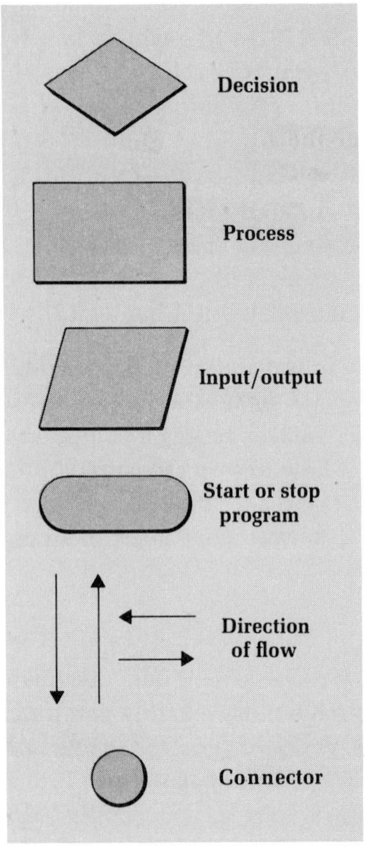

# Learning to Construct Flowcharts

As we stated, a flowchart is essentially a picture—and we all know that a picture is worth a thousand words. The flowchart consists of arrows that represent the direction the program takes and of boxes and other symbols that represent actions.

### Beginning Flowcharting: The ANSI Symbols

Some standard flowchart symbols have been established and are accepted by most programmers. These symbols, shown in Figure 8-1, are called ANSI symbols. **ANSI** stands for American National Standards Institute. Templates of ANSI symbols (Figure 8-2) are available in many office supply stores and college bookstores and are helpful in drawing orderly flowcharts. The most common symbols you will use are **decision, process, input/output, start/stop, direction of flow,** and **connector.** Let us now look at two examples.

**Preparing a Letter**  Figure 8-3 shows you how you might diagram the steps of preparing a letter for mailing. There is usually more than one correct way to design a flowchart. This becomes obvious with more complicated examples.

The rectangular **process** boxes are actions to be taken— "Address envelope," "Fold letter," "Place letter in envelope." Sometimes the

**Figure 8-1  ANSI flowchart symbols.**

Decision

Process

Input/output

Start or stop program

Direction of flow

Connector

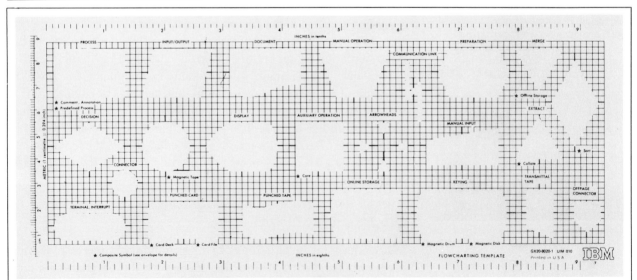

**Figure 8-2  Example of a template containing standard ANSI flowchart symbols.**  Templates like this one are used as drawing aids.

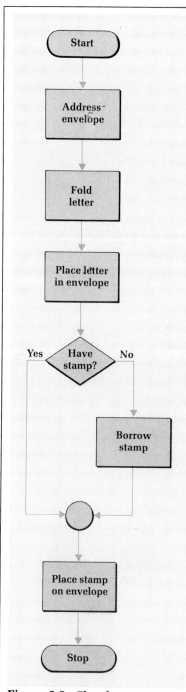

**Figure 8-3** Flowchart to prepare letter for mailing.

order in which actions appear is important, sometimes not. In this case, the letter must be folded before it can be placed in the envelope.

The diamond-shaped box ( "Have stamp?") is a **decision** box. It has two **paths** or **branches**—yes and no. Note that the decision box is the *only* box that allows a choice; no other box has more than one exit. The decision box asks a question that takes a yes or no answer. Whether you do need a stamp (and therefore have to borrow it) or do not, you take a path that comes back to a circle that puts you on a path to the end. The circle is called a **connector** because it "connects" the paths together. (This symbol can also be used as an on-page connector when transferring to another location on the same sheet of paper.) Notice that the flowchart begins and ends with the oval **start/stop** symbol.

This example of preparing a letter suggests how you can take almost any activity and diagram it in flowchart form, assuming you can always express your decisions as choices between yes and no. Now let us use flowcharting to show just what programming is all about.

**Summing Numbers from 1 Through 100** Figure 8-4 shows how you might flowchart a program to find the sum of all numbers between 1 and 100. There are a number of things to observe about this flowchart.

First, the program uses two places in the computer's memory as storage locations, places to keep intermediate results. In one location is a *counter*, which might be like a car odometer: Every time a mile passes, the counter counts it as a 1. In the other location is a *sum*—that is, a running total of the numbers counted. The sum location will eventually contain the sum of all numbers from 1 through 100: 1 + 2 + 3 + 4 + 5 + · · · + 100.

Second, as we start the program, we must initialize the counter and the sum. When you **initialize,** it means you set the starting values of certain storage locations, usually as the program execution begins. We will initialize the sum at zero and the counter at 1.

Third, note the looping. You add the counter to the sum and a 1 to the counter, and then come to the decision diamond, which asks if the counter is greater than 100. If the answer is no, the computer loops back around and repeats the process. The decision box contains a **compare** operation; the computer compares two numbers and performs alternative operations based on the comparison. If the result of the comparison is yes, the computer produces a printout of the sum. Notice that the parallelogram symbol is used for printing the sum, because this is an output process.

A **loop**—also called an **iteration**—is the heart of computer programming. The beauty of the loop, which may be defined as the repetition of instructions under certain conditions, is that you, as the programmer, have to ask something only *once*, rather than ask repeatedly. Once the programmer has established the loop pattern and the conditions for concluding (exiting from) the loop, the computer will continue looping and exit as it has been instructed to do. The loop is considered a powerful programming tool because the code is reusable and, once written, can be called upon many times.

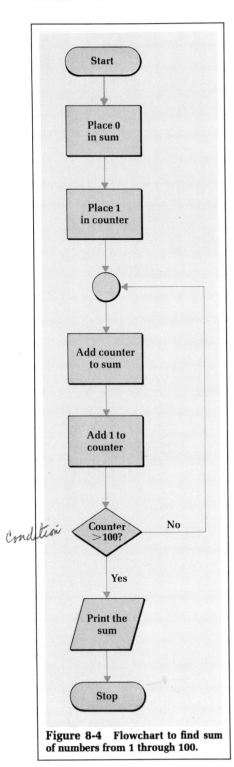

*Condition*

**Figure 8-4** Flowchart to find sum of numbers from 1 through 100.

## Structured Flowcharting

The techniques of flowcharting have been refined in a method known as **structured flowcharting,** which uses limited *control structures* to minimize the complexity of the programs and thus cut down on errors. Structured flowcharting is related to **structured programming,** an approach that emphasizes breaking a program into logical sections using certain universal programming standards.

Structured programming makes programs easier to write, check, read, and maintain. The computer industry widely accepts structured programming as the most productive way of programming. We will study structured programming in more detail in Chapter 10; that chapter provides the origin and rationale for structured programming and also places it in the broader context of structured design. For now, however, let us introduce some basic concepts of structure in this discussion of flowcharts.

There are three basic **control structures** or patterns in structured programming:

- Sequence
- Selection
- Iteration

These three are considered the basic building blocks of all program construction. You will see that we have used some of these structures already in Figures 8-3 and 8-4. The template in Figure 8-5 will be a

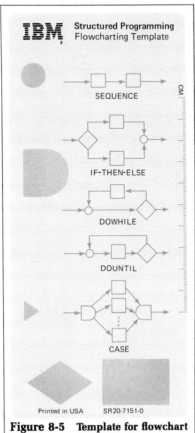

**Figure 8-5** Template for flowchart symbols for a structured program.

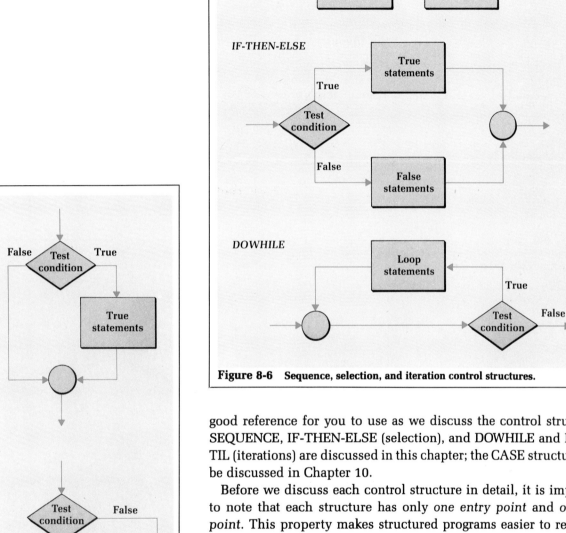

**Figure 8-6**  Sequence, selection, and iteration control structures.

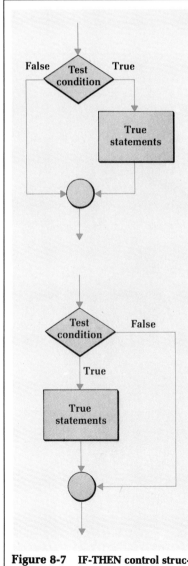

**Figure 8-7**  IF-THEN control structure.

good reference for you to use as we discuss the control structures. SEQUENCE, IF-THEN-ELSE (selection), and DOWHILE and DOUNTIL (iterations) are discussed in this chapter; the CASE structure will be discussed in Chapter 10.

Before we discuss each control structure in detail, it is important to note that each structure has only *one entry point* and *one exit point*. This property makes structured programs easier to read and to debug.

The **sequence control structure** is illustrated in Figure 8-6. One statement simply follows another in sequence. (As our discussion continues, you may find it helpful to look ahead to Figures 8-9 through 8-13 for actual examples of these control structures.)

The **selection control structure** is also shown in Figure 8-6. The IF-THEN variation is shown in Figure 8-7. IF-THEN is a special case of IF-THEN-ELSE. The IF-THEN-ELSE control structure works as follows: "IF (a condition is true), THEN (do something), ELSE (do something different)." For instance, "IF the alarm clock goes off and it is a weekend morning, THEN just turn it off and go back to sleep, ELSE get up and go to work." The IF-THEN selection is less complicated: "IF (condition is true), THEN (do something—but if it is not true, then do not do it)." Figure 8-7 gives two versions of diagramming the

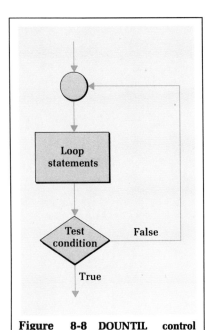

**Figure 8-8 DOUNTIL control structure.**

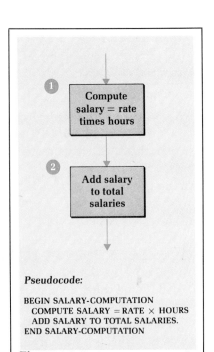

Pseudocode:

```
BEGIN SALARY-COMPUTATION
   COMPUTE SALARY = RATE × HOURS
   ADD SALARY TO TOTAL SALARIES.
END SALARY-COMPUTATION
```

**Figure 8-9 Sequence example: movie extras' salaries.** To compute total extras' wages, ❶ determine one extra's salary for that week's shooting. This is done by computing his or her hourly rate times the number of hours worked on the picture that week. ❷ Add that extra's salary to those of other extras to find the total.

same IF-THEN condition. Note that there will always be some resulting action using IF-THEN-ELSE; in contrast, the IF-THEN may or may not produce action, depending on the condition.

The **iteration control structure** is a looping mechanism. The only necessary iteration structure is the DOWHILE structure ("do . . . while"), as shown in Figure 8-6. Although DOUNTIL is not one of the three basic control structures, it is convenient to introduce the DOUNTIL structure ("do . . . until") now, as shown in Figure 8-8.

When looping, you must give an instruction to stop the repetition at some point, otherwise you will never get to the end of the program. There is a basic rule of iteration, which is related to structured programming: *If you have several statements that need to be repeated, a decision on when to stop repeating has to be placed either at the* ***beginning*** *of all the loop statements or at the* ***end*** *of all the loop statements.*

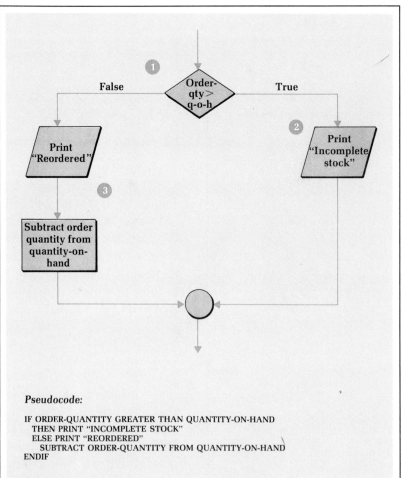

Pseudocode:

```
IF ORDER-QUANTITY GREATER THAN QUANTITY-ON-HAND
   THEN PRINT "INCOMPLETE STOCK"
   ELSE PRINT "REORDERED"
      SUBTRACT ORDER-QUANTITY FROM QUANTITY-ON-HAND
ENDIF
```

**Figure 8-10 IF-THEN-ELSE selection example: truck tires.** A trucker orders tires at a truck-tire warehouse. IF ❶ the order quantity for tires is greater than the quantity on hand, THEN ❷ the computer prints out "Incomplete stock." ELSE ❸ it prints out "Reordered" and subtracts the order quantity from the quantity on hand.

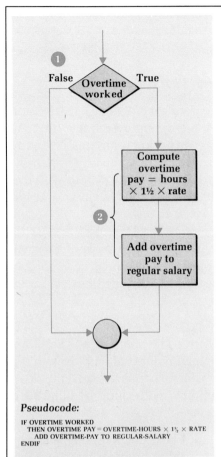

**Figure 8-11 IF-THEN selection example: Christmas season overtime.** IF ❶ department store employee worked overtime, THEN ❷ the program computes overtime pay by multiplying the overtime hours times 1½ times the hourly rate; the total is added to the employee's regular salary.

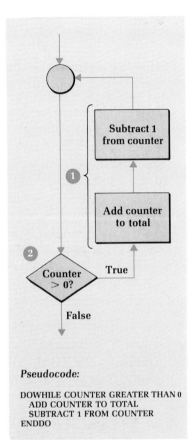

**Figure 8-12 DOWHILE iteration example.** Do ❶ add counter to total and subtract 1 from counter WHILE ❷ counter is greater than 0.

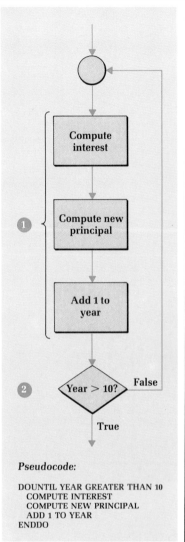

**Figure 8-13 DOUNTIL iteration example: computing loan interest and principal.** DO ❶ compute interest, compute principal, and add the number 1 to the total years. UNTIL ❷ the number of years is greater than 10.

Whether you put it at the beginning (*leading decision*) or at the end (*trailing decision*) constitutes the basic difference between DOWHILE and DOUNTIL. As Figure 8-6 shows, DOWHILE tests at the beginning of the loop; DOUNTIL tests at the end. (This means that with DOUNTIL the loop statements are guaranteed to execute at least once, because the loop statements will be executed *before* you make any test about whether to get out. Also, the test condition must be false to continue the loop.)

These basic control structures may seem a bit complex in the beginning, but in the long run they are the most efficient technique for programming, and it is worth taking your time to learn them. Figures 8-9 through 8-13 show more detailed examples of the use of the three control structures. These figures also include pseudocode as an alternative. (See the hints for writing pseudocode on p. 170.) Let us now consider two extended examples.

### Counting Salaries at Thunder Video Games

Suppose you have just been named president of Thunder Video Games Corp., which has 50 employees. You have discovered that the bookkeeper's office is so disorganized you do not know how many employees are making what salaries. You suspect the company is top-heavy with high salaries. You need to find out how many people make over $20,000 a year (high salaries), $10,000 to $20,000 (medium salaries), and under $10,000 (low salaries).

Figure 8-14 shows a solution to your problem. Note that, as the labels show, the entire flowchart is set up like a computer system, with input, process, and output operations. Now, let us go through the flowchart. The circled numbers below correspond to the circled numbers in the illustration.

We observe the following:

❶ We initialize four counters to zero. The one labeled "Employee counter" will keep track of the total number of employees in the company; the others—"High salary counter," "Medium salary counter," and "Low salary counter"—will count the numbers of employees in the salary categories.

❷ In the parallelogram-shaped input box, the computer will now read the salary. **Read** may be defined as bringing something that is outside the computer into memory; "read," in other words, means "get." The computer will get each employee's yearly salary.

❸ The first of the diamond-shaped decision boxes is a test condition that can go either of two ways—yes or no. Note that if the answer to the question, "Salary > $20,000?" is yes, then the computer will process this answer by adding a 1 to the high salary count. If the answer is no, the computer will ask, "Salary < $10,000?"— and so on ("<" means "less than," ">" means "greater than").

❹ For every decision box, no matter what decision is made, you must come back to a connector box. And, as the flowchart shows, each decision box has its own connector box. Note that, in this case, each connector box is directly below the decision box to which it is related.

❺ Whatever kind of salary, the machine adds 1 (for the employee) to the employee counter, and a decision box then asks, "Employee counter = 50?" (the total number of employees in the company).

❻ If the answer is no, the computer makes a loop back to the first connector box, and goes through the processing again. Note that this is a DOUNTIL loop, because the decision box is at the end rather than at the beginning of the computing process ("DO keep processing UNTIL the employee counter is equal to 50").

❼ When the answer is finally yes, the computer then goes to an output operation (parallelogram again) and prints out the salary count for each of the three categories. The computing process then stops.

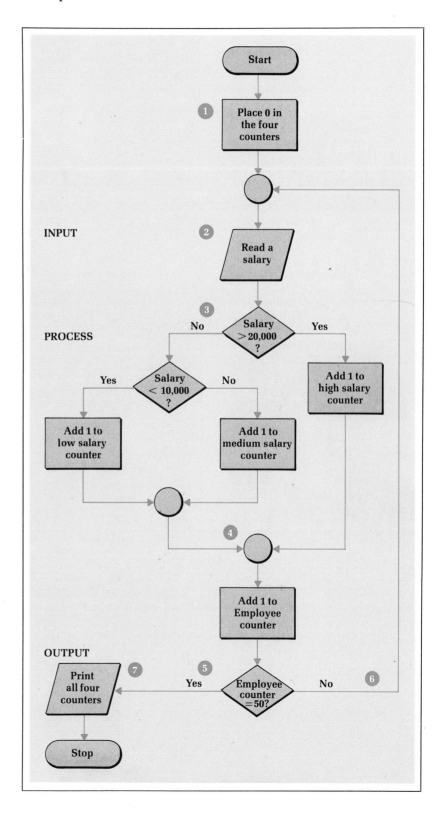

**Figure 8-14** Counting salaries at Thunder Video Games.

## HACKERS: PROGRAMMING ADDICTS

They are hardly ... the robotic, button-down androids that popular myth and the dress codes of the IBM Corporation have conditioned us to expect. On the contrary, they often seem as eccentric as their machines are logical and precise. Besides being sloppy dressers, they have been known to forget about food and sleep. Their primary interaction is with the computer, and computers have different standards from people. Computers don't care about looks or skin tone or personality. They will interface with anyone who can push a button. That's part of their appeal and also part of their curse.

"If you start off being introverted, it can suck you right in," says Jose Kalash, a self-described hacker at Berkeley. "It's like, 'Hey, I have a friend who will talk to me anytime.' You don't have to worry about somebody else laughing at you or saying no, because the computer always says yes—and it won't laugh at you unless you tell it to."

—Frank Rose,
*Science 82*,
November 1982

## The Double-Read Statement: Waldo's Big & Tall Menswear

In this example, illustrated in Figure 8-15, let us consider how to flowchart the checking of customers' credit balances at Waldo's Big & Tall Menswear. The file of customer records is kept on some computer-accessible medium, probably tape or disk. This is a more true-to-life notion than the Thunder Video Games example because, rather than a file with exactly 50 records, the file here has an unknown number of records. The program has to work correctly no matter how many customers there are.

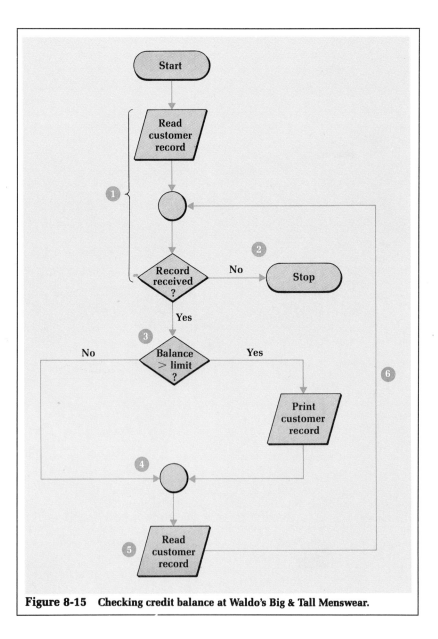

**Figure 8-15    Checking credit balance at Waldo's Big & Tall Menswear.**

As manager of Waldo's, you need to check the customer file and print out the record of any customer whose current balance exceeds his or her credit limit, so sales clerks will not mistakenly ring up sales and charges for customers over their limits. The interesting thing about this flowchart is that it has the same input operation *twice* (see the parallelograms), "Read customer record." We will see why this is necessary. Let us proceed through the flowchart:

❶ After reading the first customer record and proceeding through the connector box, you have a decision box that asks, "Record received?" This is a test to see if you have run out of all customer records (which you probably would not have the first time through, unless the store has already gone out of business).

*EOF - End of file* ❷ If the answer is no, you have reached an **end of file**—there are no more records in the file—and the processing stops.

❸ If the answer is yes, the program proceeds to another decision box, which asks, "Balance limit?" This is an IF-THEN type of decision.

❹ If the answer is yes, then the computer will print out the customer's record and move on to the connector box. If the answer is no, then the computer moves directly to the connector box.

❺ Now we come to the *second* Read statement, "Read customer record." Why are two such statements needed? Why could we not just forget the second one and loop back to the first Read statement again?

The answer lies in the rules of structure. As we stated, *a loop requires a decision either at the beginning or at the end.* If we omitted the second Read statement and looped back to the first Read statement, then the decision box to get us out of the loop ("Record received?") would be in the middle, not the beginning or the end of the loop. Why not put the decision box, "Record received?", at the end? You cannot, because then you would have done the processing *before* you were sure you even had a record to process.

In summary: The decision box cannot go at the end, the rules say it cannot be put in the middle, and therefore the decision must go at the beginning of the processing. Thus, the only way to read a second customer record after the computer has read the first one is to have the second Read statement where you see it. The first Read statement is sometimes called the *priming read*. This concept of the double-read may seem complicated at first, but it is very important. Rereading this material may help.

❻ Next, the program loops back to the connector box and repeats the processing. Incidentally, this is called a DOWHILE loop, because the decision box is at the beginning rather than at the end of the computing process ("DO keep processing WHILE records continue to be received").

## *Translating a Flowchart into a Program: Student Grades*

Now let us see how a flowchart, which is really just a kind of blueprint, gets translated into a computer program. You could type this program in on a computer terminal or key it on punched cards and then submit the cards to be read into the computer. It would deliver back to you, on a terminal screen or in printout form, the answers to the problems you seek. Figures 8-16 and 8-17, set side by side, show

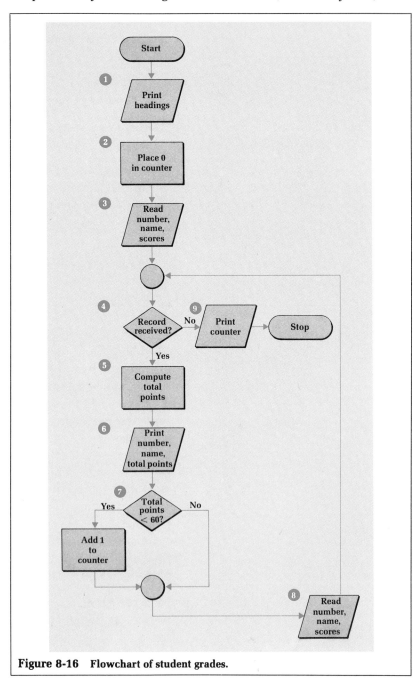

**Figure 8-16   Flowchart of student grades.**

how the flow of data and information in the flowchart translates into a similar flow in the program.

The program is written in the programming language called BASIC (described in more detail in Appendix A). BASIC is similar to English in many ways. You can understand the program even with no knowledge of BASIC.

```
10 REM PROGRAM TO COMPUTE STUDENT POINTS
20 REM
30 REM THIS PROGRAM READS, FOR EACH STUDENT,
40 REM    STUDENT NUMBER, STUDENT NAME, AND
50 REM    4 TEST SCORES. THE SCORES ARE TO
60 REM    BE WEIGHTED AS FOLLOWS:
70 REM
80 REM        TEST 1 - 20 PERCENT
90 REM        TEST 2 - 20 PERCENT
100 REM       MIDTERM - 25 PERCENT
110 REM       FINAL - 35 PERCENT
120 REM
130 REM VARIABLE NAMES USED:
140 REM
150 REM   C  COUNTER
160 REM   N  STUDENT NUMBER
170 REM   N$ STUDENT NAME
180 REM   S1 SCORE FOR TEST 1
190 REM   S2 SCORE FOR TEST 2
200 REM   S3 SCORE FOR MIDTERM
210 REM   S4 SCORE FOR FINAL
220 REM   T  TOTAL POINTS
230 REM
240 PRINT
250 PRINT "     STUDENT GRADE REPORT"
260 PRINT
270 PRINT "STUDENT", "STUDENT", "TOTAL"
280 PRINT "NUMBER", "NAME", "POINTS"
290 PRINT
300 PRINT
310 LET C = 0
320 READ N, N$, S1, S2, S3, S4
330 IF N = -9999 THEN 400
340 LET T = .20 * S1 + .20 * S2 + .25 * S3 + .35 * S4
350 PRINT N, N$, T
360 IF T >= 60 THEN 380
370 LET C = C+1
380 READ N, N$, S1, S2, S3, S4
390 GOTO 330
400 PRINT
410 PRINT "NUMBER OF STUDENTS WITH TOTAL POINTS LESS THAN 60:"; C
420 STOP
430 DATA 2164, "ALLEN SCHAAB", 60, 64, 73, 78
440 DATA 2644, "MARTIN CHAN", 80, 78, 85, 90
450 DATA 3171, "ALICE BRISTOW", 91, 95, 90, 88
460 DATA 5725, "CRAIG BARNES", 61, 41, 70, 53
470 DATA 6994, "RAOUL GARCIA", 95, 96, 90, 92
480 DATA 7001, "KAY MITCHELL", 55, 60, 58, 55
490 DATA -9999, "XXX", 0, 0, 0, 0
500 END
```

Figure 8-17   Computer program of student grades.

In Figure 8-17, the numbers in the far left column are called *statement numbers*. REM stands for a *remark statement*, which simply documents the program—a brief description of what it is supposed to do and a list of all *variable names*—symbolic names of locations in main storage. The *PRINT statement* tells the computer what message or data to print out, the *READ statement* reads the data to be processed, the *GOTO* ("go to") *statement* tells which statement the computer is to go to, and *DATA statements* list the data to be read by the computer.

Our problem is, first, to compute the student grades (ranging from 0 to 100) for six students, and, second, to count the number of students who have scored less than 60 points. The grade points are based on student performance on two tests, on a midterm exam, and on a final exam, the scores of which have been weighted in a certain way.

Once again, let us conceive of the problem in terms of input, process, and output—always a helpful way of sorting out the problems and setting up the solutions.

### Input

As before, the circled numbers in the text correspond to the circled numbers in the flowchart, Figure 8-16. Corresponding statement numbers from the program in Figure 8-17 follow in parentheses.

❶ "Print headings" (*lines 240-300*). These are the headings on the report (you can skip ahead to Figure 8-18 to see what they will look like). The first is the overall heading, "STUDENT GRADE REPORT," and the others are column headings—"STUDENT NUMBER," "STUDENT NAME," and "TOTAL POINTS." Lines that contain only the word PRINT, as line 240 does, cause blank lines to print on the output; this provides better spacing.

❷ "Place 0 in counter" (*line 310*). This is not a form of input data, but it is an initialization process required here at the outset. This counter will count the number of students who score less than 60 points, as we shall see later.

❸ "Read number, name, scores" (*line 320*). The input data is given in lines 430-490.

### Process

❹ "Record received?" (*line 330*). Note this is a DOWHILE loop, because the decision box is at the beginning of the process. In the BASIC language, DOWHILE must be implemented with IF-THEN-ELSE. The decision box asks if the particular student number, name, and scores read are the last ones in the file. How will the computer know this? Because the digits "—9999" will tell it "End of file." You will note the student numbers are four other digits (*see lines*

*430-480).* The —9999 decision instructs the computer to advance to the statement 400 when "End of file" is reached.

⑤ "Compute total points" (*line 340*). The scores are weighted 20 percent for the first test, 20 percent for the second text, 25 percent for the midterm, and 35 percent for the final exam. The total of these weighted scores gives the course grade. In the program, these percentages are documented in Remark statements, lines 30−120 and 160−220. This formula is stated in line 340. Here the expression ".20*S1" means "20 percent times first test score." (In BASIC, "*" is used as the multiplication symbol.)

⑥ "Print number, name, total points" (*line 350*). (Printing is really an output operation; we include it here for convenience because it is part of the loop.)

⑦ "Total points < 60?" (*line 360*). This decision box is given as an IF-THEN statement ("<" means "less than"). Note that we have reversed this decision in the program (>= is the reverse of <) to simplify the program. If the student's total points are at least 60, line 370, which increments counter C, will be bypassed.

⑧ "Read number, name, scores" (*line 380*). As we had in our last example, we have here an instance of a double-read statement. A GOTO statement is used to close the loop. That is, we repeat the input instruction given in number 3 above.

We now make the loop back to the first connector box and continue to DO this processing WHILE the answer to the question "Student record received?" is yes.

### Output

⑨ "Print counter" (*line 410*). When we reach the end of the file, we now also print out the total number of students with points less than 60. At this point, then, you should have the printout of results shown in Figure 8-18.

```
     STUDENT GRADE REPORT

STUDENT       STUDENT           TOTAL
NUMBER        NAME              POINTS


 2164         ALLEN SCHAAB       70.4
 2644         MARTIN CHAN        84.4
 3171         ALICE BRISTOW      90.5
 5725         CRAIG BARNES       56.5
 6994         RAOUL GARCIA       92.9
 7001         KAY MITCHELL       56.8

NUMBER OF STUDENTS WITH TOTAL POINTS LESS THAN 60:2
```

**Figure 8-18** **Printout of results of program in Figure 8-17.**

# "Unsung Heroes"

"Programmers are the unsung heroes of the computer age," write George and Victor Ledin in *The Programmers' Book of Rules.* "They are expected to produce programs that will run the first time, that can be changed easily at the whim of any user, and that are fast, well documented, and cost effective."

Moreover, they add, "professional programmers earn their pay solving problems that, even when conceptually simple, demand extreme attention to a multitude of details and that are frequently quite difficult from the programming point of view." In this chapter we have conveyed a glimpse of the "multitude of details" and the habits of mind and carefulness required to write programs. What we have described is just an overview, however; the exact process of producing a program from a flowchart is given in Appendix A.

It is important to emphasize that the programmer's chores often must be accomplished, as the Ledins note, "within the brutal but real constraints of a daily deadline"—a fact anyone contemplating a career in programming should keep in mind.

## Summary and Key Terms

- A beginning understanding of programming helps dispel the mysteriousness of the computer, and enables you to find out if programming is for you.

- Programmers work less with hardware than they do with people and software.

- There are five steps to preparing a program: (1) Define the problem; (2) plan the solution; (3) code the program; (4) test the program; and (5) document the program.

- In defining the problem, the programmer must first determine if his or her services are needed, then meet with the user to analyze the problem.

- Planning the solution can be done either by drawing a **flowchart**, which is a pictorial representation of an ordered, step-by-step solution to the problem, or by stating the solution in **pseudocode**, which is an English-like language.

- **Coding** the program means expressing the solution in a programming language, such as BASIC, COBOL, Pascal, FORTRAN, or PL/I.

- Testing the program consists of **desk-checking**, a mental checking of the program to reduce errors; **translating**, by which a program translates the programmer's program into language the computer can understand, using a **compiler** or **interpreter** that translates the entire program at one time and may give **diagnostic messages** regarding the use of the language as a by-product of the translation process; and **debugging**, in which the program is run with test data to rid the program of logic errors and other mistakes. **Documentation** is a written detailed description of the programming cycle and specific facts about the program. Some installations organize programmers into teams. Teams formally review each member's program design and coding.

- The standard symbols used in flowcharting are called ANSI symbols. **ANSI** stands for American National Standards Institute. The ANSI symbols commonly used are **decision, process, input/output, start/stop, direction of flow,** and **connector.**

- A **loop,** also called an **iteration,** is defined as the repetition of instructions under certain conditions.

- **Structured flowcharting** minimizes the complexity of programs. Structured flowcharting is related to **structured programming,** an approach that emphasizes breaking a program down into logical sections and makes programs easier to write, check, read, and maintain.

- There are three basic **control structures** or patterns in structured programming: sequence, selection, and iteration.

- In the **sequence control structure,** one statement simply follows another. The **selection control structure** is IF-THEN-ELSE: "IF (a condition is true), THEN (do something), ELSE (do something different)." The basic **iteration control structure** is DOWHILE ("do . . . while"); DOUNTIL ("do . . . until") is an alternate form of iteration.

- A basic rule of iteration that is related to structured programming is: If you have several statements that need to be repeated, a decision on when to stop repeating has to be placed either at the beginning of all the loop statements or at the end of all the loop statements. If you put it at the beginning, the loop is a DOWHILE; if you put it at the end, the loop is a DOUNTIL.

*Review*

1. Discuss the five steps needed to implement a program.
2. Define the term *flowchart*.
3. What are the phases of testing a program?
4. Draw six common flowcharting symbols.
5. What does ANSI stand for?
6. Describe initialization.
7. Give an example of a loop.
8. What are the three basic control structures of structured programming?
9. What are the two forms of the iteration control structure?

## IN THIS CHAPTER

Systems analysis and design are the processes by which a new organization or computer system supplants an old one. Using a variety of professional skills, the systems analyst—the change agent—moves through the five phases of preliminary investigation, systems analysis, systems design, systems development, and implementation and evaluation to complete a systems project.

# ch.9

# systems analysis and design

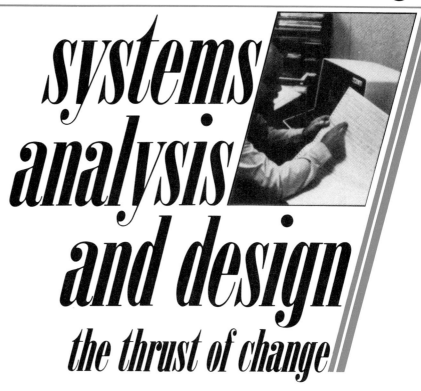

## the thrust of change

People are generally uncomfortable about change, even change in apparently minor matters. Philosopher Eric Hoffer told how, as a younger man, he spent a good part of one year as an agricultural worker picking peas, starting in southern California in January and working his way northward. He picked the last of the peas in June, then moved to another area where, for the first time, he was required to pick string beans. "I still remember," he wrote, "how hesitant I was that first morning as I was about to address myself to the string bean vines. Would I be able to pick string beans? Even the change from peas to string beans had in it elements of fear."

If small changes can cause uneasiness, large changes can cause considerable stress. And to many people the computer represents large changes.

*ch9*

## The Systems Analyst: Agent of Change

The boss tells you someone is coming to look over the work situation, ask you a few questions, "get a fix on the work flow, maybe see if we can't streamline some things and get them on a computer system."

Your ears perk up. *A computer?* Suddenly you feel very nervous. *They're going to take your job and give it to a computer!*

Congratulations. You are about to be visited by a systems analyst.

A systems analyst with any experience, however, *knows* that people are uneasy about having their job situations investigated, that they may be nervous about computers, and that they may react adversely by withholding their cooperation (sometimes subtly, sometimes quite aggressively). Attitudes depend, of course, on prior experience with computer systems. Systems author and consultant Gerald Weinberg advises, "It may be particularly useful for a would-be [systems] analyst to study people more than machines. After all, a chemical plant might be very different from an information plant, but one executive is pretty much like another executive. And more like a janitor than like a chemical plant."

What *is* a systems analyst? Let us start by defining what we mean by the words *system, analysis,* and *design.* A **system** is an organized set of related components established to accomplish a certain task. The lines you stand in, stations you go to, and forms you fill out on your college's registration day, for instance, comprise a system to get qualified students into the right classes. A computer system is a system that has a computer as one of its components.

**Systems analysis** is the process of evaluating a presently existing system to determine how it works and how it meets user needs. Systems analysis also lays the groundwork, in a broad sense, for improvements to the system. The analysis involves an investigation, which in turn usually involves establishing a relationship with the client for whom the analysis is being done and with the users of the system. The **client** is the person or organization contracting to have the work done. The **users** are people who will have contact with the system, usually employees and customers. For example, a systems analysis of college registration day requires that the analyst determine whether qualified students are enrolling in the classes they need, and whether the process is occurring at the least possible cost in time and money to both students and college administration. In this example, the client is the administration, and the user is both administration employees and students.

**Systems design** is the process of developing a plan for an improved system, based on the results of the systems analysis. For instance, the analysis may reveal that students waste time standing in lines when they register for spring semester, and that they could have done their registering in the closing weeks of the fall semester. The system design would involve making plans for the preregistration process.

The **systems analyst** normally performs both analysis and design. (The term *systems designer* is not common, although it is used in some places.) In some computer installations, a person who is officially a programmer may also do some systems analysis, and may have the title "programmer/analyst." Indeed, most persons who get into systems analysis do so by way of programming. Although some people believe that a systems analyst need not first be a programmer, it can be argued that starting out as a programmer helps one appreciate computer-related problems that arise in analysis and design work. As we shall see, programmers depend on systems analysts for specifications from which to design programs.

A systems analysis and design project does not spring out of thin air. There must be an *impetus* for change and related *authority* for the change. The systems study may be the result of an internal force, such as the organization's management deciding a computer could be useful in warehousing and inventory, or an external force, such as customer complaints about billing or government reporting requirements. But whatever the authority, it is the systems analyst who fills the role of *change agent*. That is, it is the analyst who must be the catalyst or persuader who overcomes the natural inertia and reluctance to change within an organization. The key to success is involvement of the people of the client organization in the development of the new system.

The systems analyst has three principal functions:

- **Coordination.** An analyst must coordinate schedules and system-related tasks with a number of people: his or her own boss; the programmers working with the system; the system's users, from clerks to top management; the vendors selling the computer equipment; and a host of others, such as postal employees handling mailings and carpenters doing installation.

- **Communication, both oral and written.** The analyst may be called upon to make oral presentations to clients, users, and others involved with the system. The analyst provides written reports—documentation—on the purpose and results of the analysis and the goals and means of the design. These documents may range from a few pages long to a few inches thick. Because documentation is so important in systems analysis and design, we will give it close attention in this chapter.

- **Planning and design.** The systems analyst, with the participation of the client organization, plans and designs the new system. This function involves all the activities from the beginning of the analysis until the final implementation of the system.

With these as principal functions, the kind of personal qualities that are desirable in a systems analyst must be apparent—a good analytical mind and good communication skills. Perhaps not so obvious, however, are qualities such as self-discipline and self-direction, and the ability to work well for long periods of time with few tangible results. Indeed, there will be times when the analyst feels that he or she has endured endless meetings and written numerous reports without much being accomplished. One has to have the patience to be able to survive such periods.

Let us suppose that you are blessed with these fortunate qualities and that you have become a systems analyst. You are given a job to do. How will you go about it?

# How a Systems Analyst Works: The Phases of a Systems Project

Whether you are investigating how to improve registration procedures at your college or any other task, a **systems project** may be defined as a project having five phases:

1. Preliminary investigation
2. Systems analysis
3. Systems design
4. Systems development
5. Implementation and evaluation

As you read about the phases of a systems project, follow the Portland Group Clinic case study in the adjacent boxes. Although space prohibits us from presenting a complete analysis and design project, this case study gives the flavor of the real thing.

Let us begin at the beginning.

## Phase 1: The Preliminary Investigation

The **preliminary investigation**—often called the **feasibility study** or **system survey**—is simply the initial investigation, a brief study of the problem. It consists of the groundwork necessary to determine if the systems project should be pursued further. Essentially this means you, as the systems analyst, must establish (a) the scope and (b) the true nature of the problem.

## Portland Group Clinic: Phase 1

### Preliminary Investigation

You are employed as a systems analyst by Software Resources, Inc., a company offering packaged and custom software as well as consulting services. Software Resources has received a request for a systems analyst from the Portland Group Clinic, a private medical facility. Your boss hands you this assignment, giving you the name of the clinic director, J. Scott Thompson.

In your initial meeting with Mr. Thompson, you learn that the Portland Group Clinic was established in 1976. It has grown from fewer than 100 members that first year to over 4000 members this year. Facilities and services have expanded proportionately, and the clinic has a good reputation in the community. Mr. Thompson, however, is disturbed about a growing collection of member complaints relating to the pharmacy. He has received conflicting internal reports on the nature of the problem and wants you to "start fresh" and determine the main issues. He introduces you to Gene Porter, who is in charge of pharmacy operations. Mr. Thompson also sends a memo to all pharmacy personnel, indicating the purpose of your presence and his support of the study.

In subsequent interviews with Mr. Porter and other pharmacy personnel, you find that deteriorating customer service seems to be due to overworked pharmacy staff and an inconvenient, overburdened data processing system. Together, you and the personnel further determine that the scope of this study will be limited to member prescription pro-

cessing. Mr. Thompson accepts your report, in which you outline the scope and nature of the problem and suggest a full analysis.

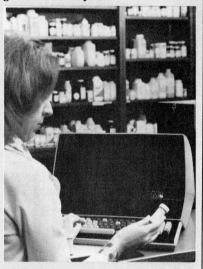

Establishing the scope of the problem is critical because problems tend to expand if no firm boundaries are established. Limitations are also necessary in order to stay within the eventual budget and schedule. To avoid trickling away energy and time, then, you must draw boundaries and decide just which part of the organization and phase of the procedures are going to be of concern. Tomorrow the world, perhaps; today the accounting department's accounts receivable . . .

As you establish the scope of the problem you should also determine its true nature. Sometimes what appears to be the problem turns out to be, or a closer look, only a symptom. For example, suppose you are examining customer complaints of late deliveries of next year's supplies of desk-calendar refills. Your brief study may reveal that the problem is not in the shipping department, as you first thought, but in the tail end of the manufacturing process at the factory.

The preliminary investigation, which is necessarily brief, should result in some sort of report, perhaps only a few pages long, telling management what you found and listing your recommendations. At this point, management has three choices: (1) drop the matter; (2) fix the problem immediately, if it is simple; or (3) authorize you to go on to phase 2.

### Phase 2: Systems Analysis

Let us suppose management has decided to continue. During the **systems analysis** phase, then, you will be concerned with (a) data gathering and (b) data analysis. Keep in mind that the system being analyzed may or may not already be a computerized system.

**Data Gathering** Data gathering is expensive and requires a lot of legwork and time—a good reason, therefore, why it is important during phase 1 that you accurately define the scope and true nature of the problem. Data gathering involves four principal sources of information:

- Written documents
- Questionnaires
- Interviews
- Observation

In the normal course of events you would pursue all four sources, but there will be times when it will be appropriate to use some and not others. All references to data gathering techniques assume that you have the proper authority and the cooperation of the client organization.

*Written documents* include procedures manuals, reports, forms, and any other kind of paper bearing on the problem that you find in the organization. Of course, some judgment is required: You will not wish to find yourself spending hours reading outdated reports or manuals no one follows. And, of course, there may not *be* any procedures manuals or helpful documentation. In any case, you should collect what you can find for use during data analysis.

*Questionnaires* can be quite useful. They save time and therefore expense. They can be used to cover large groups of people simultaneously. They allow people to respond to a question anonymously— people just complete forms and turn them in—and presumably more truthfully. Questionnaires do have drawbacks, however. A great many questionnaires will simply lie at the bottom of people's IN-baskets and never be returned. Some people will not return them no matter what kind of inducement because they are wary of putting *anything* on paper, even anonymously. And those you do get back may tend to have biased answers.

Because accurate, complete answers are so difficult to obtain, some people take classes on the subject of questionnaire construction. Although you need not go to such lengths, some reading on the subject is worthwhile. There are many types of questionnaires—for example, the box type, in which the respondent simply checks off "yes" or "no," or the qualified response, in which one rates his or her agreement/disagreement with the question on a scale from, say, 1 to 5. In general, people prefer a questionnaire that is quick and simple. If you have long, open-end questions, such as "Please describe your job functions," you should probably save them for an interview.

*Interviews,* too, have advantages and disadvantages. They are useful in that they are flexible; as the interviewer, you can change the direction of your questions if you perceive a fertile area of investigation. You can also observe the respondent's voice inflection and body motions, which may tell you more than words alone. You will find that some respondents yield more information in an interview than they would if they had to commit themselves to paper. Finally, of course, there is the bonus of getting to know clients better and

### SOME TIPS FOR SUCCESSFUL INTERVIEWING

- Plan questions in advance—even if you vary from them during the interview.
- Listen carefully to the answers, and observe the respondent's voice inflection and body movements for clues to evaluate responses.
- Dress and behave in a businesslike manner.
- Avoid technical jargon.
- Respect the respondent's schedule.
- Avoid office gossip and discussion of the respondent's personal problems.

establishing a rapport with them—important in gaining user involvement in the system from the beginning. However, interviews are unquestionably a time-consuming, and therefore expensive, method of getting information. You will not be able to do a great many interviews because you will not have enough hours in the day. Another disadvantage is that your client may not be cooperative, although you may be able to gain client trust as you go along.

Interviews are of two types—structured and unstructured. The *structured interview* includes only questions that have been planned and written out in advance. The interviewer sticks to those questions and asks no others. In other words, the structured interview resembles a written questionnaire. A structured interview is useful when it is desirable to ask the same questions of several people. However, the unstructured interview is often more productive. An *unstructured interview* includes questions prepared in advance, but the interviewer is willing to vary from the line of questioning and pursue other subjects if they seem appropriate. In both cases, however, it is important to plan questions in advance. You should never go into an interview with the idea of just chatting in hopes that something useful will turn up.

*Observation* is just that: You go into the organization and simply watch, observing the flow of data, who interrelates with whom, how paper moves from desk to desk, and how it comes into and leaves the organization. Normally you would make arrangements with a group supervisor, perhaps be given a desk, and return on more than one occasion so that the people under observation become used to your presence. The purpose of your visits is known to the members of the organization. One form of observation is *participant observation;* in this form the analyst temporarily joins the activities of the group. This practice may be useful in studying a complicated organization.

**Data Analysis** Your observations, interviews, and perusal of written documents and questionnaires completed, it is now time to turn your attention to the second activity of this phase, data analysis. What, indeed, are you going to do with all the data you have gathered? Here are some typical products:

- An organization chart
- Data flow diagrams
- Decision tables

Figure 9-1 shows an example of the first of these, an **organization chart.** Constructing such a chart is not an idle task. If you are to work effectively within the organization—especially during the systems design phase—you have to understand what the lines of authority are through the formal communication channels. The organization chart will vary, of course, with the nature of the organization.

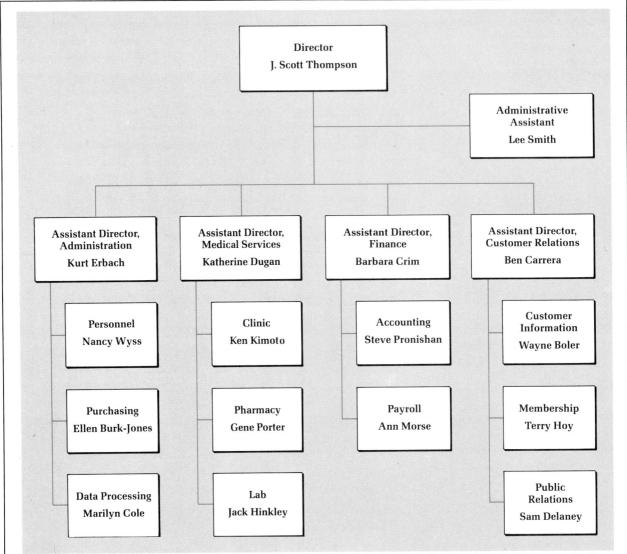

**Figure 9-1    An organization chart** shows the lines of authority and formal communications channels. This example shows the organizational setup of the Portland Group Clinic, a private medical facility whose director is J. Scott Thompson.

A **data flow diagram,** illustrated in Figure 9-2, graphically shows the flow of data through a system. This "road map" is a valuable tool for depicting present procedures and information flow. Standard practices are followed in drawing a data flow diagram. Input to the system is indicated by a rectangle. Procedural steps are indicated by boxes with rounded corners. Sources of data needed for a particular procedure are indicated by boxes that are open on the right.

A **decision table** (also called a "decision logic table") is a standardized table of the logical decisions that must be made regarding the conditions that may occur in a given system. Decision tables are useful for a series of interrelated decisions; their use helps to ensure that no alternatives will be overlooked. Programmers can code portions of programs right from a decision table. Figure 9-3(a) shows the format for a decision table; Figure 9-3(b) gives an example of one applied to a particular situation.

The table works as follows: The *heading* indicates the procedure or problem the table is set up to solve. The numbers across the top (there can be more than five numbers) are headings for the vertical columns. Each column represents a set of conditions and the corresponding actions; it shows a *rule* to be followed. The logic of the table is "If these conditions exist, then take these actions." On the left

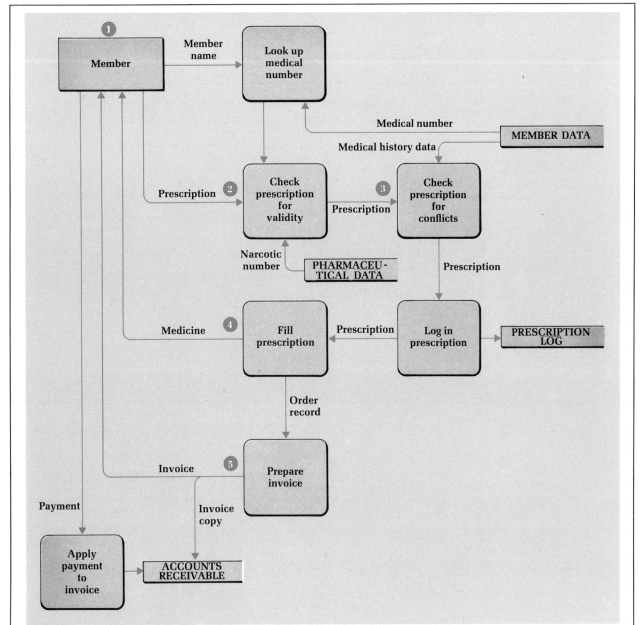

**Figure 9-2   A data flow diagram.**  This "map" shows a possible prescription refill system for the Portland Group Clinic. A patient-member ❶ may present a prescription ❷ at the clinic pharmacy, which the computer system checks for possible health conflicts with other medications ❸ and then prepares the prescribed medication ❹ and invoice ❺.

side of the table are the *condition stub*, which describes the different conditions, and the *action stub*, which describes the different actions. The *condition entries* are listed under the rule numbers and are either Y for "yes" if the condition exists or N for "no" if it does not. (A "—" means the condition does not apply.) The *action entries* indicate which actions to take under a certain set of conditions. The example given in Figure 9-3(b) is a decision table describing a prescription refill procedure, and the action entries vary according to the conditions applying to a particular prescription. Thus, if your prescription is for a controlled substance but is not class 1 or class 2, and the number of refills has not been exceeded, as indicated by the condition entries in rule 4, then your prescription will be filled.

These data analysis vehicles are typical, but the list presented here is by no means exhaustive.

 **Report to Management** When you have finished the systems analysis phase, you present a report to management. This comprehensive report, part of the continuing process of documentation, summarizes the

|  | Rules | | | | |
|---|---|---|---|---|---|
| Heading | Rule numbers | | | | |
|  | 1 | 2 | 3 | 4 | 5 |
| Condition stub (If . . .) | Condition entries | | | | |
| Action stub (then . . .) | Action entries | | | | |

**Figure 9-3(a)  Format of decision table.** The structure of the table is organized according to the logic that "If this condition exists or is met, then do this."

| Refill procedure (by drug classification) | Rule number | | | | | | |
|---|---|---|---|---|---|---|---|
|  | 1 | 2 | 3 | 4 | 5 | 6 | 7 |
| Controlled substance | Y | Y | Y | Y | N | N | N |
| Class 1: Illegal | Y | N | N | N | — | — | — |
| Class 2: Refills prohibited | — | Y | N | N | — | — | — |
| Prescription drug | — | — | — | — | Y | Y | N |
| Over-the-counter drug | — | — | — | — | — | — | Y |
| Number of refills exceeded | — | — | Y | N | Y | N | — |
| Fill prescription |  |  |  | X |  | X | X |
| Reject prescription | X | X | X |  | X |  |  |
| Call doctor |  | X |  |  |  |  |  |
| Notify authorities | X |  |  |  |  |  |  |

**Figure 9-3(b)  A decision table.** This example shows the prescription refill procedure for the Portland Group Clinic pharmacy.

# *T*he *"A*ll-*P*urpose *M*achine*"*

## The Many, Often Hidden, Uses of Computing

Computer pioneer John Von Neumann said the device should not be called the computer but rather the "all-purpose machine." It is not, after all, just a machine for doing calculations. The most striking thing about it is that it can be put to *any number of uses.* Though by no means all-encompassing, the uses presented in this double-length gallery include examples from the public sector—including government, education, the military, transportation, and science and medicine—and parts of the private sector concerned with commerce, the automated office, manufacturing, energy, and food and agriculture. Some uses may surprise you.

❶ Following the computer-generated animated figure on the screen, a ballet dancer executes a *sauté à la seconde.* Computer graphic systems permit new systems of dance notation.

The public and nonprofit sector: ❷ ❸ Students at all educational levels—including college, as shown here—are becoming involved with computers in record numbers. ❹ to ❻ State and local governments use computers in varied ways: to analyze customer electric-power demands, to assist in police communications, and to analyze unemployment data.

In peace and war: **7** to **12** The federal government is the largest computer user, whether for air traffic control, routing mail, launching the Columbia Space Shuttle, or developing fighter aircraft and new torpedos.

Transportation: **13** **14** Modern shipping, such as the "President Pierce" here, uses computerized navigation aids. **15** Airlines use computers in the cockpit and in reservations. **16** High-performance tires are computer-designed.

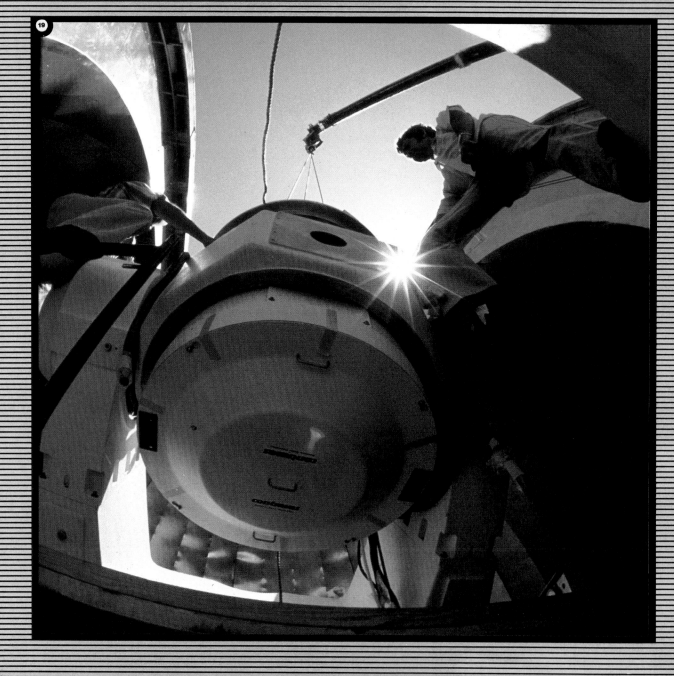

Science and medicine: **17** to **19** Science uses computers to record and analyze data, as in these experiments in chemistry and in fusion testing, or to assist in ground tracking of space vehicles. **20** The Centers for Disease Control in Atlanta, Georgia, use computers for epidemiological data. **21** A San Antonio, Texas, nursing home computerizes patient records and accounting functions.

Commerce and the automated office: **22** The New York Stock Exchange uses bar codes to provide on-line tracking of securities. **23** A regional stock exchange uses a computer-controlled information network. **24** Office automation is especially necessary in banking; here a Fort Worth, Texas, bank teller checks a transaction. **25** Ergonomics—ease of use—is important in office automation, as represented by the maneuverability of this computer keyboard. **26** An overhead view of a modern office.

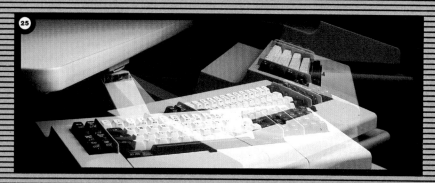

**Design and manufacturing:**
**27** A computerized drawing tablet aids in pharmaceutical research.
**28** Aerodynamics can be computer-tested prior to prototype.
**29** Computerized scheduling helps produce Fisher-Price toys.
**30** A General Motors robot paints a car.

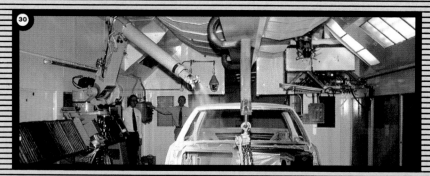

Energy and food: **31** **32** Computers help geologists evaluate exploration potential for minerals and petroleum. **33** to **35** Agriculture and food processing depend on computers for crop planning and harvesting—including new machines that pick tomatoes by computerized laser-scanning mechanisms—and scheduling and production planning, as in the bakery shown here.

**Computer beef:** 36 37 Nary a computer in sight? It takes people to herd cattle in a cattle feedlot or to erect a sign for a new McDonald's, but all the business organization of getting a hamburger into your hands is fully computerized.

## Portland Group Clinic: Phase 2

### Systems Analysis

With the assistance of Mr. Porter, you begin to learn more about the current pharmacy system. Pharmacy records are computerized, using a system established when the clinic was new. As part of your data gathering procedures, you examine the user manuals, computer-produced reports on pharmaceutical supplies and member medical histories, the manual records maintained by pharmacy personnel, and several forms used to record and input data.

Since member complaints were the impetus for the study, a member questionnaire is considered. A mass mailing is rejected in favor of having members fill out questionnaires while they wait for their prescriptions to be filled. Their replies indicate excessive waiting time and occasional lost or incorrect prescriptions. You continue to interview pharmacy personnel and also spend several hours with Marilyn Cole, head of the data processing department. You observe that members often

do not have their medical numbers available, so their records must first be looked up by name; pharmacy personnel spend most of their time cross-checking bound computer reports for member and pharmaceutical data; new prescriptions are not always logged in properly or on a timely basis; data preparation on forms is often haphazard; the pharmacy staff is rushed and under stress and often works late hours to "catch up."

During this period, you also analyze the data as it is gathered. With the help of Mr. Thompson, you construct the organization chart shown in Figure 9-1, p. 196. You obtain the additional information that the pharmacy has three full-time pharmacists, two part-time pharmacists, three assistants, and two clerks. You prepare data flow diagrams of the various activities relating to the pharmacy. Figure 9-2, p. 197, shows the general flow of data to fill a member prescription in the existing system. You prepare various decision

tables, such as the one shown in Figure 9-3(b), p. 198, for refilling prescriptions.

Your written report to Mr. Thompson includes a summary of the problems. You also recommend, in broad terms, a new system based on on-line terminal access to member and pharmaceutical data files, to improve accuracy and efficiency.

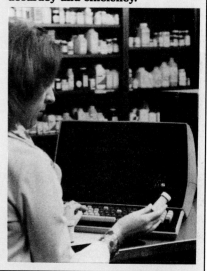

problems you found, suggests the broad outlines of alternative solutions, and makes recommendations as to what course to take next. If management decides to pursue the project, you move on to phase 3.

## Phase 3: Systems Design

Normally, in the *systems design* phase, parts of the systems are considered in this order:

- Output requirements
- Input requirements
- Files and data bases
- System processing
- System controls and backup

As you move into the systems design phases, you may become involved in possible hardware purchases—terminals, printers, even a computer. Of course, you, as the analyst, probably are not an expert in all these things. Where do you get help? One helpful publication is *DATAPRO*, a kind of consumer's guide to hardware and software. Experts evaluate user surveys on every imaginable computer-related topic, and monthly updated pages are sent to subscribers, usually libraries.

**Output Requirements** Before you can do anything, you must know what the client wants the system to produce—the *output*. You must also consider the *medium* of the output—whether paper, CRT screen, microfilm, and so on. In addition, you must determine the *contents* of the output—what types of reports will be needed (summary, exception, and so on) and what data is needed for the reports. What *forms* the output will be printed on is also a consideration; you may wish to consider preprinted forms, especially for external reports. You need to determine the *report format* using a **printer spacing chart** that shows how headings are positioned, the spacing between columns, and where date and page number are located (see Figure 9-4). You may also want to require a *user-computer dialogue* of some sort, and you may need to devise some examples of how this might work (see Figure 9-5).

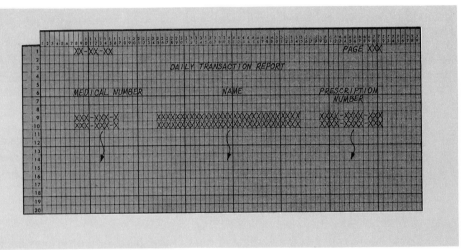

**Figure 9-4 Example of printer spacing chart.** This chart shows how a systems analyst wishes the report format to look—headings, columns, and so on—when displayed on a line printer.

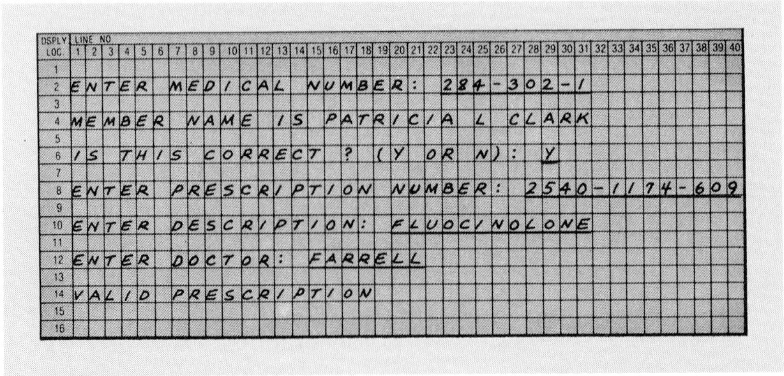

**Figure 9-5 Example of CRT dialogue.** A systems analyst might create an example such as this one to show user-computer dialogue. The data keyed in by the operator is underlined in this example.

**Input Requirements** You might have expected to have to consider *input* first, before output, but that is not so; you need to know what is wanted first. However, once output is determined, you should consider what kind of input is required to produce the output you want. First you must consider the input *medium:* Will you try to capture data at the source? Put it on floppy disks? Next you must consider *content* again— what fields are needed, the order in which they come, and the like. This in turn may involve designing *forms* for people to fill out. Like questionnaire construction, forms design is a whole subject by itself. For instance, for the sake of brevity, a form may require the person filling it out to use some *codes* (such as *F* for "female" or *M* for "male" or numbers corresponding to one's level of education). You need to plan some kind of input *editing* stage, a check as to whether the data is reasonable. A check for reasonableness can take many forms. A scrutiny of company salaries, for instance, would signal that it is reasonable for the president to earn a salary in six figures but not for someone working in the mailroom. Finally, you need to consider input *volume*, particularly at peak periods, to make sure the system can handle it; a mail order house, for instance, is apt to register higher sales of expensive toys at Christmastime than at other times of the year.

**Files and Data Bases** You need to consider how the files in your computer system will be organized, whether sequentially, directly, with an index, or by some other method. You also need to decide how the files should be accessed; they might be organized as indexed files but be accessed directly or sequentially. A helpful form is the **record layout form** (see Figure 9-6), which can be used to describe the format of records making up the data files. If the system has one

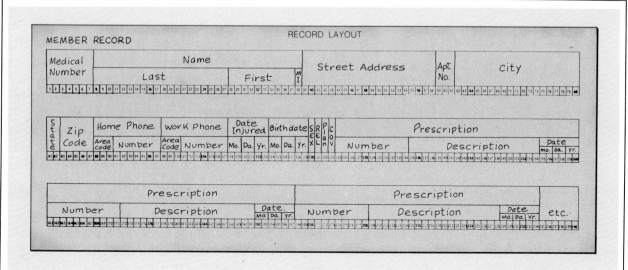

**Figure 9-6   Record layout form.** Systems analysts use this kind of form to describe the formats of records in data files.

## Portland Group Clinic: Phase 3

### Systems Design

The pharmacy staff members, who were uneasy at the beginning of the study, are by now enthusiastic participants in the design of the new system they are counting on for some relief. After designing some typical output in the form of reports (see Figure 9-4), you and some pharmacy users put together a CRT dialogue to validate and record prescriptions (see Figure 9-5). You choose to input prescription transactions using CRTs located in the pharmacy. Also needed is a plastic card containing a member's medical number, which he or she can present with a prescription

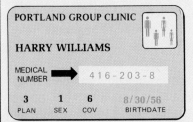

**Membership card.** Members of the Portland Group Clinic carry cards like this for presentation at the pharmacy.

order. The use of this card is expected to reduce inaccuracies significantly.

Three principal files will be needed, all on disk. The first two are the member file and the pharmaceutical file, which will be direct access files. Each new transaction will be added to the end of the transaction file, which will later be sorted by medical number for reporting purposes. The record layout for the member file is shown in Figure 9-6. Figure 9-8 shows a skeleton version of a systems flowchart for processing prescriptions. Several systems controls are planned, among them a unique numbering system for prescription forms and editing of all data input at the terminal.

You make a formal presentation to Mr. Thompson, Mr. Porter, and other members of the clinic management, using a flip chart to accent your points visually. After a brief statement of the problem, you list anticipated benefits relating to the pharmacy: faster service, improved accuracy in prescription records, better management information, and

the need for two fewer assistants and one less clerk. You explain the design and describe the expected costs and schedules. With the money saved from the reduced payroll, you project that the systems development costs will be amortized in two years. The clinic management accepts your proposal.

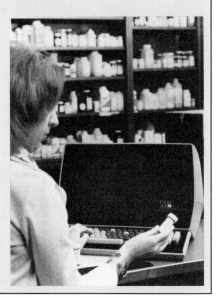

or more *data bases,* collections of interrelated data (a subject we will cover at length in Chapter 16), then you will have to coordinate your systems design efforts with the data base administrator, the person responsible for controlling and updating data bases.

**System Processing** Just as you drew a data flow diagram to describe the old system, now you need to show the flow of data in the new system. You need to choose what operations will be necessary—edit, sort, update, retrieve, report, and so on—and, using standard ANSI flowchart symbols (see Figure 9-7), put them together in a drawing that illustrates what will be done and what files will be used. Figure 9-8 shows an example of a systems flowchart. Note that a systems flowchart is not the same as a logic flowchart. The systems flowchart describes only the "big picture"; a logic flowchart (which you may have used to write programs) gives detailed program logic.

**System Controls and Backup** To make sure data is input, processed, and output correctly, and to prevent fraud and tampering with the computer system, you will need to institute appropriate system controls. We begin with the source documents, such as time cards or

**Figure 9-7  ANSI systems flowchart symbols.** These are the symbols recommended by the American National Standards Institute for flowcharts that show the movement of data through a system.

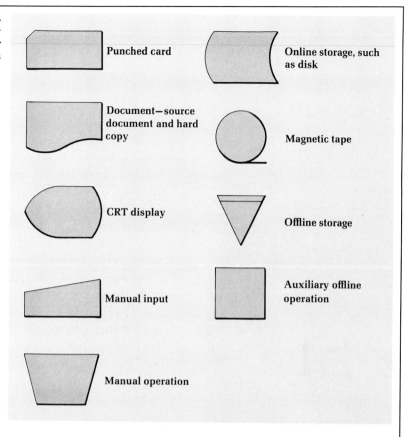

**Figure 9-8  Systems flowchart** for processing prescriptions in the Portland Group Clinic pharmacy. When the prescription is obtained from the patient ➊, the pharmacist ➋ checks the member's file ➌ to see what other medications he or she is taking. The pharmacist then checks to see if the present prescription conflicts with these other medications ➍, referring to a pharmaceutical file ➎. As the prescription is being filled, the member's file is updated ➏ and the sale of the prescription is recorded on the pharmacy's transaction file ➐. Finally, a prescription label is prepared automatically ➑ and is printed out ➒. The "lightning bolt" flowlines at the beginning and end of this flowchart indicate that the computer is accessed directly from a CRT.

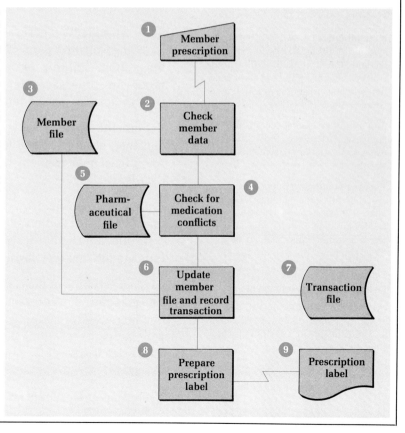

sales orders. Each document should be serially numbered and accounted for. Documents are time-stamped when received and grouped in batches. Each batch is labeled with the count of the number of documents per batch; these counts are balanced against totals of the processed data. The input is controlled to make sure data is accurately converted from source documents to machine-processable form. Processing controls include the data editing procedures we mentioned under input requirements.

It is also important to plan for backup of system files: copies of transaction and master files should be made on a regular basis. These file copies are stored temporarily to back up the originals if they are inadvertently lost or damaged.

**Making a Presentation to Management** Once you have your systems design plan in hand, you come to a step that is as critical as the plan itself: presenting it to higher management. Even if the scheme is good, it will not necessarily be adopted. Further, it does not make sense for someone else to stand up and make the presentation. You have done the systems analysis and design, so you should do it.

Consider the following for your presentation:

- **State the problem.** Although you do not want to belabor the problem part, you do want to show you understand it. Some of the people to whom you are making your presentation may already have some knowledge of the problem.

- **State the benefits.** These, after all, are a new system's whole reason for being; so your argument here should be carefully planned. Will the system improve accuracy, speed turnaround service, save processing time, save money? Whatever the benefits, the more specific you can be, the better.

- **Explain the design.** Here you should just give a general presentation and then be prepared to take questions about details. Remember that higher management will not be interested in hearing all the details.

- **Present a schedule.** How long is it going to take to carry out the plan? Give your audience the time frame. Sometimes systems analysts offer alternative design plans, with alternative schedules, and indicate the one they favor and why.

- **Give an estimate of the costs.** The costs include *development costs* (those required to construct the system) and *operating costs* (those ongoing costs of running the system). You will also need to tell your audience how long it is going to be before they get a return on their original investment—in other words, when the system is going to pay off.

- **Use visual aids.** People may not be receptive if you just talk or read to them. Therefore, arrange to present flip charts, slides, or over-

**WHAT IS ANALYSIS?**

- It certainly isn't easy. . . . In the largest systems for the most convoluted organizations, the diplomatic skills that the analyst must bring to bear are comparable to the skills of . . . negotiating for peace in the Middle East.

- The interpersonal relationships of analysis, particularly those involving users, are complicated, sometimes even hostile.

- There is nothing definite about analysis. It is not even obvious when the analysis phase is done. For want of better termination criteria, the analysis phase is often considered to be over when the time allocated for it is up!

- Largely because it is so indefinite, analysis is not very satisfying.

So analysis is frustrating, full of complex interpersonal relationships, indefinite, and difficult. In a word, it is fascinating.

—Tom Demarco,
*Structured Analysis and
System Specification*

head projector transparencies—or at the very least an illustrated handout—to help get your points across. The preparation of visual aids should be done with as much care as the preparation of the rest of the presentation.

- **Be prepared for questions.** The question-and-answer period will make you appreciate the value of having involved the system user from the very beginning. After all, the audience for the presentation *is* the user (or his or her boss), and you would hope to have resolved the stickiest questions well before this point.

After this effort, you will find that probably no one will applaud. Perhaps, however, they will say, "Yes, proceed with phase 4."

### *Phase 4: Systems Development*

Finally, the system is actually going to be developed. You will prepare a schedule to monitor the principal activities in **systems development:**

- Programming
- Testing
- Documentation

**Schedule** Figure 9-9 shows what is known as a **Gannt chart,** a bar chart commonly used to depict schedule deadlines and milestones. In our example, the chart shows the work to be accomplished over a given period of time. It does not, however, show the number of work-hours required. If you are the supervisor, it will be common practice for you to ask other people on the development team to produce individual Gannt charts of their own activities.

**Programming** Until this point there has been no programming. (Sometimes people jump the gun and start programming early, but the task will often have to be done over again because they began programming with incomplete specifications.) Before programming

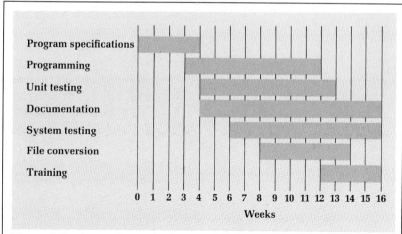

**Figure 9-9  Gannt chart.** This bar chart shows the scheduled tasks and milestones of the Portland Group Clinic pharmacy project.

## Portland Group Clinic: Phase 4

### Systems Development

Working closely with Ms. Cole of data processing, you prepare a Gannt chart, as shown in Figure 9-9. This chart shows the schedule and milestones for the pharmacy project.

Program design specifications are prepared using pseudocode, the design tool Ms. Cole thinks will be most useful to the programmers. The programs will be written in COBOL, since that is the primary language of

the installation, and it is suitable for this business application. Two programmers are assigned to the project.

Some prescription data, both typical and atypical, is prepared to test the new system. You and the programmers continue to build on the documentation base by adding the pseudocode, detailed data descriptions, logic narratives, program listings, test data results, and other related material.

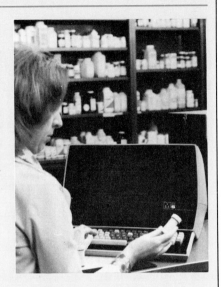

begins, you need to prepare detailed design specifications, including, of course, selecting the programming language. Design specifications can be developed through detailed flowcharts and pseudocode, among other methods. The language will be chosen for its appropriateness to the job (for example, COBOL for business uses, FORTRAN for engineering uses) or because it is standard to the installation in which you are working.

**Testing** Would you write a program and then simply turn it over to the client without testing it first? Of course not. Thus, the programmers working with you perform some *desk checking* before they run their programs on the computer; then *unit testing*, by which they individually test their own programs, using test data; and finally *system testing*, seeing that all the programs work together satisfactorily. During this process you would use test data representing as many different types of cases as possible and test every part of the programs to make sure they are in working order.

**Documentation** As in every phase of the project, documentation is required. Indeed, documentation is an ongoing activity (as the Gannt chart in Figure 9-9 showed). In this phase, however, documentation describes the program logic and detailed data formats.

### Phase 5: Implementation and Evaluation—Up and Running

Even though **implementation and evaluation** are the final phase, a good deal of effort is still required, including the following activities:

- File conversion
- System conversion
- Evaluation
- Training
- Auditing
- Maintenance

**File Conversion** This activity means that data that used to be handled manually now has to be prepared in such a way that it is accessible to computer systems. All the file drawers of folders in the personnel department, for instance, must now be converted to disk or magnetic tape files. Clearly, this step will require some time and usually the hiring of several temporary employees to do the conversion.

**Training** Often systems analysts do not give training the attention it deserves because they are so concerned about the computer system itself. But a system can be no better than the people operating it. A good time to start training is at some point during the testing, so that people can begin to learn how to use the system even as you are checking it out. An important tool in training is the *user's manual*, a document prepared to aid users not familiar with the computer system. The user's manual can be an outgrowth of the other documentation you are providing. An *operator's manual* should also be prepared; this book contains instructions to help computer personnel run the programs.

**System Conversion** This is the stage in which you actually "pull the plug" on the old system and begin using the new one. There are four ways of handling the conversion. **Direct conversion** means the user simply stops using the old system and starts using the new one—

---

**Portland Group Clinic: Phase 5**

**Implementation and Evaluation**

While the system is being developed, you take advantage of this time to write the user and operator manuals. This is done in conjunction with your plans for training pharmacy personnel (and operators) in the use of the system. The training for this project is uncomplicated for two reasons: (1) the small pharmacy staff has been involved in the project from the beginning, and (2) the CRT dialogue procedures are "user friendly"; that is, the user is instructed clearly every step of the way. You also prepare a familiarization letter to be sent to all members with their new plastic member cards. In addition, instructional signs (ALWAYS CARRY YOUR MEMBERSHIP CARD WITH YOU) are prepared for the pharmacy waiting room.

After discussing the relative merits of the various system conversion methods, you and Mr. Porter agree that a parallel period of one month is necessary. It was agreed previously that a file will be kept of all prescription transactions; this file can serve both as an audit trail and for reporting purposes.

This has been such a close work association that you expect an in-house team of, say, one of the pharmacists and a different programmer/analyst to evaluate the system. Mr. Thompson surprises you, however, by bringing in another consultant, Janna Hanson, for this function. Since your documentation is comprehensive, it is relatively easy for Ms. Hanson to check the system from stem to stern to see if it is functioning according to specifications. Her detailed report notes several positive items: Prescription wait time is a maximum of 10 minutes, prescription records are approximately 98 percent accurate, the pharmacy staff understands and accepts the new system, and an assistant position vacated through attrition does not need to be filled. Negative items are relatively minor and can be fixed as the system goes into a maintenance operation.

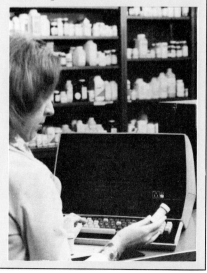

a somewhat risky method, since if anything goes wrong there is no other system to fall back on. This procedure is best followed only if the old system is nonexistent or in unusable condition. A **phased conversion** is one in which the new system is eased into, one step at a time, so that all the users are using some of the system. The reverse is the **pilot conversion,** in which the entire system is used by some of the users—and is extended to all users once it has proved successful. **Parallel conversion**—the most prolonged and expensive method—is that in which the old and new systems are operated simultaneously for some time, until users are satisfied that the new system performs to their standards.

System conversion is often a time of stress and confusion for all concerned. As the analyst, your credibility is on the line, for you must now come up with a usable system. During this time, users are often doing double duty, trying to perform their regular jobs and simultaneously cope with a new computer system. Problems seem to appear in all areas, from input to output. Clearly, this is a period when your patience and tenacity are needed.

**Auditing** Security violations, whether deliberate or unintentional, can be difficult to detect. Once data is in the system and on media such as disk or magnetic tape, it is possible for it to be altered without any trace to the original source documents—unless the systems analyst has designed an **audit trail** back to the source data. Real-time systems can be particularly elusive unless all CRT terminal transactions are recorded on disk or tape for later references by auditors. Modern auditors no longer shuffle mountains of paper; instead, they have computer programs of their own to monitor application programs and data.

**Evaluation** Is the system working? How well is it meeting the original goals, specifications, costs, timing, and so forth? Out of such evaluation will come adjustments that will improve the system. Approaches to evaluation vary. Sometimes the systems analyst and someone from the client organization evaluate the system against preset criteria. Some organizations prefer to bring in an independent evaluating team, on the assumption that the people in it will be free from bias and preconceived expectations.

**Maintenance** The maintenance process assumes that the development process is complete. Monitoring and adjustments, as necessary, are ongoing activities that ensure that computer production runs produce the expected results. Maintenance tasks also include making revisions and additions to the computer system. As more projects are implemented, organizations will obviously have an increased number of systems to maintain. In many computer installations, a very high percentage of personnel and effort is dedicated to maintenance. This necessarily limits the number of personnel available for development; the net result is often a backlog of development projects.

### SERVICE BY SYSTEMS: LESS OLD-FASHIONED PERSONAL ATTENTION, BUT MORE SPEED AND EFFICIENCY

Certainly if you still expect humble attendants to wait on you deferentially you will think service has gone to pot. The bank manager no longer greets you by name.

However, the bank does have 24-hour automatic tellers and electronic fund transfers and other striking improvements in service. The airlines have nationwide computerized reservation systems that are models of convenience and efficiency. Only a curmudgeon could argue that the American telephone system, with its direct dialing to Bangkok and its fiber-optic cables, doesn't provide service that's better than ever.

"You can't deliver service in the old way, but new systems can actually deliver it better," says Richard M. Kovacevich, a senior vice president who is using electronic razzle-dazzle to capture customers for New York's Citibank. "People tell us: don't be polite—be efficient, fast, and knowledgeable."

—Jeremy Main,
*Fortune*, March 23, 1981

## The Trials of Change: Systems Analysis and People's Lives

The preceding discussion may leave the impression that by simply following a recipe a magical system can be developed. That has certainly not been the pattern in the past.

Systems analysts have been embarrassed to find that they were not always good estimators of time, so schedules have constantly slipped. Some observers, in fact, think that systems analysis is so ambiguous that analysts do not even know when they are finished. Sometimes it seems that the definition of project completion is the point at which analysts have run out of time on the schedule.

Another problem has been failure of communication betweeen analysts and users; poor communication has resulted in poorly defined specifications, which, in turn, result in a supposedly complete system that does not do what the user expected. Budget overruns have resulted from sliding schedules. "By guess and by gosh" methods of analysis and design have often been used instead of formal tools. In the 1960s and 1970s, some systems were completed according to plan and to schedule, but many others were not.

Out of these experiences, however, have come some solutions. Managers have become more sophisticated—and more realistic—in planning schedules and budgets. Analysts have learned to communicate with users. In addition to the analysis and design approach described here, which is considered the traditional way of doing it, there are other, newer approaches, which are beyond the scope of this book. If you find yourself pursuing the occupation of systems analyst, you will no doubt encounter these approaches and find them useful.

Being a systems analyst can be important work, for you are in a position to help institute fundamental changes, altering business operations and methods, work habits, and use of time. As we suggested at the beginning, however, a systems analyst must be sensitive to the possible effects of his or her work on people's lives. The real danger, it has been remarked, is not that computers will begin to think like people, but that people will have to begin to think like computers. The best of the systems analysts try to keep this fact in mind.

- A **system** is an organized set of related components established to accomplish a certain task. **Systems analysis** is the process of evaluating a presently existing system to determine how it works and how it meets user needs, and to lay the groundwork for improvements. The **client** is the person or organization contracting to have the work done. The **users** are people who will have contact with the system. **Systems design** is the process of developing a plan for an improved system, based on the results of systems analysis. A **systems analyst** normally performs both analysis and design.

- A systems analysis and design project gets its impetus and authority for change from an internal force such as an organization's management or an external force such as customer complaints. The systems analyst fills the role of change agent, and the key to his or her success is the involvement of the people in the client organization in the development of the new system.

- The systems analyst has three principal functions: (1) coordination of schedules and system-related tasks with his or her boss and the system programmers, users, vendors, and others; (2) communication, both oral and written—with clients, users, and others involved in the system; (3) planning and design—with the participation of the client organization.

- A **systems project** is defined as a project involving five phases: (1) preliminary investigation, (2) systems analysis, (3) systems design, (4) systems development, (5) implementation and evaluation.

- Phase 1, the **preliminary investigation**—also called the **feasibility study** or **system survey**—is a brief study of the problem. It consists of the groundwork necessary to determine if the systems project should be pursued further. During this phase the systems analyst must establish (1) the scope and (2) the true nature of the problem.

- Phase 2, the **systems analysis** phase, is concerned with (1) data gathering and (2) data analysis. Once data gathering and analysis are completed, the systems analyst makes a comprehensive report to management, summarizing problems and making recommendations.

- Data gathering, the first part of phase 2, involves four principal sources of information: (1) written documents, such as the organization's procedures manuals, reports, forms, and other kinds of paper; (2) questionnaires, which allow people to respond to questions anonymously (although the questionnaires may not always be returned); (3) interviews, which, though time-consuming, permit the questioner to judge responses, explore new areas, and get to know clients and users better (interviews can be either *structured*, with the interviewer sticking to a particular list of questions—a practice useful for comparing answers from several people—or *unstructured*, with the interviewer preparing the questions in advance, but being willing to vary from them when appropriate); and (4) observation, in which the systems analyst goes into an organization and observes the flow of data and interrelations of people.

- **Data analysis,** the second part of phase 2, consists of the preparation of such products as an organization chart, data flow diagrams, and decision tables. An **organization chart** is a chart of the positions and departments within an organization; it shows the lines of authority and communication channels. A **data flow diagram** is a "road map" that shows the present procedures and information flow through an organization. A **decision table** (also called a "decision logic table") is a standardized table of the logical decisions that may be made regarding the conditions that may occur in a given system. Decision tables help ensure that no alternative will be overlooked.

- Phase 3, the **systems design** phase, usually considers the parts of the system in the following order: output requirements, input requirements, files and data bases, system processing, and system controls and backup. (1) In determining the output requirements, the analyst must know what the client wants the system to produce—the output—and the output medium—whether paper, CRT screen, or microfilm. Content of the output—what type of reports are needed (summary, exception, and so on) and what data for the reports—must also be determined. What forms the output will be printed on must be decided. The report format, perhaps using a **printer spacing chart,** which shows positioning of headings, columns, and the like, must be determined. Examples of user-computer dialogue on a CRT screen may need to be spelled out. (2) Input requirements concern the input needed to determine the desired output. This means the analyst must consider the input medium (whether to catch data at source, put it on floppy disks, or whatever), the content (the fields needed and their order), the forms people may have to fill out, editing required to check the reasonableness of the data input, and the volume of the data the system will need to handle. (3) Files and data bases need to be specified. A **record layout form** can help describe the format of records making up the data files. If the system has data bases, the systems analyst must coordinate the systems design with the data base administrator. (4) System processing describes the flow of data in the new system. The operations necessary (edit, sort, update, and so on) are indicated in a systems flowchart using standard ANSI flowchart symbols. Unlike a logic flowchart, which gives detailed program logic, a systems flowchart describes only the "big picture." (5) System controls and backup, such as numbering and time-stamping of source documents, are spelled out to prevent fraud and tampering.

- At the conclusion of phase 3, the systems design plan is presented verbally to higher management. The systems analyst states the problem, followed by the benefits of the new system, explains the design, gives an estimate of the costs, and presents a schedule.

- Phase 4, **systems development,** consists of scheduling, programming, testing, and documentation. When developing a schedule of the principal activities in systems developments, analysts often make up a **Gannt chart,** a form of bar chart depicting schedule deadlines and milestones. In the programming effort, the programming language is selected and detailed design specifications are prepared. The system is subjected to testing, using desk checking, unit testing, and then system testing, to see that all the programs work together satisfactorily. Finally, documentation is prepared to describe the program logic and detailed data formats.

- Phase 5, **implementation and evaluation,** involves six activities: (1) file conversion, by which old files are converted to make them accessible to the new computer system; (2) training, to prepare people to use and operate the new system; (3) system conversion, which may be of four types—(a) **direct conversion,** in which the user simply stops using the old system and begins using the new one; (b) **phased conversion,** in which the new system is eased in a step at a time; (c) **pilot conversion,** in which the entire system is used by some of the users and extended to the rest when proved successful; and (d) **parallel conversion,** in which old and new systems are operated concurrently for some time until the new system is proved successful; (4) auditing, in which an **audit trail** is designed so that auditors can later trace data from output back to source documents; (5) evaluation, in which the systems analyst and the client organization work out ways to evaluate system performance according to preset criteria; and (6) maintenance, in which the system is monitored and adjusted as necessary.

## Review

1. Define the following: systems, systems analysis, systems design.

2. What are the three principal functions of a systems analyst?

3. Name the five phases of a systems project.

4. What are the two parts of phase 2? The five parts of phase 3? The six parts of phase 5?

5. What problems in your own life (work or school) would benefit by a systems analysis approach?

## Selected References for Further Reading

Brooks, Frederick P. *The Mythical Man-Month.* Reading, Mass.: Addison-Wesley, 1978.

Davis, William S. *Systems Analysis and Design: A Structured Approach.* Reading, Mass.: Addison-Wesley, 1983.

Demarco, Tom. *Structured Analysis and System Specification.* Englewood Cliffs, N.J.: Prentice-Hall, 1979.

Gore, Marvin and John Stubbe. *Systems Analysis and Design.* 3rd ed. Dubuque, Iowa: Wm. C. Brown, 1983.

Jackson, Michael. *System Development.* Englewood Cliffs, N.J.: Prentice- Hall, 1983.

Leeson, Marjorie. *Systems Analysis and Design.* Chicago: Science Research Associates, 1981.

Thierauf, Robert J., and George W. Reynolds. *Systems Analysis and Design, A Case Study Approach.* Columbus, Ohio: Merrill, 1980.

Weinberg, Gerald M. *Rethinking Systems Analysis and Design.* Boston: Little, Brown, 1982.

3/25/85

**IN THIS CHAPTER**

Structured programming reduces program testing and maintenance time, increases programmer productivity, and increases clarity and readability. This chapter describes structured design characteristics such as top-down design and coupling and cohesion, and the use of these design tools: structure charts, HIPO, and pseudocode. Egoless programming and programming teams are also described.

*ch10*

# structured program design

## up from "spaghetti code"

*ch10*

In the 1950s, the programmer was hardly noticed, writes the well-known software expert Edsger W. Dijkstra. For one thing, the computers themselves were so large and so cantankerous to maintain that they attracted most of the attention. For another, Dijkstra said, "The programmer's somewhat invisible work was without any glamour: you could show the machine to visitors and that was several orders of magnitude more spectacular than some sheets of coding." Programmers flourished, nevertheless, as the demand for software grew.

In the 1960s, hardware overreached software. The development of hardware and storage capabilities proceeded apace, but software development could not keep up. Projects ran over budget, schedules slipped, and when projects were finally completed they often did not meet the users' needs.

In the 1970s, some determined attempts were made to make software development more manageable. Hardware costs had already decreased dramatically, while software costs continued to rise; it was apparent that, if money was to be saved, there would have to be considerable improvements in software. No longer would programmers be allowed to produce programs that were casually tested or that were readable only to them. The use of obscure coding in an attempt to shave a microsecond of computer time was discouraged. It became clear that, first, problem complexity had to be accepted as fact and that, second, tools had to be devised to handle it. The programmer's job was no longer "invisible work."

## "GOTO Considered Harmful"

How did people go about programming in the early 60s? One eminent computer scientist wrote: "Computer programming was so badly understood that hardly anyone even *thought* about proving programs correct; we just fiddled with a program until we 'knew' it worked." In 1966 C. Bohm and G. Jacopini published a paper in the *Communications of the ACM* (Association for Computing Machinery), a paper they had previously published in Italy. In this paper they proved mathematically that any problem solution could be constructed using only three basic control structures. These are the three structures that we have been calling **sequence, selection** (IF-THEN-ELSE), and **iteration.** It is interesting to note that the concept has been unchanged since it was proposed over a decade and a half ago.

These three control structures—sequence, selection, and iteration—were, of course, used before 1966. But other control structures were also used, notably the transfer, also known as the GOTO. Since the need for only the three basic control structures was now proven, the time had come to cut down on the number of GOTO statements.

The structure idea was given a boost in March 1968, when Edsger Dijkstra published a letter in the *Communications of the ACM* under the heading, "Go To Statements Considered Harmful." In this now-famous letter, Dijkstra contended that the GOTO statement was an

invitation to making a mess of one's program and that reducing the number of GOTOs would reduce the number of programming errors. GOTOs, he said, could be compared to a bowl of spaghetti: If a person took a program and drew a line from each GOTO statement to the statement to which it transferred, the result would be a picture that looked like a bowl of spaghetti. Since then, people have referred to excessive GOTOs in a program as "spaghetti code."

The first major project using structured programming was developed for the _New York Times._ The results were published in 1972. In this large undertaking, the newspaper's clipping file was automated in such a way that users could browse through abstracts (summaries) of all the paper's articles, using a list of index terms, and automatically retrieve the text of the article (stored on microfiche) and display it on a terminal. The project involved 83,000 lines of source code, took 22 calendar months, and involved 11 person-years, yet it was delivered under budget and ahead of schedule. Equally important, there was an amazingly low error rate: Only 21 errors were found during the five weeks of acceptance testing, and only 25 additional errors appeared during the first year of the system's operation.

In December 1973, _Datamation,_ one of the principal trade journals of the computer industry, devoted an entire issue to structured programming. This issue brought the subject to the attention of many programmers in the United States. One article hailed structured programming as a programming revolution.

In the following pages we will describe how this valuable tool works. Throughout we should bear in mind what structured programming is supposed to do:

- Reduce the time required to test programs.

- Increase programmer productivity.

- Increase the clarity and readability of programs.

- Decrease the time required to maintain programs (because increased clarity means less time spent in trying to read and understand programs).

## _Structured Design_

When the concept of program structure was first introduced, some people thought their programs would be structured if they simply got rid of GOTOs. There is more to it than that. A definition of structured design is as follows: **Structured design** is a method of designing computer system components and their relationships _to minimize complexity._ Let us consider two aspects of structured design: (1) "top-down" programming design, and (2) module independence through "coupling" and "cohesion."

**Top-down design** first identifies basic program functions. These functions are further divided into smaller and smaller subfunctions of more manageable size called modules. A **module** is a set of logically related program statements. Programmers are concerned about the relationship of these modules to each other. Top-down design is demonstrated most easily by using the structure charts described in the next section.

One relationship between modules is called **coupling.** It is the measure of the strength of the relationship between two modules. Ideally, that relationship should be weak so that the modules are independent; then, later, if a change is made in one module, it will not affect other modules. Another relationship is called **cohesion.** It is the measure of the inner strength of an individual module. The best relationship here is a strong one; a module should have a single function, although that is not always possible. An example of a single function is the computation of withholding tax. This function would not be included with other functions, such as computing credit union deductions. Strong cohesion also encourages module independence, which, in turn, makes future changes easier.

In addition, a module should have a *single entry* and a *single exit.* Single entry means that the execution of a program module must begin at the same place, usually at the beginning; the module can be entered at only a single point. Similarly, the module may be exited from only one place (see Figure 10-1). It is easier for us to keep track of what is going on in the program if there is only one way to get in and one way to get out of each module in the program.

A module should also be of manageable size. A single page of coded program instructions is often considered an ideal size.

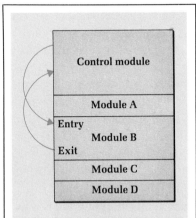

**Figure 10-1 Single entry, single exit.** The program control module executes module B by transferring to its entry point. After module B is complete, it is exited via its exit point and program control returns, in this case, to the control module.

## Program Design Tools

A good program designer will use tools to keep the design process under control. The use of such tools contributes to unity of purpose and clarity of design. More important, good design promotes software reliability. A well-designed program will not only help prevent the introduction of errors, it will also make errors easier to discover. There are several important program design tools, including:

- Structure charts
- HIPO
- Pseudocode

We will take a look at each of these.

### Structure Charts

A **structure chart** describes graphically the structure design of a program as hierarchical, independent modules. An example is shown in Figure 10-2. A structure chart is easy to make up and easy to change, and it is often used as a supplement to or even a replacement for a flowchart.

As the illustration shows, the top level of the structure chart gives the name of the program, PAYROLL PROCESS. The next level breaks

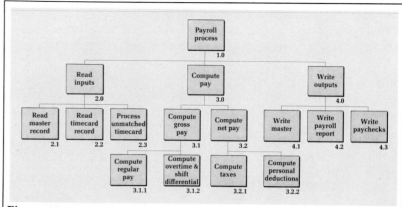

**Figure 10-2    A structure chart.** The numbers outside the boxes refer to more detailed diagrams of these functions. For instance, module 2.0 is presented in more detail in Figure 10-4.

the program down into its major functions—in Figure 10-2, these are READ INPUTS, COMPUTE PAY, and WRITE OUTPUTS. Each of these major modules is then subdivided further into smaller modules. (We could break them down even further, but space does not permit it.)

Note the relationship of the structure chart in Figure 10-2 to top-down design. The major functions are repeatedly subdivided into smaller modules of manageable size. Each of the modules is also, according to plan, as independent of the others as possible. For example, module 4.1, WRITE MASTER, will be executed independently of any activity in module 4.3, WRITE PAYCHECKS.

### *HIPO*

**HIPO**—pronounced "high po," not "hippo"—stands for Hierarchy plus Input-Process-Output. It consists of a set of diagrams that graphically describes program functions from general level to detailed level. Developed as a documentation tool by IBM, HIPO is now used for both design and documentation. As Figure 10-3 indicates, it is a visual tool.

You can see how it supports top-down development. The first of the three types of diagrams is a "visual table of contents," which presents a structure chart along with a short description and a legend explaining what the arrows on the overview and detail diagrams mean. The second diagram, the "overview diagram," shows, from left to right, the inputs, processes, and outputs. This overview diagram— there will likely be more than one—describes the processes of the program in general terms. The third diagram, the "detail diagram," also describes the inputs, processes, and outputs, but in much greater detail. There can be several detail diagrams for each overview diagram.

This HIPO visual package has developed into a popular tool for designing programs. To give you a better idea of how the overview

218

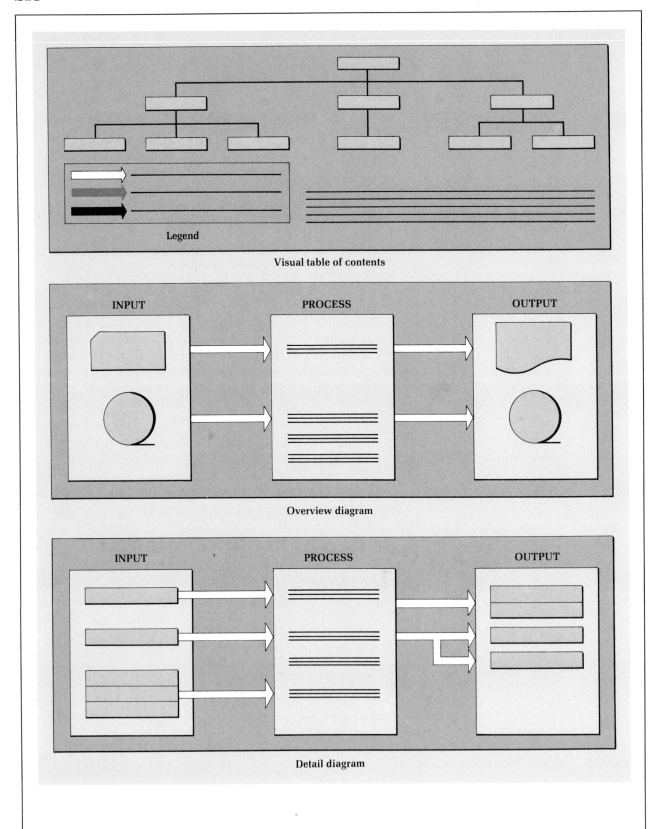

**Figure 10-3**   **A HIPO package.**

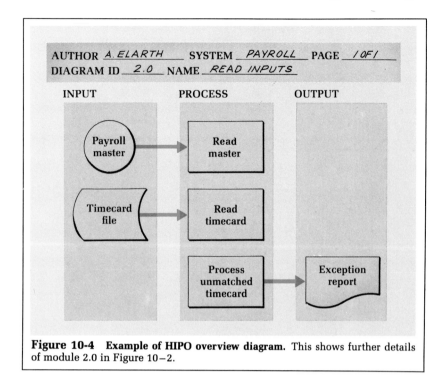

**Figure 10-4    Example of HIPO overview diagram.** This shows further details of module 2.0 in Figure 10-2.

diagram looks, see Figure 10-4, which shows how the READ INPUTS module of the structure chart in Figure 10-2 (module 2.0) would appear at the input-process-output overview level.

### Pseudocode: "Fake Code" for Control Structures

**Pseudocode** is an English-like way of representing the control structures of structured programming. It is "fake code" because, though it is English-like and has some precision to it, it does not have the very definite precision of a programming language. Also, it cannot be executed by a computer. The advantage of pseudocode is that, in using it to plan a program, you can concentrate on the logic and not worry about the rules of a specific language. It is also easy to change pseudocode if you discover a flaw in your logic, whereas most people find that it is more difficult to change the logic once it is coded in a programming language.

Before we proceed further with pseudocode, we need to pause for a moment to recall the control structures introduced in Chapter 8. The three basic structures are sequence, selection (IF-THEN-ELSE), and iteration (DOWHILE). A fourth structure, an additional form of iteration, is DOUNTIL. DOUNTIL is really just a combination of sequence and DOWHILE.

A fifth structure in common use is CASE. CASE is not considered a basic control structure because it is only a convenient substitute for a series of selections—IF statements. In languages supporting the CASE statement, different actions are taken, depending on a value in

| Flowchart format | Pseudocode format | Pseudocode example |
|---|---|---|
| 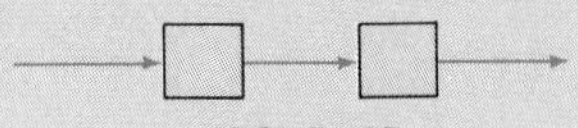 SEQUENCE | SEQUENCE<br><br>statement a<br>statement b | Write headings<br>Set counters to zero |
| 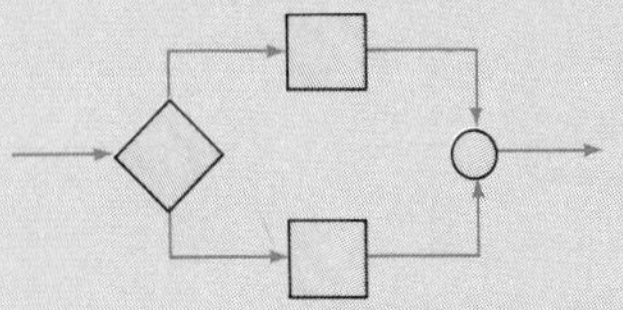 IF-THEN-ELSE | IF-THEN-ELSE<br><br>IF condition p THEN<br>  statement a<br>ELSE<br>  statement b<br>ENDIF | IF balance > 300 THEN<br>  set service charge to zero<br>ELSE<br>  set service charge to 5.00<br>ENDIF |
| 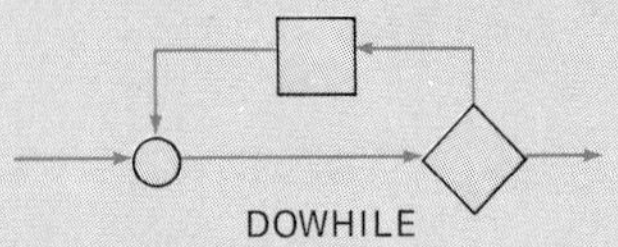 DOWHILE | DOWHILE<br><br>DOWHILE condition p<br>  statement a<br>ENDDO | DOWHILE there are more records<br>  write record<br>  read record<br>ENDDO |
| 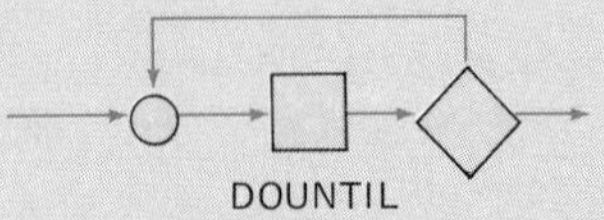 DOUNTIL | DOUNTIL<br><br>DOUNTIL condition p<br>  statement a<br>ENDDO | DOUNTIL count = 100<br>  add count to total<br>  add 1 to count<br>ENDDO |
| 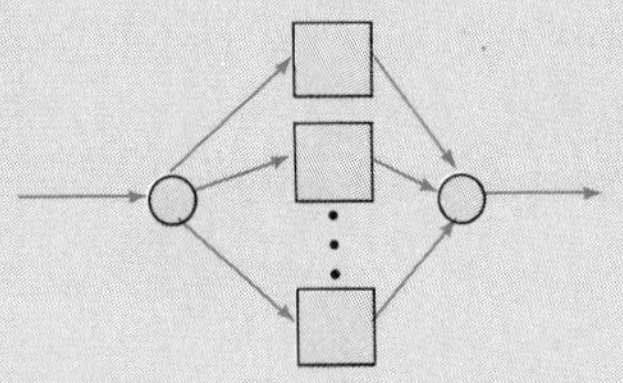 CASE | CASE<br><br>CASENTRY select value<br>  CASE a<br>    function a<br>  CASE b<br>    function b<br>  •<br>  •<br>  CASE n<br>    function n<br>ENDCASE | CASE value is 1, 2, or 3<br>  CASE 1<br>    add member record<br>  CASE 2<br>    revise member record<br>  CASE 3<br>    delete member record<br>ENDCASE |

**Figure 10-5 Control structures.** Flowchart format and equivalent pseudocode format.

```
DOWHILE THERE ARE MORE RECORDS
      IF ACCOUNT-TYPE IS BUSINESS THEN
            IF ORDER AMOUNT GREATER THAN 1000 THEN
                  SET DISCOUNT-RATE TO MAXIMUM
            ELSE
                  SET DISCOUNT-RATE TO MINIMUM
            ENDIF
      ELSE
            SET DISCOUNT-RATE TO ZERO
      ENDIF
      COMPUTE DISCOUNT
      COMPUTE AMOUNT DUE
      WRITE RECORD AND AMOUNT DUE
      READ RECORD
ENDDO
```

**Figure 10-6 Example of pseudocode.** This shows a DOWHILE loop, with ENDDO signifying the end of the loop. Note that the third line is the beginning of what is called a "nested IF"; that is, there is an IF within another IF, and each has its own ending, ENDIF.

## EGOLESS PROGRAMMING

Bill found Marilyn B. willing to peruse his code in exchange for his returning the favor. This was nothing unusual in this group; indeed, nobody would have thought of going on the machine without such scrutiny by a second party. Whenever possible an exchange was made, so nobody would feel in the position of being criticized by someone else. But for Bill, who was well schooled in this method, the protection of an exchange was not necessary. His value system, when it came to programming, dictated that secretive, possessive programming was bad and that open, shared programming was good. Errors that might be found in code he had written—not "his" code, for that terminology was not used here—were simply facts to be exposed to investigation with an eye to future improvement, not attacks on his person.

In this particular instance, Bill had been having one of his "bad programming days." As Marilyn worked and worked over the code—as she found one error after another—he became more and more amused, rather than more and more defensive as he might have done had he been trained as so many of our programmers are. Finally, he emerged from their conference announcing to the world the startling fact that Marilyn had been able to find *seventeen* bugs in only thirteen statements. He insisted on showing everyone who would listen how this had been possible. In fact, since the very exercise had proved to him that this was not his day for coding, he simply spent the rest of the day telling and retelling the episode in all its hilarious details. . . .

As an epilogue to this incident, it should be noted that when this code was finally put on the computer, no further errors were found, in spite of the most diabolical testing possible. In fact, this simulator was put into use in more than a dozen installations for real-time operations, and over a period of at least nine years no other errors were ever found. How different might have been the story had Bill felt that each error found in that code was a wound to his pride—an advertisement of his stupidity.

—Gerald Weinberg,
*The Psychology of
Computer Programming*

a variable. You may study the flowchart form of each of these five control structures in Figure 10-5.

To see how pseudocode works, look at the center column in Figure 10-5. The center column shows the standard pseudocode format for describing the control structures shown in the flowchart. An actual example of pseudocode is given in the right column, which again is still not as formal as a programming language. Figure 10-6 presents a more elaborate example of pseudocode.

## The Social Activity of Programming

Programming as a social activity? "What a strange idea," you may say. "As though writing programs were like playing cards."

As it turns out, this concept is a very useful notion. The idea was first popularized in a book by Gerald Weinberg called *The Psychology of Computer Programming,* which was published in 1971. Weinberg pointed out that though many people think of programmers as loners, programming is not really a private activity and the program itself is not private property: Unless you are totally self-employed, the program belongs to the institution for which you work. Yet, at the time, many programmers were defensive about letting other people look over their work, fearing that the others would find mistakes that would make them look "stupid." Also, some programmers were unenthusiastic about sharing their hard-earned skills and techniques. Their pride, their egos, were bound up with their programs.

### Egoless Programming

The answer to this, Weinberg said, is **egoless programming,** the adoption of the attitude that one's program is not one's personal property but is open to—indeed, benefits by—inspection by all. The idea of egoless programming sets the stage for mutual assistance. Programmers are not mad coders sitting alone in corners. Rather they should offer each other reinforcement and advice in a nonthreatening environment.

Out of the concept of egoless programming has grown another idea that is becoming standard procedure—namely, the **programming team.** The composition of a programming team varies. Often, the team members are all working on the same programming project, one requiring many programs. Team members review each other's programs both at the design level and at the coding level.

### Early Defect Removal

There is good reason for team members to review each other's work, especially at the design level. Known as **early defect removal,** this approach can save considerable time and money. It has proven far

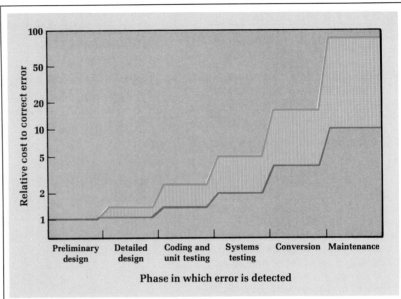

**Figure 10-7    Error versus cost.** Correcting errors late in the development process becomes very expensive and time-consuming. An error discovered during the very early stages, preliminary design, can be fixed at negligible cost. Errors found in later stages cost progressively more; during the systems testing phase, for example, an error costs 2 to 5 times more to fix and, once in maintenance, from 10 to 90 times as much!

more costly to remove program defects in the later stages of development and testing (see Figure 10-7) than in the early stages.

To encourage the early removal of defects, many programming teams have turned to the structured walkthrough.

### Structured Walkthroughs

The design review process is called a **structured walkthrough.** This is a formal process among members of a programming team, in which several team members review the design or code of an individual programmer, looking for weaknesses and errors. Managers seldom participate, since it is important that the review of the program not get entangled with notions about evaluating someone's performance. In many installations, the structured walkthrough is not for purposes of inviting comparisons. That is, a team member is not allowed to say, "I know a better way of doing this"; he or she is permitted to point out only what is not clear or what will not work. There *are* installations, however, where a suggestion is welcome.

A primary benefit of the structured walkthrough, when instituted in an organization, is that all the programs become more readable. After all, if you know that your programs are going to be reviewed by fellow programmers, you are going to try to make them comprehensible. And that is, of course, one of the main points—to make programs more understandable so they will be easier to maintain. Some managers consider the review time as "nonproductive" time, but studies usually find the effort well spent, with a payoff in reduced testing time and higher-quality programs. And, of course, programmers also learn from each other during these reviews.

Not every organization is using structured walkthroughs, not even a majority. Smaller organizations, of fewer than five people, are becoming commonplace; these organizations are less likely to use formal design reviews. There are also many large organizations that have not yet endorsed structured walkthroughs. But the adoption of this practice is clearly on the rise, and we will probably be seeing more of such "social activity" among programmers in the future.

## The "Chief Programmer" Team

Egoless programming and structured walkthroughs are all well and good, but what if we have a large system with complex software, involving a lot of people? Will too many cooks spoil the broth?

A collection of bright people working together can produce a lot of good ideas. But an excess of good ideas can lead to problems, notably a lack of conceptual integrity. *Conceptual integrity* refers to a unity of design, a consistency of purpose. A system should reflect one set of design ideas, rather than many good but independent and uncoordinated ideas. A large system requires unity of outlook, some central idea, and a leader to carry through on that central theme. Too many people may produce conflicting ideas and divergence in direction. A large system also is susceptible to communication problems, with people struggling to keep up with what everyone else is doing, staying posted on revised specifications, and so on.

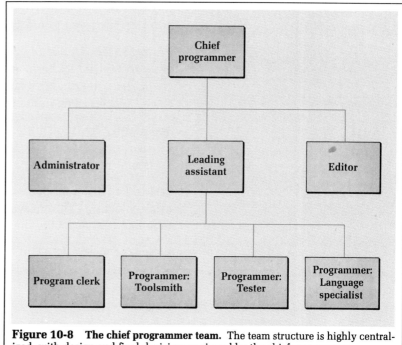

**Figure 10-8   The chief programmer team.** The team structure is highly centralized, with design and final decisions reviewed by the chief programmer.

The conceptual integrity problem was addressed, in the December 1973 *Datamation* referred to previously, by F. T. Baker and Dr. Harlan Mills, who described the **chief programmer team,** a concept used on the *New York Times* project. A formal team is headed by a chief programmer, who prepares the specifications for the systems project, prepares the program design, and oversees all the coding, testing, and documentation. The chief programmer manages all technical aspects of the project.

This effort is clearly too much for one person. Therefore, the chief programmer responsible for this effort is assisted by many people. The project then has both the resources needed and the conceptual integrity that gives it unity of purpose. The team structure is centralized, with major decisions made at the top. Team members also make decisions, as appropriate to their work; since all work is reviewed by the chief programmer, these lower-level decisions are effectively reviewed. This approach seems to work well for large projects with many people.

The chief programmer is supported by a leading assistant, who acts as the main backup person on the project. The leading assistant, who should be in communication with everyone else on the team, also acts as a sounding board for the chief programmer's ideas. These two are supported by several people acting as programmers, systems testers, documentation editors, clerical help, and so on.

A typical team has been set forth in detail by Frederick Brooks in *The Mythical Man-Month* (see Figure 10-8). In addition to the chief programmer and the leading assistant, he describes the following personnel:

- **Administrator.** The administrator handles all the nontechnical managerial details, such as money, personnel, and space. The administrator also interacts with the rest of the organization.

- **Editor.** Although documentation may be written by the chief programmer, the editor has complete responsibility for the manuscript. He or she will edit, criticize, rewrite, look up references, and oversee all phases of document production and distribution.

- **Toolsmith.** The toolsmith is a programmer who prepares special service programs to interface with the operating system. A good toolsmith may service several chief programmers.

- **Tester.** The tester prepares test data for individual programs and for system testing. The tester takes personal responsibility for challenging every aspect of the system, to make sure it works properly.

- **Language specialist.** This programmer delights in understanding all the fine points of a language. The language specialist acts as a consultant for several chief programmers and may be assigned small programming tasks for which such expertise is needed.

- **Program clerk.** The clerk is a trained secretary who keeps track of all the technical records for the team. Duties include logging in all input data and all output listings. The clerk makes copies of all recent runs readily available and files all previous runs in chronological order.

Does the chief programmer concept work? Probably it is best to say it has had mixed results. Teams are sometimes known to have low morale. However, many managers feel that a team can be an excellent training ground for programmers with less expertise than the chief programmer. Based on team learning experience, programmers can become assistants on subsequent teams and perhaps chief programmers some time in the future.

## Summary and Key Terms

- Because of difficulties during the 1960s, when hardware overreached software and projects were not completed satisfactorily, attempts were made during the 1970s to make software manageable.

- In a 1966 paper in *Communications of the ACM*, C. Bohm and G. Jacopini proved that any problem solution could be constructed using only three basic control structures—**sequence, selection** (IF-THEN-ELSE), and **iteration.**

- In March 1968 Edsger Dijkstra published a letter in the *Communications of the ACM*, under the heading "Go To Statements Considered Harmful," in which he said reducing the number of GOTOs would reduce the number of programming errors. Excessive GOTOs in a program are now referred to as "spaghetti code."

- Structured programming is supposed to accomplish the following: (1) Reduce the time required to test programs; (2) increase programmer productivity; (3) increase the clarity and readability of programs; and (4) decrease the time required to maintain programs.

- **Structured design** may be defined as a method of designing computer system components and their relationships to minimize complexity. Two aspects of structured design are "top-down" programming design and module independence through "coupling" and "cohesion."

- **Top-down design** identifies basic program functions, which are divided into smaller and smaller subfunctions called modules. A **module** is a set of logically related program statements.

- **Coupling** is the measure of the strength of the relationship between two modules. Ideally, the relationship should be weak so that if a change is made in one module, it will not affect other modules. **Cohesion** is another relationship; it is the measure of the inner strength of an individual module. The best cohesion relationship

is a strong one; a module should have a single function. A module should have a single entry and a single exit.

- Good design promotes software reliability. A well-designed program helps prevent the introduction of errors and makes errors easier to discover. There are several important program design tools, including structure charts, HIPO, and pseudocode.

- A **structure chart** describes graphically the structure design of a system as hierarchical, independent modules. The top level of the structure chart gives the name of the program; the next level breaks the program down into major functions, which are subdivided into smaller modules.

- **HIPO** stands for *Hierarchy plus Input-Process-Output.* It consists of a set of diagrams that graphically describes program functions from general level to detailed level. It supports top-down development by presenting first a visual table of contents, then an overview diagram, and then detail diagrams.

- **Pseudocode** is an English-like way of representing the control structures of structured programming. It is useful because, in planning a program, it allows one to concentrate on the logic and not worry about the rules of a specific language.

- There are five control structures to consider. The three basic structures are sequence, selection (IF-THEN-ELSE), and iteration (DOWHILE). A fourth structure, an additional form of iteration, is DOUNTIL, which is a combination of sequence and DOWHILE. A fifth structure is CASE, which is a substitute for a series of selections—IF statements.

- **Egoless programming** is the adoption of the attitude that one's program is not one's personal property but benefits from inspection by other programmers.

- Out of egoless programming has come the **programming team,** whose members review each other's programs both at the design level and at the coding level. Review at the design level encourages **early defect**

**removal,** which can save time and money. The design review process is called a **structured walkthrough;** team members review the design or code of an individual programmer, looking for weaknesses and errors. The result is that programs become more readable.

- Too many people working together on a large system can lead to a lack of conceptual integrity—to a lack of unity of design and consistency of purpose. The **chief programmer team** addresses the conceptual integrity problem by establishing a formal team headed by a chief programmer, who prepares specifications and program design, and oversees coding, testing, and documentation. The chief programmer is supported by a leading assistant. The team itself may have an administrator, editor, toolsmith (programmer who repaires special service programs), tester, language specialist and program clerk.

*prepares*
*see page*
*294*

## Review

1. Explain the contributions of C. Bohm and G. Jacopini and of Edsger Dijkstra to structured programming.

2. What are four goals of structured programming?

3. Define structured design.

4. Differentiate coupling and cohesion.

5. Explain the following important program design tools: structure charts, HIPO, and pseudocode.

6. Describe the five control structures discussed in the chapter.

7. Describe the concepts of egoless programming, the programming team, early defect removal, and the structured walkthrough.

8. What is the purpose of the chief programmer team?

## Selected References for Further Reading

Bailey, T.E., and Kris Lundguard. *Program Design with Pseudocode.* Monterey, Calif.: Brooks/Cole, 1983.

Bohl, Marilyn. *Tools for Structured Design.* Chicago: Science Research Associates, 1978.

Brooks, Frederick P., Jr. *The Mythical Man-Month: Essays on Software Engineering.* Reading, Mass.: Addison-Wesley, 1975.

Hughes, Joan K., and Jay I. Michtom. *A Structured Approach to Programming.* Englewood Cliffs, N.J.: Prentice-Hall, 1977.

Weinberg, Gerald M. *The Psychology of Computer Programming.* New York: Van Nostrand Reinhold, 1971.

Yourdon, Edward. *Structured Walk Throughs.* New York: Yourdon, 1978.

Yourdon, Edward, and Larry L. Constantine. *Structured Design.* Englewood Cliffs, N.J.: Prentice-Hall, 1979.

## IN THIS CHAPTER

Programming languages—machine, assembly, high-level, and nonprocedural—are described and seven specific languages are surveyed: FORTRAN, COBOL, PL/I, BASIC, Pascal, Ada, and RPG. Important features, program organization, and control structures are pointed out, and samples of the languages themselves are presented.

# ch 11

# languages

## communicating with the computer

You ask your friend why he is looking so excited.

"I'm mad about my flat," he says.

What does that mean? In the United States it probably means he is angry about the bad tire on his car. In England, however, it could mean he is enthusiastic about his apartment.

That is the trouble with the English language, or with any human language, for that matter. A natural language is loosely configured, ambiguous, full of colloquialisms, slang, variations, and complexities. And, of course, it is constantly changing. On the other hand, a **programming language**—a set of rules that provides a way of instructing the computer what operations to perform—is anything but loose and ambiguous: its vocabulary has specific meaning. It is not mad about its flat.

A programming language, the key to communicating with the computer, has certain definite characteristics. It has a limited vocabulary. Each word in it has precise meaning. Even though a programming language is limited in words, it can still be used, in step-by-step fashion, to solve complex problems. There is not, however, just one programming language; there are many.

## Programming Language: A Tower of Babel?

At present, there are over 150 programming languages—and these are the ones that are still being used. We are not counting the hundreds of languages that for one reason or another have fallen by the wayside over the years. Some of the languages have rather colorful names: SNOBOL, STUDENT, HEARSAY, DOCTOR, ACTORS, JOVIAL. Where did all these languages come from? Do we really need to complicate the world further by adding programming languages to the Tower of Babel of human languages?

Programming languages initially were created by people in universities or in the government and were devised for special functions. Some languages have endured because they serve special purposes in science, engineering, and the like. However, it soon became clear that some standardization was needed. It made sense for those working on similar tasks to use the same language.

The most widely used languages today are FORTRAN, COBOL, PL/I, BASIC, Pascal, Ada, RPG II, and assembly languages. We will discuss these briefly later in the chapter. Before we do so, however, we need to discuss *levels* of language.

## Levels of Language

Programming languages are said to be "lower" or "higher," depending on whether they are closer to the language the computer itself uses (0s and 1s—low) or to the language people use (more English-like—high). We shall consider these levels of language:

- Machine language

- Assembly language

- High-level language

- Nonprocedural language

Let us look at each of these categories.

### Machine Language

Humans do not like to deal in numbers alone (they prefer letters and words). But, strictly speaking, numbers are what machine language is. This lowest level of language, **machine language,** represents information as 1s and 0s—binary digits corresponding to the "on" and "off" electrical states in the computer.

An example of machine language is shown in Figure 11-1. This is a language taken from a modern computer. In the early days of computing, each computer had its own machine language, and programmers had rudimentary systems for combining numbers to represent instructions such as "add" and "compare." Primitive by today's standards, the programs were not at all convenient for people to read and use. As a result, the computer industry moved to develop assembly languages.

### Assembly Languages

Today assembly languages are considered fairly low-level—that is, they are not as convenient for people to use as more recent languages. At the time they were developed, however, they were considered a great leap forward. Rather than using simply 1s and 0s, **assembly language** uses abbreviations or mnemonic codes to replace the numbers: A for "Add," C for "Compare," MP for "Multiply," and so on. Although these codes were not English words, they were still—from the standpoint of human convenience—preferable to numbers alone.

The programmer who uses an assembly language requires a translator to convert his or her assembly-language program into machine

| | | | |
|---|---|---|---|
| FD | 71 | 431F | 4153 |
| F3 | 63 | 4267 | 4321 |
| 96 | F0 | 426D | |
| F9 | 10 | 41F3 | 438A |
| 47 | 40 | 40DA | |
| 47 | F0 | 4050 | |

**Figure 11-1   Machine language.** True machine language is all binary—only 0s and 1s—but since an example of that would take too much space here, we are showing an example of machine language in the hexadecimal (base 16) numbering system. (The letters *A–F* in hexadecimal represent the numbers 10–15 in the decimal system.) The above computer commands, taken from machine language for the IBM 360/370 series computers, are operation codes instructing the computer to divide two numbers, compare the quotient, move the result into the output area of the system, and set it up so that it can be printed.

language. A translator is needed because machine language is the only language the computer can actually execute. The translator is an **assembler program,** also referred to as an "assembler." It takes the programs written in assembly language and turns them into machine language. A programmer need not worry about the translating aspect; he or she need only write programs in assembly language. The translation is taken care of by the computer system.

Although assembly languages represent a step forward, they still have many disadvantages. One is that the assembly language varies according to the type of computer. An assembler for an IBM computer, for instance, will not run on a Univac or Honeywell, or even for a different type of IBM computer.

Another disadvantage of assembly language is the one-to-one relationship between the assembly language and machine language—that is, for every command in assembly language there is one command in machine language. Thus, assembly language is detailed in the extreme, making programming repetitive, tedious, and error-prone. This drawback is apparent from Figure 11-2, p. 231: Assembly language may be easier to read than machine language, but it is by no means crystal clear.

### High-Level Languages

The invention of **high-level languages** in the mid-1950s transformed programming into something quite different from what it had been. The harried programmer working on the nitty-gritty details of coding and machines became a programmer who could pay more attention to solving the client's problems. The programs could solve much more complex problems. At the same time, they were written in an English-like manner, thus making them more convenient to use. As a result of these changes, the programmer could accomplish more with less effort.

Of course, a translator was needed to translate the symbolic statements of a high-level language into computer-executable machine language; this translator is called a **compiler.** There are many compilers for each language, one for each type of computer. Since the machine language generated by one computer's COBOL compiler, for instance, is not the machine language of some other computer, it is necessary to have a COBOL compiler for each type of computer on which COBOL programs are to be run.

### Nonprocedural Languages: Computers for Everybody

I WANT A REPORT FOR ALL SALES PEOPLE IN REGION 20 IN ORDER BY EMPLOYEE NUMBER WITHIN DEPARTMENT, SHOWING JUNE SALES AND YEAR-TO-DATE SALES.

You cannot get much closer to English than this. This is an example of a **nonprocedural language,** a language intended primarily to help nonprogrammers access a computer's data base. For example, a cus-

# *Global Search*
## *Computer Use Around the World*

**1** How many words a minute could you type on this keyboard? It depends, of course, on how well you know Arabic.

"Global search" normally means that feature of a program that will search through an entire file looking for a particular item or word. In this gallery we use it in a different sense—literally a search of planet earth to show how computers are being used in Europe, Asia, and the Third World. North Americans have no cause to feel smug about innovation, for many exciting developments are happening elsewhere, particularly in Europe and Japan.

Europe: **2** France, a world leader in television-telephone-computer technologies, plans to have 7 million terminals hooked into the telephone system by 1990. **3** In the Netherlands, computers are used to track shipping and cargoes. **4** England, which has developed computer networks accessible through TV sets, also uses computers for a great many other services. **5** In Austria, a light pen is used in a railroad switching control system. **6** Europe has its own communications and scientific satellites; this one is the Telecom I. **7** A West German Ford dealership uses Datapoint equipment.

Asia: **8** to **11** Japan: A major computer power, Japan uses computers in its super "bullet train," in banking, and in circuit design. **12** The Philippines: A worker tests an ITT business communications system. **13** Korea: Computers are used to assist in quality control in pipe fabrication. **14** Taiwan: A tire manufacturer uses computers in production and sales analyses.

The Third World: ⑮ to ⑰ The Caribbean and Latin America: Computers are used to follow sugar prices in Jamaica, unload ship cargoes in Peru, and direct cannery operations in Uruguay.
⑱ Zambia: Computerized Braille is produced for the blind.
⑲ ⑳ Jordan: Computers are used in airline reservations and in education.

Tell me the future: **21** In India, astrology has been married to computer technology in order to provide detailed, long-term horoscopes. Here a palmist in New Delhi attempts to determine a person's future. **22** In Tokyo, a woman uses a computerized fortune-telling machine.

```
                PRINT NOGEN
PROG8           START 0
CARDFIL         DTFCD DEVADDR=SYSRDR,RECFORM=FIXUNB,IOAREA1=CARDREC, C
                      TYPEFLE=INPUT,BLKSIZE=80,EOFADDR=FINISH
REPTFIL         DTFPR DEVADDR=SYSLST,IOAREA1=PRNTREC,BLKSIZE=132
BEGIN           BALR  3,0                REGISTER 3 IS BASE REGISTER
                USING *,3
                OPEN  CARDFIL,REPTFIL    OPEN FILES
                MVC   PRNTREC,SPACES     MOVE SPACES TO OUTPUT RECORD
READLOOP        GET   CARDFIL            READ A RECORD
                MVC   OFIRST,IFIRST      MOVE ALL INPUT FIELDS
                MVC   OLAST,ILAST        TO OUTPUT RECORD FIELDS
                MVC   OADDR,IADDR
                MVC   OCITY,ICITY
                MVC   OSTATE,ISTATE
                MVC   OZIP,IZIP
                PUT   REPTFIL            WRITE THE RECORD
                B     READLOOP           BRANCH TO READ AGAIN
FINISH          CLOSE CARDFIL,REPTFIL    CLOSE FILES
                EOJ                      END OF JOB
CARDREC         DS    0CL80              DESCRIPTION OF INPUT RECORD
IFIRST          DS    CL10
ILAST           DS    CL10
IADDR           DS    CL30
ICITY           DS    CL20
ISTATE          DS    CL2
IZIP            DS    CL5
                DS    DL3
PRNTREC         DS    0CL132             DESCRIPTION OF OUTPUT RECORD
                DS    CL10
OLAST           DS    CL10
                DS    CL5
OFIRST          DS    CL10
                DS    CL15
OADDR           DS    CL30
                DS    CL15
OCITY           DS    CL20
                DS    CL5
OSTATE          DS    CL2
                DS    CL5
OZIP            DS    CL5
SPACES          DC    CL132' '
                END   BEGIN
```

**Figure 11-2 Assembly language.** This example, of the IBM Assembler Language BAL, shows a program for reading a record and writing it out again. The left column contains symbolic addresses of various instructions or data. The second column contains the actual operation codes to describe the kind of activity needed; for instance, MVC stands for "Move characters." The third column describes the data on which the instructions are to act. The far right column contains English-like comments related to the line or lines opposite. This entire page of instructions could be compressed to a few lines in a high-level language.

tomer service representative of a car-rental agency might need to know which cars are out and when they are due back. The representative would need some training in the use of the information system, but would not need formal programming training. Nonprocedural languages are thus considered to be **user friendly**—a term you will often encounter in computer and data processing circles (you will never hear "user unfriendly," however) which means no formal training in programming is required. Nonprocedural languages are often referred to as fourth-generation languages, according to the widely accepted notion that programming languages are formed into generations: machine languages—first generation, assembly languages—second, high-level languages—third. Examples of nonprocedural languages are FOCUS, RAMIS, NOMAD, INQUIRE, and MARK IV. With nonprocedural languages, it is clear that access to computer information for the masses is at hand.

## Choosing a Language

How do you choose which language to write your program in? Perhaps you will use a particular language because it is the only one available at your installation. Perhaps your manager has decreed that everyone on your project will use a certain language. Perhaps you *know* only one language!

A sensible approach is to pick the language that is most suitable for your particular program application. The following sections on individual languages will give you an overview of the languages in common use. We describe these languages in the order in which they were introduced: FORTRAN, COBOL, PL/I, BASIC, Pascal, and Ada. Then we will follow with RPG, which is a problem-oriented language. We will discuss each of these languages on the basis of its features, program organization, and control structures, that is, the types of statements available to control the flow of the program logic. Special features of each language are noted, including the types of applications for which they are often used. The brief discussions of program organization are designed to give you a general picture of how a program written in a particular language is organized.

Special attention should be given to the sections on control structures. Every language has control structures of some kind. We are

**Table 11-1   Features of Seven Important Programming Languages**

| Language | Application | Structured Features |
|---|---|---|
| FORTRAN—FORmula TRANslator (1954) | Scientific | Limited; FORTRAN 77 has some structured features |
| COBOL—COmmon Business-Oriented Language (1959) | Business | Some structured concepts |
| PL/I—Programming Language One (1964) | Scientific, business | Structured |
| BASIC—Beginners' All-purpose Symbolic Instruction Code (1965) | Education, business | Limited; Dartmouth SBASIC is structured |
| Pascal—after French inventor Blaise Pascal (1971) | Education, systems programming, scientific | |
| Ada—after Ada, the Countess of Lovelace (1980) | Military, general | Structured |
| RPG—Report Program Generator (1964) | Business reports | Not applicable |

particularly interested in identifying the languages that have the fundamental control structures mentioned in Chapter 8—SEQUENCE, SELECTION (IF-THEN-ELSE), and ITERATION (DOWHILE and DOUNTIL)—built right into the language. Using a language with structured features does not, unfortunately, guarantee that the programmer will write a structured program. Table 11-1 summarizes the important features of these languages.

Finally, a sample program is provided for each language. The applications used in the program are typical for the languages used.

## FORTRAN: The First High-Level Language

Developed by IBM and introduced in 1954, **FORTRAN**—for *FORmula TRANslator*—was the first high-level language. FORTRAN is a scientifically oriented language—in the early days, use of the computer was primarily a scientific occupation, associated with engineering, mathematical, and scientific research tasks. FORTRAN is still the most widely used language in the scientific community.

### Features

**SIX FORTRAN RELATIONAL OPERATORS**

| Operator | Meaning |
|----------|---------|
| .EQ. | Equal to |
| .NE. | Not equal to |
| .GT. | Greater than |
| .LT. | Less than |
| .GE. | Greater than or equal to |
| .LE. | Less than or equal to |

FORTRAN is noted for its simplicity and brevity, part of the reason why it remains popular. This language is very good for its primary purpose, which is execution of complex formulas, such as those used in economic analysis and engineering. It is not, however, particularly useful for file processing or data processing; its control structures are quite limited, as are its means of describing data. Consequently, it is not very suitable for business applications. Moreover, there is no requirement to define data elements before they are used. This lack contributes to the language's simplicity and brevity but also lends itself to error.

### Program Organization

Not all programs are organized the same way. They vary depending on the language used. As we shall see, in many languages (such as COBOL), programs are divided into a series of parts. FORTRAN programs are not composed of different parts. A FORTRAN program consists of a series of statements continuing one after the other. Different types of data are identified as the data is used. Descriptions for data records appear in format statements that accompany the READ and WRITE statements.

### Control Structures

As we stated in Chapter 8, the three basic control structures or patterns are sequence, selection, and iteration. FORTRAN was not designed as a structured language. FORTRAN 77, a newer version, has added some features, particularly the expanded IF (selection) statement, that enhance structured design. Other FORTRAN control structures are the GO TO statement and the DO loop.

The logical IF statement, which is a conditional transfer statement, consists of three parts: the word IF, followed by some condition in parentheses, followed by some other executable statement. For example:

```
IF (SALES.LT.10000) COMM = 500
```

This means "If sales are less than $10,000, then commission earned is $500." In the above statement, ".LT." is a relational operator that means "less than"; the computer compares the items on either side of the operator to see if the statement in parentheses is true, and if it is, executes the statement to the right of the parentheses before proceeding to the next statement in the program. If the statement in parentheses is false, the program proceeds directly to the next statement. There are six relational operators.

The GO TO statement, an unconditional transfer statement, simply transfers program control to another statement in the program, one indicated by a line number in the GO TO statement. For example,

```
GO TO 40
```

means transfer to the program statement with line number 40.

The DO loop usually is a DOWHILE loop, which means it tests first before going through the loop. For example:

```
      ISUM=0
      DO 40 I=1,100
      ISUM=ISUM+1
40 CONTINUE
```

We start with the sum ISUM equal to 0 (shown above as ISUM = 0). The second line can be translated to mean: "Proceed through all the statements from DO to line 40 and repeat 100 times, taking the sum of all the numbers from 1 to 100."

Figure 11-3 shows an example of a FORTRAN program.

## COBOL: The Language of Business

In the 1950s FORTRAN had been developed, but there was still no accepted high-level programming language appropriate for business. The U.S. Department of Defense in particular was interested in creating such a standardized language, and so it called together representatives from government and various industries, including the computer industry. These representatives formed **CODASYL**—COnference of DAta SYstem Languages. In 1959, CODASYL introduced

```
*     COMPUTE COMPOUND INTEREST QUARTERLY AT 5% INTEREST
*
*
      WRITE (6, 10)
  10  FORMAT ('1', 'ACCOUNT', 4X, 'INTEREST'/)
  20  READ (5, 30) IACCT, PRIN, IYEAR
  30  FORMAT (I4, 2X, F7.2, 2X, I2)
      IF (IYEAR.EQ.0) STOP
      AMOUNT=PRIN * (1. + .05/4.)**(FLOAT(IYEAR) * 4.)
      WRITE (6, 40) IACCT, AMOUNT
  40  FORMAT (3X, I4, 6X, F7.2)
      GO TO 20
      END
```

| ACCOUNT | INTEREST |
|---------|----------|
| 1142 | 41.20 |
| 2148 | 3271.00 |
| 3417 | 300.50 |
| 4643 | 153.27 |
| 6610 | 948.30 |
| 8190 | 51.24 |

**Figure 11-3(a)  A FORTRAN program.** This program to compute compound interest four times a year at 5 percent interest is based on the formula:

$$\text{Amount} = \text{principal} \times (1 + .05/4)^{\text{Year} + 4}$$

Except for the word FLOAT, you can understand the program from our discussion in the text. FLOAT appears for the following reason: When doing arithmetic calculations, it is more efficient to process only all integers or all real numbers. Using the word FLOAT in this example allows us to change IYEAR from an integer to a real number so that it can be used with all the other real numbers in the formula.

**Figure 11-3(b)  Output.** This shows an example of output for the compound interest program in Figure 11-3(a).

## THE COBOL–8X CONTROVERSY

Although COBOL remains the major programming language in business today, the new version being promoted by ANSI, known as COBOL–8X, encountered some resistance among potential business users.

The problem is that it does not have sufficient "upward mobility." In the past, when a new COBOL version was adopted, older programs would still run on it. COBOL–8X, however, requires that parts of old versions be revised if they are to run on the COBOL–8X compiler— an expensive proposition for, say, a collection of programs for an insurance company.

For instance, all COBOL languages have what are called "reserved words," words such as PROGRAM-ID, which have special meanings and which cannot be used by a programmer for variable names. COBOL–8X adds some *new* reserved words—which means that if old programs had used them as variable names they now must be changed.

Another change is that COBOL–8X eliminates certain features of past COBOL versions. Although many people agree in principle that these should be omitted, eliminating them in practice could cost many millions of dollars.

Recently, the DPMA, a professional organization that initially led the opposition to COBOL–8X, reversed its stand and supports the new version.

**COBOL**—for COmmon Business- Oriented Language. The U.S. government offered encouragement by insisting that anyone attempting to win government contracts for computer-related projects had to use COBOL. The American National Standards Institute (ANSI) first standardized COBOL in 1968, and then again in 1974, a version known as **ANS-COBOL.** The principal benefit of standardization is that COBOL is relatively *machine-independent*—that is, a COBOL program written for one type of computer can be run on another, for which a COBOL compiler has been developed, with only slight modifications.

### Features

The principal feature of COBOL is that it is English-like—far more so than FORTRAN or BASIC. The variable names are set up in such a way that even if you know nothing about programming you can still understand the general purpose of a program. For example:

```
IF SALES-AMOUNT IS GREATER THAN SALES-QUOTA
   COMPUTE COMMISSION = MAX-RATE * SALES-AMOUNT
ELSE
   COMPUTE COMMISSION = MIN-RATE * SALES-AMOUNT.
```

Because COBOL is so easy to read, it is said to be *self-documenting:* that is, few ongoing comments in the program are needed to explain what is being done. For this reason, it is also easy for programmers to learn to use; once you understand programming principles, it is not difficult to add COBOL to your repertoire.

COBOL can be used for just about any task related to business programming, and indeed is especially suited to processing alpha-

*(continued on page 237)*

numeric data, such as street addresses, purchased items, dollar amounts—the data of business. However, the feature that makes COBOL so useful—its English-like appearance and easy readability—is also a weakness, because a COBOL program can be incredibly wordy. It is not usual for a programmer to sit down and produce a quick COBOL program. In fact, there is hardly such a thing as a "quick COBOL program"; there are just too many program lines to write, even to accomplish a simple task. For speed and simplicity, BASIC, FORTRAN, and Pascal are probably better to use.

## Program Organization

A COBOL program is divided into four parts:

- Identification division
- Environment division
- Data division
- Procedure division

The divisions must appear in this order. Let us see how they work.

**Identification Division** COBOL has certain **reserved words**—that is, words with exact, special meanings. The programmer may not use these words for variable names. One of these reserved words is PROGRAM-ID, which is required in this first division. It is followed by a period, then by at least one space, and then by some sort of name that will uniquely identify the program, also followed by a period. For example:

```
PROGRAM-ID. ACCT-REC.
```

Other lines in the identification divisions are optional.

**Environment Division** This division has two sections, which perform specific functions. The CONFIGURATION SECTION describes the computer on which the program will be compiled and executed. The INPUT-OUTPUT SECTION relates each file of the program to the specific physical device, such as tape drive or printer, that will read or write the file. This latter section is the link between the program and the peripheral equipment used.

**Data Division** This division contains all the detailed information about all data processed by the program. It indicates field information such as type of characters (whether numeric or alphanumeric), number of characters, and placement of decimal points. It also indicates data relationships, including hierarchy. Hierarchy refers to levels of data organizations for use within the program. The type of the hierarchy is often a record name, with the next level being data fields; some data fields may be divided into even lower levels.

There are two sections in this division. The FILE SECTION contains general information about each file, such as record length, and a field-by-field description of each type of record within the file. An FD description is required for each file used. The associated record descriptions follow the FD description. The WORKING-STORAGE SECTION describes in detail data that is not directly associated with a specific file.

**Procedure Division** The stage having been set in the three preceding divisions, the data can now be acted upon. This last division contains all the statements that give the computer specific instructions to carry out the logic of the program. The instructions use specific verbs from the list of COBOL reserved words, verbs that, in keeping with the English flavor, are often self-explanatory: READ, WRITE, ADD, SUBTRACT, MOVE, DISPLAY, SORT. The procedure division is composed of paragraphs, which are in turn composed of sentences, each of which ends with a period. Each paragraph is identified by a paragraph name.

### Control Structures

COBOL was not originally designed as a structured language, but there are structures in it. For instance, there is an IF-ELSE structure, which is really the same as the IF-THEN-ELSE structure we saw in Chapter 8, except that the "THEN" is missing. There is also a PERFORM/UNTIL structure. This is the same as a DOWHILE loop; a certain set of instructions will be performed repeatedly while a condition is met, otherwise the program leaves the loop. There is also a GOTO statement, an unconditional transfer to a certain paragraph name.

Figure 11-4(a) shows a sample COBOL program; Figure 11-4(b) shows some sample output from the program.

*(continued from page 236)*

served on the ANSI X3.4 Committee on the Standardization of Computer Languages and is presently serving on the CODASYL Executive Committee. . . .

Her philosophy is . . . exemplified in her statement about Stonehenge. "I like Stonehenge," she says, "because there was this man, long before the pyramids, who had a concept. We don't know whether he was a priest or a leader, but we admire him. But then you have to stop and think. He wouldn't have gotten anywhere without the guy who moved the first stone. I tell people to be the guy who moves the first stone."

—ICP INTERFACE
*Administrative
& Accounting,
Spring 1980*

# PL/I: A Language for Both Business and Science

Introduced in 1964, **PL/I**—for Programming Language One—was sponsored by IBM and was designed as a compromise. It had been found that FORTRAN, the scientific language, did not work well in such areas as file handling, but that COBOL, the business language, was not particularly useful in scientific calculations. PL/I was introduced, therefore, as a language that would be all things to all people and would be applied to a broad number of areas. Neither scientific nor business language, it was to be a general-purpose language.

### Features

PL/I is a structured language. Actual control structures fitting the basic control structures (sequence, selection, iteration) are built right into the language. In addition, PL/I is designed to be used by both

```
010010 IDENTIFICATION DIVISION.
010020 PROGRAM-ID.              CUST-RPT.
010030 ****************************************************************
010040 * THE CUSTOMER REPORT PROGRAM READS THE CUSTOMER
010050 * NAME FILE. (CUST-IN-FILE) AND PRODUCES THE
010060 * 'CUSTOMER LISTING' (REPORT-FILE)
010070 ****************************************************************
010080 ENVIRONMENT DIVISION.
010090 CONFIGURATION SECTION.
010100 SOURCE-COMPUTER.      IBM-370.
010110 OBJECT-COMPUTER.      IBM-370.
010120 INPUT-OUTPUT SECTION.
010130 FILE-CONTROL.
010140      SELECT CUST-IN-FILE      ASSIGN TO UT-S-CUSTIN.
010150      SELECT REPORT-FILE       ASSIGN TO UR-S-SYSPRINT.
010160 ****************************************************************
010170 DATA DIVISION.
010180 FILE SECTION.
010190 FD   CUST-IN-FILE
010200                   RECORD CONTAINS 80 CHARACTERS
010210                   LABEL RECORDS ARE STANDARD
010220                   DATA RECORD IS CUST-RECORD.
010230 01   CUST-RECORD.
010240      05   FILLER                PIC X(21).
010250      05   CR-CUST-NO            PIC 9(05).
010260      05   FILLER                PIC X(15).
010270      05   CR-CUST-NAME          PIC X(15).
010280      05   FILLER                PIC X(24).
010290 FD   REPORT-FILE
010300                   RECORD CONTAINS 132 CHARACTERS
010310                   LABEL RECORDS ARE STANDARD
010320                   DATA RECORD IS REPORT-LINE.
010330 01   REPORT-LINE               PIC X(132).
010340 ****************************************************************
010350 WORKING-STORAGE SECTION.
010360 01   PROGRAM-INDICATORS.
010370      05   ARE-THERE-MORE-RECORDS  PIC X(03)   VALUE 'YES'.
010380           88 THERE-ARE-NO-MORE-RECORDS        VALUE 'NO'.
010390 01   PRINTER-CONTROL.
010400      05   LINE-COUNT            PIC 9(02)   VALUE 99.
010410      05   PAGE-COUNT            PIC 9(04)   VALUE 0.
010420      05   MAX-LINES             PIC 9(02)   VALUE 44.
010430 01   HEAD-LINE1.
010440      05   FILLER                PIC X(25)   VALUE SPACES.
010450      05   FILLER                PIC X(17)   VALUE.
010460                                             'CUSTOMER LISTING'.
010470      05   FILLER                PIC X(15)   VALUE SPACES.
010480      05   FILLER                PIC X(05)   VALUE 'PAGE'.
010490      05   H1-PAGE-NO            PIC ZZZ9.
010500 01   HEAD-LINE2.
010510      05   FILLER                PIC X(20)   VALUE SPACES.
010520      05   FILLER                PIC X(6)    VALUE 'NUMBER'.
010530      05   FILLER                PIC X(12)   VALUE SPACES.
010540      05   FILLER                PIC X(4)    VALUE 'NAME'.
010550 01   DETAIL-LINE.
010560      05   FILLER                PIC X(20).
010570      05   DL-CUST-NO            PIC 9(05).
010580      05   FILLER                PIC X(07).
```

```
010590     05  DL-NAME                    PIC X(15).
010600 ***********************************************************
010610 PROCEDURE DIVISION.
010620 *********************************************
010630 *            CONTROL MODULE                  *
010640 *********************************************
010650 A100-CREATE-REPORT.
010660     PERFORM B100-INITIALIZE-RTN.
010670     PERFORM C100-READ-RTN.
010680     PERFORM C200-PRINT-REPORT-RTN
010690         UNTIL THERE-ARE-NO-MORE-RECORDS.
010700     PERFORM E100-END-RTN.
010710     STOP RUN.
010720 *********************************************
010730 *            SUBROUTINES SECTION             *
010740 *********************************************
010750 B100-INITIALIZE-RTN.
010760     OPEN INPUT CUST-IN-FILE
010770         OUTPUT REPORT-FILE.
010780 B199-INITIALIZE-EXIT.
010790     EXIT.
010800 C100-READ-RTN.
010810     READ CUST-IN-FILE
010820         AT END
010830         MOVE 'NO' TO ARE-THERE-MORE-RECORDS.
010840 C199-READ-EXIT.
010850     EXIT.
010860 C200-PRINT-REPORT-RTN.
010870     IF LINE-COUNT > MAX-LINES
010880         PERFORM C300-HEADING-RTN.
010890     MOVE SPACES TO DETAIL-LINE.
010900     MOVE CR-CUST-NO TO DL-CUST-NO.
010910     MOVE CR-CUST-NAME TO DL-NAME.
010920     WRITE REPORT-LINE FROM DETAIL-LINE
010930         AFTER ADVANCING 2 LINES.
010940     ADD 2 TO LINE-COUNT.
010950     PERFORM C100-READ-RTN.
010960 C299-PRINT-REPORT-EXIT.
010970     EXIT.
010980 C300-HEADING-RTN.
010990     ADD 1 TO PAGE-COUNT.
020000     MOVE PAGE-COUNT TO H1-PAGE-NO.
020010     WRITE REPORT-LINE FROM HEAD-LINE1
020020         AFTER ADVANCING PAGE.
020030     WRITE REPORT-LINE FROM HEAD-LINE2
020040         AFTER ADVANCING 2 LINES.
020050     MOVE 3 TO LINE-COUNT.
020060 C399-HEADING-EXIT.
020070     EXIT.
020080 E100-END-RTN.
020090     CLOSE CUST-IN-FILE
020100         REPORT-FILE.
020110 E199-END-EXIT.
020120     EXIT.
020130 ******************** END OF PROGRAM ********************
```

```
          CUSTOMER LISTING   PAGE 1
    NUMBER              NAME

    142160              SUE BECK
    161531              ART FRANKEL
    214324              WENDY GREENOUGH
    302599              BILLIE HATCH
    416723              GARNET LONEY
    742398              DAR POPOVIC
    814622              LYNLEE RITCHIE
```

**Figure 11-4(b)  Output.** This shows an example of output from the COBOL program.

**Figure 11-4(a)  A COBOL program.** This program is designed to read a customer name file and produce a customer report. Many existing programs, incidentally, have several lines in the Identification Division to describe author, installation, date written, and so on. These lines are optional and may not be supported by newer versions of COBOL.

novice programmer and expert. The novice can write simple programs using just part, or subsets, of the language, but the expert can use all the many options available. Some critics say PL/I is so loaded down with options, however, that it loses some of its usefulness.

If, as a programmer, you are used to FORTRAN or COBOL, you will be surprised at how free-form and flexible PL/I is. There are few coding restrictions. Language statements can begin in any column and continue without any particular restrictions; nothing has to be in any certain place.

PL/I implementation requires a very large compiler, which means that it requires a lot of main storage. Therefore, it is not suitable for small computer systems with limited main storage capacity. In general, you will not find PL/I used with mini- or microcomputers.

### Program Organization

In PL/I, **data declarations**—the data statements—are made first; that is, data is described *before* the logical procedures and other activity that is applied to the data. In addition, separate logical procedures known as *blocks* enhance the possibilities for writing modular programs (as discussed in Chapter 10). As we shall see, it is a real advantage to be able to divide a program into logical pieces that make it easier to handle.

```
/*COMPUTE EMPLOYEE SALARIES*/
PAYROLL: PROCEDURE OPTIONS (MAIN);
         DECLARE NAME    CHARACTER (20);
         DECLARE RATE    FIXED DECIMAL(3, 2);
         DECLARE HOURS   FIXED DECIMAL(2);
         DECLARE SALARY  FIXED DECIMAL(5, 2);
         PUT PAGE LIST ('NAME','SALARY');
         PUT SKIP;
         ON ENDFILE END-OF-FILE=1;
         GET LIST (NAME, RATE, HOURS);
         DO WHILE (END-OF-FILE=0);
              IF HOURS > 40
              THEN SALARY = 40 * RATE + 1.5 * RATE * (HOURS - 40);
              ELSE SALARY = HOURS * RATE;
              PUT SKIP (1) LIST (NAME, SALARY);
              GET LIST (NAME, RATE, HOURS);
         END;
 END PAYROLL;
```

**Figure 11-5(a)   A PL/I program.** This program is designed to compute employee salaries. Note that data declarations come first. Also note the DO WHILE structure.

| NAME | SALARY |
|---|---|
| ROBIN CLARK | 327.50 |
| RUDY LACHOW | 250.00 |
| MARSHA ONEILL | 200.00 |
| DEE TYNDALL | 278.00 |
| LEONARD WOLF | 290.00 |

**Figure 11-5(b)   Output from PL/I program.**

### Control Structures

The control structures are the standard ones you will recognize from Chapter 8: IF-THEN-ELSE, the loops DO WHILE and DO UNTIL, and the GO TO unconditional transfer.

An example of a PL/I program is shown in Figure 11-5.

# Basic: For Beginners and Others

We have already touched on **Basic**—*Beginners' All*-purpose *Symbolic Instruction Code*—in Chapter 8 (and we go into it in some detail in Appendix A), but here we will present a quick overview. Developed at Dartmouth College, BASIC was introduced by John Kemeny and Thomas Kurtz in 1965 and was originally intended for use by students in an academic environment. In the late 1960s it became widely used in interactive time-sharing environments in universities and colleges. The use of BASIC has extended to business and personal mini- and microcomputer systems.

### Features

The primary feature of BASIC is one that may be of interest to many readers of this book: BASIC is easy to learn, even for a person who has never programmed before. Thus, the language is used often in training students in the classroom. BASIC is also used by nonprogramming people, such as engineers, who find it useful in problem solving.

### Program Organization

Unlike COBOL, BASIC has no distinct divisions; a program is all one unit. This means also that there are no separate data declarations; that is, data is simply declared as it is used.

### Control Structures

By and large, BASIC is an unstructured language, although Dartmouth BASIC is structured and BASIC-PLUS (by Digital Equipment Corp.) and UBASIC (by Sperry Univac) have structured features. Most versions of BASIC have the control structures IF-THEN and a GOTO statement. They also have a FOR/NEXT structure (explained in Appendix A), which allows repetitive execution of instructions.

# Pascal: The Language of Simplicity

Named for Blaise Pascal, the seventeenth-century French mathematician, **Pascal** was developed by a Swiss computer scientist, Niklaus Wirth, and first became available in 1971. Since that time it has become quite popular, particularly in universities and colleges offering computer science programs, first in Europe and now in the United States.

### Features

The foremost feature of Pascal is that it is *simpler* than other languages—simpler than PL/I, which has control structures built in but which is a more complicated language to code, and simpler than COBOL, which is wordy and has fewer structured features. One reason for this simplicity is that control structures are built right into the language, and by knowing only a few coding rules you can write some simple programs.

Pascal has become very popular in college computer science departments. Because of its limited input/output capabilities, it is unlikely, in its present form, to have a serious impact on the business community. Pascal is making large strides in the microcomputer market as a simple yet sophisticated alternative to BASIC.

### Program Organization

Program organization is very specific. First, you must write the program name, the name by which you can identify the program. Second, you write data declarations indicating what type a particular kind of data is— that is, integer, real number, string, array, or whatever. Third,

```
PROGRAM PASCALEX (INPUT, OUTPUT);
(*COUNT THE POSITIVE NUMBERS*)
VAR
        COUNT : INTEGER;
        NUMBER: REAL;
BEGIN
COUNT:=0;
REPEAT
        READ (NUMBER);
        IF NUMBER > 0
        THEN COUNT:=COUNT + 1;
UNTIL NUMBER=0;   (*LAST NUMBER IS ZERO*)
WRITELN ('THE COUNT OF POSITIVE NUMBERS IS', COUNT:3)
END.
```

**Figure 11-6(a)    A Pascal program.** The program counts the number of positive numbers read in and prints out that number at the end. Data declarations appear after VAR, which stands for "variable." After the BEGIN statement, COUNT is set equal (using the := sign) to zero. The REPEAT/UNTIL loop directs the computer to keep reading numbers until a number is 0, at which point it stops. Note the two comments (in parentheses and asterisks); the second comment indicates that the last number is zero, which is how the computer knows when to stop the loop. The WRITELN statement indicates the output to be written.

```
        THE COUNT OF POSITIVE NUMBERS IS 27
```

**Figure 11-6(b)    Output from Pascal program.**

you write the functions and procedures. The main part of the program actually appears last and refers back to the various functions and procedures, as needed.

### Control Structures

The beauty of Pascal is that it not only has control structures, including the loop, but that it uses the very words that emphasize how the loop works—IF/THEN/ELSE and WHILE/DO and REPEAT/UNTIL— which helps suggest why the language is easy to learn. There is also a GO TO structure, although the availability of the other control structures limits the necessity of using GO TO.

An example of a Pascal program is shown in Figure 11-6.

### Ada: The Language of Standardization?

Is any software worth over $25 billion? Not any more, according to Defense Department experts. In 1974, the U.S. Department of Defense had spent that amount on all kinds of software for a hodgepodge of languages for its needs. The answer to this problem turned out to be a new language called **Ada**—named for Lady Augusta Ada Byron, "the first programmer" (see Chapter 3). Developed as one of four competitive language designs sponsored by the Pentagon, Ada was originally intended to be a standard language for weapons systems. It has been used not only for military purposes but also for successful commercial applications. The new language, introduced in 1980, has the support not only of the defense establishment but also of such industry heavyweights as IBM and Intel, and is even available for some microcomputers. Although some industry experts have said Ada is too complex, others say that it is easy to learn and that it will increase productivity. Indeed, some experts believe that it is by far a superior commercial language to such standbys as COBOL and FOR-TRAN. The Defense Department has applied for a trademark for Ada in order to have control over its use.

### Features

Ada is a structured language. Among its features, Ada encourages modular design because it allows each specialized package or module of a large program to be written and tested separately before the entire program is put together. The modular design encourages the dividing up of various tasks and using teamwork to make them mutually compatible. Ada also requires that every data item be defined according to a certain type—an integer, character string, array, or the like—and this permits the compiler to check for errors before the entire program is run. In other words, the language makes it easier for programmers to write error-free programs.

**Figure 11-7 An Ada program** Ada allows a user to express programs in a compact, English-like notation as illustrated in this program to total coin receipts.

```
PROCEDURE count your money IS
    USE simple io;
    count, money, cents, dollars: INTEGER;
    values: CONSTANT ARRAY (1..6) OF INTEGER :=
            (1, 5, 10, 25, 50, 100);
BEGIN
    money := 0;
    FOR i IN 1 . . . 6 LOOP
        GET(count);
        money := money + values (i) * count;
    END LOOP;
    IF money = 0 THEN
        PUT ("You are broke.");
    ELSE
        dollars := money / 100;
        cents := money MOD 100;
        PUT ("dollars:"); PUT (dollars);
        PUT ("cents:"); PUT (cents);
    END IF;
END count your money;
```

### Program Organization

In its simplest form, an Ada program has two parts, a declarative part and a statement part. The declarative section comes first, beginning with the word *procedure*, to give names and types to each data variable that will be used in the statement part. The statement section starts with the word *begin* and finishes with the word *end*; the statements between these two delimiters describe the program logic—that is, actions to be taken on the data.

### Control Structures

The control structures in Ada closely parallel the basic control structures of sequence, selection, and iteration. The selection statement is IF/THEN, followed by END IF. There are two types of iteration statements, FOR LOOP and WHILE LOOP, each ending with END LOOP.

An example of an Ada program is shown in Figure 11-7.

Widespread adoption of Ada is likely to take years, as even its most optimistic advocates admit. While there are many reasons for this (the military services, for instance, have different levels of enthusiasm for it), probably its size, which may hinder its use on microcomputers, and complexity are the greatest barriers.

# RPG:
## A Language for Business Reports

All the languages discussed so far have been procedure-oriented—that is, designed to allow programmers/users to write logical sequences of instructions. However, **RPG**—for Report Program Generator—is a

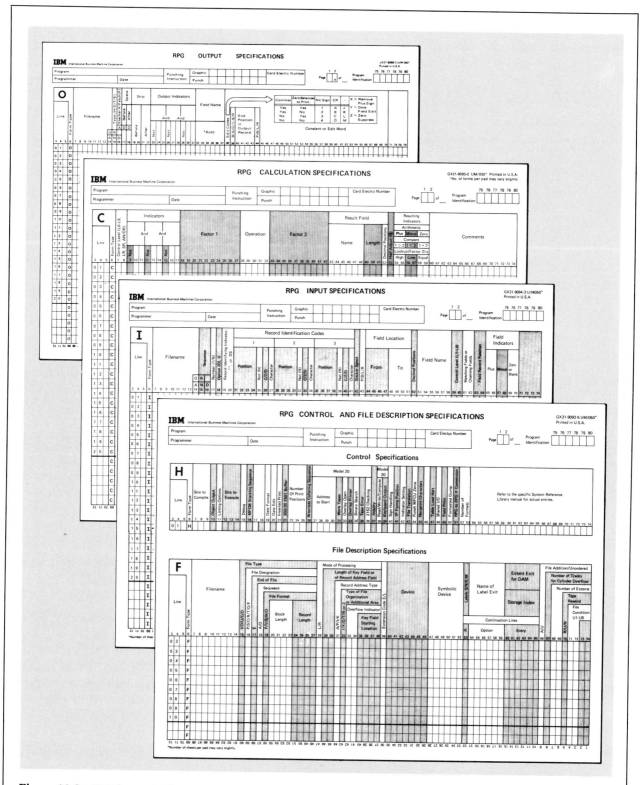

**Figure 11-8  RPG forms.** With minimal training, users can fill out specifications in these coding forms and a report will be produced with little effort. The forms are filled out in the order shown from bottom to top—file description, input, calculation, and output.

problem-oriented language designed to solve the particular problem of producing business reports. It is also capable of doing some file updating. Developed at IBM, RPG was introduced in 1964 and was intended primarily for small computer systems. An updated version called **RPG II** was introduced in 1970 and extended the language's original capabilities.

The idea behind RPG is that business reports can be produced by a person's filling out special coding forms. Indeed the forms are labeled in such detail (see Figure 11-8) that, with a minimum of training, you can fill out the forms and produce reports without having to worry about the logic involved in writing the programs.

RPG is so easy to learn that business people like it because they get the maximum return on their investment—their investment being the time their employees spend filling out the coding sheets. But RPG is necessarily limited and is suitable only for straightforward, relatively uncomplicated data processing problems. It is not used to solve the problems of the world, only to make reports about them.

## Some Other Languages

The languages just described are probably the major ones used today. But there are others that you are apt to see mentioned and that are important to know about:

**LISP** Developed in 1958 at M.I.T. by John McCarthy, **LISP** is designed to process nonnumeric data—that is, symbols, such as characters or words. LISP can be used interactively at a terminal. It is a popular language for writing programs dealing with artificial intelligence.

**ALGOL** Standing for *ALGOrithmic Language*, **ALGOL** was introduced in 1960. Though popular in Europe, it has never really caught on in the United States. ALGOL was developed primarily for scientific programming and is considered the forerunner of PL/I and Pascal. It has excellent control structures, but, like FORTRAN, it has somewhat limited file processing capabilities.

**SNOBOL** Invented in the early 1960s at Bell Telephone Laboratories, **SNOBOL** is considered quite a powerful language. Today it is the most widely used string processing language—that is, language for manipulating alphanumeric or special characters. Applications for SNOBOL include its use by text editors and language processors.

**APL** Short for *A Programming Language*, **APL** was conceived by Kenneth Iverson and was introduced by IBM in 1968. APL is interactive, easily learned by programmers, and particularly suited to table handling—that is, to processing groups of related numbers in a table. A disadvantage is that a special keyboard, which contains a rather formidable set of Greek symbols for a large group of operators, is required. Having a large number of operators means that the APL compiler must be rather large, and so it is apt to be available only on systems with large memories.

**LOGO** If you overhear a couple of programmers (or even school teachers) using the word "turtle" in conversation, it is a fair guess they are talking about **LOGO**. A dialect of LISP developed at the Massachusetts Institute of Technology by Seymour Papert, it is known at this time as a language that children can use. The "turtle" actually refers to a triangular pointer on the CRT screen that responds to a few simple commands such as FORWARD and LEFT. The language is *interactive*, which means that a person can learn to use it while sitting at the computer. Figure 11-9 gives an example of a LOGO program design.

**Smalltalk** Most interaction with a computer consists of "remembering and typing." With the **Smalltalk** language, however, you "see and print" instead. Here is the way it works: The keyboard is used to enter text into the computer, but all other tasks are accomplished with the use of a mouse, which you move around to direct the movement of a cursor on the CRT screen and on which you press a button

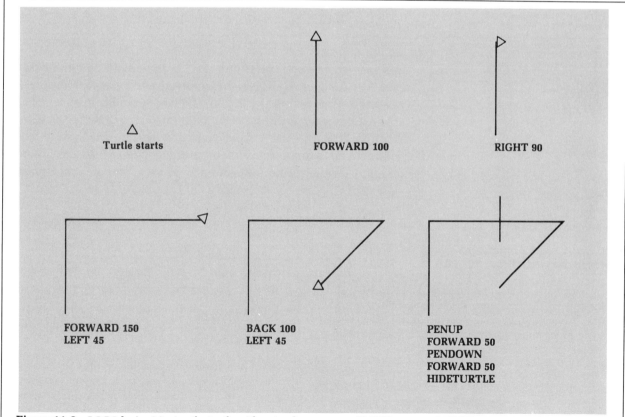

**Figure 11-9  LOGO logic.** Moving the turtle with a simple sequence of LOGO commands: FORWARD moves the turtle in the direction it is facing. RIGHT and LEFT rotate the turtle. PENUP and PENDOWN raise and lower the pen—the turtle leaves a trace when it moves with the pen down.

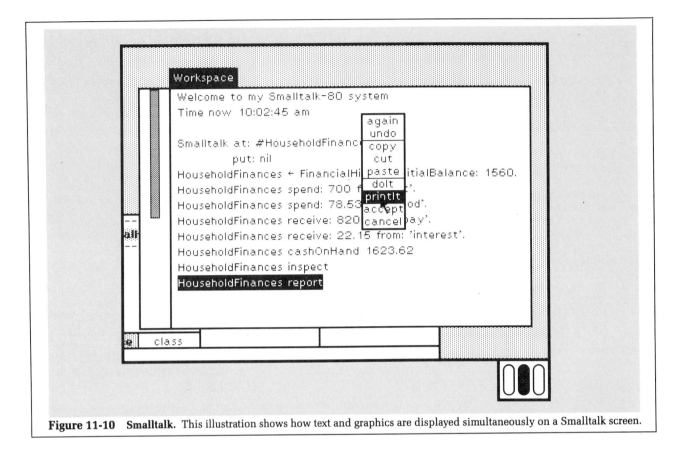

**Figure 11-10  Smalltalk.** This illustration shows how text and graphics are displayed simultaneously on a Smalltalk screen.

to select a command (see Figure 11-10). Invented by Alan Kay at the Palo Alto (California) Research Center, created by Xerox Corporation, Smalltalk represents a watershed of key ideas and concepts that constitute a dramatic departure from traditional computer science because it supports an especially visual computer system. The basis of Smalltalk is that it is an *object*-oriented language rather than a *procedure*-oriented language: the interaction is between people and things or classes of objects.

## Summary and Key Terms

- A **programming language** consists of a set of rules that can instruct the computer on what operations to perform. It has definite characteristics: a limited vocabulary; a precise meaning for each word; and the ability to solve complex problems step by step.

- There are over 150 computer languages presently being used, the most common being FORTRAN, COBOL, PL/I, BASIC, Pascal, Ada, RPG II, and assembly languages.

- Programming languages are said to be low level if they are closer to the language the computer uses (0s and 1s) or high level if closer to the language people use (English-

like). We consider four levels of language: (1) machine language, (2) assembly language, (3) high-level language, and (4) nonprocedural languages.

- **Machine language,** the lowest level, represents information as 1s and 0s—binary digits corresponding to the computer's "on" and "off" electrical states.

- **Assembly languages** use abbreviations or mnemonic codes to replace the 0s and 1s of machine language—for example, A for "Add." A translating device called an **assembler program** translates the assembly language into machine language. Assembly languages are more convenient for humans to use than are machine languages, but they have at least two disadvantages: (1) the assembly language varies according to the type of computer, and (2) assembly languages are detailed in the extreme, making programming repetitive and error-prone.

- **High-level languages** are English-like languages, making them easier to use than assembly languages. Each language has a **compiler** to translate the high-level language into computer-executable machine language. High-level languages are either **procedure-oriented,** which means they are designed for writing logical sequences of instructions, or **problem-oriented,** that is, designed to solve specific types of problems such as providing ways to generate routine business reports. Examples of procedure-oriented languages are FORTRAN, COBOL, PL/I, BASIC, and Pascal. An example of a problem- oriented language is RPG.

- **Nonprocedural languages** are intended primarily to help nonprogrammers access a computer's data base. Such languages are considered **user friendly;** that is, no formal training in programming is required.

- **FORTRAN** (for *FORmula TRANslator*), introduced by IBM in 1954, was the first high-level language and is a scientifically oriented language. It is noted for its simplicity and brevity and is good for executing complex formulas, but it is not useful for file processing or data processing.

- **COBOL** (for *COmmon Business-Oriented Language*) was introduced in 1959 by **CODASYL,** for *COnference of DAta SYstem Languages,* a group of government and industry representatives interested in creating a standardized programming language appropriate for business. The principal benefit of standardization is that COBOL is relatively machine-independent. COBOL was first standardized in 1968, and again, as **ANS-COBOL,** in 1974. The principal feature of COBOL is that it is English-like, so that a nonprogrammer can still understand the general purpose of a program.

- A COBOL program has four divisions, which must appear in order. The **identification division** identifies the name of the program. The **environment division** has two sections—the CONFIGURATION SECTION, which describes the computer on which the program will be compiled and executed, and the INPUT-OUTPUT SECTION, which relates each file of the program to the specific physical device, such as the printer. The **data division** contains all detailed information about all data processed. The data division has two sections—the FILE SECTION, which contains general information about each file, and a WORKING- STORAGE SECTION, which describes in detail data not directly associated with a specific file. The **procedure division** contains all the statements that give the computer specific instructions to carry out the logic of the program, using specific verbs from the list of COBOL reserved words such as READ, ADD, and SORT.

- COBOL has structures in it: IF-ELSE (same as IF-THEN-ELSE), PERFORM/UNTIL (same as DOWHILE loop), and GOTO statement.

- **PL/I,** which stands for *Programming Language One,* was introduced in 1964 by IBM as a compromise between FORTRAN and COBOL. Neither scientific nor business language, it was to be a general-purpose language. Control structures fitting the basic control structures (sequence, selection, iteration) are built right into the language. PL/I can also be used by both novice and expert programmers. There are few coding restrictions. The language is not usually used with mini- or microcomputers because it requires a lot of main storage. In program organization, data declarations—the data statements—are described before the logical procedures. In addition, separate logical procedures known as blocks enhance the possibilities for writing modular programs.

- **BASIC**—Beginners' All-Purpose Symbolic Instruction Code—was developed at Dartmouth College. BASIC was introduced by John Kemeny and Thomas Kurtz in 1965 and was originally intended for use by students in an academic environment. It was extended to business and personal mini- and microcomputer systems. It is easy to use, even for a person who has never programmed before. By and large, it is an unstructured language, although Dartmouth BASIC is structured and BASIC-PLUS and UBASIC have structured features. Most versions of BASIC have the structures IF-THEN, a GOTO statement, and FOR/NEXT.

- **Pascal,** named for Blaise Pascal, was developed by Niklaus Wirth and became available in 1971. It is particularly popular in universities offering computer science programs. One reason for the simplicity is that the control structures—IF/THEN/ELSE, WHILE/DO, and REPEAT/UNTIL—are built into the language. Program organization is very specific: you write the program name, then the data declarations indicating the particular kind of data, then the functions and procedures, then the main part of the program.

- **Ada,** named for the Countess of Lovelace, Augusta Ada Byron, was introduced in 1980 as a Pentagon-sponsored language intended to be a standard language for weapons systems. It also has possibilities for commercial use, although opinions differ as to whether it is too complex or easy to learn. Ada encourages modular design because each specialized part or module of a large program can be written and tested separately. Each data item may also be defined according to a certain type, allowing the compiler to check for errors before the entire program is run.

- **RPG**—for Report Program Generator—is a problem-oriented language, designed to solve the particular problem of producing business reports. Developed at IBM, RPG was introduced in 1964 primarily for small computer systems; an updated version called **RPG II** was introduced in 1970. RPG enables a person to produce business reports by filling out special coding forms.

- Other languages are **LISP,** developed in 1958, to process nonnumeric data and used with programs dealing with artificial intelligence; **ALGOL** (for *ALGO*rithmic Language), introduced in 1960 for scientific programming; **SNOBOL,** introduced in the early 1960s and used to manipulate alphanumeric or special characters; **APL** (for *A Programming Language*), introduced in 1968 and particularly suited to processing groups of related numbers in a table (although a special keyboard is required); **LOGO,** a dialect of LISP developed at M.I.T. which is particularly suited for children; and **Smalltalk,** invented at the Palo Alto Research Center in California, which is an object-oriented language rather than procedure-oriented language and allows people to interact between things or classes of objects, using a mouse to direct movements on the CRT screen.

## Review

1. How do programming languages and human languages differ?

2. What are the most widely used computer languages?

3. Differentiate machine language, assembly languages, high-level languages, and nonprocedural languages. Distinguish between procedure-oriented and problem-oriented languages.

4. Discuss the definition, purpose, control structures, principal features, and benefits and drawbacks of the commonly used high-level languages.

5. What are the names and purposes of the four divisions in COBOL?

6. Briefly describe LISP, ALGOL, SNOBOL, APL, LOGO, and Smalltalk.

## Selected References for Further Reading

Booch, Grady. *Software Engineering with Ada*. Menlo Park, Calif.: Benjamin/Cummings, 1983.

Dale, Nell, and David Orshalick. *Introduction to Pascal and Structured Design*. Lexington, Mass.: Heath, 1983.

Feingold, Carl C. *Fundamentals of Structured COBOL Programming*. 4th ed. Dubuque, Iowa: William C. Brown, 1983.

Graham, Neill. *Introduction to Pascal*. 2nd ed. St. Paul: West, 1983.

Grauer, Robert T., and Marshal A. Crawford. *The COBOL Environment*. Englewood Cliffs, N.J.: Prentice-Hall, 1979.

Kudlick, Michael D. *Assembly Language Programming for the IBM Systems 360 and 370*. Dubuque, Iowa: William C. Brown, 1980.

Nickerson, Robert C. *Fundamentals of FORTRAN Programming*. Cambridge, Mass.: Winthrop, 1980.

Page, Rex, and Rich Didday. *FORTRAN 77 for Humans*. St. Paul, Minn.: West, 1980.

Rockey, Clarence J. *Structured PL/I Programming with Business Applications*. Dubuque, Iowa: William C. Brown, 1981.

Shelly, Gary B., and Thomas J. Cashman. *Computer Programming, RPG II*. Fullerton, Calif.: Anaheim, 1976.

Wegner, Peter. *Programming with Ada: An Introduction by Means of Graduated Examples*. Englewood Cliffs, N.J.: Prentice-Hall, 1980.

Welburn, Tyler. *Structured COBOL: Fundamentals and Style*. Palo Alto, Calif.: Mayfield, 1981.

## IN THIS CHAPTER

An operating system, the set of programs that allows the computer to control resources, execute programs, and manage data, is described. Multiprocessing, time-sharing, generic operating systems such as Unix and CP/M, programmer software supports, and other special features are discussed.

# ch 12

# operating systems

## the traffic cop

All sorts of mysteries have been going on behind the scenes that we have not touched on so far. They may be summarized in two words: operating systems.

Consider the following questions:

Question: If there are several other programs in the main storage of a computer at the same time as my program, what keeps the programs from getting mixed up with one another?

Answer: The operating system.

Question: And if my program and another program both want to use the CPU at the same time, what decides which program gets it?

Answer: The operating system.

Question: And if my program gets into an endless loop, what will interrupt the program and stop it?

Answer: The operating system!

Let us look at this sophisticated concept, the operating system.

## Why Operating Systems: The Need for a Traffic Cop

In the early days of computing, only one program at a time was executed by a computer system. This meant that all the system's resources were available on demand for that program—the CPU, all the primary and secondary storage at hand, and all peripheral devices such as printers. However, it also meant that these components were idle most of the time; while a punched card was being read, for instance, the CPU and printer would be inactive.

Time was also wasted while the system waited for the computer operator to finish his or her tasks: put cards in the card reader, set up tapes, push buttons on the console, and so on. A program would come to the end of its run, and the entire system would be idled while the operator got the next job ready to run.

All this was inefficient use of an expensive machine. To improve the efficiency of computer operations, operating systems were introduced in the 1960s. An **operating system** is a set of programs that allows the computer system to manage its own resources. It handles many chores implicitly, without being told to do so by each individual programmer. An operating system has three main functions: (1) to control the computer system resources, (2) to execute computer programs, and (3) to manage data. The control programs minimize operator intervention, so that the computer operations will flow smoothly and without interruption. In addition, an operating system improves efficiency in two ways: (1) by helping users share the computer resources, such as main storage, the CPU, and peripheral devices, and (2) by invoking translators and programs to take care of certain standard tasks that everyone uses at one time or another.

The operating system is the medium for cooperation among users, helping them make the best use of computer system resources so that everyone benefits. It also helps free programmers from repetitive, machine-oriented details so that they can concentrate on solving problems for clients. (We mean here the applications programmers; the systems programmers are the ones who actually write, change, or maintain the operating systems.)

The most important program in the system is the **supervisor program,** most of which remains in main storage. It controls the entire operating system and calls in other operating system programs from disk storage as needed. These operating system programs stay in main storage while they are executing. But they do not remain in primary storage; that would be an inefficient use of space.

The operating system, in summary, is not hocus-pocus, not a collection of tricks done with mirrors. It is just a set of programs. Let us now examine some of the various ways operating systems help in sharing resources.

## Sharing Resources

A primary feature of an operating system is that you, as an applications programmer, will be able to share the resources of the computer with minimum concern about the details of how it is done. There are a number of reasons why this is so:

- Multiprogramming
- Time-sharing
- Other special features

### Multiprogramming

**Multiprogramming** means that two or more programs are being executed concurrently on a computer and are sharing the computer's resources. What this really means is that the programs are taking turns—one program is run for a while, then another one. The key word here is *concurrently* as opposed to *simultaneously.* Concurrent processing means that two or more programs are active in the same time frame—during the same hour, for instance—but not at the exact same time. Concurrent, in other words, means that one program will be using one resource while another program uses another resource. As a result, there is less idle time for the computer system's resources.

Concurrent processing is effective because CPU speeds are so much faster than input/output speeds. During the time it takes for the computer to execute a read instruction for one program, for example, the CPU can execute several calculation instructions for another program. If, instead, a program was in main storage by itself, there would be a high percentage of CPU idle time.

Multiprogramming is *event-driven.* This means that programs share resources based on events that take place in the programs. If, for example, a program instructs the computer to read a record, the computer will be interrupted to pursue this activity through the operating system. Meanwhile, the program relinquishes control of the CPU to another program; the computer may then proceed to execute calculations within this program. When the record for the first program has been read, that program may then continue to execute, subject to the availability of the CPU. Thus, although to the programmer it seems as if the program is executing continuously from start to finish, in fact it is being constantly interrupted, as the computer system resources are shared among different programs.

Programs that run in a multiprogramming environment are often batch programs. Typical examples are payroll, accounts receivable, sales and marketing analyses, financial planning, quality control, and stock reports.

### Time-sharing

**Time-sharing,** a special case of multiprogramming, is usually time-driven rather than event-driven. A common approach is to give each user a "time slice," typically 2 milliseconds, during which he or she can do whatever is required. However, the operating system does not wait for completion of the event; at the end of the time slice, the resources are taken away from the user and given to someone else. This is hardly noticeable to the user: When you are sitting before a terminal in a time-sharing system, the computer's response time will be quite speedy—a matter of a few seconds—and it will seem as if you have the computer to yourself. **Response time** is the time between your typed computer request and the computer's reply. Even if you are working on a calculation and the operating system interrupts it, sending you to the end of the line until other users have had their turns, you may not notice that you have been deprived of service. Not all computer systems give ideal service all the time, however; if a computer system is trying to serve too many users at the same time, response time may deteriorate.

Notice that, generally speaking, you as the user do not have control over the computer system. In a time-sharing environment, the operating system has actual control because it controls the users by allocating time slices. However, sometimes a particular user will, for some reason, be entitled to a higher pirority than other users. A common method of acknowledging higher priority is for the operating system to give that user more turns. Suppose, for example, that there are five users who would normally be given time slices in order: A-B-C-D-E and so forth. If user B is assigned a higher priority, the order could be changed to A-B-C-B-D-B-E-B, giving B every other turn.

Typical time-sharing applications are credit checking, point-of-sale systems, engineering design, airline reservations, and hospital information systems.

### Special Problems Relating to Shared Resources

When several programs share the same computer resources, special problems of control must be considered. There must be a method to determine which program will be executed next. A given program must be able to access needed devices. Memory space must be available to the program, and that program must be protected from inadvertent interference from other programs. We shall now consider how the operating system handles some of these types of problems.

**Resource Allocation** How does the operating system actually determine that the various resources of the computer system are allocated to the various programs as they are needed and in a fair manner?

A program waiting to be run by the computer is placed in the input queue, a file on disk, with other waiting programs. A scheduling program, part of the operating system, selects the next job from the input queue. This decision is based on such factors as memory requirements, priority, and devices needed. In other words, the selection is based to some extent on whether resources available can satisfy the needs of the waiting program.

In the course of the resource allocation, the operating system must consider the input/output devices available and their use. For example, at any given moment, the operating system knows which program is using which particular tape drive and knows which devices are free and can be allocated to a program waiting in the input queue. A job would not be allowed to begin, for example, if it needed three tape drives and only two were currently available.

**Memory Management** What if you have a very large program, for which it might be difficult to find space in main memory? Or what if several programs are competing for space in memory? These questions are related to memory management. **Memory management** is the process of allocating memory to programs and of keeping the programs in memory separate from each other.

Many computer systems manage memory using a technique called **virtual storage** (also called "virtual memory"). Virtual storage means that the user appears to have more main memory space than is actually the case; part of the program is stored on disk and is brought into memory for execution as needed. (Again, the delay in time may not be noticeable.) Since only part of a program is in main storage at any given time, the amount of memory needed for a program is minimized. Main memory, in this case, is considered **real storage,** while the secondary storage holding the rest of the program is considered virtual storage.

Virtual storage can be implemented in one of three ways:

- By segmentation
- By paging
- By a combination of segmentation and paging

Again, suppose you have a very large program, which means there will be difficulty finding space for it in the computer's main memory. Remember that main memory is shared among several programs. If your program is divided into smaller pieces, it will be easier to find places to put those pieces. This is essentially what segmentation does. **Segmentation** is the process of dividing a program into blocks of various sizes and placing these segments in main memory in *noncontiguous* locations—that is, locations not necessarily next to each other. These segments are based on the program logic. Logically related program statements, typically a program module (as discussed in Chapter 10), comprise a segment.

Even though the segments are not right next to each other in main memory, the operating system is able to keep track of them. One of the ways it does this is through a "segment table," which lists the number of segments that are part of the program and the beginning addresses of areas in main memory where they are placed.

The problem with segmentation is that it is possible to have many unused fragments of main memory. In response to this, the concept of paging was developed; this is the second method of implementing virtual storage. **Paging** is similar to segmentation, but all program blocks (which are called **pages**) and the corresponding main memory spaces (which are called **page frames**) are the same, fixed sizes—typically 2K or 4K bytes. Fixed page sizes mean the pages are not related to the program logic. The pages fit exactly into the page frames in main memory, thereby eliminating wasted space.

The third way of implementing virtual storage—and the best—is a combination of segmentation and paging. With this method, the program is first broken into segments and then the segments into pages. For the operating system to keep track of the various pieces, a segment table is needed and, for each segment, a page table. These tables have nothing in them but addresses.

Figure 12-1 shows how this system works. The example shows three segments of 20K, 30K, and 10K, respectively. Each segment is divided into pages of 4K bytes each. Note that the extra 2K in the third segment still requires a full 4K page. The pages are then distributed to various locations throughout main memory.

**Memory Protection** In a multiprogramming environment, it is theoretically possible for the computer, while executing one program, to destroy or modify another by transferring it to the wrong memory locations. To avoid this problem, the operating system confines each program to certain defined limits in memory. If the computer inadvertently transfers to some memory area outside those limits, the program execution is terminated. This process of keeping you from straying into others' programs or them into yours is called **memory protection.**

**Spooling** Suppose you have a half dozen programs active at a given moment, but your system has only one printer. If all programs take turns printing out their output a line or two at a time, interspersed with the output of other programs, the resulting printed report would be worthless. To get around this problem, a process called **spooling**

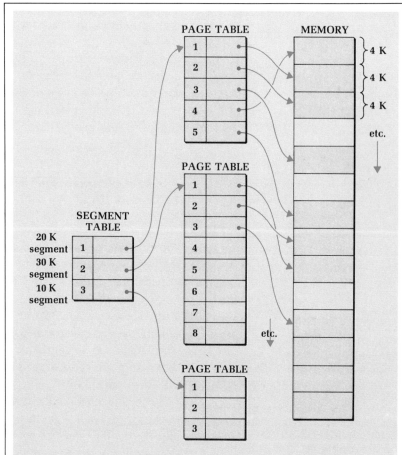

**Figure 12-1 Segmentation tables and page tables.** A program is first divided into segments, then each segment is divided into pages, which are distributed throughout main memory.

is used. Each program writes each file that is to be printed onto a disk, and when the program is completed, the disk files are printed out intact.

Spooling also addresses another problem—the relatively slow printer speeds. Writing a record on disk is much faster than writing that same record on a printer. A program, therefore, will complete execution more quickly if records to be printed are written temporarily on disk instead. The actual printing can be done at some later time. Some installations use a separate (usually smaller) computer dedicated exclusively to the printing of spooled files.

## Generic Operating Systems

Once upon a time when you bought a computer, the operating system came with the hardware. First it was free, later not free, but whether you purchased an IBM 370 with its OS (for Operating System, of course) or a Hewlett-Packard HP-3000 with its MPE (for Multiple

Programming Environment), you also bought the operating system that came with it.

Now all that is changing, and the trend is toward buying what are known as **generic operating systems**—that is, operating systems that are more general in nature, that work with more than one manufacturer's computer system, and that are frequently created by a third party that is not itself a hardware manufacturer. There are several generic operating systems, but we will discuss three that are particularly influential—Unix, Pick, and CP/M.

### For Mainframes and Minicomputers: Unix and Pick

You have just ordered a mainframe or minicomputer—say, a VAX-11/750, made by Digital Equipment Corporation (DEC), or an Eclipse, made by Data General. What kind of operating system are you going to use on it? Probably by far the best known is Unix.

**Unix** Developed in 1971 by Ken Thompson and Denis Ritchie at Bell Laboratories for use on Bell's DEC minicomputers, the designers were surprised to see Unix become the dominant operating system of the computer industry during the late 1970s and early 1980s. How did this come about?

Part of the reason may have had to do with social factors other than the software itself—namely, the "Unix graduate" phenomenon. In the late 1970s, Bell gave away Unix to many colleges and universities. Consequently, when many of these schools' graduates started entering the work force, they began agitating for the acceptance of Unix in industry. Another reason is that in 1981 Bell Labs reduced the price of executable versions of Unix to as little as $40 a copy, which set in motion a new wave of interest in the operating system.

**Unix** is considered a data processing professional's dream. A multiprogramming, time-sharing operating system, it was originally implemented for a minicomputer, but now also runs on IBM mainframes and even on some microcomputers. However, it is a very sophisticated operating system—so much so, in fact, that Unix is not considered user-friendly.

There are also some other drawbacks. Critics point to capricious use of abbreviations (such as GREP, for "global regular expression print"—whatever that may mean), inadequate documentation for general (as opposed to Bell Labs) users, and lack of support for COBOL programs. Still, today nearly all other operating systems are measured against the standard of Unix.

**Pick** One way to keep a product from becoming well known is to cleverly change its name. This has been the case with the operating system originally known as **Pick**. Developed by Dick Pick of Pick and Associates for the Microdata 16-bit minicomputer, it went under the name of Reality. Other computer companies gave it other names: Prime

---

**IN UNIX WE TRUST**

Though it hasn't aggressively marketed Unix until recently, AT&T has licensed the system to universities for a nominal fee and to some corporations for a much higher fee since the early 1970s.

As a result, thousands of university computer science students cut their teeth on Unix and became accustomed to it. Former students, now professional programmers, often describe Unix as "lovable," "accommodating" or "malleable." One compares its special language to poetry because it has "no numbers, just little commands with a lot of space on the page."

This impresses computer makers like Intel Corp. "Unix has a religious following," says William Lattin, an Intel vice president. "No other operating system has a bunch of good students that know it well and know how to make it work on other computers. We wanted to exploit that religion as part of our software offerings."

—Susan Chace,
*Wall Street Journal*,
November 8, 1982

calls it Prime-Information, Honeywell and DEC call it Ultimate, and Altos and IBM call it Pick. Take your pick.

Pick is recognized as being an easy operating system to use. It is considered to be extremely efficient for data base applications in business-oriented functions. However, it is not very efficient for scientific applications.

## THE IMPORTANCE OF CP/M

CP/M occupies a special niche in the personal computer market. By virtue of its broad vendor support and popularity with users, it is the industry's closest thing to a standard operating system.

To appreciate the importance of a standard operating system, imagine if stereo records had to be made for use only on a specific make of stereo system. Record producers would then produce records only for the most popular type of stereo systems to assure themselves of a broad market. A similar situation would exist in the computer industry if it were not for CP/M.

—Paul Kinnucan,
LIST,
Spring 1983

### For Microcomputers:
### CP/M

Like mainframes and minicomputers, microcomputers also have manufacturer-specific operating systems: Apple II has DOS (for Disk Operating System), Tandy-Radio Shack's TRS-80 has TRS-DOS, and the IBM Personal Computer has its own DOS. What this means is that the terrific piece of software you see somewhere—say, a word processing program for sale on a floppy disk at a Radio Shack store—probably will not work on another manufacturer's microcomputer. The reason: your computer (say an Apple or IBM PC) does not have the same operating system. Video game addicts who covet a friend's new acquisition on a different home computer may find this lack of standardization particularly distressing.

Happily, however, there is a generic operating system for microcomputers. Indeed, there is more than one, but the one that has become most popular by far is **CP/M**—short for Control Program/Microcomputers. If both Apple II and IBM PC users, say, have CP/M, they probably can write programs that will run on each other's computer. (There are, unfortunately, some situations where even two CP/M systems will not be compatible.)

CP/M was written in 1973 by Gary Kildall, who later went on to found Digital Research Inc., a software manufacturer in Pacific Grove, California, that now employs 155 people. Originally, CP/M was designed for 8-bit microcomputers, but now a version is available for 16-bit microcomputers. Because the operating system has been around for a while, there is a lot of off-the-shelf software available for use with it. Indeed, CP/M has become an industry standard. Many microcomputer suppliers under license to Digital Research sell a version of CP/M as an alternate operating system for their computers—Apple, Tandy-Radio Shack, and IBM are among them. DEC has taken this one step further; DEC's personal computers offer CP/M as the standard operating system, the operating system that comes with the computer. A great deal of commercially available software—business applications, games, and so on—have been written to run under CP/M.

An advantage of CP/M is that it is command driven in an interactive mode—that is, the user can sit at the terminal and carry out an interactive dialogue with the computer, issuing commands to the operating system. Yet CP/M is not considered user-friendly, and there are now some attempts to add another layer, as it were, to CP/M to make the underlying operating system more friendly. (We hasten to add, however, that adding a user-friendly software layer to CP/M might slow down the system significantly.)

CP/M is not designed for multiprogramming—that is, designed to be used by more than one user simultaneously. As microcomputers have become more popular in business, the need for this capability has developed. Enter again Gary Kildall, who has developed an operating system called MP/M, which stands for Multiuser Program/ Microcomputers. No doubt this and other similar operating systems will become more in demand as businesses increasingly use microcomputers.

## Translators and Service Programs

Most of the tasks described in sharing resources are done by the operating system without application programmer involvement. Although, as a programmer, you may need to make requests for input and output devices, generally speaking, these operating system features do not need specific instructions. Activities such as paging and spooling go on without your explicit commands. In the following discussion, however, we will describe situations that do require specific instructions to the operating systems. Since the commands vary from computer to computer, we shall make no attempt to include them here. The discussion is general and is applicable to most computer systems.

### Translators and the Link/Loader

When you write a program in BASIC, COBOL, or a similar high-level language, you need a **translator,** a program that translates your language into machine language. If you are using a high-level language, the translator program is usually a **compiler.** Sometimes, high-level languages are translated using an interpreter, as we will describe. If you are using an assembly language, the translator is called an **assembler.** It is important to note that compilers, interpreters, and assemblers are *programs,* not some sort of hardware. They are programs that use *your* programs as input data, and in this case your program is called the **source module** (or "source program").

There are three possible outputs from the compiler (or assembler) program: (1) an object module, (2) diagnostic messages, and (3) a source program listing. The **object module** is a version of your program that is now in machine language. **Diagnostic messages** inform you of **syntax errors.** These are not errors in logic but errors in use of the language, perhaps because of typing errors or because you did not understand how to use the language. If you have diagnostic messages, your program probably did not compile. (Sometimes, however, these are "warning messages," which are minor and do not prevent compilation.) The **source program listing** is a list of your program as you wrote it. You can use the source program listing to make any corrections necessary to your program.

There are many compilers: one for every language and every type of computer on which the language can be used. Thus, for any particular machine, you will have to use a COBOL compiler if you are writing a program in COBOL and a FORTRAN compiler if you are writing in FORTRAN.

Figure 12-2 shows what generally happens during the process of writing and correcting a program. The object module produced is often considered temporary, because if you are in the checkout phase of program development, the program is going to be changed, which means it will be recompiled. Notice that after the object module is ready there is a **link/load phase.** The object module of your program may be *linked* with other programs before it is run on the computer. The link/loader (also called the "linkage editor") is used to add such prewritten, standard programs to your program. These other programs are usually stored on disk in a systems library. An example of a standard program is one that computes a square root. By calling in the standard program and adding it to your own, you are spared the tedious process of writing out all the steps of computing the square root. The output from the link/load step is called the **load module.** Stored on disk, it is now ready to be read into memory and executed.

An **interpreter** translates *and* executes your program, one instruction at a time. Since the program is executed directly, neither an object module nor prior diagnostics are generated. Thus, a disadvantage of using an interpreter is that syntax errors may not be discovered until the program is executed. Interpreters are used, for the most part, with BASIC on microcomputers.

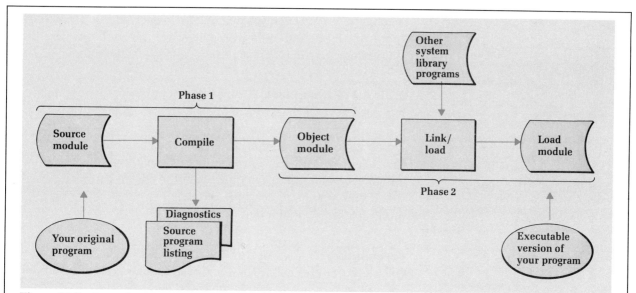

**Figure 12-2   Preparing your program for execution.** The source program is compiled into an object module, which represents the program in machine language. The compiler may produce diagnostic messages, indicating syntax errors. A listing of the source program may also be output from the compiler. After the program successfully compiles, the object module is linked with system library programs, as needed, and the result is an executable load module.

### Utility Service Programs

Why reinvent the wheel? Duplication of effort is what **utility programs** are supposed to avoid. Many repetitive file-handling tasks can be easily handled by prewritten standard programs, once certain information (such as record length) has been specified. Utility programs perform file conversions and sort/merge operations.

*File-handling* utility programs convert files from one form to another (disk to tape, disk to disk, tape to printer, and so on) and handle the general logic of reading a file from one place and writing it in another. In the course of using these utility programs you can usually specify certain options. For instance, if the utility program is concerned with printer output, you can elect to do a number of things that will improve the appearance, such as put in headings, add page numbers, and double-space the lines.

To use a *sort/merge* utility, the programmer specifies the input file name and the file output, and indicates which fields are to be sorted and where they are located in the records. The utility program then performs these operations. For instance, if you wish to sort a file by social security number, you indicate which columns the number starts and ends in and whether you wish to have records sorted in ascending or descending order. A merging operation combines two sequenced files into one file. For example, two files, each in social security number order, could be merged into a single file in social security number order.

### Software Support for Programmers

If you are entertaining the idea of becoming a programmer, you will be relieved to know that you do not have to do everything from scratch. There are numerous aids available. Here we will mention three: optimizing compilers, precompilers, and cross compilers.

**Optimizing Compilers** Ordinarily, as a programmer you might find you need several days to smooth out the rough spots in a program you are writing. An **optimizing compiler,** however, can take standard source code and generate not just object code but highly efficient object code. Although you would not use an optimizing compiler all the time, you would find it quite useful to use on a program that has already undergone most stages of testing and that you want to have running at its most efficient.

**Precompiler** If you are working in the COBOL language, you will find a **precompiler** helpful as a sort of shorthand to save time. COBOL, you will recall, is a wordy language. If you write a COBOL program in an acceptable abbreviated form, then run it through a program called the precompiler, the result will be a full COBOL program in correct syntactical form.

**Cross Compiler** Suppose you are writing a program for your microcomputer, using a complicated programming language whose compiler is so big that it does not fit in your computer's memory. What do you do? One answer is to get the help of another, bigger computer. You write your program on that bigger computer, and then, instead of using a regular compiler to make the object code, you use a cross compiler. The **cross compiler** takes the source code written on the big computer and turns it into object code that will run on your microcomputer. In other words, it allows you to *cross* from one computer to the other; the source code is run on one computer, the object code is small enough so that it fits on the microcomputer.

## *Summary and Key Terms*

- An **operating system** is a set of programs that allows the computer to manage its own resources. It is the medium for cooperation among users, helping everyone make the best use of computer system resources and helping free programmers from repetitive, machine-oriented details so that they can concentrate on solving problems for clients.

- An operating system handles many chores implicitly, without being told to do so by each individual programmer. It has three main functions: (1) to control computer resources, (2) to execute computer programs, and (3) to manage data.

- An operating system improves efficiency in two ways: (1) by helping users share the computer resources, such as main storage, the CPU, and peripheral devices, and (2) by providing translators and programs to take care of certain standard tasks.

- The most important program of the programs in the operating system is the **supervisor program,** most of which remains in main storage. It controls the entire operating system and calls in other operating system programs from disk storage as needed.

- **Multiprogramming** means that two or more programs can be executed concurrently; that is, alternating with each other during the same time frame. This feature reduces CPU idle time. Multiprogramming is event-driven; programs share resources based on events—input, processing, or output—that take place in the program.

- **Time-sharing,** a special case of multiprogramming, is time-driven rather than event-driven. That is, the various users of the system share time slices, typically 2 milliseconds each, during which they can do whatever is required. **Response time** is the time required between a user's request at the computer terminal and the computer's reply.

- Special problems relating to shared computer resources are handled by the operating system through resource allocation, memory management, memory protection, and spooling.

- **Memory management** is the process of allocating main memory to programs and keeping the programs in memory separate from each other. Many computer systems use a technique called **virtual storage,** which means that the user appears to have more main memory space than is actually the case; part of the program is stored on disk and is brought into memory for execution as needed. Main memory in this case is considered **real storage,** while the secondary storage, holding the rest of the program, is considered virtual storage.

- Virtual storage can be implemented in one of three ways: by segmentation, by paging, or by a combination of these.

- **Segmentation** is the process of dividing a program into blocks of various sizes and placing these segments in main memory in noncontiguous locations (locations not necessarily next to each other). The segments are made up of logically related program statements.

- **Paging** is similar to segmentation, but all program blocks—called **pages**—and the corresponding main memory spaces (called **page frames**) are the same, fixed sizes. The pages fit exactly into the page frames in main memory, thereby eliminating wasted space.

- The third and best way of implementing virtual storage is a combination of segmentation and paging, in which the program is first broken up into segments and then the segments into pages.

- **Memory protection,** in a multiprogramming environment, is the process of preventing accidental program destruction. The operating system confines each program to certain defined limits in memory; if there is a transfer to an area outside those limits, program execution is terminated.

● **Spooling** avoids interspersed printout from several programs. Each program writes each file that is to be printed on a disk; when the program is completed, the disk files are printed out intact. In addition, because a record may be written out more quickly on a disk than on a printer, spooling avoids the problem of slow printer speeds.

● To allocate resources of the computer to various users, the operating system puts each program waiting to be run in the input queue, a file on disk, with other waiting programs. A scheduling program, part of the operating system, selects the next job from the input queue, based on such factors as memory requirements, priority, and input/output devices needed and available.

● Unix, Pick, and CP/M are three popular kinds of **generic operating systems**—that is, operating systems that are not specific to a particular computer, will work with more than one manufacturer's computer system, and are frequently created by a third party that is not itself a hardware manufacturer. **Unix** was developed at Bell Laboratories and is used principally on mainframes and minicomputers; it is a multiprogramming, time-sharing operating system. **Pick,** also known as Reality, Prime-Information, and Ultimate, is used on mainframes and minis; though not considered efficient for scientific applications, it is efficient for business-oriented data base applications. **CP/M,** for Control Program/Microcomputers, is a popular operating system for microcomputers.

● When a programmer is writing a program in a high-level language, a **translator** is needed; this is a program that translates that language into machine language. The translator program may be a **compiler** or an **interpreter**. If an assembly language is being used, the translator is called an **assembler.** All are programs that use the programmer's program—called the **source module** or source program—as input data.

● There are three possible outputs from the compiler or assembler program: (1) an object module, (2) diagnostic messages, and (3) a source program listing. The **object module** is a version of the source module now in machine language. **Diagnostic messages** inform the programmer of **syntax errors**—errors in the use of language. The **source program listing** is a list of the program as the programmer wrote it.

● After the object module is ready, there is a **link/load phase,** which means the object module must be linked with other programs before it can be run on the computer. The output from the link/load step is called the **load module;** stored on disk, it is ready to be read into memory and executed.

● An **interpreter** translates and executes the program, one instruction at a time; neither an object module nor prior diagnostic messages are generated, so syntax errors may not be discovered until the program is executed.

● **Utility programs** prevent duplication of effort; they are prewritten standard programs that handle many repetitive file-handling tasks. File-handling utility programs convert files from one form to another (for example, disk to tape). A sort/merge utility sorts records once the programmer has specified the input and output file names and indicated which fields are to be sorted and where they are located on the record.

● Three software supports for programmers are **optimizing compilers,** which help translate source code into highly efficient object code; **precompilers,** which help turn a shorthand version of a COBOL program into a full program; and **cross compilers,** which take a source code too large and complex to run on a microcomputer, run it on a larger computer first, then turn it into object code for the microcomputer.

## REVIEW

1. What is an operating system?

2. What are the three main functions of an operating system?

3. How does an operating system improve efficiency?

4. Describe multiprogramming, time-sharing, memory management, memory protection, and spooling.

5. What are the three possible outputs from the compiler?

6. What do utility programs do?

7. Define optimizing compiler, precompiler, and cross compiler.

## Selected References for Further Reading

Calingaert, Peter. *Operating System Elements: A User Perspective.* Englewood Cliffs, N.J.: Prentice-Hall, 1982.

Cortesi, David E. *Inside CP/M: A Guide for Users and Programmers.* New York: Holt, Rinehart, and Winston, 1983.

Davis, William S. *Operating Systems: A Systematic View.* 2nd ed. Reading, Mass.: Addison-Wesley, 1983.

Lorin, H., and H. M. Deitel. *Operating Systems.* Reading, Mass.: Addison-Wesley, 1981.

Peterson, James L., and Abraham Silberschatz. *Operating Systems Concepts.* Reading, Mass.: Addison-Wesley, 1983.

Thomas, Rebecca, and Jean Yates. *A User Guide to the Unix System.* Berkeley, Calif.: Osborne/McGraw-Hill, 1982.

ch 13 computer
industry
promises:
including office
automation

ch 14 personal
computers: a
computer
of your own

ch 15 data
communications
systems:
the wired world

ch 16 management
information
systems and
data base
systems: share
and share alike

# part 4

## the new story of computing

We have arrived at a point, it has been suggested, where most of the basic inventions that make a computer work have been completed but where the general acceptance and usefulness of computers have only begun. Where are the areas in which we should look for such usefulness and acceptance in coming years? In the next four chapters we shall describe some of them. They range from personal computers to super-computers, from teleprocessing to computer net-working, from the so-called office of the future—which is already in the present—to mammoth data bases. The essence of all revolution, stated philosopher Hannah Arendt, is the start of a "new story" in human experience. When you finish reading these chapters, you will probably agree that the computer industry is writing that new story.

IN
**THIS CHAPTER**
The computer industry
includes not only manufacturers of mainframes,
minicomputers, and microcomputers, but also
peripheral equipment manufacturers, leasing
companies, service bureaus, software houses, and
independent entrepreneurs. In addition, typewriters
are yielding to word processors and other machines
making up the "automated office."

*ch 13*

# computer industry promises: including office automation

Imagine owning your own nuclear reactor. At one time, that was what it was like to own a computer. Computer systems were so complicated and expensive that only large corporations, universities, and government agencies could afford to have them.

All that has changed in less than one human generation. Owning a computer is rapidly becoming not much different from owning a television set. At the same time, the computers and computer systems that large institutions are acquiring have become awesome in their power and capabilities.

In this chapter, we will look briefly at the various classes of computers—mainframes, minicomputers, and microcomputers—at the computer industry at large, and then at what promises to be one of the major revolutions of the decade: the automated office.

*ch13*

## Mainframes, Minis, and Micros

Different users have different needs in computers. The military services, aerospace corporations, and the U.S. Weather Bureau, for example, need the large machines, the mainframes. Someone who wishes to handle personal finances at home needs only the smallest system, a microcomputer. In between are legions of retail businesses, colleges, and state and city agencies that require the intermediate-sized minicomputers. Whether you are buying for yourself or for an institution, selecting the right kind of computer is not without some risks. You may know the tasks you wish to accomplish, but it is difficult to know what kinds of equipment and systems are best suited to your special needs.

### Mainframes and "Supercomputers"

**Mainframes** are the largest, fastest, and, of course, most expensive computers. They are normally considered general-purpose computers, used by large institutions to provide comprehensive computer services. Mainframes have huge memories, normally consisting of several million bytes, or megabytes—a **megabyte** is roughly a million bytes, or exactly 1,048,576 bytes—and often process around 5 million instructions per second. Because of such size and speed, mainframes have heavy-duty cooling requirements and must be positioned on special raised floors that allow cooling ducts underneath. There can be many, even hundreds, of remote terminals.

The purchase price, which can range from a few hundred thousand dollars to $10 million or more, includes not only the mainframe but also some impressive supporting equipment and services from the vendor: 24-hour maintenance service (with very fast response—no one can afford much downtime on a million-dollar computer), extensive documentation, and a sophisticated array of supporting software systems. Needless to say, you would not buy a mainframe for just any

## THE RACE FOR THE FASTEST COMPUTER

The fastest computers in the world are today built in the United States, but these symbols of American ingenuity may soon be found only in museums. The Japanese Government last year unveiled a . . . program aimed at cornering the world market in supercomputers with machines 1,000 times more powerful.

Predictions of an American decline are voiced by academicians and scientists who fear that the race for supercomputers of the future may be somewhat lopsided. . . .

The stakes in the gamble are high. No computer is now powerful enough, for example, to simulate the airflow around an entire aircraft, so aerodynamic designs are often put together in piecemeal fashion or by the repeated processing of two-dimensional slices. The first country with computers that can design the plane as a whole, according to a recent report of the National Science Foundation, "will undoubtedly produce planes with superior performance." So, too, the Government wants bigger supercomputers for building better weapons, breaking codes, and developing new sources of energy.

Pure research, with its unpredictable rewards, also needs the machines. "The problems we are trying to address could not at this point be calculated by all the computers that have ever existed," says Dr. Bruce Knapp, a physicist at the Nevis Laboratory of Columbia University.

—William J. Broad,
*New York Times,*
February 1, 1983

purpose. The main uses are for processing vast amounts of data quickly, and so customers tend to be large mail-order houses, airlines with sophisticated reservations systems, government accounting services, aerospace companies doing complex aircraft design, and the like.

The mightiest of the mainframes are the so-called **supercomputers.** The fastest is purported to be Control Data Corporation's CYBER 205. The Cray-1 (see Figure 13-1), built by Cray Research, Inc., is available for between $6 million and $17 million. Planned for release in 1984 is the Cray-2, which is supposed to have as much as twelve times the capability of the Cray-1. Supercomputers are used for such purposes as worldwide weather forecasting and weapons research; the Los Alamos Scientific Laboratory in New Mexico, for instance, numbers five Cray-1s among its 100 mainframes, which are used for scientific computing.

A mainframe computer (see Figure 13-2) can support many peripheral devices—not only terminals but also numerous tape drives, disk drives, even other computers. Originally, a mainframe was much like the center of the universe; it was totally centralized and all work had to be brought to it. Now, in systems called "distributed data processing" systems (to be discussed in Chapter 15), minicomputers and microcomputers at distant locations can be connected to the mainframe and can operate independently of or in conjunction with the larger computer, depending on need.

### Minicomputers

A **minicomputer** (see Figure 13-3) is like a mainframe in design and concept, but it is of medium size, speed, and expense—$10,000 to about $250,000. Minicomputers receive more moderate vendor support than mainframes do. Minicomputers swept into the computer market in the late 1960s and were originally intended to be small and serve some special purpose. However, in a fairly short time they became much more powerful general-purpose machines, and the line between minicomputers and mainframes has blurred. Indeed, the appellation "mini" no longer seems to fit very well. The term **supermini** is now commonly applied to minicomputers at the high end of the size/price scale. At present, there is an annual growth rate of about 50 percent in supermini sales. Examples of some current powerful 32-bit supermini computers are the DEC VAX–11/780, Stratus/32, Data General MV/6000, Perkin-Elmer 3250, Microdata Sequel, and HP 3000/64.

Minicomputers are proof of the fallibility of human expectations. "It is hard to recall now," writes the head of a New York engineering consulting firm, "that in the '60s it was thought that the only improvement for computers was to make them bigger and faster; many at that time foresaw computer utilities that would be so superior there would be no point in using a so-called 'small computer.' They could not have been more wrong."

272

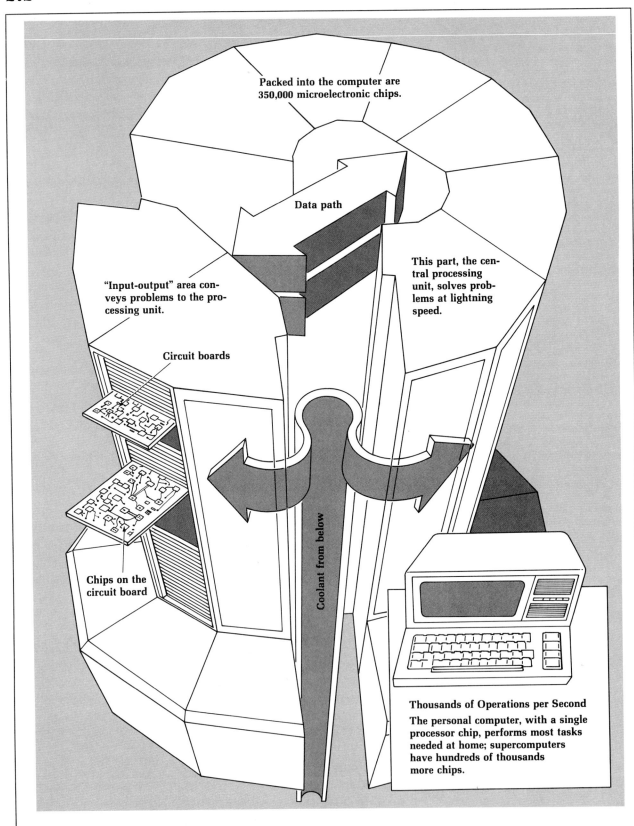

Packed into the computer are 350,000 microelectronic chips.

Data path

This part, the central processing unit, solves problems at lightning speed.

"Input-output" area conveys problems to the processing unit.

Circuit boards

Chips on the circuit board

Coolant from below

Thousands of Operations per Second

The personal computer, with a single processor chip, performs most tasks needed at home; supercomputers have hundreds of thousands more chips.

**Figure 13-1(a) Supercomputer.** The Cray-1 supercomputer operates in terms of a hundred million operations per second. By contrast a microcomputer (*see inset*) does only thousands of operations per second.

**Figure 13-1(b).** The Cray-1 in operation.

**Figure 13-2 Mainframe computers.** *Top:* An NCR 9300 mainframe that can sit on a desk and does not require special wiring or air conditioning. *Bottom:* An IBM 370/158; this is a typical size.

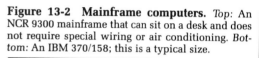

**Figure 13-3    A minicomputer.** This NCR minicomputer is designed for small business uses.

### HUNGER ORGANIZATION FINDS RELIEF WITH MINI

PHOENIX—It may not push a cart through the frozen food section, but a minicomputer here is doing some heavy-duty grocery shopping.

The processor is owned by Food for the Hungry, an international organization that provides disaster food relief and organizes food production and distribution development projects for underdeveloped countries.

"Our mission is to provide help to starving people," according to president Dr. Larry Ward. To accomplish that goal, the nonprofit organization must rely on donations. About a year ago, the organization decided to buy a computer system to help process more than 120,000 donor names and files. . . .

"By installing the [General Automation 16/470] system, we reduced our turnaround time on receipt mailing to one day, giving our donors more immediate response to their contributions. Data entry errors have been virtually eliminated since names and addresses can be verified in real time now," according to William Moy, executive director of the organization.

—*Computerworld,*
August 30, 1982

In the typical minicomputer system, input and output are through terminals, usually CRTs, but other common peripherals are printers and disk storage devices, including floppy disk drives. The uses of minicomputers range from intercity delivery services to management of country clubs, from railroad car scheduling to hospital management. Besides small business computing, minis are used for word processing (explained later in the chapter) and for data communications, including distributed data processing.

## Microcomputers

The exciting story of developments in the smallest class of computers deserves a chapter by itself, and so we shall discuss this subject in considerable detail in Chapter 14. Here let us note that the microchips that made possible the miniaturization of room-sized central processors into hand-held calculators have also made possible the production of computers that are more than a hundred times smaller than models of similar power a decade ago.

**Microcomputers** (see Figure 13-4) go by several names—personal computers, home computers, desktop computers—and cost anywhere from $100 to $10,000. There is normally only one user at a time. The compactness and standardization of hardware and software have allowed the introduction of microcomputers not only for such business purposes as accounting and inventory control but also for a variety of personal, educational, and entertainment uses.

A Buyer's Guide to microcomputers follows p. 278.

As may be apparent from our discussion, the distinctions between mainframe, mini, and micro are dissolving as the hardware evolves.

**Figure 13-4   A microcomputer.** This Hewlett-Packard HP-85 is designed for use in business and industry by professionals such as scientists, engineers, accountants, and investment analysts.

One observer has said that looking at these three types of computers is like taking a snapshot of three melting ice cubes. However, since the categories are still used throughout the industry, they are worth keeping in mind.

## BIG BLUE BUSINESS

For many years, IBM has been known as Big Blue, because the original housing for IBM's equipment was blue. Why has Big Blue been so dominant in the computer market? Many observers think it stems partly from the fact that the company gives good service.

The IBM Maintenance Agreement, for instance, provides an equipment user with a customer engineer to attend to service needs, a communications center to respond to calls, regular preventive maintenance, parts availability, engineering changes required to make the system that was delivered compatible with future programming releases and equipment upgrades, among other features.

After all, as every computer user knows, even the best equipment sometimes gives the blues.

# The Computer Industry

In the market for a computer or computer services? The companies, large and small, that are in the business to serve you are wide-ranging and continually changing. When we say "the computer industry," by and large we include:

- Computer manufacturers (including foreign firms)
- Peripheral equipment manufacturers
- Leasing companies
- Service bureaus
- Software houses
- Individual entrepreneurs

Let us look at what these sectors of the industry do.

## Computer Manufacturers

With about 70 percent of the market, IBM is still the largest manufacturer of mainframes. Behind IBM, each with less than a 10 percent share of the worldwide market, are Honeywell, Burroughs, Sperry-Univac, NCR (for National Cash Register), Control Data Corporation, and a few other American companies. The main source of income for these producers is sales of mainframes and accompanying software and peripherals. As we mentioned in Chapter 3, this elite club has remained small primarily because a gigantic capital outlay is required.

The principal companies making minicomputers are Digital Equipment Corporation (DEC—which everyone pronounces "Deck"), with about 30 percent of the market, followed by Hewlett-Packard. Other companies are Data General, Honeywell, IBM, Datapoint, Wang Laboratories, Prime, and Perkin-Elmer.

As for overseas firms, the top three revenue producers from sales of data processing equipment are all Japanese: Hitachi Ltd., Toshiba, and Fujitsu Ltd.

The manufacturers in the microcomputer market are discussed in Chapter 14.

 ## Peripheral Equipment Manufacturers

The makers of tape drives, disk drives, printers, and other peripheral equipment are larger, collectively, than any mainframe manufacturer except IBM. Among the principal **peripheral equipment manufacturers (PEMs)** are Telex, Memorex, and Ampex. The largest percentage of users' hardware budgets goes to pay for peripherals, which they must buy either from the manufacturer from whom they bought or leased their computer or from one of the peripheral equipment manufacturers. The latter companies usually have two advantages over the computer manufacturers: (1) they can sell peripherals cheaper, and (2) they can usually deliver them faster.

Peripheral equipment manufacturers are also called **plug-compatible manufacturers (PCMs)** because the peripheral devices they make are so standardized that they generally can be used ("plugged in") interchangeably with an original manufacturer's mainframe or minicomputer. For the user, of course, this plug compatibility means there are multiple sources of supply.

 ## Leasing Companies

Computers and their associated equipment are expensive. Also, computer designs change frequently. As a result, users are somewhat reluctant to buy costly equipment that they may have to keep using when newer and better hardware becomes available. In addition, companies may wish to conserve capital for other purposes or may have certain tax strategies in mind.

 Leasing companies are a direct answer to these concerns. Such companies buy hardware either directly from manufacturers or second-hand from users and lease it out to other users.

 ## Service Bureaus

Let us say you head a small company—for example, an architectural firm—that cannot justify spending money for its own computer equipment, but you still need computer services (such as for payroll or billing). Your best solution may be to call a **service bureau,** an organization selling computer services to clients. Some bureaus offer more than one service. Many of them specialize—one, for example, might provide banking services. Some of the services provided are as follows:

- **Batch processing.** A service might pick up data (such as time cards) from your office at regular intervals and return processed output (such as payroll sheets and checks).

- **Time-sharing.** Your office might have a terminal connected through communication lines to the service bureau's computer for real-time processing. Or, in a setup known as **remote job-entry (RJE),** jobs could be entered into the service bureau's regular batch processing from your office terminal.

- **Data entry.** Many bureaus will take your raw source documents and perform the data entry tasks—for example, keying them onto disk or tape—converting them to machine-readable form.

- **Software development.** The cost of employing programmers and systems analysts to develop software can be expensive—more so, perhaps, than the cost of hardware. If software needs are relatively moderate, it may not be cost-justifiable to hire your own programmers and analysts. Your office might decide to buy or lease some hardware but hire a service bureau to develop the software that fits your special needs.

- **Facilities management.** Sometimes a company will not want to manage its own computer installation. This may be the case if the computer system is inadequately staffed. In that case, an outside service bureau may provide the management. The service bureau will provide all needed personnel and services.

By 1985, the computer services industry is expected to be a $30 billion a year business.

 ### *Software Houses*

Let us suppose you have your computer hardware system in place. Where are you going to get the software for payroll, accounts receivable, and the like? You could, of course, hire programmers to develop your software packages. Many companies, however, turn to a **software house,** a business specializing in providing software and also systems analysis services.

Software houses will write, on a contract basis, software custom-tailored for you. However, the real growth area is projected to be in standard package software. Packages of standardized **applications software**—programs to solve specific business or organizational problems—are now available for an amazing variety of purposes: aircraft design, food service, even management of poultry flocks.

Often such software is available off the rack—literally. You can go into computer stores and software houses and buy cassette tapes or diskettes hanging from a rack. Such software is not tailor-made for the needs of an individual business, but it definitely is less expensive than software developed in-house. Although, as might be expected, most purchasers of packaged software are apt to be those with small computers, even mainframe users are now seeing the light, reasoning that there is no point in writing from scratch what someone else has already written.

When should you buy packaged software and what are the dangers? In general, say researchers from Auerbach Publishers, the more common the application, the more apt there is to be usable software available. For instance, over 300 packages are available for payroll/personnel applications, and 200 for accounts receivable. And the more packages that are offered, the more likely there is one that is right for you. Acquiring packaged software is not without its risks, however, including possible time wasted in the search, possible program modifications, and even poor documentation and unknown bugs in the programs. To locate applications software, you may consult vendor software lists, user group libraries, published directories, trade associations, government-supported agencies, ads in the trade press, and search publications.

### Individual Entrepreneurs

The expanding market for computer services has encouraged many computer professionals to go into business for themselves, and we will explore some of these paths in a later chapter on careers. As the box shows (see "Growing Up in Silicon Valley," pp. 280–281), many are attracted by the overnight success of computer industry millionaires.

For clients, the use of consulting or contract services offered by such computer professionals has several advantages. The user need not pay fringe benefits, and the contracted person is not on the payroll permanently. For the independent contractor, the advantages are high salary, mobility, and variety in his or her work.

## The Automated Office: From Paper to Electronics

What *is* an office—really? A farmer or a boat builder or a restaurant owner does not spend much time behind a desk. Still, each has to have a place in which to pay bills, collect money, make plans, consider proposals, and read and write and communicate—in short, some space that could be called an office. For a lot of readers of this book, however, there is a good chance they will spend most of their working lives in what we normally think of as an office—a place with desks, chairs, and filing cabinets. And while it may not be a "paperless office"—the current catch phrase for the electronic office-of-the-future—it is certain to be a "less paper" office. The new name given to this collection of electronic gadgetry is the **automated office**.

## HUNT-AND-PECK AUTHOR RAVES ABOUT WORD PROCESSING

DENVER—Author and geologist Ron Redfern found himself in a bind when he started work on *Corridors of Time* in 1979. Because of his extensive travel schedule, he was unable to engage a full-time secretary. And as a self-confessed "hunt-and-peck" typist, he had no desire to prepare the 70,000-word manuscript by himself.

Redfern found his solution at the Denver offices of his lawyer. The firm had been using an NBI, Inc. System 3000 word processor for several years and was satisfied with it. Seeing that word processing could be the answer to his problems, Redfern began to shop for a system of his own [also an NBI]. . . .

It took Redfern nearly a month to write the first chapter of his 10-chapter book. But the tenth chapter took only 10 days. Within six months, Redfern's manuscript was finished.

"There is no way I could have finished the book in under a year without the machine," said Redfern, now a word processing enthusiast. "When I bought it, I was simply trying to overcome the problem of not having a skilled secretary. But once I began using the word processor, I came to regard it as a creative tool."

Redfern said the machine "disinhibited" him as a writer. "My job is ideas and how to express them," he said. "I can use this machine creatively, playing with words and refashioning them without bothering with crossing out. If I have an idea in the middle of a page, I can simply push it down to the bottom of the page and come back to it later. Nothing I do is ever lost if I don't want it to be. As a result, the quality of my work has improved noticeably."

—*Computerworld,*
October 4, 1982

# *Buyer's Guide*

## *How to Buy Your Own Microcomputer*

We are accustomed to a great deal of freedom of choice among the products we buy. But when did you

*Computers on Main Street:* Computer stores may not be as common as dry cleaners yet, but they are becoming more and more prevalent as retailers try to make themselves accessible to the public.

ever have to choose among 150 to 200 kinds of toasters or stereos? In fact, there are at least that many kinds of microcomputers offered. Yet they can cost as little as a bicycle or as much as a car—from less than $100 to over $10,000. How, then, do you choose the right small computer for what you want? We have written this Buyer's Guide to try to deal with these concerns.

## Why Do You Need (or Want) a Computer?

We cannot pick your new computer system for you any more than we could pick a new car for you. But we can tell you what to look for. We do not mean that we can lead you to a particular brand and model—so many new products are introduced into this area every month that that would be impossible. Detailed buyer's guides are available on newsstands and in book stores, but they would probably tell you more than you want to know at this point. If you are just starting out, however, we can help you define your needs and ask the right questions.

First, though, let us point out the obvious: microcomputers are not cheap, and the initial purchase is usually only the beginnning. Just as the buyer of a sophisticated camera discovers a wonderful world of lenses, tripods, and other expensive add-ons, so the buyer of even a hundred-dollar computer finds that this is merely a down payment on an array of possible products, both hardware and software. Indeed, some computer stores sell the basic machine at substantial discount, hoping to reap profits from your future purchases. *Caveat computer emptor!*

### ■ *Sophistication and Cost*

*Shopping for software:* Be sure the software (programs) will accomplish what you want and will work on the hardware you intend to buy.

Perhaps the most important decision you need to make is to determine what price range you are in. For convenience, we can divide personal computers into two categories—less sophisticated ones, which generally cost less than $1000, and more sophisticated ones, which cost between $1000 and $10,000 (or more), excluding printers. The lower-priced computers are consumer-oriented; are in console form, containing both CPU (central processing unit) and keyboard; will attach to a TV set or monitor, cassette drive, floppy disk drive, and other peripherals that are generally optional; and have software that is oriented toward entertainment, education, or personal business. The more sophisticated ones do all of the above and also have more business software available. Any kind of personal computer can be programmed in a higher-level language, such as BASIC, and most can be attached to such peripherals as

printers, modems (telecommunications connections), additional floppy disk drives, and even hard disk drives.

The most well-known, inexpensive personal computers have names like Atari, Timex/Sinclair, Texas Instruments, Commodore, and Tandy (Radio Shack). However, the last three also offer more sophisticated personal computers. Because of its price, Apple is found in the latter category, although much Apple software has been written for entertainment and educational as well as business purposes. IBM has established a significant presence in the personal computer market with its IBM PC. Other large data processing companies making microcomputers are Digital Equipment Corp., Wang Laboratories, Burroughs Corp., and NCR Corp. *Portable computers*—machines that can be carried like an attaché case—are also sophisticated business-oriented personal computers; the pioneer of this class of computer was the Osborne 1, but there are now others, such as KayPro, Attaché, and Compaq.

### ■ *Software or Hardware First?*

After you have established your budget and delineated the reasons why you want a computer, you need to take stock of an important issue— what kind of software do you want? Indeed, it is often recommended that you *select your software before you select your hardware.* Many software manufacturers sell their programs only for certain brands of equipment. A certain word processing program, for instance, may be available for Apple or IBM computers but not for Atari or Texas Instruments. Many computers may accept business-related programs but no educational software or video games.

But now, having said that software should be chosen before hardware, let us venture another observation: Most people buy the hardware—the computer—first anyway. The main thing, then, is to make sure that the kind of hardware you buy will run software for the kinds of tasks you are interested in.

The survey at the end of this Buyer's Guide lists questions to help you identify what you want to see in a computer. Let us now run through the various possibilities of choice for hardware and software.

## Buy Now or Buy Later?

To live with a personal computer is to live with the knowledge that something will no doubt come along in a year to two (or even sooner) that will make your present equipment seem inadequate in some way. Improvements usually take the form of (1) the same kind of equipment becoming available at a lower price; (2) new models or competing equipment offering more capacity (more main memory), easier handling (such as less complicated keyboarding), or wider range of or better designed software; or (3) the quality of the new models is better for a cheaper price (for example, letter-quality printers become competitive in price with dot-matrix printers).

Yet, clearly, the longer you wait to buy, the longer you miss out on acquiring experience and expertise with microcomputers. And, of course, you miss out on the usefulness and fun. Certainly if you want a machine to do word processing or for business-related purposes, there is no point in waiting. If you want something that is easier to use than the equipment you see now, however, you may be advised to put it off a year or so.

Perhaps the best advice on the subject is given by James Edlin, president of Bruce & James Program Publishers, Inc., as quoted in *The Wall Street Journal*: "If you have a use that will justify a personal computer, buy one, knowing that things will get better. If you are just curious and have high hopes that it will change your life, you might as well wait."

## What to Look for in Hardware

The basic microcomputer system consists of a CPU (central processing unit), video display (CRT—cathode ray tube), keyboard, printer, and probably a storage device (disk drive or cassette tape drive). Unless you know someone who can help you out with technical expertise, you are probably best advised to look for a *packaged system*—that is, one in which the above components (with the possible exception of the printer) are assembled and packaged by the same manufacturer. This gives you some assurance that the various components will work together.

Let us make one more point, before we examine the various components in detail. Be sure you turn on the prospective computer system and *listen*. Any computer will make a minimum of noise, but some sound like vacuum cleaners. Remember that your house is likely to be quieter than the store, so the computer's noise will be intensified in your home.

Let us now take a quick look at the various parts of the system: CPU, video display, keyboard, secondary storage, printers, and other hardware options.

### ■ *Central Processing Unit*

Microcomputers started out with what is known as an 8-bit processor, but there are now over 100 companies making machines with 16-bit processors. More bits mean more power, faster processing speed, and a larger and more complex instruction set. How-

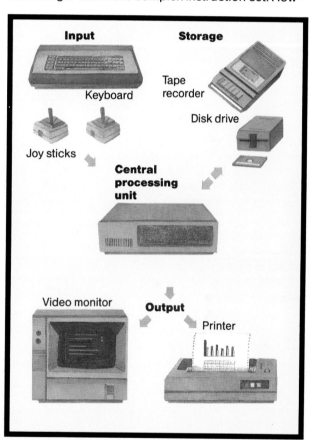

*The complete system:* This schematic of a microcomputer system shows input devices, such as a keyboard and joy sticks; storage devices, such as tape recorder and disk drive; central processing unit; and output devices, such as video monitor and printer.

ever, 16-bit processors are also more expensive; unless you have professional uses in mind for your micro, you can probably do just as well with an 8-bit processor. It should be noted that some microcomputers come with dual-processor chips, that is, both 8-bit and 16-bit chips.

**80 column screen**

**22 column screen**

**38 column screen**

### ■ *Video Display*

A great deal of publicity has been given to the notion that you can use your TV set as a monitor for your computer. This is true, if you are acquiring a lower-priced computer system. A color TV set may also be a useful adjunct if you are producing color graphics, but a color monitor will give you higher screen resolution and, therefore, a clearer picture. Let us consider several aspects of video monitors.

**Screen Width** TV sets have several drawbacks, particularly if you plan to be using the screen for close work, such as programming or word processing, over a period of time. Take the number of characters on a line. When typing a letter or term paper on a typewriter, you usually get about 70 characters per line (characters include letters, numbers, special characters, spaces). Some TV sets, however, may allow only 40 characters per line. Others may allow 80 characters, but the characters will be unreadable. An inexpensive monitor may be better than many TV sets.

**Screen Readability** Be sure to make comparisons as you shop for your video monitor for differences in readability. First, make sure the screen has minimum flicker. Next, check the shape of the characters. Some screens are difficult to read because they chop off the descenders—the tails that fall below the line—of the lowercase letters g, p, q, and y. In addition, you should look to see whether the characters appear crowded on the screen, that is, jammed together to a degree that makes them difficult to read. Glare is another major consideration: nearby harsh lighting can cause glare to bounce off the screen. There are ways to reduce glare—etched glass or chemical coatings—but these may reduce clarity.

Despite the claims of advertising copywriters, screen color has not been proven a major factor in readability. Screens may appear as gray or sort of soft black, green, or amber. Amber screens are reputed to be easier on the eyes and are, in fact, standard on European displays. More important than the color of the screen are the controls that let you adjust the contrast and brightness of screen characters.

**Screen Tiltability** You should look to see whether a video monitor is movable or tiltable, since this will remove the need to sit in exactly one position for a

*Movability:* **Many video displays tilt and swivel so that your neck does not have to.**

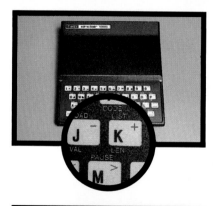

long period of time. This becomes an important consideration if there are different users for the same computer. Of course, there are trade-offs: if you need a portable computer to haul back and forth to different places, the built-in screen contributes to its portability, if not its flexibility. (However, you can buy a separate monitor to leave at home.)

Note: A color monitor may work well for games and for computer graphics, but you will probably find it leads to eyestrain if you plan to do a lot of word processing or programming.

### ■ Keyboard

**Keyboard Tactile Touch**
Keyboards vary a lot in quality. On the inexpensive end are touch-sensitive *membrane plastic keyboards.* These are just flat surfaces, with the particular parts of the surface labeled with the "keys" you are supposed to touch. These are not very satisfying—particularly if you are doing word processing—because it is difficult to know when you have made contact with a particular key because there is no tactile sensation, no "feel," as on a regular electric typewriter kind of keyboard. About the only times you should consider a membrane keyboard are (1) when you are using your computer

play games using a joy stick, and (2) when you are starting out a young child on some educational uses. In that case, your use of the keyboard is minimal and incidental.

Even beyond the membrane keyboard you will find that there can be real differences in the feel of keyboards—that is, in what are known as *full-travel keyboards,* keyboards similar to those on office typewriters. Some keyboards just feel cheap; they do not have a solid touch. It is important that you have a tactile sense with your fingers on the keys, so that you will know when you have engaged a key and released it. Make sure the keys are not cramped together, since you will find your typing is error-prone if your fingers are constantly overlapping on some of the keys. This is especially of concern if you have long fingernails.

**Keyboard Color** Ideally, keys should be gray with a matte finish. The dull finish reduces glare.

**Keyboard Slope** If you plan to use your keyboard for many hours at a time, its slope will be very important to you. A keyboard slope should be a minimum of 7 degrees and a maximum of 15 degrees. Slopes out-

### Questions to Ask the Salesperson in a Computer Store

How many units of this machine do you sell in a month? How well does the computer interface with other equipment—printers, monitors, disk drives, etc.—offered by other manufacturers? What are the names of some of your customers? Is the machine popular enough to have a user's group in my area? Is there anyone I can call after hours about problems? Does the store offer classes in how to use this computer and software of interest to me? Can you help me set up specific programs or adapt software? Do you have a maintenance contract for this machine? Does someone in your store fix the machines? Can I expand the capabilities of this machine later?

side this range can cause discomfort in the wrist and, consequently, high error rates. Some microcomputer manufacturers offer adjustable slopes.

**Keyboard Layout** Besides touch, you should look at the layout of the keyboard itself. Most follow the standard QWERTY layout of typewriter keyboards. However, some also have a separate *numeric keypad,* located to the right of the keyboard. You may find this useful if you enter a lot of numbers. In addition, some keyboards have separate *function keys.* The IBM Personal Computer, for instance, has special keys to the left of the regular keys which are used to move things around on the screen, delete, and so on. The original Apple II, on the other hand, does not have such keys, and you must accomplish movement and deletion by holding a pair of other keys (not labeled as to function) down simultaneously.

**Detachable Keyboard** Although you may be used to typing on a typewriter, where the keyboard is not separate from the rest of the machine, you may find a computer with a detachable keyboard—one that can be held on your lap, say—a desirable feature. This allows the keyboard to be moved around to suit the comfort of the user.

### ■ *Secondary Storage*

You will undoubtedly want some secondary storage—that is, some way of keeping whatever you have created on the computer, whether programs or documents you have created, usually through a word processing program. Indeed, you will probably want secondary storage even if all you want to do is play some off-the-shelf kinds of computer games. ("Off-the-shelf" means the games you can buy in a store in floppy disk or cassette form, as opposed to games you program yourself, either copying them out of a book or, if you have the programming knowledge, inventing them yourself.) You will certainly want secondary storage if you wish to take advantage of the array of software products on the market, from word processing to filing systems, for without such storage you have no way of inputting such readymade software. Software, let us not forget, covers not only any programs you write yourself and key in through the keyboard, but also programs already written and available commercially on floppy disks or cassettes. These commercial packages do require secondary storage devices such as disk drives or cassette tape recorders for their contents to be input to the computer.

*Cassette tape recorders (top):* **Inexpensive, but with cassettes they make slow storage devices.** *Disk drives (middle and bottom):* **More expensive, but with diskettes are fast and convenient.**

**Tape Cassettes** If you are starting out with an inexpensive personal computer system, want to hold your costs down, and already have a cassette tape recorder at hand, you will find cassettes a low-cost method of secondary storage. Unfortunately, cassette tapes are slow to access information, and you may find the selection of software limited in this form.

ik you for your interest in the
onal ad, the QX-10 features
ware systems which allows
eduling, calculating, filing,
hs with just a few minutes of
Epson Business Package also
e-pack of CP/M software, inclu
manager, and a spelling proof

ik you for your interest in the
ional ad, the QX-10 features the
tware system which allows you to
eduling, calculating, filing, el
hs with just a few minutes of i
v, the Epson Business Package al
e-pack of CP/M software, includ
ling list manager, and a spellir
n DX 80 printer

*Printers:* **Probably the most expensive peripheral device you will buy. Note the differences in legibility between a** *dot matrix printer* **(top) and a** *letter quality printer* **(middle).**

**Diskettes** A far more popular storage medium is diskettes, also known as floppy disks. Minifloppies, which are 5¼ inches in diameter, usually cost $3 or $4 apiece and hold the equivalent of 140 typed single-spaced pages of information. Microfloppies, which range in size from 3 to 3.9 inches, have become available for some computers.

Diskettes are run on disk drives. On some systems, the disk drives are separate components from the rest of the computer system and cost between $300 and $1000 each. On other systems, disk drives are built right into the computer console. Although not always necessary, you may find it helpful to have two (dual) disk drives to facilitate copying of disks for safekeeping.

**Hard Disks** Recently, hard disks have become available for microcomputers. Although expensive at present rates—$2000 and up—hard disk is fast and reliable and can hold lots of data. The fixed disk drive that goes with the IBM Personal Computer XT, for instance, has a storage capacity of more than 10 million characters—equivalent to 5000 double-spaced typewritten pages.

### ■ Printers

A printer is probably the most expensive piece of peripheral equipment you can buy. Although some printers are available for under $300, most likely you will find that those in the $600 to $3000 range are the ones most useful to you.

When choosing a printer, you will want to consider speed, quality, noise level, and cost.

**Electrostatic Printers** If a printer is of only minor use to you, then you should go economy class. Be aware, however, that you will have to use special paper. The least expensive printers are nonimpact electrostatic printers. Though reasonably fast and certainly quiet compared to other printers, they require a particular type of silver-like paper, much like the kind you see in some drugstore copying machines, and some people object to the glare of that kind of paper. Moreover, the print often fades from the page over time.

**Dot Matrix Printers** A better caliber of printer is the dot matrix printer, which may cost $500 to $1000. These can print as many as 250 characters per second, forming each character out of a grid of pins or dots, much like the lights on a bank temperature sign or stadium scoreboard. The appearance of the characters is not as good as those you would get from, say, an electric typewriter, which is why they are not considered "letter quality"—that is, adequate for office correspondence. Some dot matrix printers, however, can make a second pass at the characters and make the letters more fully formed, nearly resembling letter quality.

**Letter Quality Printers** Most letter quality printers use a daisy wheel, a replaceable device that can be removed, like a typewriter element, and replaced with another wheel with a different type font on it. The disadvantage of the daisy wheel printer is that it is relatively slow—often 55 characters per second or less. A letter quality printer typically costs between $1000 and $3000.

**Printer Covers** Both dot matrix and letter quality printers are noisy. Such a printer can generate about 70 decibels of sound, about the equivalent of a high-volume TV broadcast. If you will be working in an enclosed environment with your printer, the noise will soon become irritating in the extreme. First, you should consider inexpensive, sound absorbing pads to go under the printer. If the problem is extreme, plastic printer covers are available (for an additional $300), which will reduce the noise significantly.

■ *Other Hardware Options*

**Telecommunications Connections** If you wish to connect your computer via telephone lines to any number of electronic "bulletin boards" or so-called "information utilities" such as CompuServe or The Source, you will need a *modem*, a device that converts computer data into data that can be transmitted over telephone lines.

**Other Input Devices** If you are interested in games, you may wish to acquire a *joy stick*, which looks sort of like the stick shift on a car and which allows you to manipulate a cursor on the screen. A more sophisticated device is a *mouse*, a gadget with wheels on it that you can roll around on a table top and which in turn also moves the cursor on the screen.

There are several other input devices available. Ask your dealer about these for the computers you are considering.

**Graphics Display** Some computer systems have sophisticated graphic displays; others do not. Atari, for instance, is noted for its color graphics because of its heavy investment in games and recreational software. However, the IBM Personal Computer

*Joy stick:* **Most home computers are used half the time for games needing joy sticks.**

also has exceedingly good graphics capabilities.

**Sound** Be sure to check out sound effects, particularly if you are interested in games. Make sure there are different tones, that they are not unpleasant, and that you have control over starting and stopping them. Many systems also have packaged software that allows you to produce computer-generated music.

## What to Look for in Software

The first thing to understand about software on microcomputers is that standardization is nonexistent. For one thing, each microcomputer has its own *operating system.* That is, each has its own special kind of software program that determines its own internal system operations. The operating system in turn determines what other kind of software—called *applications software*—you can run on your computer. The result of this is an incredible duplication of effort throughout the industry, with many of the same types of applications software packages existing for several different microcomputers.

■ *CP/M and MS-DOS*

There are ways to get around this, however. One popular method is to use an operating system called CP/M, which stands for "Control Program for Microcomputers," developed by Digital Research of Pacific Grove, Calif. CP/M is available on most microcomputers. Though you usually have to pay extra for it, over 10,000 applications software packages become available to you. (By "package," we usually mean a 5¼-inch plastic diskette plus any documentation, which can range from a slip of paper to a vinyl binder with many pages of printed instructions.) Another approach is the operating system called MS-DOS, which is rapidly becoming a standard for 16-bit business-oriented microcomputers.

■ *Hardware Requirements for Software*

When you look at a software package in a store, whether a game, word processing program, or what have you, *be sure to read what kind of hardware it requires.* For example, you may read: "This package requires two disk drives, an 80-character display screen and printer, 64 KB of memory and the CP/M operating system." You would hate to get home with your $30 software package and find you need to spend more for a joy stick or $500 for a special circuit board that goes inside the computer. The salesperson should be able to advise you on the requirements for any particular software you might want to buy.

### ■ Software Demonstrations

Among the packaged software you can buy are word processing, data management, financial packages, personal records, home management, and the like. For children, there are all sorts of games and educational programs. Wherever you can, however, *ask to have the software demonstrated.* There is a lot of junk out there. You should not buy anything until you see that it works. Despite this admonition, we must acknowledge that approximately half of the software purchased for personal computers is ordered through the mail from advertisements in computer magazines. In some cases, you may rely on the reputation of the software manufacturer. Other useful aids are the detailed software catalogs, which sort out the "best in its class"; these catalogs are often available in computer stores and book stores.

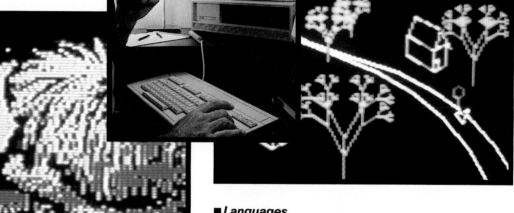

**Computer graphics:** Many home computer systems provide excellent graphics capability.

### ■ Languages

In addition, you may wish to purchase one or more languages, if you wish to write you own applications programs. BASIC is the most popular language for microcomputers, but some computers have FORTRAN, Pascal, and other languages.

## Shopping Around: Where to Buy

Where you buy is important, and usually the tradeoff is between price and service—but not necessarily.

### ■ The Dealer

You can buy a microcomputer in a computer store such as ComputerLand or Byte Shop (there are about 400 ComputerLand stores). You can buy one from a mass merchandiser such as Macy's, K-Mart, Sears, or Penney's. You can buy one from the manufacturer's own retail outlet; IBM, Tandy-Radio Shack, and Digital Equipment Corp. all have their own stores. You can buy one from a mail-order outfit, as is being done with Timex/Sinclair. You can even buy one from a door-to-door sales rep; at this time, Dynasty Computers are being sold from door to door with some success.

Which way is best? It depends first, perhaps, on where you live. If you live in a remote location, a visit to a store may be difficult, and you may indeed want to try to buy one by mail order. In addition, prices can be more favorable. The obvious disadvantage, of course, is that you do not get the support you would get from a store nearby. You also have to deal with the hassle of boxing up the computer and shipping it if it needs repairs or service.

If you do not live near a city that offers specialized computer stores, the chances are you are not far from department stores or discount stores that carry computers. Personal computers such as Atari, Timex/Sinclair, and Texas Instruments are available in many discount electronics and toy stores, and TRS-80 computers are available in Radio Shack stores. Macy's and similar department stores carry Apple, IBM, and Commodore.

### ■ Financing

The advantage of department stores in particular is that the seller can often help you finance the pur-

chase, either carrying it itself or making arrangements with a financial institution such as a bank.

### ■ *Service*

Perhaps the biggest single argument for buying at a specialized computer store—at least according to the argument offered by the stores themselves—is hand-holding and support. After all, there you are, a babe in the computer woods, presumably with no technological expertise of your own. Who is going to help you through the rough spots? Computer-store sales people are supposedly qualified to demonstrate different equipment and software, make sure everything works before it leaves the store, and help you over the phone with any glitches you later encounter at home. You will have to be your own judge of this, however, for there is a great deal of turnover among computer-store personnel; equipment and software change rapidly and you may find, in fact, that the personnel are not as knowledgeable and helpful as you had hoped. However, many stores offer training classes (free or for a price). Many will replace your computer, if there is a warranty to that effect. Some offer a loaner if it is being repaired.

*Types of software:* Software can range from games to business programs. Many users spend more on software than they did on the original equipment.

### ■ *Maintenance Contract*

When buying a computer, you may wish to check out getting a maintenance contract, which should cover both parts and labor. Such a contract has five basic levels of comprehensiveness of coverage:

1. The best offers a repair person to come out and fix your system on-site within a certain number of hours. This option is probably available only for significant business customers.

2. The next best is a courier pick-up and delivery repair service. This usually costs 25 percent less than on-site repair.

3. Carry-in service allows you to bring your machine in for repairs. With courier or carry-in service, the store may provide you with a loaner while they fix it.

4. Another provides a hot line you can call, and the person at the other end will help you troubleshoot. Clearly, this is just for basic problems of usage, not for getting inside the machine with tools.

5. The least desirable allows you to mail the machine in for repair.

### ■ Used Computers

Used car lots are common enough. Could "used computer" stores become a staple in society? Perhaps. But, if you want to pick up a bargain from an ad in your local newspaper, be careful.

There is no way, for instance, for you to know what kind of workout the secondhand computer has had. Was it merely played with from time to time or was it the office workhorse every day for two years?

Another angle, and this may be a psychological one, is that the seller may want to charge you a price which is related to the original price paid *two years ago*. Perhaps the seller paid $5000 for the system and thinks that $3000 is a fair price for the used equipment. But new comparable equipment may now

be less than $3000. Always compare the computer system with *today's* prices.

Despite these reservations, there certainly are some real bargains available in used equipment. Shop carefully.

## People Connections

"User friendly" is an overused word in the computer industry. It means how easy or difficult is it for you, the user, to learn to operate a computer or piece of software. Consider training.

### ■ Training

Can you teach yourself? Besides the documentation—the instructions that come with your computer—there are numerous books on the market that can teach you about programming and the operation of your computer. Of course, you need to check to see that the edition is up to date. Magazines are also available to help you.

As mentioned, some computer stores offer classes in the operation of computers. Other private parties do, too, although the fees are often substantial. And, of course, some local community and other colleges also offer courses, although you may want to be sure to get in line early for sign-ups. It also may be possible to get private lessons. Although this may be the most expensive method, it might be very effective.

Some manufacturers provide self-teaching materials, such as cassette tapes or training software, called *tutorials*, that work on your computer.

**Read the directions:** To make sure your hardware is adequate for the software you are buying, you should read the fine print carefully.

*Dealing with the dealer:* **It is important to check out the computer dealer as carefully as you would your computer purchases.**

### ■ Documentation

Nothing is as important as documentation, the written manuals and instructions that accompany hardware and software. Unfortunately, much of it is poor. The weakest link in personal computer systems is the documentation. Ask to see the documentation when you buy. See if you can take something from the documentation and actually try it out on a machine in the store. It should be simple to understand, have very little jargon in it, and should include simple subsets of instructions so that in short order you can actually do something. Some documentation goes on and on for many pages for a particular activity. The problem is that they have given you all the variations for all the options for each type of activity, when all you really need to get started is the simplest form of the activity.

Documentation should also have visual clarity. It should be very easy to follow the instructions. Sections in a manual should be separated with durable index tab pages. There should be lots of white space, pictures, demonstrations, and examples so that you have no trouble following what is happening. The documentation should also have attractive pack-

aging (not just be a collection of typewritten sheets), although packaging alone, of course, will not guarantee good documentation.

### The Survey

With this background, we hope you are now in a position to answer some questions as to what kind of computer you want.

### ■ *What Do You Want in a Microcomputer?*

Answer the following questions:

1. **Price Range.** I can spend ☐ under $500 ☐ up to $1000 ☐ up to $4000 ☐ up to $10,000.

2. **Peripherals Needed.** (If you checked under $500.) I have ☐ a cassette recorder (on which to keep software and data); ☐ a black-and-white TV set (to use as a monitor); ☐ a color TV set (if you wish to produce computer graphics or see video games in color).

3. **Uses for Computer.** Rank the following in order. I wish to use the computer for:

\_\_\_\_\_ Playing video games

\_\_\_\_\_ Adult educational purposes (foreign language drill, teaching self programming, etc.)

\_\_\_\_\_ Children's educational purposes (teaching arithmetic, typing, programming, etc.)

\_\_\_\_\_ Word processing (writing papers, reports, memos, letters, etc.)

\_\_\_\_\_ Business applications in office (financial spread sheets, accounts receivable, scheduling, etc.)

\_\_\_\_\_ Business or office homework

\_\_\_\_\_ Mailing lists

\_\_\_\_\_ Personal record keeping (e.g., address lists, list of insured possessions, appointment calendar, storing recipes, calorie counting)

\_\_\_\_\_ Personal finance (taxes, managing expenses, tracking stock market, etc.)

\_\_\_\_\_ Programming

\_\_\_\_\_ Information retrieval (from services such as The Source or CompuServe)

# BUYER'S GUIDE

_____ Inexpensive printer

_____ Dot matrix printer

_____ Letter-quality printer

_____ Other:_____

_____

_____

**5. Software Features Wanted.** I want the following software features (rank in order of importance):

_____ CP/M or MS-DOS compatibility

_____ Video games and recreation software packages

_____ Word processing

_____ Education packages

*Computer learning (top):* Classes are offered by dealers and independent sources. *Computer books (middle)* teach you about programming and computer operation. *Clear Documentation (bottom)* may be the biggest asset of your new system.

_____ Other:_____

_____

_____

**4. Hardware Features Wanted.** I want the following features on my computer (rate in order of importance):

_____ 16-bit processor (instead of 8-bit)

_____ 80-column screen

_____ Excellent screen readability

_____ Tiltable screen

_____ Detached keyboard

_____ Full traveling keyboard

_____ Membrane keyboard

_____ Numeric keypad

_____ Function keys

_____ Diskette storage

_____ Hard disk storage

_____ Portability

_____ Expandable memory

_____ Color graphics capability

_____ Sound

_____ Business packages

_____ BASIC

_____ Pascal

_____ FORTRAN

_____ COBOL

_____ Other:_____

**6. Other Features Wanted.** The following are also important to me (rank in order):

_____ Manufacturer's reputation

_____ Dealer's reputation

_____ Dealer financing

_____ Local service

_____ Training

_____ Documentation quality

_____ Maintenance contract

_____ Other:_____

_____

_____

## Manufacturers' Addresses and Telephone Numbers

You may wish to write some computer manufacturers for literature about their products. Some manufacturers' addresses and their telephone numbers are listed below.

**Altos Computer Systems**, 2360 Bering Dr., San Jose, CA 95131; (408) 946-6700

**Apple Computer, Inc.**, 10260 Bradley Dr., Cupertino, CA 95014; (408) 996-1010

**Atari, Inc.**, 1196 Borregas Ave., Sunnyvale, CA 94086; (408) 745-5227

**Commodore**, 487 Devon Park Dr., Wayne, PA 19087; (215) 687-4311

**Compaq Computer Corp.**, 20333 FM 149, Houston, TX 77070; (713) 370-7040

**Corvus**, 2029 O'Toole Ave., San Jose, CA 95131; (408) 946-7700

**Cromemco, Inc.**, 280 Bernardo Ave., Mountain View, CA 94040; (415) 964-7400

**Digital Equipment Corporation (DEC)**, 129 Parker St., Maynard, MA 01754; (617) 897-5111

**Dynalogic**, 141 Bentley Ave., Ottawa, Canada K2E 6T7; (613) 226-1383

**Eagle**, 11570 Martens River Circle, Fountain Valley, CA 92708; (714) 957-1711

**Epson America, Inc.**, 3415 Kashiwa St., Torrance, CA 90505; (213) 539-9140

**Fortune**, 1501 Industrial Rd., San Carlos, CA 94070; (415) 595-8444

**Franklin Computer**, 2128 Route 38, Cherry Hill, NJ 08002; (609) 482-5900

**Hewlitt-Packard**, 1601 Page Mill Rd., Palo Alto, CA 94305; (415) 857-1501

**Hitachi**, 401 West Artesia Blvd., Compton, CA 90220; (213) 537-8383

**International Business Machines (IBM)**, P.O. Box C-1645, Atlanta, GA 30301; (404) 238-3645

**Kaypro Corp.**, 533 Stevens Ave., Solano Beach, CA 92075; (619) 481-3424

**Nippon Electric Corporation (NEC)**, Five Militia Dr., Lexington, MA 02173; (617) 862-3120

**North Star**, 14440 Catalina St., San Leandro, CA 94577; (415) 357-8500

**Olivetti**, 155 White Plains Rd., Tarrytown, NY 10591; (914) 631-8100

**Otrona Advanced Systems Corp.**, 4725 Walnut St., Boulder, CO 80301; (303) 444-8100 (Attaché Computer)

**Radio Shack**, 1500 One Tandy Center, Fort Worth, TX 76102; (817) 390-3011

**Sony**, 7 Mercedes Dr., Montvale, NJ 07645; (201) 573-8899

**Televideo Systems, Inc.** 1170 Morse Ave., Sunnyvale, CA 94086; (408) 745-7760

**Texas Instruments, Inc.**, P.O. Box 73, Lubbock, TX 79408; (806) 741-2978

**Vector Graphic**, 500 N. Ventu Park Rd., Thousand Oaks, CA 91320; (805) 499-5831

**Victor**, 3900 N. Rockwell St., Chicago, IL 60618; (213) 539-8200

**Wang**, One Industrial Ave., Lowell, MA 01851; (617) 459-5000

**Zenith Data Systems**, Hilltop Rd., St. Joseph, MI 49085; (616) 982-3200

*Buyer's Notes:*_____

*Buyer's Notes:*

## WHO SHALL EDIT THE EDITOR?

Bell Laboratories, mindful of the rising tide of information that is swamping businesses, decided to do something to make the reporting of this information more readable. The culprits, Bell reasoned, were nonprofessional writers—especially technical types—who when asked to write a report or a memo would ramble on in obscure jargon. So the Bell scientists wrote a computer program called Writer's Workbench, which cleans up bad technical writing.

The Workbench program substitutes simple words, like *use* for the overused *utilize.* It shifts verbs from the passive to the active ("was done by researchers" is changed to "researchers did"). Workbench breaks up long sentences, simplifies convoluted sentence structure, corrects grammar, punctuation, and spelling—everything you'd expect from a good editor.

There are a few bugs, however. While Writer's Workbench makes bad writing better, it also makes good writing worse. As an experiment, Bell scientists fed the computer Abraham Lincoln's Gettysburg Address. "Fourscore and seven years ago, our forefathers brought forth upon this continent a new nation, conceived in liberty and dedicated to the proposition that all men are created equal . . . " was mercilessly chopped to "Eighty-seven years ago, our grandfathers created a free nation here."

Other classics fared no better. The problem seems to be that among computers—as among editors—there's no accounting for taste.

—Nick Engler,
*Omni*, August 1982

## Word Processing

In 1874, when Philo Remington began marketing a commercially useful kind of printing machine that used capital and small letters—a curious device known as a "typewriter"—it helped make business exchanges easier and began the retirement of the quill pen. Other machines introduced during the first half of the twentieth century—teletypewriters, duplicating machines, and dictating machines—also began to change the nature of office work. Recently, however, a number of machines have been introduced that may change office work more than at any other time in the past 100 years.

The first of these is the **word processor**—essentially an electric typewriter with a CRT screen attached to a computer. A word processor (see Figure 13-5) eliminates the need to retype a letter or document every time it is revised. It can also be used to send messages to other word processors—what the industry calls "electronic mail" (to be discussed further in Chapter 15). **Word processing,** a term coined by IBM in 1964, refers to electronic ways of handling the standard office activities of composing, revising, printing, and filing written material.

The reason word processing is so important is that so much office work is repetitious. The same letter is sent to different persons, with only the address and salutation changed. Drafts of a report are circulated to several people, and their changes must be pooled together in a final draft. Inquiries from outside the office by different people all require the same sort of response. For typists and secretaries, the retyping and reproofreading of such materials can be mind-deadening, tedious work. There are also related problems of duplication of

**Figure 13-5    A word processing system.** This Wangwriter features terminal and floppy disk system.

## Growing Up in Silicon Valley

It was not called "Silicon Valley" when I was growing up there in the 1940s and '50s. It was simply the Santa Clara Valley, a previously agricultural area of apricot and cherry orchards rapidly filling with suburban housing. Industrial "parks" also appeared as the postwar boom in electronics took hold in California. Blessed with a temperate climate, the valley stretches beside San Francisco Bay from the college town of Palo Alto to what was once the sleepy city of San Jose.

Today this is the nation's ninth largest manufacturing center, with the fastest-growing and wealthiest economy in the United States. In the last 10 years, San Jose has grown by over a third, jumping from 29th to 17th largest city in the United States. In the same period, the median family income in the valley went from $18,000 a year to an estimated

**Players.** The board game is "Silicon Valley: In the Chips."

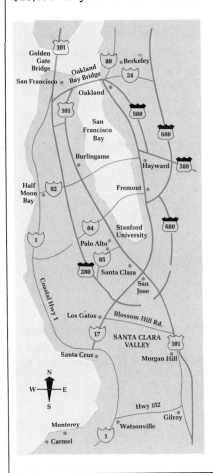

$27,000. There are 6000 Ph.D.s living here—one of every six doctorates in California—and they are a hard-working lot. Many engineers put in 15-hour days and seven-day work weeks, and talk about achieving success in 10 years. The rewards they seek are apt to be the more material badges of success, such as cars and real estate. Porsches and Mercedes abound, and one local Ferrari dealership is second in size only to the one in Beverly Hills. A Monopoly-like board game developed locally is almost a satire on this success/failure frenzy. Called "Silicon Valley: In the Chips," it has very little to do with silicon chips and computers. Rather, the object of the game is "to negotiate your way through the valley and make your wealth through proper management of your income in home purchases and business investments."

As one who has watched not a few cow pastures become parking lots, I regard all this change with a great deal of ambivalence. How did such a concentration of high-tech industry come about?

One name often mentioned as being pivotal is Frederick Terman. In the 1940s, Stanford University, located near Palo Alto, was a respectable regional university, but not yet the world-class institution of higher learning it is today. For development on its scientific and technical side, a great deal of credit must go to Terman, who in 1946 became dean of the School of Engineering. On one hand, Terman urged former students with last names like Hewlett and Packard and Varian to establish their electronics businesses locally. On the other hand, he wholeheartedly encouraged Stanford to join the effort of establishing the region as a center of advanced technology. He encouraged engineering faculty (my father among them) to go out and consult. He offered training to industry engineers. He sat on the boards of small businesses. He helped persuade the university administration and trustees to lease Stanford land to local electronics companies, thus beginning the Stanford Industrial Park, the nucleus of commercial high technology in the region.

**Stanford University, then and now.** Aerial photo shows the campus in 1947, before the university had become the techological research center it is today. Note in the second photo how open spaces have yielded to buildings.

Today the 660-acre park has some 70 advanced-technology businesses located there. Hewlett-Packard Co., Varian Associates, and other early tenants were followed into the valley in the 1950s by such large firms as Lockheed, General Electric, Ford, and GTE. The U.S. government established research facilities at Moffett Naval Air Station and nearby Berkeley and Livermore.

It has been said there would be no "Silicon Valley," however, if William Shockley's mother had not lived in Palo Alto. One of the inventors of the transistor (for which he won a Nobel Prize) while he was at Bell Laboratories in New Jersey, Shockley returned to the town where he was raised and in 1956 set up Shockley Transistor Co. Two years later, several of his associates left and set up Fairchild Semiconductors Co., which many observers believe represents the true beginning of the semiconductor industry. The 1960s became a turbulent time as many others left Fairchild to start companies with now well-known names such as National Semiconductor, Intel, and Advanced Micro Devices. Among computer manufacturers, IBM was the first to arrive in the valley, but one of its executives, Gene Amdahl, resigned in 1970 and started his own company. Tandem Computers, Inc., was founded in 1974 by several former Hewlett-Packard employees. Peripheral equipment manufacturers—makers of storage devices and media and related equipment—also sprang up. Ampex, started in 1944 and a pioneer in magnetic recording systems, was followed by companies such as Memorex, started in 1961. Electronic games began when Atari, Inc., created "Pong" in 1972. The company now makes personal computers, but it was not prepared to enter into that market when one of its employees, a young college dropout named Steve Jobs, first urged it to do so. Jobs joined forces with Steve Wozniak of Hewlett-Packard and founded Apple Computer, one of the valley's huge success stories.

Today, the Santa Clara Valley seems to an old-time resident to be strangling on its own success. Housing is among the most expensive in the country: former $25,000 homes sell for $300,000 and up. The pace and intensity of work leads to job burnout, and the divorce rate is higher than the rate for the state as a whole. Traffic chokes the eight-lane freeways. Local zoning boards and city councils are resisting further growth.

However, Silicon Valley is no longer a single region. It is a way of life. "Silicon Valley" has moved beyond Santa Clara County to the so-called 128 Belt of Boston; to the "Sci/Com" area along Route 270 outside of Washington, D.C.; to Colorado; to Oregon—and to many places overseas.

—Brian Williams

paper, storage space, lost records, and turnover in office staff because of boredom-induced job dissatisfaction. For the employer, of course, all this adds to the cost of getting work done.

The word processor is the "better mousetrap" that avoids most of this. The hardware consists basically of four components:

- The CRT terminal, the keyboard for which might look like that shown in Figure 13-6.

- The central processing unit—which in some systems may have more than one CRT connected to it.

- Either hard-disk or floppy-disk drives. Floppy-disk devices may be of two sorts: one, a master drive, which maintains the floppy disks for the documents currently being processed; another, a backup drive, used to copy documents for storage.

- A printer, usually one of fairly good quality, that has uppercase and lowercase letters. Some printers print in two directions, one line forward and the next in reverse. Printing speeds vary: 55 characters per second is typical, but some bidirectional printers produce output at 200 characters per second.

The hardware uses a special word processing program. Although other computers, notably personal computers, also have word processing software available, hardware specifically designed for word processing is more efficient for that application.

---

**Test Driving a New Word Processor for a Personal Computer**

The only way to test the roadability of a car is to take it for a drive. The only way to test the "processability" of a word processor is to run some words through it—not merely an alternate couple of lines of "The quick brown fox jumped . . . " and "Now is the time for all good men . . . ," but a real honest-to-goodness document.

What you need is something at least 2000 words long . . . to get your feel for the various software capabilities. You also need a stopwatch.

Once you have entered your test document into a word processing system, composed of a particular personal computer and its appropriate software, measure the time it takes to execute the following four moves.

First, scroll from the beginning of the document to the end, one line at a time. Think of the document as a continuous roll of film. When you request the computer to scroll the text,

the film will rise from the bottom of the screen and wind up at the top. Record how long the procedure takes.

Second, measure the time it takes to scroll from the beginning of the document to the end, one page (instead of one line) at a time.

Next, check to see how long you must wait for the cursor to advance from the start of the text to the end when you give the command "end of document" or its equivalent.

Finally, hit the repeat key or its equivalent to make the cursor move 100 characters, and time that.

Raw speed isn't everything, but it's important, particularly once you've become adroit at handling the software. The miracles of word processing soon become minor when you must wait around for the machine to perform them.

Convenience in editing is, in a sense, another function of speed. For example, if three keystrokes are

needed to switch from one preset margin to another in one system, and seven keystrokes are needed in another system, the former may well be the preferred package for applications requiring frequent margin changes.

When it comes to deleting characters, your choice in editing styles will be mainly between using a special function key provided for deleting characters, or striking the control key and then, say, the G key to make the deletion in two strokes instead of one.

Such idiosyncrasies of word processors are for you to evaluate in terms of your own personal comfort or discomfort and your own application requirements—balanced, of course, by considerations of price.

—Erik Sandberg-Diment,
*New York Times,*
April 19, 1983

**Figure 13-6** Word processor keyboard.

If you are a secretary using a word processor, sitting at your **workstation**—your work area—and doing keying (not at your "desk" doing "typing"—note how the office vocabulary is changing), you would key your document into the system, watching it on the CRT screen and making minor adjustments as you go along. Your word processor may also have that wonderful new feature, a program that will check your spelling for you. The final document would be stored on disk and after you have finished keying, could be printed out on paper. Copies of the document would be circulated to executives for comments and changes. When you received all these changes back and were ready to type the final version of the document, you would recall the original text from the disk to your CRT screen. Using a key that activates a cursor, which might be like the underscore mark ( _ ) on a typewriter, you might move to different places on the screen and add or delete characters, words, or sentences. Figure 13-7 gives an example of how insertion and deletion works.

You can also make such timesaving changes as automatically centering your text in the middle of the page, justifying your margins, and numbering the pages. An additional feature is the so-called global find, in which you can instruct the system to find every instance in the document of a particular word—say, someone's name has been misspelled throughout—and change it. When the document is printed out, you will find that the machine has already made allowances for insertions and deletions so that all margins are the same and all pages are the same length.

What we have described above is the ideal, however, for the bugs are still being ironed out in this young field. People using word processors sometimes complain that they are not given enough formal

**Figure 13-7  How a word processor revises text.** *Left,* original text. This is how a document might look as first keyboarded on the word processor. *Right,* revised text. Note that in this version the words *in large part* have been deleted and *$20* has been altered to *twenty dollars.* Yet the word processor has automatically right-justified the margins (evened them up on the right side).

## FOOT-DRAGGING KNOWLEDGE WORKERS

The availability of technology is not the stumbling block. Vendors are already offering a powerful range of electronic devices, software, and communications networks. The fact is that most decision makers are skeptical about what managerial work stations, personal computers, videoconference rooms, and the other, newer icons of office automation can do for their businesses. These executives, disenchanted by their previous exposure to ill-conceived forays into management information systems and word proocessing, doubt that knowledge workers will embrace the new technology, and they lack confidence that their organizations can channel and measure the intended benefits. In addition, members of the computer-illiterate majority are worried about whether, when, and how they themselves will deal with these new electronic tools.

—Harvey L. Poppel,
*Harvard Business Review,*
November-December 1982

training to use them, that accompanying instructions are often poor (requiring too much learning by word of mouth), that screens should be bigger, and printing of better quality. Still, there are experts who insist that word processing can boost office productivity as much as 500 percent.

### More Office Automation: Getting Executives Involved

There is much more to the automated office than just word processing. Other machines have also become commonplace: terminals that display colored graphics from data; automated forms of data entry such as optical character readers; so-called intelligent copiers that can retrieve documents from computer storage and make copies; and wall-sized projection screens that permit business people to have meetings by "teleconference networks."

For the office of the future to become the office of the present, however, one important thing must happen: acceptance not just by secretaries but by managers and professionals as well. The electronic revolution of the office will probably have to flow from the top down. Since many managers are fearful of word processor keyboards because they look too complicated, equipment manufacturers are trying other stratagems to get electronic gear onto managers' desks. For instance, in some companies, top brass are using computer terminals to send intraoffice messages—what is known as "electronic mail" (to be discussed in Chapter 15)—and what the boss finds acceptable one way or another usually is found acceptable by subordinates. A variation on electronic mail is a device that changes voices into the digital language of computers, so that messages can be stored in and retrieved from various voice "mailboxes." While this may seem somewhat frivolous at first, many executives find the slowness of interoffice mail and the tyranny of telephone synchrony—two people must be on the line at the same time to talk—a source of great frustration.

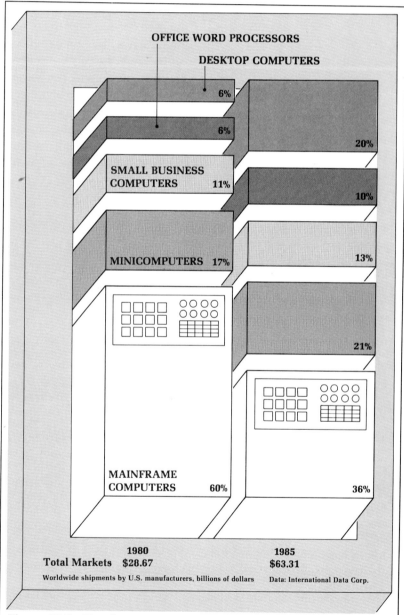

**Figure 13-8    The changing computer market.** Worldwide shipments by U.S. computer manufacturers, as expressed in billions of dollars, show that the mainframe is occupying a shrinking share of the market and desktop computers a larger share.

Some people worry that automation of the office might produce the same kinds of problems as automation of the factory: loss of jobs and further regimentation of already routinized work. In defense, it must be said that such automation—word processing in particular—actually *frees* clerical people from tedious, routinized work and makes office work easier and more pleasant.

## The Changing Hardware Mix

We shall return to the problems of automation in Chapter 19, but suffice it to say here that it does not appear as though the trend toward automating the office will be reversed. Indeed, as Figure 13-8 shows, it is likely the mix in the computer market will continue to change, with mainframes occupying a shrinking share.

Perhaps the most significant aspect of office automation is that it is not confined to large organizations. With smaller and less expensive equipment available, automation is appearing in even the smallest offices. Much of this is the result of that remarkable machine, the microcomputer—as we shall see in the next chapter.

## Summary and Key Terms

- Different users have different needs in computers. Large organizations and government departments need mainframes, individuals may need microcomputers, and those in between need minicomputers.

- **Mainframes** are the largest, fastest, and most expensive computers. They are usually considered general-purpose computers. Memories consist of several megabytes; a **megabyte** is roughly a million bytes or exactly 1,048,576 bytes. The price can range from a few hundred thousand dollars to $10 million or more.

- The largest mainframes are the **supercomputers**, the fastest being the CDC CYBER 205.

- **Minicomputers** are smaller and less powerful versions of mainframes. They cost $10,000 to $250,000. The term **supermini** is given to minicomputers on the large end of the scale, and the distinction between minis and mainframes here is no longer clear.

- **Microcomputers** are the smallest computers. They are used not only for business purposes such as accounting and inventory control, but also for a variety of personal, educational, and entertainment uses.

- The computer industry includes the following: computer manufacturers, peripheral equipment manufacturers, leasing companies, service bureaus, software houses, and individual entrepreneurs.

- Among computer manufacturers, IBM is the largest maker of mainframes, with about 70 percent of the worldwide market. Honeywell, Burroughs, Sperry-Univac, NCR, and CDC each have less than a 10 percent share. The principal makers of minicomputers are DEC, with 30 percent of the market, followed by Hewlett-Packard, Data General, Honeywell, IBM, Datapoint, Wang, Prime, and Perkin-Elmer. The top three overseas revenue producers from sales of data processing equipment are Hitachi, Toshiba, and Fujitsu.

- Among the principal **peripheral equipment manufacturers (PEMs)**—makers of tape readers, disk drives, printers, and the like—are Telex, Memorex, and Ampex. PEMs are also called **plug-compatible manufacturers (PCMs)** because the peripheral devices they make are so standardized that they can be used ("plugged in") interchangeably with an original manufacturer's computer.

- Leasing companies acquire computers and associated equipment directly from manufacturers or second-hand and lease them out to other users, thus sparing the latter the risk of buying equipment that may become obsolete.

- **Service bureaus** are organizations selling such services as batch processing, data entry, software development, facilities management, and time-sharing. Time-sharing might be via the client's terminal, which would be connected through communication lines to the service bureau's computer for real-time processing, or via **remote job-entry (RJE),** in which jobs are entered into the service bureau's regular batch processing from the client's office terminal.

- **Software houses** are businesses specializing in providing software and systems analysis services. These businesses may either write custom-tailored software for clients on a contract basis or provide packages of standardized **applications software**—programs to solve specific business or organizational problems.

- The expanding market for computer services has encouraged many computer professionals to go into business for themselves.

- The **automated office** (or "paperless office" or "office of the future") is the name given to the electronic office. One of its principal features is the use of word processing, but it also may include other machines such as terminals that display colored graphics of data, automated forms of data entry such as optical character readers, intelligent copiers that can retrieve documents from storage and make copies, and wall-sized projection screens that allow business meetings via teleconference networks.

- The **word processor** is essentially an electric typewriter with a CRT screen attached to a computer. It eliminates the need to retype a letter or document every time it is revised and can also be used to send messages to other word processors. **Word processing** refers to electronic ways of handling the standard office activities of composing, revising, printing, and filing written material. It helps cut down the repetitious retyping and reproofreading of drafted materials. A word processor consists of four components: (1) CRT terminal, (2) central processing unit, (3) hard-disk or floppy-disk drives, and (4) printer. A word processor is often considered part of a **workstation,** an office worker's work area.

- In order for the automated office to become established, it must be accepted by top-level managers as well as subordinates.

## Review

1. Differentiate mainframes, supercomputers, minicomputers, and microcomputers.

2. Name the principal manufacturers of mainframes. Of minicomputers.

3. Define PEM and PCM and name the principal companies.

4. Explain what leasing companies, service bureaus, and software houses do.

5. Explain the concept of the automated office.

6. Explain how word processing works.

## Selected References for Further Reading

Cecil, Paula B. *Office Automation.* Menlo Park, Calif.: Benjamin/Cummings, 1984.

Fishman, Katharine Davis. *The Computer Establishment.* New York: Harper & Row, 1981.

Hanson, Dirk. *The New Alchemists: Silicon Valley and the Microelectronics Revolution.* Boston: Little, Brown, 1982.

Kidder, Tracy. *The Soul of a New Machine.* Boston: Little, Brown, 1981.

Lieberman, Mark, Gerd Selig, and John Walsh. *Office Automation: A Manager's Guide for Improved Productivity.* New York: Wiley, 1982.

McWilliams, Peter A. *The Word Processing Book: A Short Course in Computer Literacy.* Los Angeles: Prelude Press, 1983.

Sobel, Robert. *IBM: Colossus in Transition.* New York: Times Books, 1981.

## IN THIS CHAPTER

Microcomputers, the fastest-growing sector of the computer industry, are available for a variety of purposes: home, educational, and business. Microcomputer software is becoming easier to use, costs of hardware are going down, and more manufacturers are entering the marketplace. This chapter describes these developments and offers consumer-related advice.

# ch 14

# personal computers

## a computer of your own

Owning your own computer is no more unlikely than owning a stereo or typewriter. As with these other devices, the range of capabilities depends on the price you want to pay—but the price is constantly coming down.

**Personal computers**—the name given to microcomputers used by individuals for various personal uses—are the fastest growing sector of the computer industry, and all the indicators point to an explosion in use. Sales may well increase 40 percent a year (some say 60 percent) through the rest of the decade. One out of two American homes, according to some predictions, will have some form of microcomputer by the end of the 1980s.

But, people say, do I really *need* a microcomputer? What would I use it for?

Before we begin to suggest the possibilities, let us consider what a microcomputer is.

## The Marvelous Microprocessor and Other Hardware

What do the following have in common? Digital watches. Videogames. Calculators. Microwave ovens. Many radios, cameras, stereo tape decks, television sets, automobiles. The answer: a microprocessor.

### The Microprocessor

People frequently confuse the terms *microcomputer* and *microprocessor*, but they are not the same. A **microprocessor** is a central processing unit manufactured on a silicon chip smaller than your thumbnail. Microcomputers have microprocessors in them. As we have seen in Chapter 4, the cost of making microprocessors has dropped dramatically since they were first introduced.

Microprocessors are classified according to the number of bits they process per operation. In the beginning there were 4 bits, then 8 bits, and now 16-bit and 32-bit microprocessors are available. Whatever the number of bits, the microprocessor is the basis for both microcomputers and an array of other items, from microwave ovens to computer-controlled cameras. Figure 14-1 shows how microprocessor-operated gadgets can be used to control many of a home's routine functions.

### The Microcomputer

In addition to the microprocessor, the microcomputer has two kinds of main storage—RAM and ROM. As you will recall from Chapter 4, **RAM** stands for **random-access memory.** This is the computer's "scratch pad," which keeps the intermediate results of calculations. **ROM** stands for **read-only memory.** ROM contents are programmed into the hardware by the microcomputer manufacturer. ROM contains systems

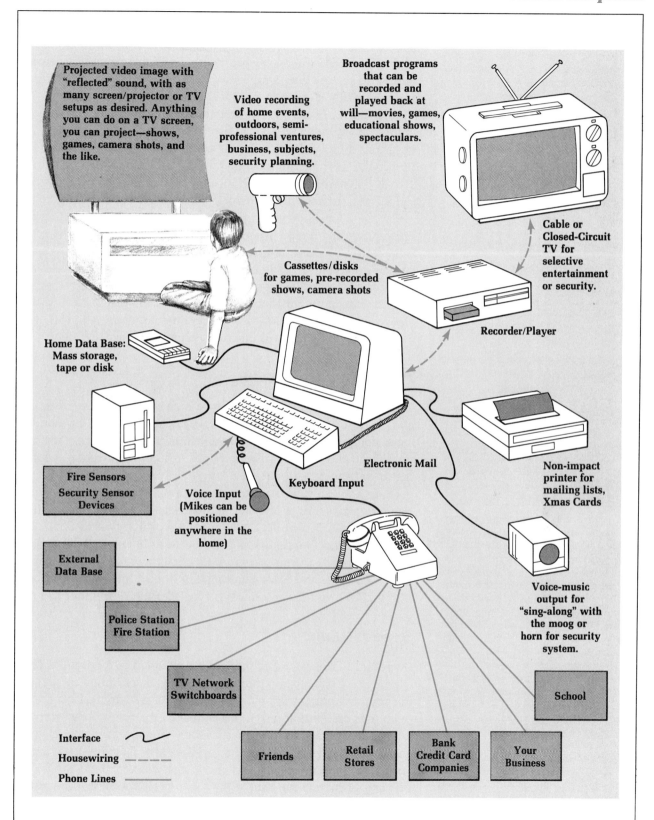

**Figure 14-1  Microprocessors in the home.** Microprocessors can be used to operate a host of items, whether in the micro-computer _(center of picture)_ or in other products.

## CHIP SHOTS

Chip numbers are often tossed into discussions in journals, but it is not always clear which computer uses which chip. Here is a list of some chips and typical microcomputers in which they are used. The first four are 8-bit chips, while the last two are 16-bit chips.

- Z80—Altos 8000, Wangwriter
- Z80A—Eagle II, NorthStar Horizon, TRS-80
- 6502—Apple II
- 8085—Microstar, Sanyo MBC 2000
- 8088—IBM PC, Hitachi Personal Computer, Toshiba America T300
- 68000—Corvus Concept, Fortune System Five, TRS-80/16

## 8 VERSUS 16: A BIT ABOUT BITS

All of the IBM PC compatible computers necessarily use the same 16-bit innards as the IBM. But does a buyer need 16 bits? The question is roughly comparable to the choice between six or eight cylinders in an automobile engine. And the answer boils down to deciding whether the speed and enhanced number-crunching power of the 16-bit machine is worth the higher price—generally at least one-third more than an eight-bit.

The choice invariably depends on how the machine is going to be used. For professional work that requires a lot of muscle—copious data storage and complicated calculations, for example—the 16-bitters will be favored. But for the home market and for personal business uses such as letter writing, budgeting and organizing a workday, eight-bit machines are more than adequate. They include old favorites such as the KayPro II, as well as several new entrants.

—Augustin Hedberg,
*Money,*
May 1983

programs that are not changeable through the keyboard. Microprocessor-controlled devices such as microwave ovens also have RAM and ROM—ROM for the stored instructions that cannot be changed and RAM for the very simple calculations such as buttons a person pushes, which constitute the "programming" in such items.

A keyboard is needed, of course, to enable you to program the computer. A video screen is also needed to display the data and programs. Many microcomputers combine keyboard and screen in a terminal, but some microcomputers use a regular television set as a screen—something to keep in mind if you are interested in keeping the initial purchase price down.

For secondary storage purposes, a disk drive is needed to read or write on floppy disks. A portable cassette recorder is needed if cassette tape is to be used. (If you already have an audio cassette recorder, you can use that—this is another way of keeping the initial cost of purchasing a personal computer system down.) Some systems also use cartridges. In addition, as we noted in Chapter 7, hard disk is also available as an option for many microcomputers. All in all, however, floppy disks are still the most common storage medium.

### Printers for Microcomputers

The basic microcomputer hardware consists of memory, terminal, and storage device. In addition, many systems have a printer. Personal computer users often want a printer quite soon after they have purchased the basic hardware; paper is a communication medium that is hard to do without.

There are many printers to choose from. On the low end, Apple offers a very small printer (8-inch carriage), which prints on heat-sensitive paper, for under $300; one of its primary assets is that it is nonimpact and therefore silent. In the middle range, there are versatile dot-matrix printers from under $1000 to $2000. The top of the line is a heavy-duty letter-quality printer used for word processing; Diablo, NEC, and Epson offer this type of printer for under $3000.

### "User Friendly"

Do not let all this talk of equipment intimidate you. A microcomputer can be quite easy to use: Step 1, plug in your machine. Step 2, slip the preprogrammed floppy disk or tape cassette into place. Step 3, push the "on" button. From that point on, the prerecorded software will lead you, asking you questions, to which you key in answers, and so on. Such software has been called **"user friendly,"** an overused term that nonetheless suggests that the software is nontechnical and that nearly anyone can use it. Writing your *own* software for a microcomputer, however, requires training and can be quite complicated.

A buyer of a personal computer is apt to find that both software and hardware are not just friendly, but possibly even addicting. Many people start out to buy what they think will be a cheap machine, then find themselves shelling out hundreds or even thousands of dollars for add-ons: printers, extra memory, telephone links, color monitors, and, of course, software of all kinds. Acquiring a personal computer is such a tricky endeavor, in fact, that as an added feature we have provided a special "Buyer's Guide: How to Buy Your Own Microcomputer," which follows p. 278.

Now let us turn back to the question so many people raise: What would I use a personal computer for?

## LEADING USES OF HOME COMPUTERS

The percentage of home-computer owners surveyed who said that they use their computer for a particular task (owners were able to give multiple responses):

| | |
|---|---|
| Video games | 51% |
| Business or office homework | 46% |
| Child's learning tool | 46% |
| Adult's learning tool | 42% |
| Balancing checkbook or budget | 37% |
| Business-in-home uses | 27% |
| Word processing | 18% |
| Mailing lists | 16% |
| Information retrieval* | 14% |
| Appointment calendar | 9% |
| Storing recipes | 9% |
| Calorie counting | 4% |

*Includes information on investing, travel and account balances, as well as paying bills by phone.
Source: Gallup Organization.
— *The New York Times*, May 11, 1983

## Why a Computer at Home?

Microcomputers in the home were originally used by computer professionals who were also computer hobbyists on the side. They wanted their own software and thrived on controlling their own machines. This scenario has evolved into something quite different. The hobbyists are still active, but today most personal computers are being used by nonprofessionals using preprogrammed software.

Home computers may seem somewhat of a luxury, but there are many uses to which they can be put—some of them quite practical, others less so.

**Entertainment and Games** Play is one of the strongest human impulses; given a choice, we would often rather play. In 1975 there were six manufacturers selling video games; now there are hundreds of companies and thousands of electronic games on the market. Games can range from the purely recreational, such as the famous Pac-Man and Donkey Kong, to such enterprising ideas as Mattel's word game that allows children to use running monkeys to grab letters to spell words and fire vowels at words with empty letters, or a game called Killer T-Cell, which shows players that they are not defenseless against cancer. While many games are based on variations of hitting a target or beating a clock, others are more sophisticated "mind games." By now the market for such educational-entertainment software for home computers alone (not counting arcade games) has topped $2 billion.

**Personal Finances** Magazines devoted to microcomputing (see the accompanying box) are full of articles and advertisements concerning software for home money management. Programs can help you compute taxes, balance checking and savings accounts, do household budgeting, record investments, and make stock market and real estate decisions.

**Records, Schedules, and Plans** Christmas and birthday lists, addresses of friends and relatives, future appointments, and warranty expiration dates—all can be made conveniently accessible and be easily updated with a personal computer. If you have a large collection of stereo tapes or LPs or a library of books, a computer can also help you organize and access them. Finally, recipes, menus, and diet and nutritional plans can be stored in the computer.

**Word Processing** Students and others who do a number of papers and reports will benefit from this use. Central to this function, however, is the quality of the printer. A letter-quality printer—that is, a

---

## An Incomplete Guide to Selected Computer Magazines

In general, the magazine-publishing business is not a healthy one—except for computer magazines. Indeed, there are about 5 million readers of microcomputer magazines. Some are as follows:

### Computerworld

Actually a newspaper, this weekly publication is the bible of the computer industry, covering all aspects from micros to mainframes. Necessary reading for all computer professionals and college instructors, this will be of only partial interest to microcomputerists.

### InfoWorld

This weekly magazine is probably on the Must Read list for any serious student of microcomputers. Attempts to appeal to a range of readers from beginners to veterans. Covers not only new-product news, conventions, philosophical issues related to the microcomputer revolution but also valuable reviews of new software, rating them according to performance, documentation, ease of use, and error handling.

### Datamation

This has been called "the *Fortune* of the computer business." Full of insider news, trends, and analysis most useful to someone in the DP field.

### Byte

A serious magazine, pretty heavy on technical issues and bulging with advertising. Of interest primarily to serious computer enthusiasts.

### Personal Computing

Probably the best-selling publication in the crowded field, this magazine is aimed primarily at generalists. Articles range from "Should You Wait to Buy a Computer?" to "Computers Let Farmers Get Back to the Soil."

### Popular Computing

Also aimed at generalists, this magazine tries to offer something for everyone, from small business people to teachers to hobbyists.

### Creative Computing

Calling itself "the #1 magazine of computer applications and software," this publication appeals to more serious computer buffs wanting detailed information on software.

### Compute!

Subtitling itself "the leading magazine of home, educational, and recreational computing," it offers program listings and hardware reviews for serious microcomputerists.

### Microcomputing

Another magazine for the serious computerist. Features in a recent issue included "How to Buy Bank Software" and an article on how to build your own personal robot with the Heath HERO 1 kit.

### Desktop Computing

Calling itself "the plain language computer magazine for business," this monthly publication offers articles for the small business person in areas of office management, telecommunications, and the like.

### Portable Computer

Debuting in February/March 1983, this bi-monthly magazine is dedicated to news, analysis, and features for people interested in portable or hand-held computers.

### LIST

The Spring 1983 premiere issue of this "software resource guide" states that it is "the only publication that takes the mystery out of personal computing" and goes on to describe over 3000 business and professional software programs for personal computer users.

In addition, there are numerous magazines designed for specific users—such as *Educational Computer Magazine* and *Classroom Computer News*—and for people owning some of the more popular personal computers. Apple users have *Softalk* and *Nibble;* IBM users have *PC, PC World,* and *PC Tech Journal.* There are other magazines for the TRS-80, Atari, and TI users.

Finally, there are magazines that are not really magazines. *Course-Ware* magazine contains a cassette with two programs, ready to run, along with user guides; the programs are educational programs for the Apple II, PET, and TRS-80 microcomputers. There are five "issues" a year.

# *Personal Computers*
## *The Personal Convenience Machine*

**1** An early start on computer literacy: Three persons try programming outside in Cullowhee, North Carolina.

If ever proof were needed that we are standing in midstream in the Computer Revolution, the evidence is in these pages. Computers have shrunk from room size to briefcase size and lap size—and even smaller. And the uses to which microcomputers may be put seem boundless—from number crunching to music making, from running a house to running a boat. The biggest trick is to figure out which of the hundreds of items is best for you.

News makers: ❷ The IBM Personal Computer XT rose rapidly to best-seller status. ❸ Apple's Lisa uses a "mouse" (table top, right) to manipulate text and graphics. ❹ The Apple II offers perhaps the widest choice of software.

Popular choices: Well-known microcomputer manufacturers include: **5** Commodore; **6** Hewlett-Packard; **7** Texas Instruments; **8** Tandy-Radio Shack; and **9** Atari.

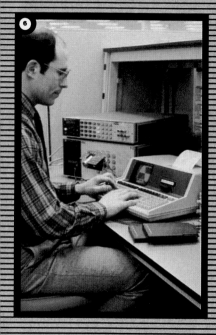

Shrinkage: The portables range from "transportable" to "hand-held": **10** Epson "lap-size"; **11** Osborne Executive; **12** Hewlett-Packard HP-75; **13** IBM's "briefcase" computer; **14** a portable capable of networking through phone links; **15** Quasar's computer-in-a-briefcase; **16** Pocket Computer, which includes a printer.

Many micro uses: Apple computers are used **17** in scientific computations; **18** to monitor home energy performance, operate security systems, and regulate room temperature in this solar house; and **19** **20** assist a dentist in his work. **21** Clarkson College of Technology, in Potsdam, N.Y., requires entering freshmen to have their own Zenith Z-100 computers. **22** A bike shop uses bytes to control inventory and accounts. **23** The joy of doing income taxes is aided with a Commodore computer. **24** Texas Instruments assists boat owners with a computerized integrated marine system.

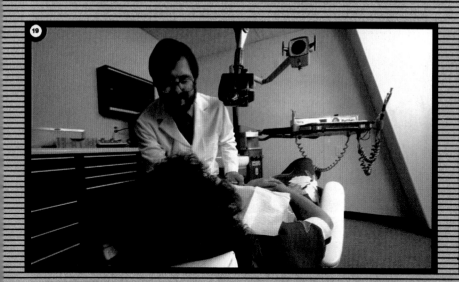

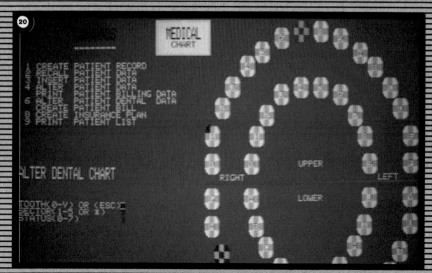

**Making music:** 25 26 **Paul Lutus is a programmer and musician who wrote the first program to play real music through the Apple II's tiny "beeper" speaker.**

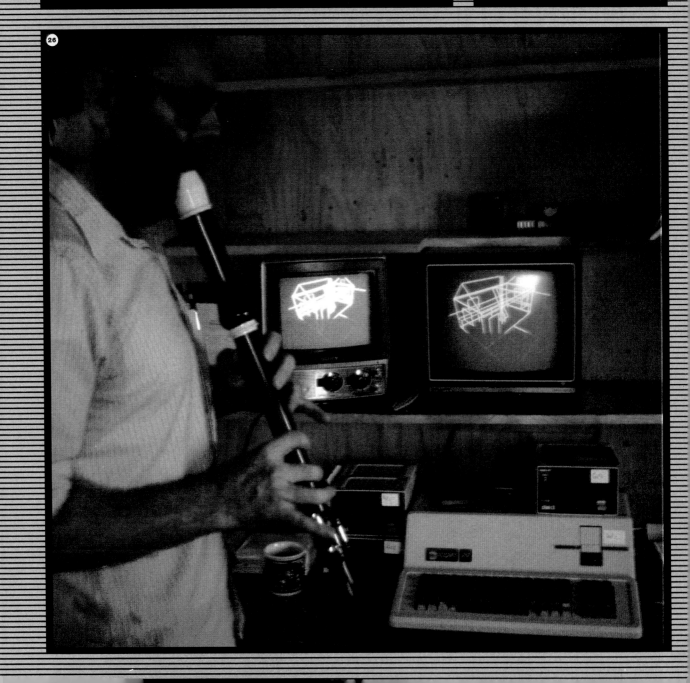

printer that produces output as good as an electric typewriter's—is usually better than a dot-matrix printer if you are concerned about the appearance of the final document.

**Home Environment Controls** Devices are available that can control temperature settings of heating and air conditioning systems, regulating fuel and electricity usage for energy efficiency. As we saw in Figure 14-1, hardware is also available for home security; sensors, which are wired to the computer, can be placed around the house on the alert for burglars and fires. A person may use the computer to turn on morning coffee or the garden sprinkler systems.

**Education** Software that produces color animation, flashing lights, sounds, and music can make learning a great deal of fun for persons of all ages. While children learn arithmetic and spelling, adults can learn typing, foreign languages, and even how to play musical instruments.

**Information Networks** We will describe various communication systems in Chapter 15. However, let us point out here that personal computerists have several mass networking systems, which connect personal computers to a large computer that acts as a massive information center. CompuServe and The Source are typical network systems. These networks offer, for a fee, an astounding variety of services: stock exchange prices, foreign language drills, wine tasting information, income tax assistance, airline and hotel reservation services, consumer guidance, home buying and selling information, daily horoscopes, gourmet recipes, sports news, and much, much more. The personal computer, through some type of network, is the key to computerized services in the home; banking and grocery shopping are two examples of routine activities that can be completed without leaving the home.

Clearly, from the previous list, nearly everyone could put a home computer to some use. To respond to the original question: No, you may not _need_ it. But it certainly can be convenient.

## _Business and Education Uses_

The microcomputer market has been considerably enriched by the continuing flood of new uses found in both business and education.

### _Microcomputers in Business_

In business, computers are no longer confined behind the castle walls of the data processing department's computer room. They appear on the desks and even in the briefcases of ordinary business people.

They speak not only BASIC and COBOL but even English. Indeed, microcomputers are forcing major changes in the dominance of traditional DP departments, which in some cases became unresponsive to the users they were supposed to serve. Business people have quickly discovered that microcomputer solutions are faster and cheaper to implement than mainframe solutions. Indeed, microcomputers are even cutting into the market for minicomputers.

Accounting, inventory, business planning, financial analysis, word processing—all the traditional business functions—can now be handled on microcomputers by small businesses and offices. There are 4 million small businesses in the United States—that is, businesses employing fewer than 200 people—and this is clearly a huge market for microcomputer hardware and software manufacturers. Many useful tools are available. Apple Computers, for instance, offers a package of business systems that is advertised as helping users control costs, identify slow payers, plan expenditures, reduce clerical time, reduce bookkeeping errors, and reduce paperwork. VisiCorp, a California software company, makes VisiCalc, an "electronic worksheet" that allows business people to ask "What if?" kinds of questions about budgets, investments, cost estimates, and the like; this program alone has been responsible for many executives seeing a need to bring microcomputers into their offices.

The presence of microcomputers in offices is not all wonderful, however. There are a number of drawbacks. First, the commercially available software is often not quite as "user friendly" or as suited to

---

## Home Computer Maintenance

Of all computer components, the terminal probably is least susceptible to failure, because it has no moving parts. Others—printers, disk drives and keyboards—are more problem-prone. These tips from Sorbus, a computer-repair company, may help:

### Printers

The printer should be vacuumed periodically and surface areas wiped clean with a light all-purpose cleaner. Do not lubricate the machine. Today's printers are designed to operate without external lubrication. Oil will only collect dust, practically guaranteeing a printer failure.

### Disk drives

To keep the read/write heads clean, use an approved head-cleaning kit about once a week or every 10 to 15 hours of use. To keep the disk head properly aligned with the disk, avoid sudden jolts of the drive. Dirt is the single most-common cause of error in disks. Store disks in their protective covers. Never touch their surfaces with your fingers.

### Keyboards

Soda, coffee, or other liquids can ruin a keyboard. Keep them away from your computer. If a spill does occur, immediately take the keyboard to a service center for a good cleaning.

### Environmental factors

Computers work best in cool temperatures—below 80 degrees Fahrenheit. Cigarette smoke doesn't bother home computers as much as it does commercial ones, but it's better to minimize smoke near the computer.

### Electrical power

Voltage variations can diminish your computer's operation. You may be able to get rid of them by switching to a power line not shared by other appliances or equipment—or use a power-surge protector.

### Static

Walking across a carpet on a cold day and touching a grounded metal surface can zap you and cause a computer error. Possible solutions: Antistatic mats and raising the humidity.

*—U.S. News & World Report,* May 9, 1983

## A VISIT WITH VISICALC

VisiCalc is an electronic "spread sheet" or financial analysis program. Spread sheets have been used in business for years, and consist essentially of columns and rows. The beauty of VisiCalc is that it allows you to make computations instantly instead of taking hours.

Suppose you are considering buying a new car. Across the top you could list different prices for different cars—say, a Pontiac Trans-Am, a Honda Accord, and a Ford van. Down the side you could list amount of down payment, bank loan interest rate, and number of months to pay. When you do your calculations across the page, you can tell what your monthly payments will be for each type of car.

Now suppose you want to change one of those elements of financing—down payment, interest rate, and number of months. In the old pencil-and-paper days you would have to start over with a fresh spread sheet. With an electronic spread sheet, however, you can change one figure, and all the other figures will change automatically and instantly.

Because such "What if . . .?" questions come up frequently in business, it is no wonder that VisiCalc has been credited with being such a powerful influence in moving microcomputers into the office.

user needs as people hope. Second, processing power and data storage capacity is, obviously, more limited than those for larger computer systems. Third, inevitably the user will want to replace his or her micro—and the old software may or may not run on the new one. Finally, unless there is some real planning within the organization, the presence of various individual microcomputers may ultimately work at cross purposes with the data processing needs of the company, for the data contained in the individual's storage may not be accessible to other microcomputers or to the DP department.

### Microcomputers in Education

Microcomputers are also attracting a great deal of attention in education, and many manufacturers consider computer-aided education a major market. Not only can such machines as Apples, Commodores, IBM Personal Computers, and TRS-80s eliminate tedious paperwork, they can also help create specialized and individualized tests and activities and inspire students to become involved in solving problems.

The most rewarding element of computers in the classroom is that students learn more through direct experience at the terminal. Passive listening in lecture environments can be supplemented with actual discovery learning experiences—one program, for instance, supposedly can speak any word you can type. The dream of computer-based laboratories for biology, physics, chemistry, and mathematics is becoming a reality.

Using computers as educational tools is not a new idea, but the availability of resources is fairly recent. Small computers are priced so reasonably that the cost per student-hour is negligible. The lack of educational software has been a problem in the past, but that gap is closing. Tutorial programs exist for languages, math, and the sciences. More specialized applications, such as chord and melodic recognition, are being produced all the time.

Teachers and school administrators stepping into the microcomputer market will find a host of vendors offering good products and services. At the college and university level, more and more institutions are even requiring that students own personal computers, among them Carnegie Mellon University, Clarkson College of Technology, Drexel University, and Stevens Institute of Technology. Ultimately, owning a computer will be as commonplace as owning a calculator.

## Micro Wars: Competition in the Small Computer Industry

Nothing we could possibly say here will remain true for long, since the one constant element in the microcomputer industry is continual change. But, having said that, let us proceed to try to describe the field anyway—at least as it exists as of this writing.

**The Macintosh.** Announced in January 1984 by Apple Computer, the Macintosh offers many of the features that Apple first put in Lisa: superb graphics, a mouse, and symbols such as trash cans that the user can manipulate on the screen. The 3½-inch floppy disk drive can store more than 400,000 characters of information.

**The IBM PC jr.** The popular IBM PC jr is based on the Intel 8088 16-bit processor, which means that some software is compatible with the original IBM PC. Expandable to 128K bytes of memory, the PC jr features connections for the IBM color monitor, an internal modem, a light pen, and two joy sticks. A cordless 62-key keyboard communicates with the computer by infrared waves from as far away as 20 feet.

## Hardware Manufacturers: A Tentative Who's Who

At present, the principal microcomputer manufacturers are American. For personal computers, firms such as IBM, Apple, Tandy-Radio Shack, Commodore, Atari, and Timex/Sinclair are probably strong. Other contenders are Hewlett-Packard, DEC, and Victor, but there are 150 to 200 manufacturers in all. Western Electric is also planning to market four microcomputers in 1984, which have to date been christened "Baby Bell."

Let us consider some of the important players.

**Apple** Apple was formed in 1977 by two college dropouts, Steven Jobs and Stephen Wozniak, working in Silicon Valley in California. They met at a club for amateur computer builders and realized their expertise was needed by others. The first Apple computers were built in that time-honored place of inventors, a garage, using the $1300 proceeds from the sale of an old Volkswagen. Designed principally for home use, Apple computers were among the first to replace complicated switches-and-lights front panels with easy-to-use typewriter keyboards. The company has been wildly successful, and when its stock was offered to the public in December 1980, it started a stampede among investors anxious to buy in. The popular Apple II, recently updated to the IIe, (see Figure 14-2) was followed by the Apple III, which was not nearly as successful. In mid-1983, Apple introduced Lisa (Figure 14-3), which uses a mouse to direct a pointer on the CRT screen; Apple says that a beginner can learn to use the computer in 20 minutes, as opposed to the usual 20 to 40 hours required of many microcomputers. The company is also offering a user-friendly computer known as Macintosh.

**IBM** "WELCOME IBM," the Apple ads said bravely when IBM introduced its personal computer in the summer of 1981. Apple hoped that IBM's shattering of its previous market boundaries would lend credibility to what until then had been considered only a market for hobbyists. Since then, the computer giant's IBM PC (Figure 14-4) has zoomed to the top in microcomputer sales. In 1983, it launched a sort of souped-up version of its PC called the IBM PC XT (Figure 14-5), which featured more power, more memory, and the availability of hard disk. In 1983, the computer industry was rife with rumors about a new IBM microcomputer. Dubbed the "Peanut" by the press, the offering was the popular PC jr, which uses the same microprocessor as the IBM PC.

**Tandy-Radio Shack** Headquartered in Fort Worth, Texas, Tandy Corp. is better known to the public as the parent company of the Radio Shack electronics stores, of which there are now some 8500 world-wide. This gives the company the widest outlet of any microcomputer manufacturer. Tandy exploited this advantage by offering

**Figure 14-2 The Apple IIe.** This model updated the bestselling Apple II (the *e* stands for "enhanced"). The standard memory is 64K, and the improved keyboard has user-programmable function keys and full cursor controls. However, it can still run software designed for the original Apple II.

**Figure 14-3 Apple's Lisa.** The mouse (*right, beside computer*) enables the user to manipulate elements on the screen without using the keyboard. *Above*, an example of a Lisa project in progress.

**Figure 14-4 The IBM Personal Computer.** Introduced in August 1981, the PC, as it is called, rose to first place in the personal computer market in just two years.

**Figure 14-5 The IBM PC XT.** A more powerful version of the Personal Computer, the computer includes a fixed disk drive with a storage capacity of more than 10 million characters—about the equivalent of 5000 double-spaced typewritten pages.

**Figure 14-6  The TRS-80 Model 16.** This computer comes with 128K bytes of RAM, which can be expanded up to 512K.

**Figure 14-7  The TRS-80 Portable Computer Model 100.** Billed as "a workstation that goes along," this "notebook-size" portable computer weighs less than 4 pounds but has an eight-line, 40-character display and 8K or 24K of RAM, expandable to 32K.

**Figure 14-8  The Commodore PET** This microcomputer has 16K to 32K of memory.

**Figure 14-9  The Commodore VIC-20.**

**Figure 14-10  The Commodore 64.** This model is an attempt to bridge the gap between low-cost home computers and low-end small business computers.

the TRS-80, which was first introduced in 1977. Its products range from the high-performance TRS-80 Model 16 computer (Figure 14-6) to the portable Model 100 (Figure 14-7).

**Commodore** Based in Norristown, Pennsylvania, Commodore Business Machines entered the personal computer market with the PET (abbreviation for Personal Electronic Transactor—see Figure 14-8). Commodore has been quite successful in Europe and is now marketing aggressively in the United States; indeed, one of the best-selling home computers world-wide is Commodore's VIC-20 (Figure 14-9). The Commodore 64 (Figure 14-10) is an attempt to bridge the gap between low-cost home computers and low-end small business computers.

**Other Manufacturers** Although the above constitute the top four manufacturers as of this writing, the market is extremely fluid, and a host of other challengers have appeared and will continue to appear. Among those with some present standing are Altos, Atari, Corvus, Cromemco, Digital Equipment, Eagle, Epson, Fortune, Franklin, Hewlett-Packard, KayPro, Nippon Electric (NEC), NorthStar, Panasonic, Timex/Sinclair, Toshiba, Vector, Victor, Zerox, and Zenith-Heath.

A Boston-based research firm, The Yankee Group, has made a distinction between personal computers and desktop computers. *Personal computers*, it states, sell for under $1000 excluding printers, are consumer-oriented, and generally useful for entertainment, education, or personal business. *Desktop computers* cost between $1000 and $10,500 (excluding printers) and are intended mainly for business uses; they can run off-the-shelf software designed primarily for business applications.

Among the personal computers, according to this distinction, are several models of Atari, Commodore, Tandy-Radio Shack, and Timex/Sinclair. These are computers that are sold in places other than the usual computer retail outlets: department stores, discount stores, even toy stores. Some machines particularly worth mentioning are the following:

- *Timex/Sinclair* entered the marketplace in 1982 with the same energy with which it had made Timex watches cheap and easily available timepieces. The Sinclair ZX81 (Figure 14-11) initially sold through the mail at $149.95, but is presently available for under $30. For this price, you get a computer with built-in keyboard, a manual, and everything you need to connect the machine to your TV.

- *Atari*, long involved with video games, offers two home computers, the Atari 400 and 800 (Figure 14-12). A great deal of software is available, especially games, such as Pac-Man, Asteroids, and Space Invaders.

**Figure 14-11 The Timex/Sinclair ZX81.** The owner needs a TV set and a cassette recorder in addition to this keyboard for the system to work.

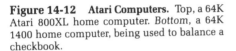

**Figure 14-12 Atari Computers.** Top, a 64K Atari 800XL home computer. *Bottom,* a 64K 1400 home computer, being used to balance a checkbook.

**Figure 14-13 The Texas Instruments TI-99/4A personal computer.** This computer became a real bargain when Texas Instruments pulled out of the computer market in 1983.

**Figure 14-14 The Osborne I.** Adam Osborne at the keyboard of his portable computer. Although Osborne pioneered the portable computer, Osborne Computer Corporation filed Chapter 11 proceedings in 1983.

- *Texas Instruments (TI)*, whose commercials long featured comedian Bill Cosby, had huge success with its TI-99/4A personal computer (16K RAM, 26K ROM) (Figure 14-13). However, the company withdrew from the home computer market in late 1983.

An interesting class of microcomputers is that known as **portable computers,** machines that can be carried like an attaché case. The pioneer in this class was the Osborne I (Figure 14-14). If there is no electrical outlet available, the portable computer can be operated with portable battery packs. Lawyers, for instance, can use portable computers in courtrooms. Many of the portables tout themselves as being able to use IBM Personal Computer software, which opens up the range of programs available because of the popularity of the IBM PC; however, most involve some extra manipulations to accomplish this.

A subset of portable computers are what are called **notebook computers** or, sometimes, **lap computers.** These are exemplified by the Tandy-Radio Shack's Model 100, which has an 8-line display built into a case the size of a 2-inch-thick notebook. The book-size Epson HX-20 contains a 4-pound package with a full-size keyboard, a screen that shows four lines of text, a microcassette tape drive, and a cash register-type printer. In addition, there are also **hand-held computers,** such as the TRS-80 PC-2 (Figure 14-15).

It is clear that the Japanese have entered the microcomputer market just as they have the calculator, television set, and other electronics applications markets. Many have recognizable brand names: Canon, Casio, Hitachi, Seiko, Sharp, Toshiba. No doubt the hardware is as good as American hardware; however, U.S. manufacturers have usually been considered superior in two areas that are considered crucial to success: (1) distribution of the machines, and (2) the software that

**SOME MAKERS OF USER-ORIENTED SOFTWARE**

- Graham-Dorian Software Systems, Wichita, Kansas

- MicroPro International Corporation, San Rafael, California

- MicroSoft, Bellevue, Washington

- MicroSource, Inc., Tempe, Arizona

- Peach Tree Software, Atlanta, Georgia

- Structured Systems Group, Oakland, California

- VisiCorp, San Jose, California

**Figure 14-15   The pocket computer.** Tandy's TRS-80 Pocket Computer PC-2 weighs 14 ounces and is just under 8 inches long, with a 2640-byte memory. It can be programmed in BASIC and displays one line at a time. Peripheral equipment, including cassette interface and printer, is available.

goes with them. Although the Japanese are designing machines to fit American-made software, the U.S. market is very strong. In Japan, on the other hand, things are changing: whereas in 1979 the market there was controlled entirely by Tandy, Apple, and Commodore, today American manufacturers control only 20 percent.

### Market Outlets: The Neighborhood Store

Mainframe and minicomputers are generally marketed by the manufacturer's sales force or by authorized dealers and distributors, but that is not quite the pattern with personal computers. For these machines, people are likely to visit a computer store.

Perhaps the world's first computer store was The Computer Store, which began in 1975 in Los Angeles (Figure 14-16). Today the number of retail outlets selling computers is in the thousands, and ComputerLand alone has 400 stores. Some outlets are office equipment stores, selling not only computers and software but also typewriters, copiers, and communications equipment. Some stores also sell video games and other electronics. Some are software-only stores (often placed strategically near a personal computer outlet, such as a Radio Shack store).

Whether the outlet is a small independent like The Computer Store or part of a large operation such as Sears, Macy's, or Radio Shack, it offers you the chance to examine different equipment before you buy. Such stores also help to keep costs down because they save manufacturers the cost of having to maintain a large sales force.

**Figure 14-16    The Computer Store.** Dick Heiser opened his small storefront operation in Los Angeles in 1975. This was probably the world's first computer store. Stores like this one allow consumers to try equipment before they buy.

### Software

A computer without software, it has been said, is like a stereo without records or a car without gas. Indeed, studies show that in an 18-month period the purchaser of a microcomputer is likely to spend as much on software (each item of which retails for between $30 and $600 apiece) as on the machine itself. There are hundreds of makers of software plying their trade for the microcomputer, and as many as 150 new programs hit the market every month. Several language translators are available. The most popular language is BASIC, but many vendors offer FORTRAN, Pascal, and other languages for microcomputers.

Nearly every expert on microcomputers urges that you consider what kind of software you want before you buy hardware, since some kinds of packaged software may not be available for the computer you are considering, or may be available but not as efficient. The truth of the matter is that many people probably are swayed by the hardware first— after all, it is the hardware rather than the software that is being pushed the hardest in TV commercials and newspaper ads— but the software-first advice is still soundest.

The variety of software available is awesome. Naturally, there are many programs for business or home finance purposes: accounting,

## 1-2-3 TO GET READY

The program clearly leading the way to the next generation of integrated software products is called *1-2-3*, produced by the Lotus Development Corporation. Its name represents its three functions: spreadsheet, data base, and graphics.

The challenge in selecting software has often been in choosing compatible applications. Can the data input through a spreadsheet be retrieved through a data base? Can data stored in a data base be retrieved and graphed into a meaningful bar chart? With this one comprehensive software package, the answer is a resounding *yes*. As a result, analysis that might have taken several hours with separate applications can now be accomplished in a few minutes with 1-2-3.

bookkeeping, inventory, payroll, income and expense logs, sales analysis and trend forecasting, and investment analysis alternatives.

Software packages are also available for many specialized business or professional purposes: real estate, medical-financial, even restaurant management. For personal use, there are, of course, programs for arcadelike computer games, such as Space Invaders. Indeed, the *leading* use of home computers is still video games. There are also education programs such as Colormath (a color/sound quiz in basic arithmetic), Spelling Rules, and The Scientific Method. A host of other programs are available for such purposes as trip planning, appointment scheduling, making personal name and phone directories, and storing and indexing recipes. The list is nearly endless. Most such software is available "off the rack" at computer stores or through mail order houses; half of all personal computer software is sold by mail order shopping through microcomputer magazine ads. Keep in mind, of course, that software is usually not interchangeable among computers; even "off the rack," many programs can be used only by a specific microcomputer.

## Computer Passions: Kits, Clubs, Fairs, Camps, Etc.

The first computer hobbyist kit came out in 1975; the MITS Altair 8800 was built around the Intel 8080 chip. A kit consists of all parts needed to construct a computer; complete, clear, step-by-step instructions are included. The kit was produced as a last-ditch effort to save the company, but it proved highly successful and has been widely imitated since. Now the best known kits are made by Heath.

The attractive feature of kits—their low cost—has now become a feature of many factory-built microcomputers, and the result has been a surge in the number of users. Indeed, microcomputer users make up their own "microcommunity" of the computer industry, and in recent years a host of groups of computer enthusiasts has sprung up. The Amateur Computer Group of New Jersey, the Chicago Area Computer Hobbyist's Exchange, and the Delaware Valley Computer Society are all examples of computer clubs organized for microcomputer hobbyists. Some clubs are organized around particular brands of computers, such as the Orange County (California) TRS-80 Users Group, the Heath Users Group, the CP/M Users Group, and such Apple clubs as Apple Core, Apple Pie, and Apple-Holics. A national association called the Personal Computing Society has been formed.

Various manufacturers publish newsletters for users of their equipment, and there are also independently published periodicals, including some catering to a particular professional orientation, such as *The Physicians Microcomputer Report* and *The Computing Teacher*. In addition, many books are published on computing and programming. Finally, for children who are computer fans there are computer summer camps, in which an outdoor program is mixed with instruction in learning how to use microcomputers.

Computer shows and fairs have become extremely popular. In California, for example, there is an annual Computer Swap Meet and also the San Francisco-area West Coast Computer Faire. Conventions such as the National Computer Conference feature exhibits and discussions not only on mainframes and minicomputers, but on micros as well.

## SECONDHAND SILICON

If you want a personal computer and are willing to settle for less than the latest technology, you can save hundreds of dollars in the fast- growing secondhand market. It's best to buy locally so that you can try out a machine before paying for it. Most used computers are mechanically sound, since there are few movable parts that can easily break. But check on some common trouble spots: keyboards, power switches and disk drives, all simple to test. . . .

If you're a neophyte user, you'll probably need assistance in learning how to operate your computer. So you should buy it from a dealer. Some retailers sell trade-ins from customers stepping up to newer equipment. Typically, retailers offer service contracts and one- to three-month guarantees, as well as help in getting acquainted with a machine.

—*Money,*
June 1983

## Yet to Come:
# The Age of the "Easy Computer"?

There are many people who think the wave of the future is embodied in Apple's Lisa computer, which, when it was unveiled in 1983, featured a 16-bit microprocessor, 5 megabytes of hard disk storage, and a one-button mouse that allows users to manipulate the cursor easily without typing on the keyboard. The significance of Lisa is the way it allows the user to interact with the software—to manipulate data, text, and graphics in a simple way with only 20 minutes of hands-on training. Thus, word processing, bar graphs and other charts, electronic spread sheets, scheduling, modeling, and other software can be mingled together.

A rival to Lisa is the software known as VisiOn, which allows IBM, DEC, Wang, and other computer users to imitate many of Lisa's features but at less cost. Indeed, one of the most important features of the micros of the future, say some industry observers, is that easier software merged with easier hardware may well produce the age of the "easy computer." Hardware will increase in power, and we can expect to see more 16-bit and 32-bit machines (the Hewlett-Packard HP-9000, for instance, is a 32-bit micro that is equivalent in power to the VAX-11 superminicomputer!). Software will become truly user-friendly (perhaps, we should say, even user-endearing), with well-thought-out self-tutoring messages on the screen, including such features as a HELP button you can push that will produce messages that will tell you how to use any aspect of the system. Software will also probably become more compatible among various computers as operating systems become standardized. Everything will become extended: high-resolution graphics will become standard on most micros, there will be more memory and hard disk will be common, input/output capabilities will be more sophisticated and will include voice, and most personal computers will be capable of forming networks both with larger machines and with other microcomputers.

Back in Chapter 1 we used the word "computerphobia" to describe the widespread fear that people have about computers. As the "easy computer" comes into being, however, we may expect to see people taking computers for granted just as they now do cars, telephones, and TV sets.

## Summary and Key Terms

- **Personal computers,** the name given to microcomputers used by individuals for various personal uses, are the fastest-growing sector of the computer industry.

- A **microprocessor** is a central processing unit manufactured on a silicon chip. A microcomputer has a microprocessor in it. Microprocessors began as 4 bits and 8 bits, and now 16-bit and 32-bit microprocessors are available. Microprocessors are used in digital watches, microwave ovens, and other items.

- Microcomputers have two kinds of main storage—**RAM,** for **random-access memory** (the computer's "scratch pad" that keeps intermediate calculations), and **ROM,** for **read-only memory,** whose contents are programmed into the hardware by the microcomputer manufacturer.

- Besides a terminal or a keyboard and a video screen (for which a TV set may be used sometimes), a microcomputer needs a disk drive or cassette recorder. It also may benefit by having a printer; these range from small heat-sensitive printers to dot-matrix to letter-quality. Micro computer software is often considered **"user-friendly";** that is, it is nontechnical and nearly anyone can use it.

- Home computers may be used for entertainment and games; for personal finances; for keeping records, schedules, and plans such as menus; for word processing; for home environment controls; for education; and for information networks.

- Microcomputers can also be used for traditional business functions— accounting, inventory, business planning, financial analysis, and word processing. "Electronic worksheets," which allow business people to ask "What if?" questions about budgets and the like, have resulted in more microcomputers being brought into offices.

- Microcomputers in offices can have three drawbacks, however: (1) Commercially available software may not be as user friendly as people hope. (2) Processing power and data storage is limited compared to that of larger systems. (3) Data contained in individual microcomputers may not be accessible to other people in the organization.

- Microcomputers are used in education to cut teacher paperwork, create specialized tests and activities, and directly involve students in learning material such as tutorial programs for languages and mathematics.

- Although the microcomputer market is in continual flux, the present major manufacturers are Tandy Corporation, which is parent company to 8000 Radio Shack electronics stores and which offers the TRS-80; IBM, which offers the IBM PC and IBM PC XT; Apple Computer, which presently manufactures the Apple IIe, Apple III, and Lisa; and Commodore Business Machines, which makes the PET and VIC-20. Other manufacturers are Altos, Atari, Corvus, Cromemco, Digital Equipment, Eagle, Epson, Fortune, Franklin, Hewlett-Packard, KayPro, Nippon Electronic, NorthStar, Panasonic, Timex/Sinclair, Toshiba, Vector, Victor, Xerox, and Zenith-Heath.

- A distinction has been made between _personal computers_, which sell for under $1000 (excluding printers), are consumer-oriented, and useful for entertainment, education, and personal business, and _desktop computers_, which cost between $1000 and $10,500 and are mainly intended for business uses. Among the personal computers are several models of Atari, Commodore, Tandy-Radio Shack, and Timex/Sinclair.

- A class of microcomputers is known as **portable computers,** machines that can be carried like an attaché case. A subset of portable computers are called **notebook computers** or sometimes **lap computers.** There are also **hand-held computers.**

- Many Japanese firms have entered the American computer market: Canon, Casio, Hitachi, Seiko, Sharp, Toshiba.

- Microcomputers are generally marketed through computer retail stores. The first such outlet was The Computer Store, which began in 1975 in Los Angeles.

- There are hundreds of makers of microcomputer software. The most popular language is BASIC, but many vendors offer FORTRAN and Pascal for microcomputers. Many software packages are available for a variety of business and home-finance purposes. Software packages are also available for specialized professional purposes.

- The first computer hobbyist kit came out in 1975, the MITS Altair 8800, built around the Intel 8080 chip. Now the best known kits are made by Heath.

- Many activities have now formed around microcomputers, such as hobbyist groups, special-interest newsletters, books, swap meets, fairs, and even computer summer camps for kids.

- There is speculation that we are rapidly arriving at the time of the "easy computer," as inspired by Apple's Lisa, in which the user will be able to interact with the software, manipulating data, text, and graphics in a simple way with little training. Software is also expected to become much more user-friendly, with well-thought-out tutoring messages on the screen and HELP buttons that will tell you how to use any aspect of the system. Software will also probably become more compatible among various computers as operating systems become standardized.

## Review

1. Distinguish between "microprocessor" and "microcomputer."

2. What do we mean when we say microcomputer software is "user friendly"?

3. Name various personal, business, and educational uses for microcomputers.

4. Who are the present principal microcomputer manufacturers? How do you think the picture might change in the near future?

5. Describe various kinds of microcomputer software. Is there any that would be of personal or professional interest to you?

6. What kinds of activities surrounding microcomputers are of interest to you?

## Selected References for Further Reading

Arca, Julie Anne. *Practical WordStar Uses.* Berkeley, Calif.: Sybex, 1983.

Herbert, Frank, with Max Barnard. *Without Me You're Nothing: The Essential Guide to Home Computers.* New York: Simon & Schuster, 1981.

Milles, Jack N. *Exploring the World of the Personal Computer.* Englewood Cliffs, N.J.: Prentice-Hall, 1982.

Osborne, Adam. *Introduction to Microcomputers.* New York: McGraw-Hill, 1980.

Prost, Stanley R. *Doing Business with VisiCalc.* Berkeley, Calif.: Sybex, 1983.

**IN THIS CHAPTER**

Systems of communicating data over telephone lines or through other channels may be centralized or decentralized or a mixture of both. This chapter describes how data is transmitted and examines the various kinds of communication networks and their uses.

# ch15

# data communications systems

## the wired world

Think of it: There are 500 million telephones installed throughout the world and, theoretically, you can call any one of them. Further, every one of these phones is a potential terminal in the home or business for data processing and telecommunications use. This combination of telecommunications (communications via telephone or television) and information processing promises revolutionary changes, particularly in office work.

# The Evolution of Data Communications

*ch15*

Mail, telephone, TV and radio, books, and periodicals—these are the principal ways we send and receive information. They have not changed appreciably in a generation. However, **data communications systems**—computer systems that transmit data over communication lines such as telephone lines or coaxial cables—have been gradually evolving through the past two decades. Let us take a look at how they came about.

In the early days, computers were often found in several departments of large companies. Any department within an organization that could justify the expenditure acquired its own computer. There could be, for example, different computers to support engineering, accounting, and manufacturing. However, because department managers generally did not know enough about computers to use them efficiently, these expenditures were often wasteful. The response to this problem was to centralize computer operations.

Centralization produced better control, and the consolidation of equipment led to economies of scale; that is, hardware and supplies could be purchased in bulk at cheaper cost. **Centralized data processing** placed everything in one central company location: all processing, hardware, software, and storage. Computer manufacturers responded to this trend by building large, general-purpose computers so that all departments within an organization could be serviced efficiently. IBM's contribution was the IBM/360 computer, so called because it provided the full spectrum—"360 degrees"—of services.

Eventually, however, total centralization proved inconvenient. All input data had to be physically transported to the computer and all processed material picked up and delivered to the users. Insisting on centralized data processing was like insisting that all conversations between people be face to face. Clearly, the next logical step was to connect users via telephone lines and terminals to the central computer. Thus, in the 1960s, the centralized system was made more flexible by the introduction of time-sharing through **teleprocessing systems**—terminals connected to the central computer via communication lines. This permitted users to have remote access to the central computer from other buildings and even other cities. However, even though access to the computer system was decentralized, all processing was still centralized, that is, performed by one central computer.

In the 1970s, minicomputers began to be used, often in locations away from the central computer. These were clearly decentralized systems, in that the smaller computers could do some processing on their own, yet they also had access to the central computer. This new setup was labeled **distributed data processing (DDP).** It is similar to teleprocessing, except that it has not only remote access, but also remote processing. Processing is no longer done exclusively by the central computer. Rather, the processing and files are dispersed among several remote locations and can be handled by smaller computers—mini- or microcomputers—or hooked up to the central **host computer.** Obviously, DDP communication systems are more complex and expensive than exclusively centralized computer systems, but they provide many more benefits to users.

The whole picture of distributed data processing is expected to change dramatically with the advent of networks of personal computers. By **network,** we mean a computer system that uses data communications equipment to connect two or more computers and their resources.

Of particular interest in today's business world are **Local Area Networks (LANs),** which are designed to share data and resources among several individual small computers, or workstations. The relatively high cost of quality disks and printers makes sharing these resources attractive.

At present, about 5 percent of the personal computers in the United States are hooked into some network, but by 1986 that number is expected to increase to 20 percent. From a people standpoint, this will have some encouraging effects: No longer will the mainframe computer room seem to be the center of the system and the individual appear at its door as a supplicant. Rather, the individual, the person, will be at the center of the system, powerfully drawing forth on the resources of various networks.

In the next two sections we will first examine the teleprocessing systems, which will give you an overview of how data communications equipment interfaces with computer equipment, and then examine distributed systems in detail.

## Teleprocessing Systems

Since the mid-1960s, the trend has been to give users access to computers in the users' locations. One application of teleprocessing, of course, is to a business or organization with many locations, branch offices, or retail outlets. It is best to input data at the source rather than mail the data to the central computer. Source input improves customer service and provides quicker cash flow for the company. (A disadvantage, however, is that if the communications lines are out of business, then so are you. Not only can telephone lines become over-

**TELECOMMUNICATIONS: GLOBAL BRAIN?**

The immense economic power of the telecommunications industry constitutes the "base camp" from which computer power will assault the old structures. One example: in the single area of "computer conferencing" (the use of computers to link people together), some scientists have already envisioned the rapid obsolescence of many education techniques, the electronic replacement of 80 percent of business mail, and a significant alteration of transportation and settlement patterns. When these effects were first suggested in a *Futurist* article in 1974, there were only about a hundred persons in the world engaging in such "computer conferencing." By the end of the decade they numbered in the thousands, and Dr. Michael Arbib suggested that the building of a "Global Brain for Mankind" was an urgent necessity. Can we build such a brain? Is it desirable to build it?

—Jacques Vallee,
*The Network Revolution: Confessions of a Computer Scientist*

311 CHAPTER 15: Data Communications Systems

burdened with heavy traffic, but the central computer can also be temporarily out of operation.)

How is teleprocessing used? In a *real-time* environment, it may be used in these ways:

- **To make queries.** For instance, a terminal in a catalog store in a rural town can be connected to a central computer in the city where the warehouse inventory file is located. The clerk in the catalog store can send a simple query—ARE CLOD-KICKER BOOTS IN STOCK—and the answer comes back from the central computer.

- **To process transactions.** You can telephone a certain number, for example, and ask to have money transferred from your savings to your checking account. The person answering your call is sitting at a terminal and has access to files at the central computer.

- **To write programs.** You are able to write programs from a remote-access terminal, using the complete facilities of the central computer, and get results while you wait.

Teleprocessing can also be used in a *batch* environment:

- **To collect data.** Data that does not have to be acted on immediately—payroll data, for instance—can be collected at local sites and then transmitted to the central computer to be processed. The processed information is then sent back and printed out on the local printer.

- **To run programs.** As with real-time processing, programming can be done with a central computer from a remote location; only in this case, processing is done on a batch basis.

### The Teleprocessing System Configuration

To see how data is transmitted from remote location to central computer and back, let us look at Figure 15-1. This gives an overview of a teleprocessing system. The components of the system may be described as follows:

1. **The terminal.** The terminal produces **digital signals,** which are simply the presence or absence of an electronic pulse. This "on" or "off" represents the binary numbers 1 and 0 used in computing. Some lines accept digital transmission directly. However, most telephone lines through which these digital signals are sent were originally built for voice transmission, which requires an **analog signal**—an electronic signal that will represent a range of frequencies. A digital signal therefore must be converted to analog.

2. **Modem.** A **modem** is a device that converts a digital signal to an analog signal or vice versa. The process of converting from digital to analog is called **modulation,** and that from analog to digital,

---

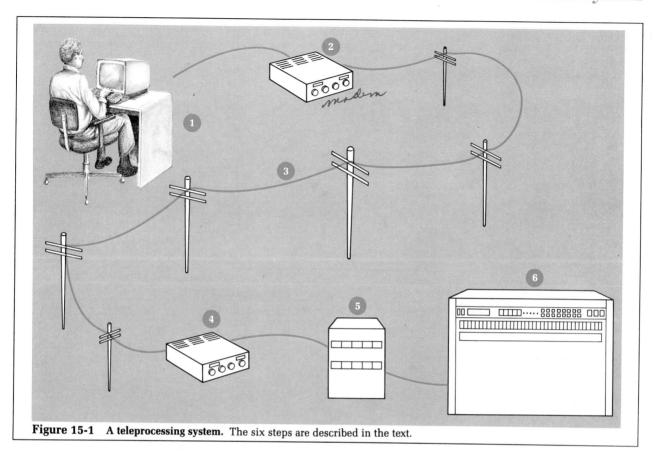

**Figure 15-1** **A teleprocessing system.** The six steps are described in the text.

**demodulation;** hence, *modem* is short for "modulate/demodulate." A particular kind of modem is the **acoustic coupler,** which allows a standard telephone receiver to be coupled to a portable computer terminal (see Figure 15-2). Some terminals have built-in acoustic couplers (see Figure 15-3).

③ **The communication channel.** No longer are computers islands unto themselves. There are various ways of connecting them over long distances. Although the cost for linking widely scattered machines can be substantial (as much as one third of the data processing budget), there are many data communications options. Telephone lines are the most convenient communication channel because the system is already in place, but **coaxial cables**—underground or undersea high-quality communication lines—are also used because they can transmit data at a much higher rate. Also popular are microwave transmission and satellite transmission. **Microwave transmission** (see Figure 15-4) uses what is called line-of-sight transmission of data signals through the atmosphere. Since these signals cannot bend around the curvature of the earth, relay stations—usually antennas in high places such as the tops of mountains and buildings—are positioned at various points to continue the transmission. (Unfortunately, there are some real problems with traffic jams in microwave transmission. In major metropolitan areas, for instance, there are horrendous difficulties

**Figure 15-2  A modem.** The modem accepts a standard telephone receiver and converts the analog signal of the telephone to the digital signal of the computer, and vice versa.

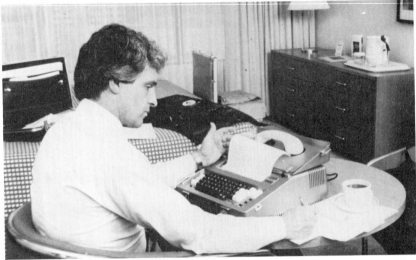

**Figure 15-3  Terminals with built-in acoustic couplers.** *Left,* the Portable Bubble Memory Data Terminal, designed by Texas Instruments, is used by the National Boy Scouts of America to transmit accounting information from the national headquarters to 35 councils across the country. *Right,* Maxine Mesinger writes her daily *Houston Chronicle* column from home on the same type of terminal.

because of electronic interference from tall buildings.) **Satellite transmission** (see Figure 15-5) uses communication satellites in space—22,000 miles above the earth—as relay stations, to amplify an electronic signal and transmit it to another station. Gaining in usage also is **fiber optics** (see Figure 15-6), which uses tubes of glass half the diameter of a human hair and connected in cables, to make a light path. Fiber optics can transmit data faster than other technology, yet the materials are lighter and less expensive than wire cables.

❹ **The second modem.** Another modem is needed at the end of the communication line to demodulate the analog signal to a digital signal again.

**Figure 15-4  Microwave transmission.** Dish-shaped antennas such as these are often located atop buildings and mountains to relay microwave signals.

**Figure 15-5  Satellite transmission.** This satellite acts as a relay station and can transmit data signals from one station to another.

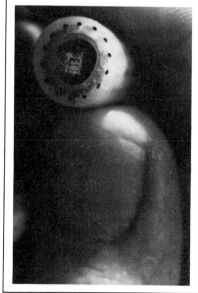

**Figure 15-6  Fiber optics.** *Near left,* hairlike glass fibers carry voice, television, and data signals, using a new technology called lightwave communication. *Far left,* fibers are held in precise alignment by honeycombs of crystal within the cable.

⑤ **The front-end processor.** From the modem, the digital signal may go through a communications processor called a **front-end processor,** which is actually a computer itself. Its purpose is to relieve the central computer of some of the communications tasks and so free it for processing applications programs.

⑥ **The computer.** The host computer at the hub of the teleprocessing configuration can vary in terms of size and capabilities, but mainframes are used in larger systems.

### Line Configurations

There are two principal line configurations or ways of connecting terminals with the computer: point-to-point and multidrop.

The **point-to-point line** is simply a direct connection between each terminal and the computer. The **multidrop line** (or multipoint line) has several terminals connected on the same line to the computer, as Figure 15-7 shows. While in many cases a point-to-point line is sufficient, in other cases it is not efficient or convenient. For instance, if the computer is at the head office in Dallas but there are several branch offices with terminals in Houston, it would not make sense to connect each terminal individually to the computer in Dallas; it is better to run one line between the two cities and hook all the terminals on it in a multidrop arrangement. On a multidrop line, only one terminal can transmit at any one time, although more than one terminal can receive messages from the computer simultaneously.

### Line Control

Several terminals sharing one line obviously cannot all use the line simultaneously. They have to take turns. Two common methods of line control are polling and contention.

**Polling** means that the computer asks each terminal on the multidrop line if it has a message to send and then allows each in turn to transmit data. This method works well unless no terminal is ready to send a message, in which case the computer's resources have been used unnecessarily.

**Contention** operates from the terminal end. A terminal that is ready to send a message "listens" in to the line to see if any other terminal is in the process of transmitting. If the line is in use, the terminal waits a given period of time, then tries again; it continues this process until it finally gets on the line. The difficulty with this technique is that, like a long-winded caller telephoning on an old-fashioned party line, one terminal can tie up the multidrop line so that other terminals cannot get their messages through. Thus, polling is probably a better method because a higher authority, in the form of the central computer, is in charge.

Interactions among components of a computer system must be done in an orderly manner. Line **protocol** is a set of rules for the exchange of information between a terminal and a computer or between two

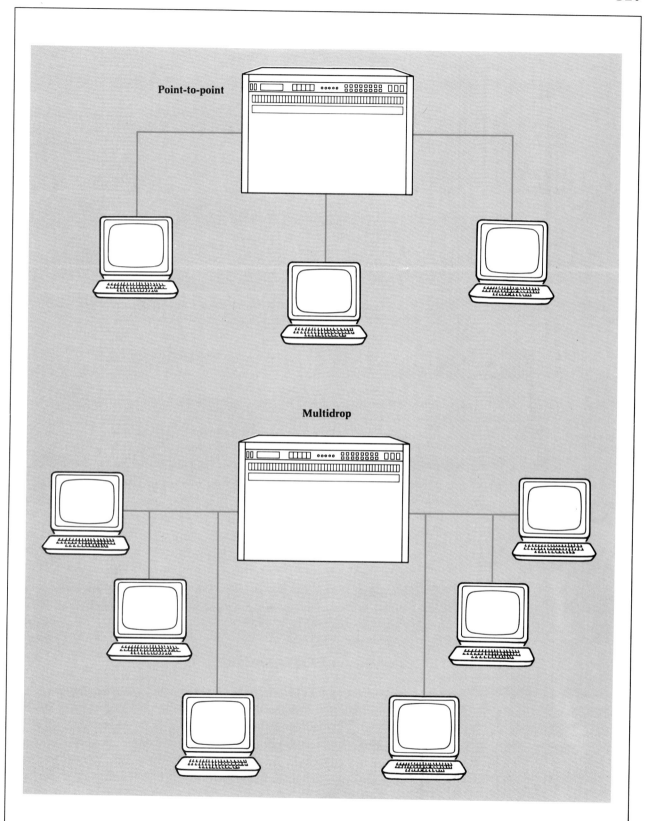

**Figure 15-7  Point-to-point and multidrop lines.** In point-to-point lines, each terminal is connected directly to the central computer. In multidrop lines, several terminals share a single line, although only one terminal can transmit at a time.

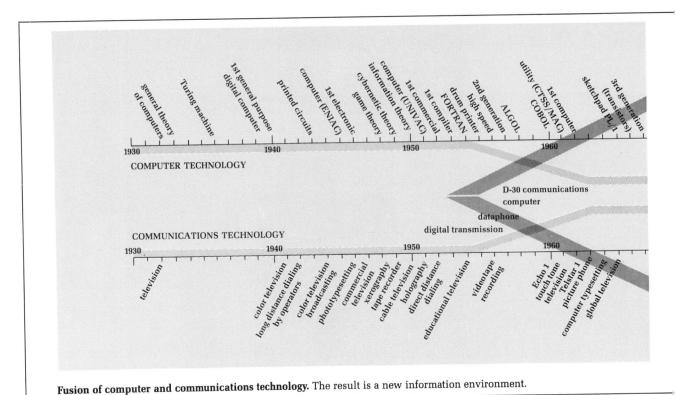

**Fusion of computer and communications technology.** The result is a new information environment.

computers. The exchange of prearranged signals is sometimes called **handshaking,** because of its introductory setup function. Protocols specify how a message is to be packaged: the sending address, the receiving address, error checks, and so forth. The prearranged signals are composed of certain combinations of bits or characters that have specific meaning. For example, "ACK" may mean that the receipt of a prior message is acknowledged. Many different sets of prearranged signals are used; these protocols are determined by the computer manufacturers, by the telephone company, and by others related to the devices that are part of the communications system. All components within the same system must use the same protocol to communicate successfully with one another.

## Carriers and Regulation

A company wishing to transmit messages may consider various sources of communications facilities. Most of the communications facilities used for data transmission were originally intended for voice transmission, such as telephone. In the United States, communications are regulated by an agency of the federal government, the *Federal Communications Commission (FCC),* and by state regulatory agencies. Any organization wishing to offer communications services must submit a tariff to the FCC. A **tariff** is a list of services and the rates to be charged for those services. The FCC, based on its commissioners' view of the public good, may or may not choose to grant a license to the organization.

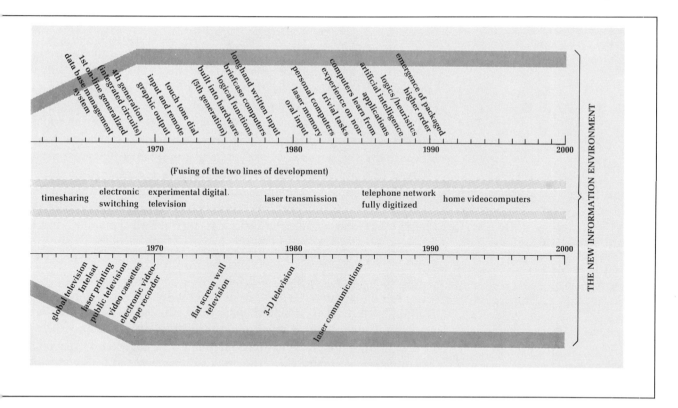

1st on-line generalized data base management system

4th generation (integrated circuits)

graphic output

input and remote touch tone dial

built into hardware (5th generation)

logical functions

briefcase computers

longhand written input

oral input

laser memory

personal computers

experience on non-trivial tasks

computers learn from

applications

artificial intelligence

logics/heuristics higher order

emergence of packaged

1970    1980    1990    2000

(Fusing of the two lines of development)

| timesharing | electronic switching | experimental digital television | | laser transmission | telephone network fully digitized | home videocomputers |

1970    1980    1990    2000

global television

Intelsat

laser printing

public television

video cassettes

electronic video-tape recorder

flat screen wall television

3-D television

laser communications

THE NEW INFORMATION ENVIRONMENT

An organization that has been approved to offer communications services to the public is called a **common carrier.** The two largest common carriers are American Telephone and Telegraph (AT&T) and Western Union.

 Common carriers offer two types of lines: switched and private. **Switched** lines, like those used with your phone service, connect through switching centers to a variety of destinations. You as the user pay only for the services used, but, as with ordinary phone use, you may find the line busy or the connection poor. **Private** (or **leased**) lines are offered for communication to fixed destinations. The advantage of this service is that the line is always available. Private lines may be "conditioned" (improved) by the carrier to reduce noise, and can use very high transmission rates.

### *Ma Bell Changes Everything*

In 1968, the FCC handed down the landmark *Carterfone decision,* the first in a series of decisions that have permitted competitors—many from the data processing industry—to enter the formerly regulated domain of AT&T. The gist of the decisions is that other companies can interface independent equipment with the public telephone network. These decisions spurred all kinds of independent activity in the communications industry. In 1972, communications companies were even permitted to launch their own satellites.

An outgrowth of this trend is the **value-added network (VAN).** In this type of system, a value-added carrier leases communication lines

## SOME LONG-DISTANCE COMMON CARRIERS WITH DATA TRANSMISSION SERVICES

- AT&T. Obviously the dominant common carrier in the U.S., if not the world, AT&T considers its Dataphone Digital Service to be its "premium" long-haul data service. . . .

- United States Transmission Systems (USTS). USTS is a subsidiary of ITT and a good example of a smaller size common carrier. . . .

- Tymnet, Inc. The Tymnet value-added . . . network is well-known for its ability to translate protocols and facilitate remote computing. . . .

- GTE Telenet Communications Corp. Telenet is another value-added . . . network with features closely paralleling Tymnet. . . .

- RCA Corp. The RCA Cylix Communications network differs from Tymnet and Telenet by its exclusive use of satellite technology. . . .

- CompuServe. Perhaps best known for its time-sharing services, CompuServe also offers its Network Services. . . .

- Western Union Telegraph Co. Among its many offerings, Western Union provides private-line service to 47 "on net" cities. . . .

- American Satellite Co. The Specialized Network Services Division stresses its pricing advantages over other common carriers for long- haul data transmission. . . .

- Satellite Business Systems. Through its private network services, SBS offers large-scale dedicated networks for very large (approximately 25) users. . . .

- American Bell, Inc. Net 1000 is billed as an intelligent . . . network that will allow on-line processing and protocol conversion. . . .

—*Computerworld*,
March 21, 1983

from a common carrier. These lines are then enhanced by adding improvements such as error detection and faster response time.

For many years, AT&T and the United States Government locked horns in an antitrust suit. Finally, in January 1982 the government agreed to drop its charges if the corporation would divest itself of the 22 local operating companies then making up the Bell System. AT&T got to keep Bell Laboratories, its research arm; Western Electric, which makes equipment; and the long-distance telephone service. Most important, it was allowed to enter areas from which it was formerly barred by federal regulations—namely, data processing, computer communications, and the manufacture of computer equipment. The result is that Ma Bell emerges as a much leaner company, free of its local telephone companies (which in turn raised their rates, since they were no longer subsidized by lucrative long-distance rates), and in a position to go head to head with such computer giants as IBM and DEC.

AT&T has long sold such computer products as the Teletype terminal, but almost all such products were designed to help computers communicate with each other rather than to do actual data processing work. The company has announced that it does not intend to become a computer company. Still, the 1982 arrangement with the government allows it to do so. And, as we have seen in Chapter 14, it has made some moves into the microcomputer market.

# Distributed Data Processing Systems

The teleprocessing system we described is the forerunner of distributed data processing (DDP) systems. The principal trouble with teleprocessing is that users at remote locations sometimes feel that the staff at the central computing site is not responsive to their needs. Often, too, the computer is overloaded, carrying too much of a processing burden. In addition, users resent having to depend on the central site, compelled to do business a certain way. Most important, remote users are at the mercy of any failures in the telephone line, central computer, or communications control unit. The answer to these problems is DDP, which gives control to users and decentralizes the computer system.

DDP allows not only remote access but also remote processing, because in addition to the centralized "host" computer, each local site has its own computer. Under this decentralized system, generalized processing is usually done at the central site, but the local sites process their own localized data. Some distributed data processing systems do not use a central host computer; instead, the local computers are linked to each other. We will discuss these concepts more fully in the DDP networks section.

### Why DDP? Why Not?

The advantages of DDP have been so readily apparent to everyone that, since its inception in the mid-1970s, its growth pattern has been explosive. An annual growth rate of 35 percent in DDP systems is expected in the immediate future. New vendors are entering the market, and even mainframe manufacturers are getting into the act and aggressively pursuing the production and marketing of DDP products.

**The Advantages** The benefits of DDP are as follows:

- *Reduced load on host.* DDP reduces the load that the host computer has to carry. Indeed, it is for precisely this reason that many computer installations have just grown into DDP: They have been forced to unburden the overworked central computer.

- *Quicker response time.* With a computer at the local site, the user does not have to wait for data and processed information to be transmitted back and forth over communication lines to a central computer.

- *Easier access.* A local computer provides easier access to data than does a computer somewhere else. Long-distance lines need not be used, and there is access competition only from local users.

- *Tailored applications.* DDP allows users to tailor their applications for the local organization rather than, perhaps, using more generalized routines on the central computer.

- *Improved management reporting.* DDP allows management reporting at lower levels of the organization to be improved, because local managers have better control of their own computerized activities. They can determine what reports will be needed and, more importantly, have better control over the timing of the reports.

- *Lower operating costs.* Clearly, not having to lease telephone lines to link local terminals with a central computer relieves the users of a big expense.

**The Disadvantages** All the advantages add up to increased productivity. However, there are some drawbacks:

- *Less on-site expertise.* Centralized processing systems have on-site experts—professionals and staff. Decentralized processing systems may have only a production manager at the local site.

- *Software and memory limitations.* The computer at the local site will not have the capability of the mainframe central computer, which can handle more sophisticated programs. The same limitations are true for memory.

- *Problems of maintaining consistency in programs.* Multiple local sites mean multiple programs. Consequently, maintaining consistency in programs for the same application is a problem. Every time a change is made in one site's program, it must be made in all the other sites that use the identical program.

- *Incompatibility in equipment.* In a DDP arrangement, an organization can find itself dealing with different vendors for different equipment such as minicomputers, modems, and front-end processors. Trying to keep vendors and their products compatible is often quite a chore.

- *Complexity.* Not only is there a multiplicity of vendors, equipment, and programs in a DDP system, there is a multiplicity of everything (including people and places). Consequently, the sum of the parts is often more complex than the sum of the parts in a strictly centralized system.

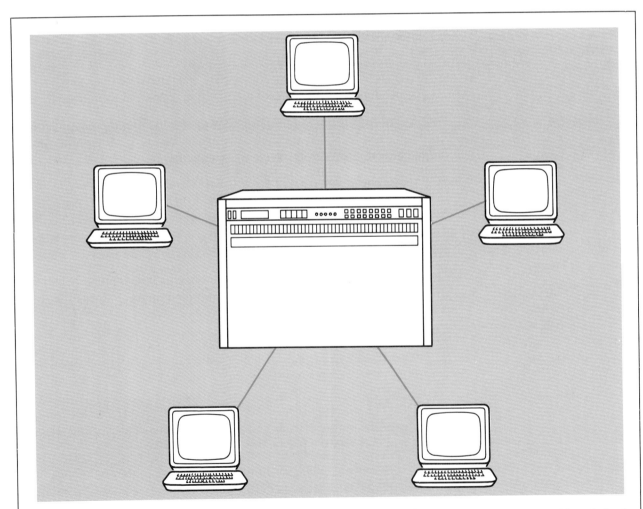

**Figure 15-8  A star network.** This distributed data processing network is like a point-to-point system, with each local computer connected to a central mainframe computer.

## DDP Networks

When its local sites are communicating with the host computer (if, indeed, a host computer is part of the system), a DDP system uses the same communications equipment and operates the same way as a teleprocessing system. Of course, much of the time each local computer may be operating by itself and not communicating with the central computer at all. The standard DDP **network**—communications system—has one of two principal designs, star or ring.

**Star Network** The pure **star network,** as shown in Figure 15-8, consists of one or more smaller computers connected to a host computer. This arrangement is suited for an organization such as a bank, with a headquarters office in which the central computer is located and with many geographically dispersed branch offices. A variation on the basic star network is the **multistar network,** as shown in Figure 15-9. In this arrangement, several host computers are tied together, but each host has its own star network of computers.

**Ring Network** The **ring network** is as simple as the arrangement shown in Figure 15-10: a circle of point-to-point connections of computers at local sites, with no central host computer. The ring network is frequently used in a decentralized organization where communication is needed between computers but not on a regular basis.

A ring network may be more expensive than a star network, but it also may be more reliable, since the star has no alternative path between locations if something should happen to interrupt a communication line with the central computer.

## What Makes a Good DDP System?

Because of the different locations, people, equipment vendors, software, and so on, putting together a DDP network can be a complicated task. Developing such a network is a delicate matter because users will promptly lose confidence if the system does not work properly, particularly if there are adverse effects on customers or clients.

Thus, if you were given the assignment of installing a new DDP system, there would be certain questions to keep in mind:

- Is the system _reliable?_ This is the prime objective. Substantial effort in planning and considerable diligence in operating the network are required for consistent reliability.

- Is it _easy to use?_ There should be clear instructions, adequate training, and easily understood documentation so that users can use the network without difficulty.

- Is it _secure?_ Users want to feel that their programs and data are safe. They are more inclined to feel that way, incidentally, with a local

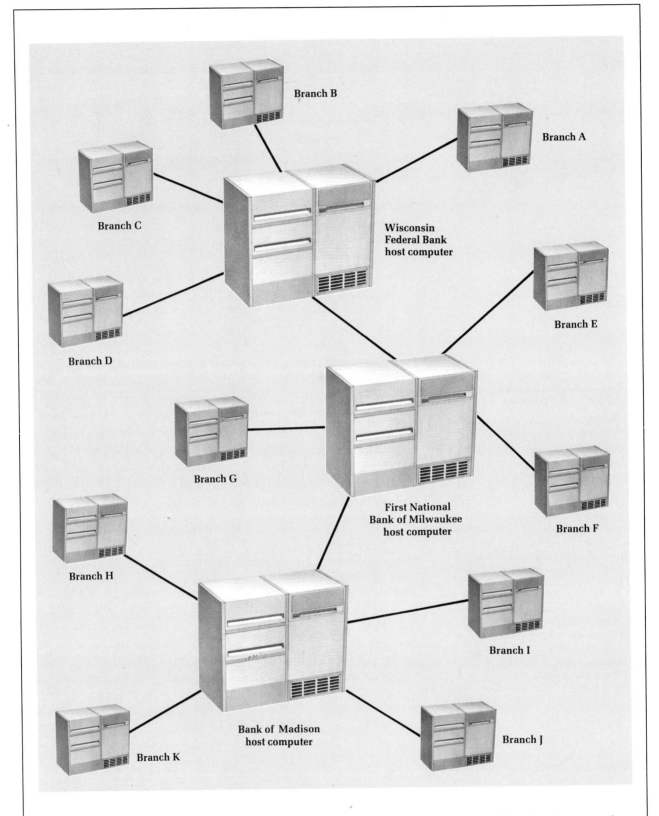

**Figure 15-9 A multistar network.** In this distributed data processing network, there are three different bank systems, whose host computers are tied to each other. Each host computer in turn has a series of branch minicomputers. In a system like this, a customer of one bank who wishes to cash a check could go to the teller window of a branch of another bank; the teller would be able to verify that there were sufficient funds in that customer's account to cover the check.

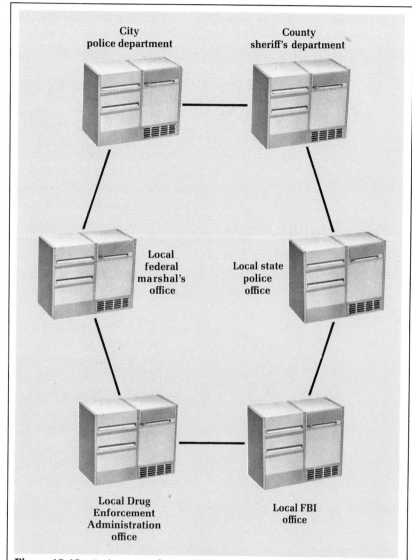

**Figure 15-10  A ring network.** Minicomputers pass messages through each other in this system. The law enforcement agencies in this hypothetical example may wish to send each other messages on occasion but not constantly.

computer than with a computer at a central site to which they must transmit their data.

• Is it *responsive?* Users may be aggravated if communication between local sites and host computer takes too long. The response time has to be reasonable.

• Is it *flexible?* The system should be able to accommodate additional sites and users without inconveniencing present users.

• Is it *economically feasible?* It should be less expensive to do processing locally than to do it at a central site, or else added benefits should offset the added costs.

## The Work of Networking

Information has become a major form of wealth, and computer networking has become a major way of communicating that information. The following are some of the ways this is coming about.

### Electronic Fund Transfers: Instant Banking

You may already be handling some financial transactions electronically instead of using checks. In **electronic fund transfers (EFTs),** people pay for goods and services by having funds transferred from various checking and savings accounts electronically, using computer technology. One of the most visible manifestations of EFT is the ATM—the **automated teller machine** (see Figure 15-11). As we mentioned earlier, an ATM is essentially a terminal (usually on a bank's exterior wall) that can be used for 24-hour banking services. Typical services would be to provide cash or inform you of your present balance. The machine is activated when you insert a specially coded plastic card and then punch in your PIN—*personal identification number*—which is, presumably, known only to you. EFT also covers automatic payment of preprogrammed bills (such as regular insurance payments), acceptance of preprogrammed deposits (such as your monthly paycheck), and transfer of funds (such as from checking to savings accounts for an automatic savings plan).

Incidentally, over 650 million social security checks have been disbursed by the government directly into the recipients' checking accounts via EFT rather than by mail. Unlike those sent via U.S. mail, no such payment has ever been lost. Moreover, such payments are also traceable—again, unlike the mail.

**Figure 15-11  An automated teller machine.** Activating the machine takes a combination of the card, and the customer's identification code, known only to him and the bank, which he must punch in using the buttons at right.

## COMPUTERIZED CONFERENCING

- Computerized conferencing will be a prominent form of communications in most organizations by the mid-1980s.

- By the mid-1990s, it will be as widely used in society as the telephone today.

- It will offer a home recreational use that will make significant inroads into TV viewing patterns.

- It will have dramatic psychological and sociological impacts on various group communication objectives and processes.

- It will be cheaper than mails or long distance telephone voice communications.

- It will offer major opportunities to disadvantaged groups in the society to acquire the skills and social ties they need to become full members of the society.

- It will have dramatic impacts on the degree of centralization or decentralization possible in organizations.

- It will have a fundamental mechanism for individuals to form groups having common concerns, interests or purposes.

- It will facilitate working at home for a large percentage of the work force during at least half of their normal work week.

- It will have a dramatic impact upon the formation of political and special interest groups.

- It will open the doors to new and unique types of services.

- It will indirectly allow for sizable amounts of energy conservation through substitution of communication for travel.

- It will dramatically alter the nature of social science research concerned with the study of human systems and human communications processes.

- It will facilitate a richness and variability of human groupings and relationships almost impossible to comprehend.

—Starr Roxanne Hiltz and Murray Turoff, *The Network Nation*

### The Stock Market

In 1969–1970, before computerization, a paper crunch nearly caused Wall Street's stock exchanges to collapse under the pressure of trading 11 million shares a day. Today, with computerization and with video terminals throughout the land, 70 million shares make an ordinary trading day. The stock market has handled nearly 170 million shares, and it can be expected to handle more.

### Teleconferencing

Jet fuel is not cheap and business travel is therefore expensive. One alternative is **teleconferencing** or **computerized conferencing,** which allows people in different geographical locations to hold conferences while sending messages back and forth to each other through a network of computer terminals. Teleconferencing has two major advantages:

- Conference participants do not need to meet in "real time." That is, they do not all have to be present simultaneously, so a person receiving a message does not have to be there when the message is sent. This does away with the headaches of trying to get a large group of people together at the same time.

- It offers an on-line memo system that records communications among the meeting participants. That is, it provides a transcript of the meeting.

The term teleconferencing is also applied to audio and television conferencing. For example, executives in New York City could take a taxi to Picturephone Meeting Service, offered by New York Telephone Company, and hold coast-to-coast meetings with other executives. The savings in time, plus travel and hotel costs, are obvious.

### Telecommunications Shopping

In recent years, there has been a trend toward nonstore retailing in such forms as telephone and mail-generated orders to department stores, offerings of records and tapes of popular music through television commercials ("Not available in any store!"), and airline in-flight shopping catalogs. One of the newest forms of retailing is interactive, two-way cable television—telecommunication merchandising. The process was described in one article (*Harvard Business Review*, July-August 1980) as follows:

Consumers with accounts at the telecommunication merchandiser will shop at home for a variety of products and services. Using an in-home video display catalog, they will order products from a participating retailer. When the order is received in the computer, this retailer will assemble the goods from a fully automated warehouse. Simultaneously, funds will be transferred from the customer's to the retailer's bank account. Customers will choose between picking up the order at a nearby distribution point or having it delivered to the door.

Warner Communications' Qube, first offered in Columbus, Ohio, is one of the first large-scale experiments in telecommunications shopping. Consumers pay a monthly subscriber cost, and retailers pay to advertise via commercials on the system.

### Electronic Newspapers

In 1981 the Newspaper Information Provider Experiment attempted to make newspaper content available electronically. The alliance was formed by CompuServe, a Columbus, Ohio, computer firm; the Associated Press; and several newspapers, including the *New York Times*, *Washington Post*, and *Los Angeles Times*. The service allows subscribers to use their home computer keyboards, connected via modems to a telephone, to request an index of the news stories, columns, editorials, and other features (but no advertisements or photographs) of the daily newspaper for the past three days.

Specific items can be selected from the index and then read on the screen. The time the consumer spends reading is computed automatically, and the bill is sent electronically to his or her credit card company. Because the system is interactive, subscribers can also write letters to the editor on their terminals, or to anyone else subscribing to the network. Similar electronic newspaper ideas are being tried elsewhere.

### Bulletin Boards, Electronic Mail, and Voice Mail

One of the newest developments is the idea of electronic **bulletin board systems,** telephone-linked networks formed by users of personal computers that constitute free public-access message systems. At first, bulletin board systems were used by computer hobbyists and club members to exchange information about computers. Gradually, new networks, consisting of people with similar interests, such as genealogical research, oceanographic information, medicine, and engineering, emerged on a nationwide basis. "What ham radio did for radio," says one writer, "bulletin board systems have done for the combination of telephone and computer, making them not only tools of academia and business but also means of personal communication and expression."

In addition, some commercial consumer-oriented communications systems have been developed, to which home computers are connected via telephone lines. Two major networks are The Source and CompuServe Information Service. The Source offers a broad range of services, including the United Press International newswire, extracts from the New York Times Consumer Data Base, and a Wall Street

## ROOM SERVICE, POOL, TV— AND COMPUTER

First came the home computer. Next it will be the computer in your home away from home.

By late March, up to 50 hotels around the nation will have installed computer terminals in many of their rooms. By pressing a few keys, guests will be able to exchange information with business colleagues and clients, get the latest stock market quotations and have a wide range of other technologically advanced amenities at their fingertips.

First to sign up for the computer service was the Midland Hotel in Chicago's financial district. Prices there for the 100 computer-equipped rooms will be the same as for the hotel's 200 other rooms. . . .

Charges will be comparable to those for a long-distance phone call—from approximately $20 per hour during peak daytime periods to $7 per hour in the early evening. Guests will pay for terminal use by typing in their credit card numbers.

Other services that will be available on the terminals:

- The latest sports scores and national weather reports.

- Airline schedules and reservations.

- Car rental arrangements.

- Restaurant and entertainment reservations.

- Ordering flowers or gifts for family and friends.

- Information on real estate and job opportunities.

- Electronic video games.

—Patricia Weiss,
U.S.A. Today,
January 26, 1983

stock index, as well as electronic games and programming languages. CompuServe offers program packages, text editors, games, a software distribution exchange, and a number of programming languages.

Out of such communication networks and bulletin boards a new form of communication is developing called **electronic mail,** in which messages intended for various users can be sent and stored and categorized by topic for later retrieval.

A further refinement in this area is **voice mail,** a computer-based system in which one person speaks into a standard telephone. The message is recorded in digital form—this is the crucial difference between voice mail and standard telephone answering machines—and can then be forwarded later to several recipients.

### The Personal Connection: Personal Networks

All these services—banking, shopping, electronic mail, and more—are available to the personal computer user. These massive communication networks are as close as your telephone. To participate in networking, you need (1) a microcomputer, (2) interfacing hardware (modem, and so on), (3) a pushbutton telephone, and (4) a subscription to an information network service such as The Source.

As we suggested earlier, it is clear that personal networks are the wave of the future. Not only will you be able to use your home computer for personal uses at home and for attaching to information networks; you will also be able to use it to communicate with your friends. Power to the people! (That is, electronic power.)

### Computer Commuting

The logical outcome of computer networks is **telecommuting,** a word coined by Jack Nilles of the University of Southern California as "the substitution of telecommunications and computers for the commute to work." According to Nilles and fellow researchers, nearly half the American work force are "information industry" workers who would be candidates for telecommuting, either by staying at home or by traveling short distances to regional offices tied by telecommunications systems to central headquarters. Those most likely to stay home would be researchers, accountants, writers, and others who usually do not need face-to-face contact in their work.

Possible problems in telecommuting are the attitudes of employers, who may feel uneasy about not being able to see their employees working, and strains brought into families and offices as a result of the relocation.

However, the benefits of telecommuting are savings in fuel costs and commuting time. Nilles found that, in some cases, worker satisfaction increased when commutes decreased, and consequently productivity was higher.

---

**THE COMING OF TELECOMMUTING**

Jack M. Nilles, director of interdisciplinary programs at the University of Southern California . . . estimates that by 1990, 15 to 20 percent of American workers will be working from their homes.

He bases his predictions on the rapid development of unique social conditions. "Personnel costs are increasing generally at a rate higher than inflation for information workers, programmers, and specialists," he says. "And I'm sure we can all expect oil shortages again. There is more demand for people not to use autos to get to work.

"Federal incentives for developing mass transit in cities have not worked very well. . . . "

Nilles also says that people are getting tired of commuting an average of 20 miles each way, spending up to two hours on the road—just to get to and from work.

—Margo Downing-Faircloth,
*Personal Computing,*
May 1982

# Networking and Security

Networks necessarily mean that information is dispersed, with valuable files in many locations, with data being transmitted over different kinds of communication lines, and with many people having access to the information. Clearly, the question of security arises: If it is so easy for authorized people to get at information, what is to stop unauthorized people from tapping into it? The safety of computers and data is of paramount importance, and deserves a chapter by itself. We will address this question in Chapter 18.

## Summary and Key Terms

- **Data communications systems** are computer systems that transmit data over communication lines such as telephone lines or coaxial cables.

- **Centralized data processing** places all hardware, software, storage, and processing in one central company location.

- Because centralized data processing is somewhat inconvenient, in the 1960s **teleprocessing systems**—terminals connected to the central computer via communication lines—were introduced. However, under this system all processing is still centralized.

- **Distributed data processing (DDP)** is similar to teleprocessing except that it has remote processing as well as remote access. The central computer is called the **host computer.**

- **Networks are** computer systems that use data communications equipment to connect two or more computers and their resources.

- **Local Area Networks (LANs)** share data and resources among several small computers.

- A teleprocessing system configuration operates as follows: A terminal produces **digital signals,** which must be converted to **analog signals.** The device that makes this conversion to or from analog or digital signals is called a **modem.** The process of converting from digital to analog is called **modulation;** the reverse is called **demodulation.**

- The communication channel in a teleprocessing system can be of several types: telephone lines, **coaxial cables, microwave transmission, satellite transmission,** and **fiber optics.** Fiber optics uses hairlike tubes of glass to make a light path.

- At the receiving end of a teleprocessing system is a second modem; a **front-end processor,** a computer whose purpose is to relieve the central computer of some of the communications tasks; and the host computer itself.

- With a **point-to-point line configuration,** each terminal is directly connected with the computer. With a **multidrop line configuration,** several terminals are connected on the same line to the computer.

- There are two common methods of line control: polling and contention. In **polling,** the computer asks each terminal on the line if it has a message to send, and then proceeds to let each in turn transmit data. In **contention,** which operates from the terminal end, a terminal that is ready to send a message waits until the line is free before transmitting.

- Interaction among components is accomplished by line **protocol,** a set of rules for the exchange of information between terminal and computer or between two computers. The exchange of prearranged signals is sometimes called **handshaking.**

- In the United States, communications are regulated by the Federal Communications Commission (FCC) and by state regulatory agencies. Companies wishing to offer communications services must submit a **tariff**—a list of proposed services and their rates—to the FCC. Organizations approved to offer communications services are called **common carriers.**

- Common carriers offer two types of lines. **Switched lines** connect through switching centers to destinations; **private** or **leased lines** offer communications to fixed destinations.

- The 1968 Carterfone decision was first in a series of FCC decisions permitting competitors to interface independent equipment with the AT&T network. The expanded activity has led to the **value-added network,** in which a value-added carrier leases communication lines from a common carrier and enhances their value by adding improvements to the lines. In 1982, AT&T was permitted to enter data processing, computer communications, and the manufacture of computer equipment in return for divesting itself of 22 local operating companies then making up the Bell System.

- Under **distributed data processing (DDP),** generalized processing is usually done at the centralized "host" computer, but local processing sites process their own localized data. Some DDP systems do not use a central computer, but rather the local computers are linked to each other.

- The advantages of DDP are reduced load on the host computer, quicker response time, easier access to data, tailoring of applications to local needs, improved management reporting, and lower operating costs.

- The disadvantages of DDP are less on-site experts, software and memory limitations, problems of maintaining consistency in programs, incompatibility in equipment, and complexity.

- The pure DDP **star network** consists of one or more computers connected to a host computer. In the **multistar network,** several host computers are tied together, but each host has its own star network of computers. A **ring network** is a circle of computers at local sites connected point-to-point, with no central host computer.

- A good DDP system should be reliable, easy to use, secure, responsive, and economically feasible.

- Computer networking communicates information in several ways. (1) In **electronic fund transfers (EFTs),** people pay for goods and services by having funds transferred from checking and savings accounts electronically. (2) The stock market on Wall Street uses computerization to expedite the trading of millions of shares of stock. (3) **Teleconferencing** or **computerized conferencing** enables business people to have meetings by being linked together by computer terminals. (4) Telecommunications shopping allows consumers to order via the computer network. (5) Electronic newspapers allow consumers to select news stories and other items through computer terminals. (6) Electronic **bulletin board systems** are telephone-linked networks formed by users of personal computers, who exchange information. (7) Electronic mail allows messages to be sent and stored for later retrieval. (8) **Voice mail** is a computer-based system in which one person speaks into a phone, the message is recorded in digital form, and the message can then be forwarded to others.

- **Telecommuting,** a logical outcome of computer networks in which telecommunications and computers may replace the daily commute, may happen more in the foreseeable future.

- A problem with dispersed information is securing the information, which becomes more accessible to unauthorized persons.

## Review

1. Distinguish between centralized data processing systems, teleprocessing systems, and distributed data processing systems.

2. Describe the steps and equipment required in a teleprocessing system configuration.

3. What are the various types of communication channels?

4. Name the two principal line configurations and describe them.

5. Describe the two common methods of line control.

6. What is a common carrier?

7. List the advantages and disadvantages of DDP.

8. Describe the types of DDP networks.

9. Describe ways in which computer networking communicates information. Do you make use of any of these methods now?

## Selected References for Further Reading

Hiltz, Starr Roxanne, and Murray Turoff. *The Network Nation: Human Communication via Computer.* Reading, Mass.: Addison-Wesley, 1978.

Hunsely, Trevor. *Data Communications and Teleprocessing Systems.* Englewood Cliffs, N.J.: Prentice-Hall, 1979.

Katzan, Harry, Jr. *An Introduction to Distributed Data Processing.* New York: Petrocelli Books, 1978.

Lientz, Bennet P. *An Introduction to Distributed Systems.* Reading, Mass.: Addison-Wesley, 1981.

Martin, James. *The Wired Society.* Englewood Cliffs, N.J.: Prentice-Hall, 1978.

**IN THIS CHAPTER**

Computer-based management information systems (MISs) help managers accomplish their tasks by providing timely and accurate information. Three additional management devices are information centers, microcomputers for executives, and the full-scale decision support system. A prerequisite to a successful MIS is a well-organized data base, which in turn requires a data base management system.

# ch 16

# management information systems and data base systems

## share and share alike

*ch16*

The view from the top—say, from a company president's office on the fortieth floor—is a lot different from the view from below. And the *viewpoint* from the top is also different: a top-level manager must have a different outlook than does a middle-level or lower-level manager. Let us show what we mean.

All managers have three main functions—planning, organizing, and controlling—but the scope of each function depends on the management level. Whether they are the head of General Electric or of an electric-appliance store, of a large company or a small one, top-level managers have to be concerned with the long-range view—with *planning*. Are American families watching less standard network television fare but going more for televised movies and miniseries? To the president of a company making videotape recorders, this fact may suggest real opportunities for expansion, since presumably people will want to preserve some of these movies for later viewing.

Middle-level managers need to take a different view; they need to be concerned principally with *organizing*. So the public is suddenly finding videotape recorders desirable if they are affordable? To a production vice-president, this may mean organizing production lines using people with the right skills for the right wage and perhaps farming out portions of the assembly that can be done by low-skilled labor.

Low-level managers are mainly concerned with *controlling*. The assembly-line supervisor need not care what kind of electrical product is being built so much as making sure that all the people, parts, and machines are available to keep the production line rolling.

To make decisions about planning, organizing, and controlling, managers need data organized into information that is right for them. An effective management information system can provide it.

## MIS for Managers

A **management information system (MIS)** may be defined as a set of formal business systems designed to provide information for decision making. Whether or not such a system is called an MIS, every company has one. Even managers who make hunch-based decisions are operating with some sort of information system (one based on their experience). The kind of MIS we are concerned with here includes a computer as one of its components. Information serves no purpose, of course, until it gets to its users. Speed and timeliness are important, and the computer can act quickly to produce information.

The extent of computerized MISs (incidentally, you may hear people use the term "MIS system," even though the "S" itself stands for "system"; this is an accepted redundancy) varies from company to company, but the most effective kinds are those that are *integrated*. An integrated MIS incorporates all three functions—planning, organizing, and controlling—throughout the company, from the most mundane typing to top executive forecasting. An integrated management computer system uses the computer to solve problems for an entire organization, instead of attacking them piecemeal. Although in most companies the completely integrated system is still only an idea, the scope of MISs is expanding rapidly in many organizations. A new type of manager is emerging, called the MIS manager, a person comfortable with both computer technology and the organization's business.

Let us see how an MIS can support managers and their management functions.

### How MIS Helps Managers Decide

As we mentioned earlier in the book, a computer system can produce three kinds of reports—detail, summary, and exception. There are also "on-demand" reports. All of these are valuable to managers, depending on their levels, as follows:

- **Low-level managers.** Concerned mainly with day-to-day operations, low-level managers need _detail_ reports—information on routine operations that will help them keep offices and plants running. Examples are overtime information from this week's payroll, spare parts that need to be ordered, shipping backlog, and quality control results of yesterday's inspections at Dock B. Many computer-based MISs are self-determining, making such preplanned decisions as automatic reordering of depleted stock as directed by an inventory management program or automatic issuing of bonuses for sales people when incoming orders reach a certain level.

- **Middle-level managers.** To do their tactical planning and organizing functions, middle-level managers need to be aware of trends; they need to know what the business is doing and where it is going. Thus, these managers are most in need of _summary_ reports and _exception_ reports. They need information quickly enough to react appropriately in a changing marketplace. Examples of summary reports showing trends are those showing past and present interest rates or sales data. Examples of exception reports are those showing depleted budgets, projects behind schedule, and expenses being paid out to temporary employees.

- **Top-level managers.** For strategic planning, high-level managers need to be able to see historic information, an analysis of data trends, not for just some parts of their business but for the total business. Moreover, such managers must be able to make decisions about things that happen unpredictably. The MIS, therefore, must be able to produce _on-demand_ reports, reports that can integrate information and show how factors affecting various departments are related to each other. An on-demand report might show the impact of strikes or energy shortages in all parts of the company.

It should be clear that an MIS must be capable of delivering information not only of the predictable, detailed sort but also of the unpredictable, general sort.

## Assembling and Using Information

Information has two sources: inside the organization and outside it. Examples of *internal* information are salary records, accounts receivable, accounts payable, inventory records, and production schedules. Much internal information is principally of concern to lower-level managers. *External* information consists of bank interest rates, government regulations, consumer preferences, competitors' marketing strategies, and similar information that is often of value to middle- and top-level executives.

How is all this computer-assembled information to be integrated and used? Suppose an American automaker decides to mount an aggressive effort to make and sell a new small car (the "S-car") overseas. How might information from each department be integrated in a useful way to make top-level decisions? The MIS manager might query purchasing agents about the acquisition of materials for manufacturing, production managers about retooling and capacity of production lines, distribution managers about shipping, personnel managers about labor pools, marketing managers about financing and return on investment, and so on. In the pre-MIS days, the automaker might have discovered—*after* the car was in production and the marketing campaign was under way—that distribution was jeopardized because of insufficient overseas warehousing in the right consumer areas. With an MIS that integrates *all* information for top managers, such pitfalls can be avoided.

# Decision Support Systems and Other Fast "What if . . ." Help

Even if an organization has a highly integrated MIS system, it may also have something else—a backlog of work. Most data processing departments are simply swamped; indeed, one recent IBM study found

that for major applications a typical DP organization was backlogged two-and-a-half years!

Imagine yourself, then, as a top-level manager trying to deal with a constantly changing environment, having to consider changes in competition, in technology, in consumer habits, in government regulations, in union demands, and so on. How are you going to make competent decisions with only old information available? More importantly, how are you going to make decisions about those matters *for which there are no precedents?* In fact, making one-of-a-kind decisions—decisions that no one has had to make before—are the real test of a manager's mettle. In such a situation, wouldn't you like to be able to turn to someone and ask a few "What if . . . " questions?

MIS is one approach to making complicated decisions, but because of backlog it may not be timely enough. Thus, business people have begun looking to other solutions. Three that we will describe here are:

- The information center
- Microcomputers for executives
- The full-scale decision support system

### *The Information Center*

As a tourist suddenly finding yourself in a strange city for a day or two, you could go about seeing the sights in one of two ways: You could simply go out and wander around, picking up whatever guides and tips you happen to come across. Or you could go to a tourist information center to get specific information tailored to your interests.

A data processing **information center** within a corporation is much the same way. Staffed by DP experts, it offers users within the organization assistance without jargon, access to reference materials, help with obtaining passwords and administrative information with which to "log on" (get access to) a computer system, and lessons in how to use existing software and work stations. However, the information center staff will not write programs for users, only provide assistance. Some users may wish to write programs, using simplified language, but in most cases they will probably make use of readymade software packages.

The information center is helpful but still only a partial solution, however. A lot of people cannot program, for instance, nor do they want to. Moreover, the center does not provide a completely integrated system. In short, users will still find themselves unable to get total access to the data they need.

### *Microcomputers for Executives*

All over this land, business executives, frustrated by the aforementioned backlog of work in their corporate DP departments, have opted for do-it-yourself, buying their own microcomputers and packaged software. Sometimes these executives are even the heads of companies.

## NO MORE DATA!! THE NEED FOR DSS

There is no shortage of evidence that management wants and is demanding more computer assistance for the more complex decision making required in business today. After two decades of waiting and hearing promises, it is growing more frustrated and angry, especially since it foots the bills for data processing. As the chief executive officer of a major food products company recently told his DP director, who was requesting a trial of a DSS, "I don't want you coming back and telling me that what we need is more data. Every time there's a problem, people come back and say, 'The answer is for us to purchase additional data.' We've got information coming out of our ears, and what we need now is some way to make sense of it!"
—Walter E. Lankau,
*Computerworld*,
September 1, 1982

One chief executive officer of a pharmaceutical company, for instance, felt he could not be sure of the information he was getting from his accounting, finance, and DP people, so he secretly purchased a TRS–80 microcomputer and studied it at home for a few months. Discovering the benefits of word processing, he then ordered 20 microcomputers for his office and began asking employees to learn to use the machines for memos and report writing. In addition, according to *Inc.* magazine, he discovered the advantages of working with Visi-Calc, the famous "electronic spreadsheet," which enabled him to examine different possible business strategies, such as the level of sales discounts and advertising support needed to reach his company's sales targets. Earlier strategic planning was fairly informal: "We just eyeballed the numbers and made our best guesses."

All this sounds wonderful, but there are definite drawbacks, particularly in large companies in which the move toward microcomputers is not organized from the top down. If many executives acquire micros on their own and build their own files of data, there may be no way for everyone to integrate and have access to that data—and what do you do when someone important leaves the company in a huff and takes along his or her floppy disks? In addition, microcomputers have limited power and are sometimes incompatible with larger computers.

### The Full-Scale Decision Support System

"What if . . . ?" That is the question business people want answered, at least for those important decisions that have no precedent. Information centers and individual microcomputers go part way toward helping users in this respect, but they basically fall into the category of self-help. Something more is needed. That something is a full-scale decision support system.

Recently, the term "decision support system" has become a buzzword, a slogan for software vendors touting individual software products. What we mean is something grander, however. A full-scale **decision support system (DSS)** is a data processing system that has the following five characteristics:

- It is fully integrated, able to obtain information from a variety of sources (the marketing department, the finance department, and so on).

- Analysis is available on a while-you-wait basis. Because managers need to make short-term, immediate decisions based on the information at hand, most DSSs are used largely to answer questions needed on a given day or given week rather than to produce a scheduled weekly or monthly report.

- It can produce "What if . . . ?" type models—that is, a variety of business scenarios or possibilities—to see which outcome you like best. This is particularly critical when dealing with the unexpected. For example, a car manufacturer having to consider issuing a recall of one of its cars because of a safety defect or a pharmaceutical company having to address a poisoning of one of its products (as in the Tylenol case) will need to consider the impact of the damage on future sales, the readiness of competitors to take advantage of the situation, and so on. A DSS can pose models of various possibilities.

- It crosses departmental functional lines—marketing, sales, finance, production, and so on—both across the width of the organization and upward and downward within the hierarchy of the organization. Information, analysis, and models from each area are all coordinated for immediate use.

- It is—that well-worn, overused term—"user friendly." The user of a DSS is a manager or executive, not a data processing specialist.

Needless to say, such a marvelous system will not come cheap. To produce a full-scale DSS, an organization will have to institute sophisticated data base management systems (a concept we will discuss shortly), have strong display and graphics capabilities that allow managers to express decision possibilities in visual form such as charts and graphs, and have modeling tools incorporated in the system such as risk analysis and forecasting programs.

Let us now turn to an important component of decision support systems, the data base.

## Before Data Base: Patchwork Files

First there was hardware, then there was software. The hardware was expensive, and had to be kept running to justify the cost and get the work done. The software had to be written to make use of the hardware. *Data*, in the early days of the Computer Age, received the least attention. If someone wanted to write a program and certain data was needed for that application, then the file or files of data were established for that particular program—data by demand. This is the background against which the need for data bases became apparent. As you might suspect, the pre–data base improvised approach led to problems.

The system of using data called **file processing** means that data is used in files—collections of records—and the files are used with programs. Before the integrated MIS approach, individuals within departments created and maintained their own files. When files of data were created on a data-by-demand basis, it led to a patchwork quilt of files, and this, in turn, caused several problems. The problems became more acute because of managerial needs for timely, interrelated information.

Duplication of files led to duplication of data—*redundancy*, in other words. For instance, a bank might have a customer's address for checking account, savings account, car loan, and so on, all on different files. Whenever the customer moved, the address on each file would have to be changed separately.

Inconsistency in data files led to problems of data *integrity*. For example, if two files were updated with the bank customer's new address, but a third file was not, the customer might be suspicious of *any* information emerging from the computer. There would be a lack of confidence in the integrity, the consistency, of the data.

With data files being developed as programs were developed, the problem of *data dependence* arose. The way the data was organized and the method of access to that data was determined by the requirements of the application program. The program logic was designed to fit the data. Programs were thus data dependent because it was impossible to change the storage structure of the data without affecting the program. This also meant data might not be easily available for another type of application program.

Such data dependence led to yet another problem—*poor data relationships*. That is, with data so rigidly structured and tied to the logic of some particular program, it was not easily shared with other programs. For instance, suppose an office supply company had developed programs and data about its customers and its sales force. The program handling customer information would use a file with the following data for each customer: account number, customer name, address, credit rating, balance owing, and the number of the sales representative servicing the customer account. There would also be a program to monitor the progress of sales representatives. The sales representative file records would contain sales representative number, sales quota, dollar volume in sales, and some personal data such as name, address, and hire date.

These two programs could process their respective files. But what if there was a need to tie this data together? Suppose, for instance, that we went to a particular customer record and found out the number of that customer's sales representative. If we now needed the address of that sales representative, we would be faced with the inconvenience of going to the other file, the sales representative file, to look up the appropriate record by the sales representative number.

This is exactly the kind of cross-relationship that managers often want to make. Data often *is* interrelated, and sometimes it is not convenient to make that relationship because the data is locked into a particular program.

Finally, poor data relationships led to the problem of *poor response to user requests*, particularly if the information cut across an organization's departmental lines. For instance, suppose the management of an office supply manufacturer wanted to consider getting into the garden furniture business. Decisions would have to be made about a sales force, local warehouse sites, manufacturing and marketing departments, and so on. To test the marketability of the new products, the management would need to have information on all these areas, and would ask the organization's data processing personnel to pull it together from the various files. Without easily accessible data, however, they would not be able to respond very quickly to this request.

As computers and data processing penetrated more deeply into organizational life, and as data files grew more haphazardly, it was clear there had to be a better way.

# Data Base Processing

The better way is a **data base** (sometimes it is spelled as one word: *database*), which may be defined as a collection of integrated data that can be used for a variety of applications. Data base processing is a method of using that data. The data in a data base is collected on a direct access device, usually a disk.

It is tempting to think that we can take all data in an organization and throw it into one pot, but that is not possible or even desirable. Most organizations have several data bases, with data from related applications placed in the same data base. The users associated with these related applications would all have access to the same data base through their application programs. For instance, an order processing data base would include all data related to the former file processing systems: systems for customer orders, warehouse tracking, invoices, shipping, and payments. A manufacturing data base could include all data related to raw materials, factory scheduling, quality control, and spare parts. A people-related data base could have information on personnel, payrolls, and union membership.

Pulling data together in this fashion has certain advantages—and disadvantages.

### IS A DREAM DATA BASE FEASIBLE?

In the late 1960s, the dream emerged of a totally integrated corporate data base. This was completely unworkable. The task of building one data base system for a corporation is unthinkably complex. It is far beyond the capability of any one team to design; and even if it could be designed, machine performance considerations would make it unworkable (except in small corporations).

—James Martin,
*Computerworld,*
October 4, 1982

## Why Data Bases?

Organizing data in data base form has several advantages, as follows.

**Reduced Redundancy** If data is stored in just one place, then the *amount* of stored data can be reduced. Although redundancy cannot usually be eliminated completely, it can be minimized. In any case, with a data base we do not have the same data scattered among numerous files.

**Data Integrity** With data centralized in one place, the updated version of the data appears on all, not just some, appropriate reports extracted from the data base. A customer notifying a bank of his or her change of address can have confidence that the new address will appear on all bank records.

**Data Independence** By its very nature, a data base system means that programs are not dependent on the storage structure of data.

## Data Base Tales

### Do You Need a Good Fullback?

OKLAHOMA CITY—It looks as if the extra points in football this year will come from having a computer in the backfield.

Thanks to the Blue Chip Bureau here, college football recruiters and coaches all over the country can obtain vital statistics on eligible athletes from across the nation with a one-time request.

The new recruitment system is based on a data base of high school seniors capable of playing collegiate football. The service . . . offers statistics on more than 4000 football players.

College recruiters can obtain the computer-generated report, which includes a table of contents listing the names carried on the data base, for $750/year. The user can then obtain information from the Blue Chip data base either by providing a specific student name or by plugging in appropriate criteria such as "quarterback, 200 lb., more than 6 ft., wants to attend school in the south."

For $1/player, a recruiter can obtain an itemized account of each player's name, position, height, weight, speed in the 40-yard dash, hometown, high school, coach's name and grade point average.

For $2/player, the recruiting school can obtain a more detailed report, which includes information on aptitude test scores, religious and ethnic background, passing percentages, receiving statistics, coach's comments and geographical preference.

—Susan Blakeney,
*Computerworld,*
August 9, 1982

### Crime Fighters' Data Bases

WASHINGTON, D.C.—The Federal Bureau of Investigation compiled its best record yet for criminal investigations and prosecutions in 1981 and 1982, and the bureau credits much of that success to a system of data bases set up in 1978.

Primary among those data bases is the Organized Crime Information System, which maintains the names of suspected mobsters along with their home and business addresses, license plate numbers and other information. "As we get into more complex cases, we find that the paperwork is tremendous, so we put the information on the data base and call it up when we need it," FBI Supervisory Special Agent Wiley Thompson said in a recent interview. . . .

To explain how the OCIS data base is used, Thompson offered as an example the case of an agent who suspects that an address is a headquarters for organized crime. By entering into OCIS the license plate numbers of the cars driven by people entering the building, the agent can find out whether they are suspected members of a criminal organization.

The data base will also tell if they have criminal records and give other information that was once difficult to compile quickly. "It provides quicker access to information and rapid transfer of that information," Thompson said. "It's faster than waiting for it in the mail."

—Jim Bartimo,
*Computerworld,*
November 22, 1982

### All-Electronic Novel
#### Available Through Data Base

*It was the day after the end of the world . . . Philip had hoped to pull off a miracle and had managed to do just the reverse. He had pitted everything on one clever move—and lost.*

*Hundreds of fashionable people—in fact, the whole artistic community of the city—had appeared in the freight elevator only a few hours before. The most important, or rather the most influential of the newspaper journalists, was the personable Suede.*

So reads an excerpt of what is thought to be the first electronically published novel, which was recently made available to subscribers of Source Telecomputing Corp.'s The Source public data base system.

*Blind Pharaoh* was written in Toronto in 61-1/2 hours on an Apple Computer, Inc. Apple III. The 20,000 word book was edited chapter by chapter on another Apple at Source's headquarters in McLean, Va., where nine Prime Computer, Inc. 750 minicomputers allow 24,000 subscribers to access the data base through modems at 1,200 bit/sec, according to a Source spokesman.

The 19-chapter book is available for as little as $2.03 by calling it up on a home computer and downloading it to a floppy disk or printer for storage, a company spokesman said.

Author Burke Campbell, a native of Texas and resident of Toronto, had previously written another three-day novel for a local contest and has also authored radio dramas for the Canadian Broadcasting Co.

"*Blind Pharaoh* is a mystery thriller," Campbell said last week. "It's the story of a mysterious man who travels around North America in his limousine manipulating the lives of other people. It's a kind of science fiction novel, but most of the technology in it already exists."

—Jim Bartimo,
*Computerworld,*
January 31, 1983

**Shared Data** With pooled resources, data can be used relatively easily for multiple applications. The data does not need to be redefined by each user; rather, the user defines the subset of the data base that is needed and the data base system will provide the data as requested.

**Fast Response to User Requests** A data base system allows a quicker response to a user request because it permits users to cross organizational lines. Files are not separated by application.

**Centralized Security** If data is all in one place, we have better control over access to it. Multiple files containing redundant information on many tapes and disks are more difficult to protect. This is particularly important with personnel files, restricted product information, customer credit ratings, marketing plans, and similar sensitive information.

### Why Not Data Bases?

Structuring data in data base form has three disadvantages: complexity, expense, and vulnerability.

**Complexity** Building a data base requires extensive planning. The ways of structuring data base files and of setting up the methods for accessing them are very complex. Once the data base is in service, it continues to be complex, and special efforts are required to monitor and maintain it.

**Expense** Complexity breeds expense. In addition to hardware considerations, more time and more people are required to plan, develop, and monitor the data base, and that costs money.

**Vulnerability** Although centralizing data in one place helps us maintain security over it, it also, paradoxically, makes the data more vulnerable. All the eggs are in one basket. And while data is theoretically more open to sabotage and theft, the vulnerability is more apt to manifest itself in loss of data due to some hardware or software problem. The people monitoring the data base must have recovery procedures available and be ready to step in should there be problems with the data base system.

Since the data on a data base is accessible by so many different types of people, it is important that only authorized persons have access to any given piece of data. This issue is addressed by having passwords associated with the data itself, so that only people who should have access can have access.

Data base systems are not for everyone, nor should they be. Many organizations have relatively simple files for which a data base system could not be cost-justified. For other organizations, however, the advantages outweigh the disadvantages, as is apparent in the steady trend toward more and larger data bases.

# Finding What You Want: Accessing the Data Base

Once the data base is in place, how do users find what they want? There are three components—a data base management system, application programs, and query languages.

**Figure 16-1  Access to the data base.** Programmers have access through application programs to the data base management system, which in turn has access to the data base. Users without programming training have access through query languages.

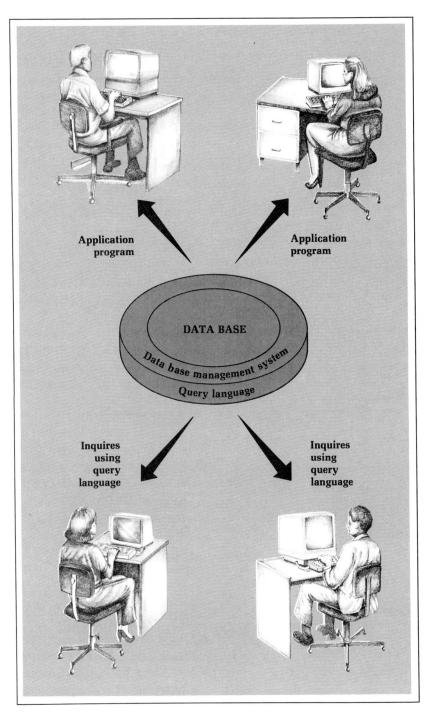

## Data Base Management System

A **data base management system,** frequently referred to by its abbreviation, **DBMS,** is a set of programs that provides access to the data base. Since we are no longer using a simple file, no simple access method such as sequential or direct access will be adequate. Instead, the DBMS—an intermediate software package that can handle input to and output from the data base—is required. Some simplified DBMSs give users access without their having to know the actual details of the data base structure. A DBMS package should not only be able to correlate data relationships within the data base, but also provide data security features and query language capability.

A DBMS package is so complicated that most users do not develop their own. Computer manufacturers and software vendors make DBMS software available in a variety of forms, from bare-bones models to sophisticated packages with many options and features. DBMS software has been available on mainframes since the early 1970s. Now DBMS software is also being offered for minicomputers and even microcomputers.

## Application Programs and Query Languages

With a data base management system in place, there are basically two ways to access the data base—through application programs and through query languages, as Figure 16-1 indicates.

Application programs can be used to call special access programs that are part of the DMBS. Instructions to access the data base can be embedded in a program language such as COBOL or PL/I. Instead of the standard COBOL READ instruction, for example, a program would use special instructions to call on the DBMS to retrieve the data. Programmers working with the data base system are, of course, taught how to use these instructions.

Most DBMSs also provide a query language, a high-level nonprocedural language that persons with no formal programming training can use to specify their requirements. A user can be taught to use a query language with minimal instruction. In response to queries, the DBMS will search the data base for the information and return it to the user (see Figure 16-2).

## Distributed Data Bases

Distributed data processing, we said in Chapter 15, is a network of decentralized local computers, possibly combined with a central host computer. Like the computers, data bases can also be distributed. This can be done in three ways:

- A data base may be centralized at the site of the host computer, but accessible to remote locations.

| English | Query Language |
|---|---|
| | **"GIS" query language** |
| Display age, name, and sex for all persons whose age is greater than 21. | LOCATE PERSON WHEN AGE GE 21 LIST NAME, AGE, SEX EXHAUST PERSON |
| | **"Image" query language** |
| Find all entries for which state is Nevada. | FIND STATE IS "NEVADA" END |
| | **"IDSQ" query language** |
| Display last name, age, and education years for all females between 25 and 35 years of age (combined college education years). | DISPLAY LAST NAME AGE EDUC YEARS IF SEX = "F" IF AGE > 25 and < 35 LET EDUC YEARS = BACHELOR + GRADUATE END |
| | **"English" query language** |
| Display inventory for items which have zero "on hand" and orders before 10/10/82. | LIST INVENTORY DESCRIPTION WITH ONHAND = "0" AND ORDER DATE BEFORE 10/10/82 |
| | **"Sequel" query language** |
| Find average salary of all clerks. | SELECT AVG(SALARY) FROM EMPLOYEE RECORD WHERE JOB = "CLERK" |

**Figure 16-2   Query languages.** Five samples of query languages are shown above. A query language permits a user to retrieve data instantly from a data base.

- Part of the data base at the central site may be duplicated at the remote site. The data chosen for duplication would, of course, be related to activities at that remote location. With this duplication of data, however, the advantage of reduced redundancy, which is one of the principal reasons for having a data base system in the first place, would be lost.

- There may be complete data bases at each remote location.

## The Data Base Administrator

The **data base administrator,** or **DBA,** is the person or group of persons responsible for monitoring and coordinating all activities related to the data base.

The DBA has five major functions:

- **To coordinate users.** The DBA helps users define data requirements and helps resolve conflicts regarding data, usually through regularly scheduled meetings. Obviously, user involvement is critical to the success of the data base, since it is the users' data and they use it.

- **To enforce standards.** The DBA makes sure the data standards of the organization are disseminated and enforced and maintains any documentation associated with them. Sample candidates for standardization are data names, data formats, record names, and access techniques.

- **To monitor data base system performance.** To keep the data base and the DBMS operating efficiently, the person or persons in charge must be alert for changes that might lower efficiency. The DBA would certainly be concerned, for example, if access time steadily deteriorated. This function involves keeping statistics, correlating information, and publishing results.

- **To plan recovery procedures.** If the data base system fails, the DBA is prepared. Contingency plans and recovery procedures have been developed so that the system can continue to operate with minimal inconvenience or disruption.

- **To monitor the security system.** As we mentioned, data is wealth, and a data base represents an organization's most important asset— its data. Consequently, the DBA must exercise considerable care to keep the system secure. The DBA ensures that the DBMS monitors system security. For instance, whenever someone wishes to gain access to the data base and gives a password, identification number, budget number, or the like, the DBMS checks to see if that person is actually authorized to use the data. Data security is discussed in more detail in Chapter 18.

## _From Computers to People_

Data bases are a very technical, complicated subject, and we have only scratched the surface here. We have tried to convey an understanding of why data bases are needed and some of the general concepts associated with them.

In the final part of this book, Part 5, we move on from hardware, software, and data to the implications of the Computer Age for people—for jobs, for security and privacy, and for society.

## Summary and Key Terms

- Managers have three functions—planning, organizing, and controlling. Top-level managers emphasize planning, middle-level managers emphasize organizing, and low-level managers emphasize controlling.

- A **management information system (MIS)** is a set of formal business systems that provide information to managers for decision making. Today an MIS usually includes the use of a computer because speed and timeliness are essential to make information useful for decision making.

- MIS is a rapidly expanding province in most organizations and has produced a new kind of manager, the MIS manager, also sometimes called the **information systems manager (ISM).**

- The kind of MIS-produced reports needed by different level managers varies. Low-level managers need detail reports, middle-level managers need summary reports and exception reports, and top-level managers need on-demand reports.

- Information in an MIS is assembled from internal sources (such as a company's salary records) and external sources (such as notices of bank interest rates).

- Even with an MIS, managers need help in making rapid "What if . . . ?" kinds of decisions. Three solutions are available: (1) the information center, (2) microcomputers for executives, and (3) the full-scale decision support system.

- A data processing **information center** is a center within a corporation which is staffed by DP experts who can offer the organization's users assistance without jargon, access to reference materials and to the computer system, and lessons in how to use existing software and workstations.

- Microcomputers for executives can allow individuals to solve many of their own DP and word processing problems, using packaged software.

- The full-scale **decision support system (DSS)** is a data processing system with five characteristics: (1) it is fully integrated with a variety of sources throughout the organization; (2) analysis is available on a while-you-wait basis; (3) it can produce "What if . . . ?" type models of various business scenarios or possibilities; (4) it crosses departmental functional lines both upward and downward; and (5) it is user friendly for executives and managers.

- In the early days of computers, files of data were established on demand. The system of **file processing**—data used in files or collections of records—when files were created on a data-by-demand basis, led to a patchwork of files.

- Duplication of files led to redundancy of data; inconsistency in data files led to problems of data integrity; programs were data dependent; data dependence led to poor data relationships, so that data could not be easily shared among programs; and poor data relationships led to poor response to user requests.

- A **data base** is defined as a collection of integrated data that can be used for a variety of applications. Data base processing is a method of using that data.

- The advantages of organizing data in data base form are reduced redundancy, increased data integrity, data independence, data that can be shared for multiple applications, fast response to user requests, and centralized security.

- The disadvantages of structuring data in data base form are the facts that the ways of structuring and accessing the data are very complex, which in turn make the system expensive to plan and monitor and the data more vulnerable to loss.

- In accessing the data base, there are three components to consider: a data base management system, application programs, and query languages. A **data base management system (DBMS)** is a set of programs that provides access to the data base; the DBMS is usually developed by computer manufacturers and software vendors. The data base is accessed through application programs, which call special programs that are part of the DBMS, or through query languages.

- Data bases can be distributed; this is done in three ways: (1) a data base may be centralized at the site of the host computer, but accessible to remote locations; (2) part of the data base at the central site may be duplicated at the remote site; (3) there may be complete data bases at each remote location.

- The **data base administrator (DBA)** is the person or group of persons responsible for monitoring and coordinating all data base–related activities. The DBA has these major functions: (1) to coordinate users; (2) to enforce standards; (3) to monitor data base system performance; (4) to plan recovery procedures; and (5) to monitor the security system.

## Review

1. Name the three levels of management, their principal functions, and the kinds of reports most useful to them.

2. What is a management information system?

3. Why is a full-scale decision support system superior to an information center or microcomputer?

4. Define "data base."

5. Describe the advantages and disadvantages of arranging data in data base form.

6. What is a data base management system?

7. Describe the three ways data bases can be distributed.

8. What are the functions of the data base administrator?

## Selected References for Further Reading

Bradley, James. _Introduction to Data Base Management in Business._ New York: Holt, Rinehart and Winston, 1983.

Curtice, Robert M., and Paul E. Jones. _Logical Data Base Design._ New York: Van Nostrand Reinhold, 1982.

Date, C. J. _An Introduction to Data Base Systems._ 3rd ed. Reading, Mass.: Addison-Wesley, 1981.

Kroenke, David. _Database Processing._ 2nd ed. Chicago: Science Research Associates, 1983.

Martin, James. _An End User's Guide to Data Base._ Englewood Cliffs, N.J.: Prentice-Hall, 1981.

Senn, James A. _Information Systems in Management._ Belmont, Calif.: Wadsworth, 1982.

Thierauf, Robert J. _Decision Support Systems for Effective Planning and Control._ Englewood Cliffs, N.J.: Prentice-Hall, 1982.

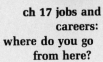

**ch 17 jobs and careers: where do you go from here?**

**ch 18 security and privacy: keeping computers friendly**

**ch 19 computers and society: the future then**

# *part 5*

# *computers and us*

Computers, says astronomer Carl Sagan, rival the invention of writing as one of the most profound innovations in human history, for they are "remaking the world at a phenomenal rate." Whereas 20 years ago a typical processor could store the equivalent of a 15-page pamphlet in a cubic meter of space, he observes, by the end of the present decade that same space will be able to contain all the information in the Library of Congress. This incredible pace of technological development is providing a completely different way of looking at the world. Computers will open up new vistas, technologies, and industries at the same time that they alter human relationships, work habits, and attitudes toward time and space. In this final part of the book, we will see how the computer is affecting our work, our security and privacy, and, finally, us as human beings.

## IN THIS CHAPTER

There is currently a shortage of qualified personnel in the computer and data processing industry. This chapter discusses the kinds of jobs available, career directions, methods of enhancing productivity, and ways of keeping current.

# ch17

# jobs and careers

## where do you go from here?

The old ways are changing and changing fast. Hardly an occupation exists that over the next ten years—or even the next five years—will not be affected by the Computer Revolution. In many manufacturing industries, such as automobiles, many jobs have been lost or upgraded. Much clerical work—filing, typing lists, sorting, and the like—is being shifted from humans to machines. Many jobs that consist mainly of providing information over a telephone, such as those of stockbrokers and airline reservations personnel, are clear candidates for change. Librarians, travel agents, employment agency personnel—all should brace for extraordinary changes in their work lives. Even those most prestigious of occupations, medicine and law, will be changed forever.

*ch17*

## Thinking about Your Work Future

Physicians, lawyers, educators, accountants, and other professionals may in some ways be as vulnerable to computer-caused change as auto workers, but for different reasons. These professionals have specialized knowledge in a particular field. Their strength is information, and their expertise rests on the rules of handling this information. But the storage and access capabilities of the computer will remove the barriers to the specialized knowledge now possessed by the professionals. Take medicine. Already computer programs have been written to aid in diagnosis and help indicate course of treatment. Most preliminary screening, interviewing, and even advice-giving could possibly be performed with physicianless computers. The complexity of the law might likewise be reduced by giving the public low-cost access to legal information. Teaching programs, such as drill-and-practice aids in languages, mathematics, typing, driving, and flying, may remove much of the teaching burden.

Some people have speculated about a society divided into two groups, the haves and the have-nots. The haves, they say, will be the people who give information to or receive information from the computer. The have-nots will be everyone else—the unemployed. While this seems a possible overstatement of things to come, it does stress the importance of your being knowledgeable about computers in whatever career you choose.

Let us turn now to a consideration of careers in computers and data processing.

## Computer Careers: The Hottest Field?

Occasionally reports appear concerning a possible oversupply of people in certain occupations—too many lawyers, for instance. Could this same thing ever happen in the computer and data processing field?

**The have-nots.** A General Motors auto worker, laid off from GM's Fremont, Calif., plant. Computers and robots have transformed the automobile industry.

Until 1982, people with experience in this area were virtually assured of being able to find a job, but the recession in that year changed the picture, with less hiring and slower salary increases. Still, the outlook through the rest of the decade seems promising. Whereas in 1980 1.5 million people were in the computer industry, by 1990, according to the U.S. Bureau of Labor Statistics, there will be 2 million. The average projected increase for all occupations during this period will be 17.1 to 25.3 percent, with some occupations even higher: programmers will increase by 28 to 49 percent, says the bureau, and systems analysts by 50 percent.

But, you may wonder, can this last? In time, advanced software may reduce the need for skilled programmers. Corporate dissatisfaction with three-year backlogs in DP departments—backlogs that exist because everything must go through programmers—may lead companies eventually to eliminate the programming function, some suggest. Instead, users may turn to microcomputers and packaged software to fill their needs. At the present time, however, the majority opinion is that computer careers are a seller's market for experienced personnel and will remain so for some time.

There are probably at least three reasons for this situation:

**More Computers** In 1970, there were 100,000 computers in use in the United States. In 1978, there were six times that many. And it is estimated that by 1985 there will be 3 million personal computers alone. More computers need more people to provide software and services.

**Job Hopping** Because there is such intense competition for their skills, experienced computer and DP people are aware of their value in the marketplace. Thus, there is a lot of moving from job to job. In fact, it has been estimated that the annual industry turnover rate is about 35 percent. The average expected length of service for a programmer is 18 months. Salary is not the only reason for job hopping, however. Forward-looking computer people are also apt to make changes whenever they feel themselves in danger of falling behind in job skills.

**Education Lag** There has been a phenomenal increase in DP education programs, and the number may well double throughout the rest of this decade. But though the American educational system continues to turn out numerous liberal arts graduates, training in computer science and data processing lags behind.

The problem of training future DPers is also aggravated by the erosion of faculty in computer and data processing departments, as faculty members are lured by industry into challenging, high-paid positions. This "brain drain" from universities and colleges is apt to continue. Another troublesome factor is maintaining state-of-the-art computer equipment in the face of tightening educational budgets.

The acute shortage of experienced computer and data processing personnel, particularly programmers, is regarded by many industry

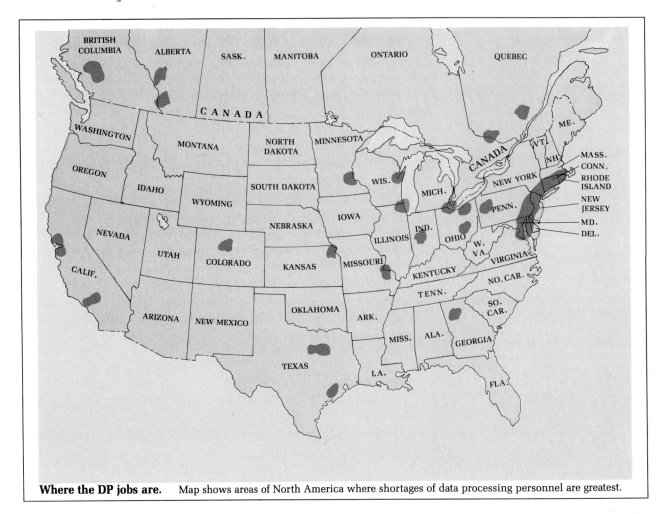

**Where the DP jobs are.**   Map shows areas of North America where shortages of data processing personnel are greatest.

executives as the biggest single problem facing them today. If, as U.S. Department of Commerce statistics show, 46 percent of the nation's gross national product is derived from information activities, then we are clearly in trouble if we cannot provide the people power to direct our information-intensive society.

Let us now examine some of the positions available and where they may take you.

## Positions in the Computer Industry

There are a great many jobs related to computers, so many, in fact, that in this chapter we can touch on only a segment of them. We will not discuss mechanical engineers, for instance, or technical draftsmen or some of the others shown in Figure 17-1. Rather, we are concerned here principally with positions related to computer-produced information—namely, data entry person, computer operator,

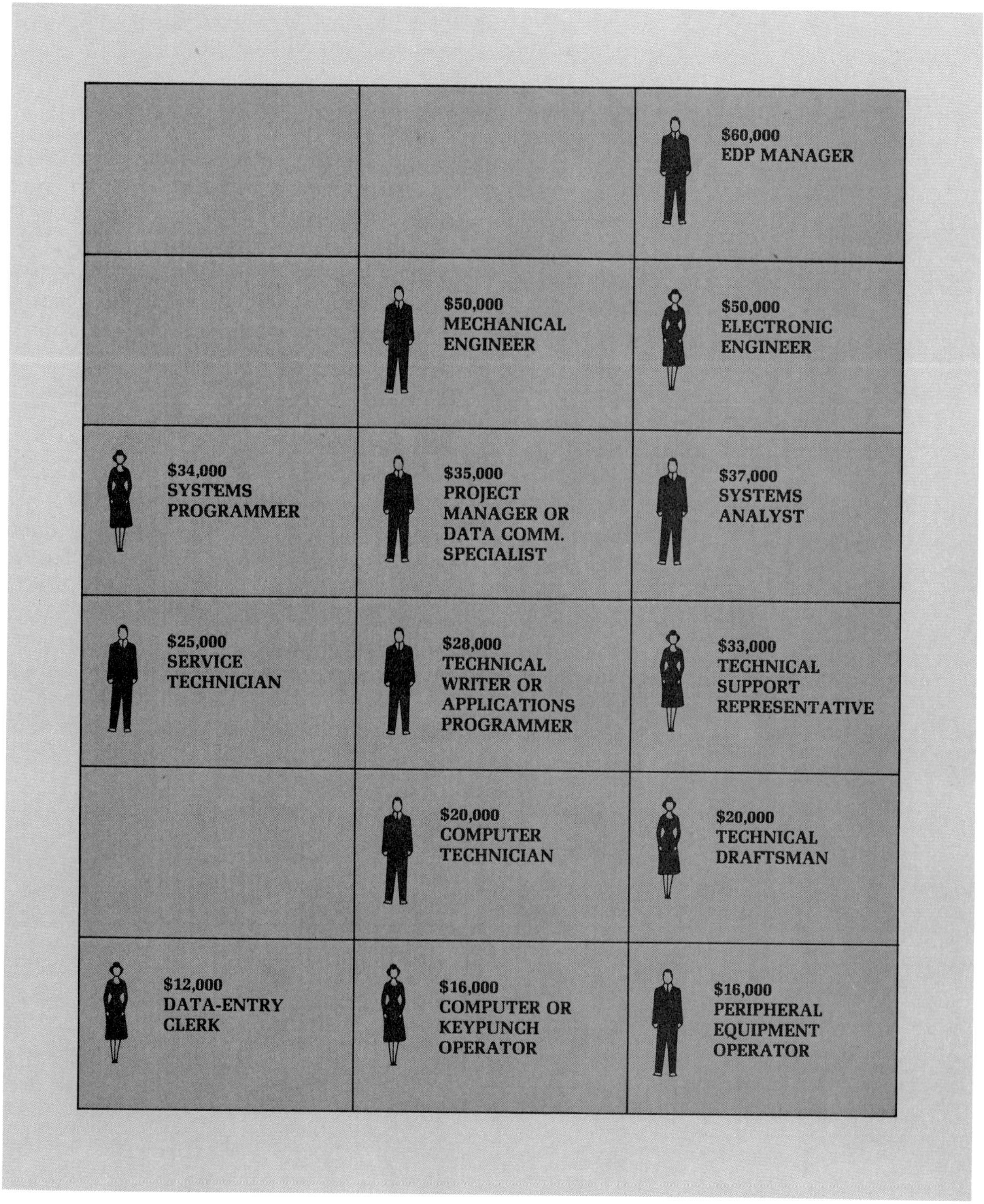

**Figure 17-1  Computer careers from bottom to top.** As this chart shows, job descriptions in computing range from data entry clerks and computer operators all the way up to data processing managers and highly trained engineers and analysts. The figures given for each position represent average maximum salaries. Actual compensation figures will vary among different companies and different parts of the country.

computer librarian, programmer, systems analyst, and manager. These are traditional positions in the data processing area that you may either be attracted to yourself or find yourself in contact with.

### Data Entry Operator

As we saw early in the book, a **data entry operator** transcribes data into a form suitable for processing by the computer. This transcription may be done on keypunching equipment, but with the decline in the use of punched cards, most data entry currently takes place on key-to-tape or key-to-disk equipment. Except for good typing skills, no formal education is necessary. A high school diploma usually is adequate. Many data entry operators are expanding their skills into careers in word processing.

### Computer Operator

A **computer operator** is a person who actually works with the computer (see Figure 17-2). The operator prepares equipment to run jobs, mounts and removes tapes or disks, and sometimes trouble-shoots programs or hardware during operation. Operator jobs are found in places ranging from the small shop to large installations. The education needed depends on the job. Few computer operators have college degrees; most receive formal education in junior college or technical school, followed by on-the-job training.

Operators are not just button pushers. They must be able to work closely with many people, including programmers, systems analysts,

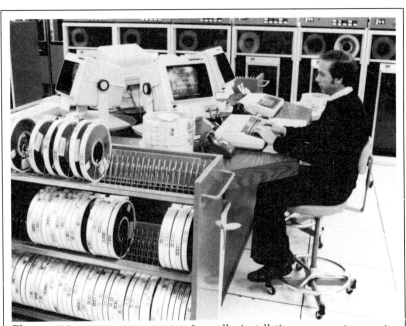

**Figure 17-2  A computer operator.** In smaller installations, a computer operator may also be a programmer.

and managers. They must have technical knowledge of the equipment—enough to keep it running—and be able to work with equipment engineers. They must be knowledgeable in many areas of data processing and know how to discuss program problems—perhaps relaying information over the phone in the middle of the night to the programmer. A good computer operator, in short, is worth his or her weight in gold.

### Computer Librarian

A **librarian** also has an important job because this person is guardian of stored data and programs. Although a high school education usually is sufficient to become a librarian, the person needs to have a basic knowledge of data processing concepts. The job consists mainly of controlling and maintaining program and data files, which are stored in the library on tapes or disks; maintaining records; weeding out old files; and preventing unauthorized persons from gaining access to data and programs.

### Programmer

**Figure 17-3    A programmer.**

Programmers are generally either applications programmers or systems programmers. **Applications programmers** (see Figure 17-3) write programs to solve specific problems for users. In general, when you hear a reference to a programmer, it means an applications programmer. **Systems programmers** are concerned with designing, developing, and maintaining system software: supervisors, control programs, utility programs, translators, and so forth. A college degree is desirable but not always essential for starting a career in computer programming. Many applications programmers have had only a few months' training or have attended community or technical colleges where programming is taught. Systems programmers, however, often have a degree in computer science.

According to industry statistics, about three-fourths of the work done by programmers involves maintenance of existing programs rather than development of new programs. Programmers performing these duties are classified in many ways. An entry-level programmer may be called a *trainee* and may then move to the classification of *junior programmer*. Other applicable names used, as a programmer moves up the organization, are *associate programmer*, *staff programmer*, *lead programmer*, and *senior programmer*. The senior programmer title is reserved for those who are very strong technically. These titles and the associated responsibilities vary somewhat among installations. Smaller organizations may use only a few such titles. Although many people remain programmers throughout their entire careers, others use the occupation as a springboard to a variety of positions. Typical positions to move to from programming are systems analyst, vendor, and technical specialist in an area such as graphics or data bases.

### Systems Analyst

We explained in considerable detail in Chapter 9 what a systems analyst does, but to repeat briefly here: A **systems analyst** (see Figure 17-4) analyzes, designs, implements, and evaluates computer-based information systems. The analyst is the link between the user, or an organization's higher management, and the computer programmers. In some organizations, the programmer and systems analyst are combined in one position, the programmer/analyst.

A programmer may become a systems analyst. Sometimes a person even begins his or her career as a systems analyst. In either case, an analyst will have the best advantage with a formal education in computer science, data processing, mathematics, management, economics, or accounting. A good systems analyst, as we mentioned in the earlier chapter, not only needs to be knowledgeable about data processing and about the organization's structure and objectives, but also must be a good planner, organizer, and communicator. A systems analyst must be capable of working with a variety of different people.

**Figure 17-4  A systems analyst,** right, discusses conversion to a new computer system with a manager. The conversion schedule appears behind them on the wall.

### Manager

All computer organizations need **managers** at various levels. The nature of the hierarchical organization and the accompanying titles vary from one organization to another. Common self-descriptive titles are data entry manager, operations manager, software development manager, and so forth.

Programmers will most commonly associate with a team leader or a project leader. A **team leader** functions primarily as a technical leader; nevertheless, he or she assumes some management responsibilities for continuing progress. A **project leader,** often called a project manager, is usually concerned exclusively with the organization, control, and progress of a specific software project involving many people. The positions of team leader and project manager are not considered permanent; they vary as the projects vary.

The **information systems manager (ISM)** manages all of an organization's information resources. A management information system may be defined as a computer-based system that is used to provide accurate information to managers to help in decision making. A person in this job will need to have a college degree, most likely in business administration, perhaps with a concentration in the area of management information systems. This person need not be computer-oriented, although some computer-related experience will be necessary. But an ISM is first and foremost a *manager.* That means he or she is a generalist rather than a technical expert, a handler of people and their grievances, a manager of budgets and costs.

### Career Directions

The world of computer technology is constantly emerging and expanding, giving rise to a host of areas in which one might specialize: data base management, computer graphics, data communications, computer security, auditing. These are five examples, but there are many others.

Some computer professionals, either by design or default, specialize in a segment of the job market. Computer-related jobs are particularly plentiful in information industries such as banking and insurance. It is common for an individual to move, for example, from one banking job to another; this person would be specializing, in effect, in the banking aspects of the computer industry. Other computer professionals prefer working for computer vendors. They are essentially acting in a sales capacity, seeking out customers for computer products, whether hardware, software, or services.

The phenomenon of microcomputer-related jobs has expanded the market considerably. Rather than pursuing a traditional computer job market such as business or aerospace, an individual could join one of the many small firms built around the use of small computers. Microcomputers have also introduced, as we have mentioned before, a variety of home-based job possibilities.

Some career counselors speak of "career paths" within the computer industry. This sort of planning used to be relatively simple—for example, programmer to systems analyst to project leader. Today, however, this type of planning has become complicated by the large number of options open to computer professionals.

## THE ENTRY-LEVEL PROBLEM: DON'T JUST STUDY PROGRAMMING

*Business Week* [in 1982] revealed that there was a glut of programmers in the job market. Personnel agencies agreed that they had few listings for beginning programmers. *Business Week* accounted for the glut by noting that over 50,000 would-be programmers had completed their training and were looking for entry-level jobs.

Yet at the same time, said *Business Week*, experienced programmers were in short supply. The real message . . . was that those applicants who found entry-level positions were the ones who had found full- or part-time jobs during their training.

"There's a real imbalance in the market," says personnel expert Bob Kvaal. He counsels first-time job hunters to find a way to draw on other experience. "For example, a job candidate might have previous publishing or marketing experience and be able to put it together with computers. Some firms are willing to compromise on technical talents if the candidate has other skills they need," he adds.

Karen Rubin, editor and publisher of *Making It*, a national career magazine, agrees with Kvaal. "I advise people to merge computing with things like commodities trading or the travel industry. Every industry has a place for computers, and the strict computer and data processing industries alone can't handle all the hopefuls. Computers will filter through music, law, and the arts."
—Rachael Wrege,
*Popular Computing,*
June 1983#

## Freelancers and Entrepreneurs

The expanding market for computer services has encouraged many computer professionals to go into business for themselves. There are, for instance, many free-lance or **contract programmers,** who are self-employed but sign a contract with a company to provide specific services, usually related to a particular user project. The programmer may contract to produce certain programs for an agreed fee, regardless of the hours actually worked. Such programmers are usually paid a wage higher than the rate paid to salaried programmers for the same kind of work. Many contract programmers like the freedom of working where they wish and controlling their own work hours.

Some independent programmers also have done well by writing programs on their own and then finding companies to market them. The well-known business program called VisiCalc, for instance, was created by two free-lance programmers, then sold to Personal Software (since renamed VisiCorp). Although the market for microcomputer entertainment and educational software is still wide open to freelancers, the business software market is increasingly dominated by large and well-funded companies.

Another path to independence is that taken by **consultants,** such as systems analysts who work for themselves or for small computer-related consulting firms. Consultants enjoy the variety provided by different types of customers, businesses, and applications and by being able to exercise different DP-related skills.

The use of contract or consulting services offers distinct advantages. The client need not pay fringe benefits, and the contracted person is not on the payroll permanently. The advantages to the independent contractor are higher salary, mobility, and variety of work. However, for the freelancer or consultant there are also disadvantages: unstable income, lack of fringe benefits, and the necessity of constantly having to "prove" oneself to an ever-changing audience.

## The Problem of Declining Productivity

A great deal of hand-wringing has been going on about declining productivity, in the United States in general and in the data processing industry in particular. Ever since the Industrial Revolution, national productivity has been rising, usually at about 3 or 4 percent per year. In 1979, however, national productivity slipped down 1.1 percent and has continued to decline since then. Although blue-collar workers have been the target of much criticism, one study found that blue-collar workers actually were 10 percent more productive than white-collar workers—and that office workers dawdle away *50 percent* of the time during an eight-hour day. Productivity, therefore, has become the buzzword for the 1980s.

## *Improving Productivity*

Computer professionals entering the field need to be aware that **productivity**—the combination of lowering the cost of computing services while maintaining acceptable quality and schedules—is the byword of the decade. Thus, they can expect their performance to be watched and measured as never before. How has this come about?

The principal reason is the end-result of the Computer Revolution. Computers have become widely accepted in business and government. The need for software is greater than ever. Therefore, the need for programmers is greater than ever. And that means that *quality* programmers have become a scarce resource. For employers, the problem is thus divided into two parts: (1) how to find good programmers, and (2) how to make better use of the people they have.

One device employers use to find good people is programmer aptitude tests. While overreliance on tests is a constant temptation, employers are generally satisfied that high test scores correlate with good on-the-job performance.

As for employers making better use of the people they already have, there has been a great deal of discussion about how to approach the problem. Some programmers argue that programming is a *creative* activity and, like the output of any kind of art, cannot be measured. But programming activities *will* be measured, if that is what it takes to improve productivity.

Here are some of the methods used for enhancing work output:

- **Structured techniques.** Studies have shown that structured programming techniques, like those discussed in Chapter 10, improve programmer productivity approximately 25 percent.

- **Workstations.** Programmers often work at a desk, using pencil and coding sheets. However, by giving programmers their own workstations—terminals with which they can enter and revise their own code—a great many trips to the data entry place, computer room, and so on, are eliminated.

- **Software aids.** Programmers need not do everything—draw flowcharts, write reports, and so on—from scratch. Software is available to assist them with these kinds of tasks.

- **Management controls.** Structured project management, including design reviews, project status reviews, code inspections—all the techniques we described in Chapter 10—help increase the quality and quantity of a programmer's work.

## 1, 2, 3, TESTING, TESTING. . .

Three companies account for the bulk of the activity in programmer aptitude testing. These are the principal tests used by most managers who wish to prescreen programmer applicants:

- Science Research Associates, Inc., produces the Computer Programmer Aptitude Battery, which is scored by managers themselves.

- Psychometrics, Inc., has two types of tests, the Berger Test of Programming Proficiency for experienced programmers and the Berger Aptitude for Programming Test.

- Wolfe Computer Aptitude Testing, Ltd., offers the Wolfe-Spence Programming Aptitude Test, the Wolfe Programming Aptitude Test, and the Aptitude Assessment Battery: Programming. Other tests are available for operators, systems programmers, and systems analysts.

• **Employee participation.** Incorporating employee suggestions into management goals can be very helpful in increasing productivity.

### Measuring Productivity

"Productivity," editorialized *Computerworld*, "has become to DP what team spirit has long been to sports: something everybody wants, but nobody knows how to measure." How, indeed, *does* a company determine if it is getting its money's worth and rewarding its productive programmers? How can it estimate programmer time for upcoming projects?

Until recently there have been problems because there has been no way to make comparisons, no units of measure. Companies have tried such systems as CPU hours per program-month or lines of code per programmer per day, but these may not correctly represent the programmer's effort. How many lines of code a programmer generates in a day, for instance, may depend on what language he or she is writing in. Also, it is difficult to know which lines to count—just the executable lines or the comments as well. (We do not wish to discourage the writing of comments.) In addition, some high-level software and nonprocedural languages make counting of lines simply useless. Further, development projects may differ from maintenance work in terms of the effort demanded because the requests of the users and the tasks undertaken vary greatly in size.

One possible measurement system is called **Halstead metrics.** In this system, instead of lines of code being counted, only the number of action statements (such as MOVE or PERFORM) and the number of data elements are counted. Experimentation has shown that there is a correlation between the productivity of a programmer and the sum of action and data statements generated.

Many installations, however, are increasingly using a standard type of measurement that weighs programmers' abilities to meet goals on time and within budget—and weighs them far more heavily than the lines of code they produce.

A discussion of productivity might, at first, seem out of place in a chapter on careers. But most of us are measured all our lives in one form or another. As students, we are measured by grades and test scores. As workers, we are measured by number of hours put in, widgets produced, employees supervised, and so on. Whatever your feelings about the creative aspects of programming, it is clear that your productivity as a programmer and how the productivity is measured will have an important effect on your career.

## Keeping Current —and Keeping Ahead

Your formal education in computers and data processing merely opens the door for you to enter the field. But your education is definitely not at an end. Perhaps it is only beginning.

The increasing rate of technological change makes education an ongoing challenge. A person contemplating a career as a computer professional, therefore, should make a firm commitment to keeping current.

## Ways of Keeping Up

There are a variety of formal and informal ways to keep current in the field:

- **Classes.** Colleges, universities, trade schools, and perhaps even your employer offer classes on topics in which you will probably want to expand your knowledge. Some classes are popular and are not always easy to get into—which may suggest their value to your career. You may also receive formal on-the-job training; that is, go to employer-provided classes during business hours.

- **Workshops and seminars.** Less formal than classes, these may be held evenings or weekends. These sessions are often sponsored by a local chapter of some professional association. Often they will feature speakers accomplished in a particular specialty; for example, a noted authority may present a Saturday seminar on structured design.

- **Conventions and exhibitions.** Also usually sponsored by professional associations are conventions and exhibitions at which professionals present papers, new equipment and software are demonstrated, and various specialists meet.

- **Magazines, books, and television.** Any topic you would care to read about has its own magazine. There are a couple of dozen magazines, for instance, relating to microcomputers alone. Professional organizations often produce their own journals. Perhaps the most widely read industry publication is *Computerworld*, published as a weekly newspaper. In addition to computer industry news, the publication also features in-depth reports on various subjects called, naturally, "In Depth." For greater in-depth treatment, there are published books. Even television can be useful occasionally; *Computerworld* sponsors a series on the world of computers.

- **Professional associations.** Becoming a member of professional associations helps you to stay current through the workshops and conferences they sponsor, and also enables you, in the course of attending regular meetings, to meet other people with the same interests. Several of these associations, notably the Association for Computing Machinery and the Data Processing Management Association, encourage the formation of student chapters.

## The Certificate in Data Processing

The **Certificate in Data Processing (CDP)** is a recognition of achievement in the computing and data processing industry. Holders of this

## ALPHABET SOUP: PROFESSIONAL ORGANIZATIONS

Some of the principal professional societies are as follows:

- *AFIPS.* The American Federation of Information Processing Societies is an umbrella-like federation of professional organizations (some of which follow) interested in information processing.

- *ACM.* The Association for Computing Machinery is the largest society devoted to developing information processing as a discipline. Among other journals, it publishes Communications of the ACM and ACM Computing Surveys.

- *ASM.* The Association for Systems Management is concerned with keeping members current on developments in systems management and information processing. It publishes the *Journal of Systems Management.*

- *AWC.* The Association of Women in Computing is open to female and male career professionals interested in promoting the entry and advancement of women in data processing.

- *DPMA.* The Data Processing Management Association, one of the largest of the professional societies in this field, is open to all levels of data processing personnel and seeks to encourage high standards and a professional attitude toward data processing.

- *ICCA.* Independent Computer Consultants Association is a nonprofit association of independent DP business people. It publishes the *National Directory of Computing and Consulting Services.*

## HOW TO BREAK INTO DATA PROCESSING

Laura Steibel Sessions, in *How to Break Into Data Processing* (Englewood Cliffs, N.J.: Prentice-Hall, 1982), offers advice on how to break into the DP job market. Excerpted and condensed, here are 10 tips on how to get your first job as a programmer:

- *Get the proper training.* This can be a four-year degree, a two-year degree or a certificate from a technical training school. Whichever method you choose must include advanced studies in at least one or more programming languages. The choice of languages should be based on their popularity in the local area.

- *Analyze your background and training and compare it with the competition.* Choose five accomplishments that can illustrate what makes you a good data processing career candidate. These five accomplishments will become your sales points. Remember, the competition doesn't have on-the-job programming experience either, so the only differences are going to be in attitude and past work experience.

- *Be determined.* Know exactly what position you want. Study the field so that you will understand what responsibilities go with each position.

- *Prepare a solid and informative resume, one that expresses your background in its most favorable light.* A resume gives you approximately two minutes to convince a manager to permit an interview. Therefore, add everything that will help make a positive impression. Don't exaggerate your skills. Exaggeration may get an interview, but it will never help get or keep the job.

- *Write an eye-catching cover letter.* Explain why your product is superior to the competition's. Use accomplishments to illustrate the benefits and features of your experience. A resume is a good place to tell what you have accomplished, but the cover letter is where you explain why these accomplishments make you best suited for the job.

- *Plan an organized job search.* Use your background. For example, if you have worked in retail, apply to retail data processing shops. Don't ignore whatever makes you unique. Also, plan job strategies the night before—what letters to write, telephone calls to make—and stick to them.

- *Apply to true hiring managers.* Call to find out the name of the data processing manager and write a personal letter. This is far more effective, especially in small and medium-size companies, than strictly applying to personnel departments.

- *Accept all interviews and consider every job offer.* You can never turn down an offer you haven't received.

- *Sell yourself in the interview.* No manager has ever learned anything about a candidate through osmosis. Tell the interviewer why you should be hired and what you can do for the company. For technical interviews, if you don't know the answer, don't fake it. Tell the truth, but in a positive way. Stress that you are eager to learn and are able to learn quickly.

- *Finally, dress professionally.* Data processing is a sensitive area. Companies do not want to hire a person who looks like a loser and give that person intimate access to the company files.

*—Computerworld,*
*September 20, 1982*

---

certificate (see Figure 17-5) have shown that they have attained certain standards of training and excellence and are presumably more attractive to employers than other applicants for a given position.

The CDP, which is sponsored by the Institute for Certification of Computer Professionals (ICCP), is granted on completion of a five-part examination. Candidates for the exam must have five years of work experience in computer-based information systems; college-level academic work may be substituted for two years' experience. The examination has five sections: (1) data processing equipment, (2) computer programming and software, (3) principles of management, (4) quantitative methods (accounting and finance, mathematics, statistics), and (5) systems analysis and design.

An announcement and study guide regarding the CDP examination is available from the Testing Office, Institute for Certification of Computer Professionals, 304 East 45th Street, New York, N.Y. 10017.

## *Careering*

You cannot just be competent in the technical skills. As the box makes clear, you also have to be competent in communication skills. In addition, you must become competent in a skill not often formally taught—finding out where good jobs are and learning how to interview for them and obtain offers of employment. For this, it is important to consult sources outside the computing field. For more on computer and DP jobs, see the selected references at the end of this chapter.

**Figure 17-5 The Certificate in Data Processing.** This certificate attests that a person has had several years of work experience and has passed a rigorous examination. Holders may enter the abbreviation CDP after their names.

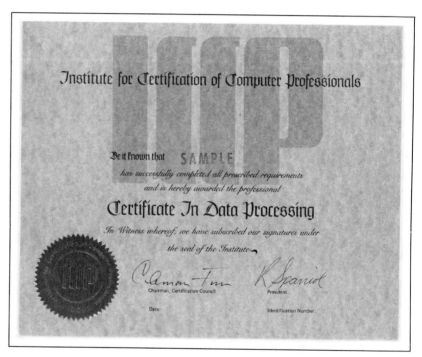

Institute for Certification of Computer Professionals

Be it known that    SAMPLE

has successfully completed all prescribed requirements and is hereby awarded the professional

Certificate In Data Processing

In Witness whereof, we have subscribed our signatures under the seal of the Institute

Chairman, Certification Council          President

Date:                    Identification Number:

## *Summary and Key Terms*

- Most jobs will be changed in some way by the Computer Revolution during the next 10 years. Even the professions, such as law and medicine, which are based on knowledge of specialized information, could be altered because computer storage and access will give more persons access to information now possessed by professionals.

- There is a shortage of experienced computer personnel for probably three reasons: (1) There are more computers—six times as many in the United States in 1978 as there were in 1970; (2) experienced computer and DP people hop from job to job, so there is an estimated 35 percent annual industry turnover; and (3) training in computer science and data processing lags behind industry need.

- Among the many computer industry jobs available are the following. (1) **Data entry operators** transcribe data into a form suitable for processing by the computer. (2)

**Computer operators** prepare equipment to run jobs and otherwise work directly with computers. (3) **Computer librarians** are guardians of programs and data files stored on cards, tapes, or disks. (4) Programmers are either **applications programmers,** who write programs to solve specific problems for specific users, or **systems programmers,** who are concerned with designing, developing, and maintaining system software. Programmers may be entry-level trainees; junior programmers; associate, staff, or lead programmers; or, at the top in technical skills, senior programmers. (5) **Systems analysts** analyze, design, implement, and evaluate computer-based information system. (6) **Managers** may be data-entry managers, operations managers, software development managers, and so on. **Team leaders** are technical leaders of programming teams; they have some management responsibilities. **Project leaders** are concerned with the organization and progress of a specific software project involving many people. The **information systems manager (ISM)** manages all of an organization's information resources.

- Careers in computing and data processing may take many directions. There are specializations in such areas as data base management, computer graphics, data communications, computer security, and auditing. There are computer-related jobs in information industries such as banking and insurance. Some people specialize in microcomputers. Many people work for computer vendors in positions such as sales. Other people free-lance, among them **contract programmers** and **consultants,** such as systems analysts, who work for themselves or consulting firms.

- There is a great deal of concern in the computer industry about improving **productivity**—the combination of lowering the cost of computing services while maintaining acceptable quality and schedules. Employers are faced with having to find good programmers and making good use of the ones they have. Ways to enhance work output include giving programmer aptitude tests, using structured techniques, providing programmers with workstations and software aids, using management controls such as design reviews and code inspections, and incorporating employee suggestions into management goals.

- One way of measuring programmer productivity is to use **Halstead metrics,** in which the number of action statements and number of data elements are counted.

- Ways to keep current in the computing field include attending classes, workshops, seminars, conventions, and exhibitions; staying familiar with new developments through magazines, books, and television; and maintaining membership in professional associations such as the Association for Computing Machinery and the Data Processing Management Association.

- The **Certificate in Data Processing (CDP),** which constitutes recognition of achievement in the computing and data processing industry, is granted by the Institute for Certification of Computer Professionals to candidates who have had five years of work experience in computer-based information systems and who have passed a five-part examination.

## Review

1. Give three possible reasons for the shortage of computer and DP personnel in the United States.

2. What kinds of computer jobs do you think that, with proper training, you could hold a year from now? Three years from now?

3. If you are considering a DP career, what are some of the directions you might like to see it take?

4. Name some ways used to improve productivity in the computer industry.

5. What are Halstead metrics?

6. At what point in your life do you think you could earn a CDP?

## Selected References for Further Reading

Brechner, Irv. *Getting Into Computers: A Career Guide to Today's Hottest New Field.* New York: Ballantine, 1983.

Editors of Consumer Guide. *Computer Careers: Where the Jobs Are and How to Get Them.* New York: Fawcett/Columbine, 1981.

Frank, A. L. *A Guide for Software Entrepreneurs.* Englewood Cliffs, N.J.: Prentice-Hall, 1982.

French, Jack. *Up the EDP Pyramid.* New York: Wiley, 1981.

*Peterson's Annual Guide to Careers and Employment for Engineers, Computer Scientists and Physical Scientists.* Peterson's Guides, P.O. Box 2123, Princeton, N.J. 08540.

Sessions, Laura Steibel. *How to Break Into Data Processing.* Englewood Cliffs, N.J.: Prentice-Hall, 1982.

Silver, A. David. *The Entrepreneurial Life.* New York: Wiley, 1983.

## IN THIS CHAPTER

The crimes called Trojan Horse, salami method, and data diddling are three by-products of the Computer Age. So are security systems, disaster recovery plans, and new protective legislation, all of which are discussed here. Privacy and the safeguarding of personal information have become legitimate worries—and we should all be concerned.

# ch18

# security and privacy

## keeping computers friendly

What if you gained access to your college's computer-produced grading system and were able to raise grades for you and your friends? A student at Queen's College in New York City did exactly that. Suppose that just before leaving a job you hated, you added instructions to a computer program to erase all the company records—two years after you left. Someone actually did that, too. What if you penetrated a railroad's computer system and ordered boxcars sent to a deserted set of tracks, where you could empty their contents at leisure? This was done to 217 boxcars through the Penn Central's computer system.

The security of computers and computer-related information is a critical issue. Let us begin by examining the most fascinating security breaches: computer crime.

## Computer Crime

Stories about computer crime have a lot of appeal. Like good detective stories, they often embody cleverness. They are "clean" white-collar crimes; no one gets physically hurt. They feature people beating the system, making the Big Score against an anonymous, faceless, presumably wealthy organization.

But computer crime is serious business and deserves to be taken seriously by everyone. After all, if computer criminals can steal money from major banks, can they not steal from you? If unauthorized persons can get at your money, can they not also get at your medical records or private family history? It is not a long step between a thief violating your bank account and an unseen "investigator" spying on your private life.

The FBI reports that whereas the average bank robbery involves $3200 and the average bank fraud $23,500, the average computer crime involves *half a million dollars*. No one knows the dollar figure of unreported computer crime, but some estimates put it as high as $3 billion a year. Whatever it is, some judge it to be 20 times the annual take of a decade ago.

Needless to say, the problems of computer crime will only be aggravated by increased access. More employees will have access to computers on their jobs. A great many more people will be using personal computers. And more students will be taking computer training.

### The Computer Criminal: A Profile

Here is what a computer criminal is apt to be like. He (we will use "he" here, but of course he could be "she") is usually someone occupying a position of high trust in the organization. Indeed, he is likely to be regarded as the ideal employee. He has had no previous lawbreaking experience and, in fact, will not see himself as a thief but as a "borrower." He is apt to be young and to be fascinated with the challenge of beating the system. Contrary to people's expectations,

## Student Scofflawry: Watching Out for Your Future

We live in a time and place when, as a *Time* magazine writer put it, "amid outlaw litter, tax cheating, illicit noise and motorized anarchy . . . it seems as though the scofflaw represents the wave of the future." Clearly, any ethic that says, in Harvard sociologist David Riesman's phrase, "You're a fool if you obey the rules" is ultimately dangerous for the society itself. It is probably also dangerous for you.

Jaywalking. Driving too fast. Smoking where there are NO SMOKING signs. How does such a scofflaw attitude manifest itself among students using computers?

There are several such transgressions that many students do not see as being outright lawbreaking, although they certainly are. The most common are:

- *Excessive use of computer time.* There are many cases of people getting access to computers to play games or to do programming or data processing beyond the time they have been officially allowed. "Borrowing" extra computer time does not sound like much, but clearly we would each feel differently if someone "borrowed" our car at night without permission on the excuse that we were not using it anyway. In any case, many educational institutions feel strongly enough about this that students caught stealing computer time automatically flunk their computer course, are liable to expulsion from college, and may even be prosecuted under the law.

- *Illegal copying of software.* Is photocopying a book stealing? Is duplicating an audio cassette tape? Is making an extra floppy disk of microcomputer software? Making a copy for a friend may seem like just a nice thing to do—except that it deprives the originator of the work (book, song, software program, or whatever) of some of the rewards of the fruit of his or her labor. And selling copies, of course, is even worse. It is like the difference between your taking two weeks to write an "A" paper for a course and someone else lifting an old paper out of a fraternity house file to get the same result.

The real question is this: What kind of habits of mind, what kind of approach to life and work, are going to be of benefit in the long run? One can cut corners, manipulate, slide by, "fake it," perhaps even cheat and steal for a long time. Ultimately, though, it is difficult to hide the scofflaw spirit from teachers, friends, employers, and others who matter.

**SUNY/Buffalo.** At State University of New York, computers link three campuses.

he is not necessarily a loner; he may well operate in conjunction with other employees to take advantage of the system's weaknesses.

What motivates him? There is no single cause; the causes can be as varied as the people. However, there is something of a pattern. Perhaps the main motivation is the nature of the crime itself. As we mentioned, it is clean and nonviolent. The crime provides a challenge, but may also be relatively easy to accomplish, fitting right in with his job. The risk is fairly low; the computer criminal thinks he can get away with it. And he does—some of the time.

### Computer Crime Types and Methods

Computer crime basically falls into three categories:

- Theft of computer time for development of software for personal use or with the intention of selling it. It is difficult to prove programs were stolen when copies are made because the originals are still in the hands of the original owners.

- Theft, destruction, or manipulation of programs or data. Such acts may be committed by disgruntled employees or by persons wishing to use another's property for their own benefit.

- Altering data stored in a computer file.

While it is not our purpose to be a how-to book on computer crime, we will mention a few criminal methods as examples. The **Trojan Horse** is the name given to the crime in which a computer criminal is able to place instructions in someone else's program that allow the program to function normally but to perform additional, illegitimate functions as well. The **salami method** describes an embezzlement technique that gets its name from taking a "slice" at a time. The salami technique came into its own with computers—the taking of a little bit at a time, such as a few cents from many bank accounts. Obviously, this activity was not worth the effort in precomputer days. **Data diddling** is a technique whereby data is modified before it goes into the computer file. Once in the file, it is not as visible.

### Discovery and Prosecution

Prosecuting the computer criminal is difficult because discovery is often difficult. The nature of the crime is such that it is hard to detect, and thus many times it simply goes undetected. In addition, crimes that are detected are—an estimated 85 percent of the time—never reported to the authorities. By law, banks have to make a report when their computer systems have been compromised, but other businesses do not. Often they choose not to report because they are worried about their reputations and credibility in the community.

Most computer crimes, unfortunately, are discovered by accident. For example, a programmer changed a program to add ten cents to every customer service charge under $10 and one dollar to every charge over $10. He then placed this overage into the last account, a bank account he opened himself in the name of Zzwicke. The system worked fairly well, generating several hundred dollars each month, until the bank initiated a new marketing campaign in which they singled out for special honors the very first depositor—and the very last. In another instance, some employees of a city welfare department created a fictitious work force, complete with social security numbers, and programmed the computer to issue paychecks, which the employees would then intercept and cash. They were discovered when a police officer found 7100 fraudulent checks in an illegally parked overdue rental car.

Even if a computer crime is detected, prosecution is by no means assured. There are a number of reasons for this. First, law enforcement agencies do not fully understand the complexities of computer-related fraud. Second, few attorneys are qualified to handle computer crime cases. Third, judges and juries are not educated in the ways of computers and may not consider data valuable. They may see the computer as the villain and the computer criminal as the hero. (Computer criminals often tend to be much like those trying to prosecute them—the same age, educational background, and social status—and may even be high up in the company and friends of top management.) Finally, the laws in many states do not adequately define computer crime.

This last point is illustrated by a famous case in which two programmers stole $244,000 worth of their employer's computer time in order to rescore music for a private business they were operating on the side. The law under which they were convicted? Mail fraud. It was the best criminal law the prosecutor could find that would apply. Although the common notion of larceny is taking goods belonging to another with the intention of depriving the owner of them permanently, this definition is not well suited to the theft of computer time. Time is not a tangible object, and it is difficult to determine its market value.

In short, the chances of committing computer crimes and having them go undetected are, unfortunately, good. And the chances that, if detected, there will be no ramifications are also good: a computer criminal may not go to jail, may not be found guilty if prosecuted, and may not even be prosecuted. You can be sure, however, that this will not be tolerated for long. One example of the countermeasures being taken is the four-week training school offered by the FBI in computer crime; the hundreds of agents that have passed through the school are now in FBI offices throughout the country.

## What Price Security?

As you can see from the previous section, it is clear that the computer industry has been extremely vulnerable in the matter of security. Until fairly recently, computer security meant the physical security of the computer itself—guarded and locked doors. But locking up and isolating the computer by no means restricts access, as we have seen. Since the mid-1970s, management interest in security has been heightened, and DP managers are now rushing to purchase more sophisticated security products. Everyone is aware that such security is not going to come cheap. Indeed, it is going to cost a lot of money—perhaps $23 billion will be spent on security devices by the computer industry by 1985.

What is security? We may define it as follows: **security** is a system of safeguards designed to protect a computer system and data from deliberate or accidental damage or access by unauthorized persons. That means safeguarding the system against such threats as burglary, vandalism, fire, natural disasters, theft of data for ransom, industrial espionage, and various forms of white-collar crime, as touched on before.

## Who Goes There?
## Authorized Versus Unauthorized People

How does a computer system detect whether you are the person who should be allowed to have access to it? It goes by one of three criteria:

- What you know. *- password - typed into keyboard*
- What you have. *- badge, card*
- What you are. *- fingerprints, facial features*

What you *know* usually involves a **password**—the secret words or numbers that must be typed in on the keyboard before the system will allow any activity to take place. Or it involves some sort of combination of cipher locks, sort of like the numbers on a safe.

What you *have* is normally some sort of badge or card that, after being shown to a security guard, lets you into a company's secured area. Or it may be the magnetized kind that, for example, gains you access to an automated teller machine.

What you *are* is a category that is becoming more and more interesting. Consider **biometrics,** defined as the measurement of individual body characteristics. By concentrating on a part of a person's body that is unique and unchanging, a security system can use that as a means of identification that cannot easily be faked. Fingerprints, of course, are one such unique identifier. In France, researchers have devised a system that records the size and shape of an ear; other systems rely on a person's eyes and facial structure. An example of how a biometric system might work is an automatic cash machine, in which you might first type in your identification number, then place your finger into a small slot in which a laser light scans your fingerprint. Needless to say, there may be some problems with public acceptance of such devices. Fingerprinting, for instance, carries associations of criminality and wrongdoing to many people.

## Security and What to Secure

In Italy, armed terrorists singled out corporate and state computer centers as targets for attack, and during a 10-month period bombed 10 such centers throughout the country. In the United States, industrial espionage has been on the rise; in a famous case, IBM security people helped the FBI arrest employees of two leading Japanese electronics firms, who were charged with conspiring to transport stolen IBM property out of the U.S. The point is that computer and DP installations can be struck by disaster, can have their security violated. What kinds of problems might the organization have?

Your first thoughts might be of the hardware, the computer and its related equipment. The actual loss of the hardware is not a major problem in itself; the loss will be covered by insurance and can be replaced. A key factor is the loss of processing ability during the time it takes to find a substitute facility and, later, to return the installation to its former state. The ability to continue processing data is critical. Some information industries, such as banking, could literally go out of business in a matter of days if their operations were suspended.

Probably a more important problem is the loss of data. Imagine trying to reassemble lost or destroyed master files of customer records, accounts receivable, or design data for a new airplane. The costs would be staggering. We consider data security in more detail in another couple of pages. First, however, let us present an overview of disaster recovery.

### Disaster Recovery Plans

Every cruise ship holds a lifeboat drill for its passengers the first or second day out. But how many companies hold disaster recovery drills for disrupted computer or data processing operations? Certainly every company should.

A **disaster recovery plan** is a scheme for providing smooth, rapid restoration of critical data processing operations in the event of physical destruction or major damage that has caused an interruption in that processing. In some organizations, a disaster recovery planning team is designated, since no one person has all the expertise that will be needed. Users of the computer system are normally included in the team. The members of the team establish priorities, that is, decide which parts of the system are critical and must be maintained.

In anticipation of a disaster such as a flood, hurricane, or earthquake damaging the organization's computer equipment and data, the team would determine the following:

- *Which application programs must be up and running first.* Since information is a corporate asset, this is a crucial decision. For instance, a bank would treat the processing of customer loans very carefully.

- *Personnel requirements.* Procedures must be established to notify company personnel during a disaster and to set up an assignment schedule, so that employees would know what their "battle stations" were.

- *Equipment requirements.* The team needs to determine what equipment would be needed and where it could be obtained if the company's own equipment was destroyed. This includes the computer itself, hardware for capturing data, and communications equipment.

- *Facilities needed.* The team must map out what buildings, floor space, air conditioning equipment, and the like would be needed, both temporarily and with an eye to rebuilding.

- *Supplies needed.* The team needs to decide what paperwork and forms would be needed to keep the organization going through the disaster recovery period.

- *Input and output distribution.* The team must determine how data is gathered, how critical reports are distributed, and the like.

Some companies have joined others in consortiums to support complete computer setups that currently go unused but that will be available in the event of disaster. A typical configuration has flooring, power, communications network, and disk drives, as well as a computer. These disaster recovery centers are tested on a regular basis. The disadvantage of such a system to the potential user is the cost—typically $1000 to $5000 a month, depending on what is available. Such disaster recovery sites may be of two types: hot sites or cold sites. **Hot sites** are fully equipped computer centers, with fire protection, security, telecommunication capabilities, and so on. **Cold sites** are basically empty shells in which a company may install its own computer, but the shell comes equipped with enough power, water cooling, and air conditioning with which to run a mainframe.

Other companies have joined forces in mutual aid pacts. They agree to lend each other computer time and facilities if one member is stricken by disaster. These arrangements have drawbacks, however. The computer facility that is physically convenient for the assisting company may not be convenient for the company being helped, which would lead to problems in moving personnel. Sharing facilities may be difficult; a company used to serving its customers on a real-time basis during the day may find itself severely handicapped if confined to another company's nighttime computer slack period. Finally, if the companies in the mutual aid pact are geographically close together, there is the possibility that a natural disaster could knock out everyone's computer facilities.

Whatever disaster recovery plan is formulated, a company's DP management is well advised to prepare a storage area away from the main computer facility. This facility will house such necessities as program and operating systems documentation, program listings, master and transaction files, hardware inventory, and the disaster plan manual. The off-site storage place can also be used to keep backup copies of other important documents and files.

### Software Piracy, Copyrights, and Other Security Matters

A pirate need not have an eyepatch and a knife between his teeth. He (or she) need only have a buccaneer's ethics and some skill at duplicating other people's property.

It happens all the time in the software industry, and it is a major problem. A skilled programmer develops a novel software product at one company, which is enthusiastically received in the marketplace; then the programmer moves on down the road to another company, which—surprise!—soon produces a very similar kind of software that it offers for a lower price. Or the Able Company gives the Baker Company a nontransferable license to use its software for internal use only—but then subsequently discovers that the Charlie Company is selling a remarkably similar software product at a lower price. It turns out the Charlie Company thought it owned the software because it had "purchased" it from the Baker Company.

Most of us would agree that this kind of piracy—really, outright fraud and theft—is dishonest. But what about when a microcomputer users' group buys one copy of a program and duplicates it for all 50 members of the group? ("It's easy to steal games," one such group member said, "without feeling that you have done anything wrong.") Or, for those who thrive on solving puzzles, what about the computer hobbyists who break the software protection codes that some software companies put into their products to prevent duplication? ("Cracking the copy protection is where the fun is," said one such person. "It's a puzzle more than anything else. They put in the copy protection routines and I try to crack them. Everybody's into puzzles. I just don't care for crosswords.") Except for the dollar amounts involved, there is no essential difference among the four kinds of piracy described above.

The issue of software security has been an industry topic for years. It was first posed as a question: Who owns a program? Is the owner the person who writes a program or the company for whom the author wrote the program? What is to prevent a programmer from taking listings of programs from one job to another? Or, even simpler, what is to prevent any user from copying microcomputer software onto a floppy disk or cassette?

These thorny questions do, however, have answers. The program belongs to the organization, not the programmer. What is more, according to a recent U.S. Supreme Court decision, software can be patented. The last questions, unfortunately, also have easy answers: Very little can be done to prevent the stealing of microcomputer software. Although it is specifically prohibited by law in some states, software continues to be copied as blatantly as music from tape to tape.

The **Copyright Act of 1976** states that flowcharts, source code, and assembly code are copyrightable. Object code has been held by the courts to be copyrightable also. In 1983 a bill was introduced in Congress, the Computer Software Piracy and Counterfeiting Amendment, that would increase the fines and imprisonment imposed on those convicted of infringing the copyrights of computer programs and data bases. The new penalties would be a *minimum* of five years in prison and/or a $250,000 fine.

Among the devices being tried by employers to restrict software piracy are (1) the requirement that employees with access to software execute security agreements, which establish contractual obligations; (2) the restriction of software distribution to those with licenses; and (3) the restriction of access to source code listings and other confidential information to employees with (in that military phrase) "need to know."

### Data Security

We have discussed the security of hardware and software. Now let us consider the security of data, which, as we said, is one of an organization's most important assets. Here too there must be planning for security. Usually, this is done by security officers who are part of top management. There are five critical planning areas for data security:

- Determination of appropriate policies and standards. A typical statement of policy might read: "All computer data and related information will be protected against unauthorized disclosure and against alteration or destruction."

- Development and implementation of security safeguards.

- Inclusion of new security precautions at the development stage of new automated systems.

- Review of state and federal laws related to security.

- Maintenance of historical records associated with computer abuse.

What steps can be taken to prevent theft or alteration of data? There are several data protection techniques; these will not individually (or even collectively) guarantee security, but at least they make a good start.

**Secured Waste** Thrown-away printouts, printer ribbons, and the like can be sources of information to unauthorized persons. This kind of waste can be made secure by the use of shredders or locked trash barrels.

**Passwords** As we mentioned earlier, passwords are the secret words or numbers that must be typed on the keyboard to gain access to the system. In some installations, however, the passwords are changed so seldom that they become well known to many people. Data protection systems change passwords often and also compartmentalize information by passwords, so that only authorized persons can have access to certain data.

**Internal Controls** Making internal controls an integral part of the computer system can also prevent security breaches. An example of internal controls is a transaction log. This is a file of all accesses or attempted accesses to certain data.

*[Handwritten margin notes:]*
*Steps prevent theft / alteration*
*1) Shred waste*
*2) Compartmentalized pass words*
*3) Internal controls as part of the computer system*
*4) Auditor checks of data*
*5) Cryptography - coded messages*
*6) Applicant screening - verify facts as presented in resume*
*7) Separation of employee functions*
*8) Built in software protection*
*9) Changing codes for programs*

**Auditor Checks** Most companies have auditors go over the financial books. In the course of their duties, auditors frequently review computer programs and data. From a data security standpoint, auditors might also check to see who has accessed data during periods when that data is not usually used and who has received unusually high overtime payments. They can also be on the lookout for unusual numbers of correction entries of data, usually a trouble sign.

**Cryptography** For data being sent over telecommunications lines, protection may be obtained by scrambling the messages, that is, putting them in code that can be broken by the person receiving the message but not by an unauthorized interceptor. The American National Standards Institute has endorsed a process called **Data Encryption Standard (DES),** a standardized public key by which senders and receivers can scramble and unscramble their messages. Although the DES has been broken, companies still use it because the method makes it quite expensive to intercept coded messages, forcing interlopers to use other methods of gathering data that carry greater risk of detection. Actually, the number of companies using encryption packages is small—under 400—and most employ them simply to avoid losing money, as with automated teller machines. Perhaps one reason there are so few users is that the stigma attached to being victimized is so great that people are reluctant to admit they have been victimized, and so others do not realize there is a need for encryption devices.

**Applicant Screening** The weakest link in any computer security system is the people in it. At the very least, employers should, during the hiring process, verify the facts that job applicants list on their résumés. This precaution would seem to be obvious, but it is remarkable how often employment applications go unchecked.

**Separation of Employee Functions** Should a programmer also be a computer operator? That would put him or her in the position of

> **★★WARNING★★**
>
> Use of this device is at your own risk. Unintended listeners can easily intercept your transmission, so you should not discuss or transmit information you would not want others to know. Use of this device releases the manufacturer or this device and the communications carrier from any liability for losses to you as a result of the interception of your transmission by others.

**Caution: This Device May Be Hazardous . . .** The above is a suggested warning label for computer communications devices.

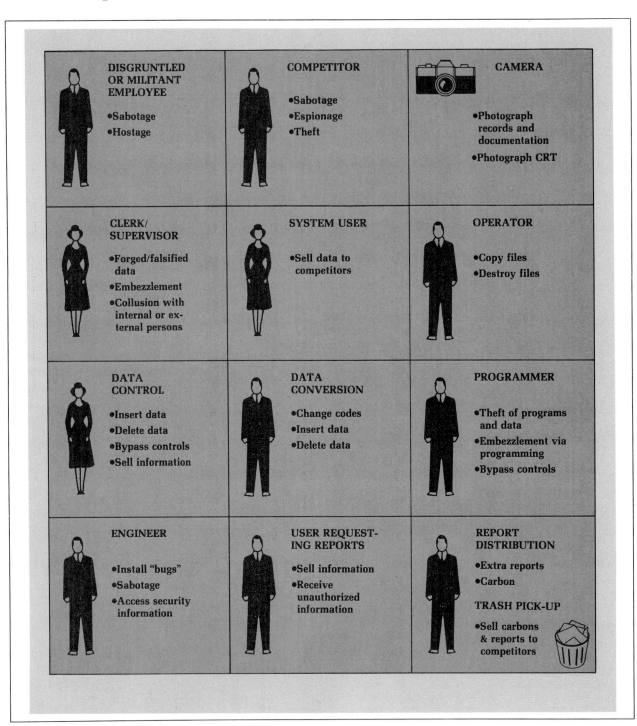

| | | |
|---|---|---|
| **DISGRUNTLED OR MILITANT EMPLOYEE**<br>•Sabotage<br>•Hostage | **COMPETITOR**<br>•Sabotage<br>•Espionage<br>•Theft | **CAMERA**<br>•Photograph records and documentation<br>•Photograph CRT |
| **CLERK/ SUPERVISOR**<br>•Forged/falsified data<br>•Embezzlement<br>•Collusion with internal or external persons | **SYSTEM USER**<br>•Sell data to competitors | **OPERATOR**<br>•Copy files<br>•Destroy files |
| **DATA CONTROL**<br>•Insert data<br>•Delete data<br>•Bypass controls<br>•Sell information | **DATA CONVERSION**<br>•Change codes<br>•Insert data<br>•Delete data | **PROGRAMMER**<br>•Theft of programs and data<br>•Embezzlement via programming<br>•Bypass controls |
| **ENGINEER**<br>•Install "bugs"<br>•Sabotage<br>•Access security information | **USER REQUESTING REPORTS**<br>•Sell information<br>•Receive unauthorized information | **REPORT DISTRIBUTION**<br>•Extra reports<br>•Carbon<br>**TRASH PICK-UP**<br>•Sell carbons & reports to competitors |

**Computer security: people threats and vulnerabilities.** By letting one's imagination run wild, one can visualize numerous ways in which people can compromise computer security. Needless to say, computer-related crime would be far more rampant if all of the people in the above positions took advantage of their access to computers.

being able not only to write unauthorized programs but also to run them. By limiting employee functions so that crossovers are not permitted, a computer organization can restrict the amount of unauthorized access. Unfortunately, separation of functions is not practical in a small shop; usually one or more employees perform multiple functions.

## BOOBY TRAPS FOR SOFTWARE

More than one clever software developer has found the solution to the "check is in the mail" syndrome.

Both to collect payment for software and to guard against piracy, software companies and independent programmers alike are planting "booby traps" in their programs that can bring them to a grinding halt.

The "booby traps" can take either of two forms. The first method involves implanting in the software a clock or timing device that goes off after a certain amount of time has elapsed, causing the software to stop executing; the second is the recurring code method, which stops all processing after a certain sequence has been repeated a predetermined number of times.

In either event, the user must contact his programmer or software house to learn how to get on-line again.

—Susan Blakeney,
*Computerworld,*
July 12, 1982

**Built-in Software Protection** Software can be built into operating systems in ways that restrict access to the computer system. One form of software protection system matches a user budget number against a number assigned to the data being accessed. If a person does not get access, it is recorded that he or she tried to tap into some area that was not authorized. Another form of software protection is a **user profile:** Information is stored about each user, including the files to which the user has legitimate access. The profile contains each person's job function, budget number, skills, areas of knowledge, access privileges, supervisor, and loss-causing potential. These profiles are available for checking if there is any problem, but they may in some ways violate a person's privacy, a subject we shall discuss shortly.

### Reactions to Security

One might wonder about the psychological effects of these security measures on employees. Do they feel threatened, spied upon? As organizations hasten to increase security, there are sometimes cries from those who have been inconvenienced, those who cannot do business quite the way they did before. In one installation, for example, security-conscious managers prohibited the lifting of sections of code from old programs for use in new programs. The managers felt this step would reduce opportunities for tampering with programs. Since "borrowing" code had been a common time-saver, the outraged programmers felt both burdened with extra work and mistrusted by their employers.

However, most computer personnel are aware of the need for security measures, and after a while they become accustomed to the minor inconveniences to themselves. More important, they become aware of the necessity of introducing security concepts into the design and implementation of computer systems.

### Security Legislation

Prosecution of computer crimes has been obstructed by laws that do not reflect the rapidly changing computer technology. Prosecutors are forced to squeeze their cases into existing laws, when it would be more appropriate to have laws relating directly to computer abuses. There have been cases, for example, where juries have puzzled over whether a computer program could really be considered stolen property. If the program was merely copied, and the original owner was not actually deprived of it, was the program really "stolen"?

In 1977, the **Federal Computer System Protection Act,** legislation aimed directly at controlling computer-related crime, was introduced in Congress. This act proposed stiff fines and heavy prison sentences for electronic burglars who misused computers and computer technology. The first section of the bill addressed unauthorized access to computers and data. The second section specifically prohibited unauthorized alteration or destruction of computers, programs, and data.

The bill was worked on for terminology problems through 1978. In 1979, 1980, and 1983, further revisions were discussed, but the bill has not yet been enacted into law. Meanwhile, approximately one-third of the states have enacted their own computer crime laws.

## Privacy: Personal Information for Personal Purposes

No matter how virtuous a life you lead, there are probably some things about it that you would just as soon not share with the world at large: past financial mishaps, youthful indiscretions, sensitive medical matters, unusual (or even usual) beliefs and opinions, embarrassing personal or family relationships, curious habits or tastes, whatever. These are matters you want to keep private. You have the right to do so.

You may, however, need to reveal some parts of your life to people such as your doctor, financial aid officer, or employer. Such information should be distributed in the limited form in which you intended it; that is, it should be kept private. **Privacy** is the assurance to individuals that personal information is used properly and protected against improper access. The question is: In the coming years, can you be assured that such information _will_ remain restricted?

### Data Banks and Other Long Computer Memories

The computer industry has collected a great deal of data. People are concerned about what all that data is, whether it is accurate, who has access to it, and how it is used.

One interesting aspect of the matter is that most of the information was handed over voluntarily. You can appreciate this if you try to recall how many times you have willingly filled out forms whose contents probably ended up in computer files. What you may not know is how much of that information about you was moved into other computer files without your knowledge. The most obvious example of this is the sale of mailing lists. If you subscribe to a fishing magazine, for instance, you will probably find yourself receiving all kinds of direct-mail ads for fishing equipment. (An interesting experiment is to subscribe to a magazine or make a charitable contribution using your name in an uncommon way—for example, using just the initial of your first name but spelling out your middle name, if this is not the way you usually do it—then see what unsolicited mail comes to you addressed in this way.)

Although you can always avoid magazine subscriptions or ask to have your name removed from mailing lists, there are new methods of capturing data about you. Some examples are: data collected from point-of-sale terminals, from teleshopping linked to your living room with two-way cable communications, from electronic banking, and

**The Internal Revenue Service.** Hundreds of workers at the IRS regional center in Memphis, Tenn., one of ten regional centers around the nation, enter data from income tax forms for data processing. Officials say that new computer systems make it harder for taxpayers to cheat on their federal income tax. The Federal Privacy Act states that government agencies cannot simply obtain and store data for no specific purpose.

from personal computer networks. Such methods could provide detailed information about you to various commercial enterprises.

Another area of concern is the many government files that can be correlated by social security number. Even though there has been resistance to identifying each person with his or her social security number, it is used as identification on many files. In 1981, the Reagan administration aroused a storm of protest when it proposed a national data bank that would, for the first time, list the names of the estimated 25 million people on public assistance. The intent of the data bank (which would include a person's name, age, address, social security number, and "benefit status") was to reduce welfare fraud. But critics pointed out that it would create a national surveillance system for keeping track of anyone receiving *any* kind of benefit from the government. It would also have violated existing privacy laws by allowing the government to monitor confidential data on citizens without their consent.

Finally, many people are concerned that erroneous or misleading information fed to data banks can be perpetuated without their knowledge. If you have had to straighten out a "computer error" (almost always a data entry error), it might make you wonder what other kinds of mistakes are in computer files that you do not know about.

Let us see what kind of protection is available to preserve privacy.

### Privacy Legislation

Significant legislation relating to privacy began with the **Fair Credit Reporting Act** in 1970. This law allows you to have access to, and gives you the right to challenge, your credit records. In fact, this access must be given to you free of charge if you have been denied credit.

Businesses will usually contribute financial information about their customers to a community credit bureau, which gives them the right to review a person's prior credit record with other companies. Before the Fair Credit Reporting Act, many people were turned down for credit without explanation because of inaccurate financial records about them. Under the act, people may now check their records (usually for a nominal fee, if they have not been turned down for credit) to make sure they are accurate. The **Freedom of Information Act** was also passed in 1970. This landmark legislation allows ordinary citizens to have access to data gathered by federal agencies (although sometimes a lawsuit has been necessary to pry data loose).

The most significant legislation in the privacy area was the **Federal Privacy Act** of 1974. Born out of post-Watergate fears, the Federal Privacy Act stipulates that there can be no secret personal files, that individuals must be allowed to know what is stored in files about them and how it is used, and that the law applies not only to government agencies but also to private contractors dealing with government agencies. These organizations cannot obtain data willy-nilly, for no specific purpose; they must justify obtaining it.

**Royal Canadian Mounted Police computer room.** All information relating to fingerprint files is being transferred to this system in Ottawa, Ontario, for easier retrieval. A concern of democratic governments is that national data banks not be misused for national surveillance systems.

This act applies to the government and its contractors, but it does not apply to the private sector. However, the last sentence of the act reads. "A commission will be formed to study privacy in the private sector." The resulting Privacy Commission that was formed published a thick document, the heart of which is some basic principles on which to build a privacy act for the private sector. The six basic principles of the Privacy Commission are as follows:

1. *The existence of all personal records must be made public.* Applying this principle to a large organization probably would mean that it would be more trouble locating information stored than notifying that person that a record exists. Enforcement of this principle would encourage centralization of information and better cross-referencing.

2. *The individual must have a way of finding out when information about him or her is stored and how it is used.* The implication of this principle is that all subjects would have to be notified annually of what is in the files about them. An organization would also have to respond to inquiries about the existence of records. (One can imagine the company switchboards lighting up with interested callers wondering if they are in a file.) In addition, companies would have to maintain record usage logs, so that there would be some sort of historical data on what records were used and for what purpose.

3. *Personal information should be used only for its intended purposes.* An organization would have to obtain a person's consent to use or transfer information (which would put a severe crimp in the distribution of mailing lists). An organization would also have to advise people of its obligation to supply data to others, such as W-2 forms to the government.

4. *Individuals must be able to correct or amend records about themselves.* An organization would have to be able to respond to complaints about data accuracy, store the complaints, and make any needed corrections.

5. *Personal information must be obtained in such a way as to ensure that it is complete, accurate, relevant, timely, and secure.* People in the industry refer to this as the CARTS principle, the acronym of these five words.

6. *All uses of personal information should be accounted for by a responsible manager.* This principle implies that there is some one person who is answerable for the handling of personal information. Thus, an individual with a grievance would not have to deal with a variety of people trying to dodge the problem by claiming it was not their responsibility. The manager would have to make sure that there were effective ways of tracing data authorizations, transactions, and so on.

The Privacy Commission also recommended that social security numbers be restricted to authorized use, that no new system should rely on these numbers for unique identification purposes, and that a separate group be established to monitor the use of social security numbers. It further recommended that the federal government not foster the development of a unique identification.

The private sector has still not been addressed with sweeping legislation from the federal level, but many states have taken up the slack. Based on the findings of the Privacy Commission, individual state legislatures have passed a variety of laws relating to specific areas: credit, insurance, medical, employment, and criminal. In each of these areas, and in others, laws address the privacy of information gathered. Such laws have been passed unevenly, however. Some states

---

## The Death of Privacy?

How close are we to losing our rights to privacy? Read the following and judge for yourself.

### Beyond the Manila Folder

CAMBRIDGE, Mass.—Government surveillance via computers is "frightening" because most victims are unaware that it is happening, Harvard Law School Prof. Arthur Miller said in a recent interview.

"Government surveillance is a part of American life. Surveillance by computers is just another way of doing it," Miller said. Court challenges have not been successful because "the right cases haven't come along."

To combat the threat of surveillance, more public awareness is needed. Reaction to government spying during the '60s and early '70s resulted in limitations on Federal Bureau of Investigation and Central Intelligence Agency activities. . . .

What happens to information about people, once gathered, is another area of concern to Miller. "The manila folder just doesn't travel as far as the computer entry," he observed.

—*Computerworld*,
March 7, 1983

### The Electronic Leash

ALBUQUERQUE, N.M.—Some misdemeanor offenders will soon be permitted to serve their sentences at home, but they must wear an electronic "handcuff" that will tell on them if they leave.

Under a 90-day pilot program, an offender normally placed on a probation where he reports to jail after work instead will go home each day. There, the electronic bracelet will keep track of his comings and goings to make sure they agree with a court-approved work schedule. . . .

The program is aimed especially toward people convicted of driving while intoxicated, said Michael T. Goss, president of the Albuquerque-based company developing the device. . . .

Each bracelet emits a digital code that is picked up by a device connected to the wearer's telephone. Information from the bracelet is fed through the phone to a computer.

If an offender tries to remove the bracelet or goes farther than 1000 feet from his telephone, a signal is sent to the computer.

"Every morning, we'll give the probation officer a list of all of their comings and goings," Goss said. "The computer will compare it to their work schedule to see if they were

where they were supposed to be. All we do is register the arrivals and departures and the rest is up to the probation officers."
—Reported by the Associated Press,
*San Francisco Chronicle*,
March 10, 1983

### Swedish ID System

STOCKHOLM, Sweden—Drinkers in Sweden have been put on notice that the days of wine and roses may have hit a sobering "STOP RUN." . . .

In an effort to quell the quaffing of excess libations, the [Swedish Parliament's ruling Center Party] is proposing to employ computer checks to limit liquor purchases in state-controlled liquor stores.

If the measure passes, drinkers will have to produce special identity cards to obtain weekly rations of their favorite spirits.

When a customer has already purchased his limit for the week or if the customer has a history of alcohol abuse, the computer at the store will spit out the card and activate a red warning light.

Those unfortunate imbibers who get the red light repeatedly could be forced to undergo treatment for alcoholism.

—*Computerworld*,
October 25, 1982

*Privacy legislation: Cost?*
*Passed on to us.*

*To ensure privacy*
*1) Labeling/storing data safely*
*2) Stating degree of confidentiality*
*of data*
*3) Recording categories of personal*
*data*
*4) Keeping up to date lists of*
*who is authorized to have*
*access to personal files*

are very up to date, while others have little or no legislation. Individual privacy is in greater danger than ever before because of the accessibility of greater numbers of people to greater numbers of computers.

What will be the side effects of privacy legislation? Will it hamper customer service, give corporations yet another set of regulations to complain about, add to the cost of doing business? Cost may indeed be the decisive factor in this matter. We all want privacy, but you can be sure private enterprise will pass the costs of ensuring it along to us. Are we prepared to pay the price?

In anticipation of further privacy legislation, some organizations in the private sector have already changed their ways of handling personal data. Among the techniques now in use are labeling and storing data safely, stating the degree of confidentiality of data, recording categories of personal data, and keeping up-to-date lists of who is authorized to have access to personal data.

## Summary and Key Terms

- Computer crime appeals to perpetrators and observers alike because it is a "clean" white-collar crime, in which no one gets physically hurt and the victim is usually perceived to be a large organization. Reported and unreported computer crime may run as high as $3 billion a year in the United States.

- There are basically three kinds of computer crime: (1) theft of computer time for personal use, (2) theft, destruction, or manipulation of programs or data, and (3) alteration of data stored in a computer file.

- Examples of kinds of computer crime are the **Trojan Horse,** in which a program is altered so that it performs normally but also performs additional, illegitimate functions; the **salami method,** an embezzlement technique in which a little bit at a time is taken from many bank accounts; and **data diddling,** in which data is modified before it goes into a computer file.

- Discovering computer crime is often difficult. Prosecution is also difficult because law enforcement agencies, attorneys, and judges and juries do not understand the complexities of computer-related fraud and may not consider data valuable. Also, laws do not adequately define computer crime.

- **Security** is defined as a system of safeguards to protect a computer system and data from deliberate or accidental damage or access by unauthorized persons.

- There are three criteria by which a computer system can detect whether people should have access to it: (1) by what they *know,* such as **passwords,** the secret words or numbers to be typed in on a keyboard before any

activity can take place; (2) by what they *have,* such as a badge or card; or (3) by what they *are,* such as being possessors of the correct fingerprints. The field of **biometrics** is concerned with the measurement of individual body characteristics such as fingerprints.

- A **disaster recovery plan** is a scheme for providing smooth, rapid restoration of critical data processing operations in the event of physical destruction or major damage that has caused an interruption in that processing. In some organizations, a disaster recovery planning team is designated to determine which programs must be up and running first after a disaster has occurred; the personnel, equipment, facilities, and supplies required; and the input and output distribution.

- Some companies have joined others in consortiums to support complete computer setups that can be available in event of disaster. Disaster recovery sites may be of two types: **hot sites** are fully equipped computer centers; **cold sites** are empty shells in which a company may install its own computer. Other companies have mutual aid pacts to assist a member stricken by disaster.

- Software piracy—unauthorized copying of software—is an important problem. The issue of software security can be formulated as the question, Who owns a program—the person who writes it or the organization he or she works for? The answer is the program belongs to the organization. The U.S. Supreme Court has also ruled that software can be patented. The **Copyright Act of 1976** states that flowcharts, source code, and assembly code are copyrightable.

- To protect data from being stolen, an organization must plan for security in five areas: (1) determine policies and standards, (2) develop security safeguards, (3) include security precautions in development of automated systems, (4) review related laws, (5) maintain records of computer abuse.

* Steps to prevent theft or alteration of data include the following: (1) using locked trash barrels; (2) frequently changing passwords; (3) instituting internal controls such as transaction logs; (4) having auditors review computer programs and data; (5) using cryptography (**Data Encryption Standard** or **DES** is a standardized public key by which senders and receivers can scramble and unscramble their messages); (6) screening applicants for DP jobs; (7) separating employee functions; (8) building software protections into operating systems to restrict unauthorized access. Another form of protection is a **user profile:** information is stored about each user and the files to which he or she has access.

* Some employees feel inconvenienced by intensified security measures, but most are aware of the importance of such measures.

* Because existing laws have made prosecution of computer-related crimes difficult, there have been attempts to introduce new laws. The **Federal Computer System Protection Act,** introduced in Congress in 1977, was aimed at stopping unauthorized access to computers and data and prohibiting unauthorized alteration of computers, programs, and data. This bill did not pass, but many states have enacted their own computer crime laws.

* **Privacy** may be defined as the assurance to individuals that personal information is used properly and protected against improper access. A great deal of information collected about people has been given out by those persons voluntarily. However, there is concern about data being collected or shared in ways that people would not approve.

* The **Fair Credit Reporting Act** of 1970 was one of the earlier pieces of legislation relating to privacy and computers. It allows people to have access to their credit records. The **Freedom of Information Act,** passed in 1970, allows ordinary citizens to have access to data gathered by federal agencies.

* The most significant legislation in the privacy area is the **Federal Privacy Act** of 1974, which prohibits secret personal files being kept on individuals by government agencies and contractors. The act also set up a Privacy Commission, which recommended six principles for a privacy act applying to the nongovernmental sector: (1) the existence of all personal records should be made public; (2) individuals must be allowed to find out when information is stored about them and how it is used; (3) personal information should be used only for its intended purposes; (4) individuals must be able to amend records about themselves; (5) personal information must be obtained in such a way so as to ensure that it is complete, accurate, relevant, timely, and secure; and (6) all uses of personal information should be accounted for by a responsible manager. Some state legislatures have passed laws based on the findings of the Privacy Commission.

## Review

1. Based on your knowledge of computers and data processing so far, do you see any aspects of your life in which you could be harmed by computer-related crime? Name the types of crime to which you might be vulnerable.

2. Why is stamping out computer-related crime so difficult?

3. Suppose you were the security officer for a new company that is just being formed. (Choose the product or service this company would provide.) What recommendations would you make to the president for protecting computers, programs, and data?

4. Name the pieces of federal legislation discussed in this chapter and describe what they do or propose to do to provide for security of information pertaining to computers and to your privacy.

## Selected References for Further Reading

*Computer Security Handbook.* Northbrough, Mass.: The Computer Security Institute, 1983.

Hoffman, Lance J. *Computers and Privacy in the Next Decade.* New York: Academic Press, 1980.

Martin, James. *Security, Accuracy, and Privacy in Computer Systems.* Englewood Cliffs, N.J.: Prentice-Hall, 1973.

Meyer, Carl and Stephen Matyas. *Cryptography.* New York: Wiley, 1982.

Parker, Donn B. *Ethical Conflicts in Computer Science and Technology.* New York: AFIPS Press, 1980.

Parker, Donn B. *Fighting Computer Crime.* New York: Scribner's, 1983.

Whiteside, Thomas. *Computer Capers: Tales of Electronic Thievery, Embezzlement, and Fraud.* New York: Thomas Y. Crowell Company, 1978.

## IN THIS CHAPTER

Computers magnify our human capabilities—and thereby magnify the potential for good or evil. The effects of computer error and breakdown, job displacement, and negative changes in the quality of life are described, but also the great promises of the future, from incredible shrinking chips to artificial intelligence. The information culture of the future, glimpsed in new developments in France, co-called "electronic cottages," and computerization of space, is considered.

*ch 19*

# computers and society

## the future then

**ch19**

"It is hard to predict, especially the future," physicist Niels Bohr is supposed to have quipped.

In Chapter 1, we wrote about "the future now," how the computer—the tool of the future—is altering the present. Now let us try to take a look at a subject that is both harder and easier, "the future then"—harder because, of course, the future is really unknowable, easier because, after all, how many futurists are held accountable for their long-range predictions?

As we have seen throughout this book, the most significant aspect of computers is *how much they extend our human intellectual capabilities*. Everything flows from the fact that computers can process data on a large scale without the involvement of a large number of people. This magnifies the capabilities for perpetrating good or evil. If, therefore, there is a single reason for continuing to stay "computer literate," it is that we should prepare ourselves to receive the benefits and avoid the dangers presented by computers.

Let us now consider some of the possible negative effects of computers that we should be alert for over the next twenty years. We will then examine the more positive ones.

## Because We Can: Some Dangers to Watch For

You switch on the TV set just before leaving home to go to the polls to vote for candidates for President and other political offices. A newscaster announces that—although only 1 percent of the nation-wide vote has been counted—the television network has predicted a winner, using computer-aided projections based on voting results of key precincts around the country. For all practical purposes, the election is over, you decide. Even though there are a couple of hours left before the polls close in your neighborhood, you decide it is not worth your while to go vote.

What is the consequence of this? In the 1980 presidential elections, NBC News did exactly this, predicting Ronald Reagan the winner over Jimmy Carter hours before polls had closed on the West Coast and in Alaska and Hawaii. The result, according to one Berkeley political scientist, was that more than a quarter million Californians alone were discouraged from voting—certainly enough to influence the outcome of many local political contests.

"This frenzied use of computers," complained another critic about the NBC predictions, "can certainly be seen as irresponsible, being another of the many examples of man using computers simply because he *can*, not because he *must*. . . . Why does anyone need to know the projected outcome of a presidential election at 8:15 p.m. EST? The answer is: Nobody does."

It can be argued, however, that most negative effects of computers, as of so much of technology in general, are not intentional. Indeed,

# *The Last Picture Show*

## *Computers and Imagination*

New machines. New ideas. New ways of seeing. The future is unknowable, but some of the shape of the future may already be evident in today's recent developments: Wider communications. Increased robotics. More computer-assisted labor-saving and entertainment devices. And new ways of perceiving the world as the computer becomes more and more a tool of the artist's and scientist's imagination.

**❶** The new nuclear family? Not likely, but in the future we may well see more personal robots—such as "Topo" here—for education and entertainment. Topo is a mobile extension of a home computer.

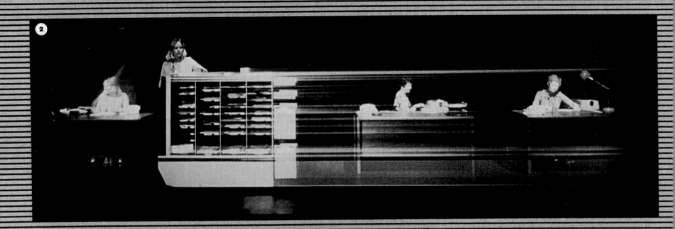

New machines... **2** The Mail-mobile can be made to roll slowly from desk to desk on a prepro-grammed course, delivering inter-office mail. **3** to **6** A vision sys-tem being developed at Stanford University can segment a raw image along its edges; knowl-edge-based robot-controlled vision has many applications, such as sorting parts. **7** This robot employed by the San Francisco Police Department can be used for removing explo-sives and other hazardous tasks. **8** Factory automation of the future was the subject of Chica-go's 1983 International Machine Tool Show. **9** This General Electric arc welding robot uses an experimental infrared sensor in its operation.

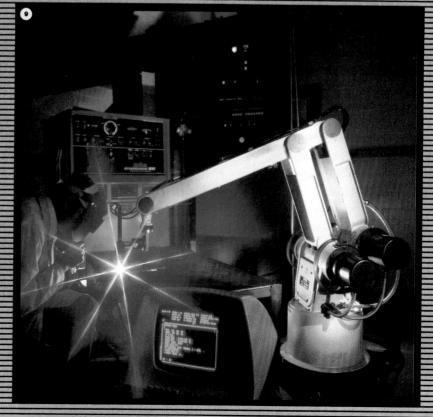

New ideas... ⑩ How do babies learn? A psychologist watches as a seven-month-old infant picks out indented lines at M.I.T. ⑪ Sun screen: Club Med offers micro-computers for interested vacationers. ⑫ ⑬ Video jukebox: Rock and roll is here to see as microprocessor-run entertainment. ⑭ Monkey do: Scientists do research into primate behavior using computers at Georgia State University and the University of Georgia. ⑮ to ⑱ Communications: Microwave and satellite transmission widen our world, as in broadcasts of winter sports and in various forms of telecommunications. ⑲ Solar power: Computer-controlled solar collectors help generate electrical energy.

New ways of seeing . . . New computer graphic artists provide fresh perspectives on fine art. ② "Tik Tak Tō" *(a portion of)* by Laurence M. Gartel. ㉑ "Ming" by David Em. ② "Organic System" by Howard Ganz. ㉓ "Q space" by Darcy Gerbarg.

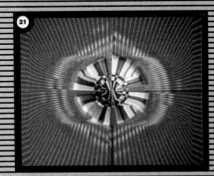

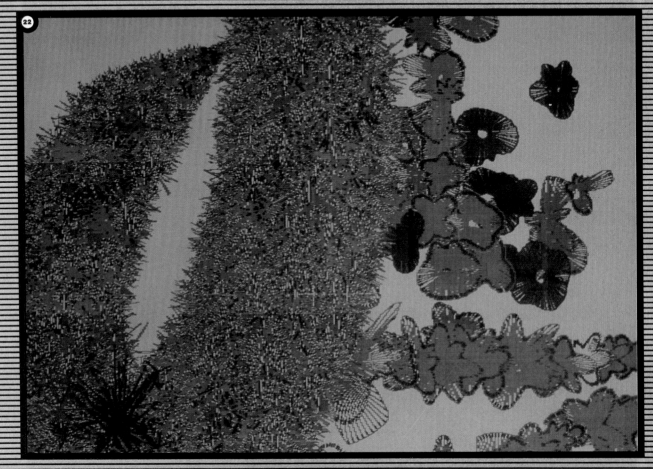

**24 25** For the young, computer camp for knowledge; for the not so young, video games for morale.

people concerned with business ethics have suggested that it is not so much greed or malice as simply negligence that is the reason for morally reprehensible computer systems.

### Mistakes, Mismatches, Breakdowns, and Brownouts

Computer professionals are fond of pointing out that mistakes often attributed to computers are really not the fault of the computers themselves. As we have seen, silicon chip manufacturers put their products through rigorous work/not work tests. However, there *are* computer mishaps of various sorts, of course, and they may have a number of causes:

- *Data entry errors.* To err is human, to forgive divine—something that is hard to remember when you have been victimized by a computer billing foul-up. But as long as humans are keying in data, there will continue to be data entry errors.

- *Programmer errors.* Although programmers have several opportunities to find and fix program errors, invariably some go undetected.

- *Equipment designer errors.* There is a story about a nuclear plant control room in which indicators used red ink to show the temperature of cold water and blue ink to show the temperature of hot gas. Because red-for-cold and blue-for-hot are the opposite of the association most people make, the staff had posted a sign in the control room: "Remember RED is COLD." Similarly, computer terminal keyboards have been designed that work quite well when used by experts but can lead to accidental erasure of data when used by ordinary people. In this sense, computers are sometimes mismatched with the way the human mind works.

- *Faulty equipment.* Errors may be caused by outdated technology, such as may be encountered when trying to send data over a public telephone system with antiquated switching plants and noise, or by deterioration in mechanical devices, such as printers that have not been adequately maintained. However, sometimes the results of such failures have been spectacular. For example, for two years, as a result of obsolete computer systems combined with poor management practices and human error, a series of false alerts occurred in the early warning defense system designed to detect invasion of United States air space.

- *Interrupted power supply.* Electrical "brownouts"—cutbacks in power—may be tolerable to appliances and other machines, but a computer can lose data under such conditions. If there is a voltage drop of 25 percent lasting one-tenth of a second, it is enough to shut down many computers. Such a drop may occur once or twice a month, and other power interference, surges, and dips may also affect semiconductor circuitry and storage disks.

---

## COMPUTER ERROR AND THE END OF THE WORLD

On June 3, 1980, a summer day unremarkable in most respects, a government computer in Colorado generated a startling message: the world was about to end.

With cold imprecision, the North American Air Defense Command (NORAD) system signaled that a wave of Russian missiles was bringing nuclear holocaust to the North American continent. But, as a retaliatory strike force warmed up on Strategic Air Command (SAC) runways around the country, the human element of the early warning system took over and recognized the situation for what it was—a false alert. . . .

The faulty component, an integrated circuit in a communications multiplexer, was eventually detected and replaced, but only after another failure that once again scrambled SAC bomber crews. . . .

Every kind of system, every kind of technology, carries its own peculiar vulnerability. Agrarian societies are completely vulnerable to the vagaries of the weather, industrial societies to the uncertain availability of energy sources.

Even the most cursory examination of computer technology shows occasional system failures are all but inevitable. If there is a vulnerability *problem*, it is that the idiosyncratic vulnerability of this new and exploding technology is not always recognized by those who control it or by those who depend on it.

—Jake Kirchner,
*Computerworld*,
January 4, 1982

**Sorry!** President Ronald Reagan laughs as he apparently makes a mistake on a computer during a visit to a private school in Chicago.

As the American space program has shown, complex systems *can* be engineered and built to perform complicated undertakings successfully. The example of the 1979 near melt-down of a nuclear reactor at Three Mile Island, on the other hand (which, it must be emphasized, was started by a jammed valve, not a computer failure) shows that we cannot allow ourselves to be too comfortable about the reliability of technological systems.

### Health and Stress

In times past it was believed that technology would make a better life for people. Now we know that is not necessarily so, but the pendulum has swung so far the other way that many people have a knee-jerk fear that technology will have unforeseen side effects, particularly in health matters. Let us take a look at some of the health consequences of computers.

Take CRTs. There are four areas of concern:

- *Visual problems.* In the early 1980s, the National Institute for Occupational Safety and Health (NIOSH) investigated several workplaces to evaluate potential health hazards of CRTs (or VDTs—video display terminals, as they are called in most of the reports). Visual difficulties—blurring, eyestrain, irritation, focusing problems, and fatigue—turn out to be common complaints among CRT operators.

In most cases, however, the source of the difficulty is that the CRT has been located in an improperly designed work area, with poor interior lighting, glare on the screen, or insufficient rest periods for operators.

- *Postural difficulties.* CRT operators report back, neck, and shoulder aches more so than do other workers. This, however, can be alleviated by frequent breaks, chairs with support for the lower back, and a keyboard that is detachable from the screen.

- *Radiation worries.* Stories have appeared about people developing cataracts or pregnant women having miscarriages, supposedly because of radiation leaking from CRTs. However, the Food and Drug Administration's Bureau of Radiological Health has concluded that CRTs emit little or no harmful radiation under normal conditions and that such emissions as are detectable are well below present international standards for low-level radiation health hazards. It is important to understand, then, that, according to present occupational standards, there is no danger of radiation hazards from current CRTs.

- *Work-related stress.* Many CRT operators have complained about the level of stress in their work lives. However, the fault is not in the CRTs themselves but rather in the structure of the job. Frequently, operators are not given enough training, or, when CRTs are introduced, jobs are degraded so that they become more monotonous. Or supervisors may set unrealistic productivity levels—levels that can be achieved technologically but that are excessive for human beings to sustain.

### Automation and Robotics: The Job Killers?

Computer technology will take its toll in the workplace. In 1980, there were about 5000 industrial robots in the United States; by the year 2000 there could be half a million, according to some predictions. The Congressional Budget Office estimates that by the end of the decade jobs representing 15 percent of today's manufacturing work force will have disappeared, owing to automation, robotization, and other microelectronic technology, as well as competition from cheaper overseas foreign labor. New jobs will be created by electronics, of course, but the question is whether older blue-collar workers will be able to make the transition. The "de-skilling" of a large segment of the work force may result in forceful demand for retraining, straining some small businesses.

Office workers, too, may find themselves threatened by automation. Unions are beginning to turn their attention toward organizing workers in automated offices. Even applications programmers, some predict, may find themselves displaced by programs that generate programs. While optimists like to stress that computers create as well as eliminate jobs, they sometimes overlook the complex effects that

**NO ROBOTS TO DARN SOCKS?**

What distinguishes man from machine? The robot revolution is providing new answers as more robots take jobs that once only people could fill. But two Carnegie-Mellon University professors have made a list of what robots probably never will be able to do.

In the near future, robots will be able to shear sheep, scrape barnacles from the hull of a ship, assemble toasters or television sets. Some day, very sophisticated robots may be able to set a table, change a tire, pick fruit or do somersaults, say Robert U. Ayers and Steven M. Miller. . . .

What will remain the province of man? Dancing a ballet, peeling a grape, darning a sock, playing championship table tennis, delivering a baby.

—Richard A. Shaffer,
*Wall Street Journal,*
June 3, 1983

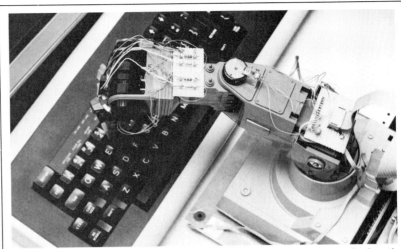

**Robot writer?** A robot arm, directed by computer, uses a computer keyboard. The robot arm was designed at Wright State University in Dayton, Ohio. Robots will be spearheading many job changes throughout the rest of this century.

computerization has on jobs—narrowing some, making others more complicated, compartmentalizing still others, and in general straining previous life and work styles.

There are, however, ways of minimizing the impact of the brave new automated world:

- Getting input from workers on implementation of new technologies in the workplace

- Having government and industry join forces to consider ideas on how jobs might be shared

- Reducing the number of work hours through shorter workweeks and longer vacations.

### Change in Quality of Life

In this book, we have maintained that the gifts computers offer generally improve the quality of life. But, as we have hinted, they can also be used to diminish it. We have alluded to the separation that the computer can impose on people, as seen in the extreme cases of alienated computer addicts, or "hackers." Some also fear that computers will reduce interpersonal relations between employers and employees, students and teachers, and so on. Some scholars speculate that computers may reduce imagination and curiosity. That is, because computers demand such absolute, "either/or" precision, because they formalize the way we need to think, computers might impair skills founded on imprecision and ambiguity, such as those required in poetry and the arts. Such observations remind us of criticisms leveled at television, though for different reasons. Moreover, computers may indeed come to alter the way we deal with others and the way we think.

Other dangers may be in the uses of computers, by society, to adversely affect our individual lives. We have already mentioned the use of data banks as instruments of control and their threat to privacy. The uses of computers for military purposes (in self-guided missiles, for example), may not be a blessing, although some suggest that automated defense systems may shift the advantage away from offensive to defensive weapons for the first time in generations.

Adam Osborne has perhaps stated the dilemma best in his book *Running Wild:*

> A computer will serve any master with equal dedication. As computers become more capable, they also become more potent as tools for anyone wishing to use or misuse the capability. We would all applaud the ability of a medical data base to provide the competent doctor with mind-jogging tidbits that lead to early diagnosis of dangerous ailments. But we should be equally afraid of the ease with which untrained personnel could access the same information. What about the profusion of charlatans and questionable characters who lurk on the fringes of the medical profession, selling services that are ineffective, questionable, or downright illegal? A medical data base would serve them as willingly as it would serve the most competent doctor.

Every use of computers implies a possible misuse.

## The Promise of the Techno-Future: Artificial Intelligence and Other Levers to the Mind

"What the lever was to the body, the computer system is to the mind," says Charles P. Lecht, president of Advanced Computer Techniques Corp. and author of *The Waves of Change.* Responding to critics of technological change, he goes on: "It is not difficult to visualize a time when people rebelled against the idea of augmenting bodily power by means of physical devices . . . but history has provided no evidence that our bodies would have been any more powerful had we not had the benefits of mechanical leverage."

Likewise, he says, computer power will lead to significant improvement in human life. Let us see what the promise of the technological future might be.

### The New Machines

Although you cannot yet pick up the computer of the future at your local store, technological developments for its various components are well under way, as described below.

**The Incredible Shrinking Chip** Tomorrow's variation on the question "How many angels on the head of a pin?" is: "How many transistors on the face of a chip?" By 1990, some engineers expect, there could be as many as ten million on a single chip. Present-day chips are made from large silicon wafers 3 to 6 inches in diameter, and many chips are made from a single wafer because it is necessary to separate out defective chips resulting from bad areas of the wafer. In the future, however, as silicon is used with fewer imperfections, it will be possible to make chips that fill entire wafers and that can be joined to others as building blocks to make "chip machines." The result, it has been predicted, may be the possibility of "component institutions": component libraries, component schools, even offices-on-a-wafer!

Other materials have also been talked about for hardware: gallium-arsenide and sapphire, which would allow higher circuit densities than now possible, and biophysical technology, which would permit revolutionary advances. Biomolecular technology, or "biochips," which would involve recombinant-DNA genetic engineering techniques, would permit computers to be "grown" as living systems.

**Storage Technology** The most immediate future direction of storage technology is miniaturization. Magnetic storage devices will continue to shrink and, at the same time, hold more data. Microfloppy disks are already available; next to emerge will be the micro-Winchester hard disk. A 4-inch Winchester hard disk will hold millions of bytes of information, yet its cost could go as low as $100.

Storage technology may also undergo change from the present magnetic media devices. Under development are optical storage devices, which record pictures, graphs, and copies of actual documents, as well as standard data, onto recordlike disks. Presently this technology has several drawbacks—information on optical disks cannot be erased, retrieval time is slow compared to current disk drive technology, storing disks is a problem, and everything so far is too expensive. However, optical disks may yet win favor with system developers.

**Graphics Display** The development that will have the most direct impact on computer users is the high-resolution graphics screen. The new screens will show finely detailed characters and graphics at the same time. The change might be compared to switching your TV viewing from a set with "snow" on the screen to one that produces an exceedingly clear, realistic picture. High-resolution displays are available now on a few computer systems, but they are still too expensive for most personal computers. As costs continue to decrease, such displays should become standard features on small computers.

**Printers** Dramatic changes in printers are about to emerge, yielding both higher quality and lower price. Letter-quality daisy wheel printers have already made some dramatic price dips. In the final stages of development are low-cost ink jet printers, which will be both fast and quiet. Just slightly down the road are low-cost laser printers that can produce outstanding graphics and print text in a variety of computer-generated type fonts.

**Networking** Future computers will also have a low-cost modem option. Technological breakthroughs include the concept of a modem-on-a-chip, a unit that contains the circuitry needed for a computer to communicate over telephone lines.

The technology for networking and data transmitting will probably also change. At present, data transmission frequencies are limited, but higher frequency satellites may be launched that will provide more communication channels. Some experts predict that advancing technology will lead to greater use of portable telephones during the next 15 years. In the 1980s we may also see a screen on one wall, and in the 21st century a holographic wall, a three-dimensional screen that would permit teleconferencing with such an appearance of reality that two physically separated groups would feel they were actually in the same room.

Many experts also forecast that the use of paper, at least in offices, will decrease to the vanishing point by the 21st century.

Feel this page and remember.

### Artificial Intelligence: Machine Consciousness?

"There are aspects to human life that a computer cannot understand," says Joseph Weizenbaum of the Massachusetts Institute of Technology. "Love and loneliness have to do with the deepest consequences of our biological constitution. That kind of understanding is in principle impossible for the computer." This is probably so, although some scientists believe that it will be possible to program a computer to at least *act* as if it had emotions—being happy or sad or loving.

Even without this aspect, however, it appears as though **artificial intelligence (AI)**—the field of study that explores how computers can be used for tasks requiring the human characteristics of intelligence, imagination, and intuition—will be superrevolutionary in its effects. "AI will change civilization in a profound way," states Nils J. Nilsson, director of the AI center at SRI International. "It will change the way we work, the way we learn, and even the way we think about ourselves."

The earliest programs of artificial intelligence involved puzzle solving, chess playing, and similar problem-solving tasks. Today, however, *knowledge-based systems* (also called "expert systems") are capable of solving complex situations involving uncertainty, human judgment, and experience. They may be used, for instance, to make medical diagnoses (one such program is called Caduceus), analyze geological data (Prospector), or help geneticists plan experiments involving structural analysis and synthesis of DNA (MOLGEN). Prospector, used to predict the location of copper deposits, has been found to be accurate within 7 percent of the experts.

A critical element of artificial intelligence is natural-language programs that can understand everyday English, which means that users do not have to learn computer syntax. A program called Intellect, for instance, uses the technology of artificial intelligence to understand

## PREDICTIONS THAT NEVER CAME TRUE

When considering the future, it is a good exercise in humility to recall some past predictions. Examples:

- When the automobile arrived, it was predicted that it would eliminate congestion (because it was only half the length of a horse and buggy).

- In 1926, Henry Ford developed plans for a personal airplane, and the federal government later began work on a "poor man's plane."

- Fascination with atomic energy in the 1950s and 1960s led to predictions that there would be atomic airplanes, trains, boats, and cars. There were plans to dig a second Panama Canal with nuclear explosions.

- In the 1960s, it was predicted that picturephones—telephones with television screens—would sweep the nation.

## Computer Innovations

The text describes uses of the computer that will have an important bearing on our lives. Some other uses are shown here—some important, some simply fanciful.

**Computers for peace.** The Disarmament Resources Peacenet in San Francisco uses networking by personal computers to keep various peace groups informed.

**Walking proudly.** Nan Davis (center) holds the hands of Dr. Jerrold Petrofsky (right), who designed a portable computer system, in bag under his arm, that controls the movements of her paralyzed legs. Davis is assisted by research assistant Don Stafford as she begins her walk to receive her bachelor's degree from Wright State University in Dayton, Ohio.

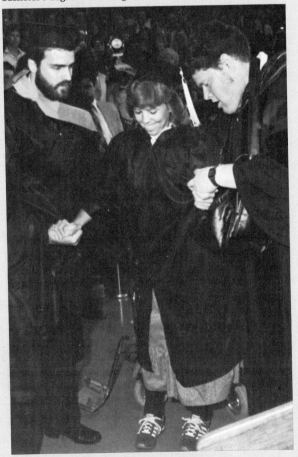

**Global data bank.** Rabbi Alan Rosenbaum (left) and Dr. Emanuel Rachman confer at the Institute for Computers in Jewish Life in Chicago, which has compiled 5000 published volumes of rabbinical opinions from Jewish communities worldwide as an aid to Talmudic and rabbinical research.

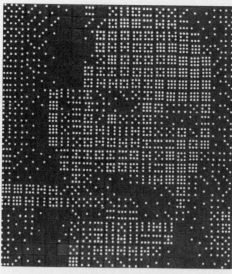

**Computer art or. . . ?** No, look carefully. These portraits of Charlie Chaplin (*left*) and Groucho Marx (with cigar) are made up entirely of *dominos*. However, the dominos were arranged with the help of a computer. The compositions were created by Ken Knowlton, who began by taking photographs of the entertainers, then putting the photographs through a computer program to digitize each area into a shade of gray. The photos were then put through a second program to establish pairings of dominos in the optimal way.

**Real robots?** *Below left,* the British robot system, Ajax Workmaster, has microprocessor intelligence and exceptional strength and dexterity that allow complex cleaning and spraying operations, multiple drilling, grinding, and welding. *Right,* Elektro, the Mechanical Man, and Sparko, the Mechanical Dog, exemplify our idea of what robots are *supposed* to look like. Built for the New York World's Fair just before World War II, Sparko was able to bark, wag his tail, sit up, and beg and Elektro was said to do "a great many things that a living man can do."

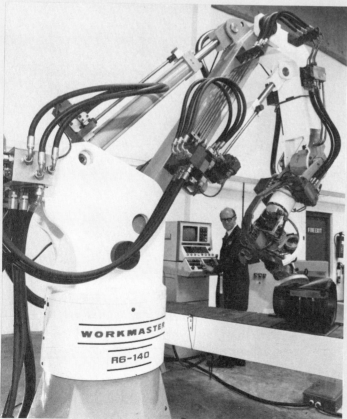

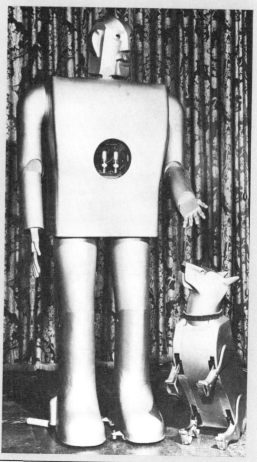

everyday, conversational English; it allows managers to call up data just by keying memolike requests.

How does AI work? The difference is in computer programming. Traditional programs follow a predetermined set of instructions step by step, but such rotelike recipes are not suitable for many kinds of problems. Artificial intelligence systems take different approaches. One way is to use stored *if-then* rules. To use a simplistic example, the computer might determine "*If* a cat is large and has stripes, *then* it is a tiger." Another way is to use *pyramid-shaped* networks of ideas to deduce facts, so that, for example, the computer can determine that dogs and elephants have four legs but only elephants have trunks. Rather than proceed according to step-by-step instructions, then, the computer sorts through all the knowledge in storage and decides on its own sequence of steps.

So far artificial intelligence has not come close to reproducing human intelligence, and there are those who doubt that it can ever do more than simulate just some of its skills—namely, data retrieval, logic, and the like. (As humanist Theodore Roszak points out, the mind can also "dream, hallucinate, tell jokes, make laws, invent fairy tales, goof off, meditate, forget, repress, lie, go crazy, and commune with God.") Yet AI promises to provide ways of duplicating many common human tasks. Today, many managers in industry face problems of overwhelming complexity that in the future could be handled by AI systems.

There are those who worry about the long-range effects of AI—that, for instance, in another 30 years the 25 million or so people currently employed in manufacturing in the United States will shrink to 3 million, victims of "AI unemployment." White-collar workers could also be displaced, for the same reasons. Others are more optimistic. Equipped with expert systems embedded in hand-held machines the size of present-day calculators, says futurist Earl Joseph, "each of us can draw upon society's amassed knowledge. Then we will have the knowledge and ability to participate in the creation of a more desirable society."

## The Uses of the Future: The Information Culture

We can glimpse the near future by developments in the present: fully automated gas stations, in which customers use magnetized credit cards similar to those used for automated teller machines; hotels with electronic mail, games, and access to data bases through terminals in the guests' rooms; medical imaging; computer programs to model the thermal behavior of solar houses; computer-generated graphics to assist athletes and dancers; computer-run offices and factories—and on and on. Another futurist use now in the development stages is computer modeling to prevent war.

As futurist John Naisbitt writes in his book *Megatrends*, these uses of computers follow the first and second stages of a new technological development. In stage 1, the new technology follows the line of least resistance (for example, microprocessors being used in toys, robots being used for unsafe jobs); in stage 2, the technology is used to improve previous technologies (for example, today's word processor is principally just an improved typewriter).

Stage 3, however, is much more interesting—and unpredictable—for it consists of new directions or uses that are created or grow out of the technology itself: "inventions and applications that are unimagined now," says Naisbitt. If they are "unimagined," we probably will not be able to imagine them here. Nevertheless, let us speculate on some possible future developments that may come to pass within our lifetimes. All of these are characterized by one fact: we are changing from an industrial society to one based on information.

### France Looks Ahead

As we mentioned in Chapter 3, Japan is moving aggressively on the technological front, with its plans for a fifth generation of computing technology. France is working on the social agenda for the computer. The country that gave the world the Concorde supersonic airliner and the first commercial breeder nuclear reactor is now working on being the leader in what they call *telematique*—**telematics,** the linkage of telephone with television and computer technologies.

By 1990, the French hope to have installed throughout France seven million terminals hooked into the telephone system. Already an "electronic directory" has allowed subscribers to use the same current phone listings as those used by telephone operators. More important, the system forms the basis for a national videotex system, with access to numerous data bases, home banking, and transaction services. Experiments are being done with a smart card—a credit-card size piece of plastic with an 8-bit microprocessor—to examine the feasibility of home banking and teleshopping. In addition, the service could provide a picturephone along with video camera, which could show faces or documents. Particularly striking is the notion that once all public records are computerized they could be made accessible to anyone with a terminal. As one writer notes, "This is freedom of information with a vengeance, for the project will deal with live administrative files."

### "The Electronic Cottage"

This is the phrase that futurist Alvin Toffler uses to describe work that has been moved from factories and offices to people's homes. Like the peasant cottage industries of 300 years ago, before the Industrial Revolution forced people to crowd into urban factories, the **electronic cottage** would allow both manufacturing and white-collar workers to perform work for employers or services for clients at home,

#### THE FRENCH AND REVOLUTION

One has to remember that France was the country of the French Revolution, which did much to transform the map of the world. The French forget little, the revolution least of all. They think they have seen what the next revolution is going to be about, that it is digital technology-based, and they believe it will have just as massive social, economic and political consequences.

What is new in France is that society is setting down the road toward organizing itself to cope with the revolution, to accommodate the technology within a short time scale.

—Rex Malik,
*Computerworld,*
May 9, 1983

## HOME WORK

...An unmeasured but appreciable amount of work is already being done at home by such people as salesmen and saleswomen who work by phone or visit, and only occasionally touch base at the office; by architects and designers; by a burgeoning pool of specialized consultants in many industries; by large numbers of human-service workers like therapists or psychologists; by music teachers and language instructors; by art dealers, investment counselors, insurance agents, lawyers, and academic researchers; and by many other categories of white-collar, technical, and professional people.

These are, moreover, among the most rapidly expanding work classifications, and when we suddenly make available technologies that can place a low-cost "work station" in any home, providing it with a "smart" typewriter, perhaps along with a facsimile machine or computer console and teleconferencing equipment, the possibilities for home work are radically extended.

—Alvin Toffler,
*The Third Wave*

while linked electronically via home computers and telecommunication networks.

Futurist Naisbitt, however, disagrees somewhat. Technological advances will not be accepted, he insists, unless there are "counterbalancing human responses." "High tech" needs "high touch"—a compensatory human element. Thus, he feels, the electronic cottage will not go far because, the more technology there is in society, the more people will want to be with other people. Therefore, they will seek ways to congregate with other people—including in offices.

### The Computerization of Space

Computers and telecommunications, it is suggested, might well allow us to reach out beyond our own planet and begin to build space platforms for exploiting the resources of space. Unclouded by the atmosphere, space stations could utilize solar power for solar-energy development, for communications, and for transportation. Facilities could exploit weightlessness and other factors for growing gallium-arsenide crystals for semiconductors, developing new drugs, and improving telecommunications.

## Computer Literacy —Continued

The phrase "computer literacy" means different things to different people. To some, it means becoming aware of how computers are used and how they affect society. To others, it means being able to use computers, to program them to solve a problem. In this book, we have tried to help readers achieve a little of both.

Computer literacy is a continuing, life-long task. In some respects it may be made easier as changing technology and software make computer use less complicated. As the computer becomes an everyday appliance like today's automobile, TV, or typewriter, it will come to be more central in our lives. Thus, being literate today does not mean being literate tomorrow. This is not the end; it is the beginning.

## Summary and Key Terms

- The most significant aspect of computers is how much they extend our human intellectual capabilities. This magnifies the capabilities for perpetrating good or evil.

- Computer error or breakdown may be caused by a number of factors: data entry errors; programmer errors; equipment designer errors; faulty equipment; interrupted power supply.

- According to present standards, CRT terminals do not present a health hazard from low-level radiation. However, CRT operators have complained of visual difficulties such as eyestrain, postural difficulties such as back and neck aches, and work-related stress arising from lack of training, job monotony, or unrealistic productivity levels.

- Computer-backed automation is displacing blue-collar production workers, and unions are concerned about the loss of employees to office automation.

- Some fear computers will alter the quality of life and thought, such as employer-employee relations, the kinds of talents founded on ambiguity such as poetry writing, and threats to privacy.

- Future computer chips may be "chip machines" filling entire silicon wafers and permitting such "component institutions" as component libraries, schools, or offices on a single chip. Chips may also be made out of new materials such as gallium-arsenide and sapphire, which would allow higher circuit densities than presently possible. "Biochips" may be built by biomolecular technology, so that, using recombinant-DNA genetic engineering techniques, chips could be grown as living systems.

- Future storage technology will continue to shrink magnetic storage devices while simultaneously enabling them to hold more data. Micro-Winchester hard disks will also emerge that will hold millions of bytes of information. Optical storage devices will become available which will record data and pictures on recordlike disks. High-resolution graphics screens will become more commonplace. Printers will become higher in quality and lower in price; low-cost laser printers will appear. Modems will be cheaper; there may even be a modem-on-a-chip. More data transmission frequencies will expand communication channels. The future may see not only more portable telephones, but also a screen on one wall and even a holographic, three-dimension wall-sized screen.

- **Artificial intelligence (AI)** is the field of study that explores how computers can be used for tasks requiring the human characteristics of intelligence, imagination, and intuition. Earlier AI programs involved puzzle solving and chess playing, but today's knowledge-based (or expert) systems are capable of solving complex situations involving uncertainty, human judgment, and experience. An element of AI is natural-language programs that can understand everyday English, so that people do not have to learn computer syntax. Unlike traditional programs, which follow a predetermined set of instructions step by step, AI programs may follow if-then rules or pyramid-shaped networks of ideas to deduce facts.

- There is some concern about "AI unemployment," in which white-collar workers could be displaced by AI programs.

- Future uses of computers will not only include variations and improvements on present technologies but also probably unpredictable and unimagined uses.

- France is working on being the leader in **telematics,** the linkage of telephone with television and computer technologies. The system now being installed throughout France consists of seven million terminals hooked into the telephone system, which will be the basis for access to numerous data bases, home banking, and transaction services.

- Some predict a rise in the so-called **electronic cottage,** in which employees perform work or services from home via computers with telecommunications links.

- Computers and telecommunications may allow us to reach out and build space platforms for exploiting solar energy and other resources of space.

## Review

1. What are your personal fears about the future dangers of computers? How can those dangers be addressed? Name other dangers described in the chapter.

2. What impact do you think computers will have on your future employment and on your future relations with people? Discuss in the light of the criticisms described in the chapter.

3. How do you think technological changes will affect what you will be doing five years from now? Ten years from now?

4. In what areas do you particularly wish you had the help of some programs in artificial intelligence?

## Selected References for Further Reading

Naisbitt, John. *Megatrends: Ten New Directions Transforming Our Lives.* New York: Warner Books, 1982.

Osborne, Adam. *Running Wild: The Next Industrial Revolution.* Berkeley, Calif.: Osborne/McGraw-Hill, 1979.

Servan-Schreiber, Jean-Jacques. *The World Challenge.* New York: Simon & Schuster, 1981.

Vallee, Jacques. *The Network Revolution: Confessions of a Computer Scientist.* Berkeley, Calif.: And/Or Press, 1982.

# appendix A
## a course of programming in BASIC

# appendix A
## a course of programming in BASIC

This appendix explains how to design and run some simple programs in BASIC, the computer language whose name is an acronym for Beginners' All-purpose Symbolic Instruction Code. To help ensure this discussion is meaningful to you, you should first read Chapter 8, "Beginning Programming," which explains how program logic is developed and what the rules of flowcharting are.

BASIC was invented in 1965 by John Kemeny and Thomas Kurtz for use at Dartmouth College as a simple language for beginners in programming. With the explosive growth of microcomputers, the language has become widely popular, and gradually more sophisticated BASIC versions have emerged. As a result of this activity, there is no one standard version of BASIC. Thus, you may find different versions at different computer installations. This diversity means we cannot be exhaustive or comprehensive here in describing BASIC. However, we will present the common features, and where there are known variations we will mention them.

## Writing Simple Programs in BASIC

Converting a flowchart to a program is usually a difficult step for beginners. It is made easier, however, with the use of the three control structures we discussed in Chapter 8— (1) **sequence**; (2) **selection,** which can be **IF-THEN-ELSE** or **IF-THEN**; and (3) **iteration,** which may be either **DOWHILE** or **DOUNTIL.** We will use these control structures extensively throughout this appendix.

Let us now consider a simple example of how to write a program. The program is a simple input/output problem, as shown in Figure A-1(a). Its purpose is to read the inventory records in a camping supplies store and print out the result. Notice the control structures in the flowchart for the program. The first part of the flowchart is a *sequence*. The second part is a *DOWHILE iteration*, because the test as to whether to stop the program (RECORD RECEIVED?) is at the beginning, rather than the end, of the iteration loop. Note also that the flowchart has a *double-read statement*: The statement, READ A RECORD, appears twice. Finally, note how the three principal parts of a program—*input, process,* and *output*— are handled in the program.

Now look at Figure A-1(b). This is the program you will write from the flowchart. Step by step, let us see what the BASIC rules are for writing this program.

### Variables: Numeric and String

**Variables** are the *names of locations* where data will be placed. There are two kinds of variables. **Numeric variables** store numbers. They must name locations for numbers that will be used in calculations. **String variables** store sequences of characters, any kind of data: digits, letters, and special characters (such as punctuation marks, asterisks, equal signs).

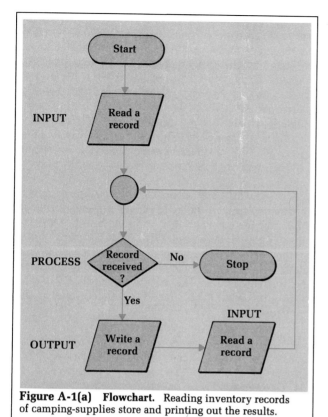

**Figure A-1(a) Flowchart.** Reading inventory records of camping-supplies store and printing out the results.

```
100 REM    INVENTORY PROGRAM  A.SCHMIDT
110 REM
120 REM    THIS PROGRAM READS AND
130 REM    PRINTS INVENTORY RECORDS.
140 REM
150 REM    VARIABLE NAMES:
160 REM        I   -INVENTORY NUMBER
170 REM        N$  -NAME
180 REM        Q   -QUANTITY ON HAND
190 REM
200        READ I,N$,Q
210 REM    BEGIN LOOP
220        IF I=9999 THEN 340
230        PRINT I,N$,Q
240        READ I,N$,Q
250        GOTO 220
260 REM
270 REM         DATA
280 DATA 1643,"FLASHLIGHT",257
290 DATA 2945,"BACKPACK",156
300 DATA 4721,"BOOTS",183
310 DATA 5091,"JACKET",261
320 DATA 6466,"LANTERN",143
330 DATA 9999,"END FILE",000
340 END
```

**Figure A-1(b) Program.**

| 1643 | FLASHLIGHT | 257 |
| 2945 | BACKPACK | 156 |
| 4721 | BOOTS | 183 |
| 5091 | JACKET | 261 |
| 6466 | LANTERN | 143 |

**Figure A-1(c) Output.**

There are special rules for forming these variable names:

- A *numeric variable* may be any letter of the alphabet or any letter of the alphabet followed by a single digit, 0 through 9. Examples are X, R, T1, and A3.

- A *string variable* is formed by a letter followed by a dollar sign. This means there are 26 possible string variables: A$, B$, C$, and so on, to Z$.

In Figure A-1(b), examples of numeric variables are shown on lines 160 and 180; an example of a string variable is shown on line 170.

### Constants: Numeric and String

**Constants** are the data that is put into variables. A **numeric constant** is simply a number. A **string constant** can be anything at all—digits, letters, special characters.

The rules for forming constants are as follows:

- For *numeric constants*, dollar signs and commas are not allowed. However, a decimal point and a minus sign in front of a number are allowed. Examples of valid numeric constants are 3, 1.6, 1000, and -8.

- *String constants* normally need to have **quotation marks** around them. Some BASIC systems use single quotation marks ('); most use double quotation marks ("). (In some versions, you can manage without quotation marks at

all.) In this appendix, we will use double quotation marks. Your instructor can tell you if the BASIC system you are using is different.

Examples of constants are given in Figure A-1(b), lines 280–330.

### Line Numbers

Every program must have *line numbers*—that is, numbers to the left of every statement, as you see in Figure A–1(b). The line numbers must be in ascending order. In theory, you could number statements consecutively from 1 to 9999, but this is not practical. You need to leave some unused numbers so that you can go back and *add* statements later, should that be necessary. Thus, if you number in increments of 10—that is, 10, 20, 30, 40, and so on—you can add statement 25 (between 20 and 30) later and not have to renumber the program.

In our program, we start with 100 and number in increments of 10. This is fairly common practice, and using three digits helps you line up your program more neatly.

### Spacing

Spacing in BASIC is not very important. In most BASIC systems, you are allowed to use any spacing you like; that is, you do not have to have a certain number of spaces between your line number, for instance, and the first character of your statement. In other words, you do not have to line up your program in certain columns.

### Statements

Let us now consider the statements in our inventory program. We have already described some of these briefly in Chapter 8, but we shall go over them again here in the order in which they appear in Figure A-1(b).

**REM Statement** The REM statement is *nonexecutable*, which means that the computer ignores it. The REM statement serves several purposes. First, it is used by the programmer in documenting the program. On the first line, for instance, the REM statement gives the program's title (INVENTORY PROGRAM) and the programmer's name (A. SCHMIDT). Often the date is also presented on this line. The REM statement is also used, as you see in lines 120 through 180, to describe the purpose of the program and the variable names (it is important to be able to remind yourself what the variable names mean in case you have to come back to the program days or weeks later).

The REM is also used as a separator, as a blank line in the program to enhance readability, as in lines 110, 140, and 190.

Note that, to make the program more readable, we have indented the non-REM lines (see lines 200 and 220–250).

**READ and DATA Statements** These two statements are very important, and we describe them together because they always go together. The READ statement indicates the variable locations where data will be placed. Variables, remember, are just *names of locations* where we are going to place data. We get that data from the DATA statement. In other words, the READ statement represents the input process; the DATA statement provides the data to be processed. In our example here, the data will be stored in the locations specified in the READ statement as I, N\$, and Q—which, as you see from lines 160–180, stand for "inventory number," "name," and "quantity on hand," respectively.

The DATA statement itself cannot be executed by the computer; it is merely a reference for the READ statement. Since DATA statements are not executable, they can be placed anywhere in the program and will be used by the READ statement in line number order.

In our program, the DATA statements are on lines 280–330. The READ statement will read the DATA statements one line at a time, the first one being statement 280. As the computer continues to go around through the loop (see the flowchart), it will move on down the DATA statements, reading new data each time.

Now let us see how the READ and DATA statements are used in this program. The READ A RECORD in the flowchart becomes, in the program, the READ statement, READ I, N\$, Q—see line 200, Figure A-1(b). That is, the READ statement reads data into three variables: I, N\$, and Q. This means that the READ statement must get data elements from the DATA statement three at a time. The I is a numeric variable that is going to hold a numeric constant from the DATA statement. The N\$ is a string variable that is going to hold a string constant of the DATA statement. The Q is a numeric variable that is going to hold a numeric constant.

Let us see what happens on the first read. The computer is instructed to read the first DATA statement, statement 280. It gets the constant 1643 and puts it in the variable I; then it gets the constant "FLASHLIGHT" and puts it into the variable N\$; and then it gets the constant 257 and puts it into variable Q. On the next read, the computer reads statement 290: 2945 goes into I, "BACKPACK" into N\$, and 156 into Q. This read process continues as the loop is executed.

**Trailer Values** The program continues this way until it reaches the last DATA statement, line 330. Actually, this is not a data line at all. The values in it, called **trailer values,** are artificial values put there to signal that we have reached the end of the data. (The computer would not know, otherwise, when it reached line 320—6466, "LANTERN," 143—that this was the last line of data.) The artificial values on line 330—that is, 9999, "END FILE", 000—are put in for the READ statement to test, as we shall see when we describe the IF statement. When the computer successfully tests for the trailer values, it stops processing.

An important note: There are exactly the same number of trailer values as there are variables in the READ statement. Here, for instance, there are three variables in the READ statement—I, N\$, and Q—and there are also three trailer values—9999, "END FILE", 000. If you do not have them, the computer may run out of data and stop processing.

**IF Statement** The IF statement is a conditional transfer; that is, the computer transfers somewhere else in the program in accordance with certain conditions. Look at line 220: IF I = 9999 THEN 340. This line means that if the condition is true, the computer will transfer to line 340, otherwise it will just continue to the next statement (line 230). Thus, if the value read into location I is 9999 (the trailer value), the computer will transfer to line 340, which is the end of the program.

**PRINT Statement** PRINT means send output to your CRT screen or to your printer terminal. Look at line 230: PRINT I, N\$, Q. This does not mean that I, N\$, and Q are literally going to be printed on the screen or paper. Rather the *contents* of these variables will be printed. You can see in Figure A-1(c) what the output of our program will be.

As you can see in Figures A-1(b) and (c), if you want the output to print out in particular columns, aligned by the letter on the left (called "left-justified"), then you have to be aware of the zone convention. There are five **zones** across the CRT screen or paper, each normally 14 characters wide. When you use the zone convention, the content of each variable is printed left-justified in each zone, as shown in Figure A-1(c). You signal the computer that you want this done by inserting commas between variables in the PRINT statement, as shown in Figure A-1(b), line 230.

There are other ways to output data using the PRINT statement. A *semicolon*, for instance, overrides the zone convention by placing the succeeding data right next to the data that came before the semicolon. We shall discuss this in more detail later.

**GOTO Statement** The GOTO ("go to") statement is an unconditional transfer of the control of the program. In our example here, Figure A-1(b), you can see that line 250, GOTO 220, completes the loop and sends control back to line 220.

**END Statement** There is exactly one END statement in every program, and it must be the last statement. If the END statement is encountered anywhere in the program in the process of running the program, the program will stop. We use the END statement here, in line 340, to do exactly that.

### Running Your Program on the Computer

How do you turn on, as it were, your computer? How do you make it work? You have to ask your instructor. He or she has to provide you with guidelines about how to use your particular computer system—to log in or "say hello" or whatever is required. Since there are so many different computer systems, there is no way we can cover them here. Thus, your instructor should advise you on required account numbers, passwords, methods of storing your programs, and methods for making changes to your programs.

Before you actually get on the computer, however, you should do some desk-checking of your program. You should prepare some test data and do some hand calculations to see what the results of the program should be, then compare them with what is actually output once you have run the program.

### Arithmetic Operations

Some people have the notion that programming is largely a mathematical skill. This is not true. Yet programming languages *can* be used to express arithmetic calculations, so let us see how these work.

**Arithmetic expressions** are combinations of numeric variables and numeric constants (both explained in previous sections) and arithmetic operations. **Operations** are

addition, subtraction, multiplication, division, and exponentiation—the last means "raising to a power," such as $2^2$. However, writing arithmetic expressions for a computer is different from doing it with pencil and paper. The reason is that, in BASIC at least, the computer prints across the page in a straight line, as opposed to stacking symbols one atop the other, as you would do when writing fractions. This requires some special rules.

**The Hierarchy of Arithmetic Operations** This hierarchy, which is shown in Figure A-2, is the order in which the computer will process an arithmetic expression: first exponentiation, then division and multiplication (at the same level), and finally addition and subtraction (also at the same level but below division and multiplication). Thus, for a particular arithmetic expression, the computer will go through it from left to right, first taking care of exponentiation, then division and multiplication, and so on. Figure A-2 also shows the symbols used to express mathematical operations—one asterisk (*) for multiplication, an upward arrow ( ↑ ) for exponentiation, and so on. (Note that some versions of BASIC also use two asterisks [**] for exponentiation.)

Figure A-3 demonstrates how to convert from algebra to BASIC, using these symbols. Notice that fractions are not written with one number above the other, but in a straight line, side by side—for example, 2/C. To write a fraction, then, you must write the numerator, then a slash (/), then the denominator.

| Operation | Symbol | Example |
|---|---|---|
| Exponentiation | ↑ or** | LET T = X↑2 |
| | | LET T = X**2 |
| Division | / | LET M = A/Z |
| Multiplication | * | LET W = X*Y |
| Addition | + | LET S = T1+T2 |
| Subtraction | − | LET D = X−10 |

**Note:** Parentheses can override the natural order in which BASIC expressions are evaluated.

**Figure A-2** Hierarchy of arithmetic operations.

| Algebra | BASIC |
|---|---|
| 3X | 3*X |
| $2Y^2 + 5Y$ | 2*Y**2+5*Y |
| $4A^3 - A^2 + 2A - 6$ | 4*A**3-A**2+2*A-6 |
| $\dfrac{C^2 - 2}{C + 4}$ | (C**2-2)/(C+4) |
| $\dfrac{A - B}{A + B}$ | (A-B)/(A+B) |
| $\dfrac{4A^2 - 2B}{3A}$ | (4*A**2-2*B)/(3*A) |

**Figure A-3** Translation of algebraic expressions into BASIC expressions.

Original algebraic expression:

$$\frac{2X^2 + 6Y - 10}{X - Y}$$

Incorrect BASIC expression:

```
2*X**2+6*Y-10/X-Y
```

Correct BASIC expression:

```
(2*X**2+6*Y-10)/(X-Y)
```

**Note:** Since the hierarchy of operations causes the BASIC language processor to evaluate division before subtraction, the *incorrect* expression will cause it to be divided by X, contrary to the intent of the algebraic expression. The correct BASIC expression contains parentheses that override the hierarchy and preserve the original intent.

**Figure A-4** Incorrect and correct translation of algebraic expression into BASIC.

Figure A-4 shows how an algebraic expression is translated into a BASIC expression—both incorrectly and correctly. Note that the use of *parentheses* is important because it can override the normal hierarchical order in which the computer will process an arithmetic expression.

**The LET Statement** The LET statement is called an **assignment statement** because its purpose is to assign a value to a variable. Here is how the LET statement works: Unlike algebraic equations, a LET statement permits only a variable to the left of the equal sign—for example, X in LET X = Y + Z. To the right of the equal sign is either another variable or an arithmetic expression. The arithmetic expression may be as simple or as complicated as you like. In BASIC, a variable name is placed on the left because that is going to be the *receiving location* of the value of the expression on the right. Thus, BASIC evaluates the expression on the right, forms a result, and places the result in the location designated by the variable name on the left. Some BASIC versions use assignment statements in the same way, without using the word LET—for example, X = Y + Z.

Some examples follow.

1. The computer moves from right to left: It evaluates the expression on the right and places the result in the variable on the left. For instance (350 is the line number):

```
350 LET X = A**2 + B
```

We evaluate A\*\*2 + B, and the result goes in X. Since A and B are variable locations that have already had some data placed in them, those data are, of course, the data evaluated in the expression A\*\*2 + B. (If you had a very simple expression such as LET T = 0, the 0 would be placed in T.)

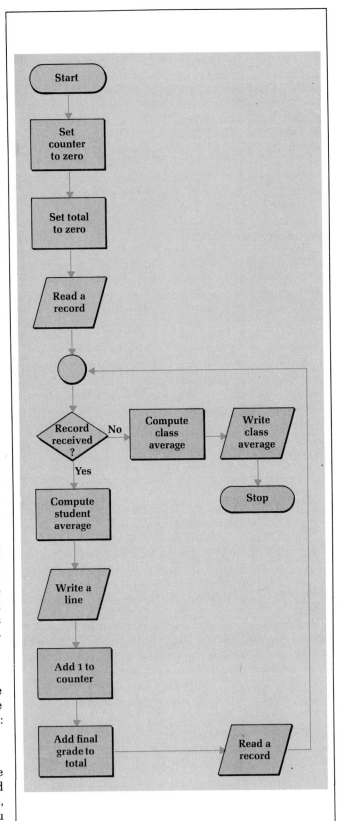

**Figure A-5** Flowchart for grade-averaging program.

```
100 REM    GRADE AVERAGING PROGRAM            N. CHAN
110 REM
120 REM    THIS PROGRAM READS STUDENT RECORDS,
130 REM    EACH OF WHICH CONTAINS STUDENT NAME
140 REM    AND 3 TEST GRADES: 2 TESTS AND A FINAL EXAM.
150 REM    OUTPUT CONSISTS OF:
160 REM             -ONE LINE PER STUDENT WITH NAME
170 REM               AND AVERAGE GRADE
180 REM             -CLASS AVERAGE ON THE FINAL EXAM.
190 REM
200 REM    VARIABLE NAMES:
210 REM          C  -CLASS COUNTER
220 REM          T  -TOTAL FINAL EXAM GRADES
230 REM          N$ -STUDENT NAME
240 REM          G1 -FIRST TEST GRADE
250 REM          G2 -SECOND TEST GRADE
260 REM          F  -FINAL EXAM GRADE
270 REM          A  -STUDENT AVERAGE
280 REM          V  -CLASS FINAL AVERAGE
290 REM
300        LET C=0
310        LET T=0
320        READ N$,G1,G2,F
330 REM    BEGIN LOOP
340        IF N$ = "END FILE" THEN 420
350        LET A = (G1+G2+F)/3
360        PRINT N$,A
370        LET C=C+1
380        LET T=T+F
390        READ N$,G1,G2,F
400        GOTO 340
410 REM    END-OF-FILE PROCESSING
420        LET V=T/C
430        PRINT
440        PRINT "CLASS AVERAGE ON FINAL IS";V
450        STOP
460 REM
470 REM            DATA
480 DATA "KIM BAUER",70,65,60
490 DATA "TIM HANSEN",92,88,94
500 DATA "PAUL OKACHI",82,80,90
510 DATA "SANDRA SHAW",100,86,94
520 DATA "ALAN STEIN",68,76,82
530 DATA "TED WARREN",65,65,78
540 DATA "END FILE",0,0,0
550 END
```

**Figure A-6** Program for grade averaging.

```
KIM BAUER              65
TIM HANSEN             91.3
PAUL OKACHI            84
SANDRA SHAW            93.3
ALAN STEIN             75.3
TED WARREN             69.3

CLASS AVERAGE ON FINAL IS 83
```

**Figure A-7** Output from grade-averaging program.

2. A LET statement is also commonly used for adding to an accumulator such as a **counter**. For instance:

```
410 LET C = C + 1
```

The number 1 is added to the current value of C, on the right; the result is replaced in C, as indicated on the left.

3. A LET statement can also be used for adding to an accumulator such as a running **total**. For example:

```
460 LET T = T + N
```

### Calculation Example: Grade-Averaging Program

Now let us look at an extended example that shows how we can use what we have learned so far. Figure A-5 shows the flowchart for a grade-averaging program. The program we will write from this flowchart is shown in Figure A-6, and the output from it is shown in Figure A-7. The purpose of this effort is to produce a program that reads student records—each of which contains a student name plus his or her scores on two tests and a final exam—and to produce output consisting of (1) one line for each student with his or her average grade and (2) the class average on the final examination. A statement of the program's purpose, you will note, is given in the program itself in the initial REM statements, lines 120–180, Figure A-6.

A glance at the flowchart, Figure A-5, shows the following features. First, there is a DOWHILE loop—the program will DO computing WHILE (that is, as long as) records are received. Second, there is a double-read statement (note the READ A RECORD parallelograms in the flowchart). Third, because the program is concerned with finding an average, we need to have a counter and a sum (or total) and these need to be initialized at zero. These activities are shown in the two rectangles at the beginning of the flowchart.

Now let us look at Figure A-6, the program stemming from this flowchart. After the documentation appearing in lines 120–180, we have the definitions of the variables, lines 200–280. You will note that all but N$ are numeric variable names. They are a letter of the alphabet or a letter followed by a number. N$ is a string variable representing the student name.

We now begin the program logic. To compute the student average, we need to use the LET statements—as you see in lines 300 and 310—which set the counter and total to zero. (You will note this corresponds to the first two boxes in the flowchart.) The READ and DATA statements and the loop mechanism are similar to those used in the previous program example. In this program the READ statements get student name and test scores. We use the LET statement again in line 350, which gives the formula by which a student's grade average is computed. Additional LET statements appear on lines 370 and 380 (these add to the counter and total) and on line 420 (this computes the class average for the final exam).

Now look at the PRINT statements. Line 360 is an instruction to print out each student name and grade average, as is shown in the output, Figure A-7. Line 430 in the program is a PRINT statement used in a new way—to produce just a blank line. As Figure A-7 shows, this line space separates the list of student names from the class average. The line 440 PRINT statement is an instruction to print the string constant shown in quotation marks—"CLASS AVERAGE ON FINAL IS"—followed by a semicolon, which overrides the zone convention, followed by the value of V. The printed value of V, like all numeric values, will be preceded by a space reserved for a minus

sign. Since V will not contain a negative number, there will just be a space in front of the number.

Now notice the STOP statement, line 450, which causes the program to stop executing. Earlier, back in Figure A-1(b), we used END for that purpose. Here in line 450, we could have said GOTO 550, but STOP serves just as well and eliminates the extra GOTO.

In the output, Figure A-7, student names are left-justified in zone 1, and each student's grade average is left-justified in zone 2.

### More on IF and PRINT

You already have a general understanding of the IF and PRINT statements. Now we shall study them more formally.

**IF Statement** The format of the IF statement is as follows:

$$\text{IF } e_1 \text{ RO } e_2 \text{ THEN } n$$

In the format, $e_1$ and $e_2$ are arithmetic expressions; RO stands for **relational operator,** which is an operator that compares the expressions. If the comparison is true, then control of the program is transferred to statement n. If the comparison is not true, then control of the program transfers to the statement following the IF statement. As Figure A-8 indicates, there are six permissible relational operations in BASIC.

We present the simplest form of the IF statement here; many versions of BASIC have expanded IF statements.

**PRINT Statement** The PRINT statement is one of the most interesting statements in BASIC because it has so much variety. Figure A-9 illustrates different uses of this statement. The five boxes in the figure represent the five zones (the boxes do not actually appear on the screen or paper, of course). Examine the five examples in Figure A-9.

1. *Using Zone Convention.* The values inside the quotation marks print as is, and they appear here in zone 1: TOTAL = . Whenever a *comma* is typed, it forces the succeeding data to print out in the next zone, so that, in this case, the value of the variable T (which we shall say is 150) is forced into zone 2, where it is left-justified. However, the appearance of the gap between the = and the 150 is not attractive.

| Operator symbol | Meaning | Example |
|---|---|---|
| = | equal to | 200 IF X = Y THEN 250 |
| < | less than | 200 IF A <6 THEN 250 |
| > | greater than | 200 IF R>10 THEN 250 |
| <= | less than or equal to | 200 IF J<=K THEN 250 |
| >= | greater than or equal to | 200 IF M>=100 THEN 250 |
| <> | not equal to | 200 IF M<>10 THEN 250 |

**Figure A-8** Relational operators.

**Using zone convention**

```
200   PRINT "TOTAL = ", T
```

| 1 | 2 | 3 | 4 | 5 |
|---|---|---|---|---|
| TOTAL = | 150 | | | |

**Overriding zone convention**

```
200   PRINT "TOTAL = "; T
```

| 1 | 2 | 3 | 4 | 5 |
|---|---|---|---|---|
| TOTAL = 150 | | | | |

**Mixture of zone and non-zone**

```
200   PRINT "A = "; A, "B = "; B, "C = "; C
```

| 1 | 2 | 3 | 4 | 5 |
|---|---|---|---|---|
| A = 6 | B = 10 | C = 24 | | |

**Column heading using zone convention**

```
200   PRINT "           INVENTORY REPORT"
210   PRINT
220   PRINT "PART", "PART", "QUANTITY", "UNIT"
230   PRINT "NUMBER", "NAME", "ON HAND", "PRICE"
240   PRINT "_____", "____", "_____", "_____"
```

| 1 | 2 | 3 | 4 | 5 |
|---|---|---|---|---|
| | | INVENTORY   REPORT | | |
| PART<br>NUMBER<br>_____ | PART<br>NAME<br>____ | QUANTITY<br>ON HAND<br>_____ | UNIT<br>PRICE<br>_____ | |

**Arithmetic operations in the PRINT statement**

```
200   PRINT N, N/2, N↑2
```

| 1 | 2 | 3 | 4 | 5 |
|---|---|---|---|---|
| 6 | 3 | 36 | | |

**Figure A-9   Some variations on the PRINT statement.** Numbers 1 through 5 refer to zones.

2. *Overriding Zone Convention.* To eliminate the excessive space between the = and the 150, we use a semicolon instead of a comma. The semicolon provides no spacing; items separated by the semicolon will be printed next to each other. However, if the data to be printed after the semicolon is numeric, a space will be reserved in front of the data for a sign. Incidentally, it is possible to print something in one zone that is longer than the number of characters (14) allowed for that zone. The additional characters simply extend into the next zone, and the use of a comma moves data into a zone still further away.

3. *Mixture of Zone and Non-zone.* It is sometimes convenient to use both semicolon and comma, as shown here. The first semicolon provides no spacing, but there will be a space for a sign in front of the 6, then the comma forces B = 10 into the next zone. Thus, we have effectively mixed zone and non-zone.

4. *Column Headings, Using Zone Convention.* This example shows how to produce attractive column headings for a report. The columns can be conveniently positioned by using the zone convention. Note here in line 200 that the report title, INVENTORY REPORT, is way over to the right, several spaces from the left quotation marks. We have, in fact, typed blank spaces after the left quotation marks, forcing the title INVENTORY REPORT to the center of the page. Line 210 leaves a blank line between the report title and the column headings below, which makes the report more readable.

Lines 220 and 230 show how two-line column headings are formed. Note that for the first heading, PART NUMBER, quotation marks are used around both "PART" and "NUMBER." As the example shows, you need to type all the first lines of these two-line column headings at one time, then type all the second lines at one time. The column headings are followed by commas to position them in the appropriate zones. The same process also takes place for the lines of dashes beneath the column headings.

5. *Arithmetic Operations in the PRINT Statement.* It is possible to have arithmetic operations in the PRINT statement. Thus, instead of writing LET X = T**2 and then printing the value for X, we can just write: PRINT T**2. Here we write PRINT N, (N/2), (N² ↑ 2). If the value of N is 6, you would have printed out the result shown in the example.

### Example: Determining Training Heart Rate for Athletes

The following is a simple example of a loop. We will use the resting heart rate and the age of athletes to determine the training heart rate—the optimum number of heart-

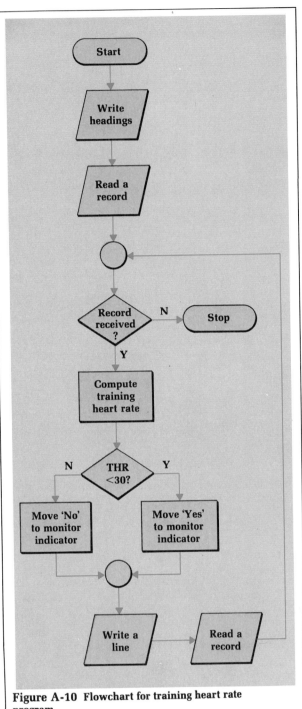

**Figure A-10 Flowchart for training heart rate program.**

beats per minute—that athletes should maintain over a given training period on a daily or thrice-weekly basis. The training heart rate is achieved by exercising oneself up to the desired heart rate, then maintaining it for about 20 minutes. The data being read into the program consist of (1) the athlete's name, (2) resting heart rate, and (3) age.

```
100 REM    TRAINING HEART RATE PROGRAM              V. HEINEMAN
110 REM
120 REM    THIS PROGRAM READS ATHLETE RECORDS, EACH OF WHICH
130 REM    CONTAINS ATHLETE NAME, RESTING HEART RATE, AND AGE.
140 REM    OUTPUT CONSISTS OF NAME, TRAINING HEART RATE, AND A
150 REM    YES/NO INDICATOR FOR MONITORING.
160 REM
170 REM    VARIABLE NAMES:
180 REM         N$ -NAME
190 REM         R  -RESTING HEART RATE
200 REM         A  -AGE
210 REM         T  -TRAINING HEART RATE
220 REM         M$ -MONITOR INDICATOR
230 REM
240        PRINT "         TRAINING HEART RATE REPORT"
250        PRINT
260        PRINT "NAME","THR","MONITOR"
270        PRINT
280        READ N$,R,A
290 REM    BEGIN LOOP
300        IF N$="END FILE" THEN 430
310        LET T=.80*(R+.75*(220-A))
320        IF T<140 THEN 350
330        LET M$="NO"
340        GOTO 360
350        LET M$="YES"
360        PRINT N$,T,M$
370        READ N$,R,A
380        GOTO 300
390 REM         DATA
400 DATA "MIRAKO OKADA",44,27,"LESLEY LEWIS",68,34
410 DATA "DIAN WELLS",48,32,"JERRY PIERCE",52,65
420 DATA "LENNY AMBAUEN",64,46,"END FILE",0,0
430 END
```

**Figure A-11** Program for training heart rate program.

| NAME | THR | MONITOR |
|------|-----|---------|
| MIRAKO OKADA | 151 | NO |
| LESLEY LEWIS | 166 | NO |
| DIAN WELLS | 150 | NO |
| JERRY PIERCE | 134 | YES |
| LENNY AMBAUEN | 155 | NO |

**Figure A-12** Output for training heart rate program.

The program example shows data for five athletes.

Two features about this program are to be observed:

1. We will write column headings, using the rules we just set forth about the PRINT statement.

2. We will have a location called the "monitor location," in which we will store the word YES or NO for each athlete. When it comes time to print the results for each athlete's record, we will print out the contents of that monitor location. Whether the word YES or NO appears in the location depends on what the training heart rate turns out to be.

If you now go through and compare the flowchart (see Figure A-10) with the program (Figure A-11), you will see the output—the various training heart rates for the five athletes (Figure A-12).

## From Flowchart to Program

If your BASIC program is fairly simple, converting from your flowchart to the program is not much of a problem. But if the logic is somewhat complicated, the conversion step may be difficult until you have had practice doing it.

Fortunately, there is a way of getting from the flowchart to the program that has proven quite effective in teaching beginning programmers, and we will explain it here. Essentially the technique is to *number the flowchart boxes, using numbers that will eventually correspond to line numbers in the program.*

First, let us identify the problem. It is: How does one translate the flowchart, which is two-dimensional, into the program, which is only one-dimensional? For instance, in the flowchart you will come to a decision box that branches off in two directions—a two-dimensional matter. How can this be reconciled with the program, which runs down the page in a one-dimensional fashion?

There are two points to remember to make programming easier:

1. Try to avoid transfers (GOTOs or IFs) to statements above the line you are presently on. Sometimes this kind of transfer is necessary, of course, as when the program returns to the top of a loop.

2. Number the boxes on the flowchart.

Let us now show, using an example, how to go from a flowchart to a program.

### Programming a Payroll System

This is the kind of problem a programmer may well encounter in the course of his or her career. The purpose of the program is to make a payroll report. You are to devise a program that will read employee records containing employee names, hourly pay rate, and the hours each employee worked during the week; compute any overtime pay (at $1\frac{1}{2}$ times the usual pay rate); and produce output consisting of (1) one line per employee, with name, pay rate, hours, and salary, and (2) total company payroll. The purpose of the program is given in Figure A-14, REM statements 120–200; the output is shown in Figure A-15.

Now let us look at the flowchart, Figure A-13. Note how the basic logic of this flowchart works. (The numbers that follow correspond to the circled numbers in the flowchart.)

❶ The first step is to set up the headings for the report. This step is shown in the first parallelogram, WRITE HEADINGS.

❷ Next we lay the groundwork for computing the total company payroll. The first rectangle initializes the counter that totals up the salaries; the rectangle near the bottom of the page accumulates individual employee salaries to yield total company salary. The loop continues until all employee salaries have been counted, whereupon (see last parallelogram before STOP) the computer writes out the total company salary.

❸ For each employee, we must determine whether he or she has worked overtime—more than 40 hours a week. This problem is handled by the decision branch. If the hours are greater than 40, the computer will compute the overtime, then set the hours of that employee to 40, to be used for computing base salary. If the employee

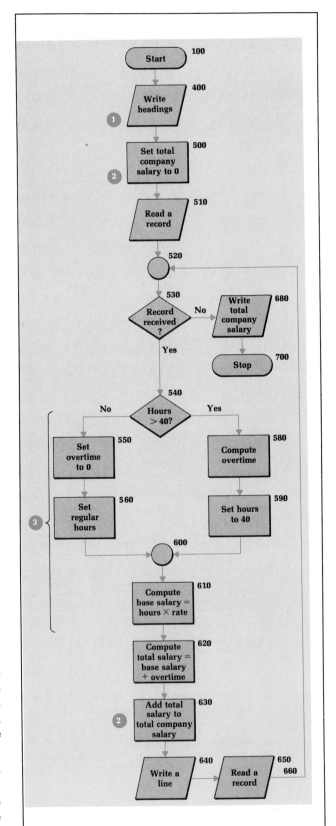

**Figure A-13 Flowchart for payroll program.**

**Laboratory session.** Students learn to use documentation tools at New York's Telephone Computer Technology Training Corporate Learning Center during a training session.

```
100 REM    PAYROLL PROGRAM             B. MCCORMICK
110 REM
120 REM    THIS PROGRAM READS EMPLOYEE RECORDS
130 REM    CONTAINING NAME, HOURLY PAY RATE,
140 REM    AND HOURS WORKED FOR THE WEEK. ANY
150 REM    HOURS OVER 40 WILL BE PAID AT ONE
160 REM    AND A HALF TIMES THE USUAL PAY RATE.
170 REM    OUTPUT CONSISTS OF:
180 REM          -ONE LINE PER EMPLOYEE WITH NAME,
190 REM           PAY RATE, HOURS, AND SALARY
200 REM          -TOTAL COMPANY PAYROLL
210 REM
220 REM    VARIABLE NAMES:
230 REM         T  -TOTAL COMPANY SALARY
240 REM         N$ -EMPLOYEE NAME
250 REM         R  -PAY RATE (HOURLY)
260 REM         H  -HOURS WORKED THIS WEEK
270 REM         H1 -REGULAR HOURS
280 REM         V  -OVERTIME AMOUNT
290 REM         B  -EMPLOYEE BASE SALARY
300 REM         S  -EMPLOYEE TOTAL SALARY
310 REM
400        PRINT "          PAYROLL REPORT"
410        PRINT
420        PRINT "NAME","RATE","HOURS","SALARY"
430        PRINT "----","----","-----","------"
440        PRINT
500        LET T=0
510        READ N$,R,H
520 REM    BEGIN LOOP
530        IF N$="END FILE" THEN 680
540        IF H>40 THEN 580
550        LET V=0
560        LET H1=H
570        GOTO 610
580        LET V=1.5*(H-40)*R
590        LET H1=40
600 REM    END-IF
610        LET B=H1*R
620        LET S=B+V
630        LET T=T+S
640        PRINT N$,R,H,S
650        READ N$,R,H
660        GOTO 530
670 REM    END-OF-FILE PROCESSING
680        PRINT
690        PRINT "TOTAL COMPANY PAYROLL=";T
700        STOP
710 REM
720 REM         DATA
730 DATA "DANA CHOY",5.46,40,"KATIE DEVOE",6.54,45
740 DATA "ED HIRSCH",5.52,36,"ERIC LARSON",8.28,40
750 DATA "PETE LEECH",9.27,40,"JOEL MORGAN",6.76,48
760 DATA "END FILE",0,0
770 END
```

**Figure A-14  Program for payroll program.**

did not work more than 40 hours, the computer will set overtime to 0. Whichever path we take, we come back to the connector box, and can then go from there to compute the total salary, which is the base salary plus the overtime.

So much for the underlying logic. We will now see what happens when we proceed to number this flowchart according to the line numbers that will appear in the program. You should refer both to the flowchart and to the program in Figure A-14 as you read the following.

**Lines 100–440** Note that we start with three digits because, as we noted earlier, the numbers line up better than they would if we started with two digits, then switched to three later. On the flowchart, we have deliberately left out numbers between 100 and 400. These will be used for comments or REM statements, as Figure A-14 shows. (If not all numbers between 100 and 400 are used, that is still proper.) Note that lines 220–300 are used to define the variable names. As Figure A-14 illustrates, the lines between 400 and 440 are used for printing headings. Note the uses of quotation marks, spaces, and commas to position the headings in the desired zones. Note also how PRINT is used to leave blank lines in the final output. We use as many 400 numbers as necessary, then proceed directly to 500.

**Lines 500–530** Line 500 initializes the accumulator of company salaries at zero; this instruction is expressed in the program as LET T = 0. Line 510 is the first of the READ statements (the other is 650), and is an instruction to read values for employee name, pay rate, and hours worked that week. Line 520 is the connector box in the flowchart; it represents the start of the loop, and so it is represented in the program as BEGIN LOOP.

Line 530 is the first place where a decision will have to be made. Note that if continued processing is required—if the answer to the question RECORD RECEIVED? is YES—we continue to move down through the flowchart, and

hence down the program. If the processing is complete—if the answer to the RECORD RECEIVED? question is NO and END FILE is encountered—then processing moves in another direction, off to the end of the program, line 680. (If you were drawing this flowchart from scratch, you would come back later and put in the 680 and 700 after you had finished constructing the entire flowchart. That is, you should fill in the number for the alternate decision paths, lines 680–700 later.)

**Lines 540–600** At line 540 we come to another decision. Generally speaking, on a decision box of this sort, which does not involve a loop, it is best to attend to the NO branch first, then the YES branch. Both paths end up meeting back at the connector box, number 600. However, note that we must leave the NO branch on the left in the flowchart to next work through the steps in the YES branch; consequently, in the program we need to devise a way to allow the NO branch to come back to the connector box. This is done with 570—GOTO 610—which in the program allows us to transfer around the information in 580 and 590, which are concerned with YES-branch information about overtime. If the particular record received is such that we must go through the YES branch of 580–590, it will take us back to the connector box at 600 without another GOTO statement. The END-IF statement in line 600 helps make the program more readable.

**Lines 610–660** These lines contain the statements to compute each employee's salary, with or without overtime, and add it to the running total (line 630). Note that, in line 640, the computer prints out a line giving each employee's name (N$), rate of pay (R), hours worked (H), and salary (S) for that week. The loop then moves on to the second READ statement (650), and then statement 660 transfers back to the top of the loop. Having used up numbers through 650, we may now use higher numbers to complete the NO branch of the decision box we encountered in line 530. This completes the program.

Now look at the output, Figure A-15. Note that the headings are written so they fall in columns (zones), with one blank line under them, and then the data, which also falls in columns. Note also that numeric data is automatically indented one space to leave room in front of the number for any minus sign that might be required. Finally, it is apparent that nonsignificant zeros to the right of the decimal point are not printed; it is understood that Dana Choy's salary, for instance, is $218.40.

### Interactive Programs

The term **interactive** means that a dialogue is taking place between the user at the terminal and the computer. The user types something and the computer "types" something back. For the computer to be able to accept the user's action, however, the INPUT statement must be used.

```
              PAYROLL REPORT

NAME            RATE    HOURS    SALARY

DANA CHOY       5.46    40        218.4
KATIE DEVOE     6.54    45        310.65
ED HIRSCH       5.52    36        198.72
ERIC LARSON     8.28    40        331.2
PETE LEECH      9.27    40        370.8
JOEL MORGAN     6.76    48        351.52

TOTAL COMPANY PAYROLL = 1781.29
```

**Figure A-15 Output from payroll program.**

### The INPUT Statement and Prompts

The INPUT statement is very much like the READ statement, except that the data comes from the user's terminal instead of from a DATA statement in the program. When the computer invokes the INPUT statement, program execution is interrupted; that is, the computer actually stops executing your program and waits for you to input some data from the terminal.

How do you know you are supposed to input data? You will know because a **prompt** will appear on the terminal screen or printout. On many systems, the prompt is a question mark (?), and that is what we will use here. The INPUT statement causes the prompt to appear. Usually, however, the prompt is preceded by information from a PRINT statement—some question or instruction such as DO YOU WANT TO CONTINUE or TYPE A NUMBER. This informs the user that he or she is supposed to input data.

An example follows that shows how prompts and INPUT statements work. Just before line 220 causes the prompt (a question mark) to print, lines 200 and 210 provides an instruction to the user. Note that the INPUT statement has variables separated by commas. Lines 230 and 240 use the input data provided by the user at the terminal.

```
200 PRINT "TYPE NUMBER OF UNITS AND"
210 PRINT "COST PER UNIT"
220 INPUT U,C
230 LET R = U * C
240 PRINT "TOTAL REVENUE IS";R
```

This is a segment of a computer program. The following is a sample of the interaction between the user and the computer as it executes this part of the program.

```
TYPE NUMBER OF UNITS AND
COST PER UNIT
?25,1.55
TOTAL REVENUE IS 38.75
```

The question mark on the third line is the prompt. It indicates that the computer is waiting for you to respond to the directions, TYPE NUMBER OF UNITS AND COST PER UNIT. In answer to the prompt, you would, as shown above in the third line, type in 25 for number of units, followed by a comma, then by 1.55 for the cost per unit. In accordance with lines 230 and 240 in the program segment, the computer prints out on the last line the total revenue, 38.75 (which was derived by the computer multiplying 25 times 1.55). So that the user knows what to do when he or she is interacting with the program, there are usually explicit instructions at the start of the program. Often the instructions are quite lengthy—line after line telling the user what questions will be asked and what to be ready for. In addition to this overview, there are brief instructions before each INPUT statement, as we just saw.

Data may be entered on a separate line, as we showed in the preceding example, or it may be entered on the same line. Consider the following program segment:

```
200 PRINT "ENTER NUMBER GALLONS";
210 INPUT G
```

Notice the semicolon at the end of line 200. That will cause the prompt from the INPUT statement (line 210) to print on the same line as the instruction. The results of executing these lines would therefore appear as follows:

```
ENTER NUMBER GALLONS?
```

You would answer the question by typing in 6 (or whatever the answer is) on the same line as the question mark, as follows:

```
ENTER NUMBER GALLONS?6
```

### Example of Interactive Program: The Square and Cube Program

Figures A-16 through A-18 show how to flowchart and write an interactive program to allow the user to input a number at the terminal and display the square and cube of that number. The program execution will continue until the user tells the computer to stop.

Note from the flowchart, Figure A-16, that this is an example of a DOUNTIL iteration. The computer will continue to DO the displaying of cubes and roots UNTIL the user tells it to stop. The flowchart is straightforward: First write general instructions (see first parallelogram) to tell the user what he or she will be asked to do. Once past the connector box, which starts the loop, the logic of the program begins: Write the short input instruction, then input a number, then produce the square and cube of that number, then ascertain if the user wishes to continue—and, if so, loop around again, or otherwise write a goodbye message and stop.

Now let us look at the program, Figure A-17. Lines 210–260 tell the user how to use the program, as diagrammed in the first parallelogram in the flowchart. (Note quotation marks at the beginning and end of each line.) Line 270 is the beginning of the loop, and we actually state this in the program: BEGIN LOOP. Lines 280–380 are concerned with interactive dialogue, and you will notice that we have printed some blank lines here and there to make the output more readable.

Line 290 instructs the user to TYPE A NUMBER NOW, after which he or she types a number (line 300). Now notice that on line 310 we provide the headings NUMBER, SQUARE, and CUBE. Line 320 instructs the program to print the number (N), square (N**2), and cube (N**3) that will appear beneath the headings.

Line 340 asks if the user wants to stop, which requires a response: Y (yes) or N (no). Notice the S$ on line 350. This is a string variable because the answer, Y or N, is a string constant, not a number. If the answer is N, the computer loops back to line 280 again; if it is Y, a goodbye message is printed, as indicated on line 380.

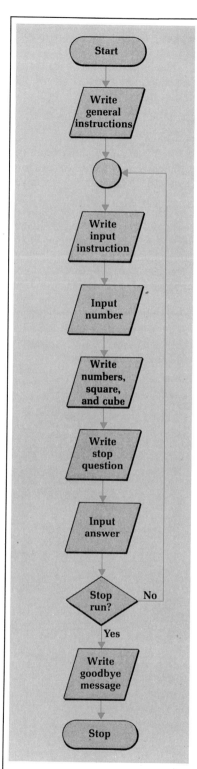

Figure A-16  Flowchart for square and cube program.

```
100 REM    SQUARE AND CUBE PROGRAM         Z. THOMPSON
110 REM
120 REM    THIS PROGRAM INPUTS A NUMBER FROM THE USER
130 REM    AT THE TERMINAL AND DISPLAYS THE SQUARE
140 REM    AND CUBE OF THE NUMBER. THIS PROCESS
150 REM    IS REPEATED UNTIL THE USER ELECTS TO STOP.
160 REM
170 REM    VARIABLE NAMES:
180 REM        N  -INPUT NUMBER
190 REM        S$ -STOP ANSWER
200 REM
210        PRINT "YOU WILL BE ASKED TO TYPE A NUMBER."
220        PRINT "THE SQUARE AND CUBE OF THE NUMBER"
230        PRINT "WILL BE DISPLAYED. YOU MAY CONTINUE"
240        PRINT "THIS PROCESS; JUST ANSWER N (FOR NO)"
250        PRINT "IF YOU DO NOT WISH TO STOP. WHEN"
260        PRINT "FINISHED TYPE Y (FOR YES) TO STOP."
270 REM    BEGIN LOOP
280        PRINT
290        PRINT "TYPE A NUMBER NOW"
300        INPUT N
310        PRINT "NUMBER","SQUARE","CUBE"
320        PRINT N,N**2,N**3
330        PRINT
340        PRINT "DO YOU WANT TO STOP? (Y OR N)"
350        INPUT S$
360        IF S$="N" THEN 280
370        PRINT
380        PRINT "END OF PROGRAM. GOODBYE."
390 END
```

Figure A-17  Program for square and cube program.

```
RUN
YOU WILL BE ASKED TO TYPE A NUMBER.
THE SQUARE AND CUBE OF THE NUMBER
WILL BE DISPLAYED. YOU MAY CONTINUE
THIS PROCESS; JUST ANSWER N (FOR NO)
IF YOU DO NOT WISH TO STOP. WHEN
FINISHED TYPE Y (FOR YES) TO STOP.

TYPE A NUMBER NOW
?6
NUMBER     SQUARE     CUBE
  6          36         216

DO YOU WANT TO STOP? (Y OR N)
?N

TYPE A NUMBER NOW
?12
NUMBER     SQUARE     CUBE
  12         144        1728

DO YOU WANT TO STOP? (Y OR N)
?Y

END OF PROGRAM. GOODBYE.
```

Figure A-18  Output from square and cube program.

The output for the square and cube program is shown in Figure A-18.

## Looping with the FOR/NEXT Statements

FOR and NEXT are two statements that go together in BASIC. You cannot use one without the other. FOR/NEXT is used as a convenience in loops in which you are using a counter (as we did earlier in counting employee salaries for the company payroll). A counting loop has three elements: First, it must be *initialized*; that is, started at a base figure, such as zero, prior to counting. Second, an *increment* is added to the counter during each loop. Third, the counter is *tested* during each loop to determine if a certain limit has been reached, in which case the counting loop stops. (The second and third steps do not necessarily occur in this order.) FOR/NEXT statements take care of these three steps. Several rules apply to the convention, however. Let us see what they are.

### The Convenience of FOR/NEXT

Figures A-19(a) and A-19(b) compare two versions of a counting loop, with and without the FOR/NEXT state-ments. Note that lines 100 to 130 are the same. We are to find the sum of five data items, variable names are listed, and we let S (which stands for sum) equal zero.

Look at Figure A-19(a). The important part here is the *counter*, which counts each data item each time we go through the loop. We *initialize* the counter—set it to one—on line 140, LET C = 1. The *increment* of the counter occurs in line 190, LET C = C + 1; here 1 is added to the counter each time we go through the loop. The *test* as to whether we have yet counted five data items occurs in line 160, IF C>5 THEN 210, which tells us to exit the loop if five items have been counted; in the latter case we go on to print out the sum.

The important point is this: In Figure A-19(a), these actions on the counter are taken care of very explicitly by you, the programmer; however, in Figure A-19(b), the FOR/NEXT statements take care of these actions. Let us look at Figure A-19(b). The program starts out the same as before, but the initialization is handled differently; that is, on line 150, we use a FOR statement: FOR C = 1 TO 5. Line 180, NEXT C, causes the counter C to be incremented and tested. In this case, when C is 5 the test will show that the loop need not be repeated again; since the loop is complete, control of the program will transfer to line 190.

```
                    100 REM   FIND THE SUM OF 5 DATA ITEMS
                    110 REM   VARIABLE NAMES:
                    120 REM   S - SUM, C - COUNTER, N - NUMBER
                    130       LET S = 0
Initialize ───────→ 140       LET C = 1
                    150 REM   BEGIN LOOP
Test ─────────────→ 160       IF C>5 THEN 210
                    170       READ N
                    180       LET S = S + N
Increment ────────→ 190       LET C = C + 1
                    200       GOTO 160
                    210       PRINT "SUM =";S
                    220 DATA 7,4,16,13,2
                    230 END
```

**Figure A-19(a)  Without FOR/NEXT.**

```
                    100 REM   FIND THE SUM OF 5 DATA ITEMS
                    110 REM   VARIABLE NAMES:
                    120 REM   S - SUM, C - COUNTER, N - NUMBER
                    130       LET S = 0
                    140 REM   BEGIN LOOP
Initialize ───────→ 150       FOR C = 1 TO 5
                    160           READ N
                    170           LET S = S + N
Test, Increment ──→ 180       NEXT C
                    190       PRINT "SUM ="
                    200 DATA 7,4,16,13,2
                    210 END
```

**Figure A-19(b)  With FOR/NEXT.**

```
100 REM    SQUARE AND CUBE USING FOR/NEXT         E. GILLICK
110 REM
120 REM    THIS PROGRAM USES FOR/NEXT TO GENERATE
130 REM    THE SQUARE AND CUBE OF NUMBERS FROM
140 REM    ONE TO TEN.
150 REM
160 REM    VARIABLE NAMES:
170 REM        N  -NUMBER
180 REM
190        PRINT "NUMBER","SQUARE","CUBE"
200        PRINT
210 REM    BEGIN LOOP
220        FOR N = 1 TO 10   STEP 1
230            PRINT N,N**2,N**3
240        NEXT N
250 END
```

**Figure A-20(a)** Program for FOR/NEXT—square and cube revisited.

## More Examples of FOR/NEXT

The following are four examples of ways FOR/NEXT may be used.

**Example 1: Square and Cube Revisited** This example is shown in Figures A-20(a) and (b). The FOR statement and its two elements (the increment, STEP 1, is the default value) appear on line 220; the body of the loop, which is indented, appears on line 230; and the NEXT statement appears on line 240. The output of this program is shown in Figure A-20(b).

| NUMBER | SQUARE | CUBE |
|--------|--------|------|
| 1 | 1 | 1 |
| 2 | 4 | 8 |
| 3 | 9 | 27 |
| 4 | 16 | 64 |
| 5 | 25 | 125 |
| 6 | 36 | 216 |
| 7 | 49 | 343 |
| 8 | 64 | 512 |
| 9 | 81 | 729 |
| 10 | 100 | 1000 |

**Figure A-20(b)** Output from the FOR/NEXT—square and cube revisited program.

**Example 2: Index Never Actually Equals Test Value** Note the value for J in the following program:

```
200 FOR J = 2 TO 12 STEP 3
210     PRINT J
220 NEXT J
```
2
5
8
11

When the STEP 3 increment is added to the J value of 2, the result is 5. Since the test for getting out of the loop is that the index (J) must be equal to or greater than the test value (12 in this case), 5 is not sufficient, and so the loop continues. On the second loop the J value of 5 added to 3 is 8—still not great enough. On the third loop, $8 + 3 = 11$; on the fourth loop, $11 + 3 = 14$, and we thereupon exit from the loop. Note that the index, J, never actually equaled the test value of 12, but it was not necessary for it to do so.

**Example 3: Negative Increment** In the following program segment, note that the increment is a *negative value*.

```
200 FOR J = 20 TO 10 STEP -5
210     PRINT J
220 NEXT J
```
20
15
10

Index J will *decrease* by 5 each time through the loop, so the values 20, 15, and 10 will be printed for J.

**Example 4: Nested Loops** It is perfectly legal to have what are known as *nested loops*—that is, one loop inside another, as the following example shows. The brackets to the left show how the FOR/NEXT statements are linked. Notice that the one inside is completely contained in the outer one. No overlapping of loops is permitted.

```
200 FOR I = 1 TO 2
210     FOR J = 2 TO 4
220         PRINT I , J
230     NEXT J
240 NEXT I
```

The output will be:

| | |
|---|---|
| 1 | 2 |
| 1 | 3 |
| 1 | 4 |
| 2 | 2 |
| 2 | 3 |
| 2 | 4 |

You will note that the inner FOR/NEXT loop must go through an entire loop while the index in the outer loop is still 1. Thus, while I remains at 1, the index J will become 2, then 3, then 4. Eventually we exit from the loop and proceed on to line 240, at which point we encounter the NEXT and start the process over again.

## FOR/NEXT

**Format:**

FOR i = e₁ TO e₂ STEP e₃

.
.
.

NEXT i

**Where:**
i is the index
e₁ is the initial value of the index
e₂ is the test value for the index
e₃ is the increment for the index

The index is a numeric variable; the three values are expressions.

**Example:**

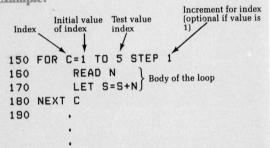

```
150 FOR C=1 TO 5 STEP 1
160     READ N          } Body of the loop
170     LET S=S+N
180 NEXT C
190     .
        .
        .
```

**Notes:**

- Use the same variable name (C in the preceding example) for both FOR and NEXT.

- The FOR statement sets the values for the initial index, index test, and index increment.

- The NEXT statement exits the loop if the index is greater than the test value. (Unless e₃ is negative; then the loop is exited if i <= e₂.) If the loop is not exited, then index i is incremented by e₃ and the loop continues.

- The loop is exited by transferring to the statement following the NEXT statement (line 190 in the preceding example).

- There must be exactly one NEXT statement for each FOR statement.

- The index, initial value, test value, and increment should not be altered in the body of the loop by statements written by the programmer.

### Processing Arrays Using FOR/NEXT

An **array** is another name for a table. Arrays in standardized BASIC can be one-dimensional or two-dimensional. A one-dimensional array is called a **list.** A two-dimensional array—with horizontal *rows* in one dimension and vertical *columns* in another dimension—is called a *table.* An individual piece of data within an array is called an item or *element.* See Figure A-21.

To reference one item of an array, a **subscript** is used. In mathematics, the subscript is expressed by a small number below the line (such as $A_5$); however, since in BASIC we can only print on the line, the subscript is placed in parentheses. Thus, $A_5$ would be represented as A(5). Subscripts can be used to indicate an individual item in an array. We shall assume, in subsequent discussions, a starting subscript of one. For instance, F$(10) could indicate the tenth item in list F$, or R(3,5) could indicate the item in the fifth column in the third row in array R. Subscripts can also be variables: X(I). This feature is particularly useful, as we shall see, for processing arrays using loops.

Array names in BASIC vary according to the variety of BASIC language one is using. Most of the time, an array name matches the standard variable-naming conventions: a letter or a letter followed by a digit for an array of numeric data, or a letter followed by a $ for an array of string data.

To inform the computer that an array will be used, we use a **DIM** statement; DIM is short for "dimension." Usually the DIM statement appears at the beginning of the program, but in any event it must occur before the array is processed. An example of a DIM statement is:

```
200 DIM X(10),R(3,5)
```

This lets the computer know that array X has a maximum of 10 elements and array R has 3 rows and 5 columns, for a maximum of 15 elements. (Remember that we have assumed a starting subscript of one.)

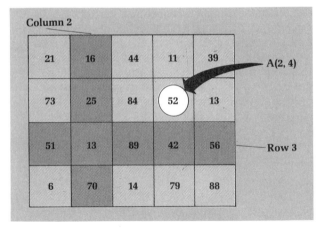

**Figure A-21** Array A with four rows and five columns.

```
100 REM     SALES COMMISSION PROGRAM          R. BURBANK
110 REM
120 REM     THIS PROGRAM READS SALESPERSON NUMBER
130 REM     AND SALES AMOUNT INTO ARRAYS AND
140 REM     COMPUTES COMMISSION, TO BE PLACED IN A
150 REM     THIRD ARRAY. THIS DATA, TOGETHER WITH
160 REM     THE TOTAL COMMISSION FOR THE SALES FORCE,
170 REM     IS OUTPUT.
180 REM
190 REM     VARIABLE NAMES:
200 REM          N  -SALESPERSON NUMBER ARRAY
210 REM          S  -SALES AMOUNT ARRAY
220 REM          C  -COMMISSION ARRAY
230 REM          T  -TOTAL COMMISSION
240 REM          I  -LOOP INDEX
250 REM
260         DIM N(10),S(10),C(10)                    ───── SETS the arrays sizes
270         PRINT "SALES","SALES","COMMISSION"
280         PRINT "NUMBER","AMOUNT","AMOUNT"
290         PRINT
300         LET T=0  ── counter
310 REM     BEGIN LOOP
320         FOR I = 1 TO 10
330             READ N(I),S(I)
340             IF S(I)>10000 THEN 370
350             LET C(I)=S(I)*.05                    } Loop
360             GOTO 380
370             LET C(I)=S(I)*.07
380             REM END-IF
390             PRINT N(I),S(I),C(I)
400             LET T=T+C(I)
410         NEXT I
420         PRINT
430         PRINT "TOTAL COMMISSION=";T
440         STOP
450 REM
460 REM         DATA
470 DATA 1146,9740,1643,11000,2167,6511
480 DATA 2461,11967,3248,8088,3945,5000
490 DATA 5155,8800,6111,12500,8140,10005
500 DATA 8490,9050
510 END
```

**Figure A-22(a)**  Program for sales commission program.

To better understand the use of arrays, let us consider three examples, the first and second in one dimension, the third in two dimensions.

**Example 1: One-Dimensional Array**  The program and output for this example are shown in Figures A-22(a) and (b). The problem here is to compute sales commissions. As lines 120–170 indicate, the computer is supposed to read the salesperson number and sales amount into two arrays and then compute the commission and place it in a third array. This data, along with the total commission for the

sales force, is then displayed as output. Note that, as indicated in lines 340, 350, and 370, if the amount of sales is over $10,000 the commission rate is 7 percent. If sales are not over $10,000, the commission rate is 5 percent. As shown in lines 200–220, the actual sales number and sales amount will be read into two arrays (N for number and S for sales), and the commission that is computed will be placed into array C. (The alert programmer will observe that the arrays are, strictly speaking, not necessary in this case; the numbers could simply be read in and processed as is.)

```
SALES         SALES       COMMISSION
NUMBER        AMOUNT       AMOUNT
  1146         9740         487
  1643        11000         770
  2167         6511         325.55
  2461        11967         837.69
  3248         8088         404.4
  3945         5000         250
  5155         8800         440
  6111        12500         875
  8140        10005         700.35
  8490         9050         452.5
TOTAL COMMISSION = 5542.49
```

**Figure A-22(b)  Output from sales commission program.**

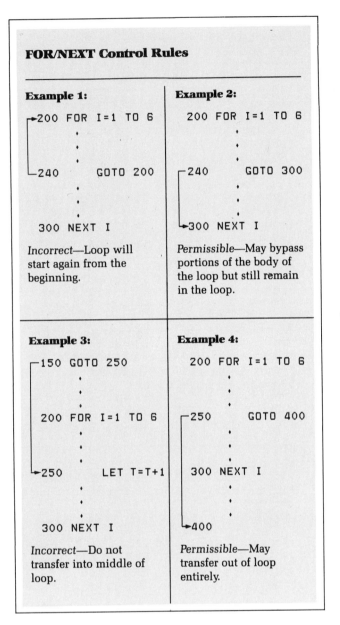

**FOR/NEXT Control Rules**

**Example 1:**

```
┌─200 FOR I=1 TO 6
│       •
│       •
│       •
└─240        GOTO 200
        •
        •
   300 NEXT I
```

Incorrect—Loop will start again from the beginning.

**Example 2:**

```
  200 FOR I=1 TO 6
        •
        •
┌─240        GOTO 300
│       •
│       •
└─300 NEXT I
```

Permissible—May bypass portions of the body of the loop but still remain in the loop.

**Example 3:**

```
┌─150 GOTO 250
│       •
│       •
│  200 FOR I=1 TO 6
│       •
└─250        LET T=T+1
        •
        •
   300 NEXT I
```

Incorrect—Do not transfer into middle of loop.

**Example 4:**

```
  200 FOR I=1 TO 6
        •
        •
┌─250        GOTO 400
│  300 NEXT I
│       •
└─400
```

Permissible—May transfer out of loop entirely.

The variables defined, let us now move into the program itself. The first statement of real interest is 260, where we give advance notice of the size of the arrays that are going to be used: 10 items in each array. After the statements to print headings (lines 270 to 290), and initialization of the total commission accumulator (line 300), the loop begins. The loop process will be repeated 10 times (lines 320 to 410): Read salesperson number and sales amount; compute commission; print salesperson number, sales amount, and commission; add commission to total commission. Finally, the loop is complete, and the computer goes to line 420 to print the total sales commission. Compare the program to the output in Figure A-22(b).

**Example 2: Sorting a One-Dimensional Array** There are many occasions when we need to sort data in order. In this example, we will input the names of six marathon runners in random order and ask that they be sorted in alphabetical order. This type of sort is called a selection sort. Figure A-23 shows the random order in which the names are input (Kakiuchi through Gattis) and how they are supposed to look after sorting (Arnold through Purrington).

Now, how do we get these names moved around? The best way is to put them in an array and then manipulate that array, using subscripts and FOR/NEXT loops. We will also use *nested loops*—inner loops within outer loops.

Let us see how this works in the program we have written in Figure A-24. Starting on line 280 and ending on line 350, we have the outer FOR/NEXT loop. Between those two lines, beginning on line 290 and ending on line 340, is another FOR/NEXT—a nested loop. This nested loop means that the inner loop will be completely exhausted on each iteration of the outer loop.

The selection sort works this way: We go through the array, comparing the first item, Kakiuchi, with each of the other items (runner names) in the array. Whenever an item

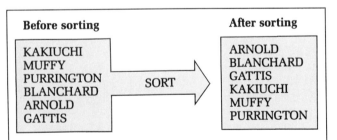

**Figure A-23  Sorting for a one-dimensional array.** Before and after arrangement of data for selection sort of names of marathon runners.

```
100 REM    SELECTION SORT                               C. NELSON
110 REM
120 REM    THIS PROGRAM USES NESTED FOR/NEXT LOOPS TO PERFORM A
130 REM    SELECTION SORT TO ALPHABETIZE A LIST OF RUNNER NAMES.
140 REM
150 REM    VARIABLE NAMES:
160 REM          N$ -NAME ARRAY
170 REM          N  -NUMBER OF ITEMS IN ARRAY
180 REM          S,S1,S2 -SUBSCRIPTS
190 REM          H$ -HOLD AREA
200 REM
210        DIM N$(100)
220 REM    READ ARRAY LENGTH AND ARRAY
230        READ N
240        FOR S=1 TO N
250            READ N$(S)
260        NEXT S
270 REM    SORT ARRAY
280        FOR S1=1 TO N-1
290            FOR S2=S1+1 TO N
300                IF N$(S1)<=N$(S2) THEN 340
310                LET H$=N$(S1)
320                LET N$(S1)=N$(S2)
330                LET N$(S2)=H$
340            NEXT S2
350        NEXT S1
360 REM    PRINT SORTED ARRAY
370        FOR S=1 TO N
380            PRINT N$(S)
390        NEXT S
400        STOP
410 REM
420 REM              DATA
430 DATA 6
440 DATA "KAKIUCHI","MUFFY","PURRINGTON"
450 DATA "BLANCHARD","ARNOLD","GATTIS"
460 END
```

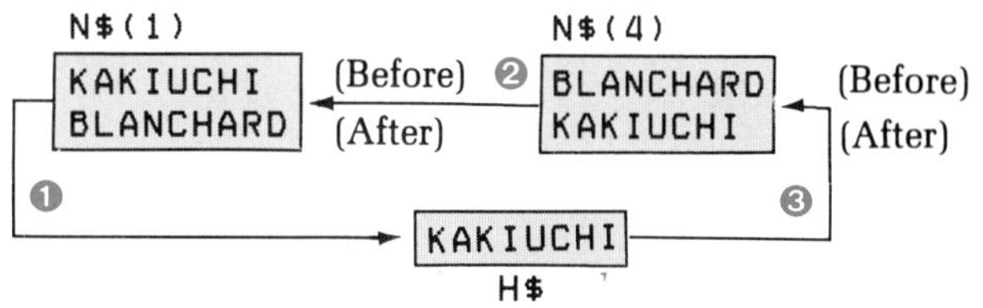

Figure A-25 **The hold area.** How exchanges are made in selection sort.

**Figure A-24** Program for selection sort of marathon runners.

in the array is encountered that is smaller than an item that is currently in the first location in the array, a change will take place. The smaller item encountered (which will be an item that is closest to the beginning of the alphabet) will be moved to the first position, and whatever item was in the first position will be put wherever that smaller item used to be. This means, of course, that there could be several exchanges before we end up with the smallest item in first place.

The above represents just one pass through the array. After the first pass, the program will look at the second item in the array and compare it with all subsequent items, again moving the smaller item, this time to the second position. On the third pass, the program will compare the third item in the array—and so on.

Now let us consider how these exchanges are made. The key to making the exchange is having a *hold area*. In this program, the hold area has been called H$ (see line 190 in the program, Figure A-24). Looking at Figure A-25, let us see how using the hold area works.

On the first pass, we will want to exchange Kakiuchi and Blanchard. That is, because we are trying to produce a list of names in alphabetical order, Blanchard should fall higher on the list than Kakiuchi (because, obviously, B comes before K). At present, Kakiuchi is in array location 1; since the array is called N$ (see line 170 in Figure A-24), Kakiuchi is in N$(1).

❶ To begin to make the exchange, we will first move Kakiuchi from N$(1) to the hold area, H$.

❷ Next we move Blanchard, which is currently at N$(4), to the first location, N$(1), replacing Kakiuchi.

❸ Finally, we retrieve Kakiuchi from the hold area, H$, and move it to Blanchard's old location, N$(4).

```
100 REM    ANNUAL SUNNY DAYS                              A, ROSARIO
110 REM
120 REM    THIS PROGRAM READS IN TWO ARRAYS: A
130 REM    ONE-DIMENSIONAL LIST WITH THE YEARS 1970-1979,
140 REM    AND A TWO-DIMENSIONAL ARRAY CONTAINING
150 REM    MAXIMUM NUMBER OF SUNSHINE DAYS PER MONTH
160 REM    (COLUMN) WITHIN YEAR (ROW), TOTAL SUNSHINE
170 REM    DAYS PER YEAR AND FOR THE DECADE WILL BE OUTPUT,
180 REM
190 REM    VARIABLE NAMES:
200 REM         Y  -YEAR ARRAY
210 REM         S  -SUNSHINE ARRAY
220 REM         I  -YEAR ARRAY SUBSCRIPT
230 REM         R  -SUNSHINE ARRAY SUBSCRIPT (ROW)
240 REM         C  -SUNSHINE ARRAY SUBSCRIPT (COLUMN)
250 REM         T1 -YEAR TOTAL
260 REM         T2 -DECADE TOTAL
270 REM
280        DIM Y(10),S(10,12)
290        PRINT "YEAR","TOTAL DAYS"
300        PRINT " ","SUNSHINE"
310        PRINT
320 REM    BEGIN LOOP TO READ YEAR ARRAY
330        FOR I=1 TO 10
340            READ Y(I)
350        NEXT I
360 REM    LOOP TO READ SUNSHINE ARRAY
370        FOR R=1 TO 10
380            FOR C=1 TO 12
390                READ S(R,C)
400            NEXT C
410        NEXT R
420 REM    ADD ITEMS IN EACH ROW TO YEAR TOTAL
430 REM    ADD YEARLY TOTAL TO DECADE TOTAL
440        LET T2=0
450        FOR R=1 TO 10
460            LET T1=0
470            FOR C=1 TO 12
480                LET T1=T1 + S(R,C)
490            NEXT C
500            PRINT Y(R),T1
510            LET T2=T2+T1
520        NEXT R
530        PRINT
540        PRINT "TOTAL DAYS OF SUNSHINE"
550        PRINT "FOR DECADE =";T2
560        STOP
570 REM
580 REM         DATA
590 DATA 1970,1971,1972,1973,1974,1975,1976,1977,1978,1979
600 DATA 16,11,14,10,20,30,31,31,30,25,18,15
610 DATA 9,14,11,11,18,30,30,30,29,24,16,16
620 DATA 10,12,5,10,19,29,31,30,28,20,16,10
630 DATA 12,9,9,6,17,30,28,30,26,22,19,12
640 DATA 11,12,10,1,20,21,26,27,27,20,14,11
650 DATA 10,16,11,14,24,25,24,28,24,19,10,12
660 DATA 9,4,5,11,22,29,30,27,25,20,17,16
670 DATA 8,5,16,9,19,30,31,28,27,18,9,8
680 DATA 7,8,19,8,18,30,27,30,29,21,14,9
690 DATA 9,11,17,6,16,26,28,31,28,22,15,10
700 END
```

Figure A-26(a)  Program for annual sunny days program.

**Example 3: Two-Dimensional Array** The input data for this example, shown in Figure A-26(b), consists of two arrays. The first array consists of a one-dimensional list with the years 1970–1979. The second array consists of a two-dimensional table containing the maximum number of sunshine days per month for each area. The purpose of this effort is to output the total number of sunshine days for each year and for the 1970–1979 decade.

The program listing in Figure A-26(a) shows separate loops to read the data. Notice that the two-dimensional array is read by row. Nested loops process the data, print the yearly total, and increase the decade total. At the end of the program, the decade total is printed. Compare the program with the output results in Figure A-26(c).

```
YEAR                    TOTAL DAYS
                        SUNSHINE

1970                    251
1971                    238
1972                    220
1973                    220
1974                    200
1975                    217
1976                    215
1977                    208
1978                    210
1979                    219
TOTAL DAYS OF SUNSHINE
FOR DECADE = 2198
```

**Figure A-26(c)  Output from annual sunny days program.**

**Array Y**

| 1970 | 1971 | 1972 | 1973 | 1974 | 1975 | 1976 | 1977 | 1978 | 1979 |
|------|------|------|------|------|------|------|------|------|------|

**Array S**
**Month**

| Year | | Jan | Feb | Mar | Apr | May | Jun | Jul | Aug | Sep | Oct | Nov | Dec |
|------|------|-----|-----|-----|-----|-----|-----|-----|-----|-----|-----|-----|-----|
| | 1970 | 16 | 11 | 14 | 10 | 20 | 30 | 31 | 31 | 30 | 25 | 18 | 15 |
| | 1971 | 9 | 14 | 11 | 11 | 18 | 30 | 30 | 30 | 29 | 24 | 16 | 16 |
| | 1972 | 10 | 12 | 5 | 10 | 19 | 29 | 31 | 30 | 28 | 20 | 16 | 10 |
| | 1973 | 12 | 9 | 9 | 6 | 17 | 30 | 28 | 30 | 26 | 22 | 19 | 12 |
| | 1974 | 11 | 12 | 10 | 1 | 20 | 21 | 26 | 27 | 27 | 20 | 14 | 11 |
| | 1975 | 10 | 16 | 11 | 14 | 24 | 25 | 24 | 28 | 24 | 19 | 10 | 12 |
| | 1976 | 9 | 4 | 5 | 11 | 22 | 29 | 30 | 27 | 25 | 20 | 17 | 16 |
| | 1977 | 8 | 5 | 16 | 9 | 19 | 30 | 31 | 28 | 27 | 18 | 9 | 8 |
| | 1978 | 7 | 78 | 10 | 8 | 18 | 30 | 27 | 30 | 29 | 21 | 14 | 9 |
| | 1979 | 9 | 11 | 17 | 6 | 16 | 26 | 28 | 31 | 28 | 22 | 15 | 10 |

**Figure A-26(b)   Input data for annual sunny days program.** Number of days of sunshine in East Newton, by month within year (1970–1979).

## Menus and Subroutines

It is interesting how people's sense of humor has become embedded in the vocabulary we use about computers and data processing. "Hardware," a flip way of referring to equipment, was followed by "software," a play on words. "Menu" is another colorful word that is now stuck in the language of computing. **Menu** is not a list of food dishes and prices, but it is like a restaurant menu in the sense that it is a list of *choices*. A menu offers an easy way for users to interact with the computer, particularly users who are only minimally trained to use existing software. For instance, a menu for a word processing program might appear on the CRT screen as follows:

```
         MENU
  1 CREATE A DOCUMENT
  2 UPDATE A DOCUMENT
  3 PRINT A DOCUMENT
ENTER YOUR CHOICE:
```

To make a selection for, say, printing a document, you would type in the number 3. The computer system would then give you other options related to printing the document.

Now let us see how menu choices are used within the program.

### ON GOTO

Let us now look at menus used with the ON GOTO statement, which is a statement used with the CASE structure that we studied in Chapter 10 (see Figure 10-5 in that chapter). Instead of having an IF statement, where there are two choices (yes or no), a CASE statement gives you several choices—a format that fits very nicely into a menu.

The format of the ON GOTO statement is as follows:

ON <u>n</u> GOTO [line no.], [line no.], [line no.], . . .

The value in location <u>n</u>—a BASIC variable—will be whatever the user places in it by typing in the menu choice. The program in turn will place that menu choice in location N by using an input statement: INPUT N. For instance, if the value in location N is 1, then the program will transfer to the first line number—[line no.]—in the list of line numbers that we separated with commas. If it has a value of 2, it will go to the second line number. If 3, it will go to the third line number—and so on. If the value is none of these numbers, then the next statement in the series of BASIC statements will be executed.

**Revolutionizing calculus.** Dr. Harry P. Allen *(left)*, associate professor of mathematics at Ohio State University, is directing a project that, he hopes, "may revolutionize the way calculus is taught." A National Science Foundation grant provides for the use of Texas Instruments programmable calculators so students can place emphasis upon practical rather than theoretical problem-solving techniques.

If you are finding this all complicated, consider the following example:

```
300 ON S GOTO 400, 420, 450, 480
310 ...
```

If the value of S is 1, then the program will transfer to line 400. If the value of S is 2, it will transfer to line 420; if 3, to line 450; if 4, to line 480. If the value of S is not 1 through 4, then the program will simply move on to the next line, which in this case is line 310.

This ON GOTO concept can appear complicated in the abstract; after the subroutine discussion, read on to the hot tub example to see how it really works.

### GOSUB and RETURN

A **subroutine** in BASIC is a sequence of statements grouped together as a unit within the program. The transfer to the subroutine is made from the GOSUB statement. The GOSUB statement specifies the line number of the statement that starts the subroutine. At the end of the subroutine, the RETURN statement transfers control back to the

statement after the GOSUB. Note how these work in the following program segment:

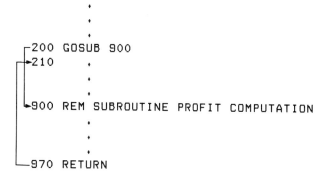

```
    .
    .
    .
┌─200 GOSUB 900
├─►210    .
│         .
│         .
└►900 REM SUBROUTINE PROFIT COMPUTATION
          .
          .
          .
 └─970 RETURN
```

The GOSUB statement causes transfer to line 900, where the subroutine is located in the program. Line 970 is the last line of the subroutine; the RETURN statement causes a transfer to line 210.

Subroutines are particularly useful for program coding that is executed more than once. Instead of repeating the code, it can be written in a subroutine; the subroutine will be invoked (GOSUB) each time it is needed. After each use, the computer will carry on from the line following the GOSUB.

**Table A-1   Summary of Elementary BASIC Statements.**

| Statement Name | Type | Purpose | Example |
|---|---|---|---|
| REM | Documentation | Add clarity to program | `200 REM COMPUTE LOAN INTEREST` |
| READ, DATA | Input | Provide data within the program | `200 READ N$,C,Q`<br><br>`500 DATA "ASPIRIN",1.98,35` |
| IF | Control | Transfer based on test condition | `200 IF T>20 THEN 250` |
| PRINT | Output | Display output results on screen or printer | `200 PRINT "TOTAL=";T` |
| GOTO | Control | Unconditional transfer | `200 GOTO 290` |
| END | Control | Mark end of program; also halt execution | `200 END` |
| LET | Assignment | Assign a value to the variable left of the equal sign | `200 LET T=0` |
| STOP | Control | Halt program execution | `200 STOP` |
| INPUT | Input | Provide data from the terminal | `200 INPUT E$,N` |
| FOR/NEXT | Control | Provide convenience in looping | `200 FOR I=4 TO 10 STEP 2`<br><br>`220 NEXT I` |
| DIM | Storage | Reserve storage for arrays | `200 DIM X (200), T(10)` |
| ON GOTO | Control | Transfer based on a value | `200 ON T GOTO 300,320,340` |

```
100 REM   HOT TUB SALES MENU                        C. CARTER
110 REM
120 REM   THIS PROGRAM USES A MENU SELECTION TO CALL SUBROUTINES
130 REM   TO PRODUCE OUTPUT RELATED TO HOT TUB SALES DATA.
140 REM
150 REM   VARIABLE NAMES
160 REM         N$ -SALESPERSON NAME ARRAY
170 REM         U  -UNITS SOLD ARRAY
180 REM         N  -NUMBER OF ITEMS IN ARRAY
190 REM         M  -MENU SELECTION
200 REM         H  -HIGH SALES HOLD AREA
210 REM         H$ -HIGH SALESPERSON HOLD AREA
220 REM         T  -TOTAL SALES
230 REM         A  -AVERAGE SALES
240 REM
250       DIM N$(100),U(100)
260 REM   READ IN ARRAYS
270       READ N
280       FOR S=1 TO N
290           READ N$(S),U(S)
300       NEXT S
310 REM   PRINT MENU
320       PRINT
330       PRINT "HOT TUB SALES MENU"
340       PRINT
350       PRINT "CODE    FUNCTION"
360       PRINT
370       PRINT "1 - TOP SALESPERSON"
380       PRINT "2 - AVERAGE SALES"
390       PRINT "3 - TOTAL SALES"
400       PRINT "4 - STOP"
410       PRINT
420       INPUT "ENTER A NUMBER, 1 THROUGH 4: ";M
430 REM   TRANSFER TO CORRECT SUBROUTINE, BASED ON MENU SELECTION
440       ON M GOTO 450, 470, 490, 510
450       GOSUB 540
460       GOTO 320
470       GOSUB 650
480       GOTO 320
490       GOSUB 740
500       GOTO 320
510       PRINT "END OF PROGRAM"
520       STOP
530 REM   TOP SALESPERSON SUBROUTINE
540       LET H=0
550       FOR S=1 TO N
560           IF U(S)>H THEN 580
570           GOTO 600
580           LET H=U(S)
590           LET H$=N$(S)
600       NEXT S
610       PRINT
620       PRINT "TOP SALESPERSON IS ";H$
630       RETURN
640 REM   AVERAGE SALES SUBROUTINE
650       LET T=0
660       FOR S=1 TO N
670           LET T=T+U(S)
680       NEXT S
690       LET A=T/N
700       PRINT
710       PRINT "AVERAGE SALES: ";A
720       RETURN
```

*continued*

_continued_

```
730 REM    TOTAL SALES SUBROUTINE
740        LET T=0
750        FOR S=1 TO N
760           LET T=T+U(S)
770        NEXT S
780        PRINT
790        PRINT "TOTAL SALES: ";T
800        RETURN
810           DATA
820 DATA 6
830 DATA "BOORD",176,"DREY",185,"FITZPATRICK",150
840 DATA "GERAMI",152,"MCGAHEY",120,"METZGER",166
850 END
```

**Figure A-27**  Program for hot tub sales menu.

```
HOT TUB SALES MENU

CODE    FUNCTION

1 - TOP SALESPERSON
2 - AVERAGE SALES
3 - TOTAL SALES
4 - STOP

ENTER A NUMBER, 1 THROUGH 4: 1

TOP SALESPERSON IS DREY
```

**Figure A-28**  Screen showing menu, selection, and output.

## Menus and Subroutines: The Hot Tub Example

Which hot tub salesperson has the hottest sales? In this example, as the remarks section (lines 120–130) of Figure A-27 indicates, we are demonstrating a program that uses a menu selection to call subroutines to produce information—such as top salesperson—related to hot tub sales data.

Each record of data (see lines 830–840) consists of the name of a salesperson followed by the number of hot tubs sold by that person in this fiscal year. The program (see lines 260–300) will read that data into two arrays: one for salespeople's names and one for the corresponding number of hot tubs sold. As lines 160 and 170 show, N$ is the variable name for the salesperson name array and U is the variable name for the units sold array. The program is made flexible because it first will read in (on line 270) the number of salespeople (6 in this example, as indicated by the data on line 820) and then (on line 280) establish a READ loop to read exactly that many salespeople.

Now that the data is available, we can print a menu, starting on line 310, to give users choices of what to do with the data. The menu gives us four choices: 1 — TOP SALESPERSON; 2 — AVERAGE SALES; 3 — TOTAL

SALES; 4 — STOP. The user looking at the menu can then type in one of the codes, 1 through 4, which will be placed in the variable M (line 420) and then, as line 440 shows, be used with an ON GOTO statement. The ON GOTO will cause the program to transfer to a line that will call the appropriate subroutine.

For instance, if the user types in a 1, then the value of M will be 1, and on line 440 the program would then transfer to line 450, because that is the first one in the list of statement numbers. At line 450, the program transfers to the subroutine that begins on line 540, which determines who the top salesperson is. When that routine is completed, there is a return statement at line 630 that causes the program to transfer back to the place where it was called.

The output for the menu is shown in Figure A-28. (The top salesperson is Drey, with 185 hot tubs.)

The program will keep looping back to allow the user to make a selection from the menu. To stop the program, the user will have to type in a 4, which indicates STOP.

## Control Breaks

The Robomatics Company has several divisions that each make separate products. Each division has several levels: a division is divided into sections, each of which is divided into departments, which are in turn divided into groups. Managers at the various levels are interested in summary data for the people, products, and services within their domains. If data is sorted in the order that fits this sort of breakdown, the managers can be given suitable totals.

Let us consider a simple example. Supose data is sorted in department order only. This means that all the records for the first department will be together, followed by all the records for the second department, and so on. When we go from the last record of the preceding department to the first record of the next department, that is known as a *control break*. The reason we wish to know about the break is that we wish to print out whatever totals we have accumulated for the preceding department. We also then have to divest ourselves of the total accumulated so far, and set the department total back to zero so that we can start totaling for the next department. In addition, we need to move the department we have just received into a *compare area* so that the department on succeeding records can be compared with the previous department. The reason we need to save the department number in a compare area is that whenever a department record is read, it is read into the location where the previous record was, and it destroys that information. That is, the act of reading one record destroys the previous record; thus, to preserve that department, it must be saved in a special place—in this program, the compare area. Notice that the program initializes the compare area (line 350) by placing the department from the first record in that location.

Figure A-29 gives a flowchart for the control break program, and Figure A-30 presents the program itself. As you can see, the data (lines 590–630) is very simple. Each record consists of the employee name, his or her department (A, B, or C), and salary. What we would like as output (see Figure A-31) is a record for each employee, consisting of name and salary; then, whenever we have finished a department, we would like to print the total salaries for that department. (In theory, we could also have control breaks at the division, section and group levels, too, adding together salaries, products sold, and so on; however, we have chosen to keep the example simple.)

## Additional BASIC Commands

What follows are some additional concepts you may find useful as you pursue the study of BASIC.

### RESTORE Statement

This statement is used whenever you wish to use the same data for DATA statements again. That is, the RESTORE statement causes the next READ statement to read data

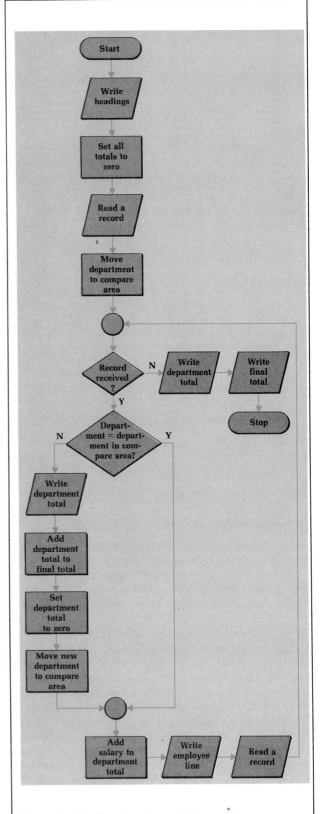

**Figure A-29  Flowchart for control group program.**

```
100 REM    SALARY TOTALS BY DEPARTMENT                    D. WELLS
110 REM
120 REM    THIS PROGRAM READS EMPLOYEE RECORDS, EACH OF WHICH
130 REM    CONTAINS EMPLOYEE NAME, DEPARTMENT, AND ANNUAL SALARY.
140 REM    THE RECORDS ARE INPUT IN DEPARTMENT ORDER.
150 REM    OUTPUT CONSISTS OF:
160 REM           -ONE LINE PER EMPLOYEE
170 REM           -TOTAL SALARY LINE BY DEPARTMENT
180 REM           -TOTAL SALARY FOR THE COMPANY
190 REM
200 REM    VARIABLE NAMES:
210 REM           T1 -DEPARTMENT SALARY TOTAL
220 REM           T2 -FINAL SALARY TOTAL
230 REM           N$ -EMPLOYEE NAME
240 REM           D$ -DEPARTMENT
250 REM           S  -EMPLOYEE SALARY
260 REM           C$ -COMPARE AREA
270 REM
280        PRINT "          SALARY REPORT"
290        PRINT
300        PRINT "NAME","SALARY"
310        PRINT
320        LET T1=0
330        LET T2=0
340        READ N$,D$,S
350        LET C$=D$
360 REM    BEGIN LOOP
370        IF N$="END FILE" THEN 510
380        IF D$=C$ THEN 460
390        PRINT
400        PRINT "TOTAL FOR DEPARTMENT ";C$,T1
410        PRINT
420        LET T2=T2+T1
430        LET T1=0
440        LET C$=D$
450 REM    END-IF
460        LET T1=T1+S
470        PRINT N$,S
480        READ N$,D$,S
490        GOTO 370
500 REM    END-OF-FILE PROCESSING
510        PRINT
520        PRINT "TOTAL FOR DEPARTMENT ";C$,T1
530        PRINT
540        PRINT
550        PRINT "FINAL TOTAL ";T2
560        STOP
570 REM
580 REM        DATA
590 DATA "KATHI WILSON","A",22000,"ZOE GROULX","A",19000
600 DATA "STEVE JONES","A",30000,"JEAN LEE","B",36000
610 DATA "ANN KOGAN","B",16500,"MIKE KEMP","C",14300
620 DATA "SHERMAN LOHN","C",25500,"PAT OHARA","C",19500
630 DATA "LYN HARTMAN","C",22700,"END FILE","X",0
640 END
```

```
              SALARY REPORT

KATHI WILSON      22000
ZOE GROULX        19000
STEVE JONES       30000

TOTAL FOR DEPARTMENT A    71000

JEAN LEE          36000
ANN KOGAN         16500

TOTAL FOR DEPARTMENT B    52500

MIKE KEMP         14300
SHERMAN LOHN      25500
PAT OHARA         19500
LYN HARTMAN       22700

TOTAL FOR DEPARTMENT C    82000

FINAL TOTAL  205500
```

**Figure A-31 Output for control break program.**

**Figure A-30 Program for control break.**

originally specified in the first DATA statement. The RESTORE statement is helpful when you have reached end-of-file. Your choice, then, is either to stop the program right there or to use the RESTORE statement and use the data over again. The statement simply uses the word RESTORE, with no other words or variables.

### TAB Function

The TAB function operates like the tab on a typewriter. By using PRINT TAB followed by a number in parentheses, followed by a semicolon and then words in quotation marks, you can indicate exactly the place on the line where you wish to have the item print. For instance:

```
200 PRINT TAB(30);"PAYROLL REPORT"
```

In this example, the words PAYROLL REPORT will begin in column 30 on your output.

The TAB function can be used in a variety of other ways. Suppose, for example, you want to write data items beginning in columns 1, 20, and 40. Your PRINT statement might look like this:

```
200 PRINT X;TAB(20);Y;TAB(40);Z
```

### PRINT USING

The PRINT USING statement gives you more control over the appearance of your output data. You have probably noticed, for instance, that BASIC will sometimes print data with a variable number of decimal places when you would prefer two decimal places, to represent dollars and cents.

PRINT USING requires two statements, one listing the variables whose contents are to be printed and the other containing the desired format (appearance) of the data. These two statements are tied together by the line number of the format statement, 250 in this next example.

**Example 1** Consider the following program statements:

```
200 PRINT USING 250,N$,C,Q
          .
          .
          .
250: ########## $##.##  ###
```

Let us say that at line 200 N$ contains BOLT, C contains 119 (two decimal places), and Q contains 98.

The output, according to the format on line 250, is as follows:

```
BOLT           $ 1.19   98
```

With the PRINT USING statement you can do the following: add commas in long numbers (to indicate thousands), add a dollar sign to the beginning of a number, change the number of decimal places, and right-justify numbers (line up a column of numbers on the right-hand side). These changes can be brought about using the # sign ("pound" sign or "number" sign), which represents the space reserved for characters in the format. Let us consider another example:

**Example 2** Consider the following:

```
200 PRINT USING 250,N,S,C
          .
          .
          .
250: ####   $##,###.##   $#,###.##
```

At line 200, N contains 1143, S contains 49143684 (three decimal places), and C contains 245718 (two decimal places).

The output is as follows:

```
1143 $49,143.68 $2,457.18
```

### Functions

Functions are precoded portions of programs. Some standard functions are available with BASIC; these are listed in Table A-2. The X in parentheses next to each function name is the argument of the function. The argument is the place holder for the data sent to the function. Functions are used either in arithmetic expressions or alone on the right side of an assignment statement. Let us look at some examples of functions to see how they work.

**SQR** Consider the first function shown in the table, SQR(X), which stands for "the square root of X" (X can represent any nonnegative number).

For example, the hypotenuse C of a right triangle, as related to sides A and B, is

$$C = \sqrt{A^2 + B^2}$$

In BASIC, this would be expressed as

```
200 LET C = SQR(A**2+B**2)
```

**Table A-2  Some Standard BASIC Functions**

| Function | Meaning |
|---|---|
| SQR(X) | Square root of X |
| RND(X) | A random number between 0 and 1 |
| INT(X) | The integer less than number X |
| ABS(X) | The absolute value of X |
| SGN(X) | The sign of X |
| LOG(X) | The natural logarithm (base E) of X |
| EXP(X) | E raised to the X power |
| SIN(X) | Trigonometric sine of X |
| COS(X) | Trigonometric cosine of X |
| TAN(X) | Trigonometric tangent of X |
| COT(X) | Trigonometric cotangent of X |
| ATN(X) | Trigonometric arctangent of X |

**RND** In another example, find a random integer number between 1 and 13 (to represent the dealing of a card in a deck):

```
200 LET C = INT(RND(X)*13)+1
```

In this example, the RND function will return a value between 0 and 1. Multiplying that value by 13 and then, using INT, taking only the integer part of it, yields a number between 0 and 12. The added 1 makes the number between 1 and 13, as desired.

**INT** INT will give you the value of the largest integer less than or equal to the argument. When the argument is 6.41, INT(6.41) = 6. However, for negative numbers it is not so obvious. For instance, INT(−2.44) = −3.

**Die Toss Example** This example uses two functions—the INT and the RND functions—which are combined to test the randomizing formula to see if the results really are equally distributed. We will simulate the tossing of a six-sided die. If we have a good randomizing program, the chances should be about equal that one of the six sides (1, 2, 3, 4, 5, or 6) could appear when we toss the die. If, as the program indicated in Figure A-32 indicates, we are going to toss the die 1000 times, then the number of times we get any of the six numbers should be about equal. We will test this proposition with our program.

Notice in Figure A-32 that we have set up a loop—a DOUNTIL loop (because the decision is at the end of the loop). In stimulating the toss of the die, we will follow the formula shown on line 320 of the program in Figure A-33:INT(RND 9X0 * 6) + 1. The RND function will return a number between 0 and 1; when we multiply this by 6, the result will be between 0 and 5.999. When we take the INT function, that will make the number an integer between 0 and 5. When we add 1 to it, then it will be an integer between 1 and 6. These two functions together will deliver some integer between 1 and 6, and that integer will be placed in location D.

To illustrate how this works, suppose the RND function gives .61. Now multiply this by 6 to get 3.66. The INT function now reduces this to 3. Add 1 and the final result, in D, is 4.

Or: if RND returns .981, then 6 times .981 is 5.886, INT(5.886) is 5 and 5 + 1 is 6, the result to be placed in D.

In either case, we got a number between 1 and 6. Try other examples yourself, but be sure your original value from the RND function is *between* 0 and 1.

Note that on line 330 D will be used as a subscript in order to add to the proper counter. For example, if 2 appeared on a particular turn, 1 would be added to the counter for 2s. The idea is that when we are done we will have six counters with six numbers corresponding to the number of times the numbers 1 through 6 were thrown by the toss of the die.

Figure A-34 shows the output for this program. If you run this program, you will find the results will probably vary from the results shown here. The only things that will be the same are that the numbers probably won't vary much from each other and that they should add up to 1000.

### E Notation

E notation can be used to represent very small or very large numbers. The number of digits in a numeric constant is limited in BASIC; on most systems the limit is seven digits. To represent a large number, you can express it as a power of 10. For instance, 2000 may be represented by $2 \times 10^3$, or, in BASIC, 2E3, in which E stands for "exponent." The number 186,000 could be represented as 186E3, and the number 0.0000001 as 1E−7.

## Summary of BASIC Statements

Table A-3 presents a list of the BASIC statements we have studied in this appendix.

**Table A-3  Summary of BASIC Commands**

| Control |
|---|
| GOTO |
| IF |
| FOR and NEXT |
| STOP |
| END |
| GOSUB and RETURN |
| ON GOTO |

| Input/Output |
|---|
| READ and DATA |
| INPUT |
| PRINT |
| PRINT USING |
| RESTORE |

| Documentation |
|---|
| REM |

| Assignment |
|---|
| LET |

| Array Storage |
|---|
| DIM |

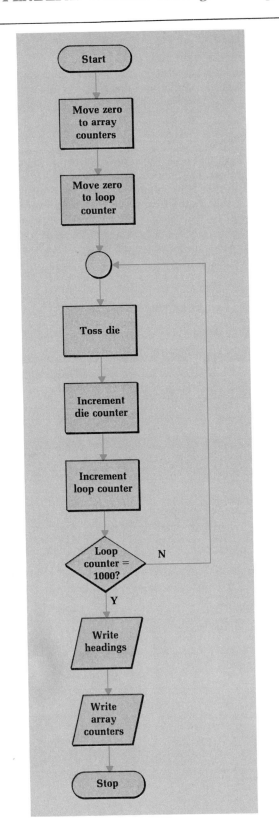

**Figure A-32** Flowchart for die toss program.

## Program Exercises

The following are programming exercises in the BASIC language arranged in order of increasing difficulty and complexity. The order in which concepts are introduced in the exercises follows the order in which they are given in this appendix.

Notice that in the beginning we provide both the input and the expected output. After Exercise 4, we leave it to you to determine the output.

1. Write a program that reads records consisting of item name, beginning quantity, and units sold this month. Display as output the item name, beginning quantity number, units sold this month, and ending quantity. Use the following input data:

| Item Number | Beginning Quantity | Units Sold |
|---|---|---|
| BAND-AIDS | 114 | 13 |
| TOOTHPASTE | 551 | 117 |
| COUGH SYRUP | 397 | 98 |
| COMB | 246 | 77 |
| MOISTURIZER | 501 | 58 |

Expected output:

```
BAND-AIDS      114    13    101
TOOTHPASTE     551   117    434
COUGH SYRUP    397    98    299
COMB           246    77    169
MOISTURIZER    501    58    443
```

2. The following inventory items are to be sold at a 15 percent discount. Read the item name and current price. Display the item name and discounted price. (Note: Your actual output may show more than two decimal places.) Use the following input data:

| Item Name | Current Price |
|---|---|
| BRUSH | 2.98 |
| CURLERS | 4.00 |
| PINS | 1.89 |
| SHAMPOO | 1.35 |
| CONDITIONER | 1.60 |

Expected output:

```
BRUSH        2.53
CURLERS      3.40
PINS         1.61
SHAMPOO      1.15
CONDITIONER  1.36
```

```
100 REM    USING RND TO TOSS DIE                        H. BJORNSON
120 REM
130 REM    THIS PROGRAM USES THE RND FUNCTION TO SIMULATE THE
140 REM    TOSSING OF A DIE 1000 TIMES. FOR EACH DIE TOSS, A NUMBER
150 REM    BETWEEN 1 AND 6 WILL BE GENERATED. THE PROGRAM WILL COUNT
160 REM    THE NUMBER OF TIMES EACH RESULT (1 THROUGH 6) APPEARS
170 REM    AND PRINT THE FINAL COUNTS.
180 REM
190 REM    VARIABLE NAMES:
200 REM          C -COUNTER ARRAY
210 REM          L -LOOP COUNTER
220 REM          D -DIE TOSS
230 REM          S -SUBSCRIPT
240 REM
250        DIM C(6)
270        FOR S=1 TO 6
280           LET C(S)=0
290        NEXT S
300        LET L=0
310 REM    BEGIN LOOP
320        LET D=INT(RND(X)*6)+1
330        LET C(D)=C(D)+1
340        LET L=L+1
350        IF L <> 1000 THEN 320
360        PRINT "DIE","COUNT"
370        PRINT
380        FOR S=1 TO 6
390           PRINT S, C(S)
400        NEXT S
410 END
```

**Figure A-33**  Program for die toss.

| DIE | COUNT |
|-----|-------|
| 1 | 158 |
| 2 | 170 |
| 3 | 175 |
| 4 | 166 |
| 5 | 160 |
| 6 | 171 |

**Figure A-34**   Output from die toss program.

3. Read values for A, B, C, and X; use this data to compute values for Y:

$$Y = A + BX + CX^2$$

Display each of the input values and each computed Y value. Use the following input data:

| A | B | C | X |
|---|---|---|---|
| 1 | 1 | 2 | 3 |
| 2 | 1 | 6 | 2 |
| 2 | 2 | 1 | 2 |
| 1 | 1 | 9 | 2 |
| 3 | 1 | 2 | 6 |

Expected output:

| | | | | |
|---|---|---|---|---|
| 1 | 1 | 2 | 3 | 22 |
| 2 | 1 | 6 | 2 | 28 |
| 2 | 2 | 1 | 2 | 10 |
| 1 | 1 | 9 | 2 | 39 |
| 3 | 1 | 2 | 6 | 81 |

4. Read data for a series of basketball games: opponent name, home score, and opponent score. Display the input data and the word WIN or LOSS for the home team. Also display the total number of wins for the home team. Use suitable headings. Use the following input data:

| Opponent | Home Score | Opponent Score |
|----------|------------|----------------|
| Danforth | 88 | 70 |
| Franklin | 67 | 65 |
| Ingraham | 68 | 70 |
| Lakeside | 60 | 58 |
| Newport | 65 | 68 |
| Rainier | 74 | 69 |

Expected output:

| OPPONENT | HOME SCORE | OPPONENT SCORE | WIN/LOSS |
|----------|------------|----------------|----------|
| DANFORTH | 88 | 70 | WIN |
| FRANKLIN | 67 | 65 | WIN |
| INGRAHAM | 68 | 70 | LOSS |
| LAKESIDE | 60 | 58 | WIN |
| NEWPORT | 65 | 68 | LOSS |
| RAINIER | 74 | 69 | WIN |

NUMBER OF HOME TEAM WINS = 4

5. Read data for product name, quantity, price, and code (1 or 2). Compute income amount by multiplying quantity by price. Then compute profit based on this amount and the code: 8 percent for code 1, 5 percent for code 2. Display product name, income amount, and profit. Use the following input data:

| Product Name | Quantity | Price | Code |
|---|---|---|---|
| STAPLER | 24 | 4.98 | 1 |
| RULER | 50 | 1.25 | 1 |
| CALCULATOR | 67 | 8.95 | 2 |
| SCOTCH TAPE | 97 | 1.00 | 1 |
| NOTEBOOK | 26 | 3.50 | 2 |

Calculate some of the expected output by hand and compare it with the computer output.

6. Read data for instructor name and three class sizes for each instructor. Display the name of any instructor with class average greater than 30. Also display the total number of students in all classes. Use the following input data:

| Instructor | Class 1 | Class 2 | Class 3 |
|---|---|---|---|
| V. Beardsley | 30 | 30 | 25 |
| M. Lafave | 35 | 31 | 30 |
| K. Lee | 40 | 41 | 30 |
| H. Pishker | 25 | 30 | 25 |
| B. Toshida | 30 | 31 | 26 |

Plan the expected output.

7. Read data for name, street address, city, state, and zip code, and display them in a format suitable for address labels. (Hint: You will need to override the print zone convention.) Make up your own data. Sample output:

```
CHRIS FITZPATRICK
10845 E. 45TH AVENUE
SYRACUSE NY 13205
```

8. Write a program to read three names (last name first) and display them in alphabetical order.

9. Write a program that will accept a number representing cents from a user at the terminal. As output, display the largest number of quarters, dimes, and pennies that can be used to make up that amount of cents. Sample dialogue:

```
WHAT IS THE NUMBER? 98
NUMBER=98 QUARTERS=3
DIMES=2 PENNIES=3

WHAT IS THE NUMBER? 61
NUMBER=61 QUARTERS=2
DIMES=1 PENNIES=1

WHAT IS THE NUMBER? 0
END OF PROGRAM. GOODBYE.
```

10. Write a program that allows the user at the terminal to input data for a relay team: the team name and run time (in seconds) for each of three runners in the relay. The four data items should be requested together, as one line of input—that is, separated by commas. For each relay team, display total run time in minutes and seconds and average run time in seconds.

Sample dialogue:

```
ENTER TEAM NAME AND RUN TIMES
?FLEETFOOT,61,47,43
```

11. Using the formula

$$C = \tfrac{5}{9} \times (F - 32)$$

convert Fahrenheit temperatures (F) to Celsius (C). Use FOR/NEXT to compute even Fahrenheit temperatures from 32 (freezing) to 212 (boiling): 32, 34, 36, ..., 212. Plan suitable headings.

12. If S represents the side of a cube, the area of the cube is $6S^2$ and the volume of the cube is $S^3$. Using FOR/NEXT, generate the area and volume for cubes with sides from 1 to 25. Use suitable headings.

13. Write a program that will read a list of 25 elements and display it in reverse order.

14. Write a program to read a 3-by-5 array (3 rows, 5 columns) and display it by column. Input is as follows:

| 14 | 6 | 11 | 3 | 10 |
|---|---|---|---|---|
| 1 | 5 | 8 | 16 | 20 |
| 7 | 4 | 2 | 18 | 9 |

Output is as follows:

| 14 | 1 | 7 |
|---|---|---|
| 6 | 5 | 4 |
| 11 | 8 | 2 |
| 3 | 16 | 18 |
| 10 | 20 | 9 |

15. Read an array of apartment complex rental prices for six units over a five-year period. Use a FOR/NEXT loop to compute the total rental income for each year and then display the percentage increase between adjacent years. (Hint: Between years 1 and 2, the percentage increase is [sum2 − sum1]/sum1.) Use the following input data:

| | | Year | | | |
|---|---|---|---|---|---|
| | 1 | 2 | 3 | 4 | 5 |
| 1 | 200 | 210 | 225 | 300 | 325 |
| 2 | 250 | 275 | 300 | 350 | 400 |
| Unit 3 | 300 | 325 | 375 | 400 | 450 |
| 4 | 215 | 225 | 250 | 250 | 275 |
| 5 | 355 | 380 | 400 | 410 | 420 |
| 6 | 375 | 400 | 425 | 460 | 480 |

16. Elements of an array can be sorted into ascending order by several methods. The easiest to program is the bubble sort, so named because smaller elements "bubble" to the top of the array. Consider sorting a one-dimensional array using a bubble sort. Examine the first two elements and exchange them if the second is smaller; repeat for the second and third, third and fourth, and so on. (Hint: A temporary hold location will be needed to complete the exchange.) Now start at the top of the array and repeat the process; this entire set of comparisons and exchanges must be repeated until one iteration produces no exchanges. Read in a list of ten data items and produce the sorted output.

17. Use PRINT TAB to print your initials with some selected character, such as X—for example:

```
XXXXX    X          X   X
    X    X          XX XX
    X    X          X X X
    X    X          X   X
    X    XXXXX       X   X
```

18. Write a program to have the user at the terminal play a guessing game with the computer. The computer displays a message indicating that a number between 1 and 10 has been selected. The user gets three chances to guess the number and is given a hint of "TOO HIGH" or "TOO LOW" if not correct. The number to be guessed can be generated by the RND and INT functions as follows:

```
LET N = INT(RND(X)*10)+1
```

An alternative method of deciding on a number to be guessed is to read it from the DATA statement, using the RESTORE statement when the data is exhausted. In either case, the user is given the option of stopping or guessing another number.

19. Solve the quadratic equation:

$$X = \left(-B \pm \sqrt{B^2 - 4AC}\right)/2A$$

Read in values for A, B, and C. Note that there are actually two values for X, based on the sign in front of the radical. (You could call them X1 and X2 in BASIC.) (Caution: The computer cannot take the square root of a number less than zero, nor can it divide by zero.)

20. Read customer name, credit limit ($500 or $1000), number of purchases (maximum six), and the purchase prices. The maximum purchase price is $1000. Display customer name, credit limit and total purchases with the PRINT USING option.

21. Write a program to input array data consisting of basketball player name, field goals attempted, field goals made, free throws attempted, free throws made. Now allow the user at the terminal to choose various statistics from a menu. For example, the first line of the menu could be:

```
1 - % FIELD GOALS
```

22. Within a loop use the RND function to determine how far to PRINT TAB; this will cause a random design to be displayed. (The actual character printed may vary—an asterisk is suggested.) If the design is to be, say, 20 characters wide, this formula will determine a number between 1 and 20:

```
LET L = INT(RND(X)*20)+1
```

You may vary this problem by using a semicolon at the end of some PRINT statements; the next character generated will print on the same line.

---

**Selected References for Further Reading**

Boillot, Michel, and L. Wayne Horn. _BASIC_, 3rd ed. St. Paul, Minn.: West, 1983.

Clark, James F., and William O. Drumm. _BASIC Programming: A Structured Approach._ Cincinnati, Ohio: Southwestern, 1983.

Davis, William S. _BASIC: Getting Started._ Reading, Mass.: Addison-Wesley, 1981.

Koffman, Elliot B., and Frank L. Friedman. _Problem Solving and Structured Programming in BASIC._ Reading, Mass.: Addison-Wesley, 1979.

Price, Wilson T. _Using Business BASIC._ New York: Holt, Rinehart and Winston, 1983.

Shelly, Gary, and Thomas Cashman. _Introduction to BASIC Programming._ Brea, California: Anaheim, 1982.

# *appendix B*
## *number systems*

Data can be represented in the computer in two basic ways: as **numeric data** or as **alphanumeric data.** The internal representation of alphanumeric data—letters, digits, special characters—was discussed in Chapter 4. Recall that alphanumeric data may be represented using various codes; EBCDIC and ASCII are two common codes. Alphanumeric data, even if all digits, cannot be used for arithmetic operations. Data used for arithmetic calculations must be stored numerically.

Data stored numerically can be represented as the binary equivalent of the decimal value with which we are familiar. That is, values such as 1050, 43218, and 3 that we input to the computer will be converted to the binary number system. In this appendix we shall study the binary number system (base 2) and two related systems, octal (base 8) and hexadecimal (base 16).

## Number Bases

A number base is a specific collection of symbols on which a number system can be built. The number base familiar to us is base 10, upon which the **decimal** number system is built. There are ten symbols—0 through 9—used in the decimal system.

Since society uses base 10, that is the number base most of us understand and can use easily. It would theoretically be possible, however, for all of us to learn to use a different number system. This number system could have a different number of, and perhaps even unfamiliar, symbols.

### Base 2: The Binary Number System

Base 2 has exactly two symbols: 0 and 1. All numbers in the **binary** system must be formed using these two symbols. As you can see in column 2 of Table B-1, this means that numbers in the binary system become long quickly; the number 1000 in base 2 is equivalent to 8 in base 10. (When different number bases are being discussed, it is common practice to use the number base as a subscript. In this case, we could say $1000_2 = 8_{10}$.) If you were to continue counting in base 2, you would soon see that the binary numbers were very long and unwieldy. The number $5000_{10}$ is equal to $10011100010000_2$.

The size and sameness—all those zeros and ones—of binary numbers make them subject to frequent error when they are being manipulated by humans. To improve both convenience and accuracy, it is common to express the values represented by binary numbers in the more concise octal and hexadecimal number bases.

### Base 8: The Octal Number System

The **octal** number system uses exactly eight symbols: 0, 1, 2, 3, 4, 5, 6, and 7. Base 8 is a convenient shorthand for base 2 numbers because 8 is a power of 2: $2^3 = 8$. As you will see when we discuss conversions, one octal digit is the equivalent of exactly three binary digits. The use of

**Table B-1**    Number Bases 10, 2, 8, 16: First Values

| Base 10 (decimal) | Base 2 (binary) | Base 8 (octal) | Base 16 (hexadecimal) |
|:---:|:---:|:---:|:---:|
| 0 | 0000 | 0 | 0 |
| 1 | 0001 | 1 | 1 |
| 2 | 0010 | 2 | 2 |
| 3 | 0011 | 3 | 3 |
| 4 | 0100 | 4 | 4 |
| 5 | 0101 | 5 | 5 |
| 6 | 0110 | 6 | 6 |
| 7 | 0111 | 7 | 7 |
| 8 | 1000 | 10 | 8 |
| 9 | 1001 | 11 | 9 |
| 10 | 1010 | 12 | A |
| 11 | 1011 | 13 | B |
| 12 | 1100 | 14 | C |
| 13 | 1101 | 15 | D |
| 14 | 1110 | 16 | E |
| 15 | 1111 | 17 | F |
| 16 | 10000 | 20 | 10 |

octal (or hexadecimal) as a shorthand for binary is common in printed output of main storage and, in some cases, in programming.

Look at the column of octal numbers in Table B-1. Notice that, since 7 is the last symbol in base 8, the following number is 10. In fact, we can count right through the "teens" in the usual manner, as long as we end with 17. Note, however, that $17_8$ is pronounced "one-seven," not "seventeen." The number 17 is followed by 20 through 27, and so on. The last double-digit number is 77, which is followed by 100. Although it takes a little practice, you can see that it would be easy to learn to count in base 8. However, hexadecimal, or base 16, is not quite as easy.

### Base 16: The Hexadecimal Number System

The **hexadecimal** number system uses exactly sixteen symbols. As we have just seen, base 10 uses the familiar digits 0 through 9, and bases 2 and 8 use a subset of those symbols. Base 16, however, needs those ten symbols (0 through 9) and six more. The six additional symbols used in the hexadecimal number system are the letters A through F. So the base 16 symbols are: 0, 1, 2, 3, 4, 5, 6, 7, 8, 9, A, B, C, D, E, and F. It takes some adjusting to think of A or D as a digit instead of a letter. It also takes a little time to become accustomed to numbers such as 6A2F or even ACE. Both of these examples are legitimate numbers in hexadecimal.

As you become familiar with hexadecimal, consider the matter of counting. Counting sounds simple enough, but it can be confusing in an unfamiliar number base with new symbols. The process is the same as counting in base 10, but most of us learned to count when we were too young to think about the process itself. Quickly—what number follows 24CD? The answer is 24CE. We increased the rightmost digit by one—D to E—just as you would have in the more obvious case of 6142 to 6143. What is the number just before $1000_{16}$? The answer is $FFF_{16}$; the last symbol (F) is a triple-digit number. Compare this with $999_{10}$, which precedes $1000_{10}$; 9 is the last symbol in base 10. As a familiarization exercise, try counting from 1 to 100 in base 16. Remember to use A through F as the second symbol in the teens, twenties, and so forth ( . . . 27, 28, 29, 2A, 2B, and so on).

### Conversions Between Number Bases

It is sometimes convenient to use a number in a base different from the base currently being used—that is, to change the number from one base to another. Many programmers can nimbly convert a number from one base to another, among bases 10, 2, 8, and 16. We shall consider these conversion techniques now. Table B-2 summarizes the methods.

### To Base 10 from Bases 2, 8, and 16

We present these conversions together because the technique is the same for all three.

Let us begin with the concept of positional notation. **Positional notation** means that the value of a digit in a number depends not only on its own intrinsic value but also on its location in the number. Given the number 2363, we know that the appearance of the digit 3 represents two different values, 300 and 3. Table B-3 shows the names of the relative positions. Using these positional values, the number 2363 is understood to mean:

$$\begin{array}{r} 2000 \\ 300 \\ 60 \\ \underline{3} \\ 2363 \end{array}$$

This number can also be expressed as:

$(2 \times 1000) + (3 \times 100) + (6 \times 10) + 3$

We can express this expanded version of the number another way, using powers of 10 (note that $10^0 = 1$).

$2363 = (2 \times 10^3) + (3 \times 10^2) + (6 \times 10^1) + (3 \times 10^0)$

### Table B-2  Summary Conversion Chart

| From Base | To Base 2 | To Base 8 | To Base 16 | To Base 10 |
|---|---|---|---|---|
| 2 | ——— | Group binary digits by 3, convert | Group binary digits by 4, convert | Expand number and convert base 2 digits to base 10 |
| 8 | Convert each octal digit to 3 binary digits | ——— | Convert to base 2, then to base 16 | Expand number and convert base 8 digits to base 10 |
| 16 | Convert each hexadecimal digit to 4 binary digits | Convert to base 2, then to base 8 | ——— | Expand number and convert base 16 digits to base 10 |
| 10 | Divide number repeatedly by 2; use remainders as answer | Divide number repeatedly by 8; use remainders as answer | Divide number repeatedly by 16; use remainders as answer | ——— |

### Table B-3  Digit Positions

| Digit | 2 | 3 | 6 | 3 |
|---|---|---|---|---|
| Position | Thousand | Hundred | Ten | Unit |

Once you understand the expanded notation, the rest is easy: You expand the number as we just did in base 10, but use the appropriate base of the number. For example, follow the steps to convert $61732_8$ to base 10:

1. Expand the number, using 8 as the base:

$$61732 = (6 \times 8^4) + (1 \times 8^3) + (7 \times 8^2) +$$
$$(3 \times 8^1) + (2 \times 8^0)$$

2. Complete the arithmetic:

$$61732 = (6 \times 4096) + (1 \times 512) + (7 \times 64) +$$
$$(3 \times 8) + 2$$
$$= 24576 + 512 + 448 + 24 + 2$$

3. Answer: $61732_8 = 25562_{10}$.

The same expand-and-convert technique can be used to convert from base 2 or base 16 to base 10. As you consider the following two examples, use Table B-1 to make the conversions. (For example, A in base 16 converts to 10 in base 10.)

Convert $C14A_{16}$ to base 10:

$$C14A_{16} = (12 \times 16^3) + (1 \times 16^2) + (4 \times 16^1) + 10$$
$$= (12 \times 4096) + (1 \times 256) + (4 \times 16) + 10$$
$$= 49482$$

So $C14A_{16} = 49482_{10}$.

Convert $100111_2$ to base 10:

$$100111_2 = (1 \times 2^5) + (1 \times 2^2) + (1 \times 2) + 1$$
$$= 39$$

So $100111_2 = 39_{10}$.

### From Base 10 to Bases 2, 8, and 16

These conversions use a simpler process but more complicated arithmetic. The process, often called the *remainder method*, is basically a series of repeated divisions by the number of the base to which you are converting. You begin by using the number to be converted as the dividend; succeeding dividends are the quotients of the previous division. The converted number is the combined remainders accumulated from the divisions. There are two points to remember:

1. Keep dividing until you reach a zero quotient.

2. Use the remainders in reverse order.

Consider converting $6954_{10}$ to base 8:

```
8|6954
 8|869    2
  8|108   5
   8|13   4
    8|1   5
      0   1
```

Using the remainders backwards, $6954_{10} = 15452_8$.

Now use the same technique to convert $4823_{10}$ to base 16:

```
16|4823
  16|301    7
    16|18    13 (=D)
      16|1    2
        0    1
```

The remainder 13 is equivalent to D in base 16. So $4823_{10}$ = $12D7_{16}$.

Convert $49_{10}$ to base 2:

```
2|49
  2|24    1
    2|12    0
      2|6    0
        2|3    0
          2|1    1
            0    1
```

Again using the remainders in reverse order, $49_{10}$ = $110001_2$.

### To Base 2 from Bases 8 and 16

To convert a number to base 2 from base 8 or base 16, convert each digit separately to three or four binary digits, respectively. Use Table B-1 to make the conversion. Leading zeros may be needed in each grouping of digits to fill out each to three or four digits.

Convert $4732_8$ to base 2:

| 4 | 7 | 3 | 2 |
|---|---|---|---|
| 100 | 111 | 011 | 010 |

So $4732_8$ = $100111011010_2$.

Now convert $A046B_{16}$ to base 2:

| A | 0 | 4 | 6 | B |
|---|---|---|---|---|
| 1010 | 0000 | 0100 | 0110 | 1011 |

Thus $A046B_{16}$ = $10100000010001101011_2$.

### From Base 2 to Bases 8 and 16

To convert a number from base 2 to base 8 or base 16, group the binary digits from the right in groups of three or four, respectively. Again use Table B-1 to help you make the conversion to the new base.

Convert $111101001011_2$ to base 8 and base 16:

In the base 8 conversion, group the digits three at a time, starting on the right:

| 111 | 101 | 011 | 011 |
|---|---|---|---|
| 7 | 5 | 1 | 3 |

So $111101001011_2$ = $7513_8$.

For the conversion to base 16, group the digits four at a time, starting on the right:

| 1111 | 0100 | 1011 |
|---|---|---|
| F | 4 | B |

$111101001011_2$ = $F4B_{16}$.

Sometimes the number of digits in a binary number is not exactly divisible by 3 or 4. You may, for example, start grouping the digits three at a time and finish with one or two "extra" digits on the left side of the number. In this case, just add as many zeros as you need to the front of the binary number.

Consider converting $1010_2$ to base 8. By adding two zeros to the front of the number to make it $001010_2$, we now have six digits, which can be conveniently grouped three at a time:

| 001 | 010 |
|---|---|
| 1 | 2 |

So $1012_2$ = $12_8$.

---

**Summary and Key Terms**

- Data can be represented in the computer as **numeric data** or **alphanumeric data**. Data to be used for arithmetic calculations must be represented numerically.

- The number system familiar to us is base 10, the **decimal** number system; it uses symbols 0 through 9.

- Base 2, the **binary** number system, uses the two symbols 0 and 1.

- Base 8, the **octal** number system, uses the symbols 0 through 7.

- Base 16, the **hexadecimal** number system, uses the symbols 0 through 9 and A through F.

- The concept of **positional notation** means that the value of a digit in a number depends on its location in the number as well as on its own intrinsic value.

- Octal and hexadecimal are convenient shorthand number systems for representing data converted from base 2.

- There are techniques for converting numbers from one number base to another. See the summary of conversion methods in Table B-2.

1. Count as follows: 25 to 61 in base 8, 10001 to 100010 in base 2, CDF to D00 in base 16.

2. Convert as follows:

   $100111_2$ to base 10; $671_8$ to base 10; $ACED_{16}$ to base 10; $1101010_2$ to base 10; $43_8$ to base 10; $1023B_{16}$ to base 10.

   Check your work by performing each conversion in reverse.

3. Convert as follows:

   $9073_{10}$ to base 2; $614_{10}$ to base 8; $591_{10}$ to base 16; $61_{10}$ to base 2; $3146_{10}$ to base 8; $157_{10}$ to base 16.

   Check your work by performing each conversion in reverse.

4. Convert as follows:

   $461_8$ to base 2; $F16C_{16}$ to base 2; $2107_8$ to base 2; $1A046_{16}$ to base 2; $111101_2$ to base 8; $110101100101_2$ to base 16; $10011001_2$ to base 8; $10101100010101_2$ to base 16.

# *credits and acknowledgments*

P. 8, excerpts headed "Burger Science" and "Monopoly" reprinted from *Made in America*, pp. 162 and 111, respectively, © 1978, by Murray Suid and Ron Harris, by permission of Addison-Wesley Publishing Company, Inc. Excerpt headed "Digital Diagnosis," by Michael Edelhart, *Omni*, October 1982, p. 24. Copyright 1982 by Omni Publications International Ltd. and reprinted by permission of the copyright owner. Excerpt headed "Brave New Music," by Mark Hunter, *California Living Magazine*, October 24, 1982, p. 20. Reprinted with permission from *California Living Magazine* of the *San Francisco Sunday Examiner and Chronicle*, copyright © 1982, San Francisco Examiner. Excerpt headed "Need a Model?" by Dennis Kneale, from "Tell the Computer What You Want on a Scale of 0–9," *Wall Street Journal*, February 15, 1983, p. 29. Reprinted by permission of The Wall Street Journal, © Dow Jones & Company, Inc., 1983. All rights reserved. Excerpt headed "Duplicating Early Scientists' Thinking," *Computerworld*, February 1, 1982, p. 10. © 1982 by CW Communications/Inc., Framingham, MA 01701. Reprinted from *Computerworld*.

P. 11, excerpt headed "Personal Computers and Personal Cars" by H.E. James Finke, *ISO World*, January 19, 1980, p. 52. Reprinted by permission.

P. 12, excerpt headed "Computer Anxiety Hits Middle Management," by Mary Bralove, *Wall Street Journal*, March 7, 1983, p. 16. Reprinted by permission of The Wall Street Journal, © Dow Jones & Company, Inc., 1983. All rights reserved.

P. 27, excerpt headed "Supercomputers: As Fast as the Entire Human Race?" by Bruce Schechter, *Discover*, January 1983. By permission of Bruce Schechter, © 1983 Discover Magazine, Time Inc.

P. 29, excerpt headed "Personal Computers Reduce TV Viewing," *Stanford Observer*, April 1983, p. 3. By permission of Stanford Observer, Stanford University.

P. 30, excerpt headed "Telecommuting and Personal Power," by Evan Peelle, *Personal Computing*, May 1982, p. 38. Reprinted with permission from *Personal Computing*, May 1982, p. 38, and copyright 1982, Hayden Publishing Company.

P. 62, excerpt headed "The Old Computers' Home," by Natalie Angier, *Discover*, February 1983, p. 97. By permission of Natalie Angier, © 1983 Discover Magazine, Time Inc.

P. 69, excerpts from Patrick Henry Winston, *Artificial Intelligence*, © 1977, Addison-Wesley, Reading, Mass., pp. 252–54. Reprinted with permission.

P. 106, excerpt headed "Computers That Listen to You—and Talk Back," by David Perlman, *San Francisco Chronicle*, September 27, 1982. © San Francisco Chronicle, 1982. Reprinted by permission.

P. 125, excerpt headed "Microfiche Discs: Manhattan Phone Books on an LP Record," by John G. Posa, *High Technology*, February 1983. Reprinted with permission, *High Technology* magazine. Copyright © 1983 by High Technology Publishing Corporation, 38 Commercial Wharf, Boston, MA 02110.

P. 129, excerpt headed "Hero the Robot Won't Wash Windows, but It Will Happily Stroll Around and Chat," by Philip Revzin, *Wall Street Journal*, January 5, 1983. Reprinted by permission of The Wall Street Journal, © Dow Jones & Company, Inc., 1983. All rights reserved.

P. 130, excerpt headed "NORMI, Call Home," reported by United Press, San Francisco Chronicle, March 24, 1983.

P. 144, excerpt headed "Gigs by Computer," by Hal Glatzer, *Frets Magazine*, March 1983. © 1983 Frets Magazine, Cupertino, CA. Reprinted by permission. Excerpt headed "Customized Vegetable Gardens," by Evelyn DeWolfe, "Seeds Planted to Cultivate Housing Sales," *Los Angeles Times*, November 29, 1981, reprinted in *San Francisco Chronicle*, January 2, 1982. Copyright, 1981, Los Angeles Times. Reprinted by permission. Excerpt headed "A Computerized Catalog of Catalogs," *Newsweek*, March 8, 1982. Copyright 1983 by Newsweek, Inc. All rights reserved. Reprinted by permission.

P. 170, excerpt headed "Learn to Type," by Richard Milewski, *Infoworld*, September 15, 1980. Copyright 1980 by Popular Computing/Inc., a subsidiary of CW Communications/Inc., reprinted from *Infoworld*.

P. 180, excerpt headed "Hackers: Programming Addicts," by Frank Rose, *Science 82*, November 1982, p. 61. Reprinted by permission of *Science 783 Magazine*; © the American Association for the Advancement of Science.

P. 204, excerpt headed "What Is Analysis?" by Tom Demarco, *Structured Analysis and System Specification* (New York: Yourdon Press, 1979), pp. 5–6. Copyright © 1978, 1979 by YOURDON, inc. Reprinted by permission.

P. 209, excerpt headed "Service by Systems: Less Old-Fashioned Personal Attention, but More Speed and Efficiency," by Jeremy Main, *Fortune*, March 23, 1981, p. 58. By permission of Mr. Jeremy Main and Fortune magazine. © Time Inc. All rights reserved.

P. 215, excerpt headed "The Software Explosion," by Herbert L. Gepner, *Computerworld*, September 17, 1980. By permission of Herbert L. Gepner, Senior Editor/Analyst, Data Decisions, Cherry Hill, N.J.

P. 221, excerpt headed "Egoless Programming," from *The Psychology of Computer Programming*, by Gerald M. Weinberg. © 1971 by Litton Educational Publishing, Inc. Reprinted by permission of Van Nostrand Reinhold Company.

P. 236-237, excerpt headed "Grace M. Hopper: 'Grandma COBOL,'" reprinted with permission from *ICP INTERFACE Administrative & Accounting*, Spring 1980, p. 18, a publication of International Computer Programs, Inc., Indianapolis, Ind., U.S.A.

P. 241, excerpt headed "Telling a Computer What to Do," reprinted from the September 1, 1980 issue of *Business Week* by special permission; © 1980 by McGraw-Hill, Inc., New York, N.Y. 10020. All rights reserved.

#P. 247, excerpt headed "Drawing with the Turtle," from "Drawing with the Turtle" by Harold Abelson appearing in the August 1982 issue of *BYTE* magazine. Copyright © 1982 Byte Publications, Inc. Used with the permission of Byte Publications, Inc.

P. 258, excerpt headed "In Unix We Trust," by Susan Chace, "AT&T's Unix a Computer's Traffic Cop, Starts Selling Fast, May Enhance Bell's Role," *Wall Street Journal*, November 8, 1983, p. 25. Reprinted by permission of The Wall Street Journal, © Dow Jones & Company, Inc., 1983. All rights reserved.

P. 259, excerpt headed "The Importance of CP/M," Paul Kinnucan, *LIST*, Spring 1983, p. 117. By permission of LIST magazine, Vero Beach, FL.

P. 271, excerpt headed "The Race for the Fastest Computer," by William J. Broad, *New York Times*, February 1, 1983, p. 19. © 1983 by The New York Times Company. Reprinted by permission.

P. 274, excerpt headed "Hunger Organization Finds Relief with Mini," *Computerworld*, August 30, 1982, p. 21. © 1982 by CW Communications/Inc., Framingham, MA 01701. Reprinted from *Computerworld*.

P. 276, excerpt headed "1990's Top Ten," *Computerworld*, April 5, 1982, p. 73. © 1982 by CW Communications/Inc., Framingham, MA 01701. Reprinted from *Computerworld*.

P. 278, excerpt headed "Hunt-and-Peck Author Raves about Word Processing," *Computerworld*, October 4, 1982, p. 34. © 1982 by CW Communications/Inc., Framingham, MA 01701. Reprinted from *Computerworld*.

P. 279, excerpt headed "Who Shall Edit the Editor?", by Nick Engler, Omni, August 1982, p. 36. Copyright 1982 by Omni Publications International Ltd. and reprinted with permission of the copyright owner.

P. 282, excerpt headed "Test Driving a New Word Processor for a Personal Computer," by Erik Sandberg-Diment, *New York Times*, April 19, 1983 (as reprinted in *San Francisco Chronicle*, April 20, 1983, p. AA–5). © 1983 by The New York Times Company. Reprinted by permission.

P. 284, excerpt headed "Foot Dragging Knowledge Workers," by Harvey L. Poppel, *Harvard Business Review*, November-December, 1982, p. 147. Reprinted by permission of the Harvard Business Review. Excerpt from "Who Needs the Office of the Future?" by Harvey L. Poppel (November-December 1982). Copyright © 1982 by the President and Fellows of Harvard College; all rights reserved.

P. 291, excerpt headed "8 versus 16: A Bit About Bits," Augustin Hedberg, *Money*, May 19, p. 156. From the May 1983 issue of MONEY magazine by special permission; © 1983, Time Inc.

P. 293, excerpt headed "Leading Uses of Home Computer," *New York Times*, May 11, 1983, p. 25. © 1983 by The New York Times Company. Reprinted by permission.

P. 296, excerpt headed "Home Computer Maintenance," from a copyrighted article in *U.S. News & World Report*, May 9, 1983.

P. 306, excerpt headed "Secondhand Silicon," from the June 1983 issue of *Money* magazine by special permission; © 1983, Time Inc.

P. 312, excerpt headed "Different Messages, Different Bits," by James Martin, *Telematic Society* (Englewood Cliffs, N.J.: Prentice-Hall, 1981). Reprinted by permission.

P. 320, excerpt headed "Some Long-Distance Common Carriers with Data Transmission Services," *Computerworld*, March 21, 1983, p. 10. © 1983 by CW Communications/Inc., Framingham, MA 01701. Reprinted from *Computerworld*.

P. 323, excerpt headed "Keeping the Blood Flowing," *Computerworld*, February 22, 1982, p. 22. © 1983 by CW Communications/Inc., Framingham, MA 01701. Reprinted from *Computerworld*.

P. 327, excerpt headed "Computerized Conferencing," by Starr Roxanne Hiltz and Murray Turoff, *The Network Nation* (Reading, Mass.: Addison-Wesley Publishing Co., 1978), pp. xxix–xxx. Reprinted by permission.

P. 328, excerpt headed "Room Service, Pool TV—and Computer," by Patricia Weiss, *U.S.A. Today*, January 26, 1983. Reprinted by permission.

P. 329, excerpt headed "Telecommunications: Global Brain?" by Jacques Vallee, *The Network Revolution: Confessions of a Computer Scientist* (Berkeley, Calif.: And/Or Press, 1982), p. 9.

P. 329, excerpt headed "The Coming of Telecommuting," by Margo Downing-Faircloth. Reprinted with permission from *Personal Computing*, May 1982, pp. 41, 44, and copyright 1982, Hayden Publishing Company.

P. 336, excerpt headed "Information Please," by Tracy Dotson, *Computerworld*, May 10, 1982, "In Depth/23." © 1982 by CW Communications/Inc., Framingham, MA 01701. Reprinted from *Computerworld*.

P. 338, excerpt headed "No More Data!! The Need for DSS," by Walter E. Lankau, *Computerworld*, September 1, 1982, Extra!," p. 6. © 1982 by CW Communications/Inc., Framingham, MA 01701. Reprinted from *Computerworld Extra*.

P. 342, excerpts from *Computerworld* headed "Do You Need a Good Fullback?" by Susan Blakeney, August 9, 1982, pp. 1, 8; "Crime Fighters' Data Bases" by Jim Bartimo November 22, 1982, pp. 1–4; and "The All-Electronic Novel Available Through Data Base" by Bartimo, January 31, 1983, p. 2. © 1982 by CW Communications/Inc., Framingham, MA 01701. Reprinted from *Computerworld*.

P. 345, excerpt headed "The Seattle Crisis Clinic," Courtesy Jean Lee for the Seattle Crisis Clinic.

#P. 362, excerpt headed "The Entry-Level Problem: Don't Just Study Programming," by Rachel Wrege, appearing in the June 1983 issue of *Popular Computing* magazine. Copyright © 1983 Byte Publications, Inc. Used with the permission of Byte Publications, Inc.

P. 366, excerpt headed "How to Break into Data Processing," by Laura Steibel Sessions, *How to Break into Data Processing* (Englewood Cliffs, N.J.: Prentice-Hall, 1982). Excerpted and condensed in *Computerworld*, September 20, 1982, p. 8. By permission of the author.

P. 374, excerpt headed "Inner Secrets," *Inc.*, February 1983, p. 111. Reprinted with permission, *Inc.* magazine, February 1983. Copyright © 1983 by Inc. Publishing Corporation, 38 Commercial Wharf, Boston, MA 02110.

P. 381, excerpt headed "Booby Traps for Software," by Susan Blakeney, *Computerworld*, July 12, 1982, p. 7. © 1982 by CW Communications/Inc., Framingham, MA 01701. Reprinted from *Computerworld*.

P. 385, excerpt headed "Beyond the Manila Folder," *Computerworld*, March 7, 1983, p. 17, and "Swedish ID System," *Computerworld*, October 25, 1982, p. 20. © 1982, 1983 by CW Communications/Inc., Framingham, MA 01701. Reprinted from *Computerworld*. Excerpt headed "The Electronic Leash," reported by Associated Press, *San Francisco Chronicle*, March 10, 1983, p. 24. By permission of the Associated Press.

P. 391, excerpt headed "Computer Error and the End of the World" by Jake Kirchner, *Computerworld*, December 18, 1981–January 4, 1982, pp. 25, 30–31. © 1982 by CW Communications/Inc., Framingham, MA 01701. Reprinted from *Computerworld*.

P. 393, excerpt headed "No Robots to Darn Socks?" by Richard A. Shaffer, *Wall Street Journal*, June 3, 1983, p. 23. Reprinted by permission of The Wall Street Journal, © Dow Jones & Company, Inc., 1983. All rights reserved.

P. 395, excerpt headed "Kids in the Future," by Doug Garr, Omni, November 1982. Copyright 1982 by Doug Garr and reprinted with the permission of Omni Publications International, Ltd.

P. 401, excerpt headed "The French and Revolution," by Rex Malik, *Computerworld*, May 9, 1983, In Depth/22. © 1983 by CW Communications/Inc., Framingham, MA 01701. Reprinted from *Computerworld*.

# Photo and Illustration Credits

We are indebted to the many people and organizations who contributed photographs and illustrations to this book. The page numbers and contributors are listed below.

2 Both, TRW Inc.
5 TRW Inc.
17 TRW Inc.
20 F2-1 Console by Sperry-Univac, a division of Sperry Corporation.
21 F2-2 3M.
21 F2-3 Right, Innovative Data Technology; left, Memorex Corporation.
22 F2-4 Sperry-Univac, a Division of Sperry Corporation.
F2-5 NCR Corporation.
23 F2-6 NCR Corporation.
F2-7 Top right, Sperry Corporation; bottom, IBM Corporation.
24 F2-8 Sperry Corporation.
F2-9 Sperry Corporation.
25 F2-10 Right, Datagraphix; left, Sperry Corporation.
26 F2-11 Left, Nashua Corporation; right, IBM Corporation.
F2-12 Left, Memorex Corporation; right, Compliments of Kennedy Company.
28 F2-13 Center, console by Sperry-Univac, a division of Sperry Corporation. Clockwise from top left: Floppy disk, 3M; magnetic tape, Memorex Corporation; disk, Nashua Corporation; CRT screen, Sperry-Univac, a Division of Sperry Corporation; printout, Datagraphix; bar code, NCR Corporation; wand reader, NCR Corporation; CRT terminal, Sperry-Univac, a division of Sperry Corporation; magnetic tape, Memorex Corporation.
29 F2-14 TRS-80 is a trademark of Radio Shack, A Division of Tandy Corporation.
42 From left to right, Intel Corporation, AT&T Longlines-Western Region Office, Wang Laboratories, Hewlett-Packard Company, Storage Technology Corporation.
45 Intel Corporation.
46 F3-1 © Merry Selk.
47 F3-2 Left, Historical Pictures Service, Chicago; right, IBM Corporation.
48 F3-3 Left, The Bettman Archive, Inc.; right, IBM Corporation.
F3-4 Historical Pictures Service, Chicago.
49 F3-5 Culver Pictures.
F3-6 Left, The Bettman Archive, Inc.; right, IBM Corporation.
50 F3-7 Left, UPI; right, IBM Corporation.
51 F3-8 All Harvard University/Cruft Laboratory.

52 F3-9 Wide World Photos.
53 F3-10 Iowa State University.
54 F3-11 UPI.
F3-12 Institute for Advanced Study, Princeton, N.J.
55 F3-13 Sperry-Univac, a Division of Sperry Corporation.
57 F3-14 Left, Smithsonian Institution Photo No. 61758E; right, Bell Laboratories.
59 F3-16 Left, Intel Corporation; right, IBM Corporation.
61 F3-17 IBM Corporation.
63 F3-18 Cray Research, Inc.
67 AT&T Longlines-Western Region Office.
74 Top left, © Ira Wyman.
F4-3 © 1983 David Cross.
78 F4-8 Bell Laboratories.
83 Wang Laboratories.
85 F5-1 Left, Culver Pictures, Inc.; right, Superscope, Inc., Pianocorder Division.
87 F5-3 NFB—Photothèque/Photo by Crombie McNeill.
F5-4 Sperry Corporation.
88 Bottom left, Dvorak keyboard, Virginia deGanahl Russell, Dvorak International Federation, 11 Pearl St., Brandon, VT 05733.
89 F5-5 Photo: U.S. Postal Service.
90 F5-6 IBM Corporation.
91 F5-7 Sperry Corporation.
F5-8 Judy Lee.
94 F5-10 and F5-11 NCR Corporation.
96 F5-12 The College Board/Educational Testing Service. Copyright © Educational Testing Service. All rights reserved.
97 F5-14 Recognition Equipment Incorporated, Dallas.
98 F5-16 National Semiconductor Corporation.
100 F5-17 NCR Corporation.
101 F5-18 Texas Instruments Incorporated.
F5-19 Bell Laboratories.
102 F5-20 NCR Corporation.
103 F5-21 Right, United States Department of the Interior, Geological Survey; left, Bausch & Lomb.
F5-22 IBM Corporation.
104 F5-23 Digital Equipment Corporation.
F5-24 Courtesy of Apple Computer, Inc.
105 F5-25 Bunker Ramo Information Systems.
F5-26 Tom Mareschal/Courtesy Interstate Electronics Corporation.

109 Hewlett-Packard Company.
110 Imaging by Samuel N. Antupit.
113 F6-2 Ring Power Corp./Courtesy Honeywell Incorporated.
115 F6-3, right, Dataproducts Corporation.
118 F6-6 Datagraphix.
119 Stanford News Service.
120 F6-7 Hewlett-Packard Company.
123 Adapted from *Potential Health Hazards of Video Display Terminals* by National Institute for Occupational Safety and Health, Cincinnati, Ohio, 1981, p. 23.
125 F6-11, left, Anacomp, Inc.; right, 3M.
126 F6-12 Tektronix, Inc.
F6-13 U.S. Department of the Interior/U.S. Geological Survey/Western Mapping Center.
128 6-15 Bell Laboratories.
6-16 BLOCPIX® image by Ed Manning.
130 F6-17, Left, Texas Instruments Incorporated; right, Chrysler Corporation.
131 F6-18 Texas Instruments Incorporated.
135 Storage Technology Corporation.
136 F7-1 © Peeter Vilms/Jeroboam, Inc.
139 F7-3, Right, Sperry Corporation.
140 F7-4 Inset, Memorex; large photo, Sperry-Univac, a Division of Sperry Corporation.
145 F7-7 Memorex Corporation.
147 F7-9 Ford Motor Company/Courtesy Control Data Corporation.
148 F7-10, Top, Storage Technology Corporation.
149 F7-11 Nashua Corporation.
150 F7-12 IBM Corporation.
158 F7-18 IBM Corporation
159 F7-19 Courtesy of Robert E. Capron.
164 From left to right, Hazel Hankin/Stock, Boston; Robert Mottar/Chase Manhattan Bank; David Powers; from Honeywell, Inc.; Bell Laboratories.
167 Hazel Hankin/Stock, Boston.
171 David Powers.
172 F8-2 IBM Corporation.
180 © Glenn R. Steiner.
184 Edu Ware Services, Inc. an MSA Company
189 Robert Mottar/Chase Manhattan Bank.
193 Mohawk Data Sciences.
194 David Powers.
199 Mohawk Data Sciences.
200 Lower right in box, Mohawk Data Sciences.
204 Bell Laboratories.

## Gallery Credits

David Cox, Randal Kleiser, Vance Loen, Jan Prins, D.L. Deas, Stan Cohen
20. Photo Courtesy of Dicomed Corporation
21. © 1980 Peter Vilms/Jeroboam, Inc.
22. 3M
23. © William Rivelli, 1981
24. Reproduced With Permission of AT&T
25. Hewlett-Packard Company
26. Sperry Corporation
27. Courtesy Intel Corporation
28. "Atlantis," Imagic, (As seen on Atari 2600)
29. © Walt Disney Productions
30. Courtesy of Marriott's Great America; Santa Clara, California
31. © 1983 Tom Zimberoff/Gamma-Liaison
32. © Kent Reno/Jeroboam, Inc.
33. © Regents of the University of California/Charles Frizzell/Lawrence Hall of Science
34. Fisher-Price Toys
35. Social Security Administration
36. Motorola Inc.
37. © Hap Stewart/Jeroboam, Inc.
38. Photo Courtesy of National Computer Systems
39. Design and execution by COLASSAL PICTURES, San Francisco
40. © 1974 Frank Balthis/Jeroboam, Inc.
41. David Weimer, Bell Laboratories

## Gallery 2

1. From Honeywell Inc.
2. Zenith Data Systems
3. From Honeywell Inc.
4. Courtesy of Bell Helicopter Textron, Inc.
5. Cray Research, Inc.
6. TRS-80 is a trademark of Radio Shack, A Division of Tandy Corporation
7. Paradyne Corporation
8. Courtesy of Burroughs Wellcome Co., Research Triangle Park, North Carolina
9. United Information Services, Inc.
10. Bell Laboratories
11. Photo Courtesy of Applicon, a Division of Schlumberger Technology Corporation
12. Memorex Corporation
13. Photo: U.S. Postal Service
14. Photo: U.S. Postal Service
15. Photo provided by courtesy of Sun Information Services Company

## Gallery 3

1. Intel Corporation
2, 3. Bell Laboratories
4. Intel Corporation
5, 6, 7, 8. National Semiconductor Corporation
9, 10, 11. Intel Corporation
12, 13. NCR Corporation
14, 15. Intel Corporation
16. Bell Laboratories

17, 18. NCR Corporation
19. National Semiconductor Corporation
20. NCR Corporation

## Gallery 4

1. Paradyne Corporation
2. Courtesy Wang Laboratories, Inc.
3. Courtesy of Electronic Data Systems Corp.
4. Disabled Student Services/Arizona State University
5. Courtesy Wang Laboratories, Inc.
6. Hewlett-Packard Company
7. Courtesy General Electric Research and Development Center
8. Metropolitan Museum of Art/NCR Corporation
9. Recognition Equipment Incorporated
10. Recognition Equipment Incorporated
11. NCR Corporation
12. Photo Courtesy of The Standard Register Company
13. INTERMEC
14. INTERMEC
15. Photograph by Richard Steinheimer, Courtesy of Exar Integrated Systems
16. TRW Inc.
17. Xerox Corporation
18. Photo Courtesy of National Computer Systems
19. Memorex Corporation
20. Sperry Corporation
21. National Semiconductor Corporation
22. Nautilus Sports/Medical Industries, Inc.
23. Nautilus Sports/Medical Industries, Inc.

## Gallery 5

1. Courtesy of Los Alamos National Laboratory
2. TRS-80 is a trademark of Radio Shack, A Division of Tandy Corporation
3. Datapoint Corporation
4. Bell Laboratories
5. 3M
6. Courtesy of Burroughs Corporation
7. Nicolet Zeta Corporation
8. CalComp
9. CalComp
10. 3M
11. Westinghouse Electric Corporation
12. ITT Corporation
13. Jerry David/U.S. Senate
14. Ramtek Corporation
15. United States Department of Interior, Geological Survey
16. Terak/Image Resource
17. Rockwell International Corporation
18. Courtesy Genisco Computers Corp.
19. Ramtek Corporation
20. Image Resource/Chromatics
21. Tripos Associates, Inc., St. Louis, MO
22. "Microsurgeon," Imagic, For Intellivision I and II
23. Ramtek Corporation
24. Image Resource

## Gallery 6

1. Photograph by Dick Zimmerman © 1983
2. Chuck Kidd/Smith College
3. Disabled Student Services, Arizona State University
4. Used with permission of SPSS Inc.
5. Pitney Bowes
6. Used with permission of SPSS Inc.
7. U.S. Department of Transportation Federal Aviation Administration
8. U.S. Department of Transportation Federal Aviation Administration
9. Used with permission of SPSS Inc.
10. Photo courtesy Martin Marietta
11. Herman Kokojam/Black Star
12. Hughes Aircraft Company
13. Courtesy of Electronic Data Systems Corp.
14. Courtesy of Electronic Data Systems Corp.
15. Sperry Corporation
16. Bridgestone Tire Co., LTD.
17. Courtesy of Burroughs Wellcome Co.
18. University of California, Lawrence Livermore National Laboratory
19. TRW Inc.
20. Centers for Disease Control
21. Courtesy of Electronic Data Systems Corp.
22. INTERMEC
23. Ampex Corporation
24. Courtesy of Electronic Data systems Corp.
25. Haworth, Inc.
26. Anacomp, Inc.
27. Photo: Merck & Co., Inc., Rahway, N.J.
28. Rockwell International Corporation
29. Fisher-Price Toys
30. General Motors Corporation, GM Assembly Division
31. IBM Corporation
32. Courtesy of Electronic Data Systems Corp.
33. Photo courtesy of Sonoma Vineyards and Unigraphics
34. © 1982 Peter Menzel
35. Courtesy of Electronic Data Systems Corp.
36. © 1983 Peter Menzel
37. © Will McIntyre/Science Source/Photo Researchers, Inc.

## Gallery 7

1. Courtesy of CPT Corporation
2. SIC-PTT
3. TRW, Inc.
4. Paradyne Corporation
5. ITT Corporation
6. Philippe Pons
7. TRW Inc.
8. © Dave Bartruff/Artistry International
9. © Dave Bartruff/Artistry International
10. Wide World Photos, Inc.
11. Hewlett-Packard Company
12. ITT Corporation
13. ITT Corporation

14. IBM Corporation
15. Jamaica Tourist Board
16. IBM Corporation
17. World Bank Photo by James Pickerell
18. ITT Corporation
19. Jordan Information Bureau, Washington, D.C.
20. Jordan Information Bureau, Washington, D.C.
21. The New York Times/William K. Stevens
22. © Dave Bartruff/Artistry International

## Gallery 8

1. © Will McIntyre/Science Source/Photo Researchers, Inc.
2. IBM Corporation
3. Courtesy of Apple Computer, Inc.
4. Courtesy of Apple Computer, Inc.
5. Commodore International Limited
6. Hewlett-Packard Company
7. Texas Instruments Incorporated
8. Radio Shack, A Division of Tandy Corporation
9. Atari, Inc.
10. Epson America, Inc.

11. Osborne Computer Corporation
12. Hewlett-Packard Company
13. IBM Corporation
14. © 1983 Photonet Computer Corporation
15. Quasar Company, Division of Matsushita Electric Corporation
16. The Panasonic Hand Held Computer
17. Courtesy of Apple Computer, Inc.
18. Courtesy of Apple Computer, Inc.
19. © Dan McCoy/Rainbow
20. © Dan McCoy/Rainbow
21. Gary Mikel
22. Courtesy of Apple Computer, Inc.
23. Commodore International Limited
24. Texas Instruments Incorporated
25. Courtesy of Apple Computer, Inc.
26. © 1981 A. Richard Immel

## Gallery 9

1. Androbot, Inc.
2. Bell & Howell Business Equipment Group
3. Alan Miller
4. Alan Miller
5. Alan Miller

6. Alan Miller
7. Courtesy of San Francisco Police Department Photo Lab
8. Allied Corp.
9. General Electric Research & Development Center
10. © Enrico Ferorelli/Wheeler Pictures
11. JANEART, for Club Med
12. Elektra-Beserkeley Records
13. Video Music International, Inc.
14. Yerkes Primate Research Center, Emory University
15. Sperry Corporation
16. Ampex Corporation
17. Courtesy of Apple Computer, Inc.
18. Hughes Aircraft Company
19. © 1982 Peter Menzel
20. © Laurence M. Gartel
21. © 1980 David Em
22. Howard Ganz, Oceanside, California
23. © 1982 Darcy Gerberg "Qspace"/ Aurora Systems, Inc., San Francisco, CA
24. The Original Computer Camp
25. Beverly Enterprises, Shore Haven Nursing Home, Grand Haven, MI

## Buyer's Guide

1. © Nita Winter, 1983/San Francisco MicroComputers
2. © Nita Winter, 1983/Èntre Computer Center sm
3. Kirk Caldwell
4. a, b © Nita Winter, 1983/Èntre Computer Center sm
5. a, b; 6. a, b © Nita Winter, 1983/San Francisco MicroComputers
7. Raytheon Data Systems

8. a, b © Nita Winter, 1983/Sunset Electronics
9. a, b; 10. a, b © Nita Winter, 1983/Èntre Computer Center sm
11. TRS-80 is a trademark of Radio Shack, A Division of Tandy Corporation
12. a, b Courtesy of Apple Computer, Inc.
13–14 Futurevision, Napa, CA
15. Courtesy of Apple Computer, Inc.

16. © Nita Winter, 1983/Pacific Stereo
19. Texas Instruments Incorporated
20. Young People's Logo Association
21. Image Resource
22–27. © Nita Winter, I 83/Èntre Computer Center sm
28. Courtesy of Apple Computer, Inc.
29–30.© Nita Winter, 1983/Èntre Computer Center sm

We are extremely grateful to the following institutions and individuals for their assistance in providing us with information or photographs.

Adage, Inc.
Aetna Life and Casualty Co.
Akron City Hospital
Allied Corp.
American Angus Association
American Dairy Association
The American Egg Board
Anacomp, Inc.
Androbot, Inc.
Apple Computer, Incorporated
Applicon, a Division of Schlumberger Technology Corporation
Atari, Inc.
AT&T
First Interstate Bank
BASF Systems Corporation
Basic Telecommunications Corporation
Belgian American Chamber of Commerce
Bell Laboratories
Bell Helicopter Textron, Inc.
Black Star

Bell Laboratories Record
Bausch & Lomb
Bell & Howell Business Equipment Group
Boeing Computer Services Company
Bridgestone Tire Co., LTD.
Bunker Ramo Information Systems
Burroughs Corporation
Burroughs Wellcome Co.
Byte Publications, Inc.
Cado Systems Corp.
Calcomp
Centers for Disease Control
COLASSAL PICTURES
Coleco
Colorgraphics Systems, Inc.
Commadore International Limited
Compushop
Computerland
Computer Camps International
Computer Faire
CompuPro, a Godbout Company

Computer Museum
Computer Transceiver Systems, Inc.
Comsat
Comshare, Inc.
Control Data Corporation
Cornell University
CPT Corporation
Cray Research, Inc.
Dave Dameron
Datapoint Corporation
Dicomed Corporation
Digital Effects, Inc.
Digital Equipment Corporation
Disarmament Resource Center/Peacenet
Reuben H. Donnelley
Edu-ware Services, Inc.
David Em
Ed Emshwiller
Environmental Research Institute
J. R. Esher
Exar Integrated Systems

**453**

*Credits and Acknowledgments*

Exploratorium
Exxon Office Systems Company
The Fine Arts Museum of San Francisco
Fisher-Price Toys
Four Phase Systems, Inc.
Gama-Liaison
Laurence M. Gartel
Howard Ganz
General Electric Research and Development Center
Genisco Computers Corp.
Darcy Gerbarg
Goldwater Memorial Hospital
Harris Corporation
Hartford National Bank
Honeywell Inc.
Hughes Aircraft Company
IBM Corporation
Image Resource
Imagic
Innovative Data Technology
INTERMEC
Intergraph Corporation
Intercolor, An Intelligent Systems Company
ITT Corporation
Jamaica Tourist Board
Janeart for Club Med
Japan Graphic Inc.
Jet Propulsion Laboratory
Jordan Information Bureau
Kaypro
Kings Island
Lawrence Berkeley Laboratory
Lawrence Hall of Science
Lawrence Livermore National Laboratory
Judy Lee
Life Scan Inc.
3M
Martin Marietta
Peter Menzel
Magnavox – N.A.P. Consumer Electronics Corp., A North American Philips Company
Magnuson Computer Systems
Benoit B. Mandelbrot
Mannesmann Tally
Marine World – Africa USA
Marriott's Great America
Mattel Electronics
Megatek Corporation
Metropolitan Museum of Art
Merck & Co., Inc.
Micropad
Gary Mikel
Mohawk Data Sciences
Motorola, Inc.
Mouse Systems Corp.
National Computer Systems
Nicolet Zeta Corporation
Nixdorf Corp.
NASA
National Semiconductor Corporation
National Center for Atmospheric Research/High Altitude Observatory
National Dynamics

Nautilus Sports/Medical Industries, Inc.
The New York Times
NCR Corporation
Nicolet Zeta Corporation
New York Institute of Technology
The Original Computer Camp
Ohio State University
Palo Alto Research Center
Photonet Computer Corporation
Photo Researchers, Inc.
Picture Group
Philippe Pons
Panasonic
Paradyne Corporation
Pitney Bowes
Plexus Computers, Inc.
Polaroid Corp.
Prentke Romich Co.
Qantas Airlines
Quasar Company, Division of Matsushita Electric Corporation
Qume Corporation – A Subsidiary of ITT Corporation
Radio Shack, A Division of Tandy Corporation
Rainbow
Ramtek Corporation
Raytheon Data Systems
RCA Satcom
Recognition Equipment Incorporated
Renssalaer Polytechnic Institute
The Robot Factory
Rockwell International Corporation
San Francisco Chronicle
The San Francisco Concert Orchestra
San Francisco Examiner
San Francisco Police Dept. Photo Lab
Sarasota Automation
Scan-Data Corporation
Scan-optics, Inc.
Research Institute of Scripps Clinic
Seattle Crisis Clinic
Sinclair Research Ltd.
Sonoma Vineyards
SIC-PTT
Siggraph Conference '81
SKS Computers
Smith College
Social Security Administration
Sony Corporation of America
The Source Telecomputing Corp.
Sperry Corporation
The Standard Register Company
Stanford University
Storage Technology Corporation
Nina Stern Public Relations
Sun Information Services Company
Sunkist Growers, Inc.
State University at Buffalo
SPSS Inc.
Tandem Computer Inc.
Televideo Systems
Terak Corporation
Texas Instruments Incorporated
Timex/Sinclair

TRW, Inc.
Tripos Associates, Inc.
Joan Truckenbrod, Northern Illinois University
TWA
United Airlines
United Information Services, Inc.
United Nations
U.P.I.
U.S. Supreme Court
U.S. Department of Transportation Federal Aviation Administration
U.S. Postal Service
United States Department of the Interior/Geological Survey
United States Department of Energy Remote Sensing Laboratory
University of California
University of Miami
University of Pennsylvania
Video Music International, Inc.
VisiCorp
Walt Disney Productions
Westinghouse Electric Corporation
Wang Laboratories, Inc.
Wheeler Pictures
Wide World Photos, Inc.
Williams & Foltz Computer Furniture
Nita Winter
The Woodworks
World Bank
U.S.A. Today
Wright State University
Unicef
Yerkes Primate Research Center
Young People's Logo Association
Yellow Phone, Inc.
Xerox Corporation
James Yudelson
Zenith Data Systems
Dick Zimmerman
Beverly Enterprises, Shore Haven Nursing Center
Pan American Health Organization
Boy Scouts of America
Communications Management Co.
San Francisco 49ers
Scott Adams, Inc.
San Francisco Bay Area Rapid Transit District
Jeroboam, Inc.
Disabled Student Services/Arizona State University
Electronic Data Systems Corp.
Chromatics
Ampex Corporation
General Motors Corporation, GM Assembly Division
Unigraphics
Artistry International
Richard Immel
David Cross
Ken Knowlton

# glossary / index

A small "f" following a page number refers to a figure; a "t" refers to a table.

imagination, and
intuition. 68–69, 80, 397–400
**ASCII:** 7–bit code adopted as a
standard to represent data
characters. 76, 77f, 81
Asimov, Isaac 11
Assembler 260
**Assembler program:** Program that
assembles programs written in
symbolic language into
machine language instructions.
There is usually a one-to-one
correspondence between
symbolic language and
machine language
instructions. 230
Assembly language 58, 65,
229–30, 231f
Astronomy, computers and 6
Atanasoff, John V. 52, 52f, 65
Atanasoff-Berry computer 52, 53f,
65
Atari 281, 298, 301, 302f
ATM; see Automated teller machine
AT&T: See American Telephone &
Telegraph
**Audio response terminal:** Terminal
that produces output with a
voice-type response.
**Audit trail:** Procedure for tracing
the path of a data transaction
from its original input
document to the final output
document on which it appears,
or vice versa. 208
Auditor checks, data security
and 379
Automated office 278–86
executives and 284–86
**Automated teller machine
(ATM):** Remote terminal,
usually in a bank's exterior
wall, that permits withdrawals,
deposits, and transfer of
funds. 105, 105f, 326, 326f
Automation, job security and
393–94

Babbage, Charles 46–48, 48f, 64
BACON program 8
Baker, F. T. 224
Band printers 115–16
**Bar code:** Code consisting of a
series of bars with varying
widths that can be read by a
light-sensitive device, such as
a wand reader, to identify an
item. Commonly used in retail
systems. 22, 23f, 28f, 40,
98–99, 107
Bar code reader 22, 23f, 40, 98,
98f, 107
Bardeen, J. 58

**BASIC:** High-level interactive
programming language that is
easy to learn and use. It is
popular with minicomputer
and microcomputer users. 170,
171, 228, 241
arithmetic operations in 409–11
compiler 260
constants in 407
control breaks in 434
flowcharting and 415–19
interactive programs and
419–22
line numbers in 407
looping in 422–29
menus and subroutines in
429–33
spacing in 408
statements in 408–9, 431t,
434–41
variables in 406–7
BASIC-PLUS 241
**Batch processing:** Processing data
in groups at specified time
intervals. 32–33, 34f, 35–36
Beginners All-Purpose Symbolic
Instruction Code; see BASIC
Bell Laboratories 58, 65, 79, 246,
258, 281, 320
Berry, Clifford 52, 65
**Binary digit:** Digit used in the
binary number system, 0 or 1.
Binary number system 442
Binary system 75, 80
Biochemistry, computers and 6–7
**Biometrics:** The measurement of
individual characteristics, such
as fingerprints.
computer security and 374
**Bit:** Binary digit, 0 or 1. 75, 81
**Block:** Group of two or more
records on a file that can be
read or written as a unit.
Usually synonymous with
physical record. 143
Blocking 142–43, 142f
**Blocking factor:** Number of logical
records in one physical
record. 143
Bohm, C. 214
bpi; see Bytes per inch
Brattain, H. W. 58
Brooks, Frederick 224
Brownouts 391
**Brush reader:** Type of card reader
that senses the holes in
punched cards by passing the
cards over metal brushes that
make electrical contacts
through the holes. 88, 107
Bubble memory storage 78–79, 81
**Bulletin board systems:** Telephone-
linked networks formed by

users of personal computers
that constitute free public-
access message systems. 328
Burroughs 63, 65, 275
**Bursting:** Process of separating
fanfold printer paper into
single sheets. 114
Business
computers and 7, 9
microcomputers and 295–97
**Bus line:** Parallel data lines used
by the control unit to to
communicate with the ALU
and primary storage. 70, 80
Byron, Augusta Ada 48, 49f
**Byte:** String of bits whose length is
the smallest accessible unit in
computer memory. Bytes are
commonly 6 or 8 bits. 75, 81
Bytes per inch (bpi) 137

**CAD/CAM:** Computer-aided
design, computer-aided
manufacturing. 121
Caduceus 397
CAI; see Computer-aided
instruction
Canon 303
Card dialers 101, 101f
Card punch; see Keypunch
Card reader 22, 23f, 40, 86–88,
87f, 107
Careering 367
Carterfone decision 319
CARTS principle 384
CASE structure 175, 219–20
Casio 303
Cassette tape, microcomputer
storage and 159
Cathode ray tube; see CRT
CDC; see Control Data Corporation
CDP; see Certificate in Data
Processing
**Centralized data processing:**
System wherein processing,
hardware, software, and storage
are all in one central
location. 310–11
**Central processing unit:** Computer
hardware that interprets and
executes program instructions
and communicates with the
input, output, and storage
devices. It consists of the
control unit and the arithmetic/
logic unit. 19, 24, 40, 68–72, 80
**Certificate in Data Processing:**
Recognition of achievement in
the computer industry, granted
by the Institute for Certification
of Computer Professionals to
candidates who have had 5
years of work experience in the

PARRY 69

**Pascal:** Structured high-level programming language. 170, 228, 241–43

output 242f

Pascal, Blaise 46, 47f, 241

**Password:** Secret word or number that must be typed on a keyboard before access to a computer account will be permitted. A password is designed to limit access to computer information to authorized persons. 374

data security and 378

Patchwork files 339–41

PATREC 129

Payroll system program 416–19, 418f, 419f

PCMs; see Plug-compatible manufacturers

PEMs; see Peripheral equipment manufacturers

**Periodic report:** Planned report, usually related to schedules or recurring events. 111

Peripheral equipment 29, 41

**Peripheral equipment manufacturers:** Manufacturers who make peripheral equipment, such as tape and disk drives, printers, and so on. 276

Perkin-Elmer 271, 276

Personal computer: Microcomputer used by individuals for various personal uses in the home. (See also Microcomputers.)

business and education uses for 295–97

competition in marketplace 297–305

hardware 290–93

reasons for buying 293–95

Personal finance, microcomputers and 293

Personal networks 329

**Phased conversion:** Systems conversion method in which the new system is eased into, one step at a time, by all users. (See also Pilot conversion.) 208

**Photoelectric reader:** Card reader that senses the holes in punched cards by passing the cards over a light source that activates photoelectric cells as light passes through the holes. 88, 107

Physical records 143

**PICK:** A generic operating system also known as Ultimate and Reality. 258–59

**Picosecond:** One trillionth of a second. 74, 80

**Pilot conversion:** Systems conversion method in which the entire system is used by some of the users and is eventually extended to all users once it has proved successful. 208

**PIN:** Personal identification number. The number an individual uses with a plastic charge card to obtain electronic fund transfer services.

**PL/I:** High-level programming language considered general purpose, that is both for scientific and business applications. 170, 228, 237–41

sample program 240f

**Plotter:** Machine that, based on computer-produced data, produces hard copy output in the form of maps, drawings, charts, and so on in two or three dimensions. 126f, 127

output 127f, 128f

**Plug-compatible manufacturers:** Manufacturers of peripheral equipment that is standardized so it can be used interchangeably with an original manufacturer's computer. 276

**Point-to-point line:** Line configuration in a data communications system in which there is a direct communication between each terminal and the central computer. 316, 317f

**Point-of-sale terminal:** Terminal used in a retail setting to act as a cash register. It may be programmable or connected to a central computer. 100, 100f, 107

Politics, computers and 10

**Polling:** In a data communications system, a line control method in which the computer asks each terminal on the system, in turn, if it has a message to send. 316

Portable computers 29–30, 303–4

POS; see Point-of-sale terminal

Positional notation: Number system characteristic in which the value of a digit and a number depends not only on its own intrinsic value but also on its location in the number.

**Precompiler:** A program that will convert an abbreviated source program into acceptable syntactical form. 262

**Preliminary investigation:** The initial investigation, a brief study of the problem, to determine if the systems project should be pursued. 192–93

**Primary storage:** Storage unit within the computer, closely associated with the CPU. All instructions and data to be processed are placed in primary storage until called for by the CPU. Processed data is returned to primary storage until sent to the output unit. (Synonymous with memory, internal storage, main storage, real storage.) 68

components of 77–79

magnetic cores and 57–58

Primary storage unit 71, 80

Prime Computer 76, 258–59, 276

Prime-Information 259

Printed reports 111–13, 112f

Printers 25, 25f, 41, 114–19

continuous form 113f

future improvements in 396

impact 114–17

mechanisms of 116f

microcomputer 292

nonimpact 117–18

paper used 113–14

speeds of 118

uses of 118–19

Printer spacing chart, systems analysis and 200, 200f

PRINT statement 408–9, 412–15, 413–15

variations on 413f

PRINT USING statement 436

Printout 28f

Privacy 382–86

legislation 383–86

**Private lines:** Communications lines to fixed destinations. Private lines are also available for use and may be improved by the carrier to reduce noise. 319

**Problem-oriented language:** Programming language designed to solve specific types of problems. 246

Process 172

Processing; see Data processing

Processor; see Central processing unit

Productivity 362–64

improving 363–64

measuring 364

**Program:** Step-by-step set of instructions that directs the